LATIN AMERICAN HISTORY

Essays on Its Study and Teaching, 1898–1965

Publication Number One
Conference on Latin American History

Latin American History

Essays on Its Study and Teaching, 1898-1965

COMPILED AND EDITED BY

Howard F. Cline, Ph.D.

VOLUME TWO

PUBLISHED FOR THE CONFERENCE ON LATIN AMERICAN HISTORY
BY THE UNIVERSITY OF TEXAS PRESS, AUSTIN AND LONDON

Conference on Latin American History Publications

This series is issued under an arrangement between the Conference on Latin American History, Inc., and the University of Texas Press. It includes works approved by the Publications Committee of the Conference and the Faculty Board of the Press. Publication funds are furnished by the Conference from a Ford Foundation grant.

CONTENTS

VOLUME TWO

VIII. THE IMMEDIATE POSTWAR YEARS, 1946–1954

BENCHMARKS

TEACHING

THE CONFERENCE ON LATIN AMERICAN HISTORY

RESEARCH PERSPECTIVES

IX. A FECUND DECADE, 1955–1965

BENCHMARKS

TEACHING

TOOLS AND RESOURCES

THE CONFERENCE ON LATIN AMERICAN HISTORY

RESEARCH PERSPECTIVES: GENERAL

Contents

VIII. THE IMMEDIATE POSTWAR YEARS, 1946–1954

54. Developments of the Past Decade in the Writing of Latin American History*

ARTHUR P. WHITAKER

1. NATURE AND SCOPE OF THIS REPORT

This report deals with the major developments of the decade 1939–1949 in historical writing about Latin America from 1492 to the present. It is an essay in historiography, not bibliography, and individual works will be cited only by way of illustrating these developments. Its chief concern is with the product, that is, original historical studies published during this decade; but some attention will also be given to historical organizations and the tools and materials available to the historian. Geographically, the report covers the whole area of significant production, which includes Spain, Portugal, France, Britain, Germany, Italy, and the United States as well as the twenty Latin American countries. Generalization about this large area is dangerous, but the prescribed brevity of this report makes it indispensable. Major exceptions and differentiations will, however, be noted in so far as space permits.

2. POINT OF DEPARTURE: THE SITUATION IN 1939

By 1939 Latin American historical writing was established on a firm academic and professional basis in several countries on both sides of the Atlantic, where universities and other institutions were giving it the same kind of recognition and support as that accorded the older fields of history. Scholars in these and other countries were by now fairly well supplied with the usual aids to study and research, such as special journals, bibliographies, documentary publications, and archival guides. A very respectable body of literature, the best of which was comparable to the best in the older fields, had been accumulated and considerable additions were being made to it every year.

Despite this achievement, much still remained to be done in order to bring Latin American historical writing up to the level of the related fields of European and United States history. The advance mentioned above had been quite uneven in various respects. Several of the Latin American countries had had little if any share in it. In these and some

* *Revista de Historia de América*, 29: 123–133 (jun. 1950). Reprinted by permission of the author and the original publisher. In preparing this report the author was greatly assisted by written and oral advice from Drs. Silvio Zavala and Ricardo Donoso; by special reports prepared at his request from Drs. Jorge Basadre and Carlos Bosch García on Spanish America and Drs. Manoel Cardozo and Alexander Marchant on Brazil; and by letters from Drs. Charles C. Griffin, Clarence H. Haring, Lewis Hanke, Irving A. Leonard, and Leslie B. Simpson. Valuable aid was also obtained from files of the *Handbook of Latin American Studies, Hispanic American Historical Review,* and *Revista de Historia de América.*

others a large part of what passed for historical writing was antiquarian, polemical, otherwise defective, or at best of purely local
interest; and the sounder part was focused
mainly upon a few periods and topics, to the
neglect of others which were no less important. The favorite periods were the two
heroic ages of the conquest and the wars of
independence; the favorite topics biographical, military, political, institutional, and
diplomatic.

This situation was in part merely a reflection of the dominant fashions in the older
fields of historical writing at that time. It
was also due, however, to a physical and financial difficulty which was exceptionally
serious in the Latin American field, namely,
the difficulty of bringing together the trained
historians and the great bodies of unpublished source materials. The trained historians were scattered over Western Europe
and North and South America, whereas the
sources for the colonial period were concentrated mainly in Spain and Portugal, and
those for the national period in the respective Latin American countries. So far as the
national period was concerned, there was
the additional handicap that the history of
these countries in the past 50 or 75 years has
always been tabu for most of the historians
who reside in them—partly, no doubt, for
prudential reasons, since in most of Latin
America political upheavals are frequent,
political passions violent, and memories
long.

3. Impact of the War and the Post-War Crisis

In varying degrees, every country that
was making contributions to Latin American history in 1939 was profoundly affected
by the six years of war and the four post-
war years of permanent political and economic crisis which followed. Yet, so far as
one can discern in the present short perspective, these harrowing events had remarkably
little effect upon historical writing about
Latin America. There were some interesting changes, which will be noted below; but
none of great importance that is directly
traceable to the war or the post-war crisis

has yet caused more than a ripple on the surface.

The decade did produce some general effects which are easily discernible. The volume of production declined to a trickle in
non-Iberian Europe, where Robin Humphreys (London) and Gonzalo de Reparaz
(University of Bordeaux) were prominent
among the few scholars who continued to
produce. By contrast, the output increased
sharply in Spain, partly as a result of the
Franco government's neo-Pan Hispanic campaign in Spanish America, and more mod-
erately in Portugal, mainly in connection
with that country's double centenary (the
eighth and the third) in 1940. In the United
States a decline in 1943–45 was followed
by a quick recovery in the rest of the decade.
Except for a reduction in Brazil after 1945,
Latin America maintained a more constant
flow of production than any other area.

There was a clearer reflection in Spain
and Spanish America than elsewhere of the
conflicting ideologies of the period—Hispanicism and Indianism, fascism and democracy—which might color one's interpretation of Latin American history. In a considerable part of Spanish America, however,
the freedom to develop the implications of
this conflict was by no means complete, for
the tensions of war-time increased the familiar hazards of dealing with recent history
or even with live issues of the remoter past.
Argentina under Peron (after 1943) illustrated this point. Brazil under the Vargas
dictatorship seemed to illustrate it too; but
Vargas's overthrow in 1945 was not followed
by any change in the character of Brazilian
historical writing. The truth seems to be that
external constraint was only a part of the
story. In fact, in both Brazil and Spanish
America there was a spontaneous and widespread turning away from the war-torn
world and all its problems and a nostalgic
flight into some fancied idyllic past.

On the negative side, this decade of world
conflict and tension did not bring about any
increase of historical interest among Latin
Americans in the relations of Russia or any
of the other great powers with their part of
the world. The rapid growth of Latin Amer-

ican studies in the United States, which had begun in the decade before 1939, continued through the early war years; but this was not reflected in any expansion of Latin American interest in the history of the United States.

4. DEVELOPMENTS OF THE DECADE

Passing from the general to the particular, let us now look at the principal features of the historical writing of this decade. Three types will be considered: revisions of earlier interpretations, shifts of emphasis, and continuations of existing trends. Attention will then be called to some large lacunae that remained unfilled at the end of the decade.

a. *Revisions*

Three examples of revisionism merit our attention here. The most striking of them was the rapid and widespread progress, in Spanish America as well as in Spain, of a more favorable interpretation of Spain's role in history, and particularly of its colonial record in America. In some quarters this was carried to the extreme of substituting a coat of whitewash for the once dominant "Black Legend"; but for the most part it was a prime illustration of the growth of sound historical method that characterized historical writing in this decade. Also, while the reaction against the Black Legend in Spanish America was due in some measure to the Hispanidad movement fostered by Franco Spain, it was due in equal if not greater measure to the presence in Spanish America in this decade of a number of outstanding Spanish historians who were enemies of the Franco regime, that is, to Spanish Republican exiles such as Rafael Altamira, José María Ots Capdequi, and Ramón Iglesia. Quite aside from their wholesome professional influence, these Spanish refugees were living reminders that Spain has a long tradition of liberalism, humanitarianism, and enlightenment as well as of authoritarianism, imperialism, and bigotry. Recognition of both traditions was the hallmark of the best revisionist writing of the decade on this subject, which is well represented by the Mexican historian Silvio Za-

vala's *La filosofía política en la conquista de América.*

The other two revisionist trends of the decade will be described more briefly since they were less widespread and less productive. There were: (1) The rehabilitation of anti-liberal leaders of the national period, such as Juan Manuel de Rosas of Argentina and Porfirio Díaz of Mexico. This probably reflected the fascist and reactionary tendencies which were strong in certain parts of Latin America during this decade. (2) The reinterpretation of the Spanish American independence movement of the early nineteenth century, particularly through a shifting of emphasis from external influences, e. g., the American and French revolutions, to domestic factors in the Spanish empire, and more particularly in Spain's American dominions. This change is well represented by the work of the Chilean historians Ricardo Donoso, Francisco Encina, and Jaime Eyzaguirre. It was probably related to the growth of Hispanicism and the revision of the Black Legend, mentioned above, but was mainly an expression of a broadening concept of the historical process and increased attention to ocial, economic, and cultural factors.

The Portuguese centenary celebration of 1940 (mentioned above) suggested the application to Brazil of the "imperial" approach to colonial history which had already been employed on a considerable scale in historical writing about other areas, notably British North America in the eighteenth century. This lead, however, was not followed up systematically in the rest of the decade.

b. *Changes of emphasis*

Our second group consists of works on a number of important themes which, though not at all new, were given much stronger emphasis in the decade 1939–1949. None of these themes aroused more widespread interest or produced more numerous or fresher studies than intellectual history; and this was one case in which the recent national period was not neglected in favor of earlier periods. Perhaps the most original and stimulating studies in this field were those which dealt with eighteenth-century currents of thought, particularly those relating to the European Enlightenment, and with the rise and decline of positivism in Latin America. The latter subject was studied by Leopoldo Zea in three notable books, the first two confined to his own country, Mexico, and the third on Spanish America at large. Mexico was indeed the most productive country in the whole field of intellectual history, though many important contributions came from other countries as well, particularly Cuba, Colombia, Argentina, Chile and the United States. Three outstanding works from the last-named country were John Tate Lanning's *Academic Culture in the Spanish Colonies*, Lewis Hanke's *The Spanish Struggle for Justice in the Conquest of America*, and Irving A. Leonard's *Books of the Brave*, an account of the romances of chivalry and the book trade in the early colonial period. Brief but authoritative accounts of the history of political ideas in Argentina and Chile were written by Jose Luis Romero and Ricardo Donoso, respectively.

The increasing contribution of literary history to intellectual and cultural history is represented by Pedro Henriquez Ureña's *Literary Currents in Hispanic America* (also published in Spanish), Mariano Picón Salas' *De la conquista a la independencia*, Alfonso Reyes' *Letras de Nueva España*, and José Torre Revello's *Orígenes de la imprenta en España y su desarrollo en la América española*. Important contributions to cultural history were also made by a number of studies of the changes that the Spanish and Portuguese languages have undergone in America.

As other disciplines, especially philosophy and literature, aided powerfully in bringing about an efflorescence of intellectual history, so a happy union of history with anthropology, ethnology, geography, and sociology gave an impetus to social history, particularly to the study, already well under way by 1939, of the Indian and negro peoples of America from remote pre-Columbian times to the present. The most important single work of this kind was the Smith-sonian Institution's monumental *Handbook of South American Indians*, a cooperative work by many scholars of South America and the United States, edited by Julian Steward. For the most part, however, production took the form of studies of smaller areas by individual authors, such as Julio Tello and Luis and Daniel Valcárcel in Peru, Gregorio Hernández de Alba in Colombia, F. Aparicio in Argentina, Pablo Martínez del Río, Wigberto Jiménez Moreno and Luis Chávez Orozco in Mexico, and George Kubler, Sylvester F. Cook, and Leslie B. Simpson in the United States. Scholars of the last-named country led in the production of geographical studies of direct utility to the historian; in scope, these ranged from Preston James's comprehensive book *Latin America* to Carl Sauer's study of Colima, Mexico, in the sixteenth century.

Fresh ground in a not unfamiliar field was broken by Silvio Zavala's publication of an extensive collection of documents on the history of labor in colonial Mexico—the first such work ever published in the field of Latin American history. Progress was also made in historiography, especially through studies published in Mexico, first by the Spanish Republican exile Ramón Iglesia and under his inspiration, and then under that of Silvio Zavala. The novelty of such studies is indicated by the fact that the revised and enlarged edition of Rómulo Carbia's *Historia Crítica de la Historiografía Argentina*, published in 1939, was at that time the only comprehensive and authoritative work on the historiography of any Latin American country.

More limited increases of emphasis took place in three other cases. In the history of Latin American art the already considerable activity of the past generation was extended and some new frontiers were opened, e.g., by Manuel Toussaint's study of Moorish art in America and by Roberto C. Smith's invaluable general bibliography of the subject, which was the first of its kind. Kurt Lange, in Montevideo, continued his important studies of the history of music in Latin America and these were supplemented by others, such as Eugenio Pereira Salas's book on the early history of music in Chile. Economic history, though still quite inadequately developed at the end of the decade, made considerable progress. In addition to the appearance of special studies of real merit, such as Alice Canabrava's *O comércio portugués no Rio da Prata,* Miron Burgin's *The Economic Development of Argentina in the Age of Rosas,* Antonio Garcia's *Bases de la Economía Contemporanea,* and new volumes in Afonso de Escragnolle Taunay's long history of coffee in Brazil, economic factors were receiving more attention than formerly in works of a more general character, such as those dealing with the post-Conquest Indians and the independence movement. Finally, the familiar theme of the Conquest received a fresh impulse from a sharp increase in the number of reprints and new editions of contemporary accounts.

c. *Continuations of existing trends*

It would be quite misleading, however, to describe the historical writing of this decade only in terms of new developments and shifts of emphasis, for much the greater part of the total output continued to flow in familiar channels. In Latin America this was true of most countries, including the largest, Brazil, where except for a few individual studies of real merit, there was a general failure to follow up the stimulating leads in economic and social history provided both shortly before and during this decade by Roberto Simonsen, Gilberto Freyre, and Caio Prado Junior. It was true also of Spain, the only European country where a large volume of production was maintained throughout the decade. Some of the Spanish product was of high quality, but it broke little new ground; Melchor Fernández Almagro's *La emancipación de América y su reflejo en la conciencia española* is exceptional in this respect. Indeed, while individual trailblazers were at work in many countries, there were only two countries in which the pioneering spirit was characteristic and dominant. These were Mexico and the United States, especially the former, which by the second half of the decade became the chief center of historical research and writing in Latin America.

One explanation of this widespread lack of response to the newer trends is suggested by the case of Brazil, which was a conspicuous illustration of it. Though Brazil now had a population of nearly 50 million, it had only one well organized center of historical research, training, and publication, the University of São Paulo; and its principal historical societies, including the Instituto Histórico e Geografico Brasileiro, continued without much vitality their accustomed activities, such as the rather irregular publication of their journals and the organizing of historical congresses in commemoration of events in Brazilian history.

In the latter connection it should be noted that in the field of Latin American history at large, a considerable fraction of the total output is published in connection with centenaries and other anniversary celebrations —a larger part, probably, than in the history of any other area in the world. This is doubtless due in some measure to the fact that in Spain, Portugal, and Latin America the cost of publishing a large fraction of all historical works is normally borne either directly by the governments or by academies or other organizations of a quasi-public character; and it is easier to get subsidies of this kind when the purpose is to commemorate a revered figure or event in the nation's history. Both this point and the continuing popularity of biography were strikingly illustrated by the avalanche of books about the Cuban patriot leader José Martí that greeted his centenary.

Among the multitude of writings on the more familiar themes were many of outstanding excellence. For the age of discovery these included S. E. Morison's splendid biography of Christopher Columbus and the works of Antonio Ballesteros y Beretta and Jaime Cortesão on the Spanish and Portuguese voyages, respectively. Notable studies in legal and institutional history were contributed by José María Capdequi, Javier Malagón, Abel Cháneton, and Julio Alemparte, and in church history by Rubén Vargas Ugarte, Pedro de Leturia, Mariano

Cuevas, José Bravo Ugarte, and Serafim Leite. The last-named and Afonso de Ecragnolle Taunay added new volumes to their works on, respectively, the Jesuits in Brazil and the *bandeirantes* which stand in the front rank of Brazilian historiography in the present generation.

Two multi-volume national histories of unusual merit were carried well on the way towards completion: the cooperative *Historia de la nación argentina* (to 1862), edited by Ricardo Levene, and Francisco A. Encina's *Historia de Chile* (to 1891). Jorge Basadre's *Historia de la República del Perú* and Clarence H. Haring's *The Spanish Empire in America* were the best works on their respective subjects ever published. Ricardo Donoso's short history of Chile since 1833 was a rare combination of courage and scholarship in dealing with recent national history. The roles of Great Britain, France, and the United States in relation to the establishment of Latin American independence were fully and authoritatively described for the first time in books by Charles K. Webster, William S. Robertson, and others. The same can be said of the history of Cuba's relations with the United States and Spain by Herminio Portell Vilá, the history of relations between the United States and Haiti by Rayford W. Logan, the international relations of Toussaint Louverture by Alfred Nemours, and the history of political parties in Uruguay by Juan E. Pivel Devoto.

A philosophical approach was followed, with stimulating results, by Edmundo O'-Gorman in his *Fundamentos de historia de América*. Interpretative essays—long a favorite form of historical writing in Latin America—were well exemplified in this decade by Natalicio González's *Proceso y formación de la cultura paraguaya* and by the books on Mexico by Jesús Silva Herzog and José Vasconcelos, on Uruguay by Alberto Zum Felde, on Peru by Jorge Basadre, and on Colombia and Spanish America at large by Germán Arciniegas. Aspects of Latin America's role in world history were considered afresh in Arnold Toynbee's *A Study of History* and F. S. C. Northrop's *The Meeting of East and West*.

d. *Lacunae*

Yet there still remained many broad lacunae which the historical writing of this decade did little or nothing to fill, and which should be indicated in order to complete the picture. The most conspicuous example is the neglect which most aspects of the history of the past half century continued to suffer. For example, J. Fred Rippy's *Latin America and the Industrial Age*, a valuable though incomplete introduction to that highly important subject, was the only book that dealt with it in a broad way. More explosive political and social questions remained virtually untouched.

Documented studies of the diplomatic history of individual countries, and of the important role of Latin America in international cooperation, were rare. The history of science was just beginning to attract serious attention, mainly in Argentina under the inspiration of an Italian scholar, Alto Mieli, and in France under that of Gonzalo de Reparaz. Contributions to the history of medicine, such as those on Venezuela and Guatemala, were few and far between and were generally confined to professional and technical matters; the only study that attempted to place medical history in a broad social setting was Aristides A. Moll's *Æsculapius* in Latin America.

Demographic studies by George Kubler, Kingsley Davis, Ramiro Guerra y Sánchez, and Gabriel Debien were interesting beginnings that left nearly everything still to be done. In the middle colonial period there were many other aspects as well that still awaited study, and even in the well-worked revolutionary period the same could be said of its economic and social aspects. In addition to all that had been left undone, much that had once seemed well done according to the standards of a generation or two ago would need to be re-examined in the light not only of changing concepts of history and new historical techniques, which historians of Latin America shared with historians in other fields, but also with the aid of the new tools, materials, and other facilities which were of special value for the writing of Latin American history.

5. Tools and Materials

The chief developments of the decade in this respect were the publication of new sources, guides to sources, and bibliographies, and increased use of microfilming. The sources consisted mainly of two types, documents and contemporary accounts. Incidental reference has already been made to important examples of both types (documents on colonial labor in Mexico, and contemporary accounts of the Conquest). Many others of comparable importance could be given, ranging from a treatise by Bartolomé de las Casas and records of *audiencias, cabildos,* and other institutions of the sixteenth century to the *Archivo Santander* and the last volume of Emilio Ravignani's monumental *Asambleas Constituyentes* (Argentina) of the nineteenth century. Sources still unpublished were made somewhat more accessible by such works as Roscoe R. Hill's *Guide to the National Archives of Latin America* and the completion of Rubén Vargas Ugarte's series of guides to Peruvian manuscript materials in European archives. Discoveries of highly important manuscript materials continued to be made; an example is the seventeenth-century "Compendio y descripción de las Indias occidentales," by Antonio Vázquez de Espinosa, in the Vatican Library.

New bibliographical aids were provided, sometimes in special periodicals such as the annuals for Argentina and Brazil. The annual *Handbook of Latin American Studies,* though established shortly before 1939, underwent a number of improvements that probably gave it its greatest usefulness after that date. Similarly, the use of microfilms became more widespread in this decade, but no guide yet existed to the formidable mass of copies of documents in the European archives already accumulated in the United States, Argentina, Mexico, and other American countries.

Among the flood of reprints of "classics" and other old books were many that were valuable as sources, such as early reports, descriptions, autobiographies, and travelers' accounts; the latter enjoyed a great vogue in Brazil. These and other works useful to historians were frequently included in the "libraries" (*bibliotecas*) or series that became a feature of Latin American publishing during this decade. Important new periodicals were the Mexican *Cuadernos Americanos* (devoted only in part to history) and two Spanish journals: *Revista de Indias* (Madrid) and *Estudios americanos,* published by the Escuela de Estudios Hispano Americanos in Seville, an institution which maintained high historical standards despite the political environment in which it had to work. Of the many private firms that made Mexico City and Buenos Aires the chief publishing centers in Latin America, the former's new Fondo de Cultura Económica was outstanding for the volume, variety, and high quality of its publications in the field of Latin American history.

6. Organizations

The principal new organization in this field was the Commission on History of the Pan American Institute of Geography and History, which included Latin American history in its broad purview. This Commission, created when the Institute was reorganized for greater efficiency in 1946, began to function the following year. Besides taking over the *Revista de Historia de América* (founded in 1938), it adopted a program which included the preparation and publication of directories of American historical societies and historians; reports on the preservation of historical monuments, missions to European archives, and the teaching of history; histories of historical writing in each American country; manuals of historical and archival method; and monographs on historical problems of inter-American interest. The vigor and success with which this program was pushed forward under the able leadership of its chairman, Silvio Zavala, promised to make the Commission a most useful agency for promoting the study of Latin American history.

The Pan American Scientific Congress of 1940 and the four International Congresses of Americanists held in the course of this decade in Mexico City, Lima, Paris, and

New York touched upon many subjects of interest to historians of Latin America.

Of the considerable number of new organizations of a national or local character, such as institutes, societies, and museums, unquestionably the most important was the Centro de Estudios Históricos of the Colegio de México (Mexico City). Offering the best training for historians available anywhere in Latin America, the Colegio de México soon attracted students from many other Spanish-speaking countries besides Mexico; it also maintained a high standard in its historical publication program.

7. CONCLUSION

Despite many adverse circumstances, the historiography of Latin America has continued during the past decade the progress which was already under way at its beginning. Most of the handicaps and defects from which it suffered then still exist, but many of them have been considerably diminished, at least in those countries which set the tone and tempo for the rest. In the area where it suffered most during the war —non-Iberian Europe—recovery is already noticeable, particularly in France and England. In many countries there was a general rise in the level of technical proficiency and a broadening and deepening of the concept of history. Interest was keen, new lines of investigation were opened up, and there was an abundance of promising new talent. All in all, considerable progress has been made towards closing the gap between Latin American history and the older and better established fields, and the outlook for continued progress is good.

55. The Tradition of Latin American History in the United States: A Preliminary View*

CLIFTON B. KROEBER

It seems somewhat risky to speak of tradition in a field of historical studies that has existed in the United States for less than half a century. Moreover, until only a short time ago North Americans dedicated to the history of Latin America have been working in relative isolation from one another. At first glance the sum total of their writings does not show an obvious distribution, since their works have covered many different topics and refer to distinct periods of historical time. However, one can show that these historians have maintained certain points of view consistently enough that we can use the word "tradition" to describe their fundamental attitudes toward historical investigation and the focus of it. This is a living tradition, given the fact that it is maintained in even the most recent North American works; it is also a living tradition because some of the men who began to formulate it and maintain it continue writing to this day.

We should like to mention four periods or stages in the development of this living tra-

* *Revista de Historia de América*, 35/36: 21–58 (ene.–dic. 1953). Reprinted by permission of the author and the original publisher. Translated by Editor. Omitted are extensive bibliographical footnotes, by permission of author. [Ed. note]

dition. In the first place are its initiators, that is to say, the historians who wrote before 1900. In the second place, what we may call the period of formation includes those who began to be considered researchers between 1900 and 1920. In the third place is the time between the two World Wars, when the study of Latin American history spread through many universities of the country, and when historical investigation in this field widened its horizons and at the same time deepened the already existing lines of investigation which had been inherited from previous eras. The fourth and final phase consists of current research and the new tendencies which may be noted among the historians of Latin America in the United States. The periods mentioned here may be considered somewhat artificial, but they will serve to illustrate how the elements of a clear and durable tradition have been selected. In discussing these periods we shall attempt to show the basis of the tradition and its duration.

Included in this tradition there are, at the least, three principal characteristics of which the first and perhaps the most notable is the firm base upon which this history rests, as to sources and as to care in interpretation. Original manuscripts are, in fact, the fundamental base of research, as they were a century ago in the hands of William Hickling Prescott. From that point onward historians in the United States have at times gone on to use other original materials: archaeological remains, iconographic materials, and even roadways have been considered as primary sources of information. At times the historians have proposed to uncover and analyze such sources even when they lack systematic training in their use; but today, as specialists in the social sciences in the United States are showing greater interest for historical research on Latin America, the historian has less need to uncover or select the type of information which can be more adequately treated by the archaeologist, the geographer, or some other specialist. Even so, whenever the historian must seek or analyze data not contained in written

testimony, in general he is better able to do so than were his predecessors of half a century ago.

Growing interest in Latin American history on the part of researchers who at the outset were trained in political science, economics, geography, and anthropology reinforces the position of the historian and permits him in a unique manner to note valid methods and points of view which he may use in the solution of the class of problems which customarily he has taken to himself. In this manner, historians in the United States have benefited from this increasing interest on the part of specialists in social sciences; and, in view of the fact that historians still continue to synthesize their own findings, the products of their own criteria and their own discipline, these syntheses more and more are developed in accord with criteria, methods, and points of view from other disciplines. It seems evident, therefore, that historians benefit not only from their established habits of validating primary information obtained from manuscript sources, but also from the stimulus they receive in work done in this field of history by North American and Latin American social scientists.

The second characteristic of this tradition is the breadth with which these researches have been undertaken. North American historians have not limited themselves to a concentration on any one area or period of time. This holds true in general not only for the group, but also for the majority of its component members. This tendency to extend their research through the whole field of Latin American history continues with considerable force to our day. As a tendency, it is opposed to a general movement in other fields of study toward greater specialization. Necessarily at the present time many specialists are orientated toward circumscribed themes, but these same historians try, in contrast, to broaden their intellectual horizons, the better to encompass and understand the development and general process of Latin American history. This second characteristic of the historiography of Latin America in the United States had its roots in the formative period, around 1900 or shortly thereafter.

The third traditional characteristic is a certain detachment, a disinterested attitude which we can suppose might be necessary and proper in those who write about traditions and cultures which differ from their own. This point of view is maintained in works concerning controversial matters such as those related to the nature of the Spanish conquest in native America, the role of the Catholic Church in Latin American history, or the relations between the Latin American nations and the United States. One may suppose that this judicious attitude results less from innate virtue on the part of the historians than from the circumstance that from the outset they have been considered partisans, in small part, of Latin culture and responsible for offering its interpretation to a large Anglo Saxon world not always inclined toward such ideas.

Moreover, it seems that the first North American historians dedicated to the field of Latin American history were for a time under the strong influence of the "scientific" European school and that their rigorous discipline, if not the equally rigid philosophy of history which accompanied it, has been transmitted to their successors.

The brief discussion of these three characteristics constitutes then a primary interpretation of the core of the tradition which is found in the works of my compatriots on Latin American history. The first two of these three characteristics have persisted, because essentially they are constructive; the third has continued to exist because it is the one which permits constructive and imaginative work and thought. Let us now turn to the way in which this tradition was formed.

A point of view and certain technical basis of research clearly appeared in writings which were published long before 1900. Among the most famous authors of that time we should mention the great William Hickling Prescott, whose works are read in the United States not only by historians but by a larger public as well. Thus he is famous

as much for his excellent writing as for his decision to use new manuscript materials, for his translation of important Spanish works, and for his sustained interest in Spanish history as well as Hispanic American.

He and other North Americans of those times did not belong to the same school of historians, nor did they work together in any one part of the country. Henry Harrisse produced one of the best critical bibliographies, a work which merits comparison with the best, as well as other monographs famous in his time. Hubert Howe Bancroft, a rich man aided in his work by various other persons, published a series of volumes which included a *History of Central America* and a *History of Mexico*. But these works, despite the richness of their sources and details, were not the product of the best research methods nor do they represent the most inspired intellectual concepts. They retain, however, great value as works of reference, with indication of a multitude of sources on nearly any theme of investigation.

Bernard Moses, on the other hand, established a high standard in his numerous books and articles written through his long and active career of more than 40 years. Like other investigators of his era he divided his efforts between Spanish and Hispanic American history. We principally recall Henry C. Lea because of his extensive works concerning the Spanish Inquisition, in which he reveals a Protestant and Anglo-Saxon prejudice; he also was the author of many other works, including some on colonial Hispanic American history. His successors assumed responsibility for correcting the tone of his research which otherwise was quite careful. At about the same time, Justin Winsor, another of the encyclopedic researchers, acted as editor of and contributed to a monumental *Narrative and Critical History of America*, which in various volumes expressed the best opinion on colonial Latin American history that the historians in the United States had developed to that point. These volumes also serve as a good indication of how limited United States interest in Latin American history then was. One may hazard the guess that a majority of North Americans considered the period of discovery and conquest in Hispanic America as little more than an adequate prelude to the history of the United States—as, for example, they also wrote in an introductory fashion concerning the redskins before commencing the tale of British colonization of the Atlantic coast. Whether or not this supposition is valid, it is obvious that some of this group of historians at the end of the 19th century took the one necessary step forward and began to investigate colonial Latin American history as such, instead of considering it as a form of introduction to the history of their own country.

Although at this distance it is difficult to draw fine distinctions in these transitions, we can indicate the work of Edward Gaylord Bourne, together with that of Bernard Moses, as the necessary bridge between the older fashion and the new. Of these two, Bourne did not live to continue at the head of an active and young group of historians in this new field of research. After writing (at the close of the 19th century) short studies concerning the period of discovery, in 1904 he published his famous work *Spain in America, 1450–1580*, perhaps the first scholarly book to attempt a general synthesis not only of the discovery and military conquest, but also of economic and political life in colonial Hispanic America. The work of Bourne was based on that of earlier North American historians and on the contemporary works of such others as Woodbury Lowery. Nonetheless, the quality of his *Spain in America* reflects his debt to the best original materials then accessible, and is a monument to his outstanding qualities as an historian.

Bourne had made great efforts to translate basic documents of the period of discovery. Another historian who contributed much to this task was James Alexander Robertson who, young in 1900, survived to be a figure of great influence in the formative period of the historiography of Latin America. Fundamentally, Robertson was, like the others, a researcher of the colonial period. His interest in colonial studies and in the translation of important narrative and accounts lasted many years.

We have now seen that the context of this period, principally the 19th century, contained mixed tendencies. Some of the principal writings still retained a marked nationalistic or religiously sectarian tone. We must credit the historians of the formative period for making use of only the most adequate points of view formulated by their predecessors. The majority of the historians in the 19th century, as we have seen, had limited themselves almost exclusively to the study of the beginning of the colonial period. We suppose that such a fact left a deep impression on the young historians who appeared afterwards, at the beginning of the present century.

The formative period of the 20th century commenced gradually. It is possible that the presence of Moses contributed to the establishment of a new tendency toward the study of the final centuries of the colonial period. Among the young men who orientated the investigation of Latin American history along new lines, we should mention four as examples. These four were not isolated figures, nor were they the only ones to achieve visible results, but they serve to illustrate the principal characteristics of growth of the historic tradition in the United States. It is important to note that they and their contemporaries had different historical training; they worked in various sections of the country distant one from another, and they dedicated themselves to different types of research so far as concerns areas, topics, and distinct time periods. But of equal importance is the fact that we may distinguish in their work similarities of methods, and a common point of view. These men were Clarence Henry Haring, Hubert Eugene Bolton, Isaac Joslin Cox, and William Spence Robertson. All of them have been dedicated to research for more than a generation and all save Bolton are still [1953] alive.

Haring has studied the administrative and economic institutions of the colony and the dichotomy between royal Spanish policy and colonial American reality. Bolton investigated a series of various problems, concentrating on the then little-known history of North American frontiers at the northern end of Spanish power. As early as 1908 Robertson had written his *Francisco de Miranda and the Revolutionizing of Spanish America.* Cox, who had visited Mexican archives even before 1900, took it upon himself to establish a solid base for investigation of the Spanish period in that region which later became the southeast of the United States.

In the various writings of these men and their companions we see how important themes were elicited: Spanish and Portuguese origins of New World institutions; colonial policy and its significance; Indian contributions to civilization, and the new creole characteristics of the population; the greatness of the men of the independence period and the firmness of their aspirations. It is true that the tone of those years a little after 1900 continued to favor colonial studies, but it is important to note that these same researchers went on to occupy themselves with new and distinct historical problems. Haring wrote extensively concerning South American history, and on contemporary affairs. Bolton contributed monographs to anthropological publications, was the author of many books, and soon developed his hemispheric thesis of American history. Robertson has passed a whole life in erudite scholarship culminating in his recent book, *Iturbide of Mexico.*

Their contemporaries wrote histories of equal calibre and during the first and second decades of this century their works appeared in such excessive numbers that it is not possible to mention them here. Much was done to write the history of colonial political and economic institutions; there appeared numerous works in the field of relations between the United States and Latin America; the colonial Spanish regimes in widely separated regions such as Louisiana, California, and Florida, were studied in great detail; important guides on materials in the archives of Spain and Hispanic America were compiled. It was in this time, also when appeared the first of the large and important volumes by Roger Bigelow Merriman, *The Rise of the Spanish Empire in the Old World and the New.*

During this period one of the major achievements was the establishment in 1918 of the *Hispanic American Historical Review,* a journal which was the vehicle for a group of investigators in the United States, constantly increasing in number, who had a common interest in the history of Latin America. Generally speaking, it is clear that in this period of formation the North American investigators occupied themselves either in the colonial or independence periods, or with those problems in the field of the foreign relations of Latin America which had most affected the United States. Although still rather limited as to topics and materials, the erudition of this period clearly demonstrates the characteristics we have indicated for the tradition of Latin American historiography in the United States. Historical studies were based solidly on manuscripts; they showed a knowledge of the many different factors in human history; and, although detailed, seldom failed to work toward a larger synthesis which would show that happenings in Latin America were part and parcel of world history. Finally, they tended to avoid nationalistic or religious prejudices.

In the period between the two World Wars one sees that this example took root. The same historians and a good number of younger ones proceeded to deepen the lines of research already established. But, and this is even more important, they widened the horizon of their research.

A brief selection from among the great number of works which began to appear would include the complementary studies of Lewis Hanke and Lesley Byrd Simpson on socio-economic institutions and policies at the beginning of the colonial period; books and articles on academic and intellectual history by Irving A. Leonard and John Tate Lanning; the diplomatic erudition of Dexter Perkins; studies of Alexander Marchant and others concerning colonial Brazil, and the works of Allan K. Manchester on the history of independent Brazil; the important colonial monographs of William L. Schurz,

Herbert I. Priestley, Charles E. Chapman, and George P. Hammond, among others. Julius Goebel wrote a volume of great merit on the Falkland or Malvinas Islands problem; Alfred Hasbrouck published his *Foreign Legionaires in the Liberation of Spanish South America*; John F. Cady utilized materials from American and European archives in outlining problems of the *Foreign Intervention in the Río de la Plata, 1838–1850*; J. Lloyd Mecham and Mary Watters wrote the earliest North American studies of consequence on the Church in the colonial and national periods of Latin America; Frank Tannenbaum issued the first of his various and well known books on modern Mexico; Charles Nowell established himself as a sharp and critical student of the period of discovery; and the excellent studies by Arthur P. Whitaker on *The Spanish American Frontier, 1783–1795*, and *The Mississippi Question, 1795–1803*, achieved a synthesis of diverse materials in relating the history of imperial rivalries in the frontier region of the Gulf of Mexico. To these John W. Caughey added his model study of *Bernardo de Gálvez in Louisiana, 1776–1783*. There were other works of no less importance during this era, on medieval and modern Spanish history.

As we said previously, some of these studies served to round out spheres of investigation already partly known. Examples would include the work by Priestley on José de Gálvez, various by Whitaker, and the continuing investigations by Bolton on the history of the frontiers. In contrast the monograph by Roland D. Hussey on the Caracas Company opened new lines, and a short volume by Whitaker on the Huancavelica mercury mine indicated new research perspectives for North Americans. Another point of departure was the careful and detailed history by Sumner Welles on the Dominican Republic. This period also brought increasing publication of essential documents; translations of important accounts continued, and bibliographies appeared in greater numbers.

On considering the contribution of this third period of Latin American historiography in the United States it would seem proper again to mention the efforts by these historians to avoid nationalistic, religious, or cultural prejudices. Concerning the Black Legend, a durable myth, the attitude of North American historians was and has been clear, and is patent in the works of Lesley B. Simpson and Lewis Hanke, among others. It suffices to say that the avoidance of that ancient prejudice is always a conscious criterion of North American historians, who today as always are interested in the problem as treated by such distinguished Latin American historians as Silvio Zavala and Edmundo O'Gorman.

On the topic of the Catholic Church in Latin America, the educative work of the Church fathers, and relations between Church and State, a majority of North American historians may take pride in avoiding a partisan religious tone. In fact, for some time now most of the strictly religious histories published in the United States have come from ecclesiastic pens, written by persons educated in North American university seminars, and many of whom are now teaching in Catholic universities in the United States.

One may expect North American writers to provide sincere interpretation of the role of the Church. In addition, as we have seen in this third period, we may expect them to display an intense and responsible sense of comprehension insofar as it is given to them to embrace this delicate topic of historical study.

The long and varied history of relations between the United States on the one hand, and Spain and the Latin American nations on the other, has become popular with North American historians. These writings are too numerous to permit adequate commentary within a brief space. As an example we mention the works of Dexter Perkins on the Monroe Doctrine, written during this period as were others by a number of public figures. At about this time such works began to lose their nationalistic tone, as did those volumes and articles inserted in the periodical press which not only preached the virtues of peace but also of conciliation and sincere friendship with neighboring republics. At times these writings still were marked by strong nationalistic prejudice, but one could note that the intellectual horizon was beginning to come clearer in this respect.

Passing now to the fourth and present period in the development of the Latin American tradition of historiography in the United States, we shall make a brief summary of recent investigations, and mention some of the apparent tendencies in these and in other writings.

During the past ten years colonial studies have been even further strengthened, with attention principally to New Spain. W. Borah has published important contributions, and the fine study by R. S. Chamberlain on the conquest of Yucatán represents only one part of his work in this general field. The new volume by Philip W. Powell concerning the northern advance of the frontier during the second half of the 16th century rests on a long and careful investigation. These books, we should add, represent a positive North American interest concerning New Spain and Mexico, and the cycle of volumes by Carlos Castañeda on the Spanish heritage of Texas is an example of that same interest.

Samuel E. Morison has written a prize book on Columbus, and has dedicated himself to other phases of the same early period. Harold Bierck is author of a study on Pedro Gual and his era. Harris Gaylord Warren has been one of the few North Americans to write a national history of a Latin American republic.

Research by Bailey Diffie has resulted, among other productions of interest, in an extended summary of the colonial period, and a long article on the ideology of Hispanidad. Gerhard Masur's new biography of Bolívar is the first important volume on the Liberator which has appeared in English since that of Víctor Andrés Belaúnde. In the same vein, Harold Davis provided an incomplete but valuable work on the principal currents in the writings of historians and social scientists in Latin America; the principal importance of his book consists in attracting attention of North Americans to

some of the main concepts and philosophic schools current among scholars and literary men of Latin America.

An active interest in relations between the United States and Latin America continues to exist. It is a field of study that now has an extensive literature. But two examples of such works are one by Rayford W. Logan on Haiti, and Dwight D. Miner's competent and well balanced treatment concerning the Panama Canal. Leaving aside for the moment the high level of scholarship which one finds in some of these volumes, perhaps the major advance is in a change of tone, gradual but easily perceptible, in writings by North American scholars who are not specialists in the history of Latin America. It is true that, as always, there yet exist some nationalistic writers in the United States, but it is obvious that the whole environment of scholarship and discussion has undergone an important and constructive change since the end of the 19th century. This tendency also probably originated among the scholars who worked before 1910. In this respect it is important to note that very few North Americans who have chosen to study Latin American history have elected one or more wars as a topic of research.

A great profusion of other studies exists, and old interests are pursued along with the new. Moreover, the larger number of works by men trained in historical disciplines is now being rapidly augmented by the growing number of excellent historical investigations occurring in other fields of study. A great part of such work is of essential value for historians of Latin America. The following examples are only a few selected from among many. Robert Redfield's *Folk Culture of Yucatan* is but one of his several important writings. The same may be said of Melville J. Herskovits' *Life in a Haitian Valley*. Charles Wagley has completed two studies on Guatemala, and the voluminous *Rural Mexico* by Nathan Whetten is of great interest for the historian of recent times.

Those who cultivate historical geography and regional history have made important contributions, combining field work with archival, especially in Mexican history. For many years the most distinguished exponent in this field has been Carl O. Sauer. The recent study of Antioquia by James J. Parsons is, among other things, a work of the highest importance for all historians of Latin America.

At the same time a group of anthropologists of Latin America and of the United States has collaborated in compiling the *Handbook of South American Indians*, in six volumes. Among these writers is John H. Rowe, and in his article concerning Inca culture in the era of the first Spanish conquest he provides us an outstanding example of the significance of this group of volumes for the student of historical problems.

The scholars who are now engaged in writing Latin American history are too numerous to be mentioned individually. Apart from this large and important group there are others who are significantly contributing to the history of literature and literary movements, to the customs and modes of life, to the history of philosophy, and to other aspects of cultural history.

In examining the recent studies mentioned, we note certain well defined tendencies. One of these is the increasing interest in contemporary politics and recent history. The attention which historians pay to publications like the new and vigorous journal, *Inter-American Economic Affairs*, is doubtless an indication of the marked zeal on the part of the historian to understand Latin American cultures of our time.

The same tendency is shown in a more specific focus on other fields of study, and in developing closer relationship with scholars in the other disciplines also interested in studying the history and affairs of Latin America. This closer contact is being brought about these days through establishment of co-operative research institutes and collaborative programs of teaching in universities. Even though the objectives of some of these programs seem to be too elevated, and to require considerable resources, they are of value to the scholar as well as to the student.

For some years historians in the United States have been undergoing a process of re-examination of their methodological and philosophical bases. At the moment it is difficult to say where this process will lead. But the modern historian in the United States seems to be taking into account economic and psychological influences in human affairs, even though the more strictly political ones are those which still enjoy the most favor.

More research is being done on the period following the wars of independence. At the same time, there is a general belief that the period of those wars ought to be re-interpreted in view both of old and new sources and of points of view also old and new. It is true, of course, that the colonial period, and in particular the 17th century and at least part of the 18th, need to be studied much more. But the North American historians of our time appear to be more convinced of the fact that there are large sectors of the independent period about which none of us has knowledge or complete comprehension. It seems safe to prophesy that research in the near future, in the United States, will be occupied principally in re-evaluating various aspects of the independence period, and will fill important gaps in our knowledge of the general history of the Latin American nations.

To point to what seems to have been a constant error of the past and of the present in writings on Latin American history by North Americans, one might first note an inclination to ignore novels, poetry, literary essays, and drama of the period being studied. Such sources offer the historian at least an opportunity to deepen his judgment and give color to his narrative. And if he is to reproduce the mood of the period about which he is writing he should not depreciate the value of such sources and their importance for history. In addition, it is clear that the North American historian very rarely takes into account Latin American philosophic concepts, or those of historians of literature or of art, in formulating his interpretive narrative of historical events. We venture to suggest that Latin America is a part of the world in which the historic sense—

what we might call the conscience of cultural experience—is of great importance and interest to a large circle of intellectuals and aesthetes. We may hope that historical writings of important perception may flow from the pens of those Latin Americans who would not be considered historians in the strict professional sense of that word.

Each of these writings can have a unique value, and, when the student does not take such works into account when developing his interpretation, he will tend for that reason to fall short of the total judgment required of an historian. In fact, it would seem that the greater the care in examination of archival materials, and the more laborious the comparison of specific information, the greater is the obligation of the historian to fulfill his other functions, not the least important of which is to penetrate into the field of concepts and ideas. It matters not whether such concepts be old or new. If the historian is to proclaim that his work is based on a solid pedestal of demonstrated fact, he ought to expose his construction of such facts through an examination of all the ideas which might affect their interpretation. Although our historiography concedes importance to these considerations, one does not find a very profound expression of them in published histories.

Despite such gaps or limitations, it seems quite clear that the traditional inclination of North American historical writings on Latin America has been toward a wider concept and a deeper and more intimate comprehension of Latin American culture. It is possible to repeat concerning this group of historians what John Franklin Jameson said at one time concerning North American historical writing in general, that it was in a state of "vigorous though raw adolescence." That is not to say that the North American students of Latin America have been adolescent from an intellectual point of view, but it does imply that maturity in a field of historical studies usually is established only through efforts of successive groups of mature students.

In order to reach the maturity of which we speak, nothing can be of greater importance for North American scholars than the repeated examples and instruction they may derive from historians in Latin America. The success of Latin Americans in the creation of a new historical literature, and the achievement of important interpretations of their own cultural tradition, are of highest interest in North America, more than they might imagine. We in the United States, if we are to remain at the level of our best historical traditions, will always direct our efforts toward the achievement of the highest accolated: to obtain the respect and approbation of Latin American historians.

56. Latin American Courses in the United States*

JORGE BASADRE

INTRODUCTION

The development of Latin American courses in colleges and universities of the United States can be divided into four periods: (1) the "pioneer period"; (2) the first expansion (1917–32); (3) the second expansion (1933–45); and (4) the present period, which should be one of evaluation and organization toward consolidating the overall program.

As a background for this study a short statement has been included on the long years during which there was a general unawareness in this country of foreign affairs. It has been considered most appropriate in this respect to unearth the remarks written some years ago by the distinguished American scholar, Professor James Shotwell, who on this particular occasion was not only applying his objective sense of historical perspective but also, in a way, reviving the memories of his own boyhood and youth, so different from those which the present generation will cherish in the years to come.

The historical aspects in the shaping of Latin American studies have been condensed in Section I of this paper. Section II is devoted entirely to an analysis of the present situation as it is shown in the detailed information assembled in the bulk of the book.

Many friends have contributed with useful suggestions and have revised the text. Among them, special acknowledgment is here given to Ronald Hilton, Stanford University; Pablo Max Ynsfran, University of Texas; Irving A. Leonard, University of Michigan; William Manger, Pan American Union and Georgetown University; Charles Wagley, Columbia University; Arthur P. Whitaker, University of Pennsylvania; and George Wythe, U. S. Department of Commerce. Some particular pieces of information are acknowledged in the text itself. All of the viewpoints and opinions expressed are the personal responsibility of the writer. Lack of time and the pressure of administrative duties prevented him from treating this subject in a more satisfactory manner. He hopes, however, that this contribution will serve a purpose in that more readers in this country and elsewhere will become aware of the significance of Latin American studies and that it will perhaps stimulate more thorough coverage and treatment of the subject. . . .

PART ONE: THE PAST
The Period of Neglect of Foreign Affairs

The two outstanding facts which have distinguished the early history of this country from that of any other, as Professor James

* Introduction, *Latin American Courses in the United States*. Pan American Union (Washington, 1949), pp. ix–lxxiii. Reprinted by permission of the author.

Shotwell points out, are its size and its isolation. He says:

It is hard today even to imagine how vast to our fathers and grandfathers were both ocean and continent. Even as recently as my own boyhood, prayers were offered in the village church for the safety of those who ventured to cross the Atlantic for a summer's holiday. The engineer has now robbed the sea of its perils and the continent of its distance. But most of those who settled in the wilderness cut themselves off doubly from the old world by the twofold migration of sea and land. Small wonder, therefore, that this nation should have made over into a general doctrine the admonitions of Washington and Jefferson that it should not involve itself in the struggle of the French revolutionary wars, or permit the establishment in this country of the reactionary state system which followed upon the Napoleonic era. Although in the century which followed, these precepts of isolation have not always been kept in mind, they were forgotten only by a generation too busily engaged upon the conquest of the continent to make any serious issue whatever of foreign affairs. It was this conquest of the continent which determined the content of American history, constituting, as it did, one of the greatest stories of achievement in the annals of any nation. As the settlements grew into commonwealths, varying according to their varying environments, the supreme interest of American politics concentrated upon the adjustment of two theories of government and two rival civilizations. This contest between North and South reached from the early decades of the nineteenth century through the Civil War and the era of Reconstruction. With such vital issues dominating the domestic scene, little attention could be paid to the far-away world of Europe. As for the countries beyond the Pacific, practically our only contact with them, after the passing of the clipper ships, was through the missionaries, whom we sent out to save the heathen.

Throughout the whole of the nineteenth century, therefore, American history and outlook remained consistent in its concentration upon home affairs. Nor was this materially changed by the war with Spain, although the acquisition of colonial responsibilities and the demonstration of the place of the United States as a world power gave a new meaning to the old phrase, "manifest destiny." For external interests had still to yield to a more fundamental problem in home affairs, one which proved even more difficult than the conquest of the continent or the elimination of slavery. It was the problem of making democracy efficient.[1]

As the role of the United States in world affairs was slowly shifting during the first part of the century, a definite change was taking place in the curricula of American universities and colleges with considerably more emphasis being placed upon the study of countries. This change was especially evident in the field of Latin American studies which has expanded steadily since that time.

The Pioneer Period

The American contribution to Hispanic studies was small but outstanding more than a century ago, through the work of George Ticknor and William H. Prescott.[2] Prescott, in particular (whose books on the conquest of Peru and Mexico were published more than a hundred years ago and are still used), deserves a testimony of recognition from the scholars of our time. Sometime afterwards, John L. Stephens published his celebrated volumes on Central America and Yucatan which are other acknowledged classics in the field, as are the books of Ephraim George Squier, *Honduras: Descriptive, Historical and Statistical* (1870) and *Peru: Incidents of Travel and Exploration in the Land of the Incas* (1877). When Justin Winsor, Librarian of Harvard University and Corresponding Secretary of the Massachusetts Historical Society, edited his *Narrative and Critical History of America* in eight volumes (1889), the first one was devoted to aboriginal America, Volume II to Spanish explorations and settlements from the fifteenth to the seventeenth century and the eighth volume to the

[1] *Courses on International Affairs in American Colleges, 1930–31*, edited by Farrell Symons, with introduction by James T. Shotwell. Boston, World Peace Foundation, 1931. pp. ix–x.

[2] For earlier relations, see Harry Bernstein *Origins of Inter-American Interest, 1700–1812*. Philadelphia, University of Pennsylvania Press, 1945. For the history of Spanish studies in the United States, see Henry Grattan Doyle, "Spanish Studies in the United States," *Bulletin of Spanish Studies*, Liverpool, Vol. II, 1925.

later history of British, Spanish and Portuguese America.

Apparently the first lectures on the history of South American diplomacy conducted in an American university were given at Columbia College by the labor leader, Daniel de León, during the years 1883–86. "They deal (at least in the manuscript copy) with Brazil and Argentina and their rival policies at the end of the Paraguayan War. He begins in the period of Independence. He lost his position at Columbia in 1886 and blamed the loss upon radical politics."[3]

In 1892 Elizabeth Wallace offered a course on Latin America at the University of Chicago, but failed to awaken enough interest to warrant the continuance of her efforts. In 1900 Frederick Starr, also connected with the University of Chicago, published in the bulletin of the Department of Anthropology, a bibliography on the native languages of Mexico, and in 1908, a description of life and customs among the Indians of southern Mexico. On January 14, 1895, Bernard Moses introduced the subject of "Spanish American History and Institutions" at the University of California where it was destined to endure and develop. Bernard Moses' books subsequently contributed a far wider significance to his efforts than did the classrooms in stimulating vocational interest and spreading a comprehensive appreciation of Spanish American history. These books were *Establishment of Spanish Rule in America* (Putnam, 1908), *South America on the Eve of Emancipation* (Putnam, 1908) and *Spanish Dependencies in South America* (Harper, 1914, 2 vols.).

The Albert Shaw lectures on diplomatic history delivered in 1899 by John H. Latané at the Johns Hopkins University, and the lectures of Hubert W. Brown on Latin America in 1901 at Princeton Theological Seminary were among the early attempts to introduce Latin American subjects in American institutions. Latané was professor of history at Randolph-Macon Woman's College and his lectures were the basis for a book which is mentioned in the list below.

The Young People's Missionary Movement of the United States and Canada published several volumes on Latin America between 1900 and 1912.

The University of Texas, with a permanent course on Spanish colonization, and Columbia University with a course, also permanent, on Hispanic America, joined the "Latin American Movement" in 1904. According to the registrar's records at the University of Texas, that course, conducted by Herbert E. Bolton, was completed by only three students the first year. Later the course was given by William R. Manning who entered the academic field in 1904 and continued to teach until 1919, holding positions in Purdue University, George Washington University and the University of Texas. In 1918 he joined the staff of the Department of State. He was perhaps best known for his work of editing and preparing for publication twenty volumes of documentary materials of the Department of State pertaining to diplomatic relations between the United States and Latin America and Canada.

Dr. William R. Shepherd of Columbia undoubtedly had a guiding influence on many generations because of his sound and realistic interpretation of Spanish American life. Shepherd was a scholar, trained in Germany. He made an important visit to Spain during which he prepared his guide to United States materials in the Spanish archives, published in 1908, and began his close friendship with the Spanish historian, Rafael Altamira. He later became deeply intrigued with Latin America and was appointed an honorary professor of the University of Chile and made a corresponding member of both the Argentine Scientific Society and the National Academy of History of Venezuela. His brief book *Latin America* (Holt, 1918), an example of his keen analysis, was read by

[3] From a letter to the present writer by Harry Bernstein, who has studied the original set of the lecture notes of the course as source material for his new book on inter-American cultural relations. Lewis Hanke has discussed the course of Daniel de Leon in *Hispanic American Historical Review*, August 1936.

thousands and was even mentioned in university catalogues in order to attract future students to this new and fascinating field. Later on he published *The Hispanic Nations of the New World* (Yale University Press, 1919, 1921).

Dr. Leo S. Rowe instilled an interest in Latin American affairs at the University of Pennsylvania. He first became a member of the faculty in 1894 and directed several courses, principally in the field of international law and municipal government. In 1907–08 he offered a course on constitutional government and constitutional guarantees in Latin America at Wharton School. After 1909–10, he discontinued this course on constitutional government and began a course on United States and Latin America which continued until 1916–17. He also taught the same Latin American subjects from 1908–09 to 1916–17 at the Graduate School. In 1908–09 Joseph Russell Smith introduced at both schools the teaching of economic conditions and of resources and industries of South America.[4] Dr. Rowe trained a number of young scholars, including Dana G. Munro, who later achieved distinction in this field. In addition, he found the time to write a book concerning the Argentine Government. Eventually he transferred his activities to other fields, though always within the realm of inter-American relations, and throughout long years as Director General of the Pan American Union, continued to promote goodwill among the Americas in universities in the United States. At his death he willed all of his books relating to Latin America to the School of Foreign Service of Georgetown University, where he had lectured for several years.

Spain in America, by Edward G. Bourne, was published in 1904. This book, unique for its shrewd criticism and stirring conclusions, was the real beginning of a re-evaluation of the work and purpose of Spain in the historiography of the United States and was received very favorably in Spain and in Spanish-speaking countries. A Spanish American history course, introduced at Yale University by Professor Bourne at the beginning of the century, was carried on after

his death in 1909 by Hiram Bingham.[5] This half-year course on the history, geography and diplomacy of South America for both undergraduate and graduate students was continued until 1917 when the course was taken over by Professor C. H. Haring who was in charge until he went to Harvard in 1923 as Robert Woods Bliss Professor of Latin American history; Yale University did not choose to carry on the teaching of the course after his departure.

At Stanford University, Percy Alvin Martin first offered in 1911–12 a two-semester course in the History Department on Spain and Spanish America, and in 1913–14 in-

[4] Information furnished by Leonidas Dodson, Archivist, University of Pennsylvania.

[5] "In 1899 I was a student of Professor Bernard Moses in the Graduate School of the Univ. of California and took his course on Spanish American History, then the only one, so far as I know, in any American university. It led me to adopt that subject as my specialty and I then went to Harvard University to get my Ph.D., hoping to be able to teach it. In conducting the final oral examination for my doctorate, Harvard called in the late Prof. E. G. Bourne of Yale, who had recently started giving a brief course on Spanish Amer. History, to examine me, as no one at Harvard felt competent.

"After securing my doctor's degree I went to Princeton as a Preceptor in History and Politics because no one wanted a teacher qualified to teach Spanish American History!

"After teaching there for a year I secured a year's leave of absence to permit me to go to South America to follow the route of General Simon Bolivar across Venezuela and Colombia to the battle field of Boyaca, which I described in my book 'The Journal of an Expedition Across Venezuela and Colombia,' published by the Yale Univ. Press in 1909. This led to my being offered a chance to teach Spanish American History at Yale. It also led to my visiting Peru as I have set forth in the first chapter of Part 2 of my recent 'Lost City of the Incas,' as you doubtless know.

"On the death of Prof. E. G. Bourne I was asked to carry on his course, which I did, frequently spending six months in South American Exploration while giving half-year courses at Yale on the history, geography and diplomacy of South America, both to undergraduates and graduate students, and occasionally publishing books and articles about South America. These courses were given every year from 1909 until 1917.

"In 1917 I was commissioned in the United States Army as a Lieut. Colonel and was sent to France as a flying officer."—Extract from letter from Dr. Bingham to the writer, July 1949.

stituted a one-semester course on Mexico and California and Brazil. Also in 1912, the Brazilian scholar and diplomat, Manoel de Oliveira Lima, delivered a short series of lectures on Brazil as compared with Spain and Anglo-Saxon America at Stanford University.[6] He later lectured at several other universities and in 1915–16 was a visiting professor of history and economics of South America at Harvard. The lectures of Oliveira Lima, and others offered by Ambassador Joaquim Nabuco, were made possible by President John Casper Branner of Stanford University, a geologist who had spent some years (1874–81) doing research in Brazil and who later undertook three expeditions to the same country (1889, 1907 and 1911). Dr. Branner completed a valuable geologic map of Brazil and published a geologic bibliography and an elementary geology, both in connection with Brazil. He also assembled an outstanding collection of Braziliana which he presented to Stanford University. His interest in the Portuguese language was so profound that he published a Portuguese grammar and translated the book of Alexandre Herculano on the inquisition in Portugal.[7]

In 1910 Professor H. Morse Stephens, Director of the Department of History, University of California, was responsible for the creation of a Fellowship by the Native Sons of the Golden West, a large California fraternity, with the objective of promoting the development of California history. As its history cannot be separated from its Spanish background, the Fellow was sent to the Archivo de Indias in Seville with $1500 per year which, at that time, constituted a large amount of money. Professor Stephens himself had first-hand experience with the resources available in the Spanish Archives during his visit to Spain in 1909–10. Lawrence Palmer Briggs was the first Fellow to benefit from this opportunity and greatly facilitated the efforts of his successors. Charles E. Chapman followed in 1912–14 and became one of the professors of the Department of History of his University. In subsequent years the Fellows of the Native Sons continued visiting Seville and their in-

fluence has been strong in American scholarship. Charles W. Hackett, John Lloyd Mecham and J. Fred Rippy were among those who received the fellowships.[8]

The University of Illinois introduced the course "History of Latin America and the Philippines," in its curriculum in the academic year 1909–10, with Assistant Professor William Spence Robertson in charge.[9]

In 1914–15 Harvard University listed a one-semester course on Latin American history conducted by Assistant Professor Felden Osgood Martin "and other lecturers assisted by Mr. Klein." The latter was Julius Klein, then an instructor in history.

As progress was becoming more evident in the Latin American movement on university campuses, some important books were being published in the United States which contributed in spreading academic interest and understanding in Latin America. On the same general subject as those of Moses, Shepherd and Bourne, previously mentioned, are the following list of books, arranged in chronological order, which

[6] Manoel de Oliveira Lima, *The Evolution of Brazil Compared with that of Spain and Anglo-Saxon America*, edited with introduction and notes by Percy Alvin Martin, Stanford University, California, 1914. See also his *Memorias*, Rio de Janeiro, 1937, p. 164, in which he says: "I learned much more of the U. S. during the two months which I spent there as a lecturer in 1912 visiting twelve universities and in the six months when I was a professor at Harvard in 1915 and 1916 than in the four years when I lived in Washington as Secretary of Legation."

[7] See introduction to Part VI, Brazil, of *Who's Who in Latin America*, 3rd ed., edited by Ronald Hilton. Stanford University, Stanford University Press, 1948.

[8] "The Archives of the Indies: Report of the Native Sons Fellow for November 1912", *Grizzly Bear*, Anaheim, California, XIII, No. 3, July 1913. p. 6. Chapman was also author of the very important *Catalogue of Materials in the Archivo de Indias for the History of the Pacific Coast and the American Southwest*, Berkeley, University of California Press, 1919. For a brief discussion on the Native Sons Fellows see Gonzalo de Raparaz-Ruiz, "Les etudes hispaniques aux Etats-Unit jusqu'en 1939" in *Bulletin Hispanique*, Bordeaux. Extract from Vols. XLVII, 1945, No. 1 and XLVIII, 1946, Nos. 1 and 2.

[9] *University of Illinois Register, 1909–10.*

gained wide reputation during this period:

Bandelier, Adolph F., *The Gilded Man and Other Pictures of the Spanish Occupancy of America* (1893).

Hancock, Anson Uriel, *A History of Chile* (1893).

Latané, John H., *The Diplomatic Relations of the United States and Spanish America* (1900).

Paxson, Frederic L., *The Independence of the South American Republics* (1903).

Dawson, Thomas C., *The South American Republics*. 2 vols. (1903–04).

Lea, Henry Charles, *The Inquisition in the Spanish Dependencies* (1908).

Bandelier, Adolf F., *The Islands of Titicaca and Koati* (1910).

Robertson, William Spence, *The Beginnings of Spanish-American Diplomacy* (1910).

Akers, Charles Edmund, *A History of South America, 1854–1904* (1912). (1912).

Bingham, Hiram, *The Monroe Doctrine, An Obsolete Shibboleth* (1913); *The Possibilities of South American History and Politics as a Field for Research* (1908).

Bishop, Farnham, *Panama, Past and Present* (1913).

Rives, George Lockhart, *The United States and Mexico, 1821–48*. 2 vols. (1913).

Bancroft, Hubert Howe, *History of Mexico* (1914).

Bowman, Isaiah, *The Andes of Southern Peru* (1916).

Priestley, H. I. (ed.), *A Californian in South America* (1917).

The potentialities for translations of Latin American literature and direct contact with Latin American songs were apparently first recognized by Elijah Clarence Hills, of Colorado College, and S. Griswold Morley, of the University of Colorado. They supplied the music, notes and vocabulary for the first book, published in 1913, containing lyrical selections from the poetry of Argentina, Colombia, Ecuador, Mexico, Nicaragua and Venezuela.

South America (New York, 1914) created a widespread interest in this country in spite of the fact that the author, James Bryce, was not an American. This was perhaps a result of his well-known studies on the American commonwealth. Another very useful book by a non-American author is *Latin America: Its Rise and Progress*, by the Peruvian writer Francisco García Calderón, translated from

French to English and published in London in 1913. It is still to be found in some colleges and universities as a reference book.

In 1915 interested readers could also find a series published by Scribner on South America and an analytical bibliography by Peter H. Goldsmith entitled *A Brief Bibliography of Books in English, Spanish and Portuguese Relating to the Republics Commonly Called Latin American, with Comments* (Macmillan); however, no textbook was published until 1919.

Even if anthropological and archaeological activities did not result in the offering of regular courses, they were significant from the point of view of the early development of American scholarly interest in Latin America. Therefore, the books of Daniel Brinton, Professor of American Archaeology and Linguistics at the University of Pennsylvania, on Mexican linguistics (1890 and 1893), the William Pepper Expedition with Max Uhle in Peru for the University of Pennsylvania Department of Archaeology in 1896, whose results were published in 1903, the archaeological research of the Peabody Museum in Yucatan in 1889–91 and in Copan in 1896–97 and the expedition to Peru in 1912 directed by Hiram Bingham under the auspices of Yale University and the National Geographic Society deserve special reference.

Bingham's books describing his trip to South America (*Across South America*, published in 1911 and *In the Wonderland of Peru*, published in 1913) heightened the interest already inspired by his statement on the possibilities of South American history and politics as a field for research and by his book suggesting the need for a new inter-American formula and understanding.

The First Expansion (1917–32)

The first World War, especially after the United States entered the conflict in 1917, was responsible for a complete change of attitude of the American people. An interest was suddenly developed in all studies which related to foreign or international affairs. In the particular case of Latin America, though it was not glamourized by the dramatic happenings surrounding the European scene and its problems of vital and immediate political and economic importance, there were many special events which attracted the attention of the public. A bulletin published by the University of Texas in 1915 and again in 1916 points out the following facts: the opening of the Panama Canal; the Pacific Exposition which took place in Panama; the Pan American Scientific Congress; the cooperation of the countries of the Western Hemisphere in Mexican affairs and the "development of a new Pan Americanism."[10] It is easy to understand how the opening of the Panama Canal greatly increased the opportunities for commerce with Latin America, and with it, the need for a better knowledge and understanding of the language, the economy, culture and the way of life of that continent. The lack of adequately prepared and specialized personnel in the consular and diplomatic staff of the United States, was a source of constant complaint; a similar situation prevailed in commercial firms of this country which found themselves faced with the necessity of employing Germans and "natives."

Furthermore, the study of Latin America seemed particularly remunerative, not only to those who were planning a government career, to lawyers in the service of manufacturing and commercial enterprises, to employees of export firms, branch banks and other agencies recently established in this continent, but also to engineers, doctors, missionaries, university professors, school teachers, and in general, to all those who simply wished to be adequately informed in order to discuss Latin America with intelligence. As a result of the first World War a large part of Latin America's former trade with Europe was transferred to the United States. This augmentation in inter-American commerce created the illusion in this country that Spanish-speaking American citizens could make a fortune in Latin America. Therefore, Spanish language courses rapidly increased in number and Hispanic studies in general were stimulated.

The teaching of languages and literature

at Yale University has been linked with the life and work of Frederick B. Luquiens, who from 1906 was professor of Spanish and other subjects. In the Graduate School he taught Spanish American literature and poetry from 1917 until his death in 1940. He was professor of Spanish American literature at Yale College in 1928, and from 1930 until his death he was Curator of Latin Americana of the Yale University Library. Professor Luquien's method of teaching Spanish was famous because it included the basic requirements that: (1) the teacher must use only Spanish in the classroom and must insist that the students do likewise; (2) the study of grammar must be rigorously insisted upon and tested frequently by short written examinations; and (3) literature must not be taught before the student attains fluency in the use of the language. As a result, Yale was the first, and for a long time the only, college to have international debating teams competing in their own language with students from other countries.

By 1917 the Universities of Colorado, Notre Dame and North Carolina, Brown, Indiana and Northwestern Universities and Goucher College,[11] had added to their subjects the study of Latin American history. It was for the encouragement and development of that study that a new journal, the *Hispanic American Historical Review* was first published in 1918 under the editorship of Dr. James A. Robertson. This journal was suspended in 1922, revived in 1926, and has been published continuously since the latter date under the successive editorship of James A. Robertson, John Tate Lanning, James F. King and (beginning this year [1949]) Charles C. Griffin.

Professor William W. Sweet of DePauw University was responsible for the first English-language college textbook relative to Latin America, published in 1919. The vol-

[10] *Bulletin of the University of Texas* No. 38, July 1915, and No. 43, August 1916.

[11] "Report of a Committee of the Pan American Union on the Teaching of Latin-American History in Colleges, Normal Schools and Universities of the United States," *Hispanic American Historical Review*, August 1927.

ume was entitled *A History of Latin America* and for three years was the only textbook available. The second textbook, written by Professor William Spence Robertson of the University of Illinois, *A History of the Latin American Nations,* was first published in 1922 and received several revisions in successive editions. In 1923 the third textbook, *The Republics of Latin America,* appeared. The authors were Professor H. G. James of the University of Texas and Professor Percy Alvin Martin of Stanford University. In 1924 the first high school text in the Latin American field, written by Professor Hutton Webster of the University of Nebraska, appeared under the title *A History of Latin America.* The first book to supply students with source material acceptable for supplementary textbooks and lectures was *Readings in Hispanic American History,* published in 1927 by Professor N. A. N. Cleven of the University of Pittsburgh. In the decade of the thirties a much larger selection of textbooks became available, beginning in 1930 with the very popular but thorough work of Professor Mary W. Williams of Goucher College, entitled *The People and Politics of Latin America.* Of considerable significance at that time also was *A Syllabus of Latin-American History,* by William Whatley Pierson, Jr., Assistant Professor of History, University of North Carolina, with editions in 1916, 1917 and 1926. The last edition, published when he was a full professor, was larger and more complete.

A symposium on the teaching of Spanish America in educational institutions of the United States published in 1918 was an excellent example of the increased interest and enthusiasm in this field.[12] Seven years later the initiative for a more comprehensive survey on the subject same from Dr. Leo S. Rowe in a letter to the American Historical Association on October 29, 1925. The proposal was accepted and a special committee was created, with Professor William Spence Robertson as chairman. At the end of January, 1926, a questionnaire accompanied by a circular letter from Dr. Rowe was sent out by the Pan American Union to 1172 educational institutions listed in the 1925 Direc-

tory of the Bureau of Education. The results of the survey showed that 175 of the higher institutions of learning included courses on Latin America in their curricula. These courses ranged from a general overall review of the subject matter to seminar courses on problems of special interest for advanced studies. Forty other colleges and universities reported that they had offered such courses at one time or another but had discontinued them for the time being. The University of California manifested the largest enrollment in Latin American courses. The texts most frequently used in introductory courses were as follows: James and Martin, *The Republics of Latin America;* Robertson, *The History of the Latin American Nations;* Shepherd, *The Hispanic Nations of the New World;* and Sweet, *History of Latin America.* In teacher-training schools Webster's *Latin America* was used considerably in addition to the texts mentioned in the above list. The committee finished its report by stating that the great variety of courses offered could indicate either that they were adapted somewhat to local circumstances, or that the subject had not yet found its proper place in the curriculum. At the same time, the committee pointed out that the steady development of interest in this subject in the United States, "indeed encourages the hope that leading educational institutions cannot much longer neglect to readjust their library and teaching facilities so as to give attention to the history of our southern neighbors."[13]

During the decade between 1920 and 1930 events were taking place, agencies were being established and books were being published which constantly encouraged, directly and indirectly, the interest of the American academic-world in Latin America. For instance, Isaac Goldberg published his *Studies in Spanish American Literature* in 1920, followed by his *Brazilian Tales* (Boston, 1921) and *Brazilian Literature* (New York, 1922). Also in 1920 the American Associa-

[12] The symposium with syllabi of courses was published in the *Hispanic American Historical Review,* August 1919.
[13] *Op. cit.,* Footnote 11.

tion of Teachers of Spanish, the Junta Para Ampliación de Estudios of the Spanish Ministry of Public Instruction, the Institute of International Education and several Spanish and American universities founded the Instituto de las Españas with headquarters at Columbia University. A quarterly review of Spanish studies (*Revista de Estudios Hispánicos*) was published by the Instituto until the spring of 1929 under the joint sponsorship of the Romance Language Department of Columbia University, the University of Puerto Rico and the Center of Historical Studies of the University of Madrid. The Instituto is still functioning as the Hispanic Institute in the United States and publishes the outstanding journal *Revista Hispánica Moderna*. The purpose of the Institute is to promote the study of Spanish and Portuguese languages and Hispanic American culture and history, and under its auspices prominent persons of Iberian and Hispanic American origin lecture in the United States.

Immediately before his death in 1928 Oliveira Lima lectured on the subject of international law at Catholic University. He presented his library, with all of its bibliographical treasures, to that university. Toribio Esquivel Obregón, well-known as a jurist and professor in Mexico, gave a series of discourses pertaining to Latin American commercial law at Columbia University during the twenties. Peter H. Goldsmith, previously mentioned in connection with his bibliography, published the *Inter-America* until his death in 1926. This magazine was unusual in that its English edition contained articles written by Hispanic Americans while its Spanish edition, translated for the benefit of Hispanic American readers, contained articles written in the United States.

In 1930 the Pan American Union announced that 34 additional colleges and universities had increased to 209 the number of institutions offering courses in the Latin American field, with a total number of 434 courses.[14]

Another survey, conducted in 1930–31 by the World Peace Foundation, independent of the Pan American Union, of courses relating to international affairs in American colleges, showed a total of 3,720 courses. Of these, the largest number (689) were on Europe, 518 on the British Empire, 436 on United States foreign relations in general, 425 on national governments and 328 on international economy. The total number of college courses on Latin America was smaller (286) but surpassed the number of courses offered on the Far East, Asia and Africa, contemporary history, international law, international organization, the World War and others.[15] It must be remembered that courses on literature and on culture in general and those of a miscellaneous character were excluded from this survey.

Of the courses mentioned by the Pan American Union in 1930, 214 were on history; 95 on literature; 34 on diplomatic relations; 18 on trade conditions; 9 on government and institutions; and 35 had a miscellaneous character. Among the latter, two were on geology, one on climatology and one on archaeology. There were others on commercial Spanish, intended for those interested in trading with Latin America, and two courses were called "Our Neighbors." Lastly, there were two courses on social problems and one isolated course on culture. Some of these courses consisted only of conferences or lectures on the various aspects of Latin American life. One of the 34 courses on international relations carried the controversial title "North American Imperialism."

Latin American studies had by 1930 made notable progress on the West Coast. Stanford was offering 10 courses; Southern California, 9; California, 6. In the History Department at Stanford, Percy Alvin Martin taught an introductory course and a seminar; Graham H. Stuart conducted the course on international law, and Chester Rowell was in charge of contemporary international relations. At the same time Stanford offered the greatest number of courses on Spanish American literature, for which Al-

[14] *Survey of Latin American Courses in American Colleges & Universities.* Washington, Pan American Union, 1930, mimeographed.
[15] *Op. cit.* Footnote 1.

fred Coester, author of *The Literary History of Spanish America* (1916), was directly responsible. There were two other subjects of a general literary nature, one course on the modernistic movement and another on Argentine literature, and one seminar.

At this time George P. Hammond, Orwin W. E. Cook and Clayton Douglas Carus were teaching at the University of California at Los Angeles in the Departments of History, International Relations and Political Science, and Trade and Transportation, respectively. These same men were also teaching at the International Relations University of Los Angeles. Roland Dennis Hussey was Assistant Professor of Latin American History at the University of California, Los Angeles, in 1930 and later became a full professor at that university. At Berkeley there was already a group of historians. Herbert E. Bolton achieved international renown with his *History of the Americas*, destined to give a fuller and more coherent view of the formation of both Anglo and Latin America. This influence was definitely felt at Northwestern University and as far away as Hawaii. Charles E. Chapman dedicated his efforts to a general survey on Spanish American history and to the ABC countries (Argentina, Brazil and Chile) and Herbert I. Priestley devoted his time to the history of Mexico.

In the Southwest the University of Texas continued in 1930 to hold a dominant position. A special course on Latin American resources and trade conducted by A. P. Winston, replaced general courses which originated in 1916 on resources and commerce with merely occasional emphasis on Latin America. In the School of Government of the University of Texas there were already two courses under the direction of John Lloyd Mecham on governments of Latin America and on inter-American relations. One general course on Latin American history had been started at Texas by Herbert E. Bolton and William Ray Manning. Charles W. Hackett was the real leader in this course of study at Texas and is one of the few survivors of the first generation of Latin American professors to whom we are so deeply indebted for the development of this field. He

first taught at the University from 1918 to 1920 in European history. In 1920 he became an Assistant Professor and devoted two-thirds of his time to Latin-American history; in 1923 he was raised to an Associate Professor but his time was still divided. In 1925–26 he was visiting lecturer in Latin-American history and economics at Harvard University, and in 1926, was promoted to a full professor in history at Texas with full time given to Latin-American history. He is still [1949] serving in this capacity.

Among the universities of the South, North Carolina, Duke and Miami have taken an active part in the organization of Latin American studies in this country. At North Carolina, William Whatley Pierson, one of Shepherd's best Columbia students, was active in the range of Latin American activities. J. Fred Rippy was doing outstanding work at Duke University and at that time had already published his books, *The Historical Background of the American Policy of Isolation* (1924), *The United States and Mexico* (1926), *Latin America in World Politics* (1928), *American Policies Abroad —Mexico* (1928), *Rivalry of the United States and Great Britain over Latin America* (1929) and *The United States and Colombian Oil* (1929). Earl J. Hamilton, also at Duke University in 1930, was Professor of Economics and it was at that time or immediately after that he conducted his research work in Spanish, French, Belgian and Italian Archives. In 1934 his book, *American Treasure and the Price Revolution in Spain—1501–1650*, appeared. John Tate Lanning was then history instructor at Duke University and has continued with this university, becoming one of the most respected scholars in the cultural history of colonial Spanish America. The Duke University Press has been publishing the *Hispanic American Historical Review* continuously since 1926. The University of Miami was then a young and relatively undeveloped university, but its Latin American studies, consisting of eight courses, had been instigated by the action of two South American professors, Victor Andrés Belaúnde and Rafael Belaúnde.

In New Orleans, Tulane University, with Newcomb College, and Loyola University formed a remarkable group. The Department of Middle American Research at Tulane was established in 1924 and later became the Middle American Research Institute which will be discussed more freely in another part of this introduction.

In the central states the University of Chicago and Northwestern University each with eight courses, Oklahoma with seven and Wisconsin with six, occupied the leading positions. Particularly influential at Chicago during the twenties were courses offered by the Mexican, José Vasconcelos, who had an outstanding command of the English language and, at that time, had the prestige of his recent campaigns as Minister of Education in his country. The Middle West was credited with men of such renown as Arthur S. Aiton of the University of Michigan, known for his book on Antonio de Mendoza, first Viceroy of Mexico (1927); Preston James, also of Michigan; Isaac J. Cox, of Northwestern, a prominent Latin American historian throughout the greater part of this period; Hayward Keniston, Chicago, whose work has been for the most part in the field of Spanish literature and in the field of bibliography of Spanish American history; Chester Lloyd Jones, Department of Economics, and Ray Hughes Whitbeck, Department of Geography, University of Wisconsin; William Spence Robertson, University of Illinois; David R. Moore, Oberlin College; and Fred A. Carlson, Department of Geography, Ohio State University. Herman James, author (with Percy Alvin Martin) of the book *The Republics of Latin America*, previously mentioned, and later of the *Constitutional System of Brazil* (1923) and *Brazil after a Century of Independence* (1925), was President of the University of South Dakota during the period 1929–34.

The East was less developed at the beginning of the thirties, in terms of the number of courses on Latin America listed, than were the West and Middle West, in spite of the ten courses offered at Columbia. Shepherd had already made his pathfinding contribution. In 1930 a Latin America-minded undergraduate student at Columbia could take his choice of a course on Pan American relations under Samuel Guy Inman, even then a veteran in the inter-American field; a course on contemporary Latin America under Paul Vanorden Shaw; a course on geography and economic geography of Latin America given by Louis A. Wolfanger or of several courses in the field of literature conducted by the Spaniards, Federico de Onís and Angel del Río. Another noteworthy professor of Latin American subjects in this period with original contributions in the somewhat neglected field of the social sciences was Frank Tannenbaum, though he did not make his appearance at Columbia until 1935, after having commenced his professional career in 1932 at Cornell in the Department of Economics. Clarence H. Haring succeeded in enhancing the respect felt for Harvard with his courses on the history and facts of present-day Latin America (one course of a general character and one on research); two additional courses given by him dealt with the history of the Republic of Mexico and the history of the ABC countries. The latter was listed in the 1930 catalogues of the Universities of California and Southern California. By 1930 Dana G. Munro had become prominent in the Latin American field, as author of a book on the five republics of Central America in 1918 and for his work with the Department of State. In 1932 he went to Princeton to teach and has remained there until the present. In the Department of History at Cornell University a young professor destined to be a leader in this field, Arthur P. Whitaker, offered a course entitled "Latin America Since 1760"; later (1936) Whitaker transferred to the University of Pennsylvania where he is presently [1949] professor of Latin American history. In the Department of Political Science of both the College and the Wharton School of Finance and Commerce of the University of Pennsylvania, courses on Latin American relations with the United States were given in 1930 by Harry Thomas Collings, economic geography of Latin America was taught by Frank Ernest Williams and Latin American and

Canadian history were included in two courses by Roy F. Nichols. At Clark University, Clarence F. Jones was Professor of Economic and Commercial Geography between 1928 and 1942.

In the Washington, D. C., area in 1930 George Washington University was outstanding for a general course, a pro-seminar and the seminars of Alva Curtis Wilgus, another hard-working pioneer in Latin American studies. In 1930 J. D. Siqueira Coutinho followed the lead of Oliveira Lima at Catholic University and offered a course on the political history of Latin America. At the School of Foreign Service of Georgetown University a course on political and diplomatic history of Latin America was offered by William Manger which served as preparation for an economic survey course on Latin America and advanced courses on outstanding problems in Latin American relations by Rowe and Manger and the Portuguese-Brazilian seminar of Siqueira Coutinho. The Walter Hines Page School of International Relations of Johns Hopkins University was an active center of research and many of its numerous publications were particularly interesting to the Latin American countries. The Johns Hopkins studies in historical and political science and the Albert Shaw lectures on diplomatic history, given in the Department of History by well-known professors, were also worthy of note in this period. In 1935 Isaiah Bowman was elected president of Johns Hopkins University. He is known as one of the more important American authorities in geography and author of several books on South America, such as *South America* and *The Andes of Southern Peru*, already mentioned, *The New World Problems in Political Geography* (1921) and *Desert Trails of Atacama* (1923). Goucher College offered the Mary Wilhelmine Williams course.

The Second Expansion

As has already been pointed out, by 1930 almost every university of any consequence in the United States had already begun to offer courses on Latin America, consisting of history, international relations, literature,

geography and other subjects. During the period from the close of the depression up to the time the United States entered the second World War inter-American activities were sufficient to promote an "inflation" within the Latin American field. The "Good Neighbor Policy" had been put into effect; Latin America for the first time was showing real warmth toward Pan Americanism; millions of dollars were spent in an effort to promote hemispheric understanding; individuals, groups and institutions in the United States, which formerly had shown indifference toward their neighbors to the south, suddenly became "hemisphere conscious"; a literary trend became apparent which was striving to find common or similar roots in both Americas.

Meanwhile, Latin America was looking on at the increasing tension of life in Europe: the Civil War in Spain uprooting the spiritual and intellectual life of that country; the fall of France which caused the interruption of a deep and old friendship; and the combined threat of a nazified Europe and Japanese imperialism. At the same time, the turn of events in Europe in 1933 and the first effects of the war in 1939 contributed, over a period of time, whether consciously or sub-consciously, to an attitude of "hemispheric isolationism" in some sections of the United States. At any rate, Latin America was "in fashion." Travelling citizens arriving from that continent, the writer for instance, can recall observations and experiences in the United States, first in 1930 and later in 1940, and the difference which existed between the two periods.

Some of the more obvious expressions of this Latin American "wave," which reached its climax during the period of 1940–41, are outlined in the following paragraphs. They are significant in that they clearly define that particular period and because of their relation to studies at university and college level, which were stimulated either directly or indirectly by these events.[16] No attempt

[16] Lewis Hanke deals with this subject from a scholarly point of view in his article "The Development of Latin American Studies in the United States, 1939–45" in *The Americas*, July

has been made to list the events in order of priority.

(1) An Official Cultural Policy.—The first concrete demonstration of interest, of an official nature, relative to the problems of cultural relations between the Americas, is found in the "Convention for the Promotion of Inter-American Cultural Relations" which was approved at the Inter-American Conference for the Maintenance of Peace, held in Buenos Aires in 1936. This convention and seven others were ratified by the United States Senate in June of the following year. Immediately following these ratifications, and perhaps of greater importance, was the "Departmental Order" of July 27, 1938, which created, at the Department of State, the Division of Cultural Relations, as had been determined by Congress a month before.[17]

This Division indicated its aims in the official order of July, 1938, and though these objectives had vast international scope, they were in reality largely concentrated on Latin America. It said in part:

The Division will have general charge of official international activities of this Department with respect to cultural relations, embracing the exchange of professors, teachers, and students; cooperation in the field of music, art, literature, and other intellectual and cultural attainments; the foundation and distribution of libraries of representative works of the United States and suitable translations thereof; the preparations for and management of the participation by this Government in international expositions in this field; supervision of participation by this Government in international radio broadcasts; encouragement of a closer relationship between unofficial organizations of this and of foreign governments engaged in cultural and intellectual activities; and generally, the dissemination abroad of the representative intellectual and cultural works of the United States and the improvement and broadening of the scope of our cultural relations with other countries.

In order to carry out its program, the Division required and often obtained the cooperation of universities and organizations, such as the Carnegie, Guggenheim and Rockefeller Foundations, as well as other agencies and private groups and individuals.

The Inter-Departmental Committee on Cooperation with the American Republics, the membership of which was comprised of representatives of thirteen agencies of the United States Government, was established in Washington in May, 1938, for the purpose of outlining a definite program designed to increase the effectiveness of friendly relations between the people of the United States and its government and their neighbors of the Latin American republics.[18]

The Office of the Coordinator of Commercial and Cultural Relations, was created in August, 1940, with a title which was later changed to "Office of the Coordinator of Inter-American Affairs" (CIAA). Within the extensive and complex work which was accomplished by the CIAA[19] there are some aspects which are directly related to the present study and to which reference will be made later. In 1946 the functions of this office were taken over by the Office of International Information and Cultural Affairs of the Department of State, formerly known as the Division of Science, Education and Arts, and which, in turn, was originally the Division of Cultural Relations.

(2) Special Funds for the Development of Academic Studies Connected with Latin America.—A subsidy was granted by the legislature of the State of New Mexico for a School of Inter-American Affairs at the

1947. The section on cultural relations of *Inter-American Affairs*, an annual survey, 1942–45, with Arthur P. Whitaker as editor and Columbia University Press as publisher, also gives valuable information. Particularly interesting and still up to date are the comments of William Rex Crawford in the 1942 issue, p. 97–130. Gonzalo de Raparaz offers a comprehensive survey of this period in his study "Les etudes hispaniques aux Etats-Unis jusqu'en 1939" in *Bulletin Hispanique*, before mentioned.

[17] *Progress Report of the Division of Cultural Relations.* Department of State, Washington, 1940.

[18] *Report of the Inter-Departmental Committee on Cooperation with the American Republics, together with the Program of Cooperation endorsed by the Committee*, Press Release, Department of State. Washington, Nov. 29, 1938.

[19] Donald Rowland, *History of the Office of the Coordinator of Inter-American Affairs*, Chapter VIII "Cultural and Educational Activities." Washington, 1947.

University of New Mexico. The Rockefeller Foundation and the CIAA gave financial aid to the North American Institute of Michigan for Future Teachers of the English Language in Latin America (now known as the English Language Institute). The CIAA helped the Law Institute under the auspices of Tulane and Louisiana State Universities. The "Latin American Artist in Residence of the Institute at the University of New Mexico" was financially supported. These are only a few of the many instances which could be cited here, but it is impossible to list them all in this introduction.

The Universities of Texas, Chicago, and California, and Harvard University and the Massachusetts Institute of Technology were assisted by the CIAA in arranging lectures, round-table discussions and courses which emphasized Latin American subjects. A special "Summer School" at the University of North Carolina in the winter of 1941 was organized for a group of students from the American republics, other than the United States. An institute for the intensive teaching of Spanish and Portuguese was held in 1941 at the University of Wyoming and in 1942 (devoted to Portuguese alone) at the University of Vermont, under the direction of Dr. William Berrien. Specially designed summer programs known as "Inter-American Workshops" were organized in cooperation with twenty-five colleges and universities for the purpose of training elementary and secondary teachers in the inter-American field.[20] Through the United States Office of Education, CIAA provided inter-American educational consultants w h o toured the workshops, teacher training colleges and other agencies. The American Council of Learned Societies (ACLS) Committee on Latin American Studies sponsored Latin American institutes at the University of Michigan (1939) and at the University of Texas (1940).[21]

(3) GRANTS FOR THE PURCHASE OF BOOKS AND MANUSCRIPTS FOR UNIVERSITIES.—Again it is impossible to enumerate each and every case in the brief space of this paper; however, an example is the grant made by the Rockefeller Foundation in 1940 to the Uni-

versity of North Carolina, and Duke and Tulane Universities for the purchase of books on Latin America. The grant given to North Carolina amounted to $25,000 annually for a five-year term, with the understanding that this university would specialize in Argentina, Chile, Paraguay, Uruguay and Venezuela. The CIAA also helped in the purchase of books, manuscripts, copies of manuscripts and occasionally in the purchase of color slides, as occurred at the University of Texas. Shortly before this the WPA assisted the Bancroft Library at Berkeley with the production of documentary historic films on Latin America.

This increase and strengthening of library and archival resources in connection with Latin America had a definite effect on the scholarship in this field.

(4) THE LIBRARY OF CONGRESS AS A SPECIAL AGENCY.—On its own initiative but with substantial aid from private sources, the Library of Congress instituted in 1939 its Hispanic Foundation which has since served as a focal point for the Library's interest in Latin American studies. In 1944, the Library established a Chair of Latin American Studies. One of its many contributions was the enlargement of its collection of books and journals related to Latin America which are available for use by scholars and students. With the help of the Inter-Departmental Committee on Scientific and Cultural Cooperation, the Library undertook the compilation of a series of basic bibliographies in art, law, music and official documents and established the photographic Archive of Hispanic Culture.[22]

(5) AGENCIES SPECIALIZING IN THE FIELD OF INTER-AMERICAN INTELLECTUAL COOPERA-

---

[20] Henry Grattan Doyle, "Practical Inter-Americanism: The Work of the Washington Inter-American Training Center," *Bulletin of the Pan American Union*, August 1944.

[21] Regarding the Institute of Texas, see the address by Charles W. Hackett on "The Proposed Institute of Latin American Studies at the University of Texas," in *The State and Public Education*, Austin, The University of Texas, May 22, 1940.

[22] *The Hispanic Activities of the Library of Congress*. Washington, 1946.

TION.—*The Study of International Relations in the United States,* by Edith E. Ware, is a 1937 survey prepared by the American National Committee on International Intellectual Cooperation which lists the following groups of organizations within the United States that were at that time endeavoring to promote cultural relations with Latin America.

a) Semi-business associations.

b) Religious groups, such as the Committee on Cooperation in Latin America, organized to interpret Latin American situations to Protestant groups in the United States.

c) Organizations within or affiliated with the university world such as Instituto de las Españas with headquarters at Columbia University; the Committee on Library Cooperation with Latin America of the American Library Association; the Latin American Division of the Institute of International Education; the Committee "L" of the American Association of University Professors, mainly interested in the interchange of professors and grant of fellowship for inter-American institutions; and the ACLS committee appointed in 1933 and again in 1935 under the direction of Clarence H. Haring.

d) Societies which promote international understanding through cultural intercourse, notably the Committee on Cultural Relations with Latin America, an organization made up of a group of American liberals headed by Hubert Herring.

e) Various activities of the Carnegie Endowment for International Peace.[23]

An outgrowth of the ACLS committee was the Joint Committee on Latin American Studies in cooperation with the ACLS, the National Research Council and the Social Science Research Council, which lasted from 1942 to 1947; Professor Robert Redfield served as chairman of this committee for the first two years. As is discussed later in this paper, this Joint Committee marked the beginning of the so-called "area study approach" because it represented various cooperating agencies and fields.

(6) BOOK EDITIONS.—This subject alone

requires much consideration; however, we may mention a few types of books:

a) *Bibliographies.* Outstanding among these is the *Handbook of Latin American Studies* which was first published in 1936 by the Committee on Latin American Studies of the ACLS. In 1945 the Library of Congress assumed the responsibility for its preparation, in cooperation with forty-odd specialists who serve as contributing editors. Other bibliographical contributions were made by Gilbert Chase regarding music (1945); by Carlos E. Castañeda and Jack Autry Dobbs concerning manuscripts at the University of Texas Library (1939); Frederick B. Luquiens on Spanish American literature in the Yale University Library (1939); Sturgis E. Leavitt and Madaline W. Nichols on materials on American Spanish (1940); Donald Pierson regarding Brazilian literature of sociological significance published up until 1940 (1945); C. K. Jones on the bibliography of Latin American bibliographies (revised edition, 1942).

Some bibliographical investigations were conducted directly by university research institutes working in the Latin American field. The Bureau for Economic Research in Latin America of Harvard University, for example, prepared a two-volume book with the title *Economic Literature of Latin America: A Tentative Bibliography*, which was published in 1935 and 1936. A Harvard Hispanic American studies group had started, in 1931, the twenty-volume *Bibliographies of Hispano-American Literature* in the Spanish and English, which was completed in 1935.

b) *Guides and reference works.* The second revised edition of Percy Alvin Martin's *Who's Who in Latin America* published in 1940 and the third revised and enlarged edition of the same work edited by Ronald Hilton for Stanford University Press; the *Handbook of Hispanic Source Materials and Research Organizations in the United States,*

[23] Edith E. Ware, ed. *The Study of International Relations in the United States: Survey for 1937.* New York, Pub. for the American National Committee on International Intellectual Cooperation by Columbia University Press, 1938. p. 204–222.

also by Ronald Hilton; the guide *The National Archives of Latin America* by Roscoe R. Hill; the *Directory of Statistical Personnel in the American Nations* and the survey *Statistical Activities of the American Nations, 1940*, prepared by the Inter-American Statistical Institute, are some of the many books and pamphlets which fall into this category.

The Pan American Union was instrumental in the publication of some guides and reference books in this field; among them the following should be mentioned: *Source Material and Special Collections Dealing with Latin America in Libraries of the United States*, by A. Curtis Wilgus (1934); *Theses on Pan American Topics Prepared by Candidates for Degrees in Universities and Colleges in the United States* (1933), *Latin American Studies in American Institutions of Higher Learning* (1936, 1940).

c) *Translations.* Numerous translations of Spanish American and Brazilian literature were carried out by private publishers with or without outside assistance.

d) *Teaching materials.* The American Council on Education appointed a committee, under the chairmanship of Arthur P. Whitaker, for the study of teaching materials on inter-American subjects. The committee selected a number of specialists who prepared a critical analysis of the treatment of Latin America in books at all levels.[24]

In 1941 the Pan American Union initiated an Editorial Project which involved close cooperation with the leading music publishers and publishers of music textbooks in the United States. This Project resulted in the publication by the United States publishers of approximately 200 pieces of Latin American music which are widely used throughout the United States, particularly in the schools. An important result of the Project was the virtual ending of piracy of Latin American rights in music by United States publishing interests. Favorable royalties for Latin American composers were obtained and copyrights of Latin American publishing houses were protected.

e) *Textbooks.* Many editions and revised editions of textbooks were found necessary. Several among them were, of course, the results of previous research. The following list of books is given in the survey which was conducted under the auspices of the American Council on Education:

Geography of Latin America, by F. A. Carlson (New York, 1936).

Colonial Hispanic America and *Republican Hispanic America*, by C. E. Chapman (New York, 1936).

A History of Latin America, by D. R. Moore (New York, 1938).

Outline History of Latin America, by A. Curtis Wilgus and Raul d'Eca (New York, 1939).

The Development of Hispanic America, by A. Curtis Wilgus (New York, 1941).

Latin America, by William L. Schurz (New York, 1941).

Latin America, by Preston James, (New York and Boston, 1942).

Economic Geography of South America, by R. H. Whitbeck, revised by F. E. Williams and W. F. Christians (New York, 1942).

The Latin American Republics, by Dana G. Munro, (New York, 1942).

The Latin American Policy of the United States, by Samuel Flagg Bemis, (New York, 1943).

Outline History of Spanish American Literature by E. Herman Hespelt and others (New York, 1941), was not included in this survey but belongs to the same period.

The *Inter-American Historical Series*, published by the University of North Carolina Press, was commenced as a one-volume translation of national histories of the Latin American nations under the general editorship of James Alexander Robertson. The first volume of the series, Levene's *History of Argentina*, was published in 1937, and was followed by volumes on Brazil, Colombia and Chile.

f) *Other books.* Popular or travel books which sought to attract the attention of the public in general are also included in this group. They were, however, too often light and inexact in character.

(7) INTER-AMERICAN CONGRESSES, INSTITUTIONS AND SPECIAL PROJECTS. — The

[24] *Latin America in School and College Teaching Materials.* Washington, D. C., American Council on Education, 1944.

Eighth American Scientific Congress of Washington, May 10–18, 1940, and numerous specialized conferences, gained exceptional importance either through direct or indirect official support.[25] The first Inter-American Congress on Philosophy was held at Yale University in 1943. A variety of organizations appeared about this time, such as the Institute of Andean Research for field work relative to the prehistoric American Indian; the Inter-American Society of Anthropology and Geography; the Committee on Pan American Relations, which originated with the Harvard Group Program of Inter-American Defense; the International Institute of Ibero-American Literature, the Inter-American Statistical Institute, etc. Most of their members were, or are, professors and they are frequently supported by universities. An independent project, the Strategic Index of the Americas, was then prepared by Yale University.

(8) TRAVELLERS BETWEEN NORTH AND SOUTH AMERICA.—This program was conducted in a very extensive manner and included professors, scholars, specialists, men and women of arts, sciences and letters, and many other groups. Visits ranged from "sightseeing" trips to assignments for the purposes of attending conferences and university courses. For less hasty travellers there were organizations such as the Inter-American Training Center, of Washington, established by the CIAA in 1942, through a contract with the ACLS to train government personnel assigned to Latin America. The increase of Latin American students in the United States was remarkable. Special housing projects, English courses and various social and personal facilities were made available to these students.

Courses on Latin America during the Period 1935–40

A survey conducted by the Pan American Union in 1935–36 on Latin American courses in American universities and colleges gave the following results: courses were offered at 335 institutions in continental United States; three in United States territories and possessions, with a to-

tal result of 875 courses. In 1935–36 the University of California listed the greatest number of courses on this subject with a total of 83. The University of Texas was in second place with 59. The State of Texas, however, had the greatest number of institutions which offered these studies (21) followed by New York (20).[26]

Another survey conducted in 1938–39 displayed the tendency of some institutions to concentrate their students in a Latin American major, which included courses of various departments (Texas, Wisconsin, Minnesota, New Mexico and others). At the University of California, Berkeley, a major in Latin American studies at the graduate level was proposed which led to the Ph.D. in Latin American civilization. Some universities in the West, South, Southwest and East of the United States opened inter-American institutes in cooperation with groups in their communities. The statistical report of the survey made in 1935–36 and 1938–39 is summarized in the following table:

In 1938–39 the survey registered a total of 729 professors, while in 1935–36 it had registered 578. It was calculated that in 1938–39 (with figures incomplete) there were 17,800 students, a considerable increase over 1935–36, which, according to figures obtained, totaled a little more than 13,300. The results of the same survey in 1930–31 manifested a tendency to give preference to history courses. At the end of the decade this situation had not changed. In 1930 literature was in second place with less than half the number of courses; in 1938–39 this lack of proportion was even greater. The most notable increase during this period was in the

[25] The proceedings of the Eighth American Scientific Congress were published in 12 volumes, Washington, Department of State, 1941–43.

[26] *Latin American Studies in American Institutions of Higher Learning, Academic Year, 1935–36*, with an introduction by Concha Romero James. Washington, Pan American Union, Division of Intellectual Cooperation, 1936. Mimeographed. *Latin American Studies in American Institutions of Higher Learning, Academic Year, 1938–39*, with an introduction by Concha Romero James. Washington, Pan American Union, Division of Intellectual Cooperation, 1940. Mimeographed.

Colleges and Universities Offering Courses on Latin America

	1935–36	1938–39
In the United States	335	381
In territories and possessions	3	2
	338	383
Courses included:		
History	395	476
Literature	199	193
Geography	145	165
International Relations	48	58
Anthropology, Ethnology, Archaeology	34	38
Economics (including Commerce)	27	31
Biography	1	5
Art	—	4
Political Science	19	4
Education	1	2
Sociology	1	2
Geology	2	1
Medicine	—	1
Agriculture	—	1
Journalism	1	—
Zoology and Botany	2	—
	875	981

field of geography with almost four times as many courses in less than ten years. The figures on international relations were probably misleading because of the strong possibility that the subject had been included in courses of a more general character.

Although proportionately small as compared to the total, the number of courses in anthropology, ethnology and archaeology, registered an amazing increase over the figures gathered in 1930–31, when only one course was in evidence. These courses in 1938–39 were slightly more numerous than those in economics.

A sub-committee on research planning and personnel of the Joint Committee on Latin American Studies of the ACLS, the National Research Council, and the Social Science Research Council initiated, at the beginning of 1942, a survey of personnel and activities in Latin American aspects of the humanities and social sciences. The task of visiting twenty representative universities was entrusted to Professor Irving A. Leonard. Leonard's report is not, nor was it intended to be, of a statistical nature. Its purpose is one of observation and evaluation,

and undoubtedly can be considered a basic document for anyone interested in the history of Latin American studies in the United States.[27] In spite of its briefness, it is a perspicuous and realistic outline of the existing situation in the first six months of 1942, which reflected the evolution that had taken place since 1930 and which remains unchanged in some respects, after seven years.

The tendency toward coordination and integration in Latin American studies was progressively more apparent in numerous universities; however, Leonard found this trend to be developing in three different directions:

a) Latin American institutes.

b) The group major leading to a Ph.D. degree.

c) A major at an undergraduate level.

The institutes which were acknowledged in the survey made by the Pan American Union shortly before, and again in Dr. Leon-

[27] Published in *Notes on Latin American Studies*, No. 1, edited by the Joint Committee on Latin American Studies. Washington, D. C., April 1943.

ard's report, appeared as a separate unit within the university with a detailed plan of cooperation between departments or disciplines bearing on Latin American problems. The only instance of a definitely established organization of this type functioning at the graduate level was, at that time, at the University of Texas, although there were other universities with plans on similar lines. The "group major" was a certain coordination of the work of departments concerned at a graduate level leading to a Ph.D. degree in a general Latin American major as distinct from the doctorate granted in a single discipline. As Leonard pointed out:

This general degree work is usually a part of the Institute where it is set up, though not necessarily included in the plan. The group major, when not comprehended in an official Institute, is usually administered by a committee of faculty members representing the various disciplines which have been coordinated. This arrangement is represented at the University of California at Berkeley where, in recent years, several doctorates in general Latin American studies have been granted. At California at Los Angeles a similar program exists theoretically, but it is not actually in operation.

The third and most common manifestation of the integrating tendency is at the undergraduate level with the creation of a "major" in general Latin American courses taken in the junior and senior years. There are sometimes "paper" plans, appearing in the university catalogue but lacking any real vitality. Increasing undergraduate interest may give them more reality. Under the administration of a faculty committee, they usually bring together the existing courses in anthropology, geography, history, languages and political science. Such programs of study are formally organized at the University of California at Berkeley, New Mexico, Texas, Minnesota, Wisconsin, Michigan, Princeton, and one is announced for Yale.[28]

He did not investigate the summer institutes which existed in 1939 and 1940 in Michigan and Texas.

As to the teaching itself, Leonard often noted a lack of administrative coordination among the courses which might have been "the core of a program of Latin American Studies," language, geography and history.

Even less effective coordination was observed in many institutions between these "core" disciplines and the "peripheral" disciplines such as anthropology, archaelogy, fine arts and political science. In history Leonard saw the beginning of the end of the brilliant generation of Martin, Chapman, Priestley, Bolton and others and the arrival of various new men with fresh archival experience abroad and a corresponding respect for documentary sources; however, in many instances courses seemed to follow in the traditional patterns which were of a more general character. He did point out that some teachers of geography had done actual field work, and he perceived marked advancement in studies on anthropology and archaeology. Instructors seemed prepared to adopt a more realistic attitude toward their program and the language difficulty was less in evidence in this field. In the universities of the West the interest was perhaps more concentrated in Mexico and Central America than in South America.

Leonard observed that the potential importance of economic studies had not been fully realized in the institutions visited by him. The studies in anthropology and sociology, even though not wholly developed, were recognized for their possibilities. In many cases the study of art appeared only as an individual hobby or as isolated or scattered efforts. One of the exceptions, he points out, was the Art School of the University of Texas, with music and plastic arts courses. General interest in art seemed to be in the following order: painting, sculpture, architecture and music.

A Summary of Latin American Studies up to the Time of the Second World War

It is possible to express in a very few words the principal trends in the development of Latin American studies up to the time of the second World War. Latin American studies began as a series of isolated and scattered efforts, but during the period from the beginning of the twentieth century un-

[28] *Op. cit.* Footnote 27.

til the first World War, their popularity grew with increasing rapidity. By the end of the decade of the twenties, over 300 courses were offered at more than 200 institutions. The majority of these courses pertained to history or literature, with a few courses in geography and almost no teaching of anthropology, ethnology or archaeology. The "boom" of Latin America during the early thirties in official circles, as well as in some literary, press and organizational groups, found a process well on its way in the academic world. The academic studies, however, obtained important benefits from the somewhat artificial stimulation which they received up until the first years of World War II. The study of history continued to flourish with increasing emphasis on documentary sources. Language and literature continued to be well cultivated and a definite improvement in geography, anthropology and archaeology was evident. It was at that time also that an increasing specialization and the first attempts at inter-disciplinary cooperation began to appear.

The Post War Period

The war interrupted or handicapped many of the purely academic studies of colleges and universities of the United States. At the same time, however, it accelerated and stimulated the study of world areas. The Army specialized training activities and the Civil Affairs Training Schools allocated special programs in area and language to the various campuses.[29] Governmental research in Washington and abroad was for the main part organized around regional specialization and not around the traditional disciplines and many university professors were "drafted" into this setup. The Ethnogeographic Board (established during the war by the Smithsonian Institution in cooperation with the American Council of Learned Societies, the National Research Council and the Social Science Research Council) and the Strategic Index of the Americas were among the attempts to make the nation's scientific and scholarly resources in area knowledge available for the emer-

gency. The mental upheaval caused by the war experience influenced the postwar area programs of some institutions. The three research councils appointed, after the close of the war, a joint exploratory committee on World Area Research with Dr. Robert B. Hall, of the University of Michigan, as chairman. A survey concerned primarily with the relation of the social sciences to the present status and prospective development of area studies was then undertaken by the Social Science Research Council which selected Dr. Hall for its execution. Dr. Hall visited twenty-four of the major universities of the country between April and September, 1946. The Hall report excluded some institutions which had only Latin American programs, because of the availability of Irving A. Leonard's report and additional information from the Joint Committee on Latin American Studies. Hall noted that there is considerable evidence that interest in the Latin American area may suffer both a relative and an absolute decline. He seems somewhat skeptical about the future of this study and declares that, in terms of the national good, we must not gamble. In other words, he does not consider that Latin American studies are "spinal." Impatiently brushing past the traditional, cultural and moral patterns of a brilliant part of the American academic output which, as we have seen, has been devoted to Latin America for so long with such encouraging results, it now seems to be in fashion to disrupt these studies, or at least to minimize their importance. The question pending is whether or not education, science and culture should be subordinated to emotional reactions or political expediency or to the fear or danger of immediate international crisis. And speaking in terms of "American national defense," who can deny that a neglected Latin America may become another China in the years to come?

[29] William N. Fenton, ed., *Reports on Area Studies in American Universities*. Washington, Ethnogeographic Board, 1945, mimeographed; and William N. Fenton, *Area Studies in American Universities*, Washington, American Council on Education, 1947.

The impracticability of ignoring Latin American studies is obvious; however, Hall adds a pessimistic note with his statement: "We appear to be the best equipped in the Latin American field although, as previously mentioned, there seems to be the beginning of a slackening of interest comparable to that which followed World War I."[30]

We cannot agree with him on the final phrase of this sentence. As has been indicated before in this paper, there was no slackening of interest in Latin America at American universities after World War I. On the contrary, they took root in their campus environment and gained a secure foothold in most institutions of higher learning, and, in fact, without the boiling-over of the days of the Coordinator of Inter-American Affairs, the study of Latin America continues under constant cultivation. At the same time, there is an increasing interweaving of hemispheric and global thinking. For example, that which during the thirties was termed "hemispheric" is now called "regional." The typical scholars of 1949 leap walls and cross borders in the landscape of knowledge laid out by more isolationist cultivators. And like some statesmen and military men of our time, they are eager to welcome the broad-based approach when and if it recognizes as universally applicable the regional quality of cultures, behaviors and institutions. In this connection, there is a far-reaching significance in the meeting of the national conference on the study of world areas which took place in New York in 1947 under the auspices of the Social Science Research Council and was financed by a grant from the Carnegie Corporation of New York.[31] A comparison between the report on the Latin American area and some of the other areas made at this conference seems to ratify the statement previously made by Professor Hall, "We appear to be best equipped in the Latin American field . . ."

With the presentation in the previous pages of the background of Latin American studies at American colleges and universities, in reality a preface to this preface, the pages that follow will discuss their present characteristics and trends.

PART TWO: THE PRESENT
Latin American Studies in 1948–49

The Pan American Union first exercised its influence in the promotion of Latin American studies during their pioneer years; later evidence of its interest is shown in the survey sponsored by Dr. Rowe in 1926 and in the compilation and dissemination of the statistical data beginning in 1930. Now with the publication of the present volume the Pan American Union renews its activity in this field and undertakes to observe, record, publicize and stimulate the development of all studies relating to Latin America at college and university level.

As a matter of fact, one of the projects to which the Division of Education of the Department of Cultural Affairs devoted the greatest amount of attention, immediately after its establishment, was that of compiling and publishing information regarding courses on Latin America in colleges and universities during 1946–47. A mimeographed report on this subject was distributed last year.[32] The results of the same study for the academic year 1948–49, are contained in the present volume, prepared again under the direction of Mrs. Estellita Hart.

At first glance, no doubt, this list of courses on Latin America for the academic year 1948–49, and of the institutions offering them, will give an impression of abundance. But the number of schools and courses recorded must not be examined solely against

[30] Robert B. Hall, *Area Studies: With Special Reference to their Implications for Research in the Social Sciences.* Social Science Research Council, Pamphlet 3, New York, May 1947, pp. 9, 23, 82, 83.

[31] Charles Wagley, *Area Research and Training: A Conference Report on the Study of World Areas*, Social Science Research Council, Pamphlet 6, New York, June 1948.

[32] *Courses on Latin America in Institutions of Higher Learning in the United States—1946–1947*, compiled by Estellita Hart, 2 vols. Washington, D. C., Department of Cultural Affairs, Pan American Union, 1948. Mimeographed.

the static background of the lists published in previous years. In the first place, it is possible that more painstaking care was shown in gathering this information, and especially it must be noted that the academic year 1948–49 is exceptional in view of the great number of students enrolled. This year there were more than 2,400,000 students in colleges and universities, while in 1947 there were 2,300,000; in 1940 there were 1,500,000, and in 1930, only 970,000. As the number and variety of courses on Latin America have increased, the number and variety of other subjects have also increased, and, in some cases, more rapidly. It is necessary, therefore, to view the figures revealed in the present study against a "moving background."

With respect to the leading trends of thought among the people of the United States, the present situation offers a paradoxical contrast. On the one hand, we clearly observe that in some sections Latin America is underestimated or ignored. This is because of a greater attraction to matters concerning the Soviet Union and its spheres of influence, and to affairs related to the United Nations and its specialized agencies. On the other hand, Latin America may profit from the fact that the people of the United States have a growing eagerness for knowledge about the rest of the world, and from the fact that this country is perceiving with increasing clarity, not only the value and meaning of its enormous abundance of natural and industrial resources, and of its own capacity, but also the actual and potential significance on a world scale of the concept that wealth and power are a "trusteeship for social service" and not the instruments for self-aggrandizement.

The Mission of Latin American Studies

Latin American studies have a mission at this moment: to continue and develop the tradition that so brilliantly justifies them, and to associate their interests with the growing preoccupation for world affairs, without being absorbed or weakened by it. "Regionalism" in academic studies must not disappear in the face of global studies. On the contrary, it could contribute to a better understanding of the different cultures of the world. Even in international politics, regionalism has not disappeared. After all, the Atlantic Pact has created a new regional group. Insofar as Latin America is concerned, colleges and universities, professors and students of the United States must not fall into the role of the "forgetful neighbor" so soon after the era of the "good neighbor" in which they played a significant part.

The general objectives of Latin American studies seems clear: to provide the fundamentals which will enable citizens of the United States to understand thoroughly and appreciate clearly the present and past life of the Latin American republics. Generally speaking, the knowledge of these republics is as yet not extensive. Noticeable progress has been made but prejudices and misconceptions are far from nonexistent. Just as in Latin America many people still believe that the people of the United States are concerned only with money and material things, in the United States the various countries of Latin America continue to be identified with revolutions, dictatorships, romantic customs, dress and dances of only folkloric interest, lack of realism, a disposition to procrastinate, cruel and systematic exploitation of Indians and peasants, and a primitive economy. The press, the radio and the ordinary people, moreover, still take merely a fleeting, perhaps a declining, interest in Latin America and sometimes then only for sensational or superficial reasons. For the most part, these are in a sense negative factors, or at least they are certainly not sufficiently constructive.

Universities should not try to take the place of other agencies, but they should give to their students the educational training necessary to break down the barriers of ignorance, prejudice or error with respect to other countries and peoples; they should, through study and research, provide a background which will assist in interpreting and evaluating objectively the problems and events of the day from the perspective of history, geography, economics, sociology, anthropology, social psychology and political science, or of the artistic or cultural patterns of the foreign groups concerned.

The study of Latin America answers the purely intellectual or cultural purposes that are the object of other academic studies, as well as having many other special reasons for being attractive. It presents a great variety and multiplicity of enigmas, archaeological and historical, which extend from the beginning of civilization in this hemisphere to the era of *caudillos* and dictators. Here the geographer may find mingled in a single locality something of the traditional patterns of Asia, of the contrast between Western civilization and the primitive atmosphere of Africa, of the youth of Australia and of the refinements of Europe. For the anthropologist and the sociologist, numerous opportunities are offered for the study of the most diverse groups, small and large, rural and urban, agricultural and industrial; of white race and black, Indian and mestizo, living side by side or together. The economist could not fail to be interested in such a singular situation where the many national economies go their separate ways, yet are often characterized by similar outlines, in transition towards industrialization; and while sometimes presenting aspects of advanced regulation by the State, they often reveal feudal and even pre-feudal aspects. The specialist in literature, art and music will find that these people are young, but that their roots extend back to the sixteenth century and even earlier. He will find that they have already produced outstanding poetry, masterpieces of essay and short stories and novels whose worth he will readily appreciate. At the same time he will see a people who are of the first rank in contemporary painting, a people who possess a rich musical folklore and first-class composers, a people who conceive of culture primarily as a way of life, as a gracious manner of daily existence.

Latin America, in other words, offers to Americans a challenge for the application of objective principles; for the practice of mental fair play in the presence of ancient prejudices of religious, racial, or political origin; for exercising the ability to adjust themselves to environments which, though near in space, are at times quite different from the American environment. These are, moreover, studies in which there is much to investigate and learn, to interpret and evaluate, to coordinate and publish; studies which call for work that is varied and difficult, meticulous and interesting. These are studies which by no means should fall into routine molds, nor can they be expressed in platitudes or approached with hasty superficiality.

The impressive figures here recorded and the numerous kinds of classes included do not justify an attitude of complacency. They should not be accepted at face value. It may be that some colleges are guilty of those characteristics so often pointed out by critics of educational life in this country; they may have a somewhat journalistic interest in things, half understanding them, and a tendency to appear up-to-date with courses which by their titles seem to offer a great deal but which in reality offer very little. No true study can be made of education without analyzing its content. Certainly it is not enough to make a list of names or titles any more than catalogue cards are enough to reveal the resources of a library. Moreover, the present directory of names and titles does not always contain the best subjects or the best textbooks available. The doubt arises as to whether all the courses on Latin America in its different phases are faithful to a coherent and constructive educational philosophy, or whether they were expanded under the influence of the interest or ideas of individual professors, or perhaps in some cases as a result of dilettantism or pressure of enrollments at the institutions themselves.

Whatever doubts may exist, however, they will not affect the deservedly high opinion we have of the American academic effort as a whole in the sphere of Latin American activity, either of the past, or especially, of the present moment. It must, moreover, be recognized (and here it may be noted that the present writer is a Latin American) that in Latin American universities the program of studies of the continent as a whole is not being carried out as intensively as in the United States. It is true that there are more courses of a national character, but there are far fewer of continental or area scope. Consequently, in any list of contemporary reference works on Latin America in general, in all languages, the greater number of them will be by American authors or used in colleges and universities of the United States. As for studies of that continent in European universities, worthy of mention are the specialized studies made in Spain of certain historical-political aspects, particularly of the colonial period, and of the lecture courses occasionally given in England and France which depend upon the personal brilliance of isolated professors.

Location of the Courses

The situation existing in universities and colleges of the United States during the academic year 1948–49 with regard to Latin American studies is very clear. In those institutions which are the wealthiest or largest, or are in closer geographic proximity to Latin America, or which have a stronger tradition in this field, the courses tend to become increasingly specialized. The specialization is not only by subject matter but also by area, as is the case at the Universities of Vanderbilt, Texas, North Carolina, and Tulane, which were recently favored with grants from the Carnegie Corporation of New York for the purpose of concentrating on Brazil, Mexico, Spanish South America, and Central America, respectively. At the same time, Latin America as a general subject has invaded the medium-sized and smaller colleges. This subject is not limited to large universities, great cities or wealthy states. Latin America has entered into the heart of the average American college.

Usually courses on Latin America are found in the colleges of liberal arts, sometimes in schools of business administration, commerce, accounts and finance, education or their equivalents, and in graduate schools. Large institutions carry them simultaneously in several schools. At Columbia University, they may be taken regularly in Barnard College, Columbia College, the School of General Studies, the School of Business, the Faculty of Philosophy, the Faculty of Political Science, the School of International Affairs and Teachers' College.

At Stanford University, Latin American courses are offered principally at the Schools of Humanities and Social Sciences under the general coordination of the Hispanic American program which gives a B.A. administered technically by special programs in humanities and an M.A. and Ph.D. in Hispanic American studies which are attached for administrative purposes to the Department of Romanic Languages.

In 1939 the University of Texas created the Institute of Latin American Studies to serve as a common center for Latin American undergraduate and graduate work, research, publication and other cultural activities at the University. It undertakes to focus attention on Latin American programs of study available in the following schools and colleges of the University: the College of Arts and Sciences, the College of Business Administration and the Graduate School.

The School of Inter-American Affairs at the University of New Mexico offers: (1) Inter-American studies with emphasis on four aspects: historical and cultural; business administration; social, economic and political affairs; and regional (the Hispanic Southwest); (2) a two-year course for secretary-interpreters specializing in inter-American relations; (3) a one-year intensive course on inter-American relations for graduate students, business men, professionals and technicians. The School of Inter-American Affairs, furthermore, has been continuing the appointments of Latin American artists in residence with the help of the cultural cooperation program of the Department of State and operates a research bureau on Latin America and cultural relations in the Southwest in cooperation with the Department of Sociology, and has employment and advisory services. It sponsors public lectures and community programs, especially in connection with the Spanish-speaking groups of the state, assisting them in several ways, particularly in the field of health. The

Inter-Americana Series, which the school publishes, has both English and Spanish editions of works by American and Mexican authors.[33] Audio-visual aids are furnished to public schools and civic groups.

In 1924 the University of Tulane established the Department of Middle American Research which was later named the Middle American Research Institute. This Institute is devoted primarily to research, education and public services in an area arbitrarily called Middle America, in order to include Mexico, Central America, the West Indies and the Bahamas. By 1948 the Institute had sponsored 26 expeditions to Middle America during a period of 23 years. These expeditions have ranged from simple reconnaissance to intensive work in the following subjects: agronomy, archaeology, art, biology, physical anthropology, ethnology, geography, bibliography, history, motion pictures and linguistics. Staff members of the Institute teach courses in the Departments of History, Sociology and Anthropology. The Institute publishes three series of monographs. The first is the regular book size series which includes the well-known philological and documentary studies. The second series, published with the title *Middle American Research Records*, consists of relatively short articles and papers issued as separates. The third is a miscellaneous series which includes administrative reports, museum guides and other releases. In the field of public services, the Institute maintains an information service and an audio-visual education program. It has an excellent library with books, manuscripts, pamphlets and maps available. A museum gallery which was remodeled and modernized in 1942 is another asset of the Institute. Maps, photographs and bibliographies are sent to requesting individuals and institutions, both in the United States and in foreign countries. Reports on Middle American subjects are prepared for them and loan exhibits from the museum are sent to many other museums every year. The Institute acts also as a depository for motion pictures on Middle America.

Vanderbilt University has a special Institute for Brazilian Studies which will be discussed later in this paper.

Studies during the regular semesters are sometimes complemented by summer schools. Authoritative courses are given in this way at the Hispanic American Institute of Stanford University. In addition, a Brazilian House will be opened soon at Stanford. At Mills College, in Oakland, California, they were, until recently, given in conjunction with a Pan American House. The summer courses of Middlebury College have also enjoyed an excellent reputation for many years. The lectures delivered before the Hispanic American Institute at the University of Miami have been published since 1939 in the *University of Miami Hispanic-American Studies* now edited by J. Riis Owre. In the summer of 1949 the University of Delaware began for the first time to offer courses and round-table discussions on art, history, and economic problems, with the participation of professors from both the United States and Latin America.

The Latin American Junior Year has a special interest for students at Wellesley and Smith Colleges. Wellesley offers an honors program in Latin American studies which combines courses relating to Latin America offered by the Department of Economics, Geography, History, Political Science, Sociology and Spanish, with a Junior Year in Mexico for qualified students. The Junior Years in Mexico for Smith students is described as follows:

October is spent in one of the smaller provincial cities, such as Puebla or Morelia, where students live with carefully selected families. About the first of November the group moves to Mexico City, where it lives in an attractive house rented by Smith College. Classes are available in Spanish literature and composition, Mexican art, archaeology and history, and various other aspects of Mexican and Latin American culture, taught by professors from different colleges and the Uni-

[33] Among the more recent publications included in the series of the University of Texas, are Charles Gibson's *The Inca Concept of Sovereignty and the Spanish Administration in Peru* (No. 4 of the Latin American Studies) and *Some Educational and Anthropological Aspects of Latin America* (No. 5), (both published in 1948).

versity of Mexico. A minimum of two years of college Spanish is required.

Opportunities for summer study in 1949 were of a wide variety. The University of Houston organized its International Study Center for the sixth year in Mexico City and for the second year in Havana in cooperation with the University of Mexico and the University of Havana respectively. Announcements were made for study in Mexico City by various organizations including the University of California at Los Angeles; Ball State Teachers College, Muncie, Indiana; and Texas Technological College, Lubbock, Texas. A Michigan Summer Study Group and an Eastern State Study Group both offered programs in connection with the summer quarter of Mexico City College. Rockford College, Rockford, Illinois cooperated with the State University of Michoacán, Morelia, Michoacán, and Sam Houston State Teachers College, Huntsville, Texas, with the University of Puebla. The University of Kentucky also announced courses in Puebla. San Angelo College, San Angelo, Texas, planned to establish a summer school in Chihuahua, Mexico, for the summer of 1949 and Florida Southern College of Lakeland, Florida, announced a summer school in Antigua, Guatemala. In addition, there were several announcements of summer sessions offered directly by Latin American institutions for American students. As is to be expected, the largest number of these opportunities came from Mexico. Among the institutions connected with these programs were the National University of Mexico, Mexico City College, the State University of Michoacán, the University of Puebla, the University of Guadalajara and the Instituto Tecnológico y de Estudios Superiores of Monterrey. Other announcements came from the University of Havana, Havana, Cuba; the University of Santo Domingo, Ciudad Trujillo, Dominican Republic; the University of San Carlos, Guatemala City, Guatemala; the National University of Colombia, Bogota, Colombia; the University of San Marcos, Lima, Peru; the University of San Andrés, La Paz,

Bolivia. Educational tours, with or without relation to the courses already mentioned, and art workshops are additional proof of the increasing popularity, especially in the southern and middle western states, of these vacation opportunities.

The Undergraduate General Course

In the majority of cases, Latin American studies tend to remain within the undergraduate level. At small colleges which cannot easily meet the expense of having several professors and an adequate library there may still be a general course. It may be called "Latin American History," continuing the traditional emphasis on the teaching of history which was initiated by Bernard Moses in 1895, although it is often described as a "Survey of Social, Economic and Political Development." Sometimes history and geography are combined in a single course; in other institutions it is likely to be called merely "Latin America," with the indication that it is concerned with the social, racial and economic development of the Latin American states, or "Twentieth Century Hispanic America," or "Contemporary Latin America," or "Cultural and Social Changes in Latin America," or some similar title. The existence of this general or isolated course in the nature of an introduction to a knowledge of Latin America is inevitable and its usefulness may be very extensive, but the difficulties of covering a subject so vast and complex are obvious. It would be profitable for professors and textbook writers to think seriously about the objectives of this course, about what to include, and especially, what not to include. They must resign themselves to the omission of many names, dates and figures. They must have compassion for their students' memories. They must limit themselves to fundamental dates and events of the multinational structure of the Latin American continent. They must try to give an idea of the essential differences that characterize each one of the twenty republics in order to be able to identify them and to distinguish one from another. If countries are considered separately this treatment must be complemented or preceded by a topical analysis. In these introductory courses, history can serve only as a background for understanding the present. Whatever the course offers, it must at the same time serve the student as a point of departure for reading and research on his own initiative.

It is the tendency of many medium-sized and large institutions to offer courses which are divided into various subjects with preference being accorded to history, geography and literature; and in some instances the subjects are even sub-divided. Despite this, however, there are institutions that give general or introductory surveys such as the very elaborate one at Stanford entitled "Hispanic World Affairs" which is sub-divided into five courses, or "Latin American Social Institutions" at the University of Washington. In other institutions there are lectures on "Introduction to Latin American Civilization" with several professors participating, each in his own field; such is the case at the University of Pennsylvania. In the catalogue of the University of Michigan a "Reading Course in Latin American Studies" is listed, which is an analysis "of important materials in the Latin American field approached from the various standpoints of anthropology, economics, geography, history, political science, literature and fine arts." Participants are Professors Arthur S. Aiton, Irving A. Leonard, Dudley M. Phelps, Harold E. Wethey; Associate Professors James B. Griffin, Horace Miner, Mischa Titiev; Assistant Professor Ferrel Heady; and Mr. Franklin M. Thompson.

The orientation of these courses is in principle quite acceptable, and they can be useful also to students who are not taking a major in this field. It is in accord with the tenet of educational philosophy to require a student to have a general idea about life and about the world as it is in his own time before undertaking a practical activity or a specialized orientation. It must be insistently repeated, however, that it is necessary to consider very carefully the criteria for selecting the fundamental information to be presented and the sufficiency of the method of coordinating it in a coherent and systematic manner.

The Latin American Majors

The tendency of American colleges to require their undergraduates to have a broad variety of knowledge is compensated for by the tendency to organize a part of their studies in a field of special interest—a major. This preference is generally grouped in a department or division, but there are also majors that are interdepartmental. As noted previously, the Latin American major made its appearance a little less than fifteen years ago. It is generally supervised by a professor or a committee and has an interdepartmental character—in some institutions, intercollegiate. Some institutions are inclined to branch out to form a Hispanic major; and in still others there is a major in one or more special fields of Latin America. A major curriculum in the economics of Latin American trade appears, for example, in the College of Business Administration of the University of Florida. At the University of Texas the College of Arts and Sciences offers a major in Latin American studies, and the School of Business Administration, the degree of Bachelor of Business Administration with a major in Latin American studies. A major program in liberal arts colleges advisable in average cases would include participation on a basis of equality, of several social science and humanistic disciplines, in other words, an introductory course, courses in Spanish or Portuguese, history, literature, culture, geography, economics, anthropology, government, sociology and art, an advanced or specialized course and a senior seminar completing at least 120 hours.

In the present trend toward undergraduate area programs, some instruments of integration of this program have been established. Among the more effective devices now in use are survey courses, cooperative courses, the block system, the single integrated course, joint seminars, group planning of the content of individual courses and integrative reading materials. At the present moment there is an increasing realization of the need to view the particular area involved in terms of its regional and world position and relationships.

The major in international relations may include Latin America as one of the regional studies group. At Stanford University it is possible to study Latin America as one of the options in the international relations program, although regional specialization occupies a secondary place in the program and a student may not specialize entirely in a region. Advanced work in international relations with Latin America is being carried on within the Hispanic American program. In the Department of Political Science, Graham Stuart gives an upper division course on Latin America and the United States, while in the Department of Romanic Languages, Ronald Hilton offers the Hispanic World Affairs Seminar for the graduate program. This seminar produces the *Hispanic World Report,* a monthly analysis of social and political developments in Spain, Portugal and Latin America.

The Area of Latin American Studies at Northwestern University

The area program in Latin American studies at Northwestern University involves the entire four years of the student's college work. This spread allows all general college requirements to be met along with the program. During the first two years the student elects such general requirements as English and a laboratory course. He also meets the language requirement by electing Spanish or Portuguese or both. Elementary, prerequisite courses in those social science fields required in the program are taken and one or two more advanced social science courses pertaining to the Latin American area can also generally be included. Hispanic American history is required in this period and can be elected without prerequisites.

In the upper division a functional field of concentration must be chosen. The student may select either geography, history, political science, or Portuguese and Spanish language and literature. The normal requirements of departmental specialization must be met. The department's offerings in the Latin American field count in this require-

ment and about one-half of the student's time is available for Latin American subjects outside the department. This program is worked out with the concentration advisor who represents both the department and the area program. All students are encouraged to continue language study throughout the four years and to elect advanced Latin American courses in each of the participating departments. Study in the Latin American area can be continued at the graduate level through specially devised seminars.

The Northwestern program attracted the attention of Professor Hall in his report already mentioned.[34] He sees an advantage in the longer exposure to things Latin American because it allows a deeper absorption. He also mentions the lack of interference with the general system and requirements of the college. The question has been asked locally, however, whether or not these advantages offset the disadvantages of such early specialization. This program has been, on the other hand, upon a voluntary basis. No concessions have been made in departmental controls and no tangible evidence of strong administrative support was found. At any rate, "Latin America is Northwestern University's best area resource."

The Subject Matter of Latin American Courses

At this point brief consideration will be given to the principal courses which constitute the Latin American program, with the object of making some observations which might possibly be of value.

HISTORY.—History is the subject that has always led, and continues to lead the list of Latin American courses given in the colleges and universities of this country. If a complete study were made of the American contribution to Latin American historiography we may be sure that it would prove to be a very important one. *The Hispanic American Historical Review* has a significant role in this connection. However, there is still room for a great deal of improvement. In an ex-

[34] Robert B. Hall, *op. cit.* Footnote 30.

amination made by James F. King and Samuel Everett a few years ago of the textbooks on Latin American history[35] they suggested some improvements, which were the following: the advantage of establishing a balance between political history and "background conditions" (social, economic, religious and cultural); the necessity of selecting the names, dates and annotations; the possibility of attempting a "horizontal" treatment by subjects instead of always blindly following a "vertical" treatment by nations; the desirability of including the study of Indian, Negro and mestizo groups, as well as immigration, industrialization and transportation, and of including an account of folk customs, and of scientific, literary and artistic development.

It is possible that substantially the same criticism could be made of the courses offered today. We must admit, however, that the suggestions are not always easy to follow.

It seems to be the common feeling among professors of history that neither the pre-Columbian era nor the colonial period are particularly difficult to handle. The first can be presented in the light of what is known from the nature of the leading Indian civilizations. For the Colonial history, it seems to be both interesting and useful to trace the voyages of discovery, the early expeditions and the political, economic, social and religious institutions developed for the government of the Spanish and Portuguese empires in America. But the problems involved in dealing with the history of 20 separate nations and their conquest of independence seem to be a real challenge for professors and students. The unstable nature of political life in these countries during much of this period creates the possibility of giving too much detail to upheavals, revolutions and changes of government, or the danger of general statements which could be a repetition of platitudes. It would be sufficient to try to explain the fundamental aspects of the creation and the evolution of each Latin American nationality. There should be a trend towards teaching the main characteristics of the history *of* the country

rather than the history of events which happened *within* the country. It is useless to try to register the pure sequence of events as a seismograph records a series of earthquakes. How and why a country came to be; which have been its main problems, international, political, economic, social; which are the landmarks of its evolution and what is the meaning of the names of the most outstanding men and women of the past: this would be enough for a historical treatment of the Latin American Republics. It is true that the main tool for any attempt at renovation of this subject will be the textbook. There are already some good textbooks available; as a matter of fact, many of them are better than the textbooks used in Latin America for the same purpose. However, professors and students observe that they need a more careful selection of names and dates, including a larger number of maps and charts and a more inspired style which could include a few selected quotations from primary sources. All of this is in addition to the other suggestions of King and Everett already mentioned.[36]

The tendency toward interpretation, evaluation and explanation seems to be gradually gaining ground in the historiography of Latin America; and it is important that American historians and professors take note of the development of this tendency. To the extent that there appears an objective and coherent treatment of national history, or of the history of areas or of the continent, in Latin America itself, the level of instruction in the United States may be improved. This does not imply, of course, any disparagement of the original contributions of Amer-

[35] James F. King and Samuel Everett, "Latin American History Textbooks" in *Latin America in School and College Teaching Materials*. Washington, D. C., American Council on Education, 1944.

[36] The writer has based this statement on his own experience as a professor of Latin American history at Swarthmore College in 1941–42, and the observations of various specialists, including some of the points of view expressed in a personal letter dated July 19, 1949, from Kenneth W. Crosby of Juniata College, Huntingdon, Pennsylvania.

ican scholars; but since the subject is so vast, and there are within it so many lacunae, any attempt at synthesis or resumé suggests the utilization of all important efforts in the different languages including the most recent contributions.

Courses in early and contemporary historiography of Latin America would be desirable in many large universities. The history course given by Dorothy Woodward at New Mexico and the several courses dealing with the history of New Mexico and of the Southwest also offered at the University of New Mexico have simultaneously, as is often the case, an American and a Spanish American character. Among these latter mentioned courses is one on research in Southwest history under the direction of France V. Scholes which uses the photostat collection of documents from the National Archives of Seville and Mexico, the Library of Congress and the Spanish Archives of New Mexico. Dr. Scholes, for many years an authority in this field, personally directed some of the "expeditions" which assembled this valuable source material.

Less obvious is the relationship existing between Mexico and Canada, two countries which in isolated cases are combined in history courses.

LITERATURE.—Literature courses seem to have received a fresh impulse in recent years. Many colleges have raised the level of this study and they have available an excellent outline and an anthology of Spanish American literature, made possible by the commendable spirit of cooperation of several distinguished specialists (E. Herman Hespelt, Irving A. Leonard, John T. Reid, John E. Englekirk, John A. Crow). Several reviews are published in this country by and for specialists (*Hispania, Hispanic Review, Revista Hispánica Moderna, Revista Iberoamericana, The Modern Language Journal* and, in the field of world literature, *Books Abroad*), and the professors of literature seem, at least to the eyes of an "outsider," to have better institutional organization than other groups. Aside from general courses in colleges and universities, courses now exist on various national literatures as well as on

literary types (the novel, poetry, the theater, the essay), sometimes within one country, and on trends (as for example "Lyrical Poetry in Latin America from Modernismo to the Present" given by the eminent Spanish poet and critic. Pedro Salinas, at Johns Hopkins), periods, school or authors. Professor José M. Arce conducts an interesting course on Sarmiento at Dartmouth College. Mention should be made here of Professor Carlos García-Prada's (University of Washington) division of courses in Spanish American literature by literary movements rather than by area, as is so frequently the case. In addition to the customary survey, his courses include those on Spanish American literature in English translation, the *costumbrista* movement, the *modernista* movement, contemporary fiction, and Latin American thought.

The level of instruction in literature depends, perhaps even more than in any other Latin American course, upon the use which students and professors are able to make of the language involved. Literature, then, is directly related to the teaching of Romance languages, and for its foundation we must look back to the elementary and high school.

The need for improvement in the methods of teaching foreign languages in this country is becoming increasingly important; indeed, it affects the whole program of international understanding. As Henry Grattan Doyle of George Washington University has pointed out:

One of the most extraordinary experiences that I imagine you teachers and future teachers of modern foreign languages will ever have, if indeed you have not already had it, is that of hearing some professional educationist deliver an address on "Education for the Air Age," or "Education for the Atomic Age," or "Education for World Citizenship," or "Education for International and Intercultural Understanding"—and never once mention the importance of foreign languages as a foundation stone of education for any of these purposes! I have in my files, I suppose, some twenty-five or thirty articles of this kind culled from educational magazines, not one of which makes the slightest reference to language barriers or the necessity for removing them.

Perhaps it is assumed that all these wonderful

results will be attained through the exclusive medium of English—a crude example of the "cultural imperialism" of which we and our British cousins are so often accused. Surely these writers and speakers can not be so naïve as to think that these desirable ends can be attained by the use of sign language, or that the machinery for almost instantaneous translation that is one of the marvels of recent international gatherings and especially of the proceedings of the United Nations at Lake Success will always and everywhere be available.

This is one of our major problems. We must arouse our people—our business and professional men, our political leaders, our citizens and taxpayers, most of all the parents of our children—to the need, now greater than ever, of increased and improved teaching of foreign languages, beginning with the elementary school. Constantly improving materials and increasingly better-prepared teachers are indispensable corollaries to such a demand —and when I say demand, I do not use the word in the economist's sense, but in the sense of something imperatively required in terms of today's world.[37]

On the other hand, some universities have a tendency to merge or combine the subject of literature with courses in Spain or Spanish literature. This is for the very purpose of placing a commendable emphasis on the language. In some cases it may be the influence of an eminent professor from Spain. In certain small institutions, which in this respect follow the example of many of the larger schools, it may be for reasons of economy. This tendency may well be favorably accepted wherever the ability and preparation of the professor are adequate to make it successful, but we would not be justified in supporting it without reservation. Whether consciously or not, it is paying homage to the doctrine of "Hispanidad." Hispanic Americans, while having reason to love and respect Spain (the present writer has for the "Mother Country" the most cordial personal memories and attachments), believe that certain definite variations have long since been produced on Hispanic America by the impact of the Indian, the Negro and the mestizo; by cosmopolitan cultural influences; by the diversity of the geographical environment; by the experience of history and by the prospects of the future. To treat

the Spanish American countries as provinces of Spain would be to destroy the educational objective of understanding their most essential and characteristic features. If an indiscriminate identification does not seem sufficient, comparative or inter-related courses such as that of Andrés Iduarte at Columbia University on "América en la literature española moderna," wherein students are acquainted with literary interpretations of America by Spanish writers from the years of independence to the present are very interesting and replete with valuable suggestions when they are, as in this case, conducted by the correct person. Courses such as "American-Spanish Divergences from Standard Castilian" at Berkeley and "Problems in American Spanish" at Tulane are useful to the purpose of preventing confused impressions. More courses in early and contemporary Spanish American literature concerned with Spain, France and/or the United States would be highly desirable ("Spanish American Critics and Apologists of the United States" offered at De Paul University for example).

In spite of the remarkable progress made recently in the study of Portuguese, the number of Portuguese classes, in comparison with the number of Spanish classes offered, is still out of proportion. The battle for Portuguese has not yet been won.[38] A similar statement could be made in connection with Portuguese literature which does not generally have in this country the same amount of outstanding European-born specialists who raise the standard of the courses on Spanish literature; men like Federico de Onís, Angel del Río, Américo Castro, Juan Ramón Jiménez, Jorge Guillén, Tomás Navarro, M. Romera-Navarro, Amado Alonso and others. A similar situation applies to Brazilian literature. The publication in 1948 of *Marvelous Journey*, a study on the development of Brazilian literature by Sam-

[37] Henry Grattan Doyle, "The Foreign Language Teacher's Challenge—and Rewards," in *Hispania*, November 1948.

[38] Manoel da S. S. Cardozo, "Portuguese in the School Curriculum," *The Catholic Educational Review*, May 1945.

uel Putnam, may be an optimistic sign in this field.

Each year *Hispania,* the journal published by the American Association of Teachers of Spanish and Portuguese, includes in its May issue a list of theses dealing with Spanish American literature.[39] In a comment preceding his 1948 list, Professor Barrett reports the existence of a certain amount of duplication, which is smaller among Ph.D. theses. It is interesting to note that these duplications are more frequent in the following subjects: the Indian in Spanish American literature, the novels of the Mexican revolution, José Enrique Rodó, Amado Nervo, Ricardo Palma, the "gaucho" in life and literature, Rómulo Gallegos, Rubén Darío, Florencio Sánchez, and Sarmiento. This may be an indication of the present trend in the teaching of literature. The only colonial work that is duplicated is *La Araucana.* However, a glance at the lists themselves for both years 1947 and 1948 shows a large and uneven variety of interests including some studies on colonial literature (*La Cristiada,* the chroniclers of the conquest of Mexico, satirical poetry, the theatre, America in eighteenth century Spanish literature).

LANGUAGE.—The teaching of language will not be discussed at length in this paper. It is perhaps enough to say that World War II revolutionized this field. The reading method became outmoded when the Army developed an intensified technique which really attained a limited conversational objective in a remarkably short time. The experience of the Army is exerting a profound effect on the teaching of modern foreign languages. Various prominent universities throughout the country, inspired by the experience of the Army, are attempting to apply its method, with the modifications made necessary by the varied conditions under which they operate.[40]

A study on the status of Spanish and Portuguese was made by Donald D. Walsh in 1947. Walsh summarizes his findings as follows:

The general situation with regard to Spanish and Portuguese in the colleges, universities, and professional schools is generally good, much better than we had been led to believe. There is no discrimination against Spanish for college admission and very little at the level of the Bachelor's and Master's degrees. The gap between the acceptance of Spanish and of Portuguese is due largely to the fact that Portuguese is still, for us, a "new" language, lacking large secondary-school enrollments and advanced courses in the colleges.

In science, the preference for German is more understandable than the preference for French, although it may be questioned whether either language is essential for contemporary research in science, engineering, or medicine. It is high time for engineering schools and medical schools to make a realistic reappraisal of their foreign language requirements, and the Johns Hopkins University Medical School requirement of French and German seems to me to place a particularly unreasonable burden upon the student.

The requirements for the degree of Doctor of Philosophy are in no less urgent need of revision, and there is evidence that such revisions are being seriously considered in several universities. They are indeed, first, so that the specialist in Romance languages will not have to add German to the French, Spanish, Portuguese and Italian that are his primary concern. In most universities, as we have reported, a substitution of Spanish or Portuguese for French or German is now possible, but it often depends upon the approval of the Dean or the Graduate Council; the requirement should be modified so that such a substitution would be granted automatically, and need not be made the subject of a special petition. Equally important is the need to liberalize and modernize the requirements for the specialist in other fields where foreign languages are not an essential tool for research.[41]

[39] Sturgis E. Leavitt commenced the compilation of these lists in 1935 and L. Lomas Barrett, Washington and Lee University, Lexington, Virginia, is continuing this work.

[40] Interesting information on present trends can be found in: Frederick Browning Agard and Harold B. Dunkel, *An Investigation of Second-Language Learning,* Boston, 1948; Robert John Matthew, *Language and Area Studies in the Armed Services: Their Future Significance.* Washington, D. C., American Council on Education, 1947; Sherman Eoff and William E. Bull, "A Semantic Approach to the Teaching of Foreign Languages," *The Modern Language Journal,* January 1948; Arthur Gibbon Bovée, "Present Day Trend in Modern Language Teaching," *The Modern Language Journal,* May 1949.

[41] Donald D. Walsh, "The Status of Spanish and

GEOGRAPHY.—The recent contribution of North American science to the geography of Latin America and related disciplines is impressive. The "millionth" map of Hispanic America completed a few years ago by the American Geographical Society, the Army Air Force maps, the reference bibliographies of that Society and the contents of its *Geographical Review*, as well as (in the inter-American field) the cooperation of the cartographers of this country in the Commission on Cartography of the Pan American Institute of Geography and History, are a challenge to improve the level of geographical studies at American colleges and universities. The Army Air Force maps are used in the course on geomorphology of South America at Colgate University. Several of the books presently used, such as those of James, Platt, Whitbeck and Jones, could be translated for students of Latin American universities. Aside from whatever might be of interest to the future specialist in geography, the undergraduate should complete his course with a fundamental knowledge of the location and distribution of natural resources and of the factors of climate and topography, as well as population, production and communication. The variety of subjects demanded by an adequate and well-balanced treatment of geography makes all the greater the scientific, pedagogic and social responsibility of the professors. The tendency to approach geography and related disciplines by area (which has led to the appearance of such novel courses as the one at Stanford: "Ecological and Areal Biogeography of Brazil"), and the emphasis on courses such as "Latin American Demography" at Vanderbilt are trends that deserve encouragement. Also to be desired, perhaps, is a greater interest in the history of geography and geographical explorations, and of the struggle to overcome the difficulties of nature and environment. The special summer school (1949) of the University of Texas which emphasized Latin American geography and related subjects is a worthy

___
Portuguese in American Colleges and Universities," *Hispania*, August 1947.

effort in this direction. Edmundo O'Gorman, of Mexico, was scheduled to give three special lectures in the field of historical geography during the session. Donald D. Brand, who has moved rapidly (within the last two years) from the University of New Mexico to the University of Michigan and then to the University of Texas, where he is Professor of Geography and Consultant in Latin American Geography, is undoubtedly instrumental in promoting interest in this field.

ECONOMICS.—Courses pertaining to Latin American economics are now offered in the colleges of liberal arts, education and others, and also in schools of business administration. This is true at the Universities of Texas, Houston, Boston and Miami; Columbia and Loyola (New Orleans) Universities; and the City College of New York. At New York University they are given in the School of Commerce, Accounts and Finance. The American Institute for Foreign Trade at Phoenix (Arizona) conducts a large variety of these courses including one on labor conditions in Latin America.

The problem of the relationship between economic and political factors in international life in general has given rise to controversies concerning courses for undergraduates in liberal arts who do not intend to become professional economists. At the University of Chicago, Professor Jacob Viner has for this reason offered two general courses, one for students concentrating in the Economics Department and another for students whose interest is in the field of international relations. The University of Pennsylvania follows the same practice, at the regional level, by offering the course "Government and Politics of Latin America" conducted by Edgar B. Cale, in both the College and the Wharton School of Finance. This solution is not practicable, however, except in a few large universities. It has been suggested, therefore, that professors of economics study national and international political conditions and that professors of political subjects emphasize the economic aspect of their work. Another example of this practice, though in the field of history rather than economics, is at the College of the City of New York where Marvin Bernstein offers "Development of Latin America: Modern Latin American Problems," in the College of Liberal Arts and Sciences, and in the School of Business and Civic Administration he offers the same course but "tied in as much as possible with the specific needs of the majority of students who are foreign trade majors."

In the sphere of international trade, attention has been traditionally given, as is logical, to the relations of Latin America *inter se* and with the rest of the world, but especially with the United States. Courses such as that at the University of Texas, "Markets for Latin American Products and Sources of Latin American Imports," should be encouraged. The inclination to use as a guide the economic principles and institutions of the United States in an environment so different geographically, economically, culturally and politically, and to neglect fundamental social and human elements must be energetically resisted.

The writer asked George Wythe to prepare a brief statement on the teaching of Latin American economic problems in American colleges and universities. The fact that Mr. Wythe is not in the teaching profession and yet has published an important contribution to one of the most modern aspects of Latin American economic life—industrialization—was taken into consideration. The statement of Mr. Wythe follows:

Specialized courses in Latin American economy may be classified as of two general types, depending on whether they are intended for students preparing for commercial work or for candidates interested in advanced economic research.

Perhaps the chief weakness of the Latin American courses that have been offered in the past has been the lack of clear understanding as to the purpose the course is to serve. Unless the students registered for the course have already completed work in elementary economics, international trade and commercial policy, it will not be practicable to expect very much original research in specifically Latin American economic problems. Some colleges and universities have met this problem by offering two different types of courses, one primarily descriptive and the other intended for

more advanced research by students specializing in economics.

Personally, I feel that there is a place in the curriculum for a good "descriptive" course on Latin American economy. However, it is not likely to be a "good" course unless the instructor has done a lot of analytical work himself and unless he has sufficient first-hand knowledge of the area to breathe the spirit of life into his lectures and discussions. One of the purposes of such a course would be to provide the students with a considerable amount of organized factual information, but equally, or even more important, it should give perspective, an understanding of relationships, familiarity with sources, and a glimpse of the history and spirit of Latin American institutions.

Such a course might also serve as an introduction for students desiring to undertake more advanced work in economics, with special emphasis on Latin American problems. Obviously, such students should have a good grounding in economic principles as a prerequisite. For advanced work, they also need a good reading knowledge of one or more of the languages of the area. Perhaps not more than a few institutions have adequate source materials, without which the work of the advanced student is further handicapped. As regards instruction, clearly the first requisite is a teacher who is a good economist. The importance of this cannot be over-estimated. At the same time, it must be recognized that an instructor with some first-hand knowledge of the area will be much better equipped to guide and inspire his students. Unfortunately, there is still a shortage in this country of adequately prepared instructors to give such courses.

I have some hesitancy in attempting to discuss what the content of these economic courses should be, other than to point out that the time has come to get away from the generalizations and clichés that have occupied such a large place in the past, for example, such statements as that transportation is deficient or that Latin America has vast stores of untouched resources. What is needed now is more concrete analysis of specific situations and a more realistic and scientific investigation of the various productive factors. We are apt to be hypnotized by phrases like "colonial economy," "economic development," and "industrialization," without adequate consideration of their real content and significance in particular situations. For example, some observers, impressed by the dependence of many of the southern republics on foreign trade are too prone to jump to the conclusion that the solution lies in reducing trade, whereas the real need is to increase production, both for export and for internal consumption. Self-sufficiency cannot solve the problem except at a greatly reduced standard of living.

Latin America has too long been a happy hunting ground for faddists and romantics (not that I object to romance in its place), but fortunately an increasing number of solid studies are coming from the presses and mimeograph machines. In this connection, I would like to call attention to the valuable documentation prepared by the Secretariat of the Economic Commission for Latin America, which was presented at the second session of the Commission held at Havana in May–June, 1949. I understand that these studies will be issued in printed form by the United Nations.

Among the topics of current interest, the following may be mentioned:

Nature of the resources of Latin American countries and the factors affecting their developments.

What type of development is best suited to the individual countries.

The respective roles of government and private enterprise in economic development.

The obstacles to local capital formation; credit and interest rates.

Technical training.

Immigration and employment policies.

Labor and industrial relations.

Taxation and fiscal policy; causes of inflation and currency instability.

The relation of bilateral, regional and Inter-American undertakings to broader international action.

GOVERNMENT.—It would not be realistic to pursue a course in government by reference exclusively to the texts of constitutions. When this is said, however, it must be added that such reference is an indispensable element of the study and it is very desirable that the texts be readily at hand. It is for this reason that the recent English edition of the twenty constitutions compiled by Professor Russell H. Fitzgibbon is worthy of high commendation. Another interesting contribution recently published is *Latin American Politics and Government*, by Austin Faulks Macdonald. What should be emphasized, without resentment or favor, is government in action.[42]

Despite the noticeable progress along these lines, a great deal remains to be done.

The most desirable objective would be to combine the theory of the basic institutions —the President of the Republic, the Ministers, Congress, local government—with a study of the salient features of their historical evolution, and a careful, objective analysis of their operation in practice. This could be done first from a national viewpoint, followed by comparative studies of the different countries. In this discipline especially, the professor and the serious student must keep in mind at all times the peculiar political structures of Latin America. The investment of time and work in the study of such topics as the structure of the federal government, the system of elections, or political parties, for example, would be useless in many countries if one were to remain unacquainted with the sociology or the social psychology of those countries. The worker in the field of the science of government in Latin America can be neither cynical nor naive; he must be, perhaps more than other specialists, a realist with the ability to see the unalloyed truth, and at the same time must have a high degree of understanding, good will and patience.

INTERNATIONAL RELATIONS.—The position of this study in the present survey appears uncertain. In the first place, there are a number of references to Latin America in general courses on international relations, not included in this directory. In the second place, the study is included by some institutions within general courses on "Latin American Affairs" (as at Swarthmore College), on history, government, politics, and at times (less understandably) on geography. It is possible that the rapid growth of studies in international relations on a world scale is tending to absorb such studies of Latin America.[43] If so, it is not a wholesome tendency.

[42] Russell Humke Fitzgibbon, *The Constitutions of the Americas, as of January 1, 1948.* Chicago, University of Chicago Press, 1948. Austin Faulks Macdonald, *Latin American Politics and Government.* New York, Y. Crowell Co., 1949.

[43] For a recent survey of problems facing educators in this field, see Grayson Kirk, *The Study of International Relations in American Colleges and*

Courses on international relations appear in this book under the greatest variety of names. It is unfortunate that the good example provided by the University of Pennsylvania is not followed more often. There Arthur P. Whitaker offers two courses, one on "The United States and Latin America" and the other on "Latin America in World Affairs." The names and content of the courses vary from "Diplomatic Issues in Latin America" (Southern California) to "Inter-American Relations in the Nineteenth and Twentieth Centuries" (Smith), and to "International Affairs of Latin America, 1935–49" (Tulane). Courses whose titles mention the Pan American Movement or the Inter-American System, however, are regrettably scarce. The "Seminar on Inter-American Organizations" conducted by William Sanders at the School of Foreign Service, Georgetown University, is one of the most authoritative of these courses. It is important that colleges and universities give more thought to the transformation that occurred in 1948 with the establishment of the Organization of American States, and to the increased activities of its General Secretariat, the Pan American Union. It would be to their advantage, also, to realize that the Pan American Union is prepared to collaborate with any academic institution.

ANTHROPOLOGY AND SOCIOLOGY. — The progress of recent years in archaeological, ethnological and anthropological studies in colleges and universities is remarkable and very gratifying and the favorable predictions for them made by Professor Leonard in his report in 1942 have been fulfilled. Some publications which have appeared in the United States recently are excellent. The first volumes of the *Handbook of South American Indians*, published by the Smithsonian Institution under the general editorship of Julian Steward, are a major event

and will provide orderly background material for classrooms. A generation which has just reached maturity and which has also worked at first hand in Latin America (often under the program of training and research of the Institute of Social Anthropology of the Smithsonian Institution) has joined the old guard in universities and colleges. In this field, one of the most interesting groups of professors is that of Yale University where men of the caliber of Wendell C. Bennett, Irving Rouse and George Kubler are found. Other interesting groups are located at Harvard with Alfred M. Tozzer (now retired) and Alfred Kidder II; at Columbia with W. Duncan Strong, Julian H. Steward, Gordon F. Ekholm, Gene Weltfish, Paul S. Wingert; and at California with John H. Rowe, Ronald L. Olson, and Robert F. Heizer at Berkeley and George W. Brainerd and Ralph Beals at Los Angeles.

"Ethnobiology of the New World," on the aboriginal utilization of plants and animals, is offered at the University of New Mexico and proves how specialized this field may become.

There are also strengthened courses in art and music.[44] The course on "Ancient Mexican and Peruvian Art" at Columbia University emphasizes interpretation and analysis of form and content as reflected against their cultural background.

Progress in social anthropology has been influenced by men like Robert Redfield, who is not presently teaching but whose studies in Mexico and especially in Yucatan are modern classics. His teaching has also been most effectual. Among others, Charles Wagley and Harry Tschopik of Columbia University, John Gillin of the University of North Carolina, Oscar Lewis of the University of Illinois, Sol Tax, Fred Eggan and Donald Collier of the University of Chicago and Allan Holmberg, who has recently joined the faculty of Cornell University, are actively engaged in both teaching and writing in the field of social anthropology.

The development of anthropology in connection with Latin America has had repercussions in that continent, and the recent growth of archaeological studies in Mexico

Universities. New York, Council on Foreign Relations, 1947.

[44] For a discussion of current problems in the study of art, with some papers on archaeology, see *Studies in Latin American Art*, edited by Elizabeth Wilder. Washington, D. C., The American Council of Learned Societies, 1949.

and of social anthropology in São Paulo, Brazil, are worthy of note. Donald Pierson's book *Negroes in Brazil*, published in this country in 1942, is the result of prolonged field study in Bahia and has been translated into Portuguese in São Paulo, where the author has taught for a number of years in the Escola Livre de Sociologia e Política.

Latin America offers an extremely rich laboratory of race mixture, a large variety of cultural contact situations and unusual opportunities for the study of great native civilizations; this accounts for the phenomenal growth in the field of anthropology mentioned above.

Among other eminent figures in the study of sociology, a subject which is gradually moving to riper maturity and a better coordinated effectiveness, is that of William Rex Crawford of the University of Pennsylvania. Nathan L. Whetten, Dean of the Graduate School of the University of Connecticut, and L. L. Bernard, Professorial Lecturer at Pennsylvania State College are also renowned sociologists in the field of Latin America. Dr. Whetten's recent book entitled *Rural Mexico* has been received with wide appreciation in that country.

Another key man in his field, Richard F. Behrendt, conducts at Colgate University a seminar in "Latin American Economic, Social and Political Thought" and a graduate seminar in "Economic, Social and Political Affairs in Latin America," which selected for its 1948–49 topic the recent events in Guatemala.[45] Recently the Committee on Latin American Anthropology of the National Research Council gave to those interested and qualified an outline for research and discussion of the problem of modern Latin American culture[46] which will be of assistance in arriving at a coordinated statement of the problem. It is hoped that this will also be reflected in the classrooms. The city and its relations to the country and the family and women in Latin America are still not receiving the emphasis they warrant; however, the University of Michigan and the University of Pittsburgh have made strides in this direction. The course "Latin American Social Systems" offered by Horace M. Miner, Associate Professor at Michigan, is concerned with the study of various types of rural communal organizations, the structure of urban communities and the nature and direction of social change. John Biesanz, now at Tulane, reported the course "Social Life and Relations among the Peoples of Middle and South America" at the University of Pittsburgh, which emphasized the contemporary aspects of marriage and family, religion, recreation, economics and education. Another interesting course in this field, which seems to be the only one of its type, is "Land-People Relations in Latin American Countries," a seminar offered by Professor Lowry Nelson at the University of Minnesota. This course deals with such topics as population trends, distribution, rural and urban; amount of agricultural land; types of farming; organization of farm enterprise; tenure, income, and level of living of the agricultural class; health and social security; agrarian reform.

The fascinating study of the Latin American Negroes has not been neglected by specialists in American universities. A course on the Negro in Africa and a seminar in Afro-American studies, conducted by a famous scholar, Melvill J. Herskovits, at Northwestern University, serve as a background for his course on the Negro in the New World. Franklin E. Frazier of Howard University should be mentioned for his work on the Negro in Latin America, as well as for his work in connection with Brazilian studies. Also worthy of note are the interdepartmental curriculum in African and Caribbean studies offered at Fisk University and the course on the Negro in Latin America at West Virginia State College.

PHILOSOPHY.—Though in an isolated way, real progress is being made in individual courses in Latin American philosophy. Ed-

[45] A very recent and useful contribution from Dr. Behrendt is his selected, annotated bibliography, *Modern Latin America in Social Science Literature*. Hamilton, N. Y., 1949. It includes books, pamphlets and periodicals in English in the fields of economics, politics and sociology of Latin America.

[46] In *Acta Americana*, Mexico, January–June 1948.

gar S. Brightman conducts such a course at Boston University and Marjorie Harris offers a similar one at Randolph-Macon Women's College. For her course she uses material supplied by Dr. José Franquiz, formerly of the University of Puerto Rico and now at West Virginia Wesleyan College. This progress in the field of Latin American philosophy is the outgrowth of first-hand contact with men and ideas of that continent by means of books and by personal relations with Latin American professors of the new generation and, in part, a result of the Inter-American Congresses of Philosophy.[47] As a result of such contacts a group of Latin American philosophers have come here under the auspices of the American Philosophical Association, with some aid provided by the Rockefeller Foundation. José Vasconcelos (Mexico) will give a tour of lectures throughout the United States in 1949–50, and Risieri Frondizi (Argentina), Clarence Finlayson (Chile) and Euryalo Cannabrava (Brazil) have been visiting professors at the Universities of Pennsylvania, North Carolina and Columbia University, respectively. An encouraging aspect of the activities in the field of philosophy is the fact that F. S. C. Northrop of Yale has included Latin American culture in his inquiries on cultural problems of our time.

FOLKLORE.—Columbia University offers a course on "Folklore hispánico" at the graduate level, conducted by Frederico de Onís, which is described as a course on the "traditional culture of established peoples with special emphasis on Hispanic music and poetry." On the other hand, the study of folk music of the Southwest at the University of New Mexico combines a Spanish American with an American subject. Professor Ralph Steele Boggs of the University of North Carolina is the individual to whom folklorists in the Americas owe perhaps more than to anyone else. In 1937 he began to publish his folklore bibliographies, and at that time there was no regular source of information about current publications in this field. In 1940, after a trip around South America, he organized a new society of folklorists called Folklore Americas, of which he is still di-

rector. With the cooperation of the members of the society he is able each year to produce a folklore bibliography listing most of the current publications in this field. Also with the annual bibliographies he includes news items of current activities of folklore scholars throughout the Americas, of new societies and periodicals, of new activities of established organizations, etc. He also publishes a bulletin with the same title, *Folklore Americas*.

OTHER COURSES.—There are great potentialities in courses such as that of the University of Wisconsin entitled "Journalism: Interpreting Hispanic Affairs." Of interest also is the course "International Good Will in the Elementary and Secondary School Programs: The Americas," found at the College of Education of Wayne University, Detroit, and in the course "Inter-American Affairs in the Secondary School Program," which exists at New Jersey State Teachers College at Upper Montclair. Indeed, at several institutions the attention on hemispheric education is worthy of note.

Graduate Studies: The M.A. and the Ph.D. in Latin America

Opportunities for Latin American graduate study are open mainly to persons preparing for business, teaching, government, religion and miscellaneous activities which theoretically require a high degree of training. As with studies in general, there are two types of graduate students in the Latin American field: those who plan to devote themselves to a teaching career or to advanced scholarly research and seek the M.A. degree or the Ph.D., and those who intend to engage in advanced work for a limited time only without being primarily interested in a degree.

[47] A new publication in this field is Arthur Berndtson's *Readings in Latin American Philosophy*. University of Missouri, Department of Philosophy, 1949. Columbia. In the book edited by F. S. C. Northrop, *Ideological Differences and World Order*, a series of studies in the philosophy and science of the world's culture, some chapters have been prepared by the Latin American philosophers, Leopoldo Zea, Manuel Sandoval and Francisco Romero.

The reports received from colleges and universities by the Pan American Union for the preparation of this directory were, for the most part, very detailed with regard to courses at the undergraduate level, but the information given throughout the text of the survey on work that may be done on Latin America toward a higher degree is admittedly spotty. Although this introduction mentions a variety of significant cases and aspects and cites examples where possible, it is felt that there may be several omissions in this section where the data were not forthcoming from the university itself nor specifically outlined in other sources of information.

Postgraduate study serves to fill in missing areas of learning, or to make up deficiencies in the undergraduate training and to carry out a serious, specialized task of research. The degrees of M.A. in International Affairs (Harvard), M.A. in Law and Diplomacy (Fletcher School of Law and Diplomacy), and those granted by the School of International Affairs of Columbia, the Princeton School of Public and International Affairs, and similar schools, refer to Latin America as a regional unit.

Latin America as a special field for the M.A. and the Ph.D. is found at several universities. At the University of New Mexico there is, as previously stated, a one-year intensive course in inter-American relations for graduate students, business men, professionals and technicians, and facilities for graduate work in the field of inter-American affairs leading to the M.A. degree have been provided through interdepartmental committees, within the Graduate School.

At the University of Pennsylvania, where the program of graduate studies is arranged individually, "Latin American History" is listed as a field of work toward the M.A. or Ph.D. degree, and "Government and Politics of Latin America" is listed as a field of work toward the Ph.D. degree. Also at Catholic University a Ph.D. degree may be obtained in the field of Latin American history.

Columbia University considers Spanish America as one of the fields of concentration for the M.A. degree in the Division of Modern Languages and Literature. Latin American history is also offered at Columbia as a major subject for candidates for the degree of Ph.D. by the Faculty of Political Science. Concentration in the Latin American area is offered, as already pointed out, in the School of International Affairs to candidates for higher degrees.

At the University of Chicago the Ph.D. degree may be obtained in six general international fields, and in seven regional fields (the United States, Latin America, the British Empire, Europe, the Slavic Countries, the Near East, and the Far East). The candidate must pass written examinations in four of the thirteen fields, three of which must be in the "general" classification. The final oral examination covers not only the dissertation, but also the field in which it was written.

The Institute of Latin American Studies at the University of Texas maintains interdepartmental committees within the Graduate School, correlating work in Latin American subjects offered by various departments and schools and suited to the individual needs of students. A graduate student, therefore, will find facilities available in the Institute for pursuing work across departmental lines that leads not only to the M.A. but also to the Ph.D. degree.

Just recently created is the Institute for Inter-American Study and Research at the University of Delaware, which, jointly with the Division of Graduate Study, administers a program leading to the degree of M.A. and M.S. in Inter-American Relations.

At the University of North Carolina a major in Hispanic American history with related work in United States history is offered for the degree of Ph.D. in History.

The degree of Ph.D. may be obtained at the University of California (Berkeley) in Hispanic Languages and Literature, with either Spanish or Spanish American literature as the field of major interest. The University of California (Los Angeles) also confers the Ph.D. degree in this feld.

Stanford University, through its Department of Romanic Languages, offers an M.A.

and a Ph.D. in Hispanic American Regional Studies.

The University of Missouri offers a concentration in Latin American affairs for the A.B. degree and through the Departments of History, Spanish and Political Science, the M.A. degree on Latin America, whereas the Department of History offers the Ph.D. degree also on Latin America. At Ohio State University "The Colonial Era of the Western Hemisphere" and "Greater Republics of Latin America" are listed among the fields of history for the degree of Ph.D. "Contemporary Spanish American Literature" is listed as a field in Spanish for the same degree.

The Institute for Brazilian Studies of Vanderbilt University presents a somewhat different program, offerinng graduate instruction leading to the M.A. and Ph.D. degrees. The Committee of Latin American Studies for Graduates offers at Syracuse University an interdepartmental program of Latin American studies for the M.A. degree.

In other words, the degrees of M.A. and Ph.D. in Latin American studies may be for special study in history, international relations, government, language or literature, or they may be obtained as a result of general study of Latin American affairs. Advanced degrees in this field are granted within already existing departments or within special programs. Special or permanent committees or members of the faculty authorize the studies and supervise their completion. Therefore, the acquisition of a broad and integrated basis in the area is generally considered a requisite for the completion of the training in a functional discipline.

At the national conference on the study of world areas held in New York in November, 1947, there was almost unanimous agreement that Ph.D. degrees in the general study of an area such as Latin America were not to be recommended but that the graduate student should be subjected to the requirements of a discipline training such as sociology, history, etc., with additional work in his area. The report states in this connection: "Graduate area study involves giving added competence to the student, rather than replacing standard disciplinary training. Area teaching programs should grant either an M.A. degree or a certificate, and there is no thought of granting the Ph.D. on an area basis."[48]

Area study focuses, as it has already been pointed out in this paper, the combined efforts of various disciplines upon one area of the earth; it becomes a common meeting ground for specialists and has, therefore, a wide significance, not only from the point of view of national or international interests but also from the purely scientific goal of an objective science of man.

What exactly does the word "area" mean? It is a geographic unit, serving as the subject of a specific interdisciplinary research project. An "area" may be a continent, a cultural group, a nation, an ecological unit or a subdivision of any of these.

The field of Latin American studies had already been developed, when the interest in the study of world areas as a whole began to attract American scholars and universities.[49] The work of the Joint Committee on Latin American Studies and other similar committees and activities, some of them already mentioned in the first section of this paper, were the first attempts of what is now known as "area studies." As the report of the national conference on the study of world areas points out, "many of the problems which face specialists in other areas have been temporarily resolved or shelved in the Latin American field."[50] Compared with other fields, Latin Americanists are relatively well equipped with specialists and have actually carried out a considerable amount of field research. However, despite this comparatively early activity, there are very few well financed and well staffed area institutes for Latin America in the United States today—none which compare in financial backing and staff resources with the Columbia University Russian Institute, with

[48] Charles Wagley, *op. cit.* Footnote 31.
[49] A description of special programs on various areas can be found in William N. Fenton's *Area Studies in American Universities.* Washington, American Council on Education, 1947.
[50] *Op. cit.* Footnote 43.

the Harvard Regional Program on Asia or with the University of Michigan Center for Japanese Studies. There is certainly the need to continue the development of Latin American area institutes.

The Costa Rican Project at Syracuse University

As has been mentioned before, Latin America as a whole is sometimes considered as an area, or the same expression could be used for one particular country. Such is the case of Costa Rica in the program of Syracuse University. The program offers integrated research in the fields of Costa Rican anthropology, geography, history, political science and literature. This simultaneous study of the five fields will be accomplished by joint planning of research projects, joint control and direction of projects, and joint presentation of the results. It is a new and fascinating experiment, worth watching.

The Institute for Brazilian Studies at Vanderbilt University

The significance and purposes of the Institute for Brazilian Studies of Vanderbilt University have been clearly presented in the following words before the President of Brazil, General Eurico Gaspar Dutra, on May 26, 1949:

The Institute for Brazilian Studies of Vanderbilt University is a center of research and studies on the social, economic, political, and cultural life of Brazil, and of the teachings of specialized courses and of the publications of the results of the studies for the American public. It forms an integral part of the University. The teachers give, each in his own department, several courses, some related to the work of the Institute, others without direct relation. The courses are open to any student of the University, or of the two neighboring universities.

One of the most important purposes of the Institute is the preparation and publication of original studies concerning the social and political institutions, the history, the economics, the literature, and the languages of the country, and it is hoped that more fields will be added in the near future.

Along with this purpose there exists that of preparing persons who will be students of the culture of Brazil, professors in the American universities, or candidates for the Foreign Service. In the courses designed for undergraduates, the field of study includes the nations of Latin America in general, but with special attention to Brazil, the largest and most populous of these nations. The similarity of language and culture, of history, and of problems, along with the variety of interests of the students themselves, indicates the propriety of this arrangement. In order to interest these students in the culture and people of Latin America, informative and descriptive courses are offered. For candidates for advanced degrees the program envisages a more intensive training in the tools and methods for projects of study relating to Brazil. They specialize in the studies and the problems in their respective majors, and later continue their work in Brazil.

Finally, an important part of the work is and will continue to be the dissemination, in and out of school, of informative material concerning Brazil, and the creation of an atmosphere of friendliness and understanding of that country among the American people.[51]

Summer school courses were offered for the first time in 1948 with a Brazilian professor, Emilio Willems, professor of sociology and anthropology of São Paulo, among the members of the faculty. It is hoped that American students who are candidates for the degree of Doctor of Philosophy will be expected to spend some months in Brazil. Brazilian students have already arrived at Vanderbilt University and more are expected in the future. At the same time, professors who form the permanent teaching staff are under the necessity of working in Brazil with relative frequency. The Institute plans also to serve as a research center. The library will be greatly increased.

Other Brazilian Studies

The Institute at Vanderbilt University certainly does not exhaust the wealth of Brazilian studies in this country. They have existed for some time and among those in the United States who were instrumental in their development were Percy Alvin Martin, Lawrence Hill, Herman James, Roy

[51] Vanderbilt University, *In Honor of the Visit of General Eurico Gaspar Dutra, President of Brazil to the Institute for Brazilian Studies.* Nashville, Vanderbilt, May 26, 1949.

Nash and Mary Wilhelmine Williams. A Brazilian "wave" is gradually becoming prominent in the academic life of this country. Stanford University should certainly be mentioned in the present discussion of Brazilian studies. Among individual scholars it is difficult here, as always, to select a few names, particularly as there are several in the field of Brazilian studies who have specialized in other fields as well. In art there are Robert C. Smith, and Helen Palmatary; in geography, Preston E. James; in history, Manoel Cardozo, Frederic William Ganzert, William B. Greenlee and Alexander Marchant; in language and literature, William Berrien, Leo Kirschenbaum and Samuel Putnam; and in sociology and anthropology, E. Franklin Frazier, Donald Pierson, T. Lynn Smith, Melville Herskovits and Charles Wagley.

Some Field Research Projects

In general, it is an acknowledged fact that students of a graduate center for area training should be trained in the techniques of field work. Usually, it is considered advisable to plan for the year preceding the granting of the doctorate but after the essential parts of classroom training have been completed.

In spite of the fact that they do not really belong to a report on courses at colleges and universities, something will be said here on field research projects conducted by professional scientists from various institutions. The Tarascan project of the University of California and the Instituto Nacional de Antropología e Historia of Mexico and the Institute of Social Anthropology is an example of such a project.

The Tarascan-speaking Indians inhabit an area west of the Valley of Mexico. The Tarascan program had the objective of learning as much as possible about them through an analysis of their contemporary culture and its relationship to the environment and through an archaeological and historical study. It was interrupted by the war and though few of the various research projects were actually accomplished, those already published are very important.[52]

There are at the present moment some projects which are not under the sponsorship of universities but are, nevertheless, conducted by scientists who work in one way or another with some of these institutions and follow the pattern of the field work of graduate centers for advanced training. Foremost among these are the large Maya project of the Historical Division of the Carnegie Institution of Washington and the Viru Valley program of the Institute of Andean Research.[53]

The Viru Valley is located in the northern section of the coast of Peru. A group of specialists in archaeology, history, geography, ethnology and sociology cooperated in studying the development of the culture of this valley from its earliest archaeological horizons to the contemporary society. The results are now in process of analysis and preparation for publication.[54]

Religion

Certain aspects of the advanced study of Latin America by subjects deserve special attention. One of these pertains to religion, a subject which cannot be ignored and has not been ignored in North American education. The surprise that Latin American observers may feel when they first note the courses given in Protestant institutions is somewhat lessened when it is recalled that at the beginning of the movement in Pan American relations initiated by private agencies in this country, Protestant missionaries or agents took an active part. At the

[52] For a description of the program itself see Daniel F. Rubin de la Borbolla and Ralph L. Beals, "The Tarascan Project: A Cooperative Enterprise of the National Polytechnic Institute, Mexican Bureau-Indian Affairs, and the University of California," *American Anthropologist*, 42 (4, Part I): 708–712 (1940); and the Introduction to Ralph L. Beals, Pedro Carrasco, and Thomas McCorkle, *Houses and House Use of the Sierra Tarascans*, Smithsonian Institution, Institute of Social Anthropology, Publication 1, (1944).

[53] The Maya project may be followed in the annual *Year Book* reports of the Carnegie Institution.

[54] See Gordon R. Willey, "The Viru Valley Program in Northern Peru," *Acta Americana*, December 1946.

Princeton Theological Seminary; at Scarritt College for Christian Workers of Nashville, Tennessee; at the Chicago Lutheran Theological Seminary in Maywood, Illinois; at the Biblical Seminary of New York; and at the Cumberland Presbyterian Theological Seminary, in conjunction with Bethel College of McKenzie, Tennessee, courses are or have been given either on Roman Catholicism in Latin America or on the Protestant influence there. In Catholic colleges and universities, on the other hand, one might expect a greater emphasis on these subjects. It is not implied here that their interest does not exist or is not important enough, for both the Catholic University and Georgetown University, as well as many others, take an active part in Latin American subjects. An excellent textbook on the history of Latin America has recently been published by two distinguished Catholic authors: John Francis Bannon of St. Louis University and Peter Masten Dunne of the University of San Francisco. Among other Catholic professors the name of the Reverend Jerome V. Jacobsen of Loyola University (Chicago) should be included in any list of leaders in the Latin American field. Loyola University publishes a quarterly journal, *Mid America*, which carries research studies in the field of Latin American history. *The Americas*, a quarterly review of Inter-American cultural history published by the Academy of American Franciscan History in Washington, D. C., with Dr. Roderick Wheeler, O.F.M., as managing editor, is well known and highly respected in the scholarly world. However, considering the interest of American Catholicism in inter-American cultural relations and the significant growth of American Catholic schools and missions in Latin America, we should perhaps expect more from Catholic colleges and universities in this country. One cannot find, for example, in a list as complete as the one published here any course on "Catholic Literature in Latin America" or on "Contemporary Catholic Thought in Latin America." There are, of course, individual studies on the subject as, for instance, the monograph of Francis Bor-

gia Steck, O.F.M., on literary contributions of Catholics in nineteenth-century Mexico.

Architecture and City Planning

The study of architecture and city planning in South America is relatively undeveloped in American universities and colleges. This is an unfortunate circumstance, as there is an increasing amount of emphasis being placed on city planning in Latin America at present and the interest in modern architecture has been amazingly active in some countries on that continent. The School of Architecture of Columbia University made plans for a course on "Contemporary Urban Planning and Development in Latin America" to be offered in the summer of 1949. These plans did not materialize but the course is to be offered again in the summer of 1951. "Architecture of the Americas" is offered at Harvard and Duke Universities. The course at Harvard is conducted by Kenneth John Conant and includes about 12 lectures on Latin America concerning pre-Columbian, colonial and more modern architecture of the Western Hemisphere. Harold E. Wethey of the University of Michigan is author of the book *Colonial Architecture and Sculpture in Peru*, published recently by the Harvard University Press, which is an additional proof of the fact that this type of study is gaining strength.

Law

The establishment in 1947 of an Institute of Inter-American Law at the New York University Law School, designed to bring together outstanding graduates of law schools in the Western Hemisphere, was certainly a step in the right direction for the stimulation of Latin American legal studies in this country.

The idea for the Institute was conceived by Arthur T. Vanderbilt, Chief Justice of the New Jersey Supreme Court and Dean Emeritus of New York University School of Law. The Director of the Institute is Dr. Miguel A. Capriles, Associate Dean of the same school. Under the program of the Institute, promising Latin American lawyers are brought to New York on $2500 scholarships

($1500 for living expenses and $1000 for tuition) financed by American business corporations. Companies currently contributing to the Institute are the American & Foreign Power Company, Creole Petroleum Corporation, Eli Lilly & Company, Radio Corporation of America, Sharp & Dohme, Inc., E. R. Squibb & Sons, Asiatic Petroleum, Standard Oil Company (New Jersey), American Smelting & Refining Company, Socony Vacuum Company, the Texas Company and the United Fruit Company. Pan American Airways also participates in the program by providing five travel fellowships yearly. All the companies have representatives on the Institute's advisory council but do not undertake to control recipients of the scholarships. In fact, they realize no direct benefits from their donations. The Institute is considered an investment in better business relations in the future for all American industries. All students are graduates of law schools in Latin America and all are practicing lawyers, selected by New York University with the assistance of the Institute of International Education. Participants are chosen for their character and personality, high academic record, adequate mastery of English and interest in and aptitude for leadership in public affairs. Over the last two years 28 students representing Argentina, Bolivia, Brazil, Chile, Costa Rica, Cuba, Ecuador, Guatemala, Mexico, Peru, Uruguay and Venezuela have enrolled in the Institute. Thirteen were enrolled in 1948–49. The course runs from September 1 to June 1. Special seminars are conducted by regular members of the New York University Law School faculty for the visiting lawyers. One of the main purposes of the course is to compare the legal structures and procedures of the Americas. Within a year after the course, the degree of Master of Comparative Jurisprudence is conferred upon the completion of a satisfactory thesis.

For many years the University of Michigan Law School has sponsored a number of legal research projects as a branch of its organized activities. By reason of an endowment provided by the late William W. Cook for legal education and research at this University, and the contributions of the Lawyers Clubs it has been possible to provide a staff of research professors, fellows and assistants to investigate problems. Research in inter-American law with specific reference to subjects of interest from the viewpoint of commercial relations is under the direction of Professor Hessel E. Yntema. This project has the cooperation of a number of scholars from the Latin American countries, some of whom are recipients of research fellowships awarded by the State Department. The research comprehends in each subject, as Professor Yntema has pointed out, detailed analysis of the pertinent laws of the Latin American countries in conjunction with those of the United States and the Dominion of Canada, comparative evaluation of their provisions in terms of practical needs and in the light of developments in other countries and, incidentally, the formulation of appropriate bases for the unification or, more precisely, the reconciliation of the subject matter. Such research will have value also for the study of international relations, for comparative legal science and, particularly, for the informed considerations of proposals to unify inter-American law.[55]

Latin American commercial law courses have begun to appear in some universities. There is one such course given at the University of Texas by Professor Pablo Max Ynsfran and another by Gordon Ireland at the Catholic University of America.

Bibliography and Graduate Library Work

The courses "Latin American Bibliography" and "Mexican Bibliography" under Nathan van Patten at Stanford University are deserving of special praise, despite the fact that sometimes they are not given for lack of students. The first offers "a general survey of current sources of information concerning Latin American bibliography and of principal publications relating to earlier bibliography of Latin American books and periodicals" and the second, "sources of information concerning Mexican books and periodicals and resources of Mexican libra-

[55] Hessel E. Yntema, "Research in Inter-American Law," *Michigan Law Review*, December 1944.

ries and archives collections." It is to be hoped that American institutions and students who plan to concentrate in the field of Latin America will realize more thoroughly the scholarly and practical value of courses in the field of bibliography, and it would be a real help to the improvement of research if there were more courses in this field with attention to other areas of Latin America. There is also great need for an institute for graduate librarians which would serve both native Latin Americans who complete their professional training in the United States and native Americans who plan to work in libraries of cultural institutions or other agencies of Latin America, or who merely desire to complete their library training. Plans are now under consideration for establishing such a center at the University of Illinois in 1950 and it is to be hoped that they may become an accomplished fact.

Cooperation in Graduate and Postgraduate Studies

The Hall report, frequently quoted in this paper, speaks of the "band wagon" technique by which some universities, for a not entirely understandable reason, feel compelled to duplicate the actions of other universities.

Universities W and X launch programs in Latin American Studies and universities Y and Z announce the same in their next catalogues. Now universities W and X may have quite sufficient reasons for entering the Latin American field. They have a strong nucleus of scholars in that field and plan to add others; through the years the library resources on Latin America have grown steadily and allocations have been made to strengthen them further; and for historical reasons of one kind or another a strong traditional interest in Latin America prevails. Universities Y and Z on the other hand, have little in the way of staff or library resources and no particular interest in the Latin American field. A professor of political science, let us say, is notoriously willing to oblige. He is asked if he would emphasize Latin America in his course on international relations. A professor of Spanish is asked to give a course in Latin American literature. A course on the geography of Latin America is discovered for the first time by the administration. An eager young man is found to give the program direction. All this is elaborately written up and when the next catalogue appears the description of the "new" program in Latin American Studies reads quite as respectably as those in the catalogues of universities W and X. Here is good publicity; something is had for nothing; and the score is even. To be sure, most programs of this type probably will die sooner or later from their own iniquities. Meantime they help to create a bad opinion of area studies in general.

All this planning is accentuated by the hope of ensnaring outside support. In one institution the Latin American resources are excellent. Those on the Far East are but mediocre and the climate for their development is distinctly unhealthy. The receipt of a small grant for Far Eastern Studies, from outside the university, and the hope for more led the administration to abandon support in the Latin American field. At a number of universities the main question seemed to be, "What areas are likely to draw the greatest support from the outside?" rather than, "In what areas are we best equipped to do a good job?"[56]

Some efforts have been made toward divisional responsibility and regional cooperation among universities within the field of Latin American studies. A good example of such a project is the Carnegie grant to North Carolina, Texas, Tulane and Vanderbilt, which called for cooperation among these universities. Particularly stressed was cooperation in the summer schools; the first on Brazil, offered at Vanderbilt in 1948 and the second on geography of Latin America, at the University of Texas. Another example of cooperation among universities is that found among the institutions in Nashville: the Scarritt College for Christian Workers, George Peabody College and Vanderbilt University.

A very gratifying development would be for the universities that have taken the lead in Latin American studies to intensify the agreements among themselves upon certain specialties to be followed in the future. This specialization might be by subjects of the curriculum, by areas or by problems. The latter two methods are not always economically feasible as it would be necessary to have a variety of specialists, but programs which would utilize individuals of different

[56] Hall, *op. cit.* Footnote 30.

disciplines in simultaneous and coherent action would very likely be beneficial to science and to the persons and institutions that participate in them. By means of conferences and joint seminars, such cooperation could be carried out very effectively. This creation, not only on the graduate level but also on a post-doctoral scale, might have very advantageous consequences. Invitations could be extended by rotation to Professors from other institutions, and to well-known specialists not active in academic life. Centers of advanced Latin American research similar to the Yale Institute of International Studies and the Princeton Institute for Advanced Study would be highly desirable. Perhaps the Washington area would be an ideal location for one of these groups.

There has been some indication of the need for a more soundly developed national program of area studies. It has even been proposed that a national organization concerned with coordinating area research might be attached to the Smithsonian Institution, as was the wartime Ethnogeographic Board, to some other quasi-governmental organization, or it might operate as an independent office.

When inter-American university cooperation is emphasized, reference should be made to the unique position which the University of Puerto Rico occupies. A Spanish-speaking center within the structure of the American educational system, it gives credit to both cultures. It is in direct contact with American universities as well as with some leading men and women of the universities of Latin American republics.

A Few Words About Professors

Before closing this introduction, which has already become so long and yet has touched only lightly upon the various problems involved, it may not be amiss to say a few words concerning professors of courses on Latin America. It may be deduced from the foregoing analysis that we have been considering as such, not only those who have contact with large groups and those who work with intermediate groups, but also those who do basic research with graduate groups. However, if a young student within one of these classifications, wishes to enter into the teaching profession in the Latin American field, what qualifications should he aspire to have aside from the usual academic requirements?

There was a time when these courses were in great demand and teaching personnel was limited; but now that the years have produced a considerable number of graduates in Latin American studies, greater selection is possible. It is undeniably of basic importance, for example, to be able at least to read Spanish, Portuguese or French well in order to keep informed at first hand in the subject taught. This language ability ought to be accompanied by actual experience in Latin America, which means contact at first hand with the people, not the incidental contact of a tourist or an acquaintance derived from books. Especially, at the graduate level, there is an increasing trend to combine teaching with occasional periods of research and field work. This traffic between the classroom and seminar and the field is one of the most healthy symptoms. Research teams might be organized, composed of staff members, advanced students and native scholars, when and if universities can afford the resources and facilities of such undertakings.

The problems here is one of integration, of giving proper emphasis to technical ability in the discipline to be taught and to the sharpness of perception or breadth of understanding provided by the study trips and contacts with the people and by the literature that exists in the native languages. Such contacts should be continuous and periodically renewed in order to avoid the stratification of judgments and opinions, and in order to keep currently informed of the changes which sometimes occur so rapidly in the Latin American scene. It is necessary to demand of the professor of Latin American subjects breadth of mind and spirit, if he is to accept and appreciate the differences in the ways of living in the two Americas, and a feeling of cordial fellowship, accompanied by a vast patience. At the same time he must have a moderate supply of skepticism or caution and be capable of his own table of values, in order to distinguish that which is fundamental from that which is of only fleeting notoriety in Latin American life, so that he will not be carried away by the influence of personal friendships or superficial impressions. He should also acquire a selective standard of preferences and tastes and he must especially avoid any "missionary complex" to participate in the internal struggles and quarrels of Latin American countries.

In general it seems that the level of the studies and of those who pursue them is uneven. In the crucial years which lie ahead this level must be raised as much as possible. The professors of Latin American courses themselves could form an association which would contribute to the improvement and supervision of this field of study, including the intellectual appraisal of projects, programs and courses.

Already remarkable progress has been observed within existing organizations. One case in point is the Association of Teachers of Spanish and Portuguese previously mentioned in this report. Another which cannot be omitted is the Conference on Latin American History, of the American Historical Association. This group has been in existence for over twenty-five years and has been formally organized for more than ten years. The session of the Conference at the coming meeting of the American Historical Association in Boston in December, 1949, will be devoted to a discussion of the general or introductory college course in Latin American history. Also, since about 1945, the American Political Science Association has had a standing Latin American Committee, under the chairmanship of Russell Fitzgibbon of the University of California at Los Angeles, which regularly organizes one or more sessions on Latin America at the Association's annual meetings. Next December there will be a session on "The Pathology of Democracy in Latin America" with three papers on that subject, one each by a political scientist, a sociologist and a historian. More of this kind of cooperation is needed, crossing the lines of departmentalization and specialization.

It is interesting to note that from the beginning of university studies on Latin America in the United States down to the present, the participation of Latin Americans themselves has been important but not exactly large, though various efforts were made in the thirties to increase it. The fact is that there are not as many instances as could be expected of outstanding professors from Latin America, who have devoted themselves definitively and exclusively to the teaching vocation. The explanation for this is obvious. In the first place, many have come for only a short time, for they have had to return to their respective countries to continue their university, political or diplomatic careers. Also, it has not always been possible to overcome the difficulties arising from differences in language, environment and ways of living. Occasionally it has surprised and troubled a university to find that some Latin Americans have a wide variety of cultural interests, but this is the influence of the tradition of humanism and of the necessities imposed by a somewhat restricted environment, and does not necessarily indicate superficiality or intellectual instability. At other times, on the contrary, when the Latin American continent is being considered as a whole, there is not so much need for the collaboration of specialists in only one country or in a particular aspect or historical period of a country. In any case the tendency to invite good Latin American professors to participate in studies on Latin America is, in principle, salutary. It might be profitable to examine in detail the possibility of continuing and augmenting their collaboration and of having conferences or round-table discussions where they and their American colleagues might exchange experiences and suggestions.

Special mention should here be made of the first meeting of United States and Mexican historians held at Monterrey, Mexico, September 4 to September 9, 1949. Another important fact in the same direction is that the United States is taking an active part in the reorganized and reinvigorated Pan American Institute of Geography and History. The United States Government has completed the appointment of its national members of the three commissions (one each on cartography, geography and history). These members are: Robert H. Randall (cartography), Preston James (geography) and Arthur P. Whitaker (history). Private institutions and individual scholars in the United States are cooperating extensively with these official members in carrying out the work of the Institute and its commissions.

The Challenge of the Future

From 1895 to the decade of 1930 was the period of the foundation of Latin American studies in colleges and universities of the United States. During the thirties and the beginning of the 1940's their development was extraordinary.

We are now at the beginning of a period of contraction which will affect the higher institutions in general because the post-war "inflation" in college and university enrollments has reached its peak. Latin American studies, in particular, will be affected because the Latin American "boom" is over and an increasing interest in other world areas is becoming more evident in recent years. On the other hand, one cannot say that the external stimulus received by Latin American studies during the past fifteen years or so was the main reason for its development. They have been officially in existence at the University of California for the past fifty-four years, at Yale University for almost fifty, at the University of Texas and Columbia University for forty-five years, at the University of Pennsylvania for forty-two years, at Illinois for forty, at Stanford and Harvard for thirty-five and at several other institutions for thirty years or slightly less.

It is true that the position of Latin American studies in the American educational system and the organization of research in the field should now be reconsidered. However, in the years to come there must not be a period of depression for these studies. On the contrary, we hope that the challenges of the future will bring greater depth and authenticity to the Latin American courses at American universities and colleges. They must be refined, adapted, tested and amplified. The level of both teaching and research needs to be raised and the unnecessary or useless eliminated. We also hope, as indicated previously, that we may see the development of increasing integration through interdisciplinary research and closer cooperation and interchange among institutions to avoid unnecessary duplication and among professors and specialists on both continents for their mutual acquaintance, for their professional stimulation, and for the progress of their studies. Furthermore, we hope to see in future years more and more effective contacts between the thousands of Latin-American-minded men and women on the campuses of this great country and the Organization of American States, through the Pan American Union, its administrative and technical General Secretariat.

57. Report of the Committee on the Twenty-Fifth Anniversary*

DONALD E. WORCESTER, JOHN P. HARRISON, BERNARD E. BOBB

This Committee has been assigned the task of evaluating the work of the Conference on Latin American History of the American Historical Association during the first twenty-five years of its existence as it appears to the current crop of younger scholars. The members of the Committee, not being able to isolate the precise factor that separates the young from the mature (they cannot be distinguished by age, number of years out of graduate school, or the quality and amount of publications), were hesitant about writing fellow Latin-Americanists who in their own minds may have made the transition from the callowness of youth to the breadth of maturity and might be indignant that we were unaware of the transformation. Operating empirically with an instinctive feeling for our own, we did correspond and talk with a number of the younger Latin Americanists, and from the answers came at least one definition of a young Latin American historian. He is one who has never held an office or administrative post in the Conference and is therefore ignorant of the basic purpose of the society. This, of course, does not preclude his having personal ideas to the functions it should perform.

The problem of evaluating the activities of the Conference in light of its stated objectives has presented some difficulties, since many of those of our own stripe—the younger set—admittedly are ignorant of both the aims and past activities of the Conference. Our report, therefore, is based on published notes in the *HAHR*, the annual programs of the AHA, and on the personal ideas of the Committee members and their correspondents as to what the Conference should be doing, ideas, it should be added, which spring from the innocence of youth and a respect for our elders. But because it is no simple task to judge the success of past activities from the brief published notes, this report can hardly be considered an evaluation.

The group that was to develop into the Conference on Latin American History sponsored its first program in the form of a symposium at the annual AHA meetings held in Rochester in 1926. The subject under discussion was "Means and Methods of Widening among Colleges and Universities an Interest in the Study of Hispanic-American History." From the account of the meeting and excerpts from correspondence received by the organizing committee published in the *HAHR* for August, 1927, it is clear that the primary concern of the group was to increase the number of courses on Hispanic-American history offered in colleges and universities as the most likely way to establish the study of Hispanic-American history

* Mimeographed. Conference on Latin American History Archives, Hispanic Foundation, Library of Congress (Dec. 1953).

as a recognized field of scholarly endeavor. It is also evident that this group believed that the most urgent matter in this regard was to improve the quality of teaching Hispanic-American history on the college level. It was in answer to this need that the series of translated national histories published by the University of North Carolina Press was undertaken. A committee on research was appointed at this meeting but there is no published evidence of its activities. If one can safely generalize from the notes in the *HAHR* and the programs of the annual AHA meetings the organized efforts to promote research were directed mainly to the publication of bibliographical tools. While much excellent work in this line appeared in the *HAHR* during the years immediately after the regeneration of the *Review* in the fall of 1926, it is important to note that although several national histories—important only as teaching aids—were published, the proposed bibliography of Hispanic-American and Spanish transcripts, facsimiles, and manuscripts in the Library of Congress has not even begun to materialize. It is also interesting to note that two of the problems most troubling historical scholarship today (methodology with its philosophical overtones, and the relationship of historical investigations to studies by geographers, anthropologists, economists, and political scientists) were not matters of vital concern when this organization was founded. They are today.

In December, 1938, the Conference formally adopted a Constitution, composed of six articles. Article 2 was concerned with the purposes of the Conferences, and will be cited below.

2. The objects of the Conference are to assist the program committee of the American Historical Association in preparing the program for a Latin American session at the annual Association meeting, to provide for a luncheon or dinner meeting of teachers, students, and others interested in Latin American history and allied fields, to be held in connection with the annual meeting of the AHA, and to take whatever action may seem desirable for furthering the interests of the Conference group.

The Constitution was amended at the December, 1947, and 1948 meetings, but the amendments did not alter the objectives as stated in 1938.

With regard to the first objects, assisting the program committee of the AHA in preparing the program for a Latin American session and providing for a luncheon or dinner meeting, the Conference has, it seems, been successful. Academic sessions and luncheon meetings have been held regularly, and to these have been added assemblies of a more convivial nature at a later hour of the day. Since the members of the Conference are widely scattered and have too few opportunities to become well-acquainted with one another, we regard all of these gatherings with enthusiasm. They are important, and serve a useful purpose.

There is, however, a widespread and, unfortunately, ill-defined feeling of dissatisfaction on the part of the younger scholars with the programs sponsored by the CLAH at the annual meetings of the AHA. Unrest may be considered a healthy condition for young minds but this particular crop of historians perhaps reflects the general state of Latin American studies in that their disturbed minds are unable to bring the various facets of the current situation into sharp enough focus to provide a positive program of their own. The one proposal in regard to the programs at the annual meetings that all of the younger men agree to—and one which this Committee endorses—is that the luncheon meetings should be free of monographic papers. We feel that they should be devoted to interpretative papers delivered by the better-established men in the field. Historiography is suggested as an ideal topic. Another possible type of paper for the luncheon meetings would be a general report on the current economic, political, and intellectual state of affairs in a particular country given by someone who has had the advantage of unofficial observation and time for reflection offered by a year or six months as an exchange professor in the country described. As a specific example we would all enjoy hearing Professor Haring give an account of the study of Latin

American history in the United States, emphasizing the major problems and landmarks as they appeared to him when they happened and as he views them in retrospect.

The feeling seems to be general that it would be a good idea to have two sessions on Latin America at the annual AHA meetings rather than the usual one. It is felt that one session should be devoted to papers that deal with philosophical orientation and interpretation and the other to papers that report the results of detailed research. The research meetings, they feel, should be organized around topics or areas. A review of the programs from 1926 through 1952 shows that this has been done much more frequently than most of the young men seem to realize. There have been programs devoted to church and state, foreign interests in the Caribbean, middle-American archeology, the development of federalism, foreign elements in the ABC states, the development of science, effects of external pressures in the seventeenth century, business enterprise, and, of course, the enlightenment, clearly the one topic most extensively treated at the annual meetings. Perhaps the most curious omission is that from 1926 to the present there has never been a luncheon talk or a program devoted to contemporary problems in Latin America. This Committee believes that when conditions justify an examination of current United States foreign policy a program of papers analyzing this policy by United States and Latin American scholars would be welcomed by the membership.

Criticism by the younger men that the programs do not have enough vitality to stimulate creative discussions and that papers read on what are supposed to be related topics are seldom complementary is probably more a criticism of the current state of Latin American historical scholarship than it is of the program committees. The tie that binds our group is a mutual interest in a defined geographical area. There is no common ground of topical interest. As long as this condition exists it is impossible to see how the program committee can be expected to arrange a group of papers that will deal with a *fresh* research topic, unless, well ahead of time, the Conference decides on some problem that needs intensive investigation and can find the men who are both prepared and interested enough to handle it. It is assumed that the program of papers on the enlightenment in Latin America was realized only by long-range planning. That the younger men recognize the difficulty of organizing research meetings around topics or problems is clear, for their suggestions favoring topical programs were usually qualified by some remark such as, "if the amount of research being done will stand the strain." Should the Conference take under consideration the planning of research on selected topics it is suggested that for the purpose of oral presentation subjects with current implications are preferable.

One situation the younger historians do not have clear in their minds is the relationship of the CLAH to the *HAHR*, other than the Managing Editor being an *ex officio* member of the General Committee. If it is not a close one they all feel that it should be. It is significant to note that the organization of this group followed immediately upon the reappearance of the *HAHR* in 1926 after a four-year hiatus. It is almost a truism that a field of scholarship well enough defined to support a Conference such as this must be able to support a journal that publishes the results of investigation, and that its standing in the world of scholarship depends to a very great extent upon the quality of that journal. The failure of the *Review* in 1922, four years after its founding, was a notice that Hispanic-American studies in the United States had not reached that stage of maturity that its founders believed it had. Its existence was dependent upon subventions from interested individuals and when this support was not forthcoming publication stopped. It is not surprising, then, that when the chairman of the 1926 symposium at Rochester opened the meeting with a plea for the support of the *HAHR* as an agency in the process of widening the interest in the study of Hispanic-American history, he emphasized the need for financial support of the *Review* in the form of subscriptions and advertisements. Today approximately 70 per cent of the membership of this conference subscribes to the *Review*. The director of the Duke University Press regards this figure as a favorable one but this Committee sees no reason why it should not be 100 per cent. It proposes that the membership fee for the CLAH be increased to $5.00 annually to include a subscription to the *Review*. It also suggests as a topic for discussion an additional assessment of 50 cents annually to go towards a prize to be awarded by a board selected for the purpose to the author of the most significant article published in the *Review* during each calendar year. The Committee believes that under the successive editorship of Professors Lanning, King, and Griffin the *Review* has become increasingly a publication in which we as scholars can take a justifiable pride. This does not mean that the level of scholarship as represented in the quality of the articles cannot be improved upon. The *Review* is unable to pay for articles as do some learned journals but the combination of honor and pecuniary reward for a prize article might stimulate more scholars to do original thinking on subjects that can be fully developed in an article, rather than writing articles that are essentially a by-product of some monograph or are narrative accounts of some little-known incident dredged up from an unused manuscript collection chanced upon by the author and which adds little if anything to the mainstreams of current investigation. In short, it is hoped that such a prize would result in the submission of a greater number of significant articles from which the board of editors could select. It seems to the Committee that if the Conference has one function other than its obvious social one it should be to support the *Review* financially and intellectually, for the quality of research everywhere is influenced by the quality of the *Review*. To a great extent it sets the tone of Hispanic-American studies in the United States. It has also been suggested that the CLAH might render a useful service by establishing liaison with Latin American scholarly organizations, and through them create more reliable channels

through which the Managing Editor may receive fuller coverage of Latin American publications and bibliographical information.

A number of the young men feel, as doubtless do many of the older members, that it would be highly gratifying if the CLAH were equipped to promote scholarship directly through grants, prizes, and publication programs. There was some expression of opinion that the large United States business concerns operating in Latin America could profitably be approached on this matter. On the probabilities of success in such a venture the Committee defers to the opinion of men with experience in this field. It does believe that if there are any members with specific ideas as to what individuals or corporations should be approached for financial aid that they be organized into a committee with authority to investigate the subject. The Committee also believes that the Conference as an organization should take cognizance of the apparent emphasis by the present administration on cultural relations with Latin America. There are indications that the Department of State is willing to consider programs presented by institutions and established organizations that have as their purpose the improvement of understanding between the United States and Latin America. Whether or not the Conference considers such matters a legitimate part of their program for the promotion of interest in Latin American studies is something about which this Committee does not presume to offer even an opinion.

The suggestion was also made that the CLAH should serve as a sort of clearing house between the individual scholar and the learned societies and foundations that support scholarly investigations on Latin American topics. The Committee members are not familiar with the way foundations operate—certainly an indication of their youth—but they do believe that some useful purpose in this line could be rendered by the CLAH as a coordinate or regulative group and as a dispenser of accurate information on available grants. The existence at many of the larger universities or institutes and other loosely organized, but nonetheless dedicated, groups whose dual function seems to be the promotion of scholarly research on Latin American topics and the building up of the universities' name through the quality of the investigations put the individual scholar not associated with these universities at a decided disadvantage in financing his personal research. Such individuals would welcome the opportunity of having an organization with the authority that could be wielded by the CLAH serve both as an advisory and evaluating agency for research topics.

A related problem is posed by the recent creation of regional groups that have been organized for the purpose of reanimating what they consider to be the sagging condition of Latin American studies. These groups, as do the university institutes, operate on inter-disciplinary lines. At a time when some universities classify history with the humanities and others consider our discipline as one of the social sciences, and when the great foundations draw a sharp distinction between the humanities and the social sciences, this Committee feels it is incumbent upon our group to do some basic thinking about and clarify its relationship with the several inter-disciplinary organizations that concern themselves with Latin American matters.

It has been pointed out that when this group was organized the primary concern of its members was with teaching problems. The correspondence and conversations of the committee members indicate that today the young men in the field are more concerned with the problems of research. One of them commented that "no organization can supply what our profession most desperately needs, namely, essential scholarship, still an individual matter." While scholarship may well be an individual matter the extent to which it is carried on and the trends it takes depend largely on the society in which the scholar lives. In matters of encouragement and direction the CLAH can, with positive action, play a decisive part in the quality and quantity of historical research on Latin American topics produced in the years to come.

The social function performed by the Conference is sufficient reason for its existence. The question is: Do the members consider this the proper organization to perform the other services suggested in this report and, if so, are the individual members willing to devote the time necessary to make an expanded program possible?

58. Research in Latin American Economics and Economic History*

MIRON BURGIN

The war years witnessed a remarkable growth of interest in Latin America. What once had been an area which only diplomats and pioneering scholars ventured to explore, became almost overnight the center of attraction to government officials, as well as to scholars and teachers. Students and statesmen, journalists and laymen embarked upon the exciting journey of discovery and exploration of the lands and peoples south of the Rio Grande. The Good Neighbor Policy, which until the end of the nineteen thirties was evident mostly in the rarefied atmosphere of diplomacy and international conferences, at long last penetrated into the lower strata of every day activities. In addition to being professed, good neighborliness began to be practiced on a large scale and in ever widening areas of human endeavor. We wanted to know more about Latin America and we wanted to know Latin America better.

It is not difficult to define the forces which conditioned this growth of interest in things Latin American. They were essentially the same forces which motivated the famous declaration by President Monroe and which kept the United States in the forefront of the Pan American movement. The Good Neighbor Policy created the proper climate in which these forces could grow and develop most fruitfully, for it emphasized the

principle that the concept of sovereignty is not incompatible with the concept of mutual assistance, such as is recognized in a community of good neighbors. But it was not until the outbreak of war in Europe and the bombing of Pearl Harbor that the spirit of collaboration implicit in the Inter-American system and the Good Neighbor Policy was transformed into living reality.

Effective collaboration against the common enemy extended beyond the area of political solidarity into economic and military cooperation. It called for detailed knowledge of the economic potential of Latin America as well as of the geographic, social and political environment in which that potential was to be realized. This in turn implied a thorough understanding of the mode of life and work in the countries to the south. It presupposed also a more than passing acquaintance with the cultural heritage of the Latin American Republics, their history and their aspirations. Hence the extension of the lines of contact between the United States and Latin America, hence also the intense need for authentic information concerning Latin America and for adequately trained personnel to serve as guides

* *Inter-American Economic Affairs*, 1/3: 3–22 (1947). Reprinted by permission of the original publisher. This article is based on a paper presented at the Conference on Latin American History Luncheon 1946 meeting.

to and interpreters of the Latin American scene.

That the needs exceeded by far the available resources in personnel and factual information was perhaps to be expected. What was not at first realized, and what later became only too painfully apparent, was the extent of the deficiency. While in some areas, notably history and ethnology, the reserve fund of manpower and information was adequate, if not abundant for the task at hand, in the field of economics the shortage of both was from the beginning rather serious. It became critical after Pearl Harbor when Washington became the center of economic defense of the Western Hemisphere.

Scarcity of information, at least basic information, could be and was remedied in time. But the problem of personnel in the field of economics and economic history was infinitely more complex, and in fact has never been satisfactorily solved. Already in the early phases of the war there developed a severe scarcity of competent economists familiar with the Latin American area and its problems. It became common practice in government agencies to fill responsible positions that called for skilled handling of complex economic material and problems with historians, anthropologists, geographers, jurists or just any one who had some sort of acquaintance with Spanish or Portuguese. The result of this practice, born of necessity, to be sure, was quite disconcerting. Mere recapitulation of readily available statistical series was only too often paraded as economic research. Economic thinking about Latin America was more often than not reduced to the level of endless repetition of worn out clichés. Even with respect to the relatively limited job of compiling and arranging factual material accomplishments left a good deal to be desired.

To be sure, a limited number of economists did enter the Latin American field. But their interest in the area was in most instances temporary. These were shot-gun weddings or marriages of conveniences, to be dissolved as soon as the emergency was no longer pressing. There can be no doubt that they contributed a good deal to our understanding of Latin American economics through proper formulation of economic problems and adaptation of appropriate techniques of economic analysis. But their contribution, however valuable, was of necessity circumscribed by their imperfect, often rudimentary, knowledge of the social, political and historical background of which the economic problems they were examining were integral parts. Moreover, their presence in the Latin American sectors of the various government agencies was too short lived to leave a permanent impress upon the quality of economic research and analysis. And most of them lost interest in Latin America upon their return to academic work.

So it is that research in the field of Latin American economics and economic history during the war period has not been as fruitful as one would expect. Preoccupation with problems arising out of the war, all of them practical and urgent, made research difficult at best. But no less important was the fact that our research apparatus in the field of Latin American economics was not sufficiently well developed to utilize to the full the opportunities created by the war. Unlike in the case of history, for example, economic research in the Latin American area was handicapped by lack of tradition, direction and personnel.

One need not be sanguine to assert that in the post war era Latin America is destined to play an increasingly active role in the affairs of the Western Hemisphere and of the world at large. Latin America has grown in stature and has become more influential not only because of the decline, political and economic, of Western Europe, but also because of the very considerable economic progress which many Latin American countries have made since the beginning of the war. Pan Americanism promises to encompass not only the political aspects of inter-American relations but economic ones as well. And precisely because the United States, a member of the American community of nations, has become the economic epicenter of a large part of the world, the specific economic weight of Latin America is likely to increase. Economic relations between the United States and Latin America will in all probability become more extensive and also more intimate, and it is not unreasonable to assume that the outside world will become increasingly concerned about economic developments in and economic policies of at least the more important Latin American countries. Accordingly, the need for competent, one is tempted to say authentic, analysis and interpretation of the ever changing economic scene south of the Rio Grande is likely to be more urgent than ever before.

It may safely be assumed that such a demand will consist not solely or even overwhelmingly of requirements of the various government agencies concerned with Latin America. Business, too, is increasingly conscious of the importance of the kind of evaluation of the economic climate of Latin America that fundamental research alone can in the final analysis provided. And last but not least there is the probability that interest in Latin American affairs on the part of the general public, though not as intense as it was during the war, will remain at a relatively high level. It is true, of course, that the general public is not a direct consumer of basic research. But this does not mean that it is indifferent to such research. On the contrary, it is not too much to expect that as the public becomes more clearly aware of the problems and issues relating to Latin America it will give increasing support to academic research in this area.

Whether economists and economic historians will heed the call, should it materialize, and take more kindly to Latin America than they have in the past is a question that cannot be readily answered. For one thing they may want to have some assurance that the propitious climate such as has been described above will endure. For it must be borne in mind that specialization in the Latin American field, as in any other area, involves a considerable investment of time and effort that in the academic field, at least, cannot be amortized easily or quickly. But even more important perhaps than the cer-

tainty and extent of returns on the investment are the questions whether such research is *per se* justifiable, and if so, whether it is feasible. The answer to the first question will depend upon the manner in which the economic problem in the Latin American area is defined. The second question involves the problem of facilities available to scholars who desire to specialize in this area.

II

It has been customary among economists in the industrially advanced countries to define the problem of research in the Latin American area in terms of the economic and socio-political development of Europe, especially Western Europe and the United States. Not without reason Latin America has been viewed as a "colonial" economy, dependent upon and subsidiary to the few commercial and industrial countries which for centuries shaped the economic destinies of the world. These "colonial" countries seemed eager to accept the economic, social and juridical institutions of Western Europe and the United States. And the more they grew in the image of the industrial societies the less attractive they appeared as objects of study to economists who were prone to view Latin American economic patterns either as anachronistic or rapidly conforming to already well known prototypes. The former are presumably outside the pale of the economist's interests; the latter, apparently, are not sufficiently challenging to arouse the interest of the scholar. As one economist put it, the problems in the field of Latin American economics are simply too thin.

Such formulation of the problem of research with respect to the Latin American area seemed all the more justified since it was seldom seriously challenged in Latin America either on theoretical grounds or by means of actual research activities. Until quite recently economics in Latin America was not only a dismal science but a neglected one as well. Even in the more advanced Latin American countries no serious effort has been made to test in terms of local experience and environment the economic theorems formulated in the industrial heartland of the world. Nor were Latin American economists interested in formulating generalizations based upon the political-economic experience of their countries. Economic thinking and teaching followed the European classical pattern, and there was little contact between it and local institutional development. Whether this divorce between economic theory and practice was the result or the cause of neglect of economic history is a question that need not concern us here. What is of moment is the fact that until recently academic economists in Latin America have not attached sufficient importance to patterns of evolution of their own economies.

The conception of Latin America as a mere appendage of the industrialized economies cannot adversely affect the scope and direction of economic research in that area. By placing undue emphasis upon selected aspects of the Latin American economy it severely limits the range of subjects considered worthy of serious study. As a rule only these sectors of the Latin American economy have come into the purview of the academic economist that were directly linked with the economic apparatus of the Western World. Certain phases of Latin America's international trade, the flow and operation of capital investments, some problems of public finance, especially those relating to the servicing and amortization of foreign indebtedness,—these, in general, were the areas which until recently have monopolized the attention of economists and economic historians in this country. With few noteworthy and instructive exceptions research in the United States made no attempt to penetrate the outer rim of the economies of Latin America, to dissect the developmental patterns of the national economies, and to examine their relations with the advanced countries of the North Atlantic in terms of internal social and economic changes. This failure is regrettable. To study Latin America solely or even largely in terms of the economic needs and aspirations of Europe and the United States is to create a partial and distorted conception of the area. Such

an approach limits the perspective and makes it impossible to bring the surface that which is perhaps most significant and also most instructive in the economic development and policies of the Latin American countries.

It should not be difficult for the economist and the economic historian to revise their position with respect to Latin America, or any area outside of the charmed circle of the community of industrial nations. Events of the past two or three decades shattered a good many of our traditional theorems concerning the structure and development of world economy. We have come to learn that the generalizations of the classical economic doctrine are not, and never were, universal either in time or space. We have become reconciled to the spectacle of large areas of the world stubbornly refusing to conform to the precepts and injunctions of the good professor of moral philosophy at the University of Glasgow and his disciples. And we are no longer certain that deviations from traditional patterns of economic development fall necessarily under the heading of economic pathology.

It is in this manner that the scope of research is broadened even for those economists who are not interested in the unusual and the freakish. For it is conceded that normal economic development need not necessarily adhere to a standard pattern, economies such as those of Latin America can claim the attention of research workers in their own right and not merely because of their ties with the industrially advanced countries. Moreover, the starting point of research must be the area itself, for it is only in terms of its historical development and objectives that the organization and functioning of the economy can be fully understood.

Thus conceived, economic research in "dependent," "colonial" areas assumes a validity all its own. The question whether the problems encountered there are thin becomes in a sense irrelevant. But even if such a question is theoretically admissible, it can scarcely apply to Latin America. The problems one will encounter there will not involve very large populations. Nevertheless the problems are real; they are complex; and they are new.

III

Few aspects of the economic development of the Latin American Republics have been studied with the thoroughness and care to which the academic economist in this country is accustomed. It should not, therefore, be difficult for the scholar to select an area or topic that has not yet been examined, or that has been only partially studied. Rather the problem is to determine the relative importance of each of the many possible topics on the basis of timeliness or relevance and in relation to the availability of statistical and other factual information. Obviously this task cannot be undertaken here, and for this reason no significance should be attached to the order in which the topics are discussed in the following pages.

For some time past Latin American countries have been acutely aware of the inherent instability of their economies. This instability is ascribed to a number of factors, the most prominent of which is excessive dependence upon the production and export of one or two staple commodities. Rightly or wrongly Latin Americans are convinced that as exporters of foodstuffs and raw materials in exchange for manufactured consumers' and producers' goods they are at a disadvantage in world markets. They consider themselves to be the victims of the "scissor" problem of prices, a problem of international ramifications and, therefore, beyond the control of any one of the countries of Latin America.

The war of 1914–18 and the disruption of the traditional pattern of international trade in the ensuing decades had taught the Latin American countries a lesson they are not likely to forget. For it was during this period that Latin America experienced the precipitous decline of prices, aggravated as it was by progressive fragmentation of world markets into bilateral barter agreements and by the accumulation of huge unsaleable surpluses and shortages of foreign exchange. World War II once again confirmed the danger of excessive integration of national economies with foreign markets and sources of supply, and the urge to circumscribe this dependence upon Western Europe and the United States became stronger than ever before.

Solution of the problem of under-development and over-dependence upon foreign trade has been sought in diversification of production, which in Latin America is almost synonymous with industrialization. Diversification of production and the resultant broadening of the economic base should, it is argued, make the economy that much more immune to the paralysing effects of the price "scissor" sickness. However, since diversification of production is at best a long term program, other measures must be invoked where the danger is more immediate. Foreign exchange controls, import quotas, barter agreements, export subsidies, and similar devices have become common instruments of economic policies in most, if not all, of the Latin American countries. And at the same time they have become useful instruments in the realization of the program of diversification.

In both the long range and short run programs governments in Latin America have played and will continue to play a preponderant role. This is almost inevitable, for governments alone could assume the responsibility of defense against the catastrophic effects of a world wide depression, or underwrite and direct programs which called for relatively large capital investments at a time when foreign capital was unavailable. But whatever the circumstances which brought forth government intervention in Latin America, it is no longer a measure of despair. More often than not it is in a very real sense a manifestation of the desire to hasten the attainment of economic maturity. It is significant that the most far reaching schemes of state intervention and control, including direct participation in or operation of industrial and commercial enterprises, have been evolved in the economically most advanced countries, such as Argentina, Chile, Mexico, Colombia and Brazil.

Although expansion of the economic

function of the state is still in its early stages of development its effect in some countries has been sufficiently far reaching to merit detailed analysis. A study of the so called Development Corporations, particularly the Corporación de Fomento de la Producción of Chile, should prove especially rewarding. The experience of Argentina in the administration of economic and financial controls as well as in the field of industrial production and management provides ample material for a broad evaluation of the system. Such a study would be justified even though some work on various phases of the activities and policies of the Argentine government has already been done. Of interest, too, would be a review of Mexico's experience, especially in the oil industry. In Brazil the great Volta Redonda project, the Companhia do Vale do Rio Doce, as well as plans for the São Francisco valley—all undertakings in which the Brazilian Government is heavily engaged—would seem to offer excellent opportunities for extensive research. The experience of the development corporations of Bolivia and Ecuador, however uninspiring, or perhaps because of that, calls for careful evaluation.

The general problem of economic development extends far beyond the activities of development corporations. In fact it is not an exaggeration to say that economic development is the central problem in Latin America today. It involves not only the question of government participation in large scale economic operations, but also the totality of long range economic policies, both domestic and foreign. Indeed, the problem has already become Inter-American and international in scope. It is probable that very large funds, both public and private, will be invested in the various projects, and whether the programs succeed or fail, they will exert a profound influence upon the economic future of Latin America. For these reasons alone the problem deserves most careful consideration and study. It is true, of course, that the general problem of economic development as well as specific projects, such as the Amazon area, for example, are receiving a good deal of attention at the hands

of the United Nations Economic and Social Council through international agencies specially created for that purpose. But there can be no doubt that independent critical studies of the problem as a whole or of individual projects should prove extremely valuable. Here is a series of problems as challenging and as urgent as any. They should satisfy the most fastidious research worker, the most demanding scholar!

In the field of money and banking a study of central banks, particularly in countries where the Kemmerer mission was active in the first half of the inter-war period should prove highly instructive. It would be especially interesting to see how well were these establishments adapted to the requirements and potentialities of the economies they were intended to serve. During the war United States assistance was requested in the organization of central banks in some Latin American countries, and in at least one country a central bank was established in accordance with specifications formulated by United States technicians. It would be worth the effort to watch how these plans withstand the test of actual operation.

Too little is known or understood about the functions and activities of the Bancos Hipotecarios which operate in almost every Latin American country. These credit institutions have long and in some instances turbulent histories, and an evaluation of the part they played in the economic development of their countries should be of considerable interest. Unlike agrarian credit, industrial banking in the strict meaning of the term has been until recently practically unknown in Latin America. For this reason industrial credit should perhaps be treated as an aspect of industrial expansion.

The organization and functioning of capital markets in Latin America are subjects about which many questions are asked. Most of these questions must for the time being at least remain unanswered. Yet these are not idle questions. If only because the climate for new foreign investments in Latin America is not propitious, mobilization of domestic capital becomes a necessity. Our understanding of the manner in which even the more important capital markets in Latin America function is rather sketchy, and a study of this sector of the Latin American economy should be particularly rewarding.

During the war economic relations between the countries of Latin America became more intimate than they had ever been before. There are good reasons to believe that in the future these relations will continue to be close, not only as a matter of routine expansion of inter-American trade, but also as a result of deliberate economic policies. Most Latin American governments are well aware of the limitations which their relatively small populations and low purchasing power impose upon industrialization. Closer cooperation among Latin American countries on a regional basis has been from time to time suggested as a means of overcoming these handicaps. Argentina has been especially active in organizing the River Plate economic area. The recent agreement between Argentina and Chile envisaging close economic cooperation and mutual assistance serves to emphasize the importance of this topic. Elsewhere in Latin America there has been talk of organizing a kind of an economic Gran Colombia, and in Central America the proposal for a confederation and a customs union has been revived in recent years.

So much has been written recently about industrialization in Latin America that to mention this field as a topic for research seems almost superfluous. If the problem is at all listed here it is because much of the current discussion is too general and too one-sided. The problem of industrialization in the social and political environment of Latin America is so complex, the effects of industrial expansion are so far reaching that detailed, monographic studies would appear to be fully justified. In this connection attention might be called to certain aspects of industrialization that so far have been largely neglected. Among these may be mentioned the impact of industrial expansion upon the social and economic fabric of the area, or the effect of industrialization on standards of living of urban and rural population.

Commercial policies, especially tariffs and other barriers to trade, assume particular significance in view of the recent conference at Geneva and the current discussions at Havana. The economist who ventures into this area will face problems as interesting and as challenging as anywhere in this world. He will find that Latin America has learned well the art of economic defense as well as aggression, and that in matters of international trade policies it is more sophisticated than its adversaries across the conference table are willing to admit. As has already been intimated foreign trade control is a particularly valuable instrument of economic policy in nearly every Latin American country, and in this respect Latin American governments are anxious to safeguard their freedom of action. It would serve an extremely useful purpose to study not only the technical aspects of trade policies as practiced by the Latin American countries, but also the broader economic issues and attitudes that condition and give meaning to specific measures.

In the field of public finance special attention should be given to taxation. However, studies of taxation in Latin America should not be confined to its relation to industrialization or public works. What is equally important is an analysis of the incidence of taxation. We should know how the burden of taxes is being distributed, how it affects economic groups, and to what extent, if any, it changes the pattern of production and distribution.

The fact that Latin America was primarily an agricultural economy lends special significance to the study of farming and stock raising. Land ownership, land tenure, methods of cultivation, costs of production, methods of marketing, agricultural credit—all these topics call for careful study. In some countries much has already been accomplished, but in others the field is still wide open. In Bolivia, for example, a very large majority of the population derives its livelihood from agriculture, yet that country is an importer of foodstuffs. The country is usually referred to as a mining economy, yet at peak production the mining industry employed less than 70,000 persons in a total population of 3.5 million. A very considerable proportion of the population is said to be living outside of the money economy of the country. Here is a topic for an economic study of an area that calls for patience and skill.

The concept of economic cooperation between the twenty American republics has in recent years come to the forefront of inter-American discussion. The Economic Charter of the Americas formulated at the Chapultepec Conference and the establishment of the Inter-American Economic and Social Council created the theoretical foundations for an extension of the scope of Pan Americanism into the sphere of economic cooperation. It is probable that the economic aspect of the inter-American system will become more pronounced in the years to come.

It may be readily admitted that this phase of Pan Americanism is still in its formative stage of development. It is not at all clear what specific form peace-time economic cooperation on a Hemisphere scale will assume. Nor is it possible at this time to define the scope of such cooperation. These and other matters will presumably be discussed and defined at the forthcoming Conference of the American States of Bogotá, and the Inter-American Technical Economic Conference now scheduled to be held during the summer of this year. When the nature and scope of the problem is determined and assuming also that the conferences lead to positive action, the area of inter-American economic relations will become an extremely fertile field for economic research. But even at this juncture the question of inter-American economic cooperation deserves careful examination, if only in order to determine the numerous issues involved and to define under given conditions the limits of such cooperation.

Closely related to the question of inter-American economic cooperation is the problem of regional organization. This problem has already been mentioned. Here it may be added that studies on this broad topic would be extremely useful, even if regional economic organization were not, for political or

other reasons, feasible for some time to come. Such studies would not only clarify the magnitude and ramifications of the problem, but they might also attempt to define the area within which regional economic organization could be successfully and advantageously accomplished.

It is not possible to exhaust the list of subjects that deserves the scholar's attention. Doubtless other equally important topics can be formulated for specific areas and with respect to specific issues. Doubtless, too, new problems will arise out of current and future experience. That experience is likely to be more complex and more varied, for unmistakably Latin America is now coming of age economically as it came of age politically some hundred and thirty years ago.

IV

The difficult task that confronts the pioneering economist who enters the Latin American area is made more formidable by the circumstance that he may expect only scant assistance from economic history. The magnificent progress in the field of historical studies which characterizes the past three of four decades has been confined largely to political history or to the colonial period. Economic history of the period since independence has been sadly neglected.

This "conspiracy of silence," regrettable and disconcerting, is not peculiar to historical research in the United States. Latin American historians appear to have been just as impervious to the charms of economic development and change as their brethren in the Anglo-Saxon part of the Hemisphere. What accounts for this curious gap in historical research cannot be easily answered. The fact that economic history is a relatively young discipline in the United States is at least partly responsible for this state of affairs. That economic historians in the United States preferred to concentrate their efforts on this country and Western Europe is quite understandable. For many reasons the axis of research in the field of economic history has run in the east-west rather than north-south direction. Again, archival and other research material relating to the economic history of the nineteenth century is not easily accessible even in Latin America. Until very recently, funds for research travel in Latin America were meager, indeed, and infinitely greater academic prestige was attached to European travel and research. In Latin America historians have been traditionally inclined to minimize the importance of the economic factor in historical evolution. They felt more at home when dealing with the vast panorama of spectacular political changes and military operations, or in the realm of juridical analyses that offered unexcelled opportunities for brilliant speculation and sweeping generalizations. By comparison economic history seemed dull, uninspiring and even unreal, for the nexus between economic processes and political changes is not always visible to the untrained eye, and cannot be easily demonstrated.

It is worth noting that historians of the colonial era have been much more conscious of the importance of economic factors than their colleagues who deal with the period since independence. This is perhaps understandable. Extended over long periods of time economic processes become more readily recognizable, and the link between political changes and their economic and social backgrounds becomes clearer and more direct. And, what is perhaps more important, the process of gathering relevant material is not as exacting.

Whatever the reasons and however valid they may be Latin America of the past 150 years is virtually a *tabula rasa* to the economic historian. Those of us who want to learn about the economic past of Latin America must go to travellers' accounts or accept generalizations formulated *ad hoc* by writers whose primary interest is political history. Neither of these alternatives is satisfactory. We cannot remain satisfied with incomplete and sketchy statements of travellers and observers, however shrewd and discriminating. Nor is it possible to tolerate generalizations that are at best brilliant hypotheses and at worst little more than verbal constructions. And it is usually the latter alternative that we are offered.

The urgency of more intensive research in the field of Latin American economic history thus becomes apparent. For it is only when the economic past of the Latin American countries is reconstructed that the processes of current political and institutional development can be fully understood. It is likely that as a result of such studies many generalizations now current may have to be discarded or seriously modified. But it is certain, too, that much of the political history of the period will assume new meaning when placed against the background of contemporary economic reality.

It is not feasible at this time to construct in detail a possible pattern of research in the field of economic history. For some countries tentative general economic histories might be attempted even now. However, for the majority of the countries much preparatory work would be necessary before a task of this magnitude could be successfully undertaken.

Attention might also be directed to periods which from the point of view of political history are of particular interest. So, for example, in Mexico the economic aspects of the Díaz administration could be profitably studied. In Colombia a study of the economic background of the civil war fought toward the end of the nineteenth century would be a welcome addition to the literature on the subject. An economic history of Gran Colombia might perhaps shed new light upon the political incompatibility of the three component states. In Uruguay an economic study of the Guerra Grande would be especially interesting in view of its international ramifications. An attempt to reconstruct the economics of Paraguay during that country's isolation would be a rewarding if difficult undertaking. These topics are offered by way of illustration, and the list of projects can easily be extended to cover a large part of the period of independence in every Latin American country.

Parallel to area studies within limited periods research should also proceed along functional lines. Here progress has been more substantial, but a good deal remains to be done. Historical monographs on various phases of economic activity, by industries, by commodities or economic institutions would provide a solid foundation for general economic histories of individual areas. They would also be extremely helpful to economists whose primary concern is analysis of current conditions and economic policies.

V

Two questions invariably crop up in any discussion of economic research in Latin America. One is what statistical material is available, and the other is how reliable it is. Unfortunately the answer to these questions, for the present at least, must be that statistical material is not abundant and that it is not always reliable. Of course, conditions vary from country to country and from topic to topic. In the more advanced countries, such as Mexico and Argentina, statistical information is relatively abundant and reliable. In most countries, however, either the volume of available information is inadequate, or the quality leaves a good deal to be desired. Again, agricultural statistics are as a rule more complete and more accurate in certain areas, while in others mining data are compiled with particular care. Statistics of foreign trade are fairly complete and detailed for all the countries. This is true also of data on public finance. Industrial statistics on the other hand are sketchy and often bear the mark of improvisation in both coverage and arrangement. Certain types of statistical information are extremely fragmentary or not at all available. Data on value of production are compiled in very few countries, and some of these compilations are hardly more than estimates. One would look in vain for reliable information on national income and its distribution. Nor are data generally available on the very important problem of capital formation.

Nevertheless, the outlook for the future is not as gloomy as might be inferred from the preceding paragraph. Since the beginning of the war, there has been continued and visible improvement in the collection and dissemination of statistical information throughout Latin America. The Inter-American Statistical Institute, which in 1940 published a rather detailed survey of statistical activities and sources in the Western Hemisphere, has had considerable success in calling to the attention of the Latin American governments the importance of organizing and maintaining adequate statistical services. Many Latin American statisticians were given the opportunity to visit the United States for training purposes. In many countries new statistical publications have been launched in recent years, designed not only to disseminate statistical information, but also to raise the standard of statistical techniques, in both compilation and presentation. But perhaps the most important single development in the statistical affairs of Latin America is the census to be taken throughout the Americas in 1950. Although the census is primarily a population census, in many countries it will cover a wide range of economic activities. Should it prove to be successful, and judging by the elaborate preparations there is good reason to believe that it will, the census will provide a wealth of data for the economist.

The economic historian is less favorably situated. As he moves back toward the beginning of the nineteenth century the volume of statistical information decreases and the quality deteriorates. Instead of continuous series he gets data for scattered periods, and the area of economic activities for which statistics are readily available is noticeably reduced. There is little that can be said to console the historian. He must be prepared to search for material in the archives, both public and private; he must continue to rely upon contemporary newspapers and periodicals for much of the information he needs; and as often as not he may have to compile his own statistical series.

Both the economist and the economic historian will find the academic climate much more favorable to research in Latin American economics and economic history than was the case ten or fifteen years ago. This is especially true of Latin America. In the last decade and a half interest in and study of economics and economic history in various Latin American countries have made notable gains. There has been a growing preoccupation with theoretical and applied economics, and the level of economic thought and analysis, especially in research organizations, improved visibly in both quality and quantity. Of particular interest to scholars in the United States is the fact that Anglo-American economic thought appears to be gaining ground in Latin America. Evidence of this may be found in the formidable list of translations into Spanish of American and English economic texts and treatises. Economic history, too, begins to lay claim to respectability. It is true that most of the research is confined to the colonial period, but it may be reasonably expected that expansion into the post-independence era will not be delayed much longer. In several Latin American countries useful work is being done on various phases of economic history. The first general economic history of Argentina appeared about three years ago. These developments would appear to suggest that students in the United States can count on an appreciative and ever growing audience in Latin America. They can also hope for competent assistance from their Latin American colleagues in the form of independent research.

In the United States the change in the academic climate is of more recent origin and conditioned by a different set of factors. But it is none the less significant. In recent years courses in Latin American economics have been initiated in a number of universities. But perhaps the most important development has been the establishment of four institutes of Latin American studies at the University of Texas (Mexico), Tulane University (Middle America), University of North Carolina (Spanish South America) and Vanderbilt University (Brazil). The institutes are now in process of organization and their effect upon research in the Latin American area is yet to be felt. It is not unreasonable to expect, however, that economic research in these institutes would be given the attention which the discipline requires. The basic impulse must, however, come from the large centers of higher education where the material and human resources are more ample, and the horizons of academic research are broader.

59. The Fall of the Spanish American Empire*

Robin A. Humphreys

At the time of the Napoleonic invasions of the Spanish peninsula in 1807–8, the Spanish empire in America stretched in unbroken line from California to Cape Horn. From Stockholm to Cape Town is less distant, and within the area ruled by Spain all western Europe from Madrid to Moscow might lie and be lost.

A hundred years earlier, at the beginning of the eighteenth century, Spain had been a major battlefield of Europe. That experience was now to be repeated, and this time foreign invasion spelt imperial destruction.

* History: The Journal of the Historical Association, n.s. 37: 213–227 (Oct. 1952). At the suggestion of the author, this essay was substituted in this anthology for his earlier parallel treatment entitled "Economic Aspects of the Fall of the Spanish Empire," Revista de Historia de América, 30: 450–456 (1950). [Ed. note] Reprinted by permission of the author and the original publisher.

The French Revolution in its Napoleonic aspect was the occasion, if not the cause, of the emancipation of Spanish America.[1] But in the years between the war of the Spanish Succession and the wars of Napoleon, Spain herself had risen with remarkable resilience from the decrepitude into which she had fallen in the seventeenth century. Her economic decline had been first arrested and then reversed, and under Charles III and during the early years of Charles IV she enjoyed what seems in retrospect to have been an Indian summer of prosperity.

What was true of Spain was true also of her empire. Of the empire during the long years of Spain's weakness and decay we know all too little. But of its material and intellectual advance during the so-called century of enlightenment there is abundant evidence. And Spain, like Britain, undertook in the eighteenth century the task of imperial reorganization and reform. At home and in the empire the administrative system was overhauled. New viceroyalties and captaincies-general were created. The establishment, in the very year of the North American Declaration of Independence, of the viceroyalty of La Plata,[2] covering the whole, indeed more than the whole, of what is now Argentina, marked a period in the history of Spanish America. And the attempt to systematize and centralize colonial government by the division of the colonies into intendancies— . . . "to unify the government of the great empires which God has intrusted to me," as Charles III expressed it in the great Ordinance of Intendants for New Spain[3]— was scarcely less important.

The reforms in the imperial economic system were equally radical. The Spanish system of colonial and commercial monopoly differed not in kind from the colonial policy of other powers, but in the extraordinary rigour with which it was applied. There were special reasons for the severity and minuteness of these economic regulations, and special reasons for the quite disastrous consequences that followed. But though the policy of colonial monopoly was never abandoned, it was, in the eighteenth century, liberalized. Slowly and cautiously the natural trade routes of the Indies were opened up. Where once Cádiz and Seville had enjoyed a monopoly within a monopoly, and the fleets and galleons had divided between them the commerce and treasure of Mexico and Perú, step by step the ports of America and the ports of Spain were opened, the age-old restrictions on inter-colonial commerce were lightened, and the tariffs and duties hampering trade revised. The so-called Decree of Free Trade[4] of 1778, by which all the more important ports of Spain and of Central and South America were allowed to trade, if not freely at least directly, with one another, was as much a landmark in the economic history of the later empire as was the establishment of the viceroyalty of La Plata in its political history.

The reasons for these striking innovations were, in the broadest sense of the word, strategic. Efficiency in administration, the rehabilitation of colonial trade, were not so much ends in themselves as means to an end; and the end was imperial defence, the protection of the empire against foreign aggression, particularly English aggression, the elimination of foreign economic competition, and the restoration of Spanish maritime and military power in Europe. And as in British colonial policy after 1763, so in Spanish, the financial problem was paramount.[5] Defence demanded revenue, "it being necessary," as Charles III instructed his visitor-general to New Spain, "on account of the large sums needed in attending to the obligations of my royal crown, to exhaust all means which may appear condu-

[1] Cf. Sir Charles Webster, *Britain and the Independence of Latin America, 1812–1830* (2 vols., London, 1938), i, 8.

[2] Made permanent in 1777.

[3] Printed in L. E. Fisher, *The Intendant System in Spanish America* (Berkeley, 1929), p. 97.

[4] Printed in *Documentos para la Historia Argentina* (Facultad de Filosofía y Letras, Buenos Aires, 1913——), vi, 3.

[5] Cf. C. H. Haring, *The Spanish Empire in America* (New York, 1947), pp. 145–6. This is the most important single volume on the history of the Spanish empire since the publication of R. B. Merriman, *The Rise of the Spanish Empire in the Old World and the New* (4 vols., New York, 1918–34).

cive to increasing as much as possible the income from the revenues."[6] This was a dominant consideration both in administrative and in economic reform. And what Britain in part proposed to effect by tightening up the acts of trade, Spain in part proposed to effect by their relaxation.

The results, or the apparent results, were remarkable. The volume of imperial trade notably increased.[7] At Buenos Aires, now the capital of the viceroyalty of La Plata and no longer a dependency of Lima, the economic life of the colony was transformed. Its customs receipts, its exports, its shipping, its population, all alike rapidly increased.[8] At Havana, Cuba, where six vessels had sufficed for the trade of Spain in 1760, two hundred were insufficient in 1778, and more than a thousand, Spanish and foreign, entered in 1801.[9] New Spain, or Mexico, repeats the same story—a larger volume of shipping, swelling revenues, greater exports.[10] In Perú, when the legislation of 1778 first came into effect, "speculations were multiplied to so extraordinary a degree" in the first fervour of novelty that the merchants resorted to the now familiar device of destroying their goods in order to maintain the price level.[11] And even remote Chile experienced a new and vigorous impulse of economic change.[12]

Whatever truth, therefore, there may be in the legend of the stagnation and decay of Spain and of the Spanish American empire in the seventeenth century, it does not hold for the eighteenth. Within Spain's transatlantic dominions the signs of an expanding economy and of a growing prosperity were everywhere, or almost everywhere, writ large. "It is just . . . to observe," wrote a competent British observer, that Perú, durin the late eighteenth century

. . . was not only in a flourishing state both in respect to her mines and to her commerce, but also as referable to the capitals possessed by individuals, to the comparative extent of her manufactures, and to her navigation. Between the years 1790 and 1800 there existed in Lima a *commercial* capital of above 15 millions of dollars; whereas in the present year [1826] it is under one million.[13]

Humboldt, in Venezuela, noted that "every-

thing seemed to announce the increase of population and industry."[14] In New Spain the public revenues increased more than sixfold in the eighteenth century, and so also did the produce of the mines.[15] And though more than half of the world output of the precious metals still flowed from Spanish America, and though there is a lively superstition that the Spanish American colonies were made of gold and silver and nothing else, agriculture as well as mining, as the great Gálvez tells us,[16] were the basis of their prosperity. The value of the gold and silver of the Mexican mines, says Humboldt, was less "by almost a fourth" than that of the agricultural produce.[17] Of Venezuela

[6] The instructions are in H. I. Priestley, *José de Gálvez, Visitor-General of New Spain, 1765–1771* (Berkeley, 1916), p. 404.

[7] For an index, but no more than an index, see the table of imports and exports in C. Calvo, *Anales Históricos de la Revolución de la América Latina,* i (Paris, 1864), cxxvii.

[8] See the figures and references assembled in my *British Consular Reports on the Trade and Politics of Latin America, 1824–1826* (Royal Historical Society, *Camden Third Series,* lxiii, London, 1940), pp. 18, 28–31.

[9] Haring, *op. cit.,* p. 342; Alexander von Humboldt, *Personal Narrative of Travels to the Equinoctial Regions of the New Continent . . .* (trans. H. M. Williams, 7 vols., London, 1818–29), vii, 228–30.

[10] The shipping figures are given in M. Lerdo de Tejada, *Comercio Esterior de México desde la Conquista hasta Hoy* (Mexico, 1853), Docs. 12 and 13, and the revenue figures in Alexander von Humboldt, *Essai Politique sur le Royaume de la Nouvelle-Espagne* (5 vols., Paris, 1811), v. 4–5.

[11] *British Consular Reports,* p. 112; *Mercurio Peruano de Historia, Literatura, y Noticias Públicas* (12 vols., Lima, 1791–5), i, 209, etc.

[12] See Diego Barros Arana, *Historia Jeneral de Chile* (16 vols., Santiago, 1884–1902), vii, 427–8. For an excellent survey of the developments described above see B. W. Diffie, *Latin-American Civilization, Colonial Period* (Harrisburg, Pa., 1945), pp. 417–40.

[13] *British Consular Reports,* p. 114.

[14] *Personal Narrative,* iv, 210.

[15] Humboldt, *Essai Politique,* v, 4–5; iv, 99. On the Mexican mines see the useful little book of C. G. Motten, *Mexican Silver and the Enlightenment* (Philadelphia, 1950).

[16] *Hispanic American Historical Review,* iv (1921), 274.

[17] *Essai Politique,* iii, 286.

and Cuba he observes that agriculture "founded more considerable fortunes" than had been accumulated by the working of the mines in Perú,[18] and in southern South America, where the mines were few, but where Buenos Aires and even Montevideo were rapidly rising in importance, the pastoral and agricultural industries, then as now, were the economic staples.

It is reasonable to conclude, with Professor Haring,[19] that as the eighteenth century closed the peoples of Spanish America were probably more prosperous than at any time in their history. True, in a colonial and developing area, there was no considerable growth of manufactures. Nor was there in the English colonies. But domestic manufacturing was in fact more widespread than is commonly supposed. True, also, the whole population of Spanish America was certainly not greater than that of the British Isles in 1811. But its increase in the eighteenth century was remarkable. In 1800 Mexico City was the leading city of the western hemisphere, larger than any city of Great Britain and Ireland except London and Dublin. Its rival, Lima, compared with Bristol and was itself outstripped by Havana. Even long-neglected Buenos Aires was as large as New York or Philadelphia in 1790.[20] And the growth and embellishment of the cities (not merely the capital cities) illustrates the same expansionist trend. Here, at least, in public buildings and public display, were the marks of opulence; and it is no accident that here also, at the end of the century, there was an efflorescence of intellectual activity, in the universities and academies, in the growth of a periodical press, in literary societies and in clubs. In Santa Fé, Perú and Mexico, observed an English merchant in 1804, there was not only a greater degree of knowledge and a greater degree of progress in civilization than was commonly supposed in Europe, but, he added, though perhaps with prejudice, "much more than exists in Old Spain."[21]

The disruption of this society by a violent cataclysm which would, within a few years, destroy much of its wealth, would seem, at first sight, an improbable event. The Conde de Aranda, one of the more far-sighted of Spanish statesmen, indeed foresaw it. "We must imagine" he wrote in 1782 "that sooner or later in [Spanish] America there will occur revolutions like those of the English colonies."[22] And Canning's retrospective judgment, on the effect of the American Revolution, that "the operation of that example" was "sooner or later inevitable,"[23] is well known. The influences of eighteenth-century rationalism and of the French Revolution were equally powerful dissolvents. The continent, despite the censorship of the Inquisition, was not closed to ideas. Forbidden literature is always the most enticing of literature. A cultivated minority was certainly acquainted with the writings of the *philosophes*, of Rousseau, of Locke, even of Adam Smith. These were to be echoed, along with the Declarations of Independence and of the Rights of Man, in the pronouncements and charters of revolutionary leaders and revolutionary governments. Yet despite the activities of an adventurer like Francisco de Miranda, who knew the "brace of Adamses" and had seen the French Revolution at first hand, despite occasional conspiracies and even outright rebellion, there was little specifically revolutionary activity in Spanish America before Spain herself fell a prey to Napoleon. The revolution, when it came, rose like a sudden tide from still, or comparatively still, waters.

Yet Spain's colonies were lost before the revolution began. The Bourbon reforms came too late, they did not go far enough, they were given insufficient time, to save the empire. And politically at least they contained no concession to the newer movement of ideas.

[18] *Ibid.*, ii, 25.

[19] *Op. cit.*, p. 344.

[20] On the population figures see Diffie, *op. cit.*, pp. 449–59.

[21] The quotation is from William Jacob, "Plan for Occupying Spanish America," 26 Oct. 1804, Public Record Office, G.D. 8/345. *Cf.* Humboldt, *Personal Narrative*, ii, 240; iii, 474.

[22] Manuel Conrotte, *La Intervención de España en la Independencia de los Estados Unidos . . .* (Madrid, 1920), p. 166.

[23] Webster, *op. cit.*, i, 6; ii, 193.

Instead of considering its colonies as a place of refuge for the idle, the profligate, and the disaffected, where they might learn to amend their lives, and, if possible, forget their errors [wrote the *Edinburgh Review* in 1806[24]] the Spanish Crown has watched over its foreign settlements with the solicitude of a duenna, and regulated their government as if they were to be inhabited by Carthusians.

The quotation, perhaps, is mainly interesting for the light it throws on the value placed on colonies in early nineteenth-century Britain. But it contains a solid grain of truth. The empire, from first to last, was built on paternalist and absolutist lines. It could not, in point of fact, be quite so centralized as theory might imply. The royal will was always limited by circumstance. But the price of paternalism was procrastination and inefficiency, a tradition of legalism and a disrespect for law, a class system which almost, but not quite, became a caste system, and a mounting jealousy between Spaniards born in Spain and Spaniards born in America, between, that is, the governors and the governed. "The most miserable European" wrote Humboldt "without education, and without intellectual cultivation, thinks himself superior to the whites born in the new continent."[25] The creoles, excluded generally from the higher administrative posts, found almost their sole representation in municipal institutions. "Even in the most despotic states" says Robertson in his famous *History* "this feeble spark of liberty is not extinguished."[26] But even here it was the local, not the representative, character of the *cabildos*, or town councils, too often close corporations, petty oligarchies, which caused them to play so prominent a part in the events of 1808 to 1810.

There was no relaxation of this paternalistic system in the eighteenth century. On the contrary, enlightened despotism sought to rationalize and simplify the machinery of imperial administration both in Spain and in America in the interests of order, uniformity, centralization, efficiency. And though, for a time, a new life was breathed into the imperial system, the political aspirations of the creoles were forgotten, or ig-

nored. In so far as the newly appointed intendants, invariably Spaniards, superseded minor, but creole, officials, and trespassed, moreover, on the functions of the *cabildos*, the Spanish American creoles were, in fact, still further removed from the work of government. "We were left" Bolivar was to say "in a state of permanent childhood."[27]

And, paradoxically enough, the measures designed to secure a still closer integration between Spain and her colonies had precisely the opposite effect. In Spanish America, as in Spain, local and regional loyalists were always strong. Customs, conditions, varied enormously. Cities and squares, law and administration, might be drawn to a pattern, but the life of the colonies flowed in its own individual channels; and at a time when the Bourbon economic reforms gave to the several regions of Spanish America a new economic autonomy, the creation of new viceroyalties and captaincies-general promoted and consolidated a growing sense of regional nationalism. Colonial self-consciousness was directly stimulated. It can be no accident that the revolution, when it came, gained its first successes in those areas whose economic and political status had thus been raised. The origins of the new Spanish American nations must properly be sought in the developing life of the eighteenth century.

Apart from a small minority, an intellectual *élite*, it is possible that the rising creole middle class of lawyers, merchants, landowners and soldiers might have reconciled themselves for some time longer to their political inferiority, however much they resented their social inferiority, to the Spaniards. The loyalists, or royalists, were always far more numerous during the Spanish American revolutions than they were dur-

[24] *Edinburgh Review*, viii (July, 1806), 383.
[25] *Essai Politique*, ii, 2.
[26] William Robertson, *The History of America* (5th edn., 3 vols., Edinburgh, 1788), iii, 262. *Cf.* Humboldt, *Personal Narrative*, iv, 102. Perhaps the best discussion of the *cabildo* is to be found in Haring, *op. cit.*, pp. 158–78.
[27] D. F. O'Leary, *Bolivar y la Emancipación de Sur-América, Memorias del General O'Leary* (2 vols., Madrid, n.d.), i, 379.

ing the revolution for North American independence. But whatever the prosperity of Spanish America, whatever the rehabilitation of Spain, in the second half of the eighteenth century, the economic foundations of the empire had been irretrievably undermined. The recovery of Spain had failed to keep pace with the expanding economy of her colonies, and the imperial economic reforms of Charles III were no more than palliatives of a condition imperfectly understood. The trade of the empire was still a closed monopoly of Spain, but the monopoly was imposed by a country which could still not successfully apply it, a country outstripped in financial and technical resources, in facilities and skills, by its greatest colonial rival, Britain. The empire, Professor Whitaker has observed, "fell not so much because of decay within as because of pressure from without";[28] and from this point of view its fall was no more than a corollary of the commercial expansion of Europe and particularly of England.

What really stimulated the economic expansion of Spanish America in the eighteenth century, indeed, were not so much the imperial economic reforms as the European search for Latin American markets and the European demand for Latin American products. And for the continued growth of European interest in Spanish America there were, apart from considerations of strategy and politics, three main reasons. First, Spanish America provided dollars, the gold and silver coin and specie which was the lubricant of international trade. The bullion supply was as interesting to the continental as it was to the British and North American merchant. Secondly, Spanish America supplied a number of raw materials, such as drugs and dyewoods, hides and skins, increasingly important for industrial and commercial purposes.[29] Thirdly, it afforded a market for manufactured goods, particularly textiles and hardware. The market, perhaps, was not so infinitely extensible as was sometimes imagined, but its potentialities were great, some English and some continental merchants knew it far better than might be supposed, and it was undoubtedly profitable.

There were, also, two ways of tapping the resources and trade of Spanish America. The first was to do so indirectly by way of Cádiz and, still more indirectly, by way of Lisbon and Rio de Janeiro. The second was the direct or contraband trade. Both had long been practised. At the end of the seventeenth century everybody knew that the fleets and galleons at Cádiz were stocked with foreign, principally French and English, not Spanish goods, that the Spanish merchants were little more than agents or shippers, and the returns which flowed to Spain immediately flowed out again. "We owe to Divine Providence" Philip V complained "the special blessing of vast dominions in America, the centre of abundant precious metals; [yet] the Crown has always seen that . . . that is the kingdom which retains the least."[30] Or, in Pufendorff's phrase, which Mr. Christelow has recently quoted, "Spain kept the cow and the rest of Europe drank the milk."[31]

Spain, in short, could not supply her colonies herself. But she maintained the pretence of so doing. What was more, she insisted that colonial products should flow only to Spain. Since the tonnage of the galleons fell by three-quarters in the seventeenth century, it is obvious that the volume of imperial trade had seriously contracted. Not only this, high duties and restrictive freights combined with the monopolistic interests of the merchant houses in Seville and Cádiz to raise the price level in America to fantastic heights. An increase of two to three hun-

[28] A. P. Whitaker, "The Commerce of Louisiana and the Floridas at the end of the Eighteenth Century," *Hispanic American Historical Review*, viii (1928), 203. See also on the above paragraph Allan Christelow, "Great Britain and the Trades from Cádiz and Lisbon to Spanish America and Brazil, 1759–1783," *ibid.*, xxvii (1947), 9, 18–21, and Ricardo Levene's introduction to *Documentos para la Historia Argentina*, v, xxiv.

[29] On the problem of raw materials see Allan Christelow, "Contraband Trade between Jamaica and the Spanish Main, and the Free Port Act of 1766," *Hispanic American Historical Review*, xxii (1942), 310–11.

[30] E. J. Hamilton, *War and Prices in Spain, 1651–1800* (Cambridge, Mass., 1947), p. 46.

[31] "Great Britain and the Trades from Cádiz and Lisbon . . .," p. 3.

dred per cent above the prices in Spain was not uncommon.[32] And if Spain could not herself supply her colonies with enough or cheap enough goods, neither could Europe obtain from Spain all that she wanted of colonial products. The result was an enormous contraband trade. This was the second method employed by the French, the English and the Dutch, the direct or contraband trade; and the more debilitated Spain became, the greater grew the contraband, the greater Spain's debility, and the weaker her empire.

Mr. Christelow has shown how the British merchants, at least, in the eighteenth century were losing their interest in the old limited commercial system based on Cádiz, how they welcomed the reforms of Charles III, and how they looked forward, indeed, to the ending of all restraints.[33] The full story of the growth of the direct or contraband trade has yet to be told. Already serious in the seventeenth century, the contraband trade grew more so in the eighteenth century. And its hold was certainly strengthened by the operations of the South Sea Company under the Asiento of 1713. The legal trade of the company in the annual ships and in the supply of negroes cloaked a still greater general but illicit trade carried on through the company's factors and agents in Jamaica, Panamá, Vera Cruz, Caracas, Santiago de Cuba, Buenos Aires, Santiago de Chile, and even in Lima and Potosí. Between 1730 and 1739, when its property was confiscated, the company realized at least five million pounds by this illicit activity.[34] Even so, it had to face the competition of private traders as well as the hostility of Spain; and it was into the hands of the private traders that the trade fell when the company's operations ceased. "This commerce in time of peace, and this with the prizes that are made in time of war" wrote the author of the *European Settlements in America* "pour into Jamaica an astonishing quantity of treasure; great fortunes are made in a manner instantly"[35]; and what Jamaica was to the Spanish Main, Colonia del Sacramento, just opposite to

Buenos Aires, was, when in Portuguese hands, to the river Plate.

The effect on Spain can partly be measured in the continued decline in the tonnage of the fleets and galleons and in the irregularity of their sailings. When the galleons sailed for the last time in 1737 they were unable to dispose of their goods because the markets were already overstocked. Royal decree after royal decree complained of the presence of foreigners and foreign goods in the Indies. Foreigners must be expelled. Officials who connived at contraband trade should be punished with death. Even their immortal souls would be imperilled, for in 1776 the Church was recommended to teach that contraband was a mortal sin.[36] Finally, of course, the great series of economic and commercial reforms which began in 1740 with the permission given to register ships to sail round Cape Horn and culminated in the legislation of Charles III, reflected the acute anxieties of the crown.

These reforms could alleviate, but they failed to remedy the situation. It is true that they did much to rehabilitate Spanish commerce. Though the old monopolists protested, new and more enterprising Spaniards and Spanish Americans entered trade. Shipping and revenue increased. But the contraband continued. To tap the trade of the Gulf of Mexico and the Spanish Main, the British, in 1766, established free ports in Dominica and Jamaica, extending the system after 1787, to other strategic points in the West

[32] See the references and figures in *British Consular Reports*, pp. 29, 30, 111, 352.

[33] "Great Britain and the Trades from Cádiz and Lisbon . . .," pp. 2–29.

[34] G. H. Nelson, "Contraband Trade under the Asiento, 1730–1739," *American Historical Review*, li (1945), 63–4. The literature on the contraband is too extensive to be cited here. The more important references, however, will be found in Nelson's article.

[35] *An Account of the European Settlement in America* (2 vols., 3rd edn., London, 1760), ii, 78. For the figures of the trade of Jamaica in the first half of the eighteenth century see Richard Pares, *War and Trade in the West Indies, 1739–1763* (Oxford, 1936), pp. 474–5.

[36] *Documentos para la Historia Argentina*, v, 380.

Indies.[37] And there is no doubt that, despite temporary vicissitudes, the free port trade, encouraged in time of peace and specially licensed in time of war, was, as the board of trade found it, when reviewing the Free Port Acts themselves, highly "beneficial."[38] The Spaniards might properly complain. But it was no part of British policy to enforce the Laws of the Indies. And whatever may have been the prospects that the imperial reforms of Charles III could have arrested foreign economic pressure upon the walls of the empire and that Spain herself could have been brought successfully to compete in the swelling volume of international trade, the doom of Spanish hopes was sealed by two events. The first was the death of Charles himself in 1788 and the accession of the incompetent Charles IV. The second was the entry of Spain into the French revolutionary wars.

The war of 1779 to 1783, when Spain had actively promoted the independence of England's colonies, had been costly enough. For the first time in Spanish history the crown was forced to issue paper money, soon to be inflated.[39] The brief war with France, from 1793 to 1795, was a further blow. But when, in 1796, Spain again went to war with England, and, with a brief interval of only two and a half years, remained at war for twelve years more, the result was disaster. This was the crisis of the empire. Spain and her colonies were severed. Spanish economy was seriously deranged. The Spanish navy was almost destroyed. And the colonies were thrown upon their own and foreign resources.

There had been occasions, in earlier years, when Spain had been compelled to tolerate the trade of friends or neutrals in Spanish America. In 1782, for example, Louisiana had been allowed to trade with France. Cuba, in 1793, was permitted to trade with the United States. In the years after 1789, moreover, the slave trade had been thrown open and foreigners allowed to engage in it.[40] But when, on 18 November 1797, the crown opened the Atlantic ports of Spanish America to neutral shipping, the measure

was one of desperation. The order was indeed revoked in 1799 because it had "redounded entirely," as the decree of revocation complained, to the injury of the state and of the interests of its subjects.[41] But what the law forbade, local regulation continued to tolerate and the crown itself to license; and though the old system was restored at the peace in 1802, with the renewal of the war once again the ports were opened.[42].

The result, or partial result, was the rapid growth of North American shipping and North American trade, from Cuba to Buenos Aires and Buenos Aires to Chile. And more than one American, perhaps, like the young Richard Cleveland of Massachusetts, carried in his cargo a copy of the Federal Constitution and of the Declaration of Independence, conveniently translated into Spanish.[43] But it was not only American trade, legitimate and illegitimate, that grew. So also did British trade. The contraband flourished at the free ports in the West Indies. It flourished at Trinidad, which alone was said to supply the Spanish colonies with goods to the value of one million pounds a year.[44] It flourished at Vera Cruz, as Vice-

[37] See, in particular, Christelow, "Contraband Trade between Jamaica and the Spanish Main . . . ," pp. 309–43, and D. B. Goebel, "British Trade to the Spanish Colonies, 1796–1823," *American Historical Review*, xliii (1938), 289–94.

[38] Minutes of the Committee of Trade, 15 March 1805, P.R.O., B.T. 5/15, p. 76.

[39] Hamilton, *op. cit.*, p. 152.

[40] Whitaker, *op. cit.*, p. 192; R. F. Nichols, "Trade Relations and the Establishment of the United States Consulates in Spanish America, 1779–1809," *Hispanic American Historical Review*, xiii (1933), 293; J. F. King, "Evolution of the Free Slave Trade Principle in Spanish Colonial Administration," *ibid.*, xxii (1942), 49–56.

[41] *Documentos para la Historia Argentina*, vii, 134, 157.

[42] A. P. Whitaker, *The United States and the Independence of Latin America, 1800–1830* (Baltimore, 1941), pp. 8–9.

[43] H. Bernstein, *Origins of Inter-American Interest, 1700–1812* (Philadelphia, 1945), p. 80. On American trade see also Goebel, *op. cit.*, pp. 295–7, and Whitaker, *United States and the Independence of Latin America*, pp. 5–16, 23–6.

[44] Minutes of the Committee of Trade, 11 June 1808, P.R.O., B.T. 5/18, p. 167; Memorandum on

roy Marquina bitterly complained. It flourished at Buenos Aires. And, even on the Pacific coast, where the South Sea whalers were
actively engaged in it, it extended and
strengthened its hold.[45]

There was still to be fought out in Spanish America the battle between monopoly
and free enterprise, between the beneficiaries of an old order and the partisans of a
new. But the issue was already resolved. It
was impossible to re-enact the Laws of the
Indies. The economic emancipation of Spanish America was determined before its political emancipation began.

And so far as political emancipation was
concerned, the years from 1796 to 1808 were
equally decisive. As Britain had formerly
wavered between plundering the Spanish
American colonies and trading with them,
so now she hesitated between their conquest
and their emancipation. In 1797 the governor of Trinidad was specifically instructed
to encourage revolution on the Mainland.
The invasion of Buenos Aires was prepared,
and cancelled, in the same years. And there
were other plans, in the mind of the British
government as well as in that of Francisco
de Miranda, so long plotting in England and
America the emancipation of Venezuela. But
fundamentally Britain was more interested
in trade than territory. Her designs were
commercial and strategic rather than imperial, and when, in 1806, Sir Home Popham
captured Buenos Aires, it was at his own
responsibility. *The Times*, indeed, rejoiced.
It knew not, it said, how to express itself in
terms adequate to the national advantage obtained.[46] But the government vacillated. It
did too little and that little too late. Buenos
Aires was recaptured and Montevideo lost.
The whole affair, said *The Times*, was "a
dirty, sordid enterprise, conceived and executed in a spirit of avarice and plunder,"
and the chief source of the calamity was the
unauthorised beginning of it.[47]

But for Spanish America its end was all
important. The viceroy of La Plata had
fled. It was the creoles who defeated the Brit-

ish, deposed the incompetent viceroy and appointed a new one. Spanish America had
seen the deposition and imprisonment of the
legal representative of the king. It had seen
a creole militia defeat a European army. It
had seen a colonial port crowded with British ships and flooded with British goods. It
was not a revolution that took place at Buenos Aires as a result of the British invasions.
But it was a political and economic transformation that contained the seeds of revolution.

Suddenly, however, the situation changed.
Napoleon invaded Spain. The crown fell
into captivity. A usurper sat upon the throne.
From an enemy Britain became, overnight,
the ally of Spain, and the army which
Wellesley was preparing in Ireland for the
liberation of Spanish America sailed, not
to emancipate Spanish America from Spain,
but to liberate Spain from France.

The news of the fall of the monarchy, and
of the invasion of the mother country, stirred
the loyalty and moved the indignation of
the colonies, and, superficially, the resistance movement in Spain was almost exactly
imitated in Spanish America. As juntas
sprang up in Spain in the name of Ferdinand VII, so in Spanish America juntas and
cabildos assumed the powers of viceroys,
presidents and captains-general, the agents,
now, of an authority which had ceased to
exist. Extraordinary circumstances called for
extraordinary measures. The colonists took
thought for their own protection and their
own future. Power reverted to the people,
though by "the people" nothing more can
be meant than a small but active creole minority: the revolutions in Spanish America
were the work of the few, not of the many.

But that a movement which began as an
assertion of independence from France

---

[45] Cf. *British Consular Reports,* pp. 256–7, 31,
127; Goebel, *op. cit.,* pp. 304–9; and see the complaints of Viceroy Marquina of New Spain (1803)
in *Instrucciones que los Vireyes de Nueva España
dejaron a sus Sucesores* (Mexico, 1867), p. 205, and
of Viceroy Abascal y Sousa of Perú in his *Relación*
printed in Manuel de Odriozola, *Documentos Históricos del Perú* (10 vols., Lima, 1863–79), ii, 23.

[46] *The Times,* 13 Sept. 1806.

[47] *Ibid.,* 14, 15 Sept. 1807.

Trinidad, C. O. 318/2, f. 275; Goebel, *op. cit.,* pp.
291–4.

should have ended as an assertion of independence from Spain was due quite as much to Spain herself as to the creole minority in her colonies whose thwarted aspirations in government and trade were thus fulfilled. For though the monarchy had collapsed, though the Peninsula was overrun, the Spaniards still clung to the principles of imperial monopoly and colonial subordination. Crown, Regency, Cortes, showed themselves equally blind, equally determined. The colonies, declared the Junta Central, in 1809, were an integral part of the Spanish monarchy, and the deduction soon followed that they owed obedience to the extraordinary authorities erected in Spain.[48] That was not the Spanish American view. Nor had it been the Hapsburg view. "Estos y esos reinos,"

"these and those kingdoms," was the famous phrase used to define the royal possessions in Spain and the Indies. The Indies had never belonged to Spain. They were the property of the crown of Castile, united to the kingdoms of Spain merely by a dynastic tie. The Bourbons forgot, or ignored this Hapsburg view; and so did the Spaniards. But the creoles remembered it. Just as the English colonies, in the eighteenth century, refused to accept subordination to the sovereignty of parliament, so the Spanish Americans refused to accept subordination to the people of the Peninsula. And in both cases what reason failed to arrange, force was left to decide.

[48] Cf. Haring, op. cit., p. 117.

60. Economic and Social Aspects of the Era of Spanish-American Independence*

CHARLES C. GRIFFIN

The revolutions which brought about the establishment of independent governments in America differed in marked degree from the classic revolutions of modern Europe—the French and the Russian—in that their primary effect was to throw off the authority of a transatlantic empire rather than to bring about a drastic reconstruction of society. In the case of the United States, however, it has long been recognized that the revolutionary struggle did not confine itself to the political sphere, i.e., to independence and the establishment of a new federal government. Almost a generation ago the late J. Franklin Jameson published his essays on *The American Revolution Considered as a Social Movement*[1] in which he suggested re-

lations between the revolution and the manifold changes of the era, some already recognized, and others destined to be more fully charted by a subsequent generation of scholars.[2] Because many of these changes were not the result of conscious revolutionary planning, but came about under the stimulus of new conditions created during and

* HAHR, 29:170–187 (May 1949). Reprinted by permission of the author and the original publisher.
[1] (Princeton, 1926.)
[2] Some idea of the quality of research that has been done in this field since Jameson wrote can be obtained by consulting the bibliography in Evarts B. Greene, *The Revolutionary Generation* (Vol. IV of *A History of American Life*, ed. by A. M. Schlesinger and D. R. Fox, New York, 1943).

after the revolution, they had not earlier been sufficiently closely related to the revolution and to each other.

It is possible that the time may be ripe for a similar shift in emphasis in the interpretation of the revolutions for independence in Spanish America. It was natural that these movements, as starting points for new national traditions, should have been regarded at first as epic conflicts. Heroism and leadership were the main themes. When this was not enough, diplomatic and constitutional history were emphasized, in consonance with the popularity of such studies in nineteenth-century European historiography.[3] Interest in political change led eventually to the study of political theories in relation to the revolutions and hence to the broader field of the history of thought. On the one hand, the background of the revolutions has been clarified by studies of the impact of the Enlightenment on Latin America; on the other, changes closely related to the triumph of new ideologies have been charted. Of these, the new status of church-state relations and the abolition of slavery can be mentioned as examples. Until fairly recently, however, the study of economic and social history has been directed primarily to the antecedents of the revolutions rather than to the developments of the era itself.[4]

There is, however, a large body of literature dealing with the socio-economic history of the revolutionary period proper. With minor exceptions, however, it is scattered through works on local history, sociological treatises, and books dealing with particular aspects of the history of individual countries. Except for travelers' accounts, the sources for such study have not as yet been classified, calendared, and made easily available. The use of such materials is laborious and general interpretation of the revolutionary era has been only slightly affected by their exploitation. Since 1935 we have had a general guide to the current historiography of Latin America in the *Handbook of Latin American Studies*. A survey of the sections of this bibliography which relate to the period of the movement for independence indicates the fragmentary character of material

published on social and economic aspects of the era. A number of articles and books have appeared on the commerce of various regions, but publications on other economic themes have been scant. In the aggregate, less than a dozen titles can be cited which deal with agriculture, industry, finance, and labor for this period, though a larger number touch incidentally on these topics. Somewhat more attention has been given to cul-

[3] A few examples may be cited to substantiate, in part, this statement. M. Torrente, *Historia de la revolución hispanoamericana* (3 vols., Madrid, 1829–1830), is almost entirely military history. Bartolomé Mitre's *Historia de San Martín . . .* and his *Historia de Belgrano . . .* (Buenos Aires, various editions), give fuller attention to political and diplomatic history and occasionally, in an incidental manner, to social aspects. Vicente F. López's *Historia de la República Argentina* (10 vols., Buenos Aires, 1833), is narrowly political, except for a chapter on the *gaucho* as a factor in the growth of a spirit of independence in Argentina. D. Barros Arana, *Historia jeneral de la independencia de Chile* (4 vols., Santiago, 1854–1856), is of little use to the economic and social historian, except for its excellent coverage of legislation related to these fields. M. Paz Soldán, *Historia del Perú independiente* (Madrid, 1923), is narrowly political in scope. J. M. Restrepo, *Historia de la revolución de Colombia . . .* (4 vols., Besançon, 1856), is somewhat broader, in the vein of Mitre. Both Restrepo and R. M. Baralt and R. Díaz, *Resumen de la historia de Venezuela desde 1797 . . .* (2 vols., Paris, 1939), give major attention to the Bolivarian epic, especially the latter. Of early historians of the revolution in New Spain, L. Alamán, *Historia de México* (Vols. I–V of his *Obras completas*, Mexico, 1940), is the most useful, far surpassing in breadth of treatment the work of C. Bustamante, *Cuadro histórico de la revolución mexicana* (5 vols., Mexico, 1926). Dates mentioned are, of course, not those of original publication in most cases.

[4] The extensive work done in the past half century in the field of the background and antecedents of the movement for independence hardly needs to be recalled, but some leading contributions may be mentioned. In the United States H. I. Priestley, W. S. Robertson, B. Moses, A. P. Whitaker, L. E. Fisher, and many others have dealt with aspects of the subject. In Argentina a whole school, led by R. Levene, has worked in the field. G. Arciniegas in Colombia and C. Parra Pérez in Venezuela have made significant contributions. Continued interest is shown by the recent publication by Salvador de Madariaga of his study, *Cuadro histórico de las Indias* (Buenos Aires, 1945).

tural subjects such as journalism, education, and religion.[5]

It may be worth while to mention, briefly, a few of the recent contributions which provide new social and economic interpretations. Rodolfo Puiggros, for Argentina,[6] and Carlos Irazábal, for Venezuela,[7] have studied the independence movement from a Marxist viewpoint, and have provided food for thought, even for those who may reject their general premises. More recently, an objective economic analysis of developments in Argentina has been presented in Miron Burgin's *Economic Aspects of Argentine Federalism, 1820–1852*.[8] Though this study centers its attention on the era dominated by Rosas, its early chapters provide a clearer view of the economics of the revolution in Argentina than any previously written. Cline's work on Yucatan in the early nineteenth century, though as yet only partly published, throws a searching light on problems of regional economy.[9]

Stimulating interpretations of social aspects of the independence movement come from the pen of the noted Aprista writer, Luis Alberto Sánchez and from that of Rufino Blanco Fombona, the celebrated Venezuelan man of letters. Both contribute to a better understanding of the part played by various social elements in the revolution.[10]

Undoubtedly, much more needs to be done in both regional and topical analysis before a really sound general interpretation can be achieved. This paper may serve, however, as a basis for discussion and may encourage further study of the field.

The presentation of a general view, however exploratory, is complicated by regional diversity in the character and course of the independence movement in its various centers. Differences in geography, in population, in tradition, as well as in the duration and intensity of military operations must be considered, together with variations in the extent of contact with Europe and the United States. These differentiating factors modified certain general tendencies: the destructive force of war, and the stimulation produced by free intercourse with foreign countries.

The immediate economic consequence of revolution, except in a few favored areas, was disaster. The prosperity of the later colonial economy of Spanish America was

[5] The scattered nature of the economic literature can easily be verified by reference to Bureau of Economic Research in Latin America, *The Economic Literature of Latin America* (2 vols., Cambridge, Mass., 1936). Few items in this extensive bibliography relate exclusively, or even primarily, to the period of the revolutions for independence. Titles listed in M. Sánchez Alonso, *Fuentes de la historia española e hispanoamericana* (Madrid, 1927), appear to be almost entirely political.

The following brief statement will give some idea of the distribution of the material on economic subjects listed in the *Handbook of Latin American Studies*, Vols. I–XI. R. A. Humphreys has edited, with great ability, a collection of invaluable *British Consular Reports on the Trade and Politics of Latin America* (London, 1940). E. Pereira Salas, C. W. Centner, and D. Amunátegui Solar have published articles relating to the foreign trade of Chile. R. S. Smith has analyzed the commerce of Veracruz. R. J. Fosalba has written an erudite and important study of currency in Colombia. J. Mancisidor Ortiz has studied Hidalgo's attitude toward agrarian reform. D. Monsalve has evaluated the contributions of Santander to Colombian agriculture. G. Hernández de Alba and E. Posada have written on slavery and abolition in Colombia. A Schaffroth has published an article on finance in the Argentine constitutional assemblies. G. Wythe's article, "The Rise of the Factory in Latin America," THE HISPANIC AMERICAN HISTORICAL REVIEW, XXV (August, 1945), is about the only contribution in the industrial field and most of the material included is devoted to a later period.

[6] Rodolfo Puiggros, *De la colonia a la revolución* (Buenos Aires, 1940), and *Los caudillos de la revolución de Mayo* (Buenos Aires, 1942).

[7] Carlos Irazábal, *Hacia la democracia* (Mexico, 1939).

[8] (Cambridge, Mass., 1946.)

[9] H. Cline, "The Sugar Episode in Yucatan, 1825–1850," *Inter-American Economic Affairs*, I (March, 1948); and "The Henequen Episode in Yucatan," *ibid.*, II, No. 2 (Autumn, 1948). See also by the same author "The 'Aurora Yucateca' and the Spirit of Enterprise in Yucatan, 1821–1847," THE HISPANIC AMERICAN HISTORICAL REVIEW, XXVII (February, 1947).

[10] Luis A. Sánchez, *El pueblo en la revolución americana* (Buenos Aires, 1942). Though the author believes that popular influences were important, he recognizes regional differences and the frequency with which the masses were exploited for the benefit of various groups. R. Blanco Fombona ("La evolución de las ideas en Venezuela durante la revolución de la independencia," *Boletín*

shattered by warfare which was everywhere waged with little regard for the rights of private property and the lives of non-combatants. It is only possible to suggest here the terrible destruction suffered by many regions. This reached its maximum in Venezuela, where both the human and the livestock population declined, the latter by more than one-half between 1810 and 1830.[11] Almost as severe were the losses in the Banda Oriental[12] and in certain parts of the Viceroyalty of New Spain.[13] New Granada and Chile represent areas which were less continuously theatres of military action, and with a consequently lighter incidence of destruction. The extreme horrors of the *guerra a muerte* in Venezuela and the slaughter in Mexico during the early stages of revolution were not often matched in scale elsewhere, but, even where loss of life was less severe, interruption of normal economic life was serious.[14] People were uprooted from their homes in various ways. Men were recruited, often by force, for the rival armies. Even when they escaped death they frequently never returned, taking up life again elsewhere. There were also many examples of emigration on a substantial scale.[15] These dislocations of population had unfavorable results for agriculture and mining, removing the necessary labor force, and on business in general owing to the flight of capital along with its owners.[16]

The interruption of normal lines of trade and communication also had serious adverse effects. Northwest Argentina suffered from the halting of trade with Peru. Montevideo, while in hands hostile to Buenos Aires, lost part of its commercial function. Guerrilla warfare in New Spain at times disrupted internal communications except by armed convoys.[17] Wartime financial exactions, ranging from confiscation to forced loans, appropriation of goods for the use of the rival armies, forced acceptance of depreciated currency, and high and arbitrary taxation

brought ruin to many.[18] Cattle-raising countries like the Banda Oriental and the Venezuelan hinterland suffered from wholesale

---

[11] A. Codazzi, *Resumen de la geografía de Venezuela* (3 vols., Caracas, 1940), II, 8, 12. Codazzi, who made the best estimate available in 1839, claims that the population of Venezuela in 1825 was 100,000 less than the figure given by Humboldt for the beginning of the century (800,000). Gil Fortoul (*Historia constitucional de Venezuela* [2 vols., Berlin, 1909], II, 67) gives a still lower figure for 1826 (659,000). Codazzi's figure for 1825 was 701,000. For the decline of livestock see Codazzi, *op. cit.*, I, 218–219.

[12] For the decline of livestock in the Banda Oriental see T. S. Hood to Canning, Montevideo, January 31, 1825, in Humphreys, *op. cit.*, p. 61.

[13] For a general view of the destructive effects of the revolution in New Spain see "Memoria, 1823, Relaciones Interiores y Exteriores," in Lucas Alamán, *Obras completas* (11 vols., Mexico, 1942–1946) IX. Detailed support is given *infra*.

[14] Buenos Aires and Peru suffered between 1810 and 1820, but not from actual devastation or loss of civilian lives. Both carried the burden of supporting armies in the field. Further, Buenos Aires was blockaded part of the time (1810–1811, and 1813–1814). Lima suffered similarly (1819–1820). Burgin (*op. cit.*, p. 27) shows the severe labor shortage in Buenos Aires. For the effect on Peru of cutting off trade with Córdoba via Tucumán, see W. R. Manning, ed., *Diplomatic Correspondence of the United States Concerning the Independence of the Latin-American Nations* (3 vols., New York, 1925), I, 404.

[15] The patriot exodus from Caracas in 1814 amounted to twenty thousand persons of all ages and sexes (Baralt and Díaz, *op. cit.*, I, 277). Over two thousand persons emigrated from besieged Cartagena in 1816 (Restrepo, *op. cit.*, I, 378–379). For the emigration of the Orientales in 1811, see T. Manacorda, *Fructuoso Rivera* (Buenos Aires, 1946), p. 19; Emilio Loza, "La campaña de la Banda Oriental, 1810–1813," in *Historia de la Nación Argentina* (ed. by R. Levene, Vols. I–X, Buenos Aires, 1939–1947), V, Part 1, 581. Other similar cases are the evacuation of Montevideo in 1815, of Lima in 1821, and of Caracas in the same year.

[16] C. M. Ricketts to Canning, Lima, December 27, 1826, in Humphreys, *op. cit.*, pp. 114–115. This flight of capital from Peru was important, reducing liquid commercial capital there from fifteen to less than two million pesos, according to this British agent. For a similar estimate of the effects of capital migration from Mexico see L. H. Jenks, *The Emigration of British Capital to 1875* (New York, 1927), p. 109.

[17] Burgin, *op. cit.*, pp. 119–120; Alamán, *op. cit.*, III, 365.

[18] For examples of forced loans see Alamán, *op.*

---

de la Academia Nacional de la Historia [Caracas], XX [1937], 409–417) analyzes the Venezuelan revolution in terms of race and class antagonisms, which, according to the author, were eventually fused and transformed by the genius of Bolívar.

robbery and expropriation of the livestock on which the economy of these regions was based.[19] Mining regions were paralyzed by flooding of the workings and destruction of equipment.[20]

It is impossible to measure exactly the total effect of these varied consequences of war, but it is probably safe to say that from 1810 to 1820 Buenos Aires and Peru, the strongholds of the rival forces in South America, were least affected. Regions like Paraguay and, to a lesser extent, Central America suffered from isolation but were little damaged. Chile, New Granada, and Mexico underwent severe destruction at times, but were not equally affected throughout the decade. On the other hand, Venezuela and Uruguay saw no real peace during the period and their normal economic activities were totally upset.

In the second decade of revolution theatres of military operations shifted. Warfare on a large scale was over in Mexico by 1821, and in Colombia after 1822. Fighting in Chile ceased, except for guerrilla warfare in the far south. On the other hand, Peru, which had previously escaped, became the center of the fighting. Though devastation here was not so widespread nor long continued as in some other areas, the burden of supporting large armies (patriot and royalist) in the field for several years was a heavy one.[21] The duration of military activity in what is now Ecuador was briefer, but this region gave a good deal of support to the later Peruvian campaigns.[22] For the war as a whole, therefore, only the province of Buenos Aires and its immediate neighbors to the north and west were able to escape

the direct scourge of war. Even here there were intermittent skirmishes between patriot factions especially after the year 1820.

The upheaval caused by war was not limited to destruction of life and property and the disorganization of business; it also brought changes in society which were not envisaged by the creole aristocrats and intellectuals who headed the revolts of the *cabildos* in 1809 and 1810. Except in Mexico, the revolutions had begun with efforts to dislodge the peninsular bureaucracy without otherwise changing relations among classes, but war unleashed forces that these early revolutionists were unable to harness.[23] Race and class antagonisms flared up which could only be brought under control by the exaltation of nationalism and a parallel minimizing of class distinctions. Without any general upset in these relations, there was a blurring of lines. None of the new independent governments recognized legal disabilities for *pardos* or *mestizos*. In Mexico, the clergy no longer kept the elaborate records of caste as a part of their parochial registers.

The "career open to talents" seems to have been the rule. A *mestizo* general might rise to the presidency of his country; a *mulato*

---

cit., III, 365; J. Henao and G. Arrubla, *Historia de Colombia* (Bogotá, 1936), p. 439. As to taxation, see Alamán, *op. cit.*, III, 400; and W. J. Miller to J. Monroe, Buenos Aires, July 16, 1812, in Manning, *op. cit.*, I, 326. For paper money, Restrepo, *op. cit.*, I, 138 and 155. For confiscation, C. M. Ricketts to Canning, Lima, December 27, 1826, in Humphreys, *op. cit.*, p. 116. See also R. J. Fosalba, "Trascendencia económica y política de las acuñaciones obsidionales y de emergencia durante la revolución por la independencia de Venezuela y Colombia," *Revista nacional de cultura*, No. 42 (1944), p. 42 and *passim*.

[19] T. S. Hood to Canning, Montevideo, January 31, 1825, in Humphreys, *op. cit.*, p. 81. For Venezuela, see note 11 *supra*.

[20] C. M. Ricketts to Canning, Lima, December 27, 1826, in Humphreys, *op. cit.*, p. 121; and for Mexico, Wythe, *op. cit.*, p. 296.

[21] C. Cortés Vargas (*Participación de Colombia en la liberación del Perú* [3 vols., Bogotá, 1946], II, 45) shows the strain on northern Peru during the preparation for the campaigns of Junín and Ayacucho. For the destruction in the Lima region, see C. M. Ricketts to Canning, Lima, December 27, 1826, in Humphreys, *op. cit.*, p. 117.

[22] Cortés Vargas, *op. cit.*, II, 46.

[23] See Irazábal, *op. cit.*, pp. 54–65, for the epoch dominated by Boves in Venezuela; and Parra Pérez, *La primera república en Venezuela* (2 vols., Caracas, 1939–1940), II, 65–67, for slave and Negro uprisings, 1810–1811. The existence of severe class antagonism in interior Argentina is clearly brought out in Mitre, *Historia de Belgrano y de la independencia argentina* (3 vols., Buenos Aires, 1886), II, 263–264, in connection with the activities of the leader of the *gauchos* in the northwest, Martín Guëmes.

colonel might become a large landowner.[24] This does not mean that an equalitarian society grew out of the wars, but it does indicate that the wars brought new blood into the ruling class and simplified the social distinctions in lower strata of the population.

The annals of revolution in Mexico and Colombia are well sprinkled with the names of prominent military officers with Indian or Negro blood in their veins, or both. Piar and Padilla in Colombia were conspicuous examples.[25] In Mexico, Guerrero and Morelos reached even higher renown.[26] In the lower ranks officers with similar racial antecedents were numerous. In Peru and Bolivia *mestizos* also held high military rank. Santa Cruz, who became president of the latter republic, was the son of an Indian woman and a Spaniard.[27] In the naval service of Colombia a number of *mulatos* held commissions.[28] The large percentage of color in the ranks of Bolívar's officers was frequently commented on by the race-conscious European officers who served in Colombia.[29]

The tendency toward greater racial tolerance was not unchecked. White creole fear accounts in part for the severe treatment meted out to such officers as Piar and Padilla. Their insubordination might well have been condoned if it had not been for their race. If there had not been great gains for the mixed bloods, such severity as that which led to the execution of both, in spite of the brilliant military services they had rendered to the cause of independence, might not have been considered necessary.

In Río de la Plata and in Chile there do not seem to have been instances of high military commanders of recognized mixed blood.[30] We can cite, however, the cases of politicians and journalists like Vicente Kanki Pazos[31] (an Indian from Upper Peru) and the meteoric career of Bernardo Monteagudo (a *mulato* from Tucumán).[32] The strength of the creole element in the population in the Viceroyalty of Buenos Aires, except in the north, and the fact that it was not heavily depleted by the wars may be one explanation for the less conspicuous place of the *mestizo* in military leadership. The relatively stable agrarian economy of Chile with its strong personal ties between landowner and *inquilino* provided fewer opportunities for social change than the more elaborately stratified population of Peru, Colombia, and Mexico. In these southern regions, however, the revolution brought increasing fluidity among economic groups. "Self-made men," among them many foreigners, began to make themselves increasingly evident, beginning the process which was to ease their way into the upper social ranks of *estancieros* and merchants. This tendency was stimulated by the procedure followed by many governments in paying off officers and men with land confiscated from royalists or from the public domain.[33] Land had been for so long

[24] Andrés Santa Cruz, a *mestizo*, became president of Bolivia (Alfonso Crespo, *Santa Cruz, el cóndor indio* [Mexico, 1944], p. 20). For an instance of a man of color who rose to high rank see references to Leonardo Infante in J. Tamayo, *Nuestro siglo XIX, La Gran Colombia* (Bogotá, 1941), pp. 205 ff.

[25] For the case of Piar see Baralt and Díaz, *op. cit.*, I, 397; also V. Lecuna, "Campaña de Guayana," *Boletín de la Academia Nacional de la Historia, XX* (1937), 445–450. There is an extensive literature on Padilla, but for a summary see E. Ortega Ricaurte, ed., *Bloqueo rendición y ocupación de Maracaibo por la armada colombiana al mando del almirante Padilla* (Bogotá, 1947).

[26] W. F. Sprague, *Vicente Guerrero, Mexican Liberator* (Chicago, 1939), p. 1. There is some doubt as to Morelos' exact racial antecedents. A recent biographer, A. Teja Zabre (*Morelos* [Buenos Aires, 1946]), follows Alamán in considering him of mixed blood.

[27] See note 24 *supra*.

[28] For a case of race feeling in the Colombian navy see testimony regarding the arrest of Teniente de Fragata José Alvarez, in the *ramo* of Guerra y Marina, Vol. 335, folio 1201, Archivo Nacional, Bogotá.

[29] A. Hasbrouck, *Foreign Legionaries in the Liberation of Spanish South America* (New York, 1928), pp. 96–97.

[30] Mitre (*Historia de Belgrano . . .*, III, 12) refers to an Indian from Misiones who was given high favor and rank by José Artigas during the latter's period of political power.

[31] Gustavo Adolfo Otero, in introduction to V. Kanki Pazos, *Memorias histórico-políticas* (La Paz, 1939), p. ix.

[32] José Vásquez Machicado, "La última palabra sobre la nacionalidad de Bernardo Monteagudo," *Boletín del Instituto de Investigaciones Históricas* (Buenos Aires), XX (1936), 35–71.

[33] One reason why this did not result in greater

a badge of social position that it proved impossible to discriminate for more than a generation against the owner of a large estate.

Another series of important social and economic changes grew out of the increasing contact with foreign lands during the course of the wars of independence. In this respect local differences are also notable. Buenos Aires, without question, developed a new economy based on foreign trade earlier than any other Spanish-American country.[34] The accumulated demand for free trade during the later years of the viceroyalty had paved the way and the absence of Spanish power to interfere, after 1810, gave the development free rein.[35] This ushered in the cattle boom which was to fix the character of the Argentine economy for generations. It led to expansion on the Indian frontier and to the rapid growth of the city of Buenos Aires, as population flowed in to serve the needs of an expanded commerce.[36] Small shops and factories on a handicraft basis multiplied and the accumulation of wealth created new luxury trades.[37] On the other hand, as Burgin has shown, free trade brought depression to Cuyo and to the northern provinces from Tucumán to Jujuy, which lost much of their market for home manufactures to foreign competition.[38]

In Chile, with interruptions due to the wars, similar changes can be seen. Free trade meant a larger market for the grain and other food surpluses which before the revolution had been shipped almost exclusively to Peru.[39] Valparaíso became a port of call for ships bound to the Orient and for the northwest coast of America. The export of Chilean silver and copper increased under the pressure of need to balance imported manufactures.[40] By 1825 a number of English mining experts were planning developments in the Coquimbo region.[41] Chilean naval activity stimulated the work of shipyards and attracted both business men and laborers to the port city, which soon lost its

sleepy colonial aspect.[42] Free trade, however, had a less violently stimulating effect on the economy of Chile than in Río de la Plata. The immediately available resources of Chile were less vast, and depended, for expanded exploitation, on growth of population and on a long-range development of mining equipment and transportation which could not be carried through at once.

The ports of Peru and Colombia were opened to world trade at a later time and these republics were less favorably situated than those of the far south from a commercial point of view. Trade did not develop here on a healthy basis. In Peru it began with a hectic wartime flush, with government purchases of munitions of war and naval stores and even of food (including flour from the United States), and with considerable speculative purchases of luxury goods.[43] This drained the country of its cur-

[34] See the statistics of British trade with Latin America, 1812–1830, in Humphreys, *op. cit.*, Appendix. British trade with Buenos Aires fluctuated violently, but except for a short period during the war between Argentina and Brazil, it was larger than that of any other Latin-American country except Brazil.

[35] The free-trade movement in colonial Buenos Aires is well summarized by E. Ravignani in *Historia de la Nación Argentina*, IV, Part 1, 129, and by R. Levene, *ibid.*, V, Part 1, 489–523.

[36] Burgin, *op. cit.*, pp. 20–30. See especially the table on p. 30 showing transactions of a Buenos Aires *estancia*, 1803–1819, and table showing population growth, p. 26.

[37] Burgin, *op. cit.*, tables 5 and 6, pp. 42–43. For the appearance of some "war industries," see Manning, *op. cit.*, I, 402.

[38] Burgin, *op. cit.*, pp. 14–15 and 119 ff.

[39] C. R. Nugent to Canning, Valparaíso, March 17, 1825, in Humphreys, *op, cit.*, p. 93. The export of agricultural products fluctuated widely during the revolution but was in general expanding. The years 1822–1825, however, were bad years and produced little grain surplus. See also Ricketts to Canning, December 27, 1826, in *ibid.*, pp. 170–171.

[40] *Ibid.*, pp. 96–97. Between 1817 and 1825 there had been an average export of 61,000 *quintales* of copper from Chile.

[41] *Ibid.*, p. 95.

[42] Travelers commented unanimously on the bustle and activity noticed in Valparaíso during these years.

[43] The ports of Callao and Huanchaco were regularly opened in 1821 (W. S. Robertson, *Hispanic-American Relations with the United States* [New

change in land ownership is suggested by the case of General Páez in Venezuela. He brought up the land scrip of his *llanero* soldiers at very low prices and acquired in this way an enormous landed estate (Irazábal, *op. cit.*, pp. 111–113).

rency and saddled it with large commercial and governmental debts. The economic situation was still further complicated by a heavy flight of capital which took the form of specie exports in British and American warships. Silver minng did not recover quickly from wartime interruption and nitrates and guano had not yet appeared on the scene to provide a temporary solution to the balance of payments problem.[44] At the same time, the domestic production of coarse textiles in Peru was largely displaced by foreign goods and did not recover after the war.[45]

Free trade in Venezuela began, except for the brief interlude of the first republic in 1810–1811, with operations which bear little resemblance to regular business. Private ownership of the livestock of the Orinoco valley was largely disregarded, and after Bolívar established himself at Angostura, the livestock resources of the region were swept up by his agents and shipped to the West Indies to pay for the war supplies sold on credit at high prices by British, Dutch, and American merchants.[46] There was no expansion of the agriculture of the coastal area of Venezuela during the period under review.[47] It continued to seek an outlet in the *colonias extrangeras* in the Caribbean, as it had under Spanish rule, though it was now a legal trade. Privileged products like Barinas tobacco and the cacao of Caracas lost the protected markets of later colonial times and production declined.[48] New Granada's economic recovery was also slow. There was a flurry of imports, chiefly for government account, from 1822 to 1825, financed by the loans floated in London. Apart from these years, foreign trade grew much more slowly than in Buenos Aires or Chile. Only in Guayaquil, in the southern part of Colombia, did a business boom develop. This

was based on the export of lumber, rice, and cacao and the exploitation of the favored situation of this port.[49]

In Mexico free trade did not actually begin until 1823. Until that time, all but a trickle of irregular trade had continued to follow traditional colonial channels to Spain and Cuba. When commerce with Spain was suspended, great difficulty arose owing to the disappearance of Spanish commercial capital at Veracruz. It was to take time to build up a new system of credit depending on agents of European manufacturers, established at Mexico City.[50] In spite of English interest in Mexican mining, production of the precious metals, which accounted for most of Mexico's export surplus, did not wholly recover in the period before 1830.[51]

---

[44] The bullion exported in British warships alone, 1819–1825, was over $26,000,000 (*ibid.*, p. 195). Mining production in 1825 was still 25 per cent below the pre-war average (*ibid.*, p. 121).

[45] *Ibid.*, p. 122.

[46] See frequent references to the exportation of livestock from the Orinoco in V. Lecuna, ed., *Cartas del Libertador . . .* (11 vols., Caracas, 1929–1948), II, 8–24. Much material on the same subject is calendared in the *Boletín del Archivo General de la Nación* (Caracas), under the heading "Gobernación de Guayana."

[47] Gil Fortoul, *op. cit.*, I, 581. Capital was lacking and interest as high as 15 per cent monthly was being charged on loans to producers. See also *Autobiografía del general José Antonio Páez* (2 vols., Caracas, 1946), I, 467, on the stagnation and poverty, especially of agriculture, in the later years of the 1820's.

[48] Irazábal, *op. cit.*, p. 96. Barinas tobacco production declined from 28,000 *quintales* before the war to 3,000 after it. Cacao exports declined from 130,000 *fanegas* (1810) to 61,000 *fanegas* (1836). On the other hand, coffee production was growing (Codazzi, *op. cit.*, II, 105, 110).

[49] For the volume of Colombian trade with Great Britain, see Humphreys, *op. cit.*, Appendix. Mining in Colombia, as in Peru, recovered slowly. A British official estimated the pre-war production, as shown by the output of the mints of New Granada at $2,141,000 *per annum* and the average from 1810–1825 at $1,760,000 (*ibid.*, p. 229, note). For the development of Guayaquil, see *ibid.*, pp. 226 ff.

[50] C. Mackenzie to Canning, Veracruz, July 24, 1824, in Humphreys, *op. cit.*, pp. 226 ff., and footnote citing H. Ward, *Mexico in 1827*, which gives a lower estimate of capital losses.

[51] *Ibid.*, p. 321. According to Ward, £3,000,000 had been invested by 1827. Coinage of silver in

---

York, 1923], p. 191). Earlier, the viceroy had permitted a small amount of licensed trade (D. B. Goebel, "British Trade with the Spanish Colonies, 1808–1830," *American Historical Review*, XLIII [January, 1938]). For the character of the early trade of independent Peru see Ricketts to Canning, Lima, December 27, 1826, in Humphreys, *op. cit.*, pp. 124, 137 (the food products imported included flour and lard).

The foregoing would appear to indicate some correlation between commercial progress and a lesser degree of severity in military operations in the different regions mentioned. This factor, however, cannot have been decisive. The extent to which free trade brought economic revolution also depended on the existence of resources in demand in the world markets and on adequate transportation facilities for bringing these to the seaports. Obviously, Buenos Aires, with its easily traversed *pampa*, and Chile, with production located never very far from the sea, had a great advantage over Peru, Colombia, and Mexico.

That the statesmen and politicians of Spanish America recognized the vital importance of transportation at this time is evident in the many efforts to develop steam navigation on South American rivers during the revolution. Plans were put forward involving the Orinoco, the Magdalena, the Atrato, and the Paraná. Several concessions were granted to foreigners, but none brought significant results until a later time.[52] Interest in road construction in Ecuador, Mexico, and Colombia also failed to bring results in view of government financial embarrassments.[53]

The rate and extent of trade expansion varied considerably from region to region, but the direction of change was the same. All the new republics headed toward a broader production of resources demanded by the world market and became increasingly intimately linked with the expanding economy of the nineteenth century, centered on and directed by Great Britain.[54] This trade expansion brought other economic developments in its wake. Taxation shifted from the complex system of colonial days, with its multiple excises, monopoly franchises, and sales taxes, toward reliance on the customs duties on imports as the all-important source of revenue.[55] Consumption of imported goods tended to outrun the ability of exports to balance them, leading to the negotiation of foreign loans on highly disadvantageous terms. Buenos Aires, Chile, Peru, Mexico, and Colombia all experienced the beginnings of their troubles with foreign creditors during this epoch.[56] The too rapid

[52] For an early abortive project see P. Gaul to W. Thornton, December 26, 1816, in Thornton Papers, Library of Congress. This project involved the Magdalena. Admiral Luis Brión was granted the exclusive right of steam navigation on the Orinoco (Baptis Irvine to the Secretary of State, July 21, 1818, Archives of the Department of State, Special Agents, Vol. 8), but the admiral never made use of this grant. J. B. Elbers also had a concession for steam navigation of the Magdalena (R. L. Gilmore and J. P. Harrison, "Juan Bernardo Elbers and the Introduction of Steam Navigation on the Magdalena River," THE HISPANIC AMERICAN HISTORICAL REVIEW, XXVIII [August, 1948], 339). Wythe (*op. cit.*) states that another contract for navigation of the Orinoco had been given in 1813 to a British subject, J. Hamilton, but that it, also, was not followed up by actual operations. W. S. Robertson mentions (*op. cit.*, p. 234), that in 1826 an American was operating a steamer on Lake Maracaibo. This is based on an article by Landaeta Rosales in the *Diario de Caracas*, July 2, 1896. Henao and Arrubla (*op. cit.*, p. 234) refer to the agitation for railroad or canal construction at the Isthmus of Panamá at this time.

[53] Gil Fortoul, *op. cit.*, II, 61. Tamayo (*op. cit.*, p. 198) gives a vivid picture of transportation difficulties in Colombia.

[54] Since the above was written, the writer is indebted to Professor Howard Cline of Yale University for a valuable comment. It is possible that in certain parts of Latin America, particularly where local regional economic initiative was important, and where there was no easy opportunity to produce goods for export on a large scale, that a transitional type of economy developed which Cline refers to as "neo-colonial." This involved development of new products for domestic use. Tariffs prohibited importation of large numbers of categories of manufactured goods capable of local manufacture. In practice, however, such restrictions were often evaded.

[55] This appears to have been gradually true. For supporting data for Buenos Aires see Burgin (*op. cit.*, p. 47) who indicates that the customs provided over 80 per cent of public revenue in the decade of the 1820's. For parallel information for Venezuela cf. Gil Fortoul, *op. cit.*, II, 52.

[56] Mexico borrowed in 1824 and 1825, Peru in 1822 and 1825, Colombia in 1820, 1822 and 1824.

Mexico, which in 1809 had been $24,000,000, fell to as low as $3,500,000 in 1823. Annual production for the period 1810–1825 was estimated at $11,-000,000, and this included bullion used for other purposes than coinage (*ibid.*, p. 318, and note there). Wythe (*op. cit.*, p. 295) refers to the difficulties encountered in reconstruction of the mining industry.

expansion of imports may have been one cause of the financial crises which contributed to wide-spread political instability after the establishment of independence.

Along with the economic liberalism, of which the removal of trade barriers was concrete evidence, there developed a broader liberalism which also influenced society. The story of the abolition of slavery has often been told and need not be repeated here. It should be remembered, however, that outright abolition in some countries and gradual emancipation in others had reduced slavery to insignificant proportions in republican Spanish America before 1830. This was, of course, preceded by the manumission of slaves on a considerable scale in the course of the revolutionary wars. Freedmen formed part of San Martín's liberating forces that fought at Chacabuco and of the army of Sucre that completed the liberation of Peru at Ayacucho.[57]

The Indian fared less well in this era. In spite of frequent references to their ancient woes in propaganda directed against the Spanish regime, the achievement of independence meant little to the native race. Though frequently involved in revolutionary fighting, Indians never wholeheartedly sided with either party in the struggle. In southern Chile they were active as royalist guerrillas. In Mexico they fought and bled with Hidalgo. In Peru and Colombia they fought on both sides, either because they were forced to do so, or because they followed some leader who had a personal reason for taking sides.[58] The lapse of colonial protective legislation exposed them to exploitation under the increasingly individualistic republican legal codes and the war of independence ruined many of the missions which had preserved their existence, even if they did not succeed in fitting them for the competitive society they now had to face.[59]

Perhaps the most marked social change of the era was the growth of the rift between the society of the seaports and capitals, on the one hand, and rural and provincial society, on the other. At the seats of government and in the ports upper and middle classes began to be affected by the streams of foreigners (diplomats, visiting scholars, pedagogues, merchants, soldiers and sailors), which began to appear on the scene. Fashions began to ape the styles of London and Paris; new sports and pastimes replaced colonial recreations; even habits of food and drink changed.[60] Provincial cities were but little affected by these newfangled notions and the countryside was largely unconscious

[57] B. Vicuña Mackenna, *Vida de O'Higgins* (Vol. V of his *Obras completas* [16 vols., Santiago, 1936–1940], p. 245.

[58] For an example of patriot identification with the cause of the Indian, see Kanki Pazos, *op. cit.*, p. 104; and by the same author, *Letters to Henry Clay on the Present State of South America* (Philadelphia, 1817). Though Indians took part frequently on the patriot side in Mexico, and conspicuously under Hidalgo, they also, at times, remained loyal to Spain (cf. Almán, *op. cit.*, III, 358). The Indians of Misiones favored Artigas and fought on his side against Portuguese and troops from Buenos Aires (Mitre, *Historia de Belgrano*, III, 12–13). In the provinces of Coro and Maracaibo (Venezuela) they were predominantly under Spanish influence (see Archivo Nacional [Bogotá], Guerra y Marina, Vol. 20, folio 194, for an example of Indian coöperation with Spanish forces, one of several such cases). Bolívar recognized this situation clearly as is shown by one of his letters (Lecuna, ed., *Cartas del Libertador*, VI, 137). On the other hand the Indians of Guayana were pro-patriot, on account of their hostility to the Spanish missionary friars (Baralt and Díaz, *op. cit.*, I, 361). For Indian activity as royalist guerrillas in Chile see B. Vicuña Mackenna, *La guerra a muerte*, Vol. V of his *Obras completas* (Santiago, 1940).

[59] For an example of eighteenth-century royal concern for Indians see J. F. Blanco and R. Azpurúa, eds., *Documentos para la vida pública del libertador de Colombia, Perú y Bolivia* (14 vols., Caracas, 1875–1877), II, 364. Colombian legislation tended to encourage individual ownership of land and to eliminate paternal restrictions (Gil Fortoul, *op. cit.*, II, 435–436).

[60] New social trends in Colombia in the years immediately after Ayacucho are described in Tamayo, *op. cit.*, pp. 145, 158, and 198–199. English influence in Chile is described by Maria Graham, *Journal of a Residence in Chile . . .* (London, 1824), p. 131. Other travelers' accounts could be cited in support of this change.

According to L. H. Jenks (*op. cit.*, pp. 45–50) £17,000,000 was invested in Spanish-American government bonds between 1823 and 1825. Most of these were in default within a few years.

of them. Thus, the wider, European outlook of the elite in almost every country began to show itself in minor ways long before it was enshrined in law, educational institutions, and in the arts.

The hypothesis suggested by the foregoing remarks may be summarized as follows: the revolutionary wars which led to independence were a profound shock to the society and to the economic life of the Spanish colonies. Wartime destruction left many countries less able to maintain traditional ways and opened the way for new developments. Ensuing changes were brought about, first of all, by the expansion of foreign trade, which, in turn, had repercussions on the whole economic and social structure. Nevertheless, only the beginnings of a basic transformation took place and there were many ways in which colonial attitudes and institutions carried over into the life of republican Spanish America. Liberal ideas, however, used at first to buttress the rising power of landowners and businessmen, weakened paternalistic aspects of colonialism.

The Río de la Plata region was most deeply changed by the revolution. Throughout the continent, too, the greater cities and the ports were more affected by the new than were the provinces and the countryside. There emerged, therefore, no single clearly identifiable pattern of change, and developments noted were not so much revolutionary as they were examples of an accelerated tempo of evolutionary transformation.

61. Latin American Economics: The Field and Its Problems*

SANFORD A. MOSK

The recent war was responsible for creating in this country a widespread interest in "area studies." During the war period, even before Pearl Harbor, it was necessary for both civilian and military branches of our government to have accurate information and informed judgments about all other countries, no matter how small or how remote. Shortages quickly appeared in the supply of trained social scientists with the knowledge required to deal with most parts of the world outside of western Europe and Canada. Such personnel as was available was not marshalled effectively among the various government agencies, as anyone with wartime experience in Washington will attest. But the main problem was one of shortage, not distribution.

The principal lacks appeared in economics and sociology, and to a lesser extent in political science. Historians, geographers, anthropologists, and linguists were available in larger numbers. Relatively they were abundant, and for that reason some of them were set to analyzing economic problems, with results that charitably can be forgotten. Economists with a working knowledge of regional conditions and institutions outside the European-North American orbit were difficult to find.

* *Inter-American Economic Affairs*, 3:55–64 (1949). Reprinted by permission of the original publisher. This paper is an outgrowth of my research on the industrialization of Mexico, made possible by a fellowship grant from the John Simon Guggenheim Memorial Foundation.

Since the end of the war a number of steps have been taken by academic and other institutions, and by some of the foundations also, to remedy the lack of regional orientation in the social sciences. Regional curricula have been devised, research institutes have been set up, funds have been made available for the purchase of books and other materials, individual scholars have been awarded grants to acquire background for regional studies through travel and research, and several meetings have been held to discuss the purpose, scope, and inter-disciplinary problems involved in creating a corps of regional specialists.

It is not my purpose to evaluate all these developments, since that is a task beyond the resources of the individual investigator. I shall deal only with one aspect of these regional studies, namely, Latin American economics. It may be useful, however, to indicate what appear to be the general characteristics of the field of regional studies as it is evolving in this country. First of all, the achievements summarized in the preceding paragraph are more impressive on paper than in substance. This is especially true of academic curricula and research institutes. The regional curriculum, graduate as well as undergraduate, is usually made up of a list of courses that happen to be given at the institution in question. What is given may be good. But usually there are gaps, and no serious effort is made to fill them.

Furthermore, there is a distinct pattern in the offerings. Because historians and geographers have specialized along regional lines, the curriculum is weighted heavily with courses in history and geography. For some parts of the world, anthropology also plays a leading role. Language training is usually featured. But offerings in such fields as economics, government, and sociology are apt to be lacking entirely, or at best meager. However competent the historians, geographers, anthropologists, and linguists may be, they cannot make up for the deficiencies in other fields, and the comparatively large attention given to their subjects necessarily makes the curriculum a lopsided one. Historians are especially likely to be active in regional programs. Thus much of the area training now available amounts to historical study embellished with language instruction, and little else.

A second main characteristic of the development of regional studies is caution. Academic people are notoriously cautious. Because of this, and also because the making of decisions in academic circles is usually diffused and decentralized, few risks are undertaken boldly in new fields. Doubtless other circumstances contribute to the same end. It is not my intention to analyze all the causes, but merely to record the fact that any new development of an academic nature, at least outside the realm of the natural sciences can be counted upon to take place by hesitant, reluctant, and therefore limited steps.

This handicap appears in aggravated form in area studies because some of the social sciences are organized so firmly along functional lines that most members of these professional groups see little point in investigations of a regional nature. Some like to think that they deal with universal ideas and truths. Others are modest about the scope of their fields of interest, but nevertheless they follow the conventional grooves of specialization found in their disciplines. Economists are probably the worst offenders in this respect. A person trained as an economist falls easily into a specialization in economic theory, or labor economics, or international trade, or banking, to cite but a few examples. A regional orientation is entirely foreign to his training. He does not know what to do with it, he views it with suspicion, and he usually calls it "overspecialization." I will deal more fully below with these tendencies of economists. Here I merely refer to them in order to illustrate how programs of regional study are handicapped by prevailing professional attitudes. Similar illustrations could be found in sociology, in political science, and, in somewhat different form, in linguistics, although probably no department in the average American university is less inclined to collaborate in regional studies than the department of economics.

The third general characteristic to be emphasized about area studies is a tendency to devote an excessive amount of time, energy, and money to the preparation of "tools of research." This observation refers to the proliferation of guides, bibliographies, handbooks, surveys of research in progress, and outlines of comprehensive research programs. Such publications have their uses, of course, and a certain amount of work of this kind is necessary in any subject. The question is, how many efforts of this kind are needed, in relation to the other work done?

There are obvious reasons why persons working in a new field are likely to turn their attention to making "tools for research." But, at least in the Latin American field, we have already gone too far in this direction. It was a common experience in Washington during the war to find a branch of a government agency, or a division, or even a whole agency so busily engaged in "tooling up" that it failed to get into production before it was abolished. We are faced with this danger in Latin American studies. It is clear that the manufacture of "tools" should now be confined to a few enterprises, such as the *Handbook of Latin American Studies,* and that most scholars in the field can spend their time more profitably in other ways than by multiplying guides which hardly anyone has the time, energy, or interest to use.

The preceding remarks about area studies in general suggest a number of issues which need to be examined in taking an inventory of the field of Latin American economics. In recent years there has been a growing number of economists interested in Latin American economic problems. Most of them are employed by the government or by one or another of the international agencies that deal with economic and financial matters, but there is also a handful of academic economists actively working in the field. The corps of economists with a principal interest in Latin America is not large, but it has been expanding, and a parallel expansion has been taking place in the output of books, brochures, and articles relating to the economy of that area. If we look at this body of literature as a whole, it becomes clear that certain kinds of questions and issues are being studied and discussed, and are apparently becoming the center of the field, while others are being pushed into the background.

Broadly speaking, the questions that are fashionable to deal with are those most likely to interest the conventional members of the economics profession, who, we must remember, are ordinarily skeptical about the value of a regional approach to economic problems. It is not amiss to suggest that those working in Latin American economics have been tempted to gain professional respectability for their subject by bringing it as close as they can to the subjects in which American economists are usually interested. Thus, much attention is paid to balance of payments problems, international trade policy (including exchange control), and inflation. Thus, too, much effort is given over to refining estimates of national income and monetary circulation. It is significant that most of the economic studies on Latin American countries deal directly with the international aspects of their economies, often specifically with their stake in an international trade program such as the I.T.O. It is even more significant that most of the remaining studies, namely those dealing with internal economic affairs—for example, inflation or government economic programs—are also oriented toward external economic relations.

To illustrate the theme of the preceding paragraph, I may refer to the session on Latin America at the most recent meeting of the American Economic Association.[1] Under the general title "Present Issues of the Latin-American Economy," two papers were presented. One of these dealt with "Some Aspects of Latin America's Trade and Balance of Payments," while the second was entitled "Inflation and Exchange Instability in Latin America." Let me hasten to say that I am not questioning the value of these papers or their quality. They were both fine papers. Furthermore, I realize that there was not

[1] See *Papers and Proceedings of the Sixty-first Annual Meeting of the American Economic Association* (May 1949), pp. 384–414.

time at one short session for more than a couple of papers. Nevertheless, I am impressed by the fact that they both were directed toward international economic questions, and that the performance as a whole can scarcely be said to have matched up to the general title, "Present Issues of the Latin-American Economy."

To point out the way in which attention is being concentrated on certain kinds of problems at the expense of others, is not to imply that the former are unimportant. On the contrary, it is obvious that the export-orientation of the commercial economies of the Latin American republics make such questions important to them as well as to academic economists in this country. Work on these topics should be carried forward by those already interested in them, and others should be encouraged to contribute new efforts. I do not advocate a cutback in these fields of investigation.

What I do advocate—and strongly, too—is that we devote an equal effort to getting an understanding of Latin American economic developments, trends, ambitions, and problems from an internal point of view. It is analysis of this kind which is virtually lacking. Without it, the field of Latin American economics is lopsided and distorted.

We need studies to show how Latin American economies function in institutional terms, for only in this way can we gain a full understanding of the problems with which they are faced. We are witnessing the early stages of an unfolding economic process in Latin America, arising out of a major effort to raise economic productivity by diversification. There are many bottlenecks and problems to be found in this process. We must evaluate these in each case. No one would deny that the balance of payments problem is important. But we must not stop there. We have to look at the process as one in which Latin Americans are mobilizing their human resources, their capital resources, and their natural resources for a new economic effort. Indeed, until we do so we cannot get a good understanding of even the balance of payments problem from the long-run point of view. We are in danger of neg-

lecting research of a fundamental character.

Let no one think that it is easy to do the kinds of studies which are urgently needed. They require not only a good working knowledge of economics but also a thorough knowledge of the social and political institutions, as well as the economic institutions, of the country or countries under study. In these institutions are found the true sources of the problems of mobilizing human, capital, and physical resources. The institutional knowledge is much more difficult to obtain than training in economics. To get it, it is necessary to read widely in history, anthropology, social conditions, literature, and geography, and it is also necessary to live and travel in the areas selected for study. All of this calls for time and for funds. Moreover, for most of the Latin American countries, it is not easy to find appropriate sources of information. There is even a scarcity of historical works that deal meaningfully with the development of institutions, in spite of the fact that there is no lack of writing on Latin American history. To cite a specific illustration, the economic history of virtually every country in Latin America since independence still remains to be written.

In Latin American economics, as in all area studies, the scholar cannot be content with serving an apprenticeship in one discipline. He must acquire maturity in other disciplines as well.

This, then, is the situation. To deal adequately with economic problems in a Latin American country, one must have a working knowledge of its whole institutional structure. Institutional assumptions which economists make in dealing with the United States, Canada, or western Europe have a limited usefulness in Latin America because of fundamentally different social and political institutions—how limited, depends on the country involved. They are farthest from relevance in the nations of Indian-Spanish culture, such as Mexico, Guatemala, Ecuador, and Peru. But even in countries with a different population composition, like Argentina, Uruguay, and Chile, they must be applied with caution because political experience, social structure, and income distribution in those countries are very different from what is found in North America or western Europe. Many economic actions in a Latin American country which appear irrational in the eyes of an American economist would seem wholly rational if he understood its institutions.

There are two further questions to be considered: who is likely to undertake the kind of work that is critically needed, and how is he to be encouraged to do so? Let us grant at the outset that there is no reason to expect most economists to be interested in Latin America, or any other region. There are plenty of intriguing and significant problems to occupy them in the more conventional aspects of economics. It is true that some economists might conceivably develop an interest in the field, but we must frankly recognize that the quest for professional security looms large in the thinking of academic economists, leading them to one of the standard grooves, such as transportation, industrial relations, or marketing, where they have a large and established audience for what they say and write, and for which they need no additional training in alien fields beyond what they acquire in graduate work.

What can we offer them in the more neglected branches of Latin American economics?—a small audience, limited teaching opportunities, the need to do much collateral work in other social sciences and in history, the assurance that most of this work cannot bear fruit in immediate publication, and meager sources of quantitative and other economic data. Surely, most economists who are tempted for a moment will take a second thought and then turn to more promising fields.

There is, however, one professional group within the broad field of economics that is more likely to respond positively to the temptation. I refer to the economic historians. The economic historian has an interest in institutions and an understanding of differences in institutional structure; otherwise, he would not be an economic historian. He must be a social scientist, and not merely a technician in economics. He has

trained himself to bring his understanding of political and social institutions to bear on his analysis of economic affairs and problems, and not to abstract from non-economic institutions, as general economists typically do in their professional work. Furthermore, he is less likely to be concerned about professional security than the average economist, because he has already chosen a marginal field in which to work. He is accustomed to getting his satisfactions in other ways. He is also accustomed to being on the peripheries of two fields—economics and history—and not quite a part of either one. Finally, he does not shrink from regional specialization, inasmuch as both his research and teaching are likely to have a regional flavor. It is a significant fact that a number of economic historians are already working in the general field of area studies.[2]

Economic history, therefore, is the most promising field in which to seek recruits for Latin American economics. The economic historian is prepared for fruitful work in Latin American economics by his interest in institutions and by his academic training, and psychologically, too, he is prepared to work in a marginal, inter-disciplinary field. Furthermore, he has been trained as an economist, and thus he is aware of interrelations to be examined and evaluated in the economic process, and also he is aware of pitfalls that he must avoid in reasoning and in the handling of quantitative material.

The preceding observations do not purport to set up the economic historian as the essence of all things that are good in social science research. They are merely intended to point out that economic history is a likely field in which to find scholars who can do good work in Latin American economics. The economic historian who makes this shift does not have to abandon economic history. On the contrary, he has an unusual opportunity to combine meaningful research in economic history with the analysis of con-

[2] Observe, too, that the *American Economic Review* uses the dual caption, "Economic History; National Economies" for one section of its book reviews.

temporary problems. But he must be willing to pioneer in both aspects, because little has been done up to now. I realize that not all economic historians have the impulse to pioneer, and I am also aware that there are some well-established, comfortable grooves of research in economic history where the going is comparatively easy. Nevertheless, I believe that a handful of able economic historians could be persuaded to shift the center of their attention to the Latin American field.

This leads us to the other question—how? So far as I can see, the only answer is support of the foundations. Only the foundations can make it possible for those who show an interest in Latin American economics to prepare themselves adequately for work in the field by means of research and travel. Obviously, not everyone who shows an interest should be encouraged. What the field needs is a handful of persons, each with comprehensive training, not a large number with a smattering. In exercising discrimination the foundations will also allay the fear, often expressed by social scientists, that area studies are apt to become a refuge for the less able scholars.

Not only can the foundations do this job,

but they have a responsibility to undertake it. What is going on nowadays in Latin America is a process of active economic change. It is part of the larger process in world economic development by which the "backward" countries are making an effort to catch up with the industrialized nations. The economic world as we have known it is being radically altered before our eyes. To study this process while it is going on certainly ranks among the more important economic questions of our day. To train scholars for this task is, therefore, an important undertaking.

I am well aware that the foundations are doing a good deal already to stimulate research in the Latin American field. My remarks are not intended to imply that they have been guilty of neglect, but rather to suggest that they re-examine what they have been doing, and, more specifically, that they ponder the problem of how to create a corps of able specialists in Latin American economics.

In writing this article of an exploratory nature, it is my hope that others interested in the field will be stimulated to express their points of view. It is time that we opened these questions for frank discussion.

62. Mexico's Forgotten Century*

LESLEY BYRD SIMPSON

A cause of speculation among amateurs of history is the unevenness with which "history" is spread; or, perhaps, I should say, the unevenness with which certain periods and very large expanses of the earth's surface are represented in historical literature. Some periods and places, one must conclude, are full of history and some are not, that is, if we

take the interest of historians as a trustworthy gauge. I refer not to those vast stretches

* *Pacific Historical Review*, 22:113–121 (1953). Reprinted by permission of the author and the original publisher. Read at the annual meeting of the Pacific Coast Branch of the American Historical Association at Vancouver on December 29, 1952.

of time before the invention of the alphabet but to periods for which abundant records are available. Evidently, the historian, like the ancient poet and the modern journalist, makes up his mind that certain times and events are "historical" and worthy of record, and others less so, if at all.

In the historiography of Latin America this kind of selection according to news value has been quite apparent. Now, "news" has to do with novel or out-of-the-ordinary happenings, the man-bites-dog theory. Thus, when Columbus performed the astonishing feat of crossing the Ocean Sea, the news gatherers promptly and properly seized upon it. It was novel, it was a "first," and beyond all question it turned out to be important or "historical." The amount of literature which it inspired, I submit, exceeds in bulk that of any other single event in the past five hundred years. The equally spectacular and, possibly, quite as important feat of Magellan a few years later received only an adequate coverage, while the amazing voyage of Andrés de Urdaneta in 1565, eastward across the Pacific, which, for better or for worse, brought Asia and America together, caused hardly a ripple of excitement among historians, then or later. It is plain, I think, that in all three of these cases the subsequent importance of the event has not been the single guiding principle of its literary exploiters.

There was, to be sure, such a bewildering wealth of novel events in the sixteenth century that the historians may be forgiven a certain hesitation in choosing among them. Extraordinary and spectacular happenings fill that century in the New World with "history" beyond any other before the nineteenth. Four years ago, in a paper read at the national meeting of this same body, I indicated that, to judge by the number of pages in the *Hispanic American Historical Review* concerned with the sixteenth century, historians evidently think it is three times as full of history as the seventeenth or eighteenth. (I hasten to add that I do not consider bulk the safest guide to go by.) Histories of Mexico in particular offer striking examples of the appeal of the novel over the humdrum. The Texas war of 1836 stimu-lated our interest in Mexico. Prescott answered the call and wrote by long odds the most stirring account of the conquest in the English language. In the bizarre adventure of 1862–1867 French archaeologists and historians belatedly discovered Mexico. They were the learned wing of Marshal Bazaine's "civilizing mission" and set out to duplicate the extraordinary exploits of Napoleon's scientific expedition into Egypt. Their researchers in Mexican archaeology have been of the utmost value to scholars, but the volume of literature which they devoted to the romantic episode of Maximilian and Carlota is immensely greater and might lead the uncritical reader to think that that theatrical and tragic adventure outweighed in importance everything that happened in Mexico before or since.

The result of this appeal of the picturesque has been the appearance of historical deserts in Mexico, periods when nothing much seemed to happen. One such relatively dead stretch, as I have suggested, is the seventeenth century. Apparently things had got shaken down into a comfortable routine: years passed, each distressingly like its predecessor. Historians can hardly be blamed for shying away from describing in detail the activities of functionaries who are as alike as the proverbial peas in a pod, and just as exciting. So we are left with the implied judgment that the seventeenth century in Mexico is comparatively unimportant, an attitude which is so marked that it has inspired the title of my paper.

I take issue with that judgment. My early schooling was much simplified by my being taught that European history ended in 476 A.D. and began again five hundred years later. The Dark Ages were a godsend to the schoolboy, although I had to learn later that they were the period of incubation of European society as we know it. The seventeenth century was a kind of Dark Age in Mexico, when, uninterrupted by major political upheavals, society was making its slow adjustment to the profound changes introduced by the Conquest. The evolution of society is, I think, the business of the historian, and we can ill afford to leave its study to ancillary disciplines. As it is, economists, geographers, social anthropologists, philologists, and biological scientists have moved into the vacuum and discovered that this quiet time was of the utmost importance in the development and composition of Mexican society. Mexico in the seventeenth century was undergoing such organic changes in form and economy that it is quite appropriate to call the period revolutionary. All its aspects are worthy of study if we wish to comprehend the Mexico that emerged a century later. Without suggesting a priority of importance and certainly without pretending to exhaust the matter, I should like to roam freely over a number of topics which I offer as fruitful lines of inquiry for our graduates to pursue.

One phenomenon in the New World that worried the folks back home from 1492 onward was the invincible Spanish centrifugalism, or the Spaniard's congenital resistance to any kind of authority. It was a retrogression into the Middle Ages. From the eleventh to the fifteenth centuries it had flourished more or less unchecked among the semibarbarous nobles of Castile and even among the townspeople, and culminated in the ferocious suppression of the *comuneros* in 1520–1522 by Charles V. The Spanish settler, once he had set foot in the New World, reverted to the type of medieval free lance which seems to have been the ideal of most, whether they were conquistadores, clerks, mechanics, priests, or peddlers. It was as if the Cid and his marauding knights of the eleventh century had returned, to plague the crown with their ancient and insolent contempt of upstart kings. The intervening centuries had done nothing to change their habits of thought or conduct. The hundreds of *probanzas*, or petitions for relief filed with the Council of the Indies by the deserving veterans of the Conquest and their somewhat less deserving offspring, fairly drip, to be sure, with avowals of undying loyalty to their sovereign, but I submit that these expressions were purely rhetorical and formalistic, and not evidence of the Spaniard's ingrained reverence for authority. The cant refrain, *Obedezco pero no cumplo,* "I obey but do not fulfill," is an accurate measure

of their feeling. This apparently nonsensical formula is, indeed, a reflection of the early feudal relationship between lord and vassal, going back possibly to Visigothic times, when the king was, so to speak, only one of the boys and not to be taken too seriously.

In New Spain this atavistic trait took the form of *criollismo*. Dating from the appearance of the first Mexican-born whites and mestizos, a rift developed between them and later immigrants from Spain. By the beginning of the seventeenth century they were calling themselves creoles (*criollos*) and their Spanish-born rivals *cachupines*, or *gachupines*, an epithet of uncertain etymology but of undisputed meaning. Writers of the day, such as Gómez de Cervantes and Thomas Gage, make it quite clear that New Spain was split by an extremely bitter, irrational, and finally sanguinary feud between the two factions. Martín Carrillo, the royal visitor who was sent over in 1625 to investigate the causes of the dangerous riots in Mexico City of the year before, gave it as his opinion that they were essentially a manifestation of the deep creole hatred of all things Spanish. The close parallel between the actions of the Mexican creoles and their Spanish forebears makes me think that *criollismo* is worth studying as the survival of an ancient folkway, the dangers of which were fully understood by the crown. It did not originate in the New World.

Conditions in Mexico in the seventeenth century were very favorable to this retrogression, for communications between the Spain of the dying Hapsburgs and her restless colony were interrupted, frequently for years on end. The settlers were able to resume the pattern of their favorite way of life with no interference to speak of. Besides, as François Chevalier brings out in his remarkable study of the early Mexican landed estate,[1] this quasi feudalism was the type of society best adapted to the primitive conditions obtaining in the vast uninhabited expanses of northern Mexico. The self-sufficient hacienda provided an ideal climate for the growth

[1] François Chevalier, *La formation des grands domaines au Mexique: Terre et société aux XVIe–XVIIe siècles* (Paris, 1952).

of separatism, but *criollismo* was equally virulent among all classes. Religious orders, merchant and trade guilds, professions, college faculties, and government bureaus, all were divided beyond hope of reconciliation into *criollos* and *gachupines,* and it is quite apparent that by the eighteenth century the creoles were by far the more numerous, wealthy, and powerful group, and, hence, the more touchy. I think it is demonstrable that Mexico was virtually independent by 1700 and that the War of Independence of 1810–1821 was hardly more than the concluding episode of two and a half centuries of retrogression among the ruling element. Luis González Obregón broached this theme some years ago,[2] but he did not carry it beyond the sixteenth century.

The countermovement to *criollismo,* that is, the loyalty to the old country professed by native-born Spaniards, should not, I think, be given undue weight. With some notable exceptions, their vociferous avowals simply do not jibe with their conduct and were, I suspect, usually a stratagem to get them preference back home over the rich, snobbish, and well-connected creoles. In any event, the loyalty of the *gachupines* could not be counted on to last beyond the moment when they had made themselves respectable in mining, trade, farming, or government jobs, and had married into creole families, after which they joined the tacit conspiracy against the crown with no discernible compunction. That conspiracy was so effective that by 1700 New Spain was firmly in the hands of a vast interlocking system of family interests, which the able servants of the later Bourbons conspicuously failed to break up. Indeed, by attempting to do so, they merely hastened the final rupture between Spain and Mexico.

An inextricable part of the conspiracy was the peculiar and all-pervading Latin American institution of *caciquismo,* or local boss rule, which, I am convinced, struck its roots deeply in the seventeenth century. *Caciquismo* came to its full flower in the rural districts, where the magistrates (*corregidores* and *alcaldes mayores,* usually Spaniards who had bought their jobs in com-petitive bidding) got rich by assessing their constituents for contributions in the form of forced purchases of salt, seeds, tools, or any commodity the supply of which they could manipulate. They made themselves solid with the landed aristocracy by peddling favors and suppressing symptoms of unrest among the peons. In a word, they joined the creole conspiracy to circumvent the Laws of the Indies. This dichotomy between Spanish written law and its practice has often been remarked, but its history has never been sufficiently explored. It deserves to be, because, without exception that I know of, all the former Spanish possessions are still governed locally by *caciques,* as, indeed, is Spain itself.

Any society may be thought of as an invention to insure the means of subsistence. Ants, bees, termites, sardines, whales, and men, all learned that they could more effectively attack the problem of getting something to eat by banding together and organizing a society fitted to do the job. Call it social ecology, which is what I am talking about in seventeenth-century Mexico.[3] The early hacienda was an effective device to insure survival in a hostile environment, or rather, I should say, to insure the survival of the "dominant minority," as Toynbee would call it. But what of the native society? At the time of the Conquest, Mexico had a large population with a highly developed culture and social habits as deeply rooted as those of the Spaniards. They became the "serfs" whom the new feudal lords counted on to man their estates. They were divided up among the *encomenderos* and adjusted themselves to the new order without intolerable friction, because their

[2] Luis González Obregón, *Los precursores de la independencia mexicana en el siglo XVI* (Paris, 1906).

[3] In addition to Chevalier's book, already cited, several other works occur to me which illuminate this theme: Johan Hjort, "Human Society and Life in the Sea," *Geographical Review* (November, 1935); Carl O. Sauer, *Man in Nature* (New York, 1939); Robert C. West, *The Mining Community in Northern New Spain: The Parral Mining District* (Berkeley, 1949); Erhard Rostlund, *Freshwater Fish and Fishing in Native North America* (Berkeley, 1952).

own ruling class was easily persuaded to become the truant officers of the Spaniards. The native serfs, however, developed a lamentable tendency to die off under the impact of the white man's culture and assorted microbes. All our records are in agreement for once, and it is clear that by the end of the sixteenth century New Spain had lost about three fourths of its aboriginal population.[4] This was a catastrophe of the first magnitude and because of it the seventeenth century presents an utterly different picture from that of a hundred years before, when the happy conquerors had settled back to enjoy the fruits of their enterprise. A deep depression had set in. Agriculture, mining, manufactures, and commerce all suffered from a want of hands and to a considerable extent from a want of customers, for Mexican economy, even in the lower ranks, was by this time on a money basis, and industries, particularly textiles, the most important, depended on the native market. Woodrow Borah was the first to point out the intimate connection between Mexico's shrinking economy and the loss of population; indeed, he was the first to call attention to the depression itself.[5]

The vanishing population meant the abandonment of very great stretches of farming land and its conversion to stock raising. In the "Indian" part of Mexico (a term I use with some misgiving in view of the current uncertainty in its meaning)—I refer to the old agricultural part of the country first overrun by the Spaniards—the social and economic consequences of the massive loss of population can only be guessed at. I recently made an attempt to determine the increase of livestock in the sixteenth century in the district of the Audiencia of Mexico[6] and derived such astronomical quantities that I hesitated to publish them, but Chevalier's scattered figures for the seventeenth century bear me out. Apparently the only thing the Spaniards could think of to do with empty land was to bring in cattle and sheep and let nature take its course. The result was a second Conquest of Mexico, by livestock. It transformed the social, political, and economic structure of the country,

which became geared to cattle and sheep, and, I might add, to horses, mules, and donkeys. Mexicans almost lost the art of walking. "To ride like a Mexican" was, by Cervantes' day, the highest compliment a horseman could receive. Wool growers organized a fraternity modeled after the ancient *mesta* of Castile, with their own laws, courts, magistrates, and special privileges. No less powerful were the *obrajeros,* or textile manufacturers. When the supply of labor ran short, the local courts could be counted on to make up the deficit out of the abundant jail population. It is not at all unlikely, indeed, that the jails were kept full for that very purpose. The court records of the seventeenth century are so crowded with complaints on this score that one gets the impression that a whole judicial system, or, rather, a conspiracy of magistrates, courts, and employers, functioned principally to keep a supply of cheap labor flowing to the *obrajes* and other worthy enterprises.

The conquest by livestock changed not only the culture of Mexico but, profoundly and even disastrously, the physical landscape. We in this country have only recently become aware of the problem created by running sheep on semi-arid land. The Navajo of New Mexico are threatened with extinction because their soil, ground into dust and mud by sharp hooves, and its cover eaten down to the roots, is being washed and blown away. Similarly, in old Mexico I think it is demonstrable that the shocking expanses of badlands on the plateau were once agricultural land which was given over to sheep running in the sixteenth and seventeenth centuries. Cattle did less damage to the soil, but their raids on native crops were a prolific source of friction for centuries. On both counts living must have become increasingly difficult for native farmers, many of whom, I suspect, took refuge in the grow-

[4] Sherburne F. Cook and Lesley Byrd Simpson, *The Population of Central Mexico in the Sixteenth Century* (Berkeley, 1948).

[5] Woodrow Borah, *New Spain's Century of Depression* (Berkeley, 1951).

[6] Lesley Byrd Simpson, *The Exploitation of Land in Central Mexico in the Sixteenth Century* (Berkeley, 1952).

ing cities, which attracted the displaced population like sinks. The miserable swarms of urban vagabonds, the plague of drunken *léperos* which so annoyed the fastidious Don Carlos de Sigüenza y Góngora, were in some degree made up of the refugee rural population whose land was running down the *barrancas* in the form of silt, or was being blown over the country in dense clouds of dust, as remarked by Juan de Torquemada at the turn of the century. The destruction of the soil and the shift of population to the cities has been accelerating ever since (for many other reasons, of course) and is today one of the gravest problems facing the harassed government of Mexico.

A while back I mentioned microbes as a major cause of the decline of the native population. The repeated and devastating epidemics of European diseases in the first two centuries after the Conquest did more, to my way of thinking, to change the face of Mexico and, indeed, of the whole New World than all other factors put together, and it is remarkable how little we know about them. Smallpox, typhus, measles, whooping cough, tuberculosis (which seems to have been unknown in aboriginal times), syphilis (which, although most likely a native of the New World, was certainly spread to uncontaminated parts by the conquerors and their Indian "friends"), new and virulent forms of malaria—all these diseases and a little known native plague called *cocolistle*, cleared the land more effectively than any amount of fighting could have done. The resulting changes were of incalculable importance to every aspect of Mexican society. To investigate them we may have to enlist the aid of geneticists and parasitologists. One striking phenomenon is that the native population did not die off entirely, but somewhere in the seventeenth century seems to have attained equilibrium. A residual group somehow developed enough resistance to these scourges to survive and slowly to recover. I suspect that the surviving group was of mixed blood. The whites, on the other hand, enjoyed relative immunity from the epidemics. They increased rapidly, until the ratio of white to native blood approached

parity. There emerged from this mingling a type which we think of as "Mexican," although it defies precise definition.

It may be, on the contrary, that the mixing of races had nothing to do with the recovery of population. The immunity of the whites was certainly owing in some degree to their better living conditions. This may be a clue to the native recovery, for during the "century of depression" the scarcity of labor forced employers to bid against each other, complaining bitterly the while, and to pay the workers a more adequate wage. Gómez de Cervantes, writing in 1599, remarks that Indian mechanics were already earning as much as six to eight *reales* a day, which is as much as free miners were making in Humboldt's time, to his great astonishment. I suggest, then, that easier living conditions, however relative, among the remnants of the native population may account for the higher survival rate in the latter part of the seventeenth century and the eventual reversal of the population trend.

One last phenomenon which I wish to bring to your attention is the stubbornness of food habits and their effect on the culture and the landscape of Mexico. One example will have to serve as an illustration. Wheat bread was the Spaniard's traditional diet, and wherever he went he insisted on having it. It was a strong link with his past and had something of magic about it. In Mexico it became a cachet of superiority to eat wheat bread, or at least to have it on the table. This irrational obsession led to the wasteful exploitation of land which could have been better employed in raising native crops. Wheat farming brought in handsome returns, for a Spaniard would pay for wheat two or three times what he would have had to pay for an equal quantity of equally nourishing maize—which meant that good wheat land was eagerly sought after and worked to death. The famous Valley of Atlixco on the eastern slope of Popocatépetl became the breadbasket of white Mexico. Juan de Torquemada observed that its soil was so rich that it never had to be fertilized! The Spanish farmers anticipated our own hardy pioneers, who could go through a given patch of land in two generations. The Valley of Atlixco was taken over by sugar cane in the seventeenth century, which may mean that it could no longer produce wheat profitably. I do not know what happened, but in traveling through it recently I was struck by the great stretches of once-cultivated land now covered with brush. I suspect there are analogies in other parts of the country where wheat was once a major crop. I suggest also that the economic and social effects of the introduction of sugar cane are worth looking into, for sugar has been one of the major determinants of important sections of the country.

By this time you will have noted the anomaly in my paper, namely, that the seventeenth century cannot properly be labeled "forgotten" if we know so much about it. It would, perhaps, have been more scholarly to have called it "the relatively forgotten, or neglected, century." In point of fact, I know only enough about it to know how little I know, an observation which my philosophical friends will approve of. Seriously, what I am proposing is that such long periods of quietness may be more meaningful for the understanding of historical processes than periods of turmoil and excitement. Their study is, to be sure, exceedingly arduous and requires the use of unfamiliar tools. It is my hope, however, that I may provoke enough interest in the matter to overcome the excruciating boredom of searching out and organizing the minute data of social change. It is the historian's job to do so, for he is trained to see events in perspective and to look for causes and processes.

63. Toward a Theory of Spanish American Government*

Richard M. Morse

1. The Viceregal Period and Its Antecedents

The purpose of this essay is neither fully to analyze the political experience of Spanish America nor to construct a mature theory which will comprehensively illuminate it. The histories of these eighteen countries are, taken singly, too fragmentary and, taken jointly, too uncorrelated to permit of so systematic a project. In this as in most areas of New World studies the elements for conclusive synthesis are still unavailable. Therefore a heuristic device will be used, which will be to examine certain formal European notions in the hope, not that they will concisely epitomize Spanish American political experience, but that they may be "played off against" that experience—contrapuntally, perhaps—in a way to evoke corresponding themes.

Professor Northrop has done something of this nature in collating Lockean philosophy with United States political history. As is suggested in the "Note" that concludes this essay, he perhaps oversimplifies the case; but a summary of his argument will be useful here as a point of departure. Professor Northrop asserts that Locke's atomistic conception of the sovereign individual squared

* *Journal of the History of Ideas*, 15:71–93 (Jan. 1954). Reprinted by permission of the author and the original publisher.

neatly with British North American conditions of life. Until the twentieth century the
United States was a laissez-faire state: not
an active intervenor assuring distribution of
limited resources among the needy many,
but a passive guarantor of private claims to
the new continent's ample wealth. Unlike
their North American counterparts, nineteenth-century British Conservatives—with
their traditions of noblesse oblige and of a
state religion—inclined toward paternalistic
social-mindedness and away from Lockean
atomism, unbridled laissez-faire and un-
qualified obeisance to rights of the sovereign
individual. British Liberals, who held closer
to Lockean ideals, eventually yielded before
a socialistic Labor Party. Locke, by this reckoning, was therefore less congenial to his
homeland than to the trans-Atlantic England which was colonized during the century into which he was born, and in 1776
the colonists' fealty to him was, for urgent
cause, consummately affirmed.[1]

The question now to be raised is: Are
there other European philosophies which
might be comparably correlated with Spanish American political history?

Spanish American preceded British colonization by more than a century, and thus
belongs to an era that antedates not only the
Lockean rights of man but also the Bossuet-
and Hobbes-type apology for the absolutist
national state. It is the Catholic kings, Ferdinand and Isabella, who symbolize Spanish
America's political heritage.

Isabella in a sense prefigures the divine-
right monarch. Her thwarting of the nobles
and of the Cortes wherein they formed an
estate; her royal agents and administrative
reforms that centralized the government;
her replacement of feudal levies with a modern army; her use of the faith to further
political unity—all have been cited to identify her as a precursor of the Hobbesian
autocrat. Yet it must be remembered that
for three centuries after Isabella's death the
Spanish empire retained, in comparison at
least with the burgeoning capitalist countries, many hall marks of the medieval, hierarchical state.

The "common law" of Isabella's Castile

was the *Siete Partidas*, drawn up c. 1260 and
promulgated in 1348. Though tinctured
with Roman law, the *Partidas* were less
Roman rules *for* conduct than medieval-type
principles *of* conduct that approached being
moral treatises. As late as the nineteenth
century Dunham found that:

. . . if all other codes [than the *Siete Partidas*]
were banished, Spain would still have a respectable
body of jurisprudence; for we have the experience
of an eminent advocate in the royal tribunal of
appeal for asserting, that during an extensive practice of twenty-nine years, scarcely has a case occurred which could not be virtually or expressly
decided by the code in question.[2]

The *Partidas* assumed the nuclear element of society to be, not Lockean atomistic
man, but religious, societal man; man with a
salvable soul (*i.e.*, in relationship with God)
and man in a station of life (*i.e.*, having mutual obligations with fellow humans, deter-
minable by principles of Christian justice).
The ruler, though not procedurally responsible to the people or the estates, was bound,
through his conscience, to be the instrument
of God's immutable, publicly ascertainable
law. The *Partidas*, in fact, specifically excoriated the tyrant who strove to keep his
people poor, ignorant and timorous and to
forbid their fellowship and assemblies.

As mistress of the hierarchical Castilian
state whose governance was largely by im-
manent justice and specially ceded privileges (*fueros*), Isabella found constant occasion to make inter- as well as intra-national
assertion of her spiritual authority. Unlike
Aragón—from whose border the Moorish
menace had been lifted in the thirteenth
century and whose rulers were therefore indifferent to the Reconquest—Castile directly
confronted Moorish Granada until 1492.
Furthermore, it was Cisneros, the Queen's
confessor, who largely animated the African
campaigns against the infidel Turks and

[1] F. S. C. Northrop, *The Meeting of East and
West* (New York, 1946), chaps. III, IV. See also
Merle Curti, "The Great Mr. Locke, America's
Philosopher, 1783–1861," *The Huntington Library
Bulletin*, 11 (April 1937), 107–151.

[2] S. A. Dunham, *Spain and Portugal*, 5 vols.
(London, 1832–1835), IV, 109.

Moslems. And it was with the Castilian sovereign that the expeditions which claimed dominion over millions of pagan Amerinds were initially associated. In her major foreign ventures, therefore, Isabella's policy reflected not only politico-military vicissitudes of statecraft but also spiritual responsibilities in the face of non-Christian multitudes. After Columbus had assigned three hundred Indians to forced labor, it was as the imperious agent of the Church Universal that Isabella demanded: "By what authority does the Admiral give my vassals away?"

If Isabella, in her enterprises to the south and overseas to the west, symbolizes the spiritualist, medieval component of the emergent Spanish empire, then Ferdinand, whose Aragón was engaged to the east and north, represents a secular, Renaissance counterpart. His holdings (the Balearics, Sardinia, Sicily, Naples) and his Italian and Navarrese campaigns confined his problems of rule, alliance and warfare to the European, Christian community. Isabella presented the unity of spiritually intransigent Christendom to infidel and pagan. Ferdinand was committed to the shifting, amoral statecraft of competing Christian princes in maintenance and expansion of a domain which, within its Christian context, was diversely composed.

Ferdinand ruled under transitional conditions which precluded resorting for authority to Isabella's Thomistic sanction or to statist apologetics. Managing with sheer personal verve and cunning, he was, in the fullest sense, Machiavellian. Indeed the Florentine, who regarded religions as instruments for political centralization and who denied that Italian well-being depended upon the Church of Rome (*Discourses*, I, xii), called Ferdinand "a new prince" who had become "the first king in Christendom" by great and extraordinary actions, "which have kept his subjects' minds uncertain and astonished, and occupied in watching their result" (*Prince*, XXI).

Spanish conquistadors, colonizers and catechizers, then, carried with them to American shores this dual heritage: medie-

val and Renaissance, Thomistic and Machiavellian. Through a close study of the letters of Cortés and the *Historia general de las cosas de Nueva España* of the missionary, Sahagún, Luis Villoro has projected the conquest as a two-way revelation. To the Indian were revealed a triumphant "universal" Church and its militant temporal agent, the Spanish crown; to Europe were revealed civilizations, fauna, flora and geography of a vast New World, which crumbled agelong sureties and challenged the imagination. The Indian, that is, was seen bifocally: through the eyes of the self-assured knight-errant or proselytizer and through those of the freely inquiring humanist. At the unspanned hiatus between these outlooks Villoro pitches the Indian's four-century tragedy.[3]

For half a century after Isabella's death in 1504 Spanish New World administration hovered between medieval and Renaissance orientations. Were men of other races, even though their hierarchical status might be politically and socially inferior, to be accorded equality as salvable souls and safeguards against exploitation? Or was amoral expediency, perhaps reinforced by the Aristotelian concept of "natural slaves," to determine their lot?

In the case of Negroes, Isabella in 1503 revoked permission to ship Christianized slaves from Spain to the Indies; but Ferdinand condoned the traffic in 1510, and, soon after, direct levies from Africa commenced. In the case of Indians, wide-ranging polemics, dating from Isabella's reprimand to Columbus, sought to fix the extent, if any, to which forced labor could be exacted of them. For decades royal decrees on the subject were a history of statement and reversal. Finally the "New Laws" of 1542-3 (modified in 1545-6 and 1548-51) definitively declared the Indians to be free persons and vassals of the crown, canceled the judicial authority of their immediate overlords (*encomenderos*) and imposed on the latter a full scale of obligations vis-à-vis the Indians. In other words, to safeguard the Indians' Thomistic

[3] Luis Villoro, *Los grandes momentos del indigenismo en México* (Mexico City, 1950), pp. 15–88.

status in society, the king was forced to curb exploitative *encomenderos* who, in earlier times would have been feudal lords more concerned than he with that status.[4]

Another question was: Would medieval exclusivism be maintained in matters of trade with and emigration to the Indies? Isabella's monopolistic contract with Columbus and her denial of emigration, except with special license, to all but Castilians and Leonese was the first answer. Ferdinand, however, extended privileges to his own subjects, and Charles I (1516–56) went much further. Of the latter's vast, pluralist, polyglot empire Spanish Europe was but a segment. Charles spoke Spanish with an accent, brought a Flemish court to Spain and played the Machiavellian cosmopolite to bring a modicum of unity to the congeries that was his realm. He even went so far as to have his delegates to the Council of Trent oppose the papal party in an effort to conciliate the Protestants. In administering overseas Spain he allowed emigration of Germans, Flemings, Italians and others of his subjects. For its economic development he enlisted aid from newly risen international commercial capitalists of northern Europe—the Welsers, the Fuggers, the Ehingers.

On the accession of Philip II (1556–98), however, the realm became somewhat less heterogeneous with the dismemberment of Bohemia, Hungary and Austria, while Philip's arduous campaigns in the Netherlands were dramatic proof of his uncompromising, militant, profoundly felt Catholicism and Hispanicism—qualities sharply intensified by the great Catholic reassertion of the period. Machiavelli went on the Index (1557), and insurgent Lutheranism restored Spain to its medieval rôle as the universal Church's knight-in-arms against the forces of darkness. It was under Philip that the structure of the Spanish American empire assumed the cast which, for purposes of this essay, it kept until c. 1810. That cast I describe as dominantly Thomistic, with recessive Machiavellian characteristics. (I use the terms "Thomistic" and "medieval" for contrast with northern Europe's emergent capi-

talist societies of 1500–1800, and not to designate a residual facsimile of the thirteenth century.)

In the 1570's, by extending the Inquisition to America and by declaring Church patronage inalienable from the crown, Philip set his governance definitively within a larger framework of divine law, imbuing his own and his agents' directives with spiritual purpose. No entry was left for the atomistic tolerance that England, despite its state religion, had already begun to evince. (England seen through Spanish perspective takes on characteristics of the United States seen through the English one—see the Northrop discussion *supra.*)

The crown considered the political and social hierarchy to be energized at every level and in every department. As Indian peoples were absorbed, for example, they were not indiscriminately reduced to a common stratum. Certain of their leaders retained prestige in the post-conquest society, and many low-born Spaniards raised their own status by marrying caciques' daughters. Unlike prim New England meetinghouses, moreover, the Spanish baroque church showed the Indian's craftsmanship (and, by the eighteenth century, his artistry); to his people it made a lavish visual, auricular, ritual appeal, while its saints tacitly reembodied his native gods. English colonists mobilized militarily *against* the Indian; Spaniards, apart from the actual conquest, mobilized socially, politically, economically, religiously and culturally *to assimilate* him.

---

[4] The historic debate (1550–1) between the humanitarian "Protector of the Indies," Las Casas, and the erudite humanist, Sepúlveda, epitomized the issue as to whether the Spanish empire should continue to expand by force and enslavement. Though the disputants hardly objectified such nebulous abstractions as medieval and Renaissance outlooks, Las Casas' view that Indians should be treated *ab initio* as catechizable souls coincided with subsequent official theory. For conflicting interpretations of the debate see: Lewis Hanke, *The Spanish Struggle for Justice in the Conquest of America* (Philadelphia, 1949), 109–132, 187–189, and Edmundo O'Gorman, "Lewis Hanke on the Spanish Struggle for Justice in the Conquest of America," *The Hispanic American Historical Review,* XXIX (1949), 563–571.

To be sure, the social hierarchy had its anomalies. Creoles (American-born whites or near-whites) rarely received the prestige and the economic and political opportunities that were officially assured them. Mestizos, mulattoes, Indians and Negroes, on the contrary, occasionally found a social fluidity that they could not officially have expected. Broadly speaking, however, a man's status was defined somewhat fixedly by his occupation and by his place and condition of birth. Transferral from one status to another (*e.g.*: an Indian who passed from mission to *encomienda*, a Negro from slave to free status, or a mestizo to the creole nobility) generally entailed official sanction and registration.

The multiplicity of judicial systems underscored the static, functionally compartmented nature of society. The fact that they—like the several hierarchies of lay and clerical administrators—constantly disputed each other's spheres of influence only served to reaffirm the king's authority as ultimate reconciler. Nuclear elements—such as municipalities or even individual Indians—as well as highly placed officers could appeal directly to the king, or to his proxy, the viceroy, for redress of certain grievances. The king, even though he might be an inarticulate near-imbecile like Charles II, was symbolic throughout his realm as the guarantor of status. In Thomistic idiom, all parts of society were ordered to the whole as the imperfect to the perfect. This ordering, inherently the responsibility of the whole multitude, devolved upon the king as a public person acting in their behalf, for the task of ordering to a given end fell to the agent best placed and fitted for the specific function.

In the economic realm, Spanish mercantilism lacked the enterprising free play of the state-guided commercial capitalism of seventeenth- and eighteenth-century England. The very anatomy of the economy showed the impress of medievalism: primary dedication to extractive pursuits; confusion between bullion and real wealth; dogged (but ineffectual) prohibition of foreign and even intercolonial trade; a multiform, burdensome tax structure; monopolis-

tic merchant- and craft-guilds (*consulados* and *gremios*); lack of credit and banking facilities; use of the simplest forms of partnership (*commenda, societas*); scarcity of currency (and in outlying areas the use of pre-Columbian tokens, such as cacao beans); commercial exchange through annual fairs; municipal price control.

The Spanish empire, to be sure, could scarcely avert contagion from the post-medieval world in which it existed and for which it was in part responsible. The Jesuits, who had received extensive privileges overseas for the very purpose of bolstering the empire's moral and religious base, were outstandingly versed in modernism. An "enlightened" Bourbon regime expelled them in 1767 less for their reactionary perversity than for their shrewd, disciplined commercial activities and their faith-defying "probabilist" dialectics.

Spanish American bullion was a lodestar for foreign merchants. Introduced as contraband or else covertly within the Spanish system itself, the wares of Dutch, French and English were temptingly cheap, well-made and abundant. They, like the fiscal demands of the mother country, were a constant incentive for creoles to organize local economies from which bullion and exportable surplus might readily be factored out. The calculating acquisitiveness of capitalism, if not its institutions for unlimited accrual, was frequently in evidence.

Moreover, Indian and Negro burden-bearers were, unlike the medieval serf, never fully identified with the historical and cultural ethos of their masters. For this reason they suffered more from the emergent exploitative psychology than, perhaps, post-medieval peasants who remained bound to the land. The African received no comprehensive protective code until 1789. And the very laws that assured the Indian status in return for fixed services could in practice be perverted, rendering him servile to an *encomendero* or a royal agent (*corregidor*). Indeed, the existence of Thomistic guarantees for the common man can be confirmed only by examining Spain's New World experience in selected eras and locales, or by comparing it en bloc with other European ventures in the Antilles and North America.

Yet however strongly such "recessive" Machiavellian, protocapitalist or secularistic traits might erupt, the underpinning of the empire—social, economic, political, intellectual—bore a rubric of the earlier era. Eighteenth-century Bourbon reforms (the notable ones being those of Charles III, 1759–88) did little to alter this generalization. Some reforms—like the intendant system—were superimposed on the old structure, caused added confusion and were revoked. Others—like the Caracas Company, a more modern and enterprising trade monopoly—found harsh opposition because their services entailed strict enforcement of regulations which a more adaptive, personalistic regime of local control had traditionally winked at.

The hierarchical, multiform, pre-capitalist Spanish America of 1800 was ill prepared for the ways of enlightened despotism, still less for those of Lockean constitutionalism.

2. THE REPUBLICAN PERIOD

That the heterogeneous Spanish American realm was for three centuries relatively free from civil strife and separatist outbreaks must largely be explained by a steadfast loyalty to the politico-spiritual symbol of the crown. Even the sporadic Indian revolts of the eighteenth century were directed not against the Catholic sovereign and imperium but against malfeasance of local agents. Daniel Valcárcel says of Túpac Amaru, the Inca scion who led an abortive uprising in 1780:

And when the decision to fight is made, the cacique already has in his spirit a clear purpose to achieve: he must eliminate the evil functionaries who with their venality and greed for riches corrupt the wise laws of the monarch, run against the precepts of religion and ruin the life of the Indians, *cholos* and mestizos. His rebellion will be more apparent than real. . . . Túpac Amaru is the most distinguished champion of His Majesty; fidelity is his principal virtue. A fervent Catholic and vigorous monarchist, his attitude is wholly normal for a mestizo of the 18th century in indirect contact with the new ideas of the era of Enlightenment.[5]

Not until 1809, during Spain's Napoleonic interregnum, did local juntas appear overseas. Yet even then their autonomy, in expectation of a legitimist restoration, was provisional. Only when the ad hoc "liberal" Cortes, established in unoccupied Spain, tried to reduce Spanish America from viceregal to colonial status did the independence campaign, championed by a few firebrands, gather momentum.

Ferdinand VII was restored in 1814. But in the face of the independence movement, his character and policy discredited both himself and the Church, whose support he retained. For Spanish America the Thomistic keystone had been withdrawn. Efforts to supplant it, on a continental basis or even within regional blocs, were vain. No creole caudillo and no prince of European or Inca lineage could command universal fealty or age-old spiritual sanction. A Thomistic sovereign could not be created *ex nihilo*, and Spanish America's centrifugal separatism was for the first time unleashed.

Another idiom than the Thomistic is therefore needed to be played off against the republican experience. Hitherto the most satisfying analyses have been those that attribute Spanish American instability to the imposition of French-, British- and American-type constitutions upon peoples whose illiteracy, poverty, provincialism, political inexperience and social inequalities rendered ineffectual the mechanisms of constitutional democracy. This somewhat negative view, however, does not fully draw one into the fabric of Spanish American politics. If postulates of the Enlightenment were not relevant to that milieu, how, in a positive sense, may we comprehend it?

The answer this essay proposes is that at the moment when the Thomistic component became "recessive," the Machiavellian component, latent since the sixteenth century, became "dominant."

This circumstance was sensed by Keyserling, the perceptive (if unnecessarily occult) philosopher-voyageur: ". . . in the undisciplinable revolutionary and the un-

[5] D. Valcárcel, *La rebelión de Túpac Amaru* (Mexico City, 1947), p. 180.

scrupulous *caudillo* of all South American States survives the son of Machiavelli's age."[6] A Venezuelan cosmopolite in a novel by Manuel Díaz Rodríguez (1902) remarked on a similarity between his country and fifteenth- and sixteenth-century Italy: "Are not our continual wars and our corruption of customs . . . the same continual wars and depraved customs of the Italy of those times, with its multiple small republics and principalities? There were then in Italy, as among us, brutal condottieri and rough captains, exalted overnight, like the first Sforzas, from the soil to the royal purple."[7]

Machiavelli was born into an "Age of Despots." Italian city states had lost their moral base; they no longer shared a common Christian ethos. The pope had become one of many competing temporal rulers. Machiavelli perceived that the mercenary "companies of adventure" of his time, unlike national militias, were undependable since they lacked any larger loyalty. They could be used to further intrigues of statecraft, but not to wage open and steady warfare. The Italian was effective only in duelling and individual combat.

Like Machiavelli, the Spanish American nation-builder of c. 1825 had to contend with nucleated "city states," the rural masses being passive and inarticulate. The absence of any communities intermediate between such nuclei and the erstwhile imperium had been revealed by the autonomous urban juntas of 1809–10. Only the somewhat arbitrary boundaries of colonial administration defined the new nations territorially. Only virulent sectionalism could define them operatively. The Church, once coterminous with the State, had become the intruding handmaiden of a hostile sovereign power (Spain). For lack of a politico-spiritual commonalty, sources and directions of leadership were wholly fortuitous. The consequent emergence of opportunist caudillos —as of Italy's city tyrants—deranged the predictable interplay of hierarchical class interests.

The Spanish American who held to constitutionalism and avowed the existence in fact of a state-community was swept away before winds of personalism. Mexico's Gómez Farías, vice-president under Santa Anna, was a statesman who, despite his energy and dedication, would not infract "the principles of public and private morality," before which, wrote his contemporary, Mora, vanished "his indomitable force of character." Why did he not cast out the treacherous Santa Anna? "Because the step was unconstitutional [:] . . . a famous reason which has kept the reputation of Señor Farías in a very secondary place at best and caused the nation to retrogress half a century."[8]

A similar case was Rivadavia, Argentina's first president and proponent of bourgeois democracy and economic liberalism. His plans and principles had been no match for provincial *caudillismo*. The exiled statesman wrote sadly from Paris in 1830 (shortly before the personalist tyranny of Rosas):

In my opinion what retards regular and stable advance in those republics stems from the vacillations and doubts that deprive all institutions of that moral force which is indispensable to them and can be given only by conviction and decision. It is evident to me, and would be easy to demonstrate, that the upheavals of our country spring much more immediately from lack of public spirit and of cooperation among responsible men in sustaining order and laws than from attacks of ungovernable, ambitious persons without merit or fitness and of indolent coveters.[9]

Machiavelli's writings are the handbook *par excellence* for the leader who could cope with "lack of public spirit and of cooperation among responsible men." Just as Lockean precepts were more congenial to the British-American than to the European scene, so the Florentine seemed to write for the New World. For the latter's detailed counsels regarding personalistic rule were of

[6] H. Keyserling, *South American Meditations* (New York, 1932), p. 103.

[7] Manuel Díaz Rodríguez, *Sangre patricia* (Madrid, n.d.), p. 169.

[8] José María Luis Mora, *Ensayos, ideas y retratos* (Mexico City, 1941), pp. xx, 184.

[9] Bernadino Rivadavia, *Páginas de un estadista* (Buenos Aires, 1945), p. 137 (letter to a politician of Upper Peru, 14 March 1830).

secondary importance to European monarchs who would soon find sanction in the traditions, panoply and universal acceptance of a Divine Right.

The embryonic nature of New World political forms, the lack of state traditions and state mysticism, were observed by Hegel (c. 1830):

In South America ... the republics depend only on military force; their whole history is a continued revolution; federated states become disunited; others previously separated become united; and all these changes originate in military revolutions. . . .

 . . . As to the political condition of North America, the general object of the existence of this State is not yet fixed and determined, and the necessity for a firm combination does not yet exist; for a real State and a real Government arise only after a distinction of classes has arisen, when wealth and poverty become extreme, and when such a condition of things presents itself that a large portion of the people can no longer satisfy its necessities in the way in which it has been accustomed so to do. . . . North America will be comparable with Europe only after the immeasurable space which that country presents to its inhabitants shall have been occupied, and the members of the political body shall have begun to be pressed back on each other.[10]

Another European, Carlyle, in an essay on Paraguay's Francia (1843) described with certain envy the free-acting caudillo, unfettered by traditions of the national community: "Such an institution of society, adapted to our European ways, seems pressingly desirable. O Gauchos, South-American and European, what a business is it, casting out your Seven Devils!"[11]

Locke and Machiavelli both wrote for peoples who were without an organic, pre-existing state. The former, however, addressed an articulate, relatively homogeneous bourgeoisie that was free to ascertain and pursue private interests, economic and otherwise; the latter addressed the leader who with craft and foresight was to unite an inchoate, inarticulate populace whose only claim was that it be not too heavily oppressed.

On nearly every page of Machiavelli appears practical advice which almost seems distilled from the careers of scores of Spanish American caudillos. Of crucial importance is the leader's commanding physical presence. In time of sedition he should: ". . . present himself before the multitude with all possible grace and dignity, and attired with all the insignia of his rank, so as to inspire more respect. . . . [For] there is no better or safer way of appeasing an excited mob than the presence of some man of imposing appearance and highly respected" [Discourses, I, liv]. Among countless leaders and incidents one recalls the moment when Bolivia's ruthless Melgarejo, with six men, entered the palace where his rival, Belzu, was celebrating a coup d'etat. The intruder, icily calm, shot the President, then with imperious presence faced and overawed the mob in whose throats the shouts of victory for Belzu had scarcely died away.

The personalist leader must be physically disciplined, skilled in warfare, and "learn the nature of the land, how steep the mountains are, how the valleys debouch, where the plains lie, and understand the nature of rivers and swamps" (Prince, XIV; see also Discourses, III, xxxix). This is almost a page from the autobiography of Páez, who knew Venezuela's vast llanos (inland plains) like the palm of his hand, a knowledge that confounded the royalists in 1817 and later earned respect for him as caudillo of the new republic. Writing of an assault against the Spaniards, Páez recalled:

Necessity obliged us not only to fight men but to challenge the obstacles opposed by nature. Counting on these, we proposed to turn to our advantage the impediments that gave the enemy surety and trust in his position, for to no one would it occur that in that season cavalry troops could sortie from the lower Apure to cross so much inundated terrain and especially the many streams and five rivers, all at the period of overflow.[12]

[10] G. W. F. Hegel, Lectures on the Philosophy of History (London, 1894), pp. 87–90.
[11] Thomas Carlyle, Critical and Miscellaneous Essays, 5 vols. (London, n.d.), IV, 316.
[12] José Antonio Páez, Autobiografía, 2 vols. (New York, 1946; re-issue of 1869 edition), I, 132.

This telluric, earthbound quality so vital to Spanish American leaders was matched in Argentina's Quiroga and San Martín, Uruguay's Artigas, Mexico's Pancho Villa, Venezuela's Bolívar, Peru's Santa Cruz and innumerable others. Their guerrilla warfare was a far cry from the chessboard strategy and diplomatic power alignments of Europe.

Space does not permit analysis of the host of Machiavelli's dicta empirically confirmed by caudillos. It remains, however, to emphasize that he was concerned not merely with leadership per se but with state-building. His ideal was a republic with "laws so regulated that, without the necessity of correcting them, they afford security to those who live under them" (*Discourses*, I, ii). Significantly, the most difficult time to preserve republican liberties is when a people, accustomed to living under a prince who binds himself "by a number of laws that provide for the security of all his people" (cf. Spanish colonial experience), recovers "by some accident" its freedom. Such a people, "ignorant of all public affairs, of all means of defense or offense, neither knowing the princes nor being known by them, . . . soon relapses under a yoke, oftentimes much heavier than the one which it had but just shaken off" [*Discourses*, I, xvi].

Government, to be created in such cases *ex nihilo*, is most expediently organized by a single leader of strength and sagacity. Yet "it will not endure long if the administration of it remains on the shoulders of a single individual; it is well, then, to confide this to the charge of the many, for thus it will be sustained by the many" (*Discourses*, I, ix).

If at length a republic is established, that very fact certifies a fundamental "goodness" and certain "original principles" conducing to its "first growth and reputation." To maintain republican vigor and repress "the insolence and ambition of men" those principles must find periodic reassertion through "extrinsic accident" or, preferably, "intrinsic prudence" (*Discourses*, III, i). The Machiavellian leader, therefore, is to be bound by *original principles* (environmental, human and customary components) generic to the nascent nation-community.

Writing in about 1840 the Argentine socialist, Echeverría, diagnosed and prescribed for his country's political chaos in identical terms. He found it impossible to organize a people without a constitution rooted in "its customs, sentiments, understandings, traditions." If the sole credentials of a nation-building legislator are those bestowed by electoral victory, his official acts will be no more in the public interest than the activities of a private business man. The indwelling fact of commonalty is not externalized in a manner that automatically informs such a legislator. Eschewing solutions of other nations, he must himself actively sound out the "instincts, necessities, interests" of the citizens and, through laws, reveal to them their own will and communal identity. Only on this preliminary basis of wise and public-minded paternalism may one hope for an eventual "faculty of perpetual communication between man and man, generation and generation—the continuous embodiment of the spirit of one generation in the next."[13]

The general cast of Spanish America's "original principles"—its "instincts, necessities, interests"—is inherent in Keyserling's perception of a ubiquitous *gana*—or loosely, "urge." By this he meant a raw, telluric spirit: formless, unchanneled, diffuse, self-sustaining; lacking past traditions or future hope. Sarmiento had expressed himself similarly almost a century earlier in describing the nomadic yet earthbound life of the pampas, having a morality unto itself and calling Asiatic comparisons frequently to mind. And in 1821 Bolívar, criticizing Colombia's lawmakers, wrote:

These gentlemen believe that Colombia is filled with dullards who sit around the firesides of Bogotá, Tunja, and Pamplona. They have not troubled to notice the Caribs of the Orinoco, the herdsmen of the Apure, the seamen of Maracaibo, the boatmen of the Magdalena, the bandits of Patia, the indomitable citizens of Pasto, the Guajibos of Casanare, and all the savage hordes from Africa

[13] Esteban Echeverría, *Dogma Socialista; Edición crítica y documentada* (La Plata, 1940), pp. 206–212.

and America who, like deer, run untamed in the solitudes of Colombia.[14]

Not only the peons and gauchos but the bourgeoisie has shared in this New World atomism, as evidenced in Thoreau's *Civil Disobedience* (1849): "Thus the State never intentionally confronts a man's sense, intellectual or moral, but only his body, his senses. It is not armed with superior wit or honesty, but with superior physical strength. I was not born to be forced. I will breathe after my own fashion. Let us see who is the strongest."[15]

The meaning of *gana* in relation to the pampas, the Chaco, the *llanos* or Mexico's arid northland—or to jungle-dwellers of Panama and the Amazon—is perhaps clear. But is there a counterpart among the nucleated, tradition-bound communities descended from highly organized Aztec, Maya and Inca civilizations? Some writers assert that these areas are still distinguished for elaborate functionalism, for concentrated and well integrated communalism; whereas it is in Portuguese (and British) America that one finds "gangliated" rural settlement and, until recent times, a locality group structure remaining in the "neighborhood" stage.[16]

That Brazilian settlements, rural and urban, were not by and large as cohesive as those of Spanish America is true. Yet the compactness of, say, the Andean *ayllu* (rural Indian community) is misleading. Once the conquerors removed the ruling Inca, the tribes and nations of his empire "dispersed like the beads of a necklace whose thread has been broken. Each community returned, politically and economically, to the pre-Incaic stage. Thousands of communities, isolated, strangers each to the other, could thus be conquered one at a time."[17] The Indian was turned earthward by the Spaniard, made an instrument of production for a vast imperial community which, despite its proselytizers and Indianist legislation, the Indian could not feel himself purposefully a part of. When in the 1920's Mariátegui applied Marxian analysis to the Peruvian scene, he reformulated it to make

allowance for this "earth-consciousness" of the Indian.[18]

How is it, then, that Spanish American caudillos or governments have, in certain countries and eras, achieved political stability in the face of this New World brand of social and moral centrifugalism? I define three essential modes of stability, which are categorized here merely for schematic purposes and with the understanding that the "pure" type never occurs. By way of further analogy I suggest a correspondence between these types and the three "legitimations of domination" which Max Weber distinguishes in his essay "Politics as a Vocation."[19]

The first mode of stability is furnished by the Machiavellian leader who asserts himself by dynamic personalism and shrewd self-identification with local "original principles," though without ever relinquishing government, as Machiavelli would have wished, "to the charge of many." The system remains subordinate to the man and unless a suitable "heir" is available, which happens infrequently, it falls with him. Here we perhaps have Weber's charismatic leader with the personal gift of grace, who flouts patriarchal traditionalism and the stable economy, whose justice is Solomonic rather than statutory, who maintains authority "solely by proving his strength in life." One recent writer, Blanksten, holds that the cau-

[14] Harold A. Bierck, Jr. (ed.), *Selected Writings of Bolívar*, 2 vols. (New York, 1951), I, 267–268 (letter to F. de P. Santander, 13 June 1821).

[15] *The Writings of Henry David Thoreau*, 20 vols. (Cambridge, 1906), IV, 376.

[16] F. J. de Oliveira Vianna, *Instituições políticas brasileiras*, 2 vols. (Rio de Janeiro, 1949); T. Lynn Smith, "The Locality Group Structure of Brazil," *American Sociological Review*, IX (February, 1944), 41–49.

[17] Luis E. Valcárcel, *Ruta cultural del Perú* (Mexico City, 1945), pp. 143–144. See also Charles Gibson, *The Inca Concept of Sovereignty and the Spanish Administration in Peru* (Austin, 1948), pp. 88–100.

[18] José Carlos Mariátegui, *Siete ensayos de interpretación de la realidad peruana* (Lima, 1928).

[19] H. H. Gerth and C. W. Mills (ed.), *From Max Weber: Essays in Sociology* (London, 1947), pp. 78ff.

dillo and charismatic types correspond.[20] George S. Wise, on the other hand, claims that "the stratagem and chicanery" of at least one caudillo (Venezuela's Guzmán Blanco) revealed an insecurity and lack of purpose precluding the oracular, prophetic qualities that he attributes to charismatic legitimacy.[21] Weber's specific consideration of the condottiere type leads me to feel, however, that charisma need not invariably imply "anointment."

The charismatic leader may be dedicated to molding the self-perpetuating traditions of a state-community—for example, Bolívar's vision of federated Andean republics, Morazán's Central American union, the constitutionalism of Mexico's Juárez and perhaps the quasi-theocracy of Ecuador's García Moreno. Or, which is more usual, he may set about exploiting the country as his private fief. In the decades after independence such a caudillo would win the army's allegiance (or create his own plebian militia), then assert control over the several classes by blandishment, personal magnetism or threat of force—the method depending, in the case of each segment of society, on "original principles" and the leader's own antecedents. Examples are Argentina's Rosas, Mexico's Santa Anna, Guatemala's Carrera, Paraguay's Francia. (Venezuela's Páez seems to fall between the two sub-types.)

Toward the end of the century the exploitation of new sources of mineral and agricultural wealth, together with a strong influx of foreign investments, gave caudillos more dependable leverage for control. Though force and personalism did not go in the discard, financial resources and the protective favor of foreigners allowed the leader to govern by "remote control." He adopted bourgeois bon ton and even paid lip service to constitutionalism. Such men were Venezuela's Guzmán Blanco, Mexico's Porfirio Díaz, Guatemala's Barrios.

Intensified economic activity might also give rise to a second type of state: a modified version of laissez-faire democracy. This development, which Weber calls legitimation through bureaucratic competence and public respect for rational legal statutes, has

been rare in Latin America, even in hybrid form. Argentina affords an example. In that country after 1860, and especially after 1880, the pampas experienced a torrential land rush, occasioned by a world demand for meat and grains and by improved methods of husbandry, transportation and refrigeration. Though the lion's share of the benefits accrued to an oligarchy of large proprietors, many immigrants took small homesteads in the northern provinces; moreover, the expanding economy created niches for articulate, middle-class city dwellers. Argentines were, relative to Latin America, homogeneous and white. A growing nucleus identified its interests with the stability and prosperity of the nation-community, even though the positions of highest socio-economic authority were already pre-empted.

Given Argentina's economic direction and momentum, it remained for a series of statesmen-presidents merely to encourage and guide its development, in tolerable conformance with the Lockean Constitution of 1853. Eventual malfeasance in high office led, not back to tyranny, but to the emergence in 1890 of the Radical (liberal, middle-class) Party, to free suffrage and the secret ballot, and finally to Radical control of the presidency (1916–1930). Twentieth-century Radical leaders, however, reined back certain socio-economic forces from a natural course by acquiescing in the continued entrenchment of the landowning oligarchy. Only then did thwarted urban classes fall prey to demagoguery of an ominous breed—and to Juan Domingo Perón.

A third solution for anarchy has been a full-scale implementing of the Machiavellian blueprint. A personalist leader emerges (as in the first case), but goes on successfully to create a system, larger than himself, that is faithful to "original principles." In Spanish America such a system is larger than the leader, to frame a paradox, only when it

[20] George I. Blanksten, *Ecuador: Constitutions and Caudillos* (Berkeley and Los Angeles, 1951), pp. 35–36.

[21] George S. Wise, *Caudillo: A Portrait of Antonio Guzmán Blanco* (New York, 1951), pp. 161–163.

recognizes the leader to be larger than itself. This statement has Thomistic implications, and the more successful Spanish American constitutions have translated into modern idiom certain principles under which the viceroyalties enjoyed three centuries of relative stability.

This solution, insofar as it reinvigorates the body social by setting its classes, or "estates," into centrally stabilized equilibrium, is a neotraditionalism reminiscent of Weber's third category: "the authority of the eternal yesterday." Of Mexico's present Constitution—brought into being in 1917 by Carranza, a shrewd, opportunist caudillo—Frank Tannenbaum has written:

By implication, the Constitution recognizes that contemporary Mexican society is divided into classes, and that it is the function of the State to protect one class against another. The Constitution is therefore not merely a body of rules equally applicable to all citizens, but also a body of rules specially designed to benefit and protect given groups. The community is not made up of citizens only; it is also made up of classes with special rights within the law. What has in fact happened is that the old idea of the "estates" has been re-created in Mexican law. The pattern of the older Spanish State, divided into clergy, nobility, and commons, has been re-created in modern dress, with peasants, workers, and capitalists replacing the ancient model. This is not done formally, but it is done sufficiently well to make it evident that a very different kind of social structure is envisioned in the law, even if only by implicit commitment, than that in a liberal democracy. . . .

The Revolution has certainly increased effective democracy in Mexico. It has also increased, both legally and economically, the dependence of the people and of the communities upon the federal government and the President. The older tradition that the king rules has survived in modern dress: the President rules. He rules rather than governs, and must do so if he is to survive in office and keep the country at peace.[22]

I have reserved any mention of Chile until now because its history usefully illustrates our three political types as well as a twentieth-century variant which has yet to be considered. Like its sister nations, Chile fell after independence into anarchic factionalism. A revolution of 1829–30, however, brought the conservatives into power; at their head was Diego Portales who, as a business man, was atypical among Spanish American nation-builders. Portales appreciated more keenly than most the need for disciplined, predictable conditions of life and was more empirical in perceiving that liberal slogans and mechanisms were meaningless within an aristocratic, agrarian society. His views were reflected in the centralized, quasi-monarchic Constitution of 1833 which, by recognizing Chile's hierarchic social anatomy and at the same time guaranteeing status and justice for the component members, lent the government a supra-personalist sanction. Portales himself did not become president, but wisely designated a military hero, General Prieto, whose prestige, aristocratic bearing and benevolence, traditionalism and religiosity further enhanced the office with an aura of legitimacy.[23] None of Chile's presidents was overthrown for sixty years, while the Constitution lasted nearly a century.

Portales, alone among his Spanish American contemporaries, brought to fulfillment the policy of "the compleat Machiavellian." As the century advanced, however, a leavening took place within the system he had fathered. A law of 1852 abolished primogeniture, infusing new blood and interests into the landed oligarchy. Mineral exploitation in the north and the activities of German immigrants in the south posted new directions for economic change and opportunity. The consequent desire for more effective economic competition provided a rallying cry for enthused liberals emerging from the new (1843) University. So too did growing dissatisfaction with the constitutional ban on public exercise of non-Catholic religions.

At length the Chilean élite, larger and more diversely composed than in 1833, revolted against centralized, one-man rule by

[22] Frank Tannenbaum, *Mexico: The Struggle for Peace and Bread* (New York, 1950), pp. 101, 118.

[23] Ricardo Donoso, *Las ideas políticas en Chile* (Mexico City, 1946), pp. 64–114; Alberto Edwards Vives, *La fronda aristocrática en Chile* (Santiago, 1936), pp. 39–47.

ejecting President Balmaceda from office in 1891. This élite then governed through its congressional representatives, and the fitfulness of public policy for the next thirty years reflected the jostling of private economic interests.

As in Argentina, however, the modified laissez-faire state could not indefinitely subsist if it was to victimize the increasingly self-aware lower classes, such as, in Chile's case, the copper and nitrate workers. The little man eventually found his champion in President Arturo Alessandri (1920–1925, 1932–1938).[24]

Alessandri's and subsequent administrations represent an attitude toward government that has in this century become universal throughout Spanish America. It has in varying degrees infiltrated the three earlier systems, or combinations thereof, wherever they exist. Essentially, it is a recognition of the need to build into public policies a dynamics for socio-economic change. This need stems from two interrelated phenomena: first, the urbanization and industrialization of hitherto extractive economies; second, the growing self-awareness and articulateness of the citizenry at large.

The Spanish American leader, whether dictator or democrat, is fast adopting a broader, more sophisticated view of how modern political power must be won, maintained and exercised. He also knows that, regardless of any nationalistic rhetoric to which he may be committed, he must import more and more blueprints and technical solutions from abroad. Such solutions, however—whether socialism, fascism, exchange control or river valley authorities— take on a new complexion as they flash into amalgam with conditions of life wholly different from those by which they were engendered. Not only is the receiving ethos broadly speaking *sui generis*, but in a strictly technological sense the particular juxtapositions of ancient and modern in Spanish America are quite beyond the experience of any of the capitalist countries. Therefore slogans of foreign systems ring far differently upon Spanish American ears than their originators imagine.

In fact, Peru's *Aprista* movement and Mexico's forty-year-long "Revolution" attest that Spanish America is starting to generate its own credos. Sometimes, as with Perón's *justicialismo*, they are heartlessly cynical rhetoric. At best they designate, as did our own New Deal, a piecemeal pragmatism, uncommitted to the mysticism or fixed morality prescribed for the New World by Hegel. Yet the fact that Spanish America is by tradition accustomed and by economic necessity forced to rely heavily on official planning, intervention and protection has on occasion led its statesmen to a "total view" (to be distinguished carefully in nature and intent from a totalitarian view). From such views flow social, economic and cultural agenda which, however imperfect of execution, uniquely contribute to an understanding of man-in-community.

Co-existent, indeed, with Spanish America's atomism, or *gana*, is a sense of commonalty, however latent, deriving in large part from its Catholicity (in the ingrained, cultural sense) and from its agrarian, Negro and Indian heritage. Native to this commonalty is an ethic upon which the hyper-rationalist logos of the industrial world seems able to make only limited and conditional encroachments. The prediction is sometimes heard among Spanish Americans that this logos will in the long run exhaust itself; that their descendants will be freer to weave certain principles of a pre-Machiavellian age into the new patterns of an entering one; that the promise which erratically flashes in the travail of twentieth-century Mexican democracy is yet to be realized.

[24] The dictatorial interregnum of Carlos Ibáñez (1925–1931) can be considered as Chile's nearest approach to the first, or pure caudillo type of rule. His advent is partially explained by the post-World War I collapse of the world nitrate market, which impaired the mainspring of parliamentary, laissez-faire government and left Chile (since Alessandri had not yet given shape and momentum to his social democracy) in its primordial anarchy. Ibáñez, though sometimes referred to as a "man on horseback," effectively used modern technocratic methods and was not a caudillo of the old stamp—to which his re-election in 1952 bears witness.

3. A NOTE ON PORTUGUESE AND BRITISH AMERICA

The theme that has emerged from our analysis of Spanish American government is that the sense of moral community imparted by Spain to its New World colonies lost its staying power in the early nineteenth century and could no longer yoke the amoral, anti-traditional atomism of the American hemisphere. It is logical to ask whether a similar process occurred in other American areas. The following remarks on Brazil and the United States, while suggesting this to be the case, are too sketchy to be conclusive and will chiefly serve to place the Spanish American experience in broader perspective.

The course of Portuguese colonization differed from that of the Spanish in many respects. The mother country was more restricted in resources and population, politically more centralized, more strongly commercial and agricultural, less militantly religious. Brazil itself lacked the densely settled, highly civilized Indian peoples of Spanish America and, for the first two centuries, its abundant supply of precious gems and metals. These factors inhibited the growth of a multiform politico-ecclesiastical hierarchy with sophisticated urban centers of radiation. Political control and initiative were more fully diffused among slave-owing seigneurs of the sugarfields and among hardy municipalities of the poorer backlands. Even so, Portugal's empire bore enough similarities to Spain's to make the two comparable for present purposes. Both participated in a quasi-feudal, pre-capitalist, Catholic ethos.

The transition to independence, however, was another matter, for the Portuguese king, João VI, fled overseas to Brazil upon Napoleon's invasion of his country. When summoned home in 1821 by the Portuguese Cortes, he left his son, Pedro, in Rio de Janeiro as Brazilian Regent. The following year the latter declared Brazil's independence, and the transition was relatively peaceful; for since he was of the royal line accredited by the creoles, Pedro's accession to the new Brazilian emperorship went unchallenged.

The benevolent, paternalistic reign of João's grandson, Pedro II (1840–1889), convincingly demonstrated the stabilizing effect of the transferral of the ruling lineage to the New World. These years were, within Latin America, a political golden age. Using the "moderative power" of the conservative 1824 Constitution, Pedro II counteracted the separatism and political inarticulateness of his nation by careful manipulation of elections, ministries and policy changes. Yet he never originated policies or intervened in the affairs of the two political parties. Joaquim Nabuco described him as merely making "soundings on either side of the channel being navigated." His power was rigorously exercised: "1st.) within the Constitution; 2nd.) in accord with the fictions and uses of the English parliamentary system, which were even observed by our parties themselves; 3rd.) in constant obedience to public opinion and sentiment."[25]

Beneath the parliamentary trappings one senses Thomistic vestiges. Pedro's legitimacy was unquestioningly recognized by the people, while he in turn felt morally, if not procedurally, responsible to them. So it is the republican coup d'état of 1889, rather than independence (as in Spanish America), which most clearly defines the post-Thomistic watershed. The presidential regime which supplanted the Emperor was, to be sure, more stable and constitutional and less a prey to disruptive localism than the Spanish American governments of two generations previous. Yet its slogans were those of a somewhat cynical positivism, and it signalized the triumph of city over country, of materialism over traditionalism, of industrialized coffee over patriarchal sugar, of European fashion over native custom. In the conscience of the new bourgeois generation that destroyed the paternal symbol one writer discovers a gnawing "complex of remorse."[26]

[25] Joaquim Nabuco, *Um estadista do Império*, 4 vols. (São Paulo, 1949), IV, 108.

[26] Luis Martins, "O patriarca e o bacharel," *Revista do Arquivo Municipal* (São Paulo) LXXXIII (1942), 7–36. For the anti-traditionalist spirit of the early republican period see Gilberto

For the United States, Professor R. G. Mc-Closkey has already shaped a perspective comparable to my own for Spanish America, one which refines the analysis of Northrop referred to at the start of this essay. McCloskey maintains that the American Constitution and Jeffersonian democracy drew upon "a diverse array of abstract doctrines, semireligious convictions, and economic motivations." This tradition enshrined economic freedom for individuals and Lockean sanctity of property rights without discarding the humane, Christian values derived also from Locke and from England's seventeenth-century leftist Puritans.[27] Just as in colonial Spanish America, moral rather than economic man was society's nuclear element.

An eloquent expression of this tradition is Calhoun's *A Disquisition on Government*.[28] Showing nostalgia for a monarchy in which a king's interests are hereditarily identified with those of his subjects to form a kingdom-community, Calhoun affirms society to be organic and "man so constituted as to be a social being." A constitution: "must spring from the bosom of the community, and be adapted to the intelligence and character of the people, and all the multifarious relations, internal and external, which distinguish one people from another." Not from the will of a "numerical, or absolute majority" but from that alone of a *concurrent majority* may "the sense of the community" be taken. Only when the vox populi proceeds out of natural communities and through the permanently empowered "appropriate organ" of each one will anarchy and despotism cease to threaten, private and public morals become one, all elements of the nation-community achieve a "disposition to harmonize," and the people's voice become God's. With few changes Calhoun's principles become Thomistic, or those of modern Mexico.[29]

The Civil War is, symbolically at least, the watershed corresponding to Spanish American independence and the exile of Brazil's Emperor. It marks the dominance of industrial and monopolistic over mercantile capitalism, and the eclipse of Calhoun's agrarian, patriarchal South as a determinant in national policy. The moral, humane, Christian component of Locke becomes recessive; the Lockean sanction for atomistic economic individualism—which had been less strong in the earlier period than Northrop suggests—becomes dominant. McCloskey writes that "a new conservative rationale develops on the moribund body of Jeffersonian liberalism."[30] He develops his case by examining three representatives of the late nineteenth century: William Graham Sumner, who as a sociologist urged "the frank espousal of a social norm based on material utility"; Stephen J. Field, who as a jurist argued "that democratic freedom and economic freedom are one"; Andrew Carnegie, who as a captain of industry, and despite his vaunted humanitarianism, felt that capitalism and democracy "cannot be disjoined."[31]

Henry Adams had received his mind-set by the 1860's and could never to his own satisfaction address these new conditions of post-bellum democracy. Of that period he later wrote:

The system of 1789 had broken down, and with it the eighteenth-century fabric of *a priori*, or moral,

---

[27] Robert Green McCloskey, *American Conservatism in the Age of Enterprise* (Cambridge, 1951), pp. 1–8.

[28] John C. Calhoun, *A Disquisition on Government* (New York, 1854).

[29] Like Argentina's Echeverría, Calhoun espoused a Machiavellian rather than an artificial social-contract theory of how governments are formed: "It would thus seem almost necessary that governments should commence in some one of the simple and absolute forms, which, however well suited to the community in its earlier stages, must, in its progress, lead to oppression and abuse of power, . . . unless the conflicts to which it leads should be fortunately adjusted by a compromise, which will give to the respective parties a participation in the control of the government; and thereby lay the foundation of a constitutional government, to be afterwards matured and perfected. Such governments have been, emphatically, the product of circumstances. And hence, the difficulty of one people imitating the government of another" (*Ibid.*, p. 79).

[30] McCloskey, *op. cit.*, p. 15.

[31] *Ibid.*, p. 167.

Freyre, "O período republicano," *Boletim bibliográfico* (São Paulo) I, 2 (1944), 61–72.

principles. Politicians had given it up. Grant's administration marked the avowal. . . . Darwinists ought to conclude that America was reverting to the stone age, but the theory of reversion was more absurd than that of evolution. Grant's administration reverted to nothing. One could not catch a trait of the past, still less of the future. It was not even sensibly American.[32]

With Lincoln Steffens, however, born a generation after Adams, we find a mind from the Far West, cast in the flux of the new period and with the self-confidence to cope with it. Steffens shrewdly perceived the disparity between constitutional morality and the structure and exercise of power to be no different in Europe than in the United States. The French, however, do not face the moral dilemma of American democracy because they "have not called good or right the evil that they have done, and so they have that charm which I felt always in 'bad men' in America, in the 'honest crooks' in politics and business."[33] Lincoln Steffens' lesson to America, to the Americas, is that a meaningful political morality issues only from American experience, that it is a lived morality and that it must be recognized as being lived.

[32] Henry Adams, *The Education of Henry Adams* (Cambridge, 1918), pp. 266, 280–281.

[33] Lincoln Steffens, *The Autobiography of Lincoln Steffens* (New York, 1931), pp. 705–711.

IX. A FECUND DECADE, 1955–1965

64. Trends of United States Studies
in Latin American History*

CHARLES GIBSON AND BENJAMIN KEEN

I

When United States historians in the first half of the nineteenth century began to give attention to Latin America, professional and public interest in the subject was confined almost wholly to the colonial period. The Latin American independence movements and the creation of new national states received notice in United States political and journalistic writing but remained largely unattractive to historians until the twentieth century. Within the colonial period, United States preferences were expressed in the selection of a limited number of themes, among which the discovery by Columbus and the two conquests by Cortés and Pizarro predominated. These lent themselves to the prevailing romanticism of United States historical writing. In the hands of Washington Irving and William H. Prescott they achieved a remarkable popularity.[1] It may be suggested that the reception accorded to these topics coincided with an effort to disassociate America from the more complex history of Europe, where in the absence of clear-cut starting points no such dramatic or episodic reconstruction at a point of origin could be achieved. In practice, discovery and conquest were far more accessible, bibliographically speaking, than were any subjects of the later colonial or postcolonial periods, and they fit more easily the sense of nostalgic admiration for the Hispanic past that characterized United States romanti-

cism. The first two United States historians to deal seriously with topics outside the United States—Irving in the *Life of Columbus* and Prescott in *Ferdinand and Isabella* —both selected Hispanic themes and both wrote of the American discovery.[2] A compatibility between the subjects chosen and

* *American Historical Review*, 62: 855–877 (Jul. 1957). This article combines papers read by the two authors at the session on "Latin American Historiography: A Progress Report" of the meeting of the American Historical Association on December 28, 1955. The session was arranged by Dr. Howard F. Cline, to whom the authors express their thanks for a critical reading of the first version of this combined paper. In the light of other commentaries made upon this presentation it seems appropriate to state explicitly that (1) no serious student of Latin American history should depend exclusively upon work written in the United States, and (2) the authors' emphases and critical observations in this article depend upon evaluations that are in part subjective and with which there is not a universal agreement. Reprinted by permission of the authors and the original publisher.

[1] Irving, *A History of the Life and Voyages of Christopher Columbus*, 3 vols. (New York, 1828); Prescott, *History of the Conquest of Mexico, with a Preliminary View of the Ancient Mexican Civilization, and the Life of the Conqueror, Hernando Cortés*, 3 vols. (New York, 1843), and *History of the Conquest of Peru, with a Preliminary View of the Civilization of the Incas*, 2 vols. (New York, 1847).

[2] Irving, *op. cit.*; Prescott, *History of the Reign of Ferdinand and Isabella, the Catholic*, 3 vols. (Boston, 1839). See Prescott's own remarks on

the wider ambient of United States literary taste is suggested further by the fact that Irving and Prescott, each independently of the other, undertook researches on the conquest of Mexico in the 1830's. Only after Irving relinquished the topic did Prescott complete his famous work.[3]

The tendency to concentrate upon the spectacular and early themes of Latin American history survived the romantic age and remained dominant through the first years of scientific historiography in the United States. The writings of Justin Winsor, John Fiske, and John Boyd Thacher at the turn of the nineteenth century illustrate the application of scientific, or incipiently scientific, methods to standard romantic themes. Even Hubert Howe Bancroft, from whose monumental work much of the twentieth-century historical writing on Mexico and Central America has derived, devoted more attention to the period of Cortés' lifetime than to the whole of the remainder of pre-revolutionary New Spain.[4] Discovery, conquest, and exploration—the last reflecting interests in areas of the United States previously under Spanish authority—were topics wholly suited to scientific research. They possessed apparently controllable bibliographies; their historiographical tradition included much nonsense that could be satisfactorily debunked; they comprised that portion of colonial Latin American history of which everyone had heard. Conquest especially fit the familiar conception of Hispanic America as a land that had never fully emerged from the brutality of its colonial past. And the continued dependence of United States students upon the themes of the romantic age goes far to explain their nearly absolute neglect of Brazil.

In the early twentieth century the first major United States scholar in the study of the Latin American sixteenth century was Edward Gaylord Bourne. He designed Spain in America primarily to inform the American reading public on those features of Hispanic colonial history pertinent to the his-

tory of the United States. Bourne's emphasis, like that of his predecessors, lay in Spanish North America, but he was additionally concerned with the transmission and modification of European institutions, topics that were then at the forefront, significantly, in Anglo-American colonial history as well.[5] With Bourne the continuity of subject matter from the nineteenth century was not wholly broken, nor were Bourne's researches conducted in isolation, as the contemporaneous work of Woodbury Lowery and George Parker Winship testifies.[6] Bourne's merit lay in the originality and acumen with which he interpreted sources, in the objectivity of his observation, and in the critical insights he applied to Spanish colonization prior to 1580. He did not pursue his subject in detail beyond the sixteenth century, but he did succeed, through an unequivocally scholarly presentation, in laying a positive assessment of early Hispanic colonization before the American public. He may justifiably be

[3] See the correspondence exchanged between Irving and Prescott in 1838–1839 and further commentary in George Tichnor, Life of William Hickling Prescott (Philadelphia, 1875), pp. 157–63.

[4] Winsor, ed., Narrative and Critical History of America, 8 vols. (Boston and New York, 1884–1889); Fiske, The Discovery of America, with Some Account of Ancient America and the Spanish Conquest, 2 vols. (Boston and New York, 1892); Thacher, Christopher Columbus: His Life, His Work, His Remains, As Revealed by Original Printed and Manuscript Records . . ., 3 vols. (New York and London, 1903–1904); Bancroft, History of Mexico, 6 vols., The Works of Hubert Howe Bancroft, IX–XIV (San Francisco, 1883–1888).

[5] Bourne, Spain in America, 1450–1580, The American Nation: A History, III (New York and London, 1904), and "The Relation of American History to Other Fields of Historical Study," in H. J. Rogers, ed., Congress of Arts and Science, Universal Exposition, St. Louis, 1904 (New York, 1906), II, 172–82.

[6] Lowery, The Spanish Settlement within the Present Limits of the United States, 1513–1561 (New York and London, 1901), and The Spanish Settlements within the Present Limits of the United States: Florida 1562–1574 (New York and London, 1905); Winship, ed., The Journey of Coronado, 1540–1542, from the City of Mexico to the Grand Cañon of the Colorado and the Buffalo Plains of Texas, Kansas, and Nebraska, as Told by Himself and his Followers (New York, 1904).

this coincidence in the preface of Ferdinand and Isabella.

termed the first scientific historian of the United States to view the Spanish colonial process dispassionately and thereby to escape the conventional Anglo-Protestant attitudes of outraged or tolerant disparagement.

Bourne was the author of a single major work. Following his death in 1908, leadership in Hispanic colonial history shifted from the east to the west coast, and its character underwent some changes. Bernard Moses, whose early study (1898) of Spanish rule in America had been undistinguished, later made an admirable effort in the *Spanish Dependencies in South America* and *Spain's Declining Power in South America* to establish a chronological structure for the entire colonial period as soundly developed as that for the sixteenth century.[7] Moses, to be sure, lacked the perspicacity of Bourne. He offered the first course in Latin American history in the United States, and his writings betray a classroom proclivity hardly comparable with the erudition and maturity of Bourne. It is true that he embraced a large subject with enthusiasm and fortitude, but it is equally true that his writings are no longer read; subsequent monographic studies have corrected and complemented them at many points. A large part of the monographic literature of Moses' later period continued to reflect particular interests in areas of the United States previously under Spanish authority: the eighteenth-century Texas of Herbert E. Bolton,[8] Spanish California of Irving B. Richman and Charles E. Chapman,[9] Louisiana and the Philippines of James A. Robertson,[10] and the Louisiana-Texas frontier of Isaac J. Cox.[11] Two of the monographs of this same period, moreover, remain among the foremost ever produced in the United States: Herbert I. Priestley's *José de Gálvez*[12] and Clarence H. Haring's *Trade and Navigation*.[13]

Separating Hispanic American history as an autochthonous entity, disciplining its method, and educating the historical profession to regard it seriously were the tasks confronting the United States Latin Americanists of the second decade. The process in its early stages was part and parcel of a broad-

ening of American, i.e. United States, history in several new directions. The relation of those labors of Bolton, Chapman, Robertson, and Cox to the prevailing regionalism of United States history is close and evident. The United States connection may as clearly be seen in the bibliographies of the period, beginning in 1907 with William R. Shepherd's *Guide* to Spanish archives and the similar work of J. A. Robertson for American transcripts, through the Bolton *Guide* to Mexican archives, Roscoe R. Hill's compilation for Cuban material on the United States, and the Chapman *Catalogue* for the Southwest and Pacific coast.[14] Only follow-

[7] *The Establishment of Spanish Rule in America: An Introduction to the History and Politics of Spanish America* (New York and London, 1898), *The Spanish Dependencies in South America: An Introduction to the History of Their Civilization* (New York and London, 1914), and *Spain's Declining Power in South America, 1730–1806* (Berkeley, 1919).

[8] *Texas in the Middle Eighteenth Century: Studies in Spanish Colonial History and Administration*, Univ. of California Pubs. in Hist., III (Berkeley, 1915).

[9] Richman, *California under Spain and Mexico, 1535–1847* (Boston and New York, 1911); Chapman, *The Founding of Spanish California: The Northwestward Expansion of New Spain, 1687–1783* (New York, 1916).

[10] Robertson, *Louisiana under the Rule of Spain, France, and the United States, 1785–1807*, 2 vols. (Cleveland, 1911); Emma H. Blair and J. A. Robertson, eds., *The Philippine Islands, 1493–1803*, 55 vols. (Cleveland, 1903–1909).

[11] *The Louisiana-Texas Frontier*, 2 vols. (Austin, 1906–1913).

[12] *José de Gálvez, Visitor-general of New Spain (1765–1771)*, Univ. of California Pubs. in Hist., V (Berkeley, 1916).

[13] *Trade and Navigation between Spain and the Indies in the Time of the Hapsburgs* (Cambridge, Mass., 1918); see also his pioneering work, *The Buccaneers in the West Indies in the XVII Century* (London, 1910).

[14] Shepherd, *Guide to the Materials for the History of the United States in Spanish Archives*, Carnegie Inst. of Washington Pub. No. 91 (Washington, 1907); Robertson, *List of Documents in Spanish Archives Relating to the History of the United States, Which Have Been Printed or of Which Transcripts Are Preserved in American Libraries*, Carnegie Inst. of Washington Pub. No. 124 (Washington, 1910); Bolton, *Guide to Materials for the History of the United States in the Principal Archives of Mexico*, Carnegie Inst. of Washington Pub. No. 163 (Washington, 1913); Hill,

ing this bibliographical preparation, organized principally under the direction of J. Franklin Jameson and the Carnegie Institution Department of Historical Research and focused on United States history in regions or as a whole, did the exclusively Hispanic American bibliographies—first of R. Hayward Keniston and then of Cecil Knight Jones—make their appearance.[15] The transition from a domestic to a borderland to an exclusively Latin American context characterized United States research of the first quarter of the twentieth century and set it sharply apart from the work of Europeans and Latin Americans.

The act that most strikingly signalized the separation of professional Hispanic American history—particularly, at first, in its colonial aspects—as a specialty in United States scholarship was the founding of the *Hispanic American Historical Review* at the meeting of the American Historical Association in Cincinnati in 1916.[16] The publication of this periodical from 1918 to 1922 and from 1926 continuously to the present ranks as an achievement of the Hispanic Americanists of the United States equaled by those of no other non-Hispanic nation. The *Review's* early issues, corresponding to the interests of its editors, were concerned to a large degree with colonial subjects. The articles and book reviews of the first issues reveal the historians' professional attitudes at this critical moment. They express the enthusiasm aroused by the discovery and demarcation of a new historical field, a field, however, that in its practical cultivation was not yet clearly separated from the Hispanic antecedents of the United States. A preponderant

interest in Latin America still depended—and would for many years continue to depend—upon the connection with Florida or Georgia, Texas or California.

Encompassing this regionalism, seeking to identify its common denominators, and relating it to the totality of America, there appeared in the 1920's the only over-all interpretation of Hispanic American history ever devised in this country. The celebrated unitary hemisphere thesis of Herbert E. Bolton was developed during its author's early years at the University of California. Bolton's publications of the period dealt principally with colonial Hispanic America in relation to areas of the modern United States. *The Colonization of North America*, written in collaboration with T. M. Marshall, appeared in 1920, shortly after Bolton began his lectures on the history of the Americas, and this work was followed by a series of monographic and documentary publications on the Spanish borderlands, Georgia, the Pacific coast, the Southwest, and northern Mexico in late colonial times. Bolton's *History of the Americas: A Syllabus with Maps* (Boston, 1928) and his "Epic of Greater America"[17] presented the doctrine of hemispheric homogeneity. Argued principally in terms of the colonial materials of his specialization and resembling to some degree the Turner thesis of frontier history (with which it has

---

Descriptive Catalogue of the Documents Relating to the History of the United States in the Papeles procedentes de Cuba Deposited in the Archivo general de Indias at Seville, Carnegie Inst. of Washington Pub. No. 234 (Washington, 1916); Chapman, Catalogue of Materials in the Archivo general de Indias for the History of the Pacific Coast and the American Southwest, Univ. of California Pubs. in Hist., VIII (Berkeley, 1919). See also Hill, American Missions in European Archives, Pan American Inst. Geog. and Hist., Commission on Hist., Pub. 22 (Mexico, 1951).

[15] Keniston, *List of Works for the Study of Hispanic American History* (New York, 1920); Jones, *Hispanic American Bibliographies, Including Collective Biographies, Histories of Literature and Selected General Works* (Baltimore, 1922). The second edition of the latter, greatly expanded, is entitled *A Bibliography of Latin American Bibliographies*, Library of Congress, Hispanic Foundation, Latin American Ser., 2 (Washington, 1942).

[16] Charles E. Chapman, "The Founding of the Review," *Hisp. Amer. Hist. Rev.*, I (1918), 8–20; William Spence Robertson, "Introduction," in Ruth Lapham Butler, *Guide to the Hispanic American Historical Review, 1918–1945* (Durham, N.C., 1950); Lesley Byrd Simpson, "Thirty Years of *The Hispanic American Historical Review*," *Hisp. Amer. Hist. Rev.*, XXIX (1949), 188–204; Howard Cline, "Reflections on Traditionalism in the Historiography of Hispanic America," *ibid.*, pp. 205–12.

[17] *American Hist. Rev.*, XXXVIII (1933), 448–74.

frequently been compared and with which it was not unrelated), the unitary hemisphere thesis depended for its acceptance upon definition, upon selected levels of generalization, and upon a philosophical interpretation of unity and diversity in history, problems in which Bolton himself was not profoundly interested. His own forte, continuously demonstrated until his death in 1953, lay in vivid narrative history. His achievement is measurable in a lengthy series of historical writings and in his wide influence and inspiration, to which more than a generation of historical students have given repeated testimony.[18] The influence concentrated heavily on the sixteenth and eighteenth centuries. Its geographical concern was principally with Mexico and the United States Southwest. Topically, it emphasized exploration and the institutions of the Hispanic colonial frontier. Thus though the followers of Bolton accepted the doctrine of American unity, they did not in their monographic writing, any more than Bolton himself in his, explore the Hispanic portion of the hemisphere systematically or uniformly through space and time. Neither did the Bolton thesis receive that detailed critical reexamination at the hands of Bolton's students that might otherwise have been expected, nor were effective rebuttals forthcoming from other, alternatively oriented, students of the area. It is symptomatic of the condition of American history in the 1920's and 1930's that the major critiques of the Bolton thesis came from Latin America itself.

The first two decades of the *Hispanic American Historical Review*, the period of the editorship of J. A. Robertson, formed a period of concentration, specialization, and elaboration in monographic work on the colonial period. Political biography appeared in Arthur S. Aiton's study of Viceroy Antonio de Mendoza and Arthur F. Zimmerman's study of Viceroy Francisco de Toledo.[19] The institutional history of sixteenth-century Spain received the close documentary attention of L. B. Simpson, whose studies of encomienda and repartimiento initiated a new and exceptionally productive series of publications at the University of California.[20]

The important researches of the period between the two World Wars included the political studies of Charles H. Cunningham and Lillian Estelle Fisher on audiencias, viceroyalties, and intendancies, and the financial and commercial documentation provided by E. J. Hamilton and Roland Dennis Hussey on price systems and the Caracas Company. Intellectual and literary history was represented in the work of Irving Leonard, particularly in his biography of Sigüenza, and in John Tate Lanning's study of

[18] Bolton's writing to 1940 and the writings of his students to 1944 are listed in *Greater America: Essays in Honor of Herbert Eugene Bolton* (Berkeley and Los Angeles, 1945), pp. 537–672. It should be added that modern hemispheric histories, to a greater or lesser degree influenced by the Bolton theses, combine Latin American and Anglo-American materials. Outstanding examples are John F. Bannon, *History of the Americas* (New York, 1952); Harold E. Davis, *The Americas in History* (New York, 1953); Vera Brown Holmes, *A History of the Americas from Discovery to Nationhood* (New York, 1950); Robert S. Cotterill, *A Short History of the Americas* (New York, 1939). Further, the Commission on History of the Pan American Institute of Geography and History has since 1947 undertaken a comprehensive "Program of the History of America," with the collaboration of historians in Europe, the United States, and Latin America. See "The Problem of a General History of the Americas," *Rev. hist. América*, No. 34 (Dec., 1952), 469–89; Silvio Zavala, "Colaboración internacional en torno de la historia de América," *ibid.*, Nos. 35–36 (1953), 209–26; "El programa de historia de América," *ibid.*, No. 39 (June, 1955), 133–214.

[19] Aiton, *Antonio de Mendoza, First Viceroy of New Spain* (Durham, N. C., 1927); Zimmerman, *Francisco de Toledo, Fifth Viceroy of Peru, 1569–1581* (Caldwell, Idaho, 1938).

[20] *The Encomienda in New Spain: Forced Native Labor in the Spanish Colonies, 1492–1550*, Univ. of California Pubs. in Hist., XIX (Berkeley, 1929) and *Studies in the Administration of the Indians in New Spain*, 3 vols., *Ibero-Americana*, 7, 13, 16 (Berkeley, 1934–1940) (Vol. II, Pt. III concerns repartimiento). Simpson's *Encomienda in New Spain: The Beginning of Spanish Mexico* (Berkeley and Los Angeles, 1950) is an extensive revision of his 1929 volume; see the review article by Robert S. Chamberlain in *Hisp. Amer. Hist. Rev.*, XXXIV (1954), 238–50, evaluating Simpson's volume and other contributions to encomienda literature.

academic culture in the Spanish Colonies.[21] The same period witnessed the concluding volumes of Roger B. Merriman's history of the Spanish empire, a work falling in an older tradition, with emphasis upon royalty and political and military narrative, and almost unique among United States scholarly writings for its perception of Old World Spanish and Spanish American relations.[22] Among textbook writers, whose growing numbers called attention to the acceptance of the subject in United States colleges and universities, the individual who expressed the most sympathetic feeling for the colonial period was C. E. Chapman. His *Colonial Hispanic America* was a text in the Bolton manner, the foremost single volume on its subject for a number of years and still, despite some peculiarities, far from a worthless book.[23]

As a group, the leading monographs and general works of the twenties and thirties explored Hispanic America less superficially than their predecessors. They escaped the connection with the United States more successfully, and in several instances their historiographical contributions are of enduring value. They still concentrated heavily on selected political and economic institutions; they barely touched seventeenth-century history; and despite the many endorsements of the term "Hispanic" America,[24] colonial Brazil remained for them a peripheral area, remote and unexplored.

During the past fifteen years in the United States, new students have been attracted to colonial Latin American studies in large numbers, but the claims of the national period now far exceed those of any previous era, and as a result, interest in colonial history has proportionately declined. The fact that the time span of colonial history remains static, whereas that of national history becomes greater with each passing year has contributed to a relative recession in colonial studies. "The time should be approaching," in the words of a recent text, "when less attention need be given to . . . the colonial era."[25] Many colonial subjects, in other words, are becoming antiquarian from a textbook point of view, and the accelerating

pace of modern Latin America tends to place colonial history progressively farther in the background. There is an unmistakable tendency to locate the three colonial centuries in a category of the antecedent.

On the other hand, the positive achievements in colonial scholarship of the past fifteen years have been impressive. A new journal, *The Americas*, began publication in 1944. A series of extraordinary illuminating studies by Lewis Hanke was climaxed in 1949 by *The Spanish Struggle for Justice in the Conquest of America* (Philadelphia), a fundamental work in imperial socio-intellectual history and one that has already gone far to modify the traditional American susceptibility to the anti-Hispanic "Black Legend." The work of Whitaker, Hussey, Lanning, and others opened another socio-intellectual subject, that of the Enlightenment.[26]

[21] Cunningham, *The Audiencia in the Spanish Colonies as Illustrated by the Audiencia of Manila (1583–1800)*, Univ. of California Pubs. in Hist., IX (Berkeley, 1919); Fisher, *Viceregal Administration in the Spanish-American Colonies*, Univ. of California Pubs. in Hist., XV (Berkeley, 1926) and *The Intendant System in Spanish America* (Berkeley, 1929); Hamilton, *American Treasure and the Price Revolution in Spain, 1501–1650*, Harvard Econ. Stud., XLIII (Cambridge, Mass., 1934); Hussey, *The Caracas Company, 1728–1784: A Study in the History of Spanish Monopolistic Trade*, Harvard Hist. Stud., XXXVII (Cambridge, Mass., 1934); Leonard, *Don Carlos de Sigüenza y Góngora, a Mexican Savant of the Seventeenth Century*, Univ. of California Pubs. in Hist., XVIII (Berkeley, 1929); Lanning, *Academic Culture in the Spanish Colonies* (New York, 1940). See also in this period Philip Ainsworth Means, *Fall of the Inca Empire and the Spanish Rule in Peru: 1530–1780* (New York and London, 1932).

[22] *The Rise of the Spanish Empire in the Old World and the New*, 4 vols. (New York, 1918–1934).

[23] *Colonial Hispanic America: A History* (New York, 1933). The development of textbooks and teaching in Latin American history is treated in Jorge Basadre's introduction to *Courses on Latin America* (Washington, 1950), pp. v–lxxiii.

[24] "The Term 'Latin America'," *Hisp. Amer. Hist. Rev.*, I (1918), 464–67. The point here is that "Hispanic" refers to both Spain and Portugal rather than to Spain alone.

[25] Mary W. Williams, Ruhl J. Bartlett, and Russell E. Miller, *The People and Politics of Latin America* (Boston, 1955), p. vi.

[26] Arthur P. Whitaker, *et al.*, *Latin America*

R. H. Barlow's important researches in the codex literature of Mexico were the first in the United States to combine ethnological and historical techniques after the manner

---

and the Enlightenment (New York and London, 1942).

[27] Barlow, The Extent of the Empire of the Culhua Mexicana, Ibero-Americana, 28 (Berkeley and Los Angeles, 1949). Barlow's extensive periodical writings occur in the Memorias de la Academia mexicana de la historia, Tlalocan, and other journals.

[28] Smith and Elizabeth Wilder, A Guide to the Art of Latin America (Washington, 1948); Elizabeth Wilder Weismann, Mexico in Sculpture, 1521–1821 (Cambridge, Mass., 1950); Wethey, Colonial Architecture and Sculpture in Peru (Cambridge, Mass., 1949); Kubler, Mexican Architecture of the Sixteenth Century, Yale Hist. Pubs., Hist. of Art, V, 2 vols. (New Haven, Conn., 1948).

[29] Cook and Simpson, The Population of Central Mexico in the Sixteenth Century, Ibero-Americana, 31 (Berkeley and Los Angeles, 1948); Cook, Soil Erosion and Population in Central Mexico, Ibero-Americana, 34 (Berkeley and Los Angeles, 1949); Borah, New Spain's Century of Depression, Ibero-Americana, 35 (Berkeley and Los Angeles, 1951).

[30] Morison, Admiral of the Ocean Sea: A Life of Christopher Columbus, 2 vols. (Boston, 1942); Wagner, The Rise of Fernando Cortés, Documents and Narratives Concerning the Discovery and Conquest of Latin America, New Ser., No. 3 (Los Angeles, 1944); Chamberlain, The Conquest and Colonization of Yucatan, 1517–1550, Carnegie Inst. of Washington Pub. No. 582 (Washington, 1948), and The Conquest and Colonization of Honduras, 1502–1550, Carnegie Inst. of Washington Pub. No. 598 (Washington, 1953).

[31] From Barter to Slavery: The Economic Relations of Portuguese and Indians in the Settlement of Brazil, 1500–1580 (Baltimore, 1942).

[32] Ralph L. Roys, The Indian Background of Colonial Yucatan, Carnegie Inst. of Washington Pub. No. 548 (Washington, 1943); France V. Scholes, et al., The Maya Chontal Indians of Acalan-Tixchel: A Contribution to the History and Ethnography of the Yucatan Peninsula, Carnegie Inst. of Washington Pub. No. 560 (Washington, 1948); George Kubler, "The Quechua in the Colonial World," Handbook of South American Indians, Julian H. Steward, ed., 6 vols., Smithsonian Inst., Bureau of American Ethnology, Bull. 143 (Washington, 1946–1950), II, 331–410; Charles Gibson, Tlaxcala in the Sixteenth Century (New Haven, Conn., 1952); Howard Cline, "Mexican Community Studies," Hisp. Amer. Hist. Rev., XXXII (1952), 212–42; Mathias C. Kiemen,

---

of Seler, Aubin, and other European scholars.[27] The history of colonial art in the works of Robert C. Smith, Elizabeth Wilder Weismann, Harold E. Wethey, and George Kubler is principally the accomplishment of the last fifteen years.[28] The California historians, Sherburne F. Cook, Lesley Byrd Simpson, Woodrow W. Borah, and others, have recently exposed a whole new world to colonial Latin Americanists in their analyses of population, economy, and human ecology in early colonial Mexico, demonstrating scholarship of a type unique in this country, without counterparts in Latin America or Europe, informed by the "auxiliary" techniques of economics, demography, and anthropology.[29] Discovery, exploration, and conquest, of course, continue to be reexamined, as in Samuel E. Morison's work on Columbus, Henry R. Wagner's biography of Cortés, and Robert S. Chamberlain's meticulous studies of Yucatan and Honduras.[30] The recent period has seen also the first serious monographs on colonial Brazil, beginning with Alexander N. D. Marchant's From Barter to Slavery.[31] Many additional scholars are currently active; their numbers do not appear to have been depleted, and the omission of their names here carries no disrespect. Their over-all tendencies appear to be in the direction of rectifying long-standing prejudices against Spain, of detailing actual colonial behavior in the New World (as against the "ideal" behavior of the laws), and of understanding Indian-Spanish or Indian-Portuguese relations in local American environments.[32]

The period since 1940 has also provided new occasions for surveys of the total colonial scene. For colonial Hispanic America, two general works represent the mid-twentieth-century achievement. The Latin-American Civilization, Colonial Period of Bailey W. Diffie is the first successful attempt in the United States to see colonial history in the large, to analyze and detail its underlying principles, and to incorporate its cultural expression in an historical synthesis. The Spanish Empire in America of Clarence H. Haring offers our soundest and most comprehensive formulation of the institutional history of colonial times.[33] There is a sense in which such general treatments depend upon the continued publication of special studies, but there is a sense also in which this is not true, and the original research and comprehensive orientation of the works mentioned render each an independent scholarly production. As single-volume interpretations of the entire colonial period, they meet simultaneously the needs of the specialist and the nonspecialist for accurate summary information.

II

We have noted that the modern period of Latin American history held little interest for United States historians until the twentieth century. Actually, if we exclude two marginal fields within this period that have perhaps received their fair share of attention—the revolutionary era and the diplomatic relations of Latin America with the United States—it may be said that intensive study of modern Latin American history in the United States is a development of only the last few decades. The reasons that have led North American scholars to neglect the modern and favor the colonial period of Hispanic history are not difficult to enumerate. The colonial period has enjoyed the advantage of those romantic themes of discovery, conquest, and exploration indicated above. The geographic unity and continuity in time of the colonial period have also caused historians to favor it over the republican era, whose "turbulence and kaleidoscopic political changes make it difficult to find a continuity in development and to appraise the long-run significance of individual events."[34] Finally, for a variety of reasons, the colonial historian, especially of the sixteenth century, has enjoyed a decided advantage in respect to published and unpublished source materials. In part, at least, this last condition has had its roots in the traditionally aristocratic structure of Latin American society and politics. "A sense of loyalty to political and family con-

nections has unquestionably made its influence felt in the selection of records to be preserved and to be made available to scholars."[35]

The first three decades of this century produced little significant writing on the modern period of Latin American history by United States authors. The few notable works that come to mind, such as Justin H. Smith's *The War with Mexico* and Dana G. Munro's survey of the Central American area,[36] were generally confined to regions in which the United States had large interests; occasionally, as in the case of Smith's book, they displayed a certain nationalistic bias. A unique exception was the sturdy monograph by John F. Cady on Argentina's mid-century troubles with Europe.[37] Research in the revolutionary era, on the other hand, made a promising debut in this period with the publication in 1908 of William S. Robertson's monograph on Miranda, the foundation for his later superb biography of the Venezuelan hero.[38]

The appearance of the *Hispanic American Historical Review* in 1918 did not materially alter the balance between the colonial and modern periods in United States historiography dealing with Latin America. A survey of the contents of this review between the two World Wars reveals a continuing

---

[33] Diffie, *Latin-American Civilization, Colonial Period* (Harrisburg, Pa., 1945); Haring, *The Spanish Empire in America* (New York, 1947).

[34] Sanford A. Mosk, "Latin America and the World Economy, 1850–1914," *Inter-American Econ. Affairs*, II (1948), No. 3, 54.

[35] *Ibid.*

[36] Smith, *The War with Mexico*, 2 vols. (New York, 1919); Munro, *The Five Republics of Central America, Their Political and Economic Development and Their Relations with the United States* (New York, 1918).

[37] *Foreign Intervention in the Rio de la Plata, 1838–1850: A Study of French, British, and American Policy in Relation to the Dictator Juan Manuel Rosas* (Philadelphia, 1929).

[38] "Francisco de Miranda and the Revolutionizing of Spanish America," *Annual Report of the American Historical Association for the Year 1907* (Washington, 1908), I, 189–539; *The Life of Miranda*, 2 vols. (Chapel Hill, N. C., 1929). His interest in this period also produced *Iturbide of Mexico* (Durham, N. C., 1952).

The Indian Policy of Portugal in the Amazon Region, 1614–1693 (Washington, 1954).

overwhelming emphasis on colonial, revolutionary, and diplomatic topics. It was perhaps symptomatic of the state of affairs that as late as 1930 Percy Alvin Martin had to deplore the tendency of some critics to declare that "the Hispanic American republics have no history worthy of the name," and that "the task of the historian . . . is finished when he has adequately investigated the colonial period and the wars of independence."[39] Martin practiced what he preached, contributing to the *Review* articles on such varied modern topics as the career of José Batlle y Ordóñez and the causes of the fall of the Brazilian Empire, but few followed his example.[40]

Nevertheless, historical writing on modern Latin America could record certain advances in the period between the two World Wars. Progress was made in detaching the field from the orbit of United States diplomatic and regional history and in developing some understanding of the economic and social factors in Latin America's historical evolution. In the twenties appeared the first scholarly national histories—Herbert I. Priestley's *The Mexican Nation* (New York, 1923), Charles E. Chapman's *A History of the Cuban Republic* (New York, 1927), and Sumner Welles's *Naboth's Vineyard: The Dominican Republic, 1844–1924* (2 vols.; New York, 1928). As was to be expected, these pioneer works dealt with countries in the United States sphere of interest and were rather heavily weighted on the diplomatic or political side. It was also natural that Mexico, not only for reasons of proximity but because its history seemed to reveal most clearly a true clash of political and social ideals, should attract the largest share of scholarly attention. Wilfrid H. Callcott's *Church and State in Mexico, 1822–1857* (Durham, N. C., 1926), followed by his *Liberalism in Mexico, 1857–1929* (Stanford, 1931), and two socio-economic studies written with much historical perspective, George M. McBride's *The Land Systems of Mexico* (New York, 1923) and Frank Tannenbaum's *The Mexican Agrarian Revolution* (New York, 1929), were among the important contributions in this field. To these should per-

haps be added the studies by Lillian Fisher on the marginal zone between the late colonial and early republican periods in Mexico.[41] Another group of books, departing from the academic formula of emphasis on diplomatic relations, subjected to critical analysis the record of United States economic dealings with selected Latin American countries; these "Studies in American Imperialism" included Leland H. Jenks, *Our Cuban Colony, A Study in Sugar* (New York, 1928); J. Fred Rippy, *The Capitalists and Colombia* (New York, 1931); and Charles D. Kepner and Jay Soothill, *The Banana Empire* (New York, 1935).

The coming of age of Latin American history in the United States in a certain sense may be said to date from the thirties, a decade that saw the launching of the indispensable annual *Handbook of Latin American Studies* (1936–   ) and a general increase of bibliographical activity in the Latin American field.[42] This intensified bibliographical effort made possible more adequate study of the national period of Latin American history, an area in which great confusion and obscurity had prevailed even in respect to printed, not to mention unpublished, sources. Simultaneously, historians began to accord a somewhat greater share of attention to the period since independence. The appearance of two collaborative works edited by Alva C. Wilgus, *Argentina, Brazil and Chile since Independence* (Washington, 1935) and *South American Dictators during*

---

[39] *Hisp. Amer. Hist. Rev.*, X (1930), 413.

[40] These few, however, included such distinguished names as C. E. Chapman, C. H. Haring, A. K. Manchester, W. W. Pierson, and M. W. Williams.

[41] See in addition to the works cited above (fn. 21) her volume on *The Background of the Revolution for Mexican Independence* (Boston, 1934).

[42] Among the bibliographical aids published in this period, *The Economic Literature of Latin America*, 2 vols. (Cambridge, Mass., 1935–1936) was of special interest to students of modern Latin America. For a useful survey of activity in the late thirties, see M. M. Wise, "Development of Bibliographical Activity during the Past Five Years: A Tentative Survey," in *Handbook of Latin American Studies: 1939* (Cambridge, Mass., 1940), pp. 13–26.

the First Century of Independence (Washington, 1937), suggested a laudable desire to provide serviceable works of synthesis on the national period. The same tendency was reflected in a well-intentioned but not altogether felicitous project for translation into English of selected Latin American national histories. Within the national period, some improvement in areal and topical emphasis became evident in the publication of J. Lloyd Mecham's massive study of Church and State in Latin America (Chapel Hill, N. C., 1934) and Mary Watters' History of the Church in Venezuela (Chapel Hill, N. C., 1933)—the first serious studies of an important subject. The curtain of neglect that had hidden modern Brazil from historical view began to rise with the publication of Alan K. Manchester's British Preëminence in Brazil, Its Rise and Decline (Chapel Hill, N. C., 1933) and Mary W. Williams' life of Dom Pedro the Magnanimous, Second Emperor of Brazil (Chapel Hill, N. C., 1937). Within the modern period, however, attention continued to center heavily on diplomatic and revolutionary topics. Particularly fruitful work was accomplished in the thirties in the investigation of foreign influence on the Spanish American revolutions, a subject which John Rydjord, Charles C. Griffin, and William S. Robertson cultivated with distinction.[43]

Despite these advances, it must be said that as of 1940 the literature in English on the history of modern Latin America was pitifully meager, the great bulk of this writing was devoted to diplomatic or revolutionary topics, and much of it was narrowly political in scope or superficial in treatment. Fortunately, students could supplement the purely historical material with the works of anthropologists, economists, and other social scientists whose researches in this period often illuminated aspects of Latin American reality ignored by the professional historians. Some of these valuable studies were Mark Jefferson's Peopling the Argentine Pampa (New York, 1926), George M. McBride's Chile: Land and Society (New York, 1936), Robert Redfield's Tepoztlán, A Mexican Village (Chicago, 1930),[44] João F. Nor-

mano's Brazil: A Study of Economic Types (Chapel Hill, N. C., 1935), Eyler N. Simpson's The Ejido: Mexico's Way Out (Chapel Hill, N. C., 1937), and Simon G. Hanson's Utopia in Uruguay (New York, 1938).

Only since 1940 can a major shift in emphasis and interpretation in the writing of United States historians on Latin America be detected. A statistical analysis of the material published since that date would almost certainly show a relative decline in the number of books and articles dealing with colonial and revolutionary topics and a corresponding increase in the volume of writing on the national period. Such an analysis would probably also show some movement of historical attention from Mexico and Middle America to South America. Equally important, but less susceptible to measurement, there is evidence of a growing awareness of economic, social and cultural factors on the part of United States historians who specialize in the modern period of Latin American history.

This tendency is even apparent in writing on the revolutionary era, in which not long since political, military, and diplomatic themes held absolute sway. Charles C. Griffin has broken new ground here with a broadly suggestive essay on the economic and social aspects of the era of Spanish American independence.[45] Harold A. Bierck has described the struggle for the abolition of slavery in Gran Colombia.[46] Arthur P. Whitaker devotes considerable attention to economic and intellectual factors in The United

---

[43] Rydjord, Foreign Interest in the Independence of New Spain: An Introduction to the War for Independence (Durham, N. C., 1935); Griffin, The United States and the Disruption of the Spanish Empire, 1810–1822 (New York, 1937); Robertson, France and Latin-American Independence (Baltimore, 1939). In this tradition also is Benjamin Keen, David Curtis DeForest and the Revolution of Buenos Aires (New Haven, Conn., 1947).

[44] Oscar Lewis has challenged some of Redfield's main conclusions in his Life in a Mexican Village: Tepoztlán Restudied (Urbana, Ill., 1951).

[45] Hisp. Amer. Hist. Rev., XXIX (1949), 170–87.

[46] Hisp. Amer. Hist. Rev., XXXIII (1953), 365–86.

States and the Independence of Latin America, 1800–1830 (Baltimore, 1941), and Gerhard Masur takes note of these influences in his life of Bolívar[47]—the best biography of the Liberator available in English up to the present time.

Turning to the historiography of the national period since 1940, we note that Mexico continues to lead in the number of investigations. The vast panorama of the Mexican Revolution has proved a particularly alluring subject to North American scholars. The extremely divergent conclusions reached in such notable works as Frank Tannenbaum's *Mexico: The Struggle for Peace and Bread* (New York, 1950) and Howard F. Cline's *The United States and Mexico* (Cambridge, Mass., 1953) illustrate the controversial nature of this topic. Biographical studies of leading Mexican personalities have multiplied. The versatile Ralph Roeder has written a distinguished but not definitive account of *Juárez and His Mexico* (2 vols., New York, 1947); the martyred Madero has received sympathetic as well as scholarly treatment at the hands of Charles C. Cumberland and Stanley R. Ross.[48] Even lesser figures have found their competent biographers.[49] Walter V. Scholes brings a stimulating sociological approach to the Mexican *Reforma* in his article, "A Revolution Falters: Mexico, 1856–1857."[50] Other North American scholars who have written on modern Mexican topics in recent years include N. L. Benson, R. W. Frazer, C. H. Gardiner, and R. B. McCornack.

The interest aroused by the dramatic course of events in Argentina since the Nationalist Revolution of 1943 has focused historical attention on that country in the past decade. Ysabel F. Rennie's *The Argentine Republic* (New York, 1945) lucidly sketches the economic and social background of political developments. A book of major importance, perhaps comparable in significance to Charles A. Beard's *Economic Interpretation of the Constitution* for the historiography of the United States, is Miron Burgin's heavily documented study of *Economic Aspects of Argentine Federalism, 1820–1852* (Cambridge, Mass., 1946). We have acquired a life of Sarmiento by Allison W. Bunkley and a study of Mitre by William H. Jeffrey,[51] but definitive biographies of these two makers of modern Argentina still need to be written. The interest and controversy engendered by *Peronismo* find expression in recent studies by Robert Alexander and George I. Blanksten.[52] Arthur P. Whitaker has written a brief but penetrating survey of *The United States and Argentina* (Cambridge, Mass., 1954)—a book of broader scope than its title suggests—that is now supplemented by his *Argentine Upheaval: Perón's Fall and the New Regime* (New York, 1956).

Harris G. Warren has told the Paraguayan story in a readable book that does not neglect social history, and Russell H. Fitzgibbon includes much historical matter in his genial portrait of Uruguay.[53] We still lack an adequate history of Brazil, but various aspects of this vast field have been studied in recent years by A. K. Manchester, Alexander Marchant, Richard Morse, T. W. Palmer, and Stanley Stein, among others. The Andean region—virtually a *terra incognita* to United States historians before 1940—has only begun to obtain the recognition that it merits. Arthur P. Whitaker, *The United States and South America: The Northern Republics* (Cambridge, Mass., 1948), is a useful survey of the area. David Bushnell's

[47] *Simon Bolivar* (Albuquerque, N. M., 1948).

[48] Cumberland, *Mexican Revolution: Genesis under Madero* (Austin, 1952); Ross, *Francisco I. Madero, Apostle of Mexican Democracy* (New York, 1955).

[49] See for example T. E. Cotner, *The Military and Political Career of José Joaquin de Herrera, 1792–1854* (Austin, 1949), and Frank A. Knapp, *The Life of Sebastián Lerdo de Tejada, 1823–1889: A Study of Influence and Obscurity* (Austin, 1951).

[50] *Hisp. Amer. Hist. Rev.*, XXXII (1952), 1–21.

[51] Bunkley, *Life of Sarmiento* (Princeton, 1952); Jeffrey, *Mitre and Argentina* (New York, 1952).

[52] Alexander, *The Perón Era: An Interpretation* (New York, 1951); Blanksten, *Perón's Argentina* (Chicago, 1953).

[53] Warren, *Paraguay: An Informal History* (Norman, Okla., 1949); Fitzgibbon, *Uruguay, Portrait of a Democracy* (New Brunswick, N. J., 1954).

The Santander Regime in Gran Colombia (Newark, Del., 1954) illustrates the kind of careful, intensive investigation that is needed in all aspects of modern Latin American history. A work of much value to historians is James J. Parsons, *Antioqueño Colonization in Western Colombia* (Berkeley, 1949). We possess only one substantial work on Venezuela—George S. Wise's study of Antonio Guzmán Blanco.[54] The situation with respect to Ecuador and Peru is equally unsatisfactory. George I. Blanksten's book on *Ecuador: Constitutions and Caudillos* (Berkeley, 1951) deals mainly with the very recent period. Only one aspect of Peru's history—the *Aprista* movement—has received serious attention from United States scholars; the literature of the subject includes contributions by Frank Tannenbaum, Robert E. McNicoll, and Harry Kantor.[55] For material on Bolivia, one must look almost exclusively to nonhistorical writings, notably Olen E. Leonard's sociological study, *Bolivia: Land, People, and Institutions* (Washington, 1952). United States historians have sadly neglected Chile; we can cite only one outstanding monograph, John R. Stevenson, *The Chilean Popular Front* (Philadelphia, 1942).

A most significant development in United States historical writing on modern Latin America since 1940 has been the rapid growth of economic history, which before 1940 could boast only of such isolated achievements as Hanson's book on Uruguay and Normano's study of economic Brazil. This trend reflects in some degree the interest aroused in recent decades by the energetic efforts of some Latin American countries to transform their economies; it has certainly been stimulated by the writings of historically minded economists like Sanford A. Mosk, George Wythe, and Henry W. Spiegel.[56] Much credit in particular is due the journal *Inter-American Economic Affairs*, edited since 1947 by S. G. Hanson, which has encouraged this type of research by publishing articles of historical as well as current interest. Miron Burgin summed up the point of view of this new school in 1947: "It is only when the economic past of the Latin

American countries is reconstructed that the processes of current political and institutional development can be fully understood."[57] J. F. Rippy made an even more ambitious claim for the economic interpretation when he wrote in the preface to his *Latin America and the Industrial Age*: "Science and technology largely determine the rise and fall of nations. The impact of foreign science and technology upon Latin America is a major episode in modern history which no one who aspires to understand world history can afford to ignore."[58]

Since those words were written in 1944, a small army of researchers has joined Rippy in the work of unearthing the buried facts of Latin American economic history and appraising their significance. The variety of topics studied appears from the following sampling: as noted above, Miron Burgin has explored the economic background of Rosas' Argentina; George Wythe has described the beginnings of the factory system in Latin America;[59] David M. Pletcher has written on "The Building of the Mexican Railway";[60] Howard Cline has investigated the manufacturing, sugar, and henequen episodes in Yucatecan economic history;[61] Wil-

---

[54] *Caudillo: A Portrait of Antonio Guzmán Blanco* (New York, 1951).

[55] Tannenbaum, "Agrarismo, Indianismo, y Nacionalismo," *Hisp. Amer. Hist. Rev.*, XXIII (1943), 394–423; McNicoll, "Intellectual Origins of Aprismo," *ibid.*, 424–40; Kantor, *The Ideology and Program of the Peruvian Aprista Movement* (Berkeley, 1953).

[56] Mosk, *Industrial Revolution in Mexico* (Berkeley, 1950); Wythe, *Industry in Latin America* (New York, 1945); Spiegel, *The Brazilian Economy: Chronic Inflation and Sporadic Industrialization* (Philadelphia, 1949). To these should perhaps be added H. Foster Bain and Thomas Thornton Read, *Ores and Industry in South America* (New York, 1934), and the series written for the United States Tariff Commission, *The Foreign Trade of Latin America*, 3 pts. (Washington, 1940–1941).

[57] "Research in Latin-American Economics and Economic History," *Inter-American Econ. Affairs*, I (1947), No. 3, 3–22.

[58] (New York, 1944), p. viii.

[59] "The Rise of the Factory in Latin America," *Hisp. Amer. Hist. Rev.*, XXV (1945), 295–314.

[60] *Hisp. Amer. Hist. Rev.*, XXX (1950), 26–62.

[61] "The *Aurora Yucateca* and the Spirit of En-

liam H. Gray has told the story of "Steamboat Transportation on the Orinoco";[62] John J. Johnson has recorded the beginnings of telegraphy in Chile;[63] Robert L. Gilmore and John P. Harrison have studied early steam navigation on the Magdalena River;[64] J. P. Harrison has traced "The Evolution of the Colombian Tobacco Trade to 1875";[65] Stanley Stein has probed into the causes of the decay of the coffee industry in the Paraiba Valley of Brazil;[66] and Watt Stewart has employed a biographical approach to Peruvian economic and social history.[67] In the light of these studies and others not cited, we suggest that Burgin would even now need to qualify his statement, made nine years ago, that "Latin America of the past 150 years is virtually a *tabula rasa* to the economic historian."

In the field of social history, almost everything remains to be done. Tom B. Jones has illuminated life and manners in nineteenth-century South America from travelers' accounts in his *South America Rediscovered* (Minneapolis, 1949); Madaline Nichols has written a pioneer study of the gaucho;[68] Watt Stewart has recorded the tragic plight of Chinese coolies in Peru.[69] A notable study is Sidney W. Mintz's reconstruction of the culture history of a Puerto Rican plantation— a good illustration of the use of anthropological techniques in the writing of social history and of the general utility of cross-fertilization in the social sciences.[70] On the margin between social and intellectual history lies Richard Morse's article on the changing cultural climate of São Paulo since independence—an essay that treats with a rare sophistication the relation of intellectual to economic and social phenomena.[71]

The history of ideas—a field of study for which Latin American historians have shown a distinct affinity—has been strangely neglected by North American scholars working in the modern period. We lacked even

an introduction to the subject until the appearance of William R. Crawford's *A Century of Latin-American Thought* (Cambridge, Mass., 1944). Only with difficulty can one compile a list of more than a few significant contributions to this field: these include Morse's above-mentioned article on São Paulo, Philip D. Curtin's fine study of "The Declaration of the Rights of Man in Saint-Domingue, 1788–1791," and Patrick Romanell's somewhat technical study of the Mexican mind.[72] Providing a corpus of source material for the study of Latin American historical evolution in a wide range of fields is the collection of translated sources brought together by Benjamin Keen.[73]

Among works of synthesis published since 1940, we must single out Harry Bernstein's *Modern and Contemporary Latin America* (Philadelphia, 1952), which documents in a very careful way the impact of regional economic rivalries upon the political development of the countries with which it deals. If one had to level any criticism against an

[62] *Hisp. Amer. Hist. Rev.*, XXV (1945), 455–69.

[63] *Pioneer Telegraphy in Chile, 1852–1876* (Stanford, 1948).

[64] "Juan Bernardo Elbers and the Introduction of Steam Navigation on the Magdalena River," *Hisp. Amer. Hist. Rev.*, XXVIII (1948), 335–59.

[65] *Hisp. Amer. Hist. Rev.*, XXXII (1952), 163–74.

[66] "The Passing of the Coffee Plantation in the Paraiba Valley," *Hisp. Amer. Hist. Rev.*, XXXIII (1953), 331–64.

[67] *Henry Meiggs, Yankee Pizarro* (Durham, N. C., 1946).

[68] *The Gaucho, Cattle Hunter, Cavalryman, Ideal of Romance* (Durham, N. C., 1942).

[69] *Chinese Bondage in Peru: A History of the Chinese Coolie in Peru, 1849–1874* (Durham, N. C., 1951).

[70] "The Culture History of a Puerto Rican Sugar Cane Plantation: 1876–1949," *Hisp. Amer. Hist. Rev.*, XXXIII (1953), 224–51.

[71] "São Paulo since Independence: A Cultural Interpretation," *Hisp. Amer. Hist. Rev.*, XXXIV (1954), 419–44.

[72] Curtin, *Hisp. Amer. Hist. Rev.*, XXX (1950), 157–75; Romanell, *Making of the Mexican Mind* (Lincoln, Nebr., 1952). Curtin has recently published *Two Jamaicas: The Role of the Ideas in a Tropical Society, 1830–1865* (Cambridge, Mass., 1955).

[73] *Readings in Latin-American Civilization, 1492 to the Present* (Boston, 1955).

terprise in Yucatan, 1821–1847," *Hisp. Amer. Hist. Rev.*, XXVII (1947), 30–60; "The Sugar Episode in Yucatan, 1825–1850," *Inter-American Econ. Affairs*, I (1948), No. 4, 79–100; "The Henequen Episode in Yucatan," *Inter-American Econ. Affairs*, II (1948), No. 2, 30–51.

exploratory work of such solid worth, it would be to note its failure to give adequate attention to the influence of European and North American technology and capital in the shaping of modern Latin America and its relative slighting of cultural factors in the modern history of this area.

III

The present needs and future prospects of Latin American studies in this country will probably bear more significantly upon the national than upon the colonial period. Without carrying the emphasis to extremes, the present authors believe that today's tendencies in national history are salutary and that the long tradition of colonial concentration has not yet been redressed in modern times.

That the colonial tradition was itself unbalanced goes without saying. Probably most Latin Americanists of the United States would agree that the heavy stresses of that tradition upon conquest, upon exploration, and upon "borderland" areas, while wholly understandable, need not qualify as directional guides for the future. So far as the detail and chronology of historical research are concerned, these subjects come as close to being "exhausted" as any in Latin American history.

In what Hispanic Americanists habitually indicate as "background" studies, the researches of United States students have concentrated on the American aborigines at the expense of the Hispanic peninsula. For the former, the historical profession must acknowledge a long-standing debt to archaeology and anthropology and to the vast organized labors of such bodies as the Carnegie Institution and the Smithsonian Institution's Institute of Social Anthropology. The impressive gains in twentieth-century knowledge of the American preconquest "background" have not stimulated historians to comparable researches in postconquest aboriginal history, where great lapses in knowledge extend through both colonial and national periods. As for the peninsular "background," the record of American historians is fragmentary at best, and no associated

disciplines have come forth to fill this breach. The tendency is still to regard American history from the fixed starting point of the discovery and to depend upon selected and outmoded categories of preliminary peninsular material. This tendency has been conspicuously reversed among some historians in Spain and Portugal and to a certain extent among historians in Latin America, but United States scholars have made only a bare beginning at following their example.[74]

United States contributions to encomienda studies have been impressive, but we are still far from a thorough understanding of that institution. Individual encomiendas need to be examined in their operating detail over long periods, when possible, and at carefully chosen geographical locations. The related subject of tribute, both in its encomienda form and in its royal form, is capable of sustaining a far more intense scrutiny than any yet accorded it in the United States or elsewhere. The entire problem of postconquest relations between Spaniards and Indians, of which encomienda and tribute are two aspects, stands in need of systematic, precise examination. The subject comprehends political rule, economic interchange, acculturation and deculturation, peonage, and a variety of other labor institutions, as well as rates of change in spatial and temporal dimensions.

In political and social history, colonial studies suffer from a neglect of the seventeenth century. The convention is to dwell on the beginning and the end, to pass rapidly from the aftermath of conquest to the precursors of independence. The convention

[74] Henry C. Lea, *The Inquisition in the Spanish Dependencies: Sicily—Naples—Sardinia—Milan—the Canaries—Mexico—Peru—New Granada* (New York, 1908); Julius Klein, *The Mesta: A Study in Spanish Economic History, 1273–1836* (Cambridge, Mass., 1920); Charles Julian Bishko, "The Iberian Background of Latin American History: Recent Progress and Continuing Problems," *Hisp. Amer. Hist. Rev.*, XXXVI (1956), 50–80. For United States Luso-Brazilian trends see *Proceedings of the International Colloquium on Luso-Brazilian Studies, Washington, October 15–20, 1950* (Nashville, 1953), especially pp. 167–335.

is natural and by no means confined to the Latin Americanists of the United States. In Anglo-American history, a compressed but otherwise equivalent period falls roughly between the 1690's and the Great Awakening. Such periods cannot conveniently be attached either to the colonial foundations or to the independence movement, and in Latin America, where colonial foundations occurred early and independence occurred late, the intermediate vacuum is the more pronounced. United States students have deplored this situation, but sound seventeenth-century studies remain rare.[75] If, as is frequently stated, the seventeenth century served as a period of test for socio-political experiments undertaken in the sixteenth century, that proposition itself remains untested. The seventeenth century's basic demographic trends are still matters of conjecture. Its urban-rural relationships are vague. Its social classes and family structure and the extent of its ethnic fusion are unknown. The seventeenth century as a whole —and to it we may add large portions of the eighteenth century—needs all its particular data enlarged and all its generalizations reexamined.

The present situation in colonial economic history may be described as respectable but erratic. Imperial commerce, selected industries, and price systems have been the objects of some excellent studies. Local economies, land utilization, urban markets, plantation systems, and private fortunes are examples of subjects imperfectly examined or wholly neglected. Existing studies in local economies relate predominantly to Mexico, and abundant research needs to be accomplished in the remainder of Latin America. Here as in political history it is the colonial scene itself, rather than the imperial supervision of it, on which our knowledge is most deficient. United States students have been less guilty than their colleagues in Spain and Latin America of identifying the imperial legislation with the colonial reality, but they have not been wholly innocent nor has confusion been wholly eliminated. It appears increasingly likely that dependence upon the *Recopilación de leyes* and other

pancolonial digests has created an overestimation of the uniformities in the American scene. Equivalent dangers lurk in studies of colonial intellectual history, where peninsular impositions in a less codified form have surely diverted attention from the manifold colonial varieties. In all these topics, the situation in Brazilian studies may be said to be similar to those of Spanish America but more acute.

We believe that the evidence of recent years justifies a modest satisfaction with the present trends and future prospects of historical writing on modern Latin America in the United States. But only a beginning has been made; the list of problems that call and compete for attention is endless. Our comprehension of the process of Latin American independence is still inadequate; the causal factors and particularly the economic and social aspects of this great movement are still poorly understood. In the national period, there is a serious need for more intensive study of the economic and geographic bases of regional rivalries, *caudillismo,* and the Liberal-Conservative cleavage so characteristic of nineteenth-century Latin America— phenomena that the textbooks too often explain with political clichés.

In view of the great importance attached to the problem in contemporary Latin America, a high order of priority should perhaps be assigned to the study of the influence for good and evil of foreign capital and technology on Latin America during the past century. In this connection, there is a clamorous need for company histories and biographies of entrepreneurs like Minor C. Keith and Percival Farquhar, written with the candor, objectivity, and thoroughness that the sensitivity of the subject requires. Again, in view of the current agitation over land reform in Latin America, studies are needed on the historical evolution of land systems in the national period—as has been done to

[75] See L. B. Simpson, "Mexico's Forgotten Century," *Pacific Hist. Rev.,* XXII (1953), 113–21; Howard F. Cline, "The Terragueros of Guelatao, Oaxaca, Mexico: Notes on the Sierra de Juárez and its XVIIth Century Indian Problems," *Acta Americana,* IV (1946), 161–84.

some extent for the colonial period by Silvio Zavala, François Chevalier, and others. In the field of social history, themes still awaiting intensive investigation include European immigration since independence and its varied effects, the history of the modern Latin American city and of urbanization in general, the development of trade unionism, and the sociological effects of the shift from the nineteenth-century patriarchal estate to the impersonal, corporation-owned plantation of today.

In addition, we should like to call attention to one of the greatest voids in historical writing on modern Latin America—cultural or intellectual history. United States historians seem to have ignored the fact that in Latin America, even more than in some other parts of the world, the writer and artist have consciously employed books, paintings, and philosophies as weapons in political and social struggles and have often themselves been statesmen and even warriors. To be sure, we have some excellent histories of Latin American literature,[76] music, and art, but they approach their subjects principally from an aesthetic point of view. What are needed are studies along the lines of those made by Alejandro Korn, José Ingenieros, and José Luis Romero in Argentina, Ricardo Donoso in Chile, and Leopoldo Zea in Mexico—studies that would relate the movement of literature, art, and ideas to their political, economic, and social background.

In both the colonial and the national history, students continue to confront the problems of travel, of time, of linguistic and other training, and of admission to archives. Problems of travel and time surely account in part for the preference of colonial students for "borderland" studies and for the relative neglect of large parts of South America. Few students enter the colonial field sufficiently grounded in the medieval and Renaissance history of the Hispanic peninsula, in anthropology, in paleography, or in the Indian languages in which much of the early local history is recorded. The Portuguese language is itself an obstacle for those who halt their training with Spanish. A large number of historical subjects require research not only in Latin American but in Hispanic peninsular depositories. In the one as in the other, the student has at his disposal a growing but still meager collection of catalogues and guides to assist his practical work. Latin American archives tend to be labyrinthine and chaotic beyond the imagination of scholars accustomed to the orderly bibliographical habits of the United States. Hours are short, national holidays are frequent, and access often depends upon the cultivation of personal connections. Students of the modern period feel even more acutely, perhaps, than their colonialist colleagues the lack of adequate guides and archival materials, since the well-known traditional preference of Latin American historians, bibliographers, and archivists for colonial and revolutionary topics has seriously hindered the preservation and organization of archival records and the publication of guides to printed or manuscript materials dealing with the modern period. Progress is being made in this direction,[77] but much more remains to be done. It is almost unnecessary to add that students of modern Latin American history would be greatly aided by some acquaintance with the economic history, sociology, anthropology, and geography of the area—qualifications which relatively few of them possess at the present time.

Finally, mention may be made of a traditional ideological obstacle to research in the modern period: the view that the history of the Latin American republics since independence is drab, confused, and pointless by contrast with the glamorous epic of the mighty Spanish empire with its well-defined lines of institutional development. In part this belief reflects the lingering influence of nineteenth-century romanticism, with its stress on exotic themes of a bygone age; in part it stems from a certain aristocratic tra-

[76] See especially Samuel Putnam, *Marvelous Journey: A Survey of Four Centuries of Brazilian Writing* (New York, 1948).

[77] See the valuable work of Roscoe R. Hill, *The National Archives of Latin America* (Cambridge, Mass., 1945).

dition in Latin American historiography—happily now in decline—which views with nostalgia the glories of *La Colonia* and *La Independencia* and turns its back on almost all that has occurred since the death of Bolívar. Fortunately, this belief in the general insignificance of modern Latin American history is rapidly disappearing. In recent decades at least, some Latin American states have begun to grapple vigorously with their problems, as a result of which their history has gained in interest, and intensive investigations have begun to show that the apparent anarchy and futility of much nineteenth-century Latin American history conceal meaningful economic and social conflicts and the stirrings of a new life.

65. History: Needs and Prospects*

Robert N. Burr

The marked ebb of teaching and research interest in the general area of Latin American studies in the United States which was noted in the report of the Conference on Latin American Studies of April 13, 1958, has been typical also of the field of Latin American History. Although the number of university course offerings in Latin American History seems to have increased over the past decade, there appears to have been a decline in enrollments in these courses. Several universities, with either a tradition of work in the field or a hope to give greater emphasis to it at the beginning of the decade, now seem to have dropped the field as one of serious study. More important, graduate work in Latin American History has suffered a decline in its relative importance with respect to other areas of history. A comparison of the doctoral dissertations accepted at American universities in the five-year period 1947–51 with the number accepted in the five-year period 1952–56 reveals that in the earlier period dissertations on Latin American topics made up 10.1 per cent of the total dissertations in history, while in the later period dissertations on Latin American subjects accounted for only 5.6 per cent of the total.

Numerous reasons have been advanced to account for the declining interest in Latin American studies. In addition to those set forth at the ACLS Conference on April 13 and which affect the entire area of Latin American studies, I would like to suggest two other possible reasons for declining interest which derive from the current state of the field of Latin American History.

The first is that the discipline of Latin American History does not appear to have shown its usefulness in contributing to an understanding of contemporary Latin American society and its rôle in the modern world. The second is an apparent failure on the part of the historians of Latin America in the United States to make clear that their

* *Latin American Studies in the United States: Proceedings of a Meeting Held in Chicago, November 6–8, 1958, Sponsored by the American Council of Learned Societies and the Newberry Library (assisted by the Hispanic Foundation)*, edited by Howard F. Cline. Hispanic Foundation, *Survey Reports*, 8: 57–62 (Washington, 1958). Reprinted by permission of the author.

area of study offers real intellectual challenges either within the framework of contemporary historical thinking or in opening up new currents of historical thought. Although there is undoubtedly a relationship between these two conditions, they are not identical. All worthy intellectual challenges do not directly relate to the solution of contemporary problems.

These two conditions, which in my opinion have contributed to a decline of interest in Latin American history, have developed as a result of a variety of interrelated factors, a few of which I mention because they point up certain urgent needs in the field. The first is the fact that until recent years the bulk of historical production has been concerned with the Colonial period or with the movements of independence. Specialists in these periods have pointed out that there remain many major problems to be dealt with. In particular it has been suggested that more attention be paid to various aspects of the American scene in the Colonial period as opposed to the imperial structure, and to the economic and social aspects of the movements for independence.

In spite of the inadequacies of our knowledge about these periods, it is nevertheless true that the major gap in our understanding relates to the period since independence. The work that has been done in this period is for the most part in the areas of political and diplomatic history or biography. With rare exceptions, studies of this period have done little to explore themes important for an understanding of contemporary Latin America—themes such as the growth of nationalism; the impact of technology and science, foreign investment, immigration and other similar factors on the development of Latin America; or the history of ideas and of the social structure in Latin America. Studies such as these would serve not only to link our knowledge of the earlier periods to the contemporary world; they would also bring the Latin American historians into the mainstream of historical thought. Both of these results should tend to increase interest in the field.

This post-independence field has not been explored along the lines indicated above for many reasons. The bewildering political shifts of the area may have led to the opinion that its history was meaningless and turned attention from the interior workings of the society. The emphasis placed upon national history has tended to make historians overlook broader socio-economic forces which have an effect on an international level. Moreover, source materials for the history of the period have been located either in badly organized archives and libraries in Latin America or in private hands where they are inaccessible. Travel to Latin America has been expensive. There has been a lack of adequate guides to both published and unpublished materials relating to the period.

Many historians are aware of these difficulties. Much of what I have said, or will say has already been stated in articles by Griffin, Cline, Burgin, Gibson, Keen and others. Moreover, historians have already taken steps to expand our knowledge of the period. A number of younger historians are now working intensively in the history of the national period. The *Hispanic American Historical Review* is planning to publish a series of historiographical articles on the period since 1830 which should give us some idea of what has been done and what needs to be done. The Editorial Board of the *HAHR*, the Hispanic Foundation, and Professor R. Humphrey of London, have been discussing the possibilities of several new guides, the most important of which would be a General Guide to the Historical Literature of Latin America along the lines of the *Harvard Guide to United States History*. Yet the number of scholars working in the field is relatively small and the job is to take an inventory of what has been done up to now, then to select the areas which most urgently need further exploration, and to find ways of stimulating research and writing.

The first step, in my opinion, should be the preparation of the Guide to historical literature mentioned above, which in addition to strictly historical materials would also include contributions of other disciplines which are so important to understanding Latin America's past. Other steps which might be taken are the following: (1) the preparation of an analysis of the historiography of Europe and the United States with the dual purpose of (a) discovering significant approaches employed in those fields which might profitably be employed in the Latin American area and (b) of evaluating the contributions of Latin American historians to the general historiographical movement; (2) the preparation of a volume of essays which might be called "New Viewpoints in Latin American History," the purpose of which would be to stimulate research in unexplored areas of Latin American history. Included would be several significant articles already published along with specially prepared articles suggesting new approaches; (3) the preparation of selected bibliographies on a topical as opposed to national basis, with the aim of

stimulating comparative studies in the national period and (4) examination of the possibility of preparing an Abstract of Historical Statistics on Latin America which would throw into relief quantitative changes which have taken place over periods of time and provide bibliographical information as to sources of more detailed information.

Finally, because these suggestions would obviously involve cooperative action, both among historians and on an interdisciplinary level, I would second the recommendation of the Conference of April 13 concerning the need for the establishment of a Joint Committee on Research and Training in the United States on Latin America. In addition I would suggest that a permanent subcommittee of historians be formed to work in cooperation with the proposed Joint Committee.

66. The Tasks Ahead for Latin American Historians*

STANLEY J. STEIN

1

Latin America stands today at a watershed in its history, comparable to the year in which it began its anticolonial struggle, or to the revolutionary years 1889 to 1891, or to that *annus terribilis*, 1930. The degree of tension throughout Latin America, to use a recent observation in the *New Statesman*, suggests that the "time is coming when its peoples will step onto the world stage in their own right, and play the massive part to which their economic wealth entitles them." Despite the long period in which the area has enjoyed political independence, tension is everywhere and its forms are

many. In Mexico it is evident in the heated discussion over what constitutes "judicious Leftism"; in Colombia it is the fragile nationalized stalemate of the National Front; in Venezuela it is seen in the snail's pace of reform and the creeping insolvency of an oil-rich country; since Perón's overthrow it is etched in the widespread pessimism and cynicism of Argentina; and, it has reached a peak in the Cubans' decision to cast off

* *HAHR*, 41: 424–433 (Aug. 1961). Reprinted by permission of the author and the original publisher. This paper was read at the luncheon session of the Conference on Latin American History of the American Historical Association, December, 1960.

from the past and embark upon uncharted seas.

The novelty of the Cuban case derives not as much from the elements that have made it explosive as from the combination of all the elements found scattered throughout Latin America. It has long been assumed that the major problems of Latin America would be solved somehow by evolutionary methods; but Cuba's instability suggests that this assumption is erroneous. The historian's task is not to perpetuate error but to enlighten, and it is clear that what brought Cuba to its present situation, mal-distribution and under-utilization of land and other natural resources, economic nationalism, the inadequacy of parliamentary government to solve effectively and demonstrably the principal national problems—in sum, the juxtaposition of traditional and ultra-modern institutions, needs re-examination. The analysis of these and related themes constitutes the tasks ahead for the Latin American historian everywhere.

2

Ever since West Europeans came to Latin America, the dominant feature of Latin America's culture and society has been the large landed estate and its labor force. This has been recognized but superficially studied. For the early colonial period there exist literally only a handful of studies and these focus largely on Mexico. For the era since the middle of the seventeenth century, and in particular since independence, there are equally few studies. Again, most of these concern Mexico and with few exceptions are legalistic in approach. During the 1920's and 1930's a number of publications seemed to indicate sustained interest in agrarian history; it is no exaggeration to state that the postwar emphasis upon industrialization and the interrelated problems of international trade, balance of payments, and capacity-to-import have diverted attention from the land. For the republics of Latin America there is no documented synthetic view such as that prepared by Marc Bloch for France thirty years ago.

Despite the absence of detailed studies, a model or highly generalized pattern of Latin American agrarian history is possible, at least for heuristic purposes. By the middle of the eighteenth century, the basic agricultural unit was the estate worked by peons bound by debt, or by chattel slaves. In the last decades of the colonial era, population growth and improved communications both within the colonial world and with metropolitan centers led to intensified land utilization, the opening of new zones, and the expansion of old and new crops. Rising volume of output of cotton and sugar in Brazil and Mexico, sugar in Cuba, Chilean wheat, Argentine hides and tallow, were a response to the expansion of both domestic and foreign markets. The era of independence and the decades of adjustment that followed down to about 1850 caused apparent reduction of the rate of growth. It was the era of the international division of labor in the eighty years after 1850, closing with the Great Depression of 1929, that saw the heyday of the Latin American landed estate. The basis of these prosperous years was the reciprocal relationship between an area producing primary materials and the industrializing North Atlantic basin which furnished capital, and capital and consumer goods in return. In this fashion capitalism came to an essentially agrarian Latin America, and in almost every area it occurred while colonial or neo-colonial institutions and attitudes were still vigorous. Only in Mexico after 1910 did a violent reaction to the prevailing system of land tenure and land utilization occur.

From the examination of this simplified "construct" a number of questions are derived. In the first place, was there a causal relationship between the expansion of agriculture at the close of the colonial era and pressures to eliminate the controls of the Spanish and Portuguese colonial system on the one hand, and on the other, the outbreak of the anti-colonial wars? Where small holdings appeared on the periphery of large estates (ranchos in the Mexican *Bajío*, grain farmers on the outskirts of Buenos Aires) or where estate owners encroached upon the lands of nearby communities in Indo-

America, did the small proprietors join the anticolonial movement because of land hunger? To pursue this line of reasoning, perhaps the conflict between estate owners and small proprietors may explain the attempts found sporadically throughout Latin America in the 1820's and 1830's to eliminate the entailed estate, to turn communal holdings into small free holds, and to dispose of large blocks of public lands in small sections, often to imported colonists. Land as a factor in Liberal-Conservative factionalism of these decades has yet to be fully explored.

Until the diffusion of industrialism to Latin America, the major channel of modernization in this area particularly after about 1850 was the nexus between landed estate and European or North American markets, or the large cities of Latin America. Put in other terms, was the landed estate an effective instrument for transforming traditional society in rural areas into a more modern society and culture? It would appear that in areas where production was geared to domestic consumption as in the highlands of Peru and Bolivia, on the Mexican plateau, or in the central valley of Chile, the large estate perpetuated landlordism and peonage, or what Latin Americans tend to term "semi-feudalism." It may be argued that where estates produced for an overseas market—for instance, the Brazilian coffee or Cuban sugar plantation—slavery was indeed perpetuated. Yet after abolition these areas, plus Argentina, developed perhaps the most capitalistic agriculture in Latin America—Argentina and Brazil with the aid of European immigrants. Perhaps a factor to be considered is that in areas of export agriculture, the merchants who acted as commission agents and ultimately as bankers gradually acquired ownership of large estates and tended to apply capitalistic incentive, innovation, and careful bookkeeping practices. Or, is it more accurate to assume that massive foreign investment in agriculture as in the Cuban *central*, the Brazilian coffee *fazenda*, or the Argentine *estancia* brought capitalistic policies and attitudes? Not without significance is the fact that the two most powerful social movements of modern Latin America were the Mexican Revolution and Peruvian Aprism, both of which proposed to make the hacienda productive by eliminating peonage and introducing rational for traditional modes of operation. Recent analyses of Mexico's agrarian reform indicate that capitalistic rather than collectivistic utilization of the land has been the end product, along with the creation of an ever-growing internal market and a source of cheap, mobile labor for a capitalistic industry.

Finally, historians have yet to assess the impact of the landed estate upon industrialization, hastening or retarding it. By controlling the banking systems to obtain mortgage loans, by preventing land taxation or keeping such taxes ridiculously low, by employing income from the land in nonproductive channels or investing in overseas enterprises, did estate owners through their rural associations force governments to depend upon customs duties? This has been offered as one reason for inadequate tariff protection for infant industry until recent decades. On the other hand, it may well be that the development of export agriculture in Cuba, Argentina, and Brazil created the basic preconditions of industrialism, that is, social overhead capital in the form of railroads, highways, portworks, and communications systems. On balance, then, the historian may well ask whether the agrarian history of Latin America since 1750 is merely the extended transition from subsistence to capitalistic agriculture, from debt bondage or chattel slavery to salaried rural worker, without substantial improvement of rural living conditions. Fleeing the land, the rural dweller has moved toward the city and the attraction of wage labor and personal liberty in industrial and service employment.

3

The migration of rural population to towns and cities, or what we call the rural exodus, is no novelty in the history of Latin America. It was evident in the immediate post-conquest years and in the appearance of mining camps and commercial and bureaucratic nuclei during the colonial era. Towns and cities were modernizing centers amid the imperceptibly changing traditional culture of the rural countryside. In the variety of employment offered, in wages and salaries, and in the opportunity of anonymity, personal liberty, and social mobility could and can still be found in the magnetism of the city.

For the study of industrial growth in Latin America, the importance of urban development lies in the multiple economic enterprises and employment found there. It is in the cities of late colonial and neo-colonial Latin America, 1750–1850 or thereabouts, that the roots of contemporary economic nationalism are probably to be found. In the last decades of the colonial period, local demand as well as the wider inter-colonial market created an incipient industrial complex of sheep-farming, cattle-raising, and cotton production, woolen and cotton manufacture, and the processing of iron and leather. In the Iberian colonial world there developed regional specialization of production as well as nuclei of distribution. The Mexican Bajío and the Argentine northwest or interior provinces are but two examples of this type of complex. Simultaneously, pressure appeared for intercolonial trade and then for trade outside the colonial world. The long-smouldering conflict between incipient industrializing sectors and mercantile interests flared up in the early decades of independence in the controversy over free trade versus protection.

Historians have until recently neglected the field of urbanization, economic growth, regional specialization, and free trade as factors not only in the revolution against the Iberian colonial system but also in the centralist-federalist conflicts that furnish the major theme of Latin American political history until the middle of the nineteenth century. The concept of economic nationalism, the desire to reduce the economic dependence of one region or area upon another to provide full employment of human and natural resources, is dimly visible in Argentina, Mexico, Chile, and Brazil in the century following 1750. Economic nationalism may explain the measures of early republi-

can regimes to foment industry through exemptions of import duties on capital equipment, tax exemptions, and subsidization of technically trained personnel. And we have yet to explore why these efforts were premature—the role of imports of British manufactures and local merchant oligarchs in industrial failures, and the contribution of the early protectionist controversy to later economic nationalism.

One may concede that the study of Latin American economic nationalism before 1880 is a form of antiquarianism and that subsequent widespread and intensive commitment of the nations of this area to the international division of labor, to economic specialization, and to the uninhibited acceptance of foreign developmental capital only proves this. It is a mistake, however, to entertain the hypothesis that economic nationalism and the drive toward industrialism can be adequately studied only in the period of the past thirty years. To do so would overlook an explanation of the generalized intensity of economic nationalism throughout Latin America today.

Recent exploratory monographs suggest that economic nationalism was a factor in the tariff controversies in several Latin American countries during the 1870's, 1880's, and 1890's. More to the point are indications that economic nationalism, i.e., a reaction to the international division of labor and to the role of foreign capital, was a common theme in Brazil, Argentina, and Chile between 1889 and 1891—not to mention the now classic example of the Mexican Revolution. Why this phase of economic nationalism did not produce a sustained drive toward economic diversification through industrialism may find an explanation in the rise in output as well as the material gains from the high rate of foreign investment between 1890 and 1930 in agriculture, mining, and related transport facilities, and in particular, in the spectacular flow of United States capital, technology, and technicians, first to the Caribbean basin and later to South America.

It is no exaggeration to state that one of the principal features of Latin American history in the twentieth century has been the influence of the United States, especially "corporate" United States. It is inseparable from analysis of economic nationalism. Yet historians have so far failed to provide either a balance-sheet of the role of United States investment, portfolio and direct, or—what is perhaps more essential—the Latin American "image" of the multi-national United States corporation. To be sure, the volumes published in the 1920's under the editorship of Harry Elmer Barnes and built around the theme of American imperialism furnished at best an interim assessment. The Good Neighbor Era and post-war developments seem to have diminished interest in this theme of historical study.

A list of questions that Latin American historians may pose with respect to the role of the United States in Latin America is readily prepared, but three general formulations seem the most important at this juncture. In the first place, did the United States corporation in Latin America modify its philosophy and labor-management relations to the extent that it did so in the United States after 1933? Next, is the attack upon what are considered the shortcomings of United States corporations operating in Latin America traceable to the belief of United States investors and management that United States contributions to economic growth through portfolio or direct investments in agriculture, mining, utilities, and recently, industry, would automatically modernize predominantly traditional cultures? Or—and this is my third question—has economic nationalism in Latin America been directed against the United States corporation as part of the reaction against the monopolistic or oligopolistic structure and practices of Latin American industry?

It would seem logical to assume that economic nationalism would diminish as Latin American nations developed the industrial sector of their economies, most notably in Mexico, Brazil, and Argentina, where direct investments by United States industrial corporations have been considerable since 1945. What seems to lie at the heart of this problem is the role of the state in economic growth, a field historians have notoriously neglected. Whether the state has been the most decisive factor in the past three decades of economic growth is debatable; what seems beyond question is that the state has stimulated economic activity at various points, if not at all simultaneously: by the creation of a capital goods industry, oil refineries, chemical plants, power, transport, and protective tariffs. In Cuba's case, a combination of state intervention and foreign and domestic investment forged perhaps one of the most efficient sugar producing areas in the world. That the state threw its resources behind economic growth after 1930 grew out of the public mandate that the state maintain and expand the national economy providing full employment and a stable or rising level of real wages. The public expected a dividend which either has not materialized or has not matched the rising level of aspirations, and it has pressured the state to intervene for higher wages, social security benefits, and stable prices.

Traditionally, Latin American business has insisted upon laissez faire at this point, and Latin American businessmen since 1945 have pointed to the role of laissez faire in creating and maintaining the United States economy. Their arguments have been buttressed by United States public and private emphasis upon neoclassical economic liberalism in dealing with foreign governments. Here the historian has an excellent opportunity for research on the evolution of industrial enterprise in Latin America, and its attitude toward labor, consumers and government. In this process the historian may also cast light upon the goals of economic nationalism, collectivism or socialism, or merely a more effective capitalism that rejects a revived social Darwinism or neopositivism. He should also try to explain why economic nationalism, and industrialism, or excessive specialization have failed as signally as the landed estate to narrow the chasm between the living standards of the elite and the mass, between capital cities and the countryside, and between traditional and ultramodern sectors of Latin America.

4

This analysis of certain essential factors of Latin American history, namely selected economic features, suggests that the process of change, the spread of a modern culture throughout a traditional one, has been surprisingly slow there. In the century and a half since independence, this area has had only two major social upheavals, the Mexican Revolution and the as-yet-unfinished Cuban Revolution. It is no hasty judgment, then, for the Latin American historian to conclude that effective change has come by working outside democratic, parliamentary institutions, that is, by revolution. He may also conclude that the detailed study of Conservatism is far from fruitless dedication to lost causes, and is indeed a long overdue antidote to Liberal literature. Liberals may have won debates over anachronistic institutions, but the Conservatives have consistently gathered the spoils of battle.

As children of our times, we historians have searched so eagerly for the outcrops of change that we have ignored the hard bedrock of Latin American political history, theory, and practice. Since independence this bedrock has been the control of politics by an elite which had to accept a republic but was never committed to a democracy. The Conservative tradition has been far from pathological; it has shown extraordinary vitality. But despite the role of Conservatism in Latin American political history, scholarly studies of Conservatism are notable by their absence. Aside from unsubstantiated generalizations, we know little of sources of recruitment of its leadership or of its flexibility in adapting to changing times. It is assumed that its core consisted of landlords and Roman Catholic churchmen in the decades before 1850, but did it include that other important sector of neo-colonial society, the mercantile community? As for the other block of Conservative support, the Roman Catholic clergy, during the anticolonial struggle and through the neo-colonial decades of the nineteenth century, a highly vocal segment of Catholic clergymen opposed the Conservatives.

There is a curious coincidence between the peak of the Liberal anticlerical cycle in the latter half of the nineteenth century and the superficially monolithic adherence of the clergy to the Conservative tradition. Perhaps even more curious and still unexplored, is the gradual shift of one-time Liberals into the Conservative camp once the clerical issue was resolved. It can be argued that Conservatism displayed remarkable plasticity in providing a congenial home for the parvenus among the elite—financiers, corporation executives, miners, bureaucrats—who became prominent between 1880 and 1930 and whose earlier allegiance, we may assume, was probably given to Liberalism. The compromise or conciliation of apparently bitterly partisan groups is one of the main features of the political landscape of Latin America of the past eighty years. In short, was the magnetism of western Liberalism as molded to Latin American conditions the promise of economic liberty and a secular and stable society, rather than massive modernization of a society that was not "born free" at the close of the anticolonial struggle? The Conservative-Liberal fusion implies that Liberals accepted one of the major tenets of Conservatism, namely "authoritarian," "directed," "caesaristic" democracy, that is, government by the elite; it implies too that Liberals as well as Conservatives were unprepared to cope with the novel, indeed revolutionary feature of Latin American political life in the twentieth century, the participation of the masses in the political process.

Periodization of historical development, weaving together the distinguishing strands of an era to establish form and structure, is one of the basic tools of the historian's craft. To this point the term neocolonial has been used without adequate clarification. It has been implicit that neocolonial institutions dominated Latin America until the close of the last century and that they have eroded rapidly in the twentieth. The year 1930 may turn out to be a major indicator to historians of the degree of erosion. Almost everywhere in Latin America after 1930 parties of mass rather than minority appeal and participation have revolutionized political life. This phenomenon poses a number of problems for the historian. Does it reflect merely the efficiency of public health services which have reduced mortality rates and stimulated high rates of population growth? Or does it demonstrate the formation of integrated national communications systems? How can the historian classify movements whose common ideological fundament consists of anti-imperialism, nationalism, state intervention, capitalism, and mass political participation, and which in at least three cases —Argentina, Brazil, and Venezuela— clearly achieved political control by rejecting parliamentary procedures for revolutionary ones? The Cuban Revolution with its frank abandonment of political evolutionism for revolution, and its equally frank appeal to the peasantry and rejection of the middle class, suggests to historians that a revolutionary cycle already three decades old has reached its apogee. Or, on the contrary, will future historical investigation indicate that the cycle begun in 1930 merely sought more rapid modernization under capitalist auspices and that the modernization of Cuba since 1959 under social "humanism" has inaugurated a new cycle in the evolution of Latin America?

5

By concluding this lengthy statement, a word about methodology is in order. For too long we Latin American historians have focused upon major developments—a majority of them political phenomena. The utility of these studies is not questioned, but they should be supplemented by studies based upon two criteria: (1) can a major theme be approached through the examination in depth of a key aspect and, (2) can the battery of techniques developed in the social sciences be brought to bear for optimum results. The precepts of the "New History," the interdisciplinary method that ethnohistorians promise to use effectively, seemed on the way to wide application for a short period after the last war, particularly in the field of community and regional studies. Regrettably this interest has waned. The field of Latin American history requires careful study of haciendas and communities, banks and industrial corporations, specific interest groups and their aggregation in political parties in each country and over extended periods of time. Only in this fashion will the broad generalizations be tested, refined, and recast. Moreover, since fellow historians in Latin America and elsewhere share increasingly mutual interests, we Latin American historians in the United States should strive for closer, sustained contact with them. The community of scholars is, after all, an international one.

No doubt it will be charged that in this approach Latin American history has been forced into the Procrustean bed of generalization and hypothesis. I would be the first to admit this. But I can take some consolation in the thought that history thrives on controversy, and in the hope that a somewhat unorthodox probing of the commonplace may be useful.

67. Research Opportunities: Mexico and Central America*

Robert A. Naylor

If by opportunity we mean "a favorable juncture of circumstances" then the picture which emerges is not exactly propitious. The Latin American Conference held this year in Los Angeles reflected the concern about the post World War II decline of interest in Latin America and the prevailing indifference of students, the public, and many academic institutions toward Latin America, past and present.[1] Contributing to this general apathy were both the general cultural orientation of the United States and Latin America toward Europe, and the general shift of American emphasis after 1945 to "crisis areas" which reduced Latin America to a minor position since it appeared to be neither threatened nor threatening in the polarized world. (In this respect, Castro remains our greatest benefactor.) Futhermore, the more obvious availability of funds, both public and private, for studies of these "crisis areas" tended to confirm the seeming unimportance of Latin America. The failure to attract the needed personnel, recognition, and support, coupled with the dissipation of current resources for the study of Latin America in the United States have, with few exceptions, prevented Latin American programs from developing momentum and visibility.[2]

When the special problems of the Latin Americanist are considered in the larger academic context of mushrooming college enrollment, heavier teaching loads, sagging standards, efforts to supplement low salaries, less time for research and a deteriorating intellectual climate in which to conduct it, the difficulties increase. Finally, the mounting pressure to "publish or perish" in order to secure professional advancement has a tendency to lure scholars into reappraisals and revisions of the safe and the familiar.[3] There is little incentive among Latin American-ists to turn out the needed specialized monographs as long as they can look forward only to having them mimeographed and circulated among themselves for mutual elucidation. The demand of publishers for broad, interpretative studies indicates an unrealistic desire to build the house without making the bricks.[4]

* *Americas*, 18: 352–365 (Mar. 1962). Reprinted by permission of the author and the original publisher. This paper, as well as the following two, was presented at the twenty-seventh annual meeting of the Southern Historical Association held at Chattanooga, Tennessee, November 9–11, 1961.

[1] Summary of Discussion, Conference on the Status of Latin American Studies in the United States, February 9 and 10, 1961, UCLA, Los Angeles, California, sponsored by the University of California at Los Angeles, and by the Council on Higher Education in the American Republics (CHEAR).

[2] A notable exception would be the Inter-American program centered at the University of Florida which maintains a good undergraduate and graduate Latin American program, sponsors the Annual Conference on the Caribbean—the one held in December, 1961, dealt with the Central American area—publishes a monographic series, and houses the new multi-lingual *Journal of Inter-American Studies*.

[3] Since writing this observation I noticed a similar appraisal by Frank Knapp in his review of the historical literature of nineteenth and twentieth century Mexico in the 1960 issue of the *Handbook of Latin American Studies*: "In choice of subject matter, there appears to be a preference among historians to retrace old steps already well travelled without adding new facts or interpretation, and a concomitant reluctance to explore the many rich fields open for pioneer research in the nineteenth and twentieth centuries."

[4] Although this attitude can be understood for commercial publishers, it is less appropriate for the university presses that often receive financial assistance for scholarly publications. This attitude is evident in correspondence with the University of North Carolina Press when it rejected a specialized study on the grounds that although "excellent in concept and execution" it was "quite narrow in

If, however, one transcends the immediate mundane circumstances and approaches the problem on a more Platonic level as a seeker after historical truth, then one is confronted with horizons unlimited. The consensus of professional opinion among scholars in the Mexican and Central American fields is that for the nineteenth and twentieth centuries the field is virtually wide open, with very few segments of it developed beyond the rudimentary stages. Bibliographically there exists a vast amount of material for modern Mexico and a considerable number of works on Central America, as attested by the recent articles by Robert Potash of the University of Massachusetts and William J. Griffith of Tulane.[5] When the mass is sifted carefully, however, the residue reveals few studies which meet even modest historical standards. With the partial exception of Daniel Cosío Villegas, there was little quarrel with the views expressed by Howard Cline that in very general terms all social history, all economic history, and most of political and intellectual history remain to be written on nineteeenth and twentieth century Mexico.[6] With the exception of the monumental contribution of the Cosío group on the Restored Republic and the Porfirian period, no substantial studies based on documents, apart from those found in United States repositories, have been done. With the partial exception of United States-Mexican relations, the field of international affairs remains wide open. No suitable history of any sort exists of the Church, and the military is virtually blank except for a few minor memoirs. With

few exceptions no useful biography has yet been done of any major figure that would meet current professional standards. With regard to the Central American area no one would deny the broad generalization of William Griffith that practically the whole field is wide open for research at almost any point any one wants to begin.[7]

The analysis by Stanley Stein in his paper on "The Tasks Ahead for Latin American Historians" is certainly relevant to Mexico and Central America.[8] The economic problems pinpointed and the questions posed with regard to what he terms "the juxta-

scope and, while it undoubtedly contains information about its subject which is not elsewhere available, it does not, I am afraid, have that wider significance that we must now look for. . . . You see that what the readers want is a widened scope." Howard R. Webber to Naylor, Chapel Hill, October 9, 1961. A similar attitude exists on the part of Duke University Press: "Our own experience with several titles in a similar vein has proved that the market for such books is a limited one at best." Ashbel G. Brice to Naylor, Durham, August 18, 1961. Yet the said study, "British Commercial Relations with Central America, 1821–1851," would seem from the forthcoming discussion to be of the type that most scholars in the field are advocating.

[5] Robert A. Potash, "Historiography of Mexico Since 1821," *HAHR*, XL (August, 1960), 383–424. William J. Griffith, "The Historiography of Central America Since 1830," *HAHR*, XL (November, 1960), 548–569.

[6] Daniel Cosío Villegas of the Colegio de México would take exception to the above generalizations. He believes that the study made by his group on the period of the Restored Republic and the Díaz era, 1867–1910, and their present investigation of the contemporary period 1911–1950 goes a long way toward filling this gap. He indicates, furthermore, that there are many works, albeit partisan, already done in these areas. He admits, however, that numerous specific studies remain to be written. I expect all of us would agree that the Cosío volumes constitute a major and monumental contribution to Mexican history, both in the quality of scholarship applied and in the broad scope of the undertaking. But even the Cosío volumes, substantial as they are, are not definitive in the sense that they contain exhaustive analysis of the topics treated. Potash, while strongly commending the Cosío study, points out, for example, that the volumes rest heavily on contemporary newspapers and public documents, and that there are bodies of archival material in manuscript form that could not be employed because of their uncatalogued, disordered state. These materials, Potash believes, could provide the basis for interesting studies in the field of administrative and economic history which might alter to some extent the views presented in the Cosío series.

[7] The following, some with slight reservations, concur with Cline's generalization on modern Mexico: Charles Cumberland, Charles Hale, C. Harvey Gardiner, Alfred Jackson Hanna, Paul Murray, David Pletcher, Robert Potash, Stanley Stein, Alfred Tischendorf, Stanley Ross, A. W. Bork, David Waddell, and R. A. Humphreys. Franklin D. Parker and Gordon Kenyon concur absolutely with Griffith's statement.

[8] *HAHR*, XLI (August, 1961), 424–434.

position of traditional and ultramodern institutions" point the way to a variety of themes that could profitably be investigated in the fields of modern Mexican and Central American history. The general impression that emerges from my discussions with prominent scholars in these fields is that we are in dire need of a thorough analysis of nineteenth and twentieth century economic developments, and more importantly the economic and social thought behind these developments. Although this need is in part being met for Mexico by the efforts of Calderón in the Cosío series, nothing of this sort has been attempted in the Central American field.[9]

Charles Cumberland at Michigan State and Charles Hale at Lehigh agree that the crying need for nineteenth-century Mexico is a sophisticated study of the hacienda as an institution. They suggest that Frank Tannenbaum's assertion that the hacienda was the predominant institution in nineteenth-century Latin America might not hold true. Despite general evaluations of the hacienda in innumerable accounts, the fact that no historian really has any sound information of the social, political, and economic, not to mention religious, functions performed by the hacienda. Such a study properly done, Hale and Cumberland propose, should shed considerable light on regionalism and political instabilty, to say nothing of society in general. Cumberland further insists that a good study of what the ejidos have meant in the twentieth century is overdue. Most of the material on twentieth century agricultural development, he charges, has been "glandular nonsense" and that we are all guilty somewhat of stating hypotheses as if they were established facts.

An institution requiring similar investigation is the Church. Stanley Ross at the University of Nebraska cites especially the need to bring judicious scholarly judgment to bear on the emotion-packed area of Church-State relations. Cumberland agrees with this emphasis but remains doubtful about the "opportunities" in this area because of the unavailability of pertinent materials.[10] Robert Potash holds that it is for the period 1821–1857 and since 1917 that studies of the Mexican Church are urgently needed. He cites two studies, as yet unpublished, made by Karl Schmitt and Robert Quirk on the Church in the Díaz and early revolutionary periods as an indication of what can be done. Charles Hale insists that specifically we must learn more of the economic status and power of the Church in the nineteenth century. The need for comprehensive studies of institutions like the hacienda and the Church are even more pressing for Central America, where even less has been done.[11]

Another challenging subject in the economic sphere is that of foreign economic penetration into Mexico and Central America. David Pletcher at Hamline University praises Alfred Tischendorf's recently published study of British capital in Mexico during the Díaz period but believes that British capital was less important than that from the United States—a field that still requires considerable work.[12] Cosío concurs that a

[9] Daniel Cosío Villegas (ed.), *Historia moderna de México. La república restaurada.* Tomo II, *La vida económica* by Francisco R. Calderón (Mexico, 1955). Potash remarks that this well-documented volume has the distinction of being the first comprehensive study of the economic life of a significant period of Mexican history, and that another volume is projected in this series to carry the economic study through the Porfiran era.

[10] Cumberland claims that he has been through all the available documentation in the Archivo de Historia in Defensa Nacional, the Archivo Nacional, and the National Archives dealing with the Church-State conflict in the early twentieth century without finding the kind of evidence he would like to have to substantiate some of the charges made by both sides. This evidence, he suspects, will be hard to come by since he cannot exactly picture the Church archives being thrown open to a historian trying to determine whether anti-clericalism was justified.

[11] A beginning has been made with Mary Holleran, *Church and State in Guatemala* (New York, 1949). Although not meant to be definitive, this well-documented study presents the main problems of Church-State relations during the administrations of Morazan, Carrera, and Barrios.

[12] Alfred P. Tischendorf, *Great Britain and Mexico in the Era of Porfirio Díaz* (Duke University Press, 1961). David Pletcher is the author of the prize-winning study of *Rails, Mines, and*

solid study of foreign investments during the Díaz era is still needed. Most of the original materials he claims are in the United States, but English, French, German, and Swiss sources would have to be consulted also. Pletcher and Cosío agree that even if the subject were limited to American investments, it would still be worthwhile. Unfortunately, neither Pletcher nor Tischendorf are now working in Mexican history.[13] Except for rudimentary beginnings, little effort has been expended investigating foreign economic penetration of Central America.[14]

Research possibilities arise also with regard to the labor movement and the role and ideology of both Marxism and Communism, as well as to the economic problems surrounding transportation and communication, trade, finance, and irrigation, both in Mexico and Central America. Schneider's book and Bernstein's article on Communism point the way into this tangled area.[15] Hale points to Stanley Stein's study, now underway, of the merchants before and after the War for Independence, and to Potash's excellent study of the Banco de Avío as indications of what could emerge from further research in the specifics of economic history.[16]

In the fields of social history, developments in Mexico and Central America remain virtually untouched except for the volumes in the Cosío series.[17] In this forsaken area Hale draws attention to the whole problem of the structure of nineteenth-century society as being of particular significance. The Indian and his status after independence could be investigated profitably following the pioneer efforts of González Navarro.[18] Hale believes that Cline's excellent, and as yet unpublished, work on the Mexican Caste Wars of 1847 could well be extended to the outbreaks in the Huasteca region at the same time. Hale suggests that historians might be attracted to the purely historical side of recent anthropological community studies— if source material could be found.[19] He mentions also that a study of the expulsion of

the Spanish might serve as an indication of the attitude of independent Mexico and Central America toward their Spanish heritage.

Although stressing the needs in the social

[13] Pletcher reports that in recent years he has been moving from Latin American history into U. S. foreign relations. Walter Scholes is another, formerly working on foreign influences in Mexico in the 1850's and 1860's, who has shifted his interest to American diplomacy in the twentieth century. Tischendorf writes that although he became interested in British activities in Mexico some time ago, his interests are now in countries other than Mexico. Currently, he is enmeshed in Argentine and Colombian bibliography.

[14] With the exception of passing references in the Isthmian canal studies, and the somewhat dated works of Chester Lloyd Jones of United States interests in Central America, the question of the role of foreign enterprise has been neglected. Brief economic surveys like Valentín Solórzano, *Historia de la evolución económica de Guatemala* (Mexico, 1947) barely touch the subject, and pioneer studies have been generally limited to works like William J. Griffith, *Santo Tomas: Anhelado emporio de comercio en el Atlántico* (Guatemala, 1959); the article by Robert A. Naylor on "The Mahogany Trade as a Factor in British Expansion in the Bay of Honduras" and the latter's investigation of "British Commercial Relations With Central America, 1821–1851," both of which remain unpublished. Although the United Fruit Company has long been a popular target of writers, no penetrating historical analyses have yet appeared.

[15] Ronald M. Schneider, *Communism in Guatemala, 1944–1954* (New York, 1958) is regarded as a major and exemplary study, whereas the brief article by Harry Bernstein, "Marxismo en México, 1917–1925," *Historia Mexicana* (abril-junio, 1958), pp. 497–516, is a mere introduction, of interest partly because the author points out the difficulty of securing source material.

[16] Robert A. Potash, *El banco de avío de México. El fomento de la industria, 1821–1846* (Mexico, 1959).

[17] Daniel Cosío Villegas (ed.), *Historia moderna de México. La república restaurada*. Tomo III, *La vida social* by Luís González (Mexico, 1956); and *Historia moderna de México. El Porfiriato*. Tomo IV, *La vida social* by Moisés González Navarro (Mexico, 1957).

[18] M. González Navarro, "Mexico independiente," *Métodos y resultados de la política indigenista en México* (Mexico, 1954).

[19] He refers specifically to Oscar Lewis' successful effort to give his study of Tepoztlan historical depth. Oscar Lewis, *Life in a Mexican Village. Tepoztlan Restudied* (Urbana, Ill., 1951).

Progress: Seven American Promoters in Mexico, 1867–1911 (Ithaca, 1958). His book is a major contribution to the study of the role of foreign entrepreneurs in late nineteenth-century Mexico.

and economic fields, most of the men consulted were aware of a continuing need for a variety of political studies. Despite the traditional political emphasis little has been accomplished beyond distorting past events to justify present policies. Hale, Ross, and Cline agree that regionalism as a force and factor in Mexico's independent existence in the nineteenth century is certainly a fruitful area for investigation. Local institutions such as a municipal government should be afforded more attention. If local government is universally weak in Latin America today, and if it apparently flourished during the Revolutionary period, Hale asks what accounts for its decline? Cosío cites a need for a study of factional politics, during the Restored Republic, especially at the local levels, in order to test his hypothesis that Mexico was then a true democracy. The material for such a study does exist, he adds, although only or largely in Mexico. Cumberland, Potash, and Ross concur that the changing role of the military in politics over the past hundred years would be another area of fruitful investigation. Regionalism, political factionalism, and the military are themes which are especially appropriate for Central America, where additional scholarly works are needed along both the general and specific lines laid out by Thomas Karnes, Joaquín Chamorro, and Tobar Cruz.[20]

Efforts could well be expended on the development of the nineteenth-century liberal movement both in Mexico and Central America. Ross states that scholarly biographical, intellectual, and political appraisals in this area remain scanty despite the increasing availability of Mexican materials.[21] Indicative of what can be accomplished in the field of Mexican liberalism are Hutchinson's unpublished manuscript on Gómez Farías, Harry Bernstein's forthcoming book on Matías Romero, Leopoldo Zea's provocative intellectual analysis, and Reyes Heroles' philosophical treatise on the struggle between Mexican liberalism and conservatism.[22]

Hale and Paul Murray agree that further efforts must be made to reassess both liberalism and conservatism, especially the intellectual framework. They argue that perhaps continuity may be a more important theme in recent Mexican history than has been recognized and that possibly conservatism played a more constructive role than is usually indicated. Laissez-faire liberalism of the nineteenth century may have been an aberration from the conservative tradition of state intervention beginning in colonial times, reappearing with the nationalization of Church properties, the Banco de Avío, and the consolidation of power under Díaz, and finally completed with the state as the

[20] Thomas Karnes, *The Failure of Union: Central America, 1824–1960* (Chapel Hill, 1961); Pedro Joaquín Chamorro, *Historia de la Federación de la América Central, 1823–1840* (Madrid, 1951); Pedro Tobar Cruz, *Los montañeses* (Guatemala, 1958). The latter study, although displaying a Liberal bias, does a reasonable job, based on extensive use of materials in the Archivo Nacional and the Biblioteca Nacional, with the Galvez reforms, 1831–1840, and the Carrera upheaval. In Mexican history a good introduction and background to a study of nineteenth century federalism is Nettie Lee Benson, *La diputación provincial y el federalismo mexicano* (Mexico, 1955), and a well-documented, lucid analysis of factional politics is Walter V. Scholes, *Mexican Politics during the Juarez Regime, 1855–1872* (Colombia, 1957).

[21] Ross states that here has been considerable material made more readily available by the publications in Mexico resulting from the centennial celebration of the Constitution of 1857. He urges, however, that a study of liberalism will necessitate that a real effort be made to preserve and organize the mass of nineteenth-century documentation housed in the Casa Amarilla in Mexico.

[22] C. A. Hutchinson, "Valentín Gómez Farías and the Secret Pact of New Orleans," *HAHR*, XXXVI (1956), 471–489, affords an introduction to his subject, and Harry Bernstein's *Modern and Contemporary Latin America* (New York, 1952) is indicative of the high quality work of this author. Leopoldo Zea, *Del liberalismo a la revolución en la educación mexicana* (Mexico, 1956) offers a sound analysis of the intellectual and political development surrounding the clash of liberal and conservative ideas in the nineteenth century. Jesús Reyes Heroles, *El liberalismo mexicano*; 2 vols. (Mexico, 1957–1958) is considered by Potash as the most impressive study of nineteenth-century liberal ideology in Mexico, but Hale charges that the work is too concerned with discrediting conservatism. Potash has some interesting comments on studies of Mexican liberalism in his bibliographical article. *Supra*, note 5.

agent of social reform and industrial development after 1910. Further insight could probably be gained by trying to identify Mexican liberalism and conservatism in terms of comparable European intellectual currents.[23]

The field of foreign relations has proven a popular target with historians, but few bulls' eyes have been tallied to date. Opportunities still exist, especially in Mexican and Central American relations with countries other than the United States. Pletcher points out that although the Rippy and Callahan books and several other limited monographs do a reasonably good job with diplomacy between Mexico and the United States, they fail to relate it to domestic affairs in either country—a weakness discernible in the studies of the United States and Central America as well.[24] He would like to see a triangular study of Britain, the United States, and Mexico from about 1820 to 1870 which would combine diplomacy, politics, and economics —a rather large order! Potash agrees that the international field remains relatively wide open.[25] Cosío suggests that a study of American public opinion toward the Mexican Revolution, especially in its early stages, would be welcome. His research on French and English reactions has proved highly interesting. A topic that has captured the popular imagination, but has failed to attract a corresponding amount of scholarship, is that of the French intervention. The efforts of the Hannas at Rollins College hold promise for a clearer insight into the interplay of international cross-currents permeating the Maximilian venture.[26]

An area in which quantity has far outweighed quality is that of biography. Lesley Simpson declares we have given too much weight to biographical studies, interesting as they are, and important as some of them may be, but C. Harvey Gardiner argues that biography has and always should command

the historian's attention.[27] Gardiner, however, does criticize the many biographies which produced "stiff sticks stomping through time in lonely isolation." They too often fail because the living man never

[23] Hale was working on such an exploratory venture last summer with José María Luis Mora. Although the area is vague, difficult to pinpoint, and involving a familiarity with much European writing, he reported before his departure that the project should prove definitely worthwhile.

[24] J. Fred Rippy, *The United States and Mexico* (New York, 1931); J. M. Callahan, *American Foreign Policy in Mexican Relations* (New York, 1932). Stanley Ross urges that in the area of United States-Mexican relations historians of both countries make a more conscientious effort to utilize documents and other sources from across the border.

[25] In his bibliographical article, however, he cites what he considers some solid studies on Mexican relations with other countries during the independence and intervention period. Cosío's latest volume, furthermore, treats in great detail Mexican relations with Central America, especially Guatemala, during the Porfirian era. He also discusses the increasing availability of additional materials in the field of diplomatic history.

[26] Alfred J. Hanna and his wife have been pursuing this topic for fifteen years. He writes that their search has been confined primarily to the Foreign Office Archives of Mexico, the Maximilian Papers left in Mexico by the Emperor (papers which were lost but re-located by them over a ten-year period), the excellent collection of newspapers of the period, and some published documents compiled by Mexicans. In analyzing the impact of foreign influences on Mexico they have worked on the valuable Mexican materials in the archives of France, England, the United States, and have had access to materials in the Austrian archives. They have examined less important materials in the archives of Colombia and Venezuela, as well as other materials bearing on the subject, such as the Seward Papers at the University of Rochester, the Henry S. Sanford Papers at Florida, and special collections at Harvard, Yale, the New York Historical Society Library, and the Bigelow Papers in the New York Public Library. Robert A. Naylor has combed the pertinent volumes of Genaro García, *Documentos inéditos o muy raros para la historia de Mexico* (Mexico, 1905–1911), in an effort to unravel the role of the Mexican exiles in initiating the Maximilian enterprise. See his thesis done for the University of Western Ontario, "Preludes to Two Mexican Empires" (1952).

[27] Simpson is of the opinion that Roeder's "*Juarez* misses the boat, Beal's *Díaz* is undiluted journalism, and Ross' *Madero* tries to build up a hero where no hero is discernible." Cumberland declares that none of the Santa Anna biographies fill the bill, principally in that they portray him too much apart from his milieu and consequently explain neither the central figure nor Mexico. He adds that the Díaz biographies are worse. Being more familiar with Ralph Roeder, *Juarez and His*

emerges and he is insufficiently related to his time. Many would agree with Cline that generally no very useful biography exists of any major nineteenth-century Mexican figure, including Juárez and Díaz, and very little has been done for twentieth century figures with the exception of Ross' study of Madero and Quirk's projected study of Carranza. Potash insists, however, that the biographical field is not this bad for Mexico.[28] For Central America, on the other hand, the picture is much worse.[29]

Although studies are still needed for most of the major leaders, the secondary figures that usually surrounded them should not be neglected. Ross and Murray emphasize particularly some of the intellectuals who helped to formulate programs and point the direction of Mexican development—Andrés Molina Enríquez, Luís Cabrera, José Vasconcelos; and Cosío stresses the importance of

José Limantour, who as Díaz's Finance Minister was certainly the most powerful political factor during the last eighteen years of the regime. Gardiner believes that twentieth-century Mexican biographical studies could easily become almost a monopoly of American scholars if they desire to do the work. He visualizes, for instance, a clearly formulated series of biographies on key figures of the Mexican Revolution. Although the pertinent papers are often in the hands of former associates and not presently available for consultation, Cosío suggests that Mexicans sometimes appear more willing to make them available to foreign historians in the belief that they would treat them more impartially.

The foregoing symposium indicates that the opportunities for research in the field of modern Mexico and Central America are almost unlimited, especially in the economic, social, and intellectual fields—providing the source material can be found. In this respect the picture is less encouraging. Tischendorf remarks that after examining the Mexican

---

Mexico; 2 vols. (Mexico, 1947), I inquired about its reception because although very illuminating it makes absolutely no reference to source material and no citation even of direct quotations—a practice that is not limited in the Latin American field to Roeder's study. Simpson dismissed it as being too long by half, too windy, and too allusive. Cumberland argues that in spite of the lack of citations, it appeared to be a work of considerable stature although one could quarrel with some of his interpretations. Why Roeder failed to cite his sources is a mystery to Cumberland. Hanna knew Roeder when he was in Mexico writing the biography. Hanna has the impression that the research was exhaustive but believes that it was extremely unfortunate that the work was not documented. Potash claims that whatever the deficiencies in scholarly apparatus and in overwriting, it is still an impressive piece of work as far as it goes. He admits that "it slights the Intervention from the Republican side" but thinks that the void is partially filled by the studies of Scholes and Knapp. Gardiner is of the opinion that Roeder's study put Scholes out of business in that it was good enough to discourage another study. Unfortunately, the "magnificent amateurs" like Roeder will never do their work to the complete satisfaction of the scholars, Gardiner argues, but so many scholars do their work in such stodgy fashion as to invite the activity of the amateurs. Ross states that Roeder's biography of Juarez is the best available, certainly in English and probably in Spanish also, although he did rely very heavily on the contemporary press, and the first volume is vastly superior to the second.

[28] Stanley R. Ross, *Francisco I. Madero, Apostle of Mexican Democracy* (New York, 1955). An interesting study encompassing a broader area with a somewhat novelistic and interpretative approach is Jose Vasconcelos, *Don Evaristo Madero, Biografía de un patricio* (Mexico, 1958). Further examples of what can be accomplished in the field of biography were indicated by Gardiner's references to the as yet unpublished studies by Hutchinson of Gómez Farías and Bernstein of Matías Romero, and by Cumberland's references to Thomas E. Cotner, *The Military and Political Career of Jose Joaquin de Herrera, 1792–1854* (Austin, 1949), and Frank Knapp, *The Life of Sebastian Lerdo de Tejada, 1823–1899* (Austin, 1951).

[29] Gordon Kenyon comments that certainly Morazan begs for an analytical biographer. "Rafael Carrera, the Son of God, Perpetual President of Guatemala, etc." needs careful examination. Justo Rufino Barrios is another. Kenyon's grandfather served as a colonel under Barrios during an attempt to control a cholera outbreak, and Kenyon recalls some interesting comments he made. Encouraging efforts at filling the biographical void occur with David Vela, *Barrundia ante el espejo de su tiempo*; 2 vols. (Guatemala, 1956–1957). This well-documented analysis of the political role, theories, and writings of the liberal statesman José Francisco Barrundia is relatively thorough and balanced.

archives and talking to various persons about the situation, he is convinced that some of the problems will not be solved for some time. Furthermore, there are too many people who control papers and letters in Mexico who are not about to give them up. Gordon Kenyon at Pueblo College holds similar opinions with regard to Central America. He believes that extensive work must be done in modernizing the archives and rearranging materials. Until that is done the work on official records will remain herculean, expensive, and frequently too time-consuming to attract any except the most dedicated. Ross regrets that no systematic effort has been made to record and catalogue the papers in the hands of surviving participants of the Mexican Revolution. He is encouraged, however, by the efforts of various governmental agencies in Mexico to obtain and preserve basic documentary materials which will facilitate the task of the historian working in Mexican history, especially in the period of the Revolution, where certain prerequisites for adequate scholarship are in the process of being fulfilled.[30]

With bibliographical aides increasingly available and documentary collections in the preliminary stages of conservation and organization, the next important step, according to Ross, is the preparation of a broad range of monographic studies which will place the multiple aspects of Mexican and Central American history in balanced historical presentation and provide the basis for sound, generalized works of interpretation. Gardiner warns, however, that the historiographical pattern must not be allowed to follow that of the colonial period, where the concentration was heavily on political history with social, economic, and intellectual studies trailing far behind. This approach resulted in colonial stereotypes being established on a frightfully unbalanced and incomplete analysis of colonial life. The history of the modern era, Gardiner argues, must be a "simultaneous assault," written from the beginning with a breadth that never attended that of the colonial period.

Gardiner charges that the historical profession is insufficiently disciplined and needs more planning in its production. In military terms he emphasizes that our current attack on history is that of the tactician, insufficiently that of the strategist. He would have us concentrate more on a basic formulation of research programs and less on hit and miss isolated contributions. For departments offering doctoral programs this means, positively, the formulation of a long range pattern of thesis labors—not the narrow pursuit of the interest of the directing professor, nor the narrow interest of the immature student, and not the narrow range tailored to the holdings of the library.

Simpson urges us to pay less attention to geographical boundaries, or even to temporal

[30] These include the creation of basic bibliographical guides through the Seminar on Contemporary Mexican History at El Colegio de Mexico. In the process of publication are a three-volume critical guide to books and pamphlets prepared by Luís González y González and associates, and Ross' three volumes on historical materials contained in the press and periodical sources. Analyses have been prepared also of the documentary collections in the Secretariats of National Defense and Foreign Relations. Also worthy of mention is the publication of documentary, broadside and other sources by Manuel González Ramírez of the Patronato de la Historia de Sonora. In addition to the publication of various materials as a result of the centennial celebration of the Constitution of 1857, a wealth of new materials has been published in connection with the recent fiftieth anniversary of the Mexican Revolution. This and the effort of various agencies of the Mexican government to obtain and preserve basic documentary materials should facilitate the task of the scholar, although much still remains to be done to prevent considerable material from becoming fragmented and lost. The gradual availability of Diaz' personal papers, now approaching thirty volumes, Ross believes should open up a substantial amount of materials on administrative procedures as well as political events and social and economic conditions. A useful bibliographical tool is scheduled to appear with the projected eight-volume detailed cataloguing of travel literature in modern Latin America under the editorship of C. Harvey Gardiner. The massive, analytical appendices and indices in this series are intended to help the researcher in a wide variety of fields. Gardiner is preparing the volume on Mexico, and Franklin D. Parker, currently in Peru, will do the volume on Central America. Present plans call for publication of the first two volumes in 1962–1963. Thereafter it is hoped that the project can be completed at the rate of two volumes a year.

ones, but rather to pursue topics that are common to the whole culture, such as the migration of plants, animals, and diseases; the heritage of Rome, and the astonishing impact of urbanism. Potash suggests that there may be a timeliness in taking a fresh look at the early decades of Mexican and Central American independence in the light of difficulties that new Afro-Asian nations are currently experiencing. The older assumption that the relatively peaceful experience of the United States was the norm from which Mexico and Central America perversely deviated is hardly tenable today. This realization should permit a sympathetic yet searching approach to the problems of Mexico and Central America during their formative decades as independent nations.

William Griffith believes the greatest need is for works—they could deal with almost any pertinent subject—that try to get at the issues to discover the active forces in Central American life that propelled Central American history in the direction it took. His comments are just as applicable to Mexico. He agrees with the general consensus that the socio-economic field is the one that deserves a great deal of study because many of the most significant forces, whether active or passive, are to be found there. Political studies will be valuable to the degree that they show these forces in action. A study of the motivation and the forces to which the regimes of the political leaders gave expression would be a far more profitable approach to their careers than the traditional efforts to account for events in terms of a Zoroastrian struggle between the powers of good and evil. Specifically, studies of the ways in which certain socio-economic groups have been able to maintain their control of the social, political, and economic life of the country to the detriment of the major-

ity of the population, of the rising groups in society such as the nascent middle class and particularly organized labor which have challenged the dominant groups, and of the special role that foreigners, whether capitalist, communist, or other, have played in this development would be far more revealing than the traditional sort of drum-and-bugle histories.

Finally, in conclusion, Edmundo O'Gorman of Mexico City criticizes current historical trends in general. One of his main points is that the major assumption in all past historical writings consists in thinking that historical entities such as Mexico and Central America are ready-made and that, therefore, history is something that happens to them but does not and cannot affect them in their being. O'Gorman argues that such entities have no being in themselves and that which is said to happen to them is really what constitutes them ontologically. In his view historical entities are nothing but transient inventions man made and which reflect man's concept of himself at a given moment. He insists we must purge historical thinking of that archaic Greek substantialist notion of being which has dominated our culture for centuries.[31]

Generally and specifically, then, this is the salutation to scholars as they amass themselves for a frontal assault on the ramparts of ignorance that still surround the modern era of Mexican and Central American history. The challenge may appear slightly overwhelming but the opportunities are, nevertheless, there.

[31] O'Gorman's provocative views have been expressed in his *Crisis y porvenir de la ciencia histórica* (México, 1947). His most recent book, *The Invention of America* (Bloomington, Ind., 1961), expresses his views more effectively because instead of simply preaching and criticizing, he has attempted to write a historical work according to those views.

68. Research Opportunities: The Bolivarian Nations*

J. León Helguera

Defining, for the purposes of this paper, modern Latin American history as the period following 1830, and the Bolivarian nations as Colombia, Ecuador, Venezuela, and Peru, the spectrum of research opportunities is very broad. As is well known, the modern period is the step-child, in respect to historical interest and production, of the colonial, in most of Latin America. In the Bolivarian nations, this tendency is made worse by the exaggerated devotion of historians there to the independence struggle, notably in Colombia and Venezuela.

The frontier of historical knowledge in the modern period is limited, too, by economic, social, and political factors generally no longer found in Western Europe or in the United States. In most of the Bolivarian nations, since no widespread historical profession scientifically oriented or trained exists, the writers about the past are drawn largely from amateurs from within the upper classes and reflect their partisan bias or economic interests in the interpretation they give. With very few exceptions, such as Orlando Fals Borda in Colombia, Pedro Grases in Venezuela, and Jorge Basadre and Alfonso Tauro in Peru, the resultant product can only with charity be termed historical.

The opportunity, then, for historians in this country and in Western Europe for historical research in the Bolivarian nations is limited only by lack of materials (certain archival collections being destroyed or closed to the investigator), or, what is perhaps even worse, the dearth of even the barest guides and indices to the archival and printed materials. Very few usable guides to even officially controlled manuscript collections exist in the Bolivarian nations today.

In view of the dearth of real historical production in the Bolivarian nations, so much

historical earth lies untilled as to satisfy the most greedy historical entrepreneur. Even in the much-worked, though hardly cultivated, field of basic narrative political history, none of the four nations, with the possible exception of Peru,[1] can point to an adequate broad general history of its political genesis and development.

Leaving aside manuscript sources for narrative political history, much can be done in defining certain areas of policy by means of printed public documents. Some headway has been made in Peru, where a collection of presidential messages saw print in 1943,[2] and in Colombia, where a similar compilation appeared in 1954.[3] These are, however, largely executive messages to the congress, and neither collection includes the many incidental special presidential pronouncements which are so characteristic of both time and area, and which can be readily found in the various official gazettes or *boletínes* of the respective countries up to the present day. Until a truly concerted effort is made to collect the public papers of the chief executives of the Bolivarian nations, our view of public policy will remain fragmentary at best. The same type of compilation should be attempted of the mes-

* *Americas,* 18: 365–374 (Apr. 1962). Reprinted by permission of the author and the original publisher.

[1] Jorge Basadre's *Historia de la República, 1822–1899* (Lima: Librería e imprenta Gil, 1939) serves as an able synthesis.

[2] See Pedro Ugarteche and Evaristo San Cristóval (compilers) *Mensajes de los presidentes del Perú. Vol. I. 1821–1867* (Lima: Imprenta de Gil, 1943).

[3] The Colombian collection, badly mutilated by poor editing, is limited to inaugural addresses. See Manuel Monsalve Martínez (ed.), *Colombia. Posesiones presidenciales, 1810–1954* (Bogotá: Editorial Iqueima, 1954).

sages and papers of the principal cabinet members, though, admittedly, this is a much more ambitious undertaking.

Another area of narrative political history which can be studied from public documents is that of the voting behavior, from 1830 to recent days, of individual cantons and/or districts in the four nations. Despite electoral frauds and fraudulent returns, certain patterns of political and regional voting could be approximated, were students to compile the voting records of departments, provinces, prefectures, and their subdivisions from officially printed returns. How much more understandable certain official policies of the past 150 years, with respect to certain regions of the Bolivarian nations would be, if we had maps of their voting behavior!

Partisan political behavior and thought, too, need careful examination. As yet, no history of the Venezuelan "Oligarquía" or the Liberal Party has appeared to show the ideological evolution of these parties and the personalism that characterized them in the 1830–1899 period.[4] The same is true of the Colombian scene, despite the intensive use of liberal-conservative labels there, from the 1849's up to our own days.[5] Ecuador's historians are possibly even less cognizant of party designations and still more ponderously weighted by the personalities of Flores, Rocafuerte, García Moreno, or Alfaro, from whom they cannot yet disassociate their modern history.[6] The historians of Peru have only recently devoted much effort to the modern period because of the persistence of intellectual obeisance to colonial traditions.

If the bulk of the narrative political history is yet to be written, so too is the evolution of the concept of governmental administration and the meaning and use of power in all of the Bolivarian nations. Monographs concerning the actual functioning of government during the past century and a half, or even for small periods of rule, have not been produced, except by foreign scholarship in very small quantity. Bushnell's excellent *Santander Regime in Gran Colombia*[7] might serve as a model, but is limited to the late independence period, and no one has continued the story further, except for my incomplete study of the brief 1845–1849 first presidency of General Mosquera.[8]

Nor has the vital matter of bureaucracy and its relationship to the actual power structure been studied. The hierarchy of clerks and administrative quill-sharpeners and the persistence of certain of these persons in the middle and power echelons of governments, despite frequent radical changes at the top of the ruling pyramid,

[4] Ramón Díaz Sánchez, *Guzmán, elipse de una ambición de poder* (Caracas: Ediciones del Ministerio de Educación Nacional, 1950), a brilliant, but unbalanced study of the careers of Antonio Leocadio Guzmán (1801–1884), and his son, Antonio Guzmán Blanco (1828–1899), is a striking example of Venezuelan history viewed over-much through the lives of two personalist figures. It should be noted that a great compilation of Venezuelan political thought, in more than ten volumes, is nearing completion. Its compilers are Pedro Grases and Manuel Pérez Vila, its title, *Pensamiento político venezolano del siglo XIX: textos para su estudio.*

[5] A massive list of names, dates, statistics, and odd information is Gustavo Arboleda's *Historia contemporánea de Colombia* (*Desde la disolución de la antigua república de ese nombre hasta la época presente*), 6 vol. (Bogotá and Cali: Editorial Arboleda y Valencia and Others, 1918–1935). The six published volumes—two still in manuscript are apparently lost—carry the Colombian narrative from 1830 to 1861, but do little to clarify ideological differences between the two major parties.

[6] The enigmatic personality of Gabriel García Moreno (1821–1875) has attracted no less than twelve works over the past dozen years, at least six of which, may be called major efforts. See Luis Robalino Dávila, *García Moreno* (Quito: Talleres Gráficos Nacionales, 1949); Wilfrido Loor (ed.), *Cartas de García Moreno*, 4 vols. (Quito: La Prensa Católica, 1953–1955); Severo Gómez Jurado, S.J., *Vida de García Moreno*, 4 vol. (Cuenca and Quito: Editorial "El Tiempo" and Others, 1954–1957); Wilfrido Loor, *García Moreno y sus asesinos* (Quito: La Prensa Católica, 1955), and the same author's *La victoria de Guayaquil* (Quito: La Prensa Católica, 1960); and finally, Benjamin Carrión, *García Moreno, el santo del patíbulo* (México, D.F.: Fondo de Cultura Económica, 1959).

[7] Published as Number 5 of the University of Delaware Monograph Series (Newark, Delaware: The University of Delaware Press, 1954).

[8] "The First Mosquera Administration in New Granada, 1845–1849" (Ann Arbor: University Microfilms, 1958). The writer plans to complete and revise this study for eventual publication in book-form.

over decades of the past century and a half, deserves serious consideration by scholarship.

Certain aspects of administration have, it is true, been studied. A stimulating monograph by Ospina Vázquez relates the history of the tariffs and Colombian industrialism from 1810 to 1930.[9] John P. Harrison's important history of the Colombian tobacco industry from 1776 to 1876 is basic to an understanding of the government-controlled monopolies in the national period.[10] Other sources of government revenues—substantial ones—like the *aduanas, aguardientes*, and salt need investigation in all of the four countries. In this connection, the relationship between regionalism and certain government revenues should not be overlooked. George Kubler's *Indian Caste of Peru, 1795–1940*[11] is an outstanding example of this type of work.

Regionalism, localism, particularism, or federalism, too, need careful historical scrutiny. Robert Gilmore's study of Colombian federalism,[12] especially his treatment of the period following 1830, is trail blazing at its purest, since he reveals an enormous body of printed materials, and concludes honestly that he has barely touched upon his topic. What Gilmore has begun for Colombia finds no repetition in Venezuela, none in Ecuador, Peru, or Bolivia. Yet all of the Bolivarian nations in the early national period, indeed until about 1930, are deeply affected by the pulls and twists of regionalism, and even today the local allegiances are by no means moribund.

All four nations—as is true of other Latin American countries—suffer from the exaggerated role of their respective capital cities. The over-concentration of political power, national wealth, and intellectual resources in the capital, aside from being economically and socially burdensome, has had profound historiographical repercussions. This process of over-concentration into the capitaline districts over the past century has led many writers in the Bolivarian nations to duplicate it historiographically. A lack of national sense, or perspective, is characteristic of many authors who, since they live in the

capital, cannot really divorce themselves from the glitter that blinds them to an understanding or even an awareness of regional developments and historical aspirations.

An obvious case in point is the production of Peruvian history—or rather, Lima—in the modern period. The Colombians are little better. The role of Bogotá looms paramount in almost every treatise. The dominance of Caracas has, in the past sixty years, been somewhat lessened by an increase in historical attention directed toward Venezuela's western states.[13] The eastern states, however, still suffer neglect. Ecuador, despite its relative smallness, follows a line of *Quito es la Patria*, like her two immediate neighbors.

Distinct from any other ethno-political group in the Colombian cosmos of regions are, of course, the Antioquians. These western Andean highlanders are probably the best socially integrated people in South America. Their strong pride of achievement has developed into a state within a non-state. The region—really a miniature nation—thus has attracted studious attention. Its ethnic virility has been well described by James J. Parsons who has shown the expansion of the *antioqueños* from the late colonial period into surrounding and distant parts of

---

[9] Luis Ospina Vázquez, *Industria y protección en Colombia: 1810–1930* (Medellín: Editorial Santa Fe, 1955). Also valuable is David Bushnell's article, "Two Stages in Colombian Tariff Policy: The Radical Era and the Return to Protection (1861–1885)," *Inter-American Economic Affairs*, IX, No. 4 (Spring 1956), 3–23.

[10] John Parker Harrison, "The Colombian Tobacco Industry from Government Monopoly to Free Trade, 1776–1876." Unpublished doctoral dissertation, University of California at Berkeley, 1951.

[11] The full title is: *The Indian Caste of Peru, 1795–1940. A Population Study Based upon Tax Records and Census Reports*. Smithsonian Institution. Institute of Social Anthropology Publication No. 14. (Washington: Government Printing Office, 1952).

[12] Robert Louis Gilmore, "Federalism in Colombia, 1810–1858." Unpublished doctoral dissertation, University of California at Berkeley, 1949.

[13] This can be partially accounted for by the fact that from 1899 to 1958 Venezuela's dominant military leadership was of Andean origin.

Colombia.[14] Again unlike any comparable region, Antioquia and her people are both literate and introspective. Besides his research in archives, Parsons was able to make use of considerable printed material which can be considered monographic.

The dearth of real monographic material not only for regional studies but also for those of a more general nature is apparent to all in the Latin American field, and especially those in the Bolivarian area. However, it is a deficiency which is not as critical as might be supposed in certain aspects of regional history. A great many minor catch-all-type provincial descriptions, atlases, memoirs, and descriptive geographies have been produced in Colombia, Ecuador, and Venezuela, in the past decade.[15] In Peru, a definite trend of regionalistic re-valuation may be discerned. The Sierra is awakening to itself, after long Lima-inspired neglect.[16] The new, more virulent Latin American nationalism demands more than merely capitaline allegiance—the example of certain hirsute Cuban provincials is well known.

The problems presented by regional history are many, but the opportunities are equally so. The modern period of the Bolivarian nations can not be truly recorded without an examination of the role of regionalism. Peru offers a convenient case in point: why does the city of Arequipa, from 1829 to 1930, invariably mother all or nearly all of the successful revolutions aimed at seizing power away from those in Lima? What role does Popayán play in the first half-century of Colombian national life? What causes Pasto to play its rebellious role in almost all of Colombian history since (and including) independence? What factors account for Guayaquil's persistent liberalism as opposed to the conservatism of Quito, since 1821? Cannot the Federal Wars of 1858–1868 in Venezuela be seen as an effort by the westerners of Coro and Trujillo to achieve political prestige in Venezuela, after having been pushed aside by the easterners and the llaneros during three previous decades? Is the basis for such conjecture merely contained in abstract psycho-sociological concepts of prestige?

Another aspect of the modern period, much discussed and the victim of millions of verbal essays, is the problem of the caudillo and his lesser satellite, the cacique. Here again, persistent and careful study might be directed toward an examination of the rise of provincial education in the Bolivarian nations during the 1830–1850 period, its gradual eclipse in the late 1850's and 1860's, and its replacement by capitaline secondary schools of nationally accepted preeminence. Is there not a definite abandonment of provincial towns and country-estates by the creole aristocracy in the 1860's in all the countries? In part, this has been explained as a search for the security of numbers in the larger cities and the capitals, away from the depredating civil (Federal) wars. In part, however, the oligarchy left its landed estates in order to secure better education for its young—many of whom, reared in urbis, never return to seats of ancestral leadership and prominence in the countryside."[17] The power vacuum is filled, I believe, by the members of lesser provincial families to begin with, and then, by the dawn of this century, by self-made men, either mestizos or mulatos—well-known stereotypes of caciques.

If the opportunity for study of caudillism and caciquism exists, so too, serious appraisal should be given to the intellectual history of the area. No really careful study has yet appeared of the impact of Bentham in early republican Colombia,[18] or of the

---

[14] In his *Antioqueño Colonization in Western Colombia.* Ibero-Americana, 32 (Berkeley and Los Angeles: University of California Press, 1949).

[15] Numerous examples of this type of literature have been noted and reviewed by the writer in "National Period. Colombia, Ecuador, Peru and Venezuela," *Handbook of Latin American Studies.* Nos. 20–23 (Gainesville: University of Florida Press, 1958–1961).

[16] See, especially, Carlos Núñez Anavitarte, *Mariátegui y el descentralismo* (Cuzco: Editorial Garcilaso, 1958).

[17] This point is well made by Eduardo Caballero Calderón in his *Historia privada de los colombianos* (Bogotá: Imprenta Antares, 1960), p. 92.

[18] Julio Hoenigsberg, *Santander, El Clero y Bentham* (Bogotá: Editorial ABC, 1940), is an

equally contentious intellectual warfare revolving around the transcendentalism of Victor Cousin which took place in Venezuela in the decade of the 1840's,[19] and whose echoes were heard in both Colombia and Peru throughout much of the 1850's. Nor have the theories of Bastiat, Blanqui, Blanc, and even Karl Marx been assessed in regard to their reverberations among the intellectuals of northern South America during the 1840–1860 period. [20] Yet an abundant body of source material for such investigation exists. Newspapers, public documents, pamphlets and books in impressive quantities, to say nothing of private and public archives, bear ample witness to the real passion and wide reading of many important nineteenth-century Bolivarian figures.

Oblivion has, however, overtaken many men of ability and intellect of the first half of the modern period. Unjust as this seems, it is almost diabolic in effect for the scholar, since no adequate biographical dictionaries exist. Collective biography has attracted little attention and small honest effort, if we except Perú's Mendíburu[21]—slanted toward the colonial-independent periods—and Ospina's hodge-podge of borrowed or plagiarized *Diccionario biográfico* for Colombia.[22] Neither Venezuela nor Ecuador have done even as well. Norwithstanding this, there are an infinity of resources in print which, if properly known and utilized, would provide a firm basis for biographical data on many, if not most, of the leading historical, political, intellectual, and military personalities of the nineteenth and early twentieth centuries. Aside from geneologies, both provincial and national, numerous necrologies in pamphlet form, civil and military service records in manuscript and biographical sketches in newspapers all add up to abundant materials for this important but neglected aspect of Bolivarian national history.

The reasons for the neglect have been alluded to previously in this paper. To correct the situation, much needs to be done. In the first place, guides to the major and minor newspapers of the area are an implicit necessity. Some work, like that of Grases in Venezuela,[23] has been of great benefit in covering the enormous resources of periodical literature. But nothing as extensive as Brigham's *History and bibliography of American Newspapers . . .* has been prepared for any one of the four countries, to list together all the printed newspapers of the 1830–1930 century. Here is a task, large certainly, but not impossible, for the well-equipped scholar. An annotated Union Catalogue of northern South American Newspapers, 1830–1930, their history, editorial policies, and duration, would be a priceless stimulus to native and foreign scholarly production.

So too, would be lists of ephemera (broadsides, handbills, announcements, decrees, bulletins) and pamphlets, over the same century. This problem could be handled on a yearly basis, that is to say that, starting with 1830–1831, the work could proceed until the major library resources in the South American nations as well as in this country and in Europe had been surveyed, comments

---

able, but superficial essay, based primarily on secondary sources.

[19] See Manuel Ancízar's "Filosofía. Método" in *El Liberal* (Caracas), July 28, 1840, an espousal of Cousin, and Rafael Acevedo's vigorous rebuttal in "Remitido. Sr. Editor del Liberal" in *El Liberal* (Caracas), September 8, 1840, and Ancízar's equally vigorous reply and reaffirmation of Cousin, "Filosofía. Método. Sr. Rafael Acevedo" in *El Correo de Caracas* (Caracas); September 29, 1840.

[20] Although Robert Louis Gilmore, "Nueva Granada's Socialist Mirage," *HAHR*, XXXVI (May, 1956), 190–210, is a valuable indication of the ferment these ideas caused in Colombia in the 1850's; an important earlier effort, William Whatley Pierson, "Foreign Influences on Venezuelan Political Thought, 1830–1930," *HAHR*, XV (February, 1935), 3–42, reveals the variety of European and United States ideologies on Venezuelan thinkers.

[21] Manuel de Mendiburu, *Diccionario histórico-biográfico del Perú.* 8 volumes (Lima: Imprenta de J. F. Solis, 1874–1890). A second edition in 11 volumes edited and added to by Evaristo San Cristóval was published by the Lima Imprenta "Enrique Palacios," 1931 to 1935.

[22] Joaquín Ospina (compiler), *Diccionario biográfico y bibliográfico de Colombia,* 3 volumes (Bogotá: Editorial Cromos and Editorial Aguila, 1927–1939).

[23] Pedro Grases, *Materiales para la historia del periodismo en Venezuela durante el siglo XIX* (Caracas: La Central de Venezuela, Escuela de Periodismo, 1950).

written, and rough chronology fixed—often difficult in the case of ephemera—before the results were drawn up in printed form.

With these basic tasks of surveying in hand, annual bibliographies from 1830 to 1930 of all larger printed works, including public documents—those of the states and provinces are frequently overlooked in the guides we have today—might be taken up for each of the countries. Some countries, like Venezuela,[24] Peru,[25] and, recently, Colombia,[26] have been publishing useful *Anuarios bibliográficos* over the past two decades. From these guides, it becomes apparent that much valuable historical material sees print in the form of articles in Sunday literary and magazine supplements to leading newspapers like *El Tiempo* of Bogotá, *Universal* of Caracas, or *El Comercio* of Lima.

A collective effort in the direction of preparing bibliographies of travel literature is underway. Colombia, Venezuela, Peru and Ecuador are being surveyed, both as to native and foreign travel accounts.[27] In this regard, the work of Giraldo Jaramillo[28] for Colombia and the older work of Venezuela's great Manuel Segundo Sánchez[29] show the wealth of works written by foreigners about parts of the area, as does Larrea's *Bibliografía científica del Ecuador.*[30]

The very important and fascinating but also neglected area of intra-Bolivarian diplomatic relations must be also studied. Robert Burr's brilliant but all too brief article on the balance of power in nineteenth-century South America,[31] is but an indication of what can be done. Without even considering the largely restricted archival materials, the printed materials on, say, the Venezuelan-Colombian frontier dispute in the nineteenth century are more than sufficient for an appreciation of the conflict of interests of the two sister nations, and, when used with archival materials from the British Public Records provide an excellent example of British *divide et impera* tactics during the last century.

Detailed studies on cultural history, architecture as reflecting social or political trends,

decorative arts and caudillism, verse and literary vilification, the role of the "Academic" historians and dictatorship, or of intellectuals generally as politicians are all other topics and research possibilities in the area.

This paper does not pretend to be more than an arbitrarily limited over-view of research horizons as seen by one student of the Bolivarian area. It is merely intended as a rough *Guía de Forasteros* to the very real numerous research opportunities that the nations freed from Spanish rule by the Liberator, Simón Bolívar, offer to serious

[24] First issued as a separate publication of the Biblioteca Nacional, the *Anuario bibliográfico venezolano* (Caracas: Tipografía Americana, 1944), has in recent years formed a bibliographic appendix in the issues of the *Revista Nacional de Cultura* published by the Ministerio de Educación Nacional in Caracas.

[25] The Peruvian *Anuario bibliográfico*, edited by Alfonso Tauro, first appeared in 1944 as a publication of the Lima Biblioteca Nacional.

[26] The first *Anuario bibliográfico colombiano*, for 1951, was issued by the Biblioteca Jorge Garcés B. of Cali in 1952; since then it has been produced by the Instituto Caro y Cuervo's Departamento de Bibliografía. Rubén Pérez Ortiz has compiled those published so far: *Anuario bibliográfico colombiano 1951–1956* (Bogotá: Imprenta del Banco de la República, 1958), and *Anuario bibliográfico colombiano 1957–1958* (Bogotá: Prensas del Instituto Caro y Cuervo, 1960).

[27] Under the general editorship of C. Harvey Gardiner (Southern Illinois University), travel literature from 1800 to 1920 is to be inventoried. Professor J. Preston Moore (Louisiana State University) is preparing the volume covering Ecuador and Peru. J. León Helguera (North Carolina State College) is responsible for Colombia and Venezuela.

[28] Gabriel Giraldo Jaramillo, *Bibliografía colombiana de viajes*, Biblioteca de Bibliografía Colombiana, II (Bogotá: Editorial ABC, 1957).

[29] *Bibliografía venezolanista. Contribución al conocimiento de los libros extranjeros relativos a Venezuela y sus grandes hombres, publicados o reimpresos desde el siglo XIX* (Caracas: Empresa El Cojo, 1914).

[30] Carlos Manuel Larrea, *Bibliografía científica del Ecuador* (Madrid: Ediciones Cultura Hispánica, 1952).

[31] Robert N. Burr, "The Balance of Power in Nineteenth-Century South America: An Exploratory Essay," *HAHR*, XXXV (No. 1, February, 1955), 37–60.

scholarship. It seems to me that what is most needed are the historical craftsmen to make effective use of the opportunities and thus help bring modern scholarly production to an area undeservedly neglected by its own as well as foreign historians.

69. Research Opportunities: Southern South America*

Thomas F. McGann

There is no egoism or special virtue in the fact that all of us on this program have numerous research possibilities to suggest. The plain truth is that the field of Latin American history bulges with first-class topics for historical writing. In this respect I am sure that we Latin Americanists are more fortunate than colleagues in some other historical fields where, it is my impression, there is a good deal of trampling of each other's grapes. But historical research is not the contemplation of ideas, no matter how promising they may be, and in Latin America the investigator confronts notorious difficulties in obtaining orderly source materials. Therefore, before turning to some of the research possibilities, I should touch briefly on several underlying assumptions. The first is that the investigators working on these topics shall be qualified linguistically, technically, and intellectually to accomplish their work in Latin America and in the United States. Unhappily, this has not always been the case in this underdeveloped field. Second, for all of these topics I estimate that there exists a sufficiency of source materials, although in some cases that assumption has not been fully tested in the field. (This is the point at which field research in Latin America takes on a more colorful aspect than research, let's say, in the British Museum.) Finally, an investigator engaged in research in Latin America must have, or quickly develop, a

hunter's ability to move rapidly yet sure-footedly after his quarry, tracking down private and even public archives which, at the outset of his adventure in research, may be completely unknown to him. And he must be tough, and his topic sufficiently adaptable, so that both can withstand the shock of discovering, as may happen, that promised or rumored depositories are non-existent or, worse fate, that the documents which they contain are declared to be unavailable for some reason or other—perhaps because of an exaggerated sense of privacy on the part of the controlling authority, perhaps because of embarrassment over the chaotic conditions in which the documents may be found, or, a still worse fate, because of personal dislike taken to the would-be researcher.

I favor the big topic, the vital, central subject, but with the reservation that the young scholar, and perhaps the old scholar too, should grapple piecemeal with his big idea, working at sections of it before attempting to master the entire theme.

What sort of big topic? Daniel Cosío Villegas, in a recent lecture at the University of Nebraska, while discussing another matter, referred in passing to just such a subject when he said, "some day an intelligent

* *Americas*, 18: 375–379 (Apr. 1962). Reprinted by permission of the author and the original publisher.

man will do a study of the history of liberalism in Latin America." In a few words this
great Mexican intellectual has sketched out
work for a dozen historians. There may be
debate as to whether or not any historian is
ready to tackle this intriguing subject in its
entirety. I tend to think that none is, but it
is obvious that liberalism can and should
be studied now on the national level, then
on an inter-regional level, that is, comparing
developments within a group of nations, as
in the area of the Río de la Plata and Chile,
until finally there will be some day a book
entitled *A History of Liberalism in Latin
America*—from which even European historians may learn.

The nations of southern South America,
Uruguay, Paraguay, Chile, and Argentina,
offer excellent opportunities for national
and regional histories of liberalism. Think
of the range in time and in men from the
political theorizing and building of the
years from 1810 to 1830 on through a turbulent century to the apparent accomplishments of liberalism in the years 1910 to
1930—and on further, if the sources become
sufficiently exposed, to the collapse of liberalism after 1930. Consider the great careers
of Artigas, San Martín, and O'Higgins, and
their inchoate political theories; study Moreno, Belgrano, and Henríquez; examine the
evolution of ideas over a century; end with
consideration of Irigoyen, Batlle, and Alessandri. There you have the complexity within unity which is the warp and woof of a
powerful historical subject.

The sources, both contemporary and
monographic, for a study of liberalism are
ample; the subject is one of profound significance. Who will commence the work?

Only a few shafts have been sunk in the
mine of Latin American economic history.
I want to mention two topics in the economic sector. One is in the sector of agriculture: the history of the latifundio, or perhaps more precisely, of a latifundio. True,
there is an apparent scarcity of documentary
materials derived directly from the ownership and operation of great *estancias* or *fun-
dos*, but is the scarcity not more apparent
than real, more the result of a lack of initia-

tive in digging out such documents than a
matter of their unavailability? I have indications from each of the four countries
about which I am talking that important collections of *latifundio* papers may be available to investigators. Certainly there are
plentiful supporting public records, including provincial and municipal archives, and
memoirs, newspaper accounts, and other
materials available for rewarding investigations of what was in the nineteenth century
the most important institution in Latin
America. And is not the great estate also the
most dramatic theme in Latin American history—rich in the colors which a good historian must try to seize? American historians have given us good accounts of the working cowboy and the working ranch in the
United States. Who will tell us more about
the working gaucho, or, rather, the working
peon, and the working *estancia* or *fundo?*

A second topic of equal interest in the
field of Latin American economic history
has international as well as national character, that is, the history of foreign business
enterprise. The time has come to examine
further the establishment, the growth and
the impact of foreign business in Latin
America. Among the enterprises which
might be investigated are the first United
States—or European—overseas banks; mining companies; shipping firms, and, closely
related to the investigation of the great estates which I have just discussed, foreign-
owned latifundi. Admittedly, there are
thorny aspects to obtaining access to some
business records. But with tactful persever-
ance, sufficient records may be made available to illuminate the history of some of the
major business operations in southern South
America in the nineteenth and early twentieth centuries. There are also ample materials to be utilized in public legislative
and other records, in consular reports, and
in newspapers (not forgetting that instructive newspaper source, its advertisements),
both in the Latin American country where
the business was located and in the foreign
country where the enterprise originated.
(Let me emphasize here that I have not forgotten that there have been significant books

done in the field of the economic history of southern South America. Two scholars of this field have been Miron Burgin and Simon Hanson, but they have had few successors.)

In social history the opportunities for fresh and rewarding work are equally great. One subject of overwhelming interest, as I see it, is urban history. In this area I freely—but with some twinges of regret—grant my unstable claim to the richest of these topics: the history of Buenos Aires since the year 1805. The sources for that history are numerous and to bring to life the dazzling past of a city of six million people is a commanding challenge. If one does not wish to write on Buenos Aires, why not Montevideo or Santiago de Chile or Concepción or Rosario? The urban centers—lively inheritances from Spain, vastly enlarged by Spanish Americans—need their historians.

Intellectual history is unexplored territory. Almost nothing has been written, objectively, about the major men and movements in Latin America's cultural past. There are dozens of leaders in southern South America whose careers, combining ideas with action, warrant study. Some of the first-rank figures, Mitre and Sarmiento for example, still lack that comprehensive, balanced, and imaginative treatment which modern historical biographers have mastered. If one shys away from biography, there are intellectual generations to be portrayed: the generation of '42 in Chile, or Rodó's generation, or the generation of 1910 in Argentina. In the important newspapers and journals of each age and in the writings by and about the leaders there are ample sources for the historian. One need not write on the most famous figures or movements: there are critically important men of secondary fame but primary influence who deserve study. One who comes to mind is the Argentine statesman, author, and university founder, Joaquín V. González, who had great influence on many men now in key positions in Argentina. European and indigenous philosophical and esthetic currents, transmitted and transmuted by such Latin American leaders into past and present realities,

provide dozens of exciting themes for future historians.

Another topic begging for its historians is immigration. We need an Oscar Handlin for Latin America. This is particularly true for Argentina, a nation which in its ratio of natives to immigrants was more heavily affected by immigration than our own country. Uruguay, too, is a challenge to the potential historian of immigrants and Chile, in lesser but distinct measure, of course, also should have the unifying and independent treatment which a foreign scholar may bring to a study of the role of that country's immigrants. For all these nations, primary material is abundant, including government documents, foreign language newspapers, private letters, and the files of immigrant aid societies.

A few more topics may be mentioned to show the expanse of possible topics calling the future explorer of southern South American history. There is the frontier, and there are the Indians—vigorous forces in the history of southern South America about which enormous amounts of material have accumulated while very little real work has been done, and that little, certainly, not from a comparative basis by scholars versed in the highly developed genre writing done in the United States.

Regional history has never been able to raise its head in southern South America for many reasons, principally the weakness of the region itself in the face of the core area. But this weakness does not make less significant the need to understand the regional problem; rather, the reverse is true. We need scholarly definitions of the role of up-country Uruguay versus Montevideo; northern—or southern—Chile in its relation to the Central Valley; the opposition of any and all the Argentine provinces to the city of Buenos Aires; finally, and frankly, the position of Paraguay as a region, rather than as a nation, in the Río de la Plata complex.

The political, economic, social, and cultural forces at work in each country are the matrix from which its foreign policy is formed; studies of such interrelationships have been few. A recent example is the good job done by the Englishman, Ferns, in his book *Britain and Argentina in the Nineteenth Century*. There are sound topics in the history of right-wing movements in the southern South American countries, while the popular front and the left-liberal movement in Chile calls for further study. There are ample sources for such work.

Let me end my list of suggestions at this point with the observation that a lively scholar can make a classic out of what seems to be a hopelessly worked-over subject. With this in mind, my closing suggestion is that

there is a need to tackle the most-studied yet least-synthesized of all periods of Latin American history: the wars for independence. I recently returned from a congress of historians held in Caracas, which was concerned with the independence period, convinced that there are now rich printed sources, accessible unpublished sources, and many capable hands ready to assist the historians who will analyse the causes and the processes of Latin America's birth of freedom—if only in southern South America.

70. United States Historiography of Latin America*

Howard F. Cline

When the Associate Editor of *ABS* solicited a contribution to this special issue on "Social Research on Latin America" he wrote that "Historical research on Latin America is sometimes slighted for its unwarranted assumptions or selection of topics supposedly irrelevant to present concerns." He thought that readers of this journal might be particularly interested in "views of the state of historical research, topics which most need attention, appropriate methods or approaches, and inter-disciplinary implications." In the brief space allotted, some casual comments can be made on these matters; no very comprehensive summary of each is possible.

The indication that the work of historians on Latin America is slighted brings to mind an anecdote that touches the whole range of behavorial sciences. Some months ago when I was testifying as an expert witness in an Indian Claims Act case, the Chief Commissioner, a grizzled old Texas lawyer, told me during a recess in the hearing, "There are

two kinds of people whom we hear. There are lawyers, and you can trust them. Then there are anthropologists, economists, psychologists, historians, and a whole lot of other 'ologists.' I just call them all *phrenologists* and you don't have to worry too much about them." Perhaps from the vantage point of one's own specialty all others seem less important, and are slighted to a greater or lesser degree. So with historians among fellow-phrenologists.

Before essaying even tentatively the state of historical research on Latin America, a word about historical research in general seems appropriate. Several features are noteworthy and relevant to the task at hand.

The discipline itself is well-established, with better than a century of thought and

* *American Behavioral Scientist*, 7/1:15–18 (Sept. 1964). Reprinted by permission of the author and Sage Publications, Inc. The original article contained two introductory paragraphs, which were omitted in the printed version. They are here restored. [Ed. note]

writing about proper historiography since attempts were first made to develop a scientific basis for the work of the professional historian. In the United States the principal learned body, the American Historical Association, was founded in 1884, now has about 11,500 members. As a branch of knowledge the study of history has gone through various stages of evolution and change, generally tending to become more specialized as historians' interests have grown to embrace more world areas and topics.

With this wider variety of problems, the historian has over the years evolved a rather formidable arsenal of techniques and approaches to aid his study of the past, within a broad general framework that often is more implicit than explicit, the boundaries of which are shifting and occasionally ill-defined. The key concept of history is change in human activity over time, comparable to culture as the key in anthropology, or area for geographers. The temporal elements run through historiography, however limited its topic, period, or area.

The prime concern of historians is the identification of major changes and multicasual explanations of them. To provide the perspective necessary to isolate and evaluate trends, the time spans in which we work customarily exceed a decade, and may stretch to centuries. Within the selected span we deal with social mechanisms and structures, noting and evaluating their endurance, adjustments under varying actual conditions, and their interrelationships. Proper historiography always attempts as much to answer "why" as "how" for any of the innumerable changes that have taken place throughout the world during Man's long past.

Concern for the longer range implications also plays a part in the study of history. Largely inductive, often empirical, historiography places much stress on identifying what are the meaningful questions that recur over a wide panorama of periods, civilizations, cultures. Several other matters might be mentioned, but the above are sufficient to provide some base for noting briefly how the historian's work seemingly differs from the concerns of other behavioral scientists.

As we see the latter, their objectives are usually short-term research on relatively recent or current problems. This contemporaneity lends itself admirably to the use of questionnaires, which have no relevance to the normal work of historiography. Historical studies, draw on other, usually written, sources for prime data. Seemingly also a considerable effort on the part of other behavioral scientists is related to policy-oriented matters, especially United States foreign policy. Subject to both domestic and international political considerations, the questions to which alternative answers are sought often appear of minor concern in the longer trends with which the historian generally hopes to deal.

LATIN AMERICAN HISTORICAL RESEARCH

Turning to the stated topic, historiography in the United States on Latin America, it can be said that its trends parallel those of the larger guild of historians, in this country and abroad. As an area specialization it has a respectable, if somewhat short, tradition. About 1900 it began to emerge and coalesce as those interested in regional overseas aspects of European nations. Their joint concerns broadened as they explored a then almost unknown area. By 1918 many of the basic general historical monographs had sketched out problems, and sufficient numbers of specialists had been produced to warrant founding the *Hispanic American Historical Review*, now in its 44th volume. Increasing interest and incremental growth of specialists led in 1928 to the establishment of the Conference on Latin American History, a professional body affiliated with the American Historical Association. Its membership now is about 400 persons, a majority of the approximately 500 historians in the United States with a Ph.D. or its equivalent who have specialized competence on Latin America. Of these a small proportion, perhaps 100, are actively producing published studies of history.

Trends in the study of Latin American history and in the training of students show a broadening and diversification. In very sweeping terms, it can be said that preoccupation with the colonial period at the outset has, over the past 25 years, been balanced and even exceeded by writings on post-colonial matters. In line with shifts of emphasis in the general field of historiography, especially the so-called movement toward New History, topical coverage has expanded from an almost exclusively political and administrative base to envelop more and more social and economic phenomena, and their interrelationships.

There is some measure and documentation of what in recent years the Latin Americanists judge to be significant historical research. The Conference on Latin American History has, since 1954, awarded a series of annual prizes for books and articles within the specialty. Each year the membership of the various Prize Committees, drawn from the Conference, changes. Each Committee sets its own specific criteria for selection among the several nominations for each prize. The works which have won or received honorable mention from them reveal some patterns or trends in the current studies of Latin American history.

In 1953 the Conference established the Robertson prize for the best article "on a topic related to Latin American history." After some initial confusion over terms it has been awarded annually for work published in the *Hispanic American Historical Review*. The Bolton Prize is awarded annually "for the most worthy book in English . . . on any aspect of Latin American history." Its terms also provide that "Grace of style as well as sound scholarship are criteria which will be used in making the decision." Yet another prize, the Conference Prize, was established in 1961 and is awarded to the best article on Latin American history appearing in a journal other than the *Hispanic American Historical Review*.

A total of 28 awards for winners and honorable mentions have been made over the decade since 1954. A study of the titles and authors shows that three winners had made a general sweep of history, both colonial and

national; ten fell into the colonial period category, while 15 dealt with matters since 1821. Topically, there is a massing on economic, social, and demographic aspects, in varying combinations. These findings corroborate earlier descriptions of the main trends within the specialty.[1]

Various sources indicate a rising quantity of books and articles as the corps of specialists interested in Latin American history slowly expands. Annually the *Handbook of Latin American Studies* reports and annotates a highly selected group of titles, usually about 1,000 in its History section and subsections, drawn from the world literature. In general, historians in the United States continue to be the single largest national group of Latin American specialists, but the excellent works occasionally coming from France, Great Britain, Scandinavia, Germany, the Iberian Peninsula, serve to add new data and viewpoints, as do a small stream of professionally acceptable studies from the Latin American area itself. The study of Latin American history is an international enterprise. The extra-national writings aid in keeping U.S. parochialism in check.

On the quality of work there is more diversity of opinion than on the increased quantity and broadened scope. It must be said that at any time, in any field, there is only a small proportion of absolutely first-rate or outstanding work, with a larger proportion of competent studies, and then a

[1] Clifton B. Kroeber, "La tradición de la historia latinoamericana en los Estados Unidos, apreción preliminar," *Revista de Historia de América*, 35/36:21–58 (ene.-dic. 1953); Charles Gibson and Benjamin Keen, "Trends of United States Studies in Latin American History," *American Historical Review*, 62:855–877 (July 1957); Charles Gibson, *The Colonial Period in Latin American History*, American Historical Association, Service Center Pamphlets, 7 (Washington, 1961); Arthur P. Whitaker, *Latin American History since 1825, ibid.*, Pamphlets, 42 (Washington, 1961); Stanley J. Stein, "Historiography of Latin America" Palo Alto Conference on Latin American Studies, 1963 (in press); Howard F. Cline, "Study and teaching of Latin American history in the United States, 1898–1964," University of Iowa, Spring Conference, 1964, MS.

fairly substantial range of poor, uninspired, or even ridiculous scholarly output. Historiography of Latin America has all these elements.

Its best ranks favorably with the production from other historiographical specialties, both in books and articles. The proportion of good to excellent work has risen since World War II, partly as a result of the survival of the fittest in an era when Latin American studies in general were starved for support in relation to the newer area specialties. But all would agree that there are never enough top-flight publications. Constant efforts are being made by the Conference on Latin American History and other bodies to provide means and mechanisms to increase it. The productive core is rather small to cover the range of topics and areas yet uninvestigated.

FUTURE INQUIRIES

Another query this article was asked to answer relates to lacunæ, "topics which most need attention." Historians habitually are concerned with this matter, and the Latin Americanists are no exception. From time to time they publish "benchmark" or "state of the art" inventories to ascertain what we have done, and what we should be doing.[2] From these and other data, it is quite clear that no topic is exhausted; any and all can with profit be elaborated further, and many remain to be covered in preliminary fashion.

As an aid to research, the Conference on Latin American History and the Hispanic Foundation (Library of Congress) recently initiated a joint project, funded by the Ford Foundation. A group of historians will prepare and publish a volume, *Latin America: A Guide to the Historical Literature*, under the editorship of Charles C. Griffin, assisted by an Advisory Editorial Board. Aimed at the non-specialist and graduate student, divided into perhaps 20 main sections, the Guide will obviously be highly selective. One of its purposes will be to state on what topics, periods, and areas the available historiographical writings are insufficient or inadequate.

Even without the details which we hope the Guide will provide, certain gaps are a matter of common professional lore among Latin Americanists. We are aware that in the colonial period we are less informed about the seventeenth century and early eighteenth than we are about the sixteenth and later eighteenth. Further, much of the earlier work on the whole period was prepared within the limitations of the epoch and is relatively narrow in outlook. Nearly any colonial topic can be re-examined in light of later advances in knowledge and broadened contexts which current historiography demands.

Similarly the national period, the years since about 1825, is quite open to pioneering, both through study of topics not previously covered at all, or re-examination and extension of traditional ones. To aid further investigations by providing some guide-lines as to what had been written, and perhaps more illuminating, what the principal lacunae are for the National Period, the Editors of the *Hispanic American Historical Review* have undertaken an inventorying program, still in progress. For the various regional units of Latin America they commissioned a series of bibliographical articles by recognized specialists; when the series is completed, it is expected the articles will

[2] Samples include W. R. Shepherd, "Brazil As a Field for Historical Study," *Hispanic American Historical Review* [hereafter abbreviated *HAHR*], 13:427–436 (1933); John Tate Lanning, "Research Possibilities in the Cultural History of Spain in America," *HAHR*, 16:129–161 (1936); Miron Burgin, "Research in Latin American Economics and Economic History," *Inter-American Economic Affairs*, 1/3:3–22 (1947); A. P. Whitaker, "Developments of the Past Decade in the Writing of Latin American History," *Revista de Historia de América*, 29:123–133 (1950); L. B. Simpson, "Mexico's Forgotten Century," *Pacific Historical Review*, 22:113–121 (1953); Robert N. Burr, "History," in H. F. Cline, ed., *Latin American Studies in the United States*, Hispanic Foundation Survey Reports, 8 (Limited circulation), pp. 57–62 (Washington, 1958); Stanley J. Stein, "The Tasks Ahead for Latin American Historians," *HAHR*, 41:424–433 (1961); Robert A. Naylor, "Research Opportunities in Modern Latin America," *The Americas*, 18:352–365 (1965).

be up-dated and then be issued in a single volume. To date coverage has been given the Iberian Backgrounds (1956), Spanish American Revolutions for Independence (1956), Río de la Plata area since 1830 (1959), Brazil, 1808–1889 (1960), Mexico since 1821 (1960), Central America since 1830 (1960), Colonial and Modern Bolivia (1962), Twentieth Century Cuba (1964), with several others now scheduled for early publication.

Historians in general are reluctant to develop elaborate programmatic lists of topics which they think some other scholar should investigate. There is therefore no agreed view on the priorities which should govern the individual work of a specialist. He should decide that. Nor, without elastic limits, is there outside specification on how he should approach a new topic with tested techniques, or re-examine an older one with a fresh viewpoint or conceptual tools. Fortunately, history is a house of many mansions.

METHODOLOGY AND TRAINING

This leads us to consideration of "appropriate methods or approaches" mentioned in the opening paragraph. To the historian's mind, the appropriate methods are those which an historian would find useful to the solution of a meaningful problem. Redundant as this may sound, it can be translated to say that in techniques, even methodology, historical study is eclectic, and non-exclusivist; this lack of a tight theoretical context has advantages as well as disadvantages.

Apart from the absolute prerequisites to have a meaningful problem whose solution will aid in illumination of human behavior over a time period, to utilize as comprehensively as possible the appropriate sources available, and to distinguish between testimony and historical evidence, the historian is relatively free to synthesize his materials along lines he deems professionally proper. He may, and even should, adapt from related fields those data and concepts needed for his own purposes.

Thus the ethnohistorian may well be required to have a nearly professional grasp of certain anthropological materials, or the intellectual historian a firm hold on some tools forged by philosophers or others. The historian's end-product, however, is historiographical. It is not necessarily directed toward the goals set by the disciplines whose information and concepts he may find useful.

The advantages of this *laissez-faire* approach are many. The general spirit of tolerance it breeds among historians for each other and for other scholarly colleagues is not the least of them, abating unseemly polemics over disputed theoretical points. Connected with such tolerance is lack of dogmatism or over-reliance on unilinear explanations for complex phenomena. The lack of theoretical prescriptions opens up broad avenues for experimentation both in the selection of problems and the combinations of techniques to provide partial solutions to them.

The disadvantages arise chiefly in relation with other disciplines. The Aristotelian inductive man and the Platonic deductive one have been at odds intellectually since Western thought entered the literature; these ancient divisions mark one group of scholars from another. The inductive historian may have some difficulty communicating with the deductive behavioral scientist, but usually the best of each crowd manage to create a common universe of discourse.

To return to approaches for filling the gaps in the historical literature on Latin America, perhaps a brief word on training of graduate students is relevant. They are the ones who will rectify the shortcomings of their mentors.

The expectations for graduate work have altered in the past two decades, and are fairly general in major departments of history. We expect the graduate student to know and then learn quite a lot of history, from ancient times to the present. He is also expected to master the elementary tools of his trade, notably general and specialized bibliography and the literature of historiography. Beyond that he begins to make real inroads on his specialty, whether this is an area, a period, or a combination of them. For the Latin Americanist, functional language abilities in Spanish, and hopefully, Portuguese, are common requisites, plus whatever other language skills are germane (Dutch, native Indian, Papiamento, etc.). Normally, after his qualifying exams he will spend at least one year in the area gathering data not available in the United States for his dissertation, and another year in its preparation. He is encouraged, and in some cases required, to work in at least one other discipline in the social sciences or humanities, whose subject matter and techniques relate to his particular historiographical interests. After all this, or as part of it, he should be prepared to begin his professional career as an historian.

Interdisciplinary Implications

This brings us to the final point, "interdisciplinary implications." That is a vast and unruly sphere, in which overgeneralization is seductively easy. It can be said, however, that through the half century that Latin American history has been evolving as a specialty, it has shared with other Latin American studies a general acceptance of interdisciplinary cooperation and approach.

The statement about cooperation must be qualified immediately to indicate that traditionally historians have had closer relationships with the field of geography and of anthropology, and to lesser extent with historically oriented humanists in art and literature, than with a number of other social sciences: economics, political science, psychology, sociology, among others.

To recent times, and perhaps even at present, the latter have limited their investigations to Europe and the United States, on whose experiences they have constructed their theoretical apparatus and have assumed it to be applicable universally. As distinct from anthropology and geography, whose inductive emphasis and area catholicity has many parallels for historical studies, the other social sciences have only recently begun to evolve a body of verified Latin American data. Eventually it may be invaluable to future generations of histor-

ians, but much of it is only marginally relevant to the study of the Latin American past.

The proposition that theoretical social science approaches fully applicable to the United States and Europe are equally valid outside those areas, and particularly in Latin America, has often been asserted, but has yet to be proved to the historian's satisfaction. A small but apparently growing group of historians has in recent months published articles in which they have tested social science "models" against historical situations in Latin America, without conclusive results.[3] If continuing evidence mounts that such models do indeed aid real understanding of historiographical problems of Latin America, it will inevitably erode the historian's understandable and almost ingrained skepticism of their easy transfer. In general, the most fructifying influences for study of Latin American history have come from the occasional and rare individual who has personally combined and integrated various approaches and transmits these through teaching and publication.

Resulting from trends over the past two decades in academic circles, the crossing of interdisciplinary boundaries is relatively commonplace, even for historians. The utilization in area analysis of combinations of skills drawn from various academic departments now is certainly not as revolutionary as it seemed in immediate post-war years. Two rather clear lessons have emerged from the accumulated experience with area studies, whether the area is Africa, the Orient, or Latin America.

One is that no one discipline is sufficiently omniscient to provide full explanations or descriptions for a total culture. Almost a

---

[3] John L. Phelan, "Authority and Flexibility in the Spanish Imperial Bureaucracy," *Administrative Science Quarterly*, 5:47–65 (1960); Lyle N. McAlister, "Civil-Military Relations in Latin America," *Journal of Inter-American Studies*, 3:341–350 (1961), and his "Social Structure and Social Change in New Spain," *HAHR*, 43:349–370 (1963). For the important theoretical and expository works on 16th-century Mexican demography by Woodrow W. Borah and S. F. Cook, see under authors, *Handbook of Latin American Studies*, 1960 ff. (Gainesville, annually).

corollary is that varying degrees of immersion in that culture by those who deal with it are requisite for meaningful generalizations about it. Testing an hypothesis abroad is not "area" study.

A second induction is that successful "area" work rests on full disciplinary competence of the investigator, be he historian, anthropologist or sociologist. Total immersion in the rigors of the discipline is an absolute necessity, independent of the "area" component. The latter is additional, not a substitute for disciplinary training and continuing participation in disciplinary concerns. In short, one can be a practitioner of a discipline without being an "arealist" (i.e., his area is U.S. or Europe), but one cannot be an "arealist" without disciplinary qualifications.

It is the combinations of discipline-area competence that are hardest to come by, or to produce. As Latin American specialists in history, we have found from experience that our most productive studies are those which are interdisciplinary and international, but directed toward objectives commonly agreed to enrich the historian's attempts to unravel the past. We do not claim to have found the mystic balances among disciplinary, cross-disciplinary, and area components, but we do think all are important for our studies.

CONCLUSION

A final word. Part of the historian's credo is that he seeks wisdom, as well as knowledge. It is that effort, whether or not ever fully successful, that may link him to day-to-day policy matters, whose correct determination usually requires judgment more than manipulated data. Apart from their role as prime policy-makers, such diverse figures as Theodore Roosevelt, Woodrow Wilson, Herbert Hoover, Winston Churchill, Franklin Roosevelt, Dwight Eisenhower, and John F. Kennedy also had in common some experience as historians, and shared the deep conviction that historical knowledge and a sense of history were *sine qua non* in formulation and execution of plans and policies, large and small. Most historians echo those views. As a group we do not absolutely guarantee to each Ph.D. in history that he will develop into a wise man, or become President, but it has happened. Our particular branch of learning is not far enough advanced technically to predict when it will occur again, a viable problem we gladly turn over to our colleagues in the other behavorial sciences.

71. Latin American Historiography:
Status and Research Opportunities*

STANLEY J. STEIN

Among the disciplines that have been focused upon Latin America in the nineteenth and twentieth centuries, history has attracted the largest number of scholars and achieved the greatest volume of output. Within the field of history, the period drawing the most scholarly attention has been the colonial, from pre-Conquest to the beginning of the independence movements

(1810), or if one accepts a modern tendency to call the immediate post-independence dec-

* *Social Science Research on Latin America: Report and Papers of a Seminar on Latin America Studies in the United States Held at Stanford, California, July 8–August 23, 1963*, edited by Charles Wagley (New York, 1964), pp. 86–123. Copyright © 1964 Columbia University Press. Reprinted by permission of the author and the original publisher.

ades "neocolonial," to the middle of the nineteenth century (1850–70). Broad scholarly interest in the post-1850 years, the "national" or "modern" period, is largely a phenomenon of the last twenty-five to thirty years. Such are the conclusions drawn from recent surveys of Latin American historiography.[1]

THE COLONIAL PERIOD, 1450–1850

Interest has not been spread evenly over the four colonial centuries. Historians have tended to cluster their studies around three colonial eras: (1) discovery, Conquest, and settlement to roughly 1570; (2) the antecedents of independence movements, 1763–1810; (3) the anti-colonial surge against Iberian imperialism and the decades of postwar adjustment, 1810–50. The reasons for this distribution of time-interest are fairly clear. Nineteenth-century scholars in the United States and Latin America were naturally interested in the origin of their New World cultures, partly from the natural bent of historians to seek the beginnings of a process, partly from their viewpoint of the whole colonial experience. Latin American scholars, such as Bustamante, Alamán, Orozco y Berra, García Icazbalceta, Varnhagen, Barros Arana, and Amunátegui, often examined the colonial period, and in particular the sixteenth century, because they wished to extol or deprecate the colonial heritage.[2] North American scholars from Irving and Prescott to Bancroft and Bourne looked to the era of discovery and conquest with the romantic "nostalgia for the Hispanic Past," or, as in the case of Winsor, Fiske, and Thacher, because they saw in nineteenth-century Latin America the survival of colonial institutions and values or because of Spanish contacts on the rim or approaches to the continental United States (Gibson and Keen 1957: 855–57). While nineteenth-century U.S. historians limited their attention to discovery, Conquest, and exploration, their Latin American counterparts also wrote about the bloody and dramatic debacle of Iberian colonialism, the wars of independence, origins, evolution, and end. From 1910 to 1922 centennial ceremonies

commemorating the independence movements reinforced this aspect of Latin American historiography. By 1918, U.S. scholars had produced a few outstanding monographs on the colonial period, Prescott's *History of the Conquest of Mexico* (1843), Bancroft's *History of Mexico* (1883–88), Bourne's *Spain in America* (1904), Priestley's *Gálvez* (1916), and Haring's *Trade and Navigation* (1918), not to mention the bibliographical tools of Shepherd (1907), Robertson (1910), Bolton (1913), Hill (1916), and Chapman (1919).[3]

The founding of the *Hispanic American Historical Review* (1918) helped establish Latin American history as a field of professional activity among U.S. scholars of Latin America. The next two decades were a period of "concentration, specialization and elaboration" (Gibson and Keen 1957: 860–61) leading to the publication of monographs on colonial political institutions and economic, intellectual, and literary history textbooks; and Bolton's controversial hemispheric view of historical development, "The Epic of Greater America" (1933, 1939). After 1940 the growth of scholarly interest in the recent, i.e., nineteenth-century, origins of Latin American problems detracted from the formerly overriding emphasis upon colonial history. None the less, in quality, theme, and synthesis, there has been in fact a renaissance in colonial studies. Pre-Conquest and Conquest periods in Meso-America and Andean America have been reexamined and reinterpreted;[4] neglected aspects of the sixteenth and seventeenth centuries have been

[1] The references for this paper are only suggestions. The following have been consulted in preparation for this survey: Gibson and Keen (1957: 855–57), Cline (1959), Simpson (1949), Barager (1959: 588–642), Potash (1960: 383–424), Griffith (1960), Naylor (1962), Zavala (1962), Griffin (1961), Gibson (1958), Whitaker (1961a), Burgin (1947), Mosk (1949).

[2] See particularly Bustamante (1829, 1836), Alamán (1844–49, 1849–52), Orozco y Berra (1880, 1938), García Icazbalceta (1886, 1858–66), Varnhagen (1854–57, 1871), Barros Arana (1874, 1884–1902), Amanátegui (1862).

[3] See also Keniston (1920), Jones (1922), Gibson and Keen (1957: 858–59).

[4] Especially useful from this point of view are

illuminated by studies of demography and social, economic, and intellectual history and by analyses of political theory and institutions;[5] there has been more interest in economic and intellectual developments of the eighteenth century.[6] Certain institutions and social forms—*encomienda*, the hacienda, peonage, mestization, Indian aristocracy —have been traced through the colonial centuries and beyond.[7] Particularly promising have been essays in comparative colonial history in which authors of monographic studies have tried to look beyond the particular to broad historical patterns (Chamberlain 1954; Mauro 1961: 571–85). It is not surprising to note that since 1940 broad syntheses of the colonial period by Haring (1947), Diffie (1945), and Picón-Salas (1944) have appeared. On a more limited scale, Chaunu (1955–60), Arcila Farías (1946), and Mauro (1960) have focused upon economic aspects and Borah (1956) on sixteenth-century institutions. Finally, a number of scholars have stressed economic and social aspects of the independence movements in general, as well as the over-all significance of the movements in such areas as Mexico and Argentina (see Griffin 1949, 1962; Humphreys 1950, 1952).

In sum, it is evident that although colonial historians have broken new ground and ably synthesized the growing monographic literature, lacunae are numerous. First of all, colonialists are testing colonial codes against colonial practice. The most notable gap concerns the "formative" seventeenth century, when many enduring colonial institutions, it is now argued, were forged (Simpson 1949: 189–90; Gibson and Keen 1957: 862). Other gaps are those institutions and attitudes that characterized the eighteenth century and endured into the nineteenth. Griffin's article (1949) on the economic and social aspects of the era of independence has suggested that the conflict accelerated "evolutionary" rather than "revolutionary" change. Scholars interested in modern Latin America, the decades following 1850, have

an unparalleled opportunity to bridge the late colonial and early modern periods (1750–1850) by examining such institutions as hacienda and plantation, mestization, family structure, and elitism; the relationships among economic development, demographic growth, and the desire for economic liberty and social mobility; the varying patterns and consequences of independence movements in Mexico, Argentina, and Brazil; and the factors insuring continuity of colonial rule in Cuba and Puerto Rico.

THE MODERN PERIOD, 1850 TO THE PRESENT

Sustained interest in the historiography of modern Latin America has been largely the result of U.S. political and economic expansion, the economic crises of the 'thirties, the stresses and strains of World War II, and the problems of economic growth, social change, and political stability since 1945. The problems of the student of the modern period are, however, far more complex than those of the colonialist. The colonial era has unity of time, a beginning and an end; colonial Latin America was subject to uniform codes of law, in theory applied throughout the colonies; the materials and tools of research are, relatively speaking, well organized and accessible; and change occurred almost imperceptibly after 1570. Consequently, the task of the colonial historian is relatively simple when compared with that of the historian of modern Latin America, who must deal with twenty different states, scattered sources, and the absence of tools of research and who must respond to

[5] Important for this subject are Cook and Simpson (1948), Borah and Cook (1963), Gibson (1952), Kubler (1946), Cline (1949), Chevalier (1952), Marchant (1942), Rowe (1957), Zavala (1943a), Hanke (1949), Leonard (1949), Miranda (1952), Gibson (1948), Borah (1956), Góngora (1951), Parry (1957).

[6] About this subject see Hussey (1934), Smith (1944, 1948), Céspedes del Castillo (1945), Arcila Farías (1950), Levene (1927), Whitaker (1941), Howe (1949), Whitaker, ed. (1942), Lanning (1940).

[7] On this subject see Zavala (1943b), Mörner (1960), Konetzke (1946: 7–44, 215–37), Gibson (1955, 1960), Kubler (1952).

Armillas (1951, 1962), Rowe (1946), Morley (1956), Thompson (1954), Palerm (1955).

rapidly changing pattern of contemporary events raising new questions about a very superficially known past. Whereas colonialists are checking their syntheses by examining the specific operation of institutions at local levels, students of the modern period have yet to make the detailed national studies to justify syntheses. It is not intended to deprecate the useful syntheses proposed by Humphreys (1946), Mosk (1948), Bernstein (1952), Worcester and Schaeffer (1956), Johnson (1958), and Griffin (1961), but merely to point out how much there remains to be done on the historiography of modern Latin America and how weak are the bases of our generalizations.

Obviously one difficulty in synthesis and generalization is the complexity of Latin American history in the modern period.[8] The complexity may be traced to a number of related factors: (1) the shortened perspective; (2) the increase in the size of the literate population, and the corresponding increase in publications dealing with historical themes; (3) the shift from political, military, and diplomatic to economic, social, and intellectual history, which make great demands on the training of scholars and their ability to integrate; (4) the dispersal of manuscript sources and the absence of catalogues of manuscript and printed collections; (5) the varying impact of external phenomena—the fluctuations of a world market, two world wars, and post-1945 international tensions; and (6) the overriding dedication of Latin American scholars to national historical questions.

It is possible, however, to indicate certain historiographical trends in the treatment of modern Latin America. Although Whitaker's *Latin American History since 1825* limits its discussion to materials available in English, its topical organization suggests the principal trends among both U.S. and Latin American scholars. With some fusion of Whitaker's major categories, the broad trends are (1) greater interest in social, economic, and intellectual history, supplementing the traditional politico-military-diplomatic focus; (2) within the still paramount political emphasis, the theme of democracy

versus dictatorship and the issue of the state versus clericalism; (3) a broad conception of international relations going beyond diplomatic exchanges between the United States and individual Latin American republics to include Latin America's involvement in the United Nations and the Latin American process of economic development in an international context.

These trends require further elaboration. Professionalization of the historian's craft is occurring among both U.S. and Latin American scholars, and Latin American scholars' output naturally exceeds that of their U.S. colleagues. The appearance of excellent scholarly journals has acted as both a stimulus and a response to the growth of the community of scholars in the social sciences.[9] Despite the publication of several heuristic syntheses covering Latin America as a whole, such as Johnson's politico-social view of the middle classes and politics in his *Political Change in Latin America* (1958), Prebisch's *The Economic Development of Latin America and Its Principal Problems* (1950), Zea's pioneer study of *The Latin American Mind* (1963), and Beal's "Social Stratification in Latin America" (1953), the principal contributions have been made in nationally oriented studies. In the largely neglected specialization of intellectual history there have appeared the studies by Ramos (1934), Zea (1944), and Romanell (1952), the Brazilian studies of Cruz Costa (1956) and Miguel Pereira (1952), and the Argentine studies of Martínez Estrada (1933) and Romero (1946). Historically oriented economists have made the most significant contributions to economic history in the form of highly original essays: Pinto's *Chile: Un caso de desarrollo frustrado*

[8] As Griffin (1961) has phrased it, "For the national period the plethora of data is overpowering. . . . More important . . . is the rapidity of historical change and the more exact knowledge available as to how and why these changes occurred."

[9] For example, *Revista de historia de America* (Mexico), *Historia Mexicana, Trimestre Economico* (Mexico), *Revista de história* (São Paulo), *Revista de historia* (Buenos Aires), *Revista de Indias* (Madrid), *The Americas* (Washington, D.C.).

(1958) and Furtado's *The Economic Growth of Brazil* (1963). Finally, the outstanding contributions to historiography have been either single-volume national studies, such as Cline's *The United States and Mexico* (1953) and *Mexico: Evolution to Revolution* (1962), Rennie's *The Argentine Republic* (1945), and Whitaker's brief *The United States and Argentina* (1954), or the multi-volume series organized by Cosío Villegas for Mexico (1955–63), Buarque de Holanda for Brazil (1960–), Levene for Argentina (1936–50), and Guerra y Sánchez and associates (1952) for Cuba. Few will cavil with the statement that the volumes in the *Historia moderna de Mexico*, prepared under the editorship of Cosío Villegas and the auspices of the Colegio de Mexico, constitute the most notable historical publications of the last decade in Latin American historiography.

No doubt the complexity of modern Latin American history and the corresponding difficulty of synthesis are also partly due to the fact that the clusters of topics that interest historians vary from country to country. As recent historiographical articles on the history of modern Mexico, Brazil, and Argentina indicate, only in the broadest of senses are the historical "questions" of these countries comparable.[10] Scholars of Argentine history have debated the age of Rosas, the *Unicato* and the revolution of 1890, the trajectory of Radicalism—party, personalities, and program—the Revolution of 1930, and the Peron era. Brazilianists have re-examined the last four decades of the monarchy, the origins of the republic, abolitionism and the process of integration, and the Vargas "revolution" (1930–45). For the Mexicans the questions have turned on the Reforma, the Díaz era, and the Revolution to 1940 and on the evolution of Mexico's liberal tradition. As might be expected, the authors of the historiographical articles differ on lacunae. Potash recommends analyses of Mexico's local and regional electoral processes in 1867 and 1871, the role and function of the *jefe político*, the utilization of hacienda and factory records for economic history, dispassionate biographies of leading

political figures of the revolution, the roots of nationalism, and nineteenth-century Mexican conservatism. Barager urges specialists to study the Argentine "agrarian revolution" after 1880, immigration (1870–1914) and urbanization in a "socio-political framework," trade unionism, and social welfare organizations. Even from this brief review it is clear that the leading areas of historiographical interest and production are Mexico, Brazil, and Argentina and that scholars' interests, and lacunae awaiting treatment, vary markedly. Equally manifest is the fact that the historians whether colonialists or students of the modern period are specialists in the history of one, or at most, two areas, on the basis of which they risk generalization and heuristic syntheses (see Dore, 1963). Perhaps the most ambitious synthesis of this type, continental rather than Latin American in scope, is Griffin's *The National Period in the History of the New World: An Outline and Commentary* (1961). Based upon preliminary outlines of collaborators in the program of the history of the New World, Griffin's periodization, skillful weighting of extra continental, continental, and regional phenomena, and judicious bibliography render the volume a godsend to textbook writers and a boon to the research-oriented seeking the macrocosm in the microcosm.

RESEARCH OPPORTUNITIES

This summary review of Latin American historiographical trends of the near and distant past comes at an appropriate moment. In the first place, the historian heeding the precepts of what was once termed the "New History," an interdisciplinary and multicausal view of the historical process, can and indeed must now call upon research tools, analytical approaches, and the findings of scholars in allied disciplines—economics, sociology, anthropology, psychology, art, and literary history—in unraveling the complexity of modern, i.e., post-1850, Latin America's historical evolution. Probing for the economic and social roots of political in-

[10] On this subject see Potash (1960), Stein (1960), Barager (1959).

stability since the onset of the great depression, perceptive social scientists examining Latin American phenomena have implicitly forced historians to modify what was until then a generally purblind adherence to the tradition of political, military, diplomatic, and bad biographical history. A start in this direction has been made, but historians have a long road to travel. In the second place, the decade since the end of the Korean conflict has undoubtedly been one of great transition in the evolution of Latin America as remnants of the "old," or "neocolonial," order crumble swiftly under rising pressure from hitherto submerged, unrecognized, and neglected classes. Visible are the vestiges of obsolescent tradition as well as the spearheads of change. Historians now have an unparalleled opportunity for a multilateral approach to their craft, by developing tools of research (guides to historical literature, specialized bibliographies, and catalogues of manuscript and printed source materials) and through improved graduate training. Above all, this historical moment of almost cataclysmic change in Latin America obliges the historian to isolate the key problems and issues of contemporary developments and to subject them to macro- as well as micro-analysis—in effect to do what the craft has always considered its ideal, to eschew anti-quarian interests and to reinterpret the past that is relevant. No doubt historians differ on what is relevant, and consensus among historians diverges from generation to generation. The relevance of the past to the present is a personal matter, to be sure, and the following tasks for the Latin American historian today in both national and international perspective and in terms of a broad research "design" have the merit only of suggestive probes in a limited number of areas.

Mexico

Mexico's pre-Conquest background of high Stone Age cultures, phases of the Conquest, its economic importance to Spain in the eighteenth century, its bitter drawn-out civil war for independence, and its turbulent history of modernization since the 1850's

have produced perhaps the most voluminous body of historical literature. To the historian of modern Mexico, the Revolution of 1910 is the great watershed of Mexican history and the first social revolution of modern Latin America. First of all, the historian must raise the broadest question, why was there a great upheaval in Mexico in 1910 rather than in so comparable an Indo-American area as Peru? In evaluating the independence struggle, what relative weight should be given to (1) Mexico's relatively close communications with the countries bordering on the North Atlantic and Caribbean basins; (2) the economic expansion of Mexico at the end of the eighteenth century, the stagnation of the Peruvian economy, and the Spanish government's readiness to make in Mexico a last-ditch stand against anti-colonialism; and (3) the relative "openness' or mobility of Mexican society, the spirit of nationalism, and the early emergence of Mexican insurgent leadership? (See McAlister, 1963). In Mexico this conflict apparently forged an abiding Hispanophobia and an attempt to expel Spaniards judged to be security risks, i.e., whose loyalty to the republican regime was questionable in the 1820's. Hispanophobia may have led to broader criticism and rejection of Spanish traditions inherited from colonial times, whereas republican Peru seems to have kept a Hispanophile tradition. In sum, historians have to ransack archives in the search for material on the struggle against Spanish hegemony as a social movement. Beyond doubt, however, the independence movement laid the basis for the deep liberal-conservative cleavage that apparently subsided in the 1880's, after Mexico's mid-century liberal surge associated with the figure of Juárez had swept conservatives from political, if not from social and economic, power. Curiously, historians on both sides of the border have failed to assess the impact of the Mexican-U.S. war that preceded the Reforma and which may have induced the liberals to modernize to prevent further dismemberment. Research on Mexico's neocolonial decades from 1821 to 1867 must go beyond Cosío Villegas' (1955: I, 45-

107) introduction to post-1867 developments, Potash's pioneer economic study of the Banco de Avío (1959), Chávez Orozco's analysis (1938), and the political treatment of Scholes' *Mexican Politics under the Juárez Regime* (1957).

To what may be conceived as the background of the Mexican revolution of 1910, perhaps the first stage in Mexico's modernization, or what Cosío Villegas has termed the Porfiriato (1876–1910), historians have devoted considerable attention. Admirably detailed as are the numerous studies available, they have left unanswered certain key questions.

It must be recalled that in justifying the Mexican revolution, muckraking liberal historians have peopled the Mexican cosmography with an underworld of Porfirio Díaz, José Limantour, Bernardo Reyes, and others, involved in a vast conspiracy to exploit the Indian masses. No one denies the facts of exploitation, yet historians may more profitably investigate this and related aspects as part of a stage of modernization of an underdeveloped area, as a syndrome of agricultural change, early industrialization, mobilization of unskilled rural and urban labor, social mobility, and pragmatic liberalism whose tenets did not include economic democracy (see Bazant 1960). Since Díaz and his associates were products of the Reforma and never repudiated the liberal tradition, Hale has questioned Reyes Heroles' interpretation that "Porfirism . . . is not a legitimate descendant of liberalism" (Hale 1963: 460). Historians must re-examine the stage in the development of Mexico's nineteenth-century liberalism that produced the pleiade of the Reforma and then evolved into the Porfirian oligarchy which abandoned the earlier emphasis upon political liberalism for rapid economic growth. Assuming that the major characteristic of the Porfirian decades was growth rather than stagnation, treatments of agrarian problems of that era are inadequate. What happened to the confiscated landed property of the Roman Catholic Church, urban and rural, after 1859? More specifically, who obtained what, how much, where? Analyses of the Mexican hacienda

before 1910 have emphasized its "semifeudal" aspects, its reliance upon minimal capital inputs, extensive cultivation, and labor immobility (Tannenbaum, 1929). On the other hand, it is now becoming evident that certain agricultural sectors—for example, those producing *pulque* near railroads or the Morelos and Puebla sugar *ingenios*— were modernizing rapidly. Was the modernization of the sugar sector of Morelos and Puebla agriculture a principal element of social disequilibrium there and consequently an explanation of the intensity of Indian peasant revindications under Zapata after 1910 (Chevalier 1961: 66–82)? Did Mexican peasants revolt in 1910 because their standards of living as well as level of aspirations were significantly or measurably higher than those of their counterparts in Peru? It may be concluded that in 1910 Díaz' authoritarian handling of the political process sparked a revolution because Mexican society was far more "open" than that of Indo-America, because (1) the struggle for independence and the Reforma were more than political upheavals; (2) wage labor in Mexican mining, consumer industry, and railroad construction siphoned labor from isolated rural communities and haciendas, thereby undermining the traditional hacienda complex; and (3) landowners and mine operators, too, were dissatisfied with the Porfiriato's post-1907 fiscal policy (Rosenzweig Hernandez 1962: 519–24; Vernon 1962).

Regardless of how historians interpret the Porfiriato's decades, no one questions the role of the Revolution in accelerating modernization by destroying the hacienda, the core institution of "semifeudal" Mexico. The revolution has been characterized as lacking ideology, as a response to intermittent pressures that force revolutionary governments to respond in piecemeal, pragmatic fashion with the sole goal of social betterment for all Mexicans whether they be the new elite, the middle classes, the "transitional" groups (Cline 1962: Chap. XI), or the rural and urban underdogs who constitute the human material of the "culture of poverty" (Lewis 1959). Some Mexicans now argue that there were purposeful currents in their Revolution and that its success in toppling the Porfiriato came from a marriage of convenience, so to speak, a pragmatic collaboration among dissatisfied elements of a small but vocal middle class and an oppressed peasantry (Flores Olea *et al.* 1959). This interpretation opens the way to a series of hitherto neglected aspects of the Revolution. First, what lessons may students of Latin American agrarian reform learn from (1) the Madero administration's efforts to institute a moderate program of land reform through full compensation for selected haciendas or (2) the proposals of liberals such as Luís Cabrera to maintain the hacienda while granting hacienda workers ownership of subsistence plots (*pegujales*)—neither of which succeeded? Next, what was the long-term influence of U.S. government policy upon the course and duration of agrarian reform and indeed upon the Mexican Revolution itself? Still unevaluated is Tannenbaum's provocative thesis of 1933 that "fear of the United States" had led the Mexican government after 1917 to avoid confiscation of large estates, thereby "protracting" the Revolution. Was this, rather, one of the results of a moderate middle-class orientation, of the Bucareli treaties that "put a complete stop to the Revolution," or of Ambassador Morrow's friendship with President Calles (Tannenbaum 1933: 172, Castañeda 1963: 403)? More to the point, what was the background of the decision to nominate Cárdenas for the presidency in 1933? Little has been published on the ideological cross currents sweeping Mexico between 1930 and 1934. In many respects, the most radical phase of the revolution came two decades after its outbreak, in the six years of the Cárdenas administration (1934–40), when the spine of the hacienda complex was finally shattered by massive, albeit hasty, land redistribution. This was a radical solution, but was it socialistic? Was the ideology of the Cárdenas government basically compounded of New Deal-type reform, in which the state would act merely as a balance wheel, creating opportunities for all interest groups and favoring none? The ideological premises of

the Cárdenas regime would then not differ markedly from those of the Vargas government in Brazil, the Aprista movement in Peru, or the Chilean popular front—all contemporaneous.

There is no disagreement that immediately following the end of the Cárdenas administration the incoming administration chose to de-emphasize radical agrarianism and to put its human and natural resources behind industrialization. Still subject to debate is whether this decision terminated the Mexican revolution. Awaiting historical investigation are careful analysis of how the great decision to industrialize was made and whether it was at this crucial point or in the last years of Cárdenas' regime that middle-class interests and orientation came to predominate over those of the Mexican peasantry and industrial workers. Without employing the terminology of economic or social class, Cline (1962: Chap. III) has contended that the direction of the revolution changed after 1940, and he has termed this latter phase the era of the "institutional revolution."

At this point, historical perspective and insight indicate that the "institutional" phase of the revolution is analogous to liberalism under the Porfiriato when the political elite rationalized that the returns of economic growth would seep downward and that authoritarian political practices within the form of the Constitution of 1857 were required to mold a favorable climate for domestic and foreign investment. Certainly this has been done in Mexico since 1940, as is evidenced by the statistics of the growth of volume and value of output, urbanization, private and public investment, and the industrial labor force. Economic historians have yet to assess the role of government planning and investment and the relative contributions of private U.S. and Mexican investors to industrialization since 1940. Has the state been the principal motor of economic growth? In a society of revolutionary traditions how has Mexican industrial labor been made to accept a reduced slice of the national income pie? What is the significance for the history of labor in Mexico of the career of the secretary-general of the CTM, Fidel Velázquez, now a senator? Finally, what lessons may be drawn from two major phases of the revolution, anticlericalism and agrarian reform, in the light of the contemporary resurgence of clerical influence and the twin phenomena of renewed concentration of agricultural properties and millions of landless peasants?

Brazil

It is difficult to define what is most relevant to the historian today reviewing the history of Brazil of approximately the past century, far more so than in the case of Mexico. Mexico's history can be written in terms of dramatic upheavals against entrenched conservatism: liberation from Spanish tutelage, the Reforma and anticlericalism, the Revolution. Similar mass movements of wide and deep repercussion do not seem to have punctuated Brazilian history; their absence supports those who hold that its history is monotonous (Marchant 1951: 37–51; Morse 1962: 159–82). This may be traced to the continuity of Brazilian conservatism, to an oligarchy whose temper has been "more restrained, its techniques less brutal,"[11] to a frequently cited national spirit of providential compromise, or merely to the fact that neither Brazilians nor foreigners have produced a large corpus of historiographical literature. Cynics may dismiss the problem by citing space, "windows" on the Atlantic coast, and fertility rates. Whatever the causes, the historian must still account for Brazil's high rate of sustained economic growth accompanied by relative political stability (or continuity) since 1850.

Historians must test what is perhaps the most general theory of Brazilian evolution, a tradition of determined yet intelligent conservatism which has known when and where to yield to pressures for change. Independence from Portuguese colonialism came late, twelve years after the Argentine May revolution, after the spectacular military campaigns of Bolívar and San Martín. It was a relatively bloodless movement, almost a *coup d'état*, despite bloody episodes in Pernambuco and Baía; it left intact planta-

tions, livestock, mining installations, and human lives and human property, namely, chattel slaves. Just as republican Mexico preserved and indeed expanded from colonial times its major rural labor institution, debt slavery, or peonage, independent neocolonial Brazil maintained zealously chattel slavery. Rodrigues (1961) argues cogently that in 1822 Brazilian slaveholders accepted an independent monarchy primarily to insulate themselves from British pressure on the Portuguese metropolitan government to abolish the African slave trade. To pursue further the political role of slavery in neocolonial Brazil, was the unity as well as the monarchical institutions of the huge Brazilian land mass preserved despite section uprisings (many with republican overtones) because slaveholders gave massive support to a monarchy promising the maintenance of aristocracy and privilege and of the "contract between masters and slaves"?

Williams (1930: 313–336), Tannenbaum (1947), Elkins (1959), and Freyre (1945: 49, 1959: 79), among others, have claimed that Brazilian (and by extension Hispanic American) slavery was more humanitarian than the U.S. variety. Only Boxer (1963) has offered a dissident view. Perhaps the bases of such comparisons should be reviewed judiciously, for analysis requires the use of comparable criteria, such as (1) phase of agricultural development, whether expanding or stagnating, and the corresponding role of slave labor; (2) size, function, and location of plantations as well as the labor force utilized; (3) availability of a slave labor supply. Have modern students of slavery, like colonial historians, confused the humanitarianism of legal codes with the raw hell of practices? It is also premature to believe that Brazilian emancipation was unaccompanied by violence. Was slavery abolished in 1888, as the monarchy was in 1889, because the Brazilian elite finally recognized that semifeudal or neocolonial institutions impede economic growth at a certain

[11] On this subject see Lambert (1953: 70–77, 118–36), Lipson (1956: 183–84). On the Brazilian conservative tradition and the "social dilemma," see Fernandes (1963: 31–71).

historical juncture? Understandably the apparently peaceful integration of Negroes and non-Negroes in post-abolition Brazilian society has intrigued U.S. scholars tracing the persistence of the Ku Klux Klan and of Jim Crowism. Recent studies suggest that Negro freedmen and their descendants in Brazil until recently stayed at the lowest, most unskilled occupation levels, abandoning to the more skilled and more market-oriented immigrant laborers the better employment opportunities (Fernandez 1960; Ianni 1962; Wagley, ed., 1952). An explanation may perhaps be found in (1) the tradition of miscegenation in the lowest strata of Brazilian colonial and neocolonial society and the formation of a large body of free colored artisans and (2) consequently the relative lack of friction in incorporating freedmen into the rural and urban labor force (Cardoso 1962: Chap. VI, 299–305). Is it verifiable that lacking a tradition of communal landholding as existed in pre-1910 Mexico, Negro freedmen in Brazil accepted their new role as wage laborers or sharecroppers instead of forming a *Jacquerie*, as some have characterized the early phases of the Mexican revolution?

Normano and others have noted that waves of economic specialization—dyewood, sugar, gold, cotton, coffee, rubber, ferrous ores—have highlighted Brazil's economic history.[12] Is the secret of Brazil's social evolution, rather than revolution since 1850, the succession of internal economic frontiers of enterprise in coffee, cacao, sugar, and cotton cultivation, supplemented by recurrent attempts at economic diversification? For example, what is the significance of the "big spurt" of growth, 1850–64, when investment was redirected from the profitable slave trade into the infrastructure of development—turnpikes, coach lines, railroads, urban services (gas, sewage, illumination, trolleys), portworks, textile mills, iron foundries, and banking and insurance companies? After the rate of growth had slumped in the 1880's, the new republican regime in the 1890's almost immediately on taking control stimulated new economic sectors in industry to create sectors of allegi-

ance to republican rather than imperial institutions. Here historians have noted but not investigated an effort to accelerate the "Anglo-Saxonization" of Brazil, using not only Great Britain but also the United States as prototypes (Freyre 1949: 447–51). Should the historian introduce into this model of socio-economic growth the hypothesis that the slow but uninterrupted growth of the Brazilian economy until 1930 was in no small measure due to the influx of millions of immigrants between 1880 and 1934, whose rearing, education, skills, and levels of aspiration were subsidized by the European countries of origin and who provided a market for Brazilian industrial output? Thus, when the Vargas regime in the 1930's sought frantically to stabilize the national economy during the great depression, when overseas markets for Brazil's raw materials production slumped disastrously, it attempted to preserve a small but promising industrial sector-in-being. How this decision was made historians still must speculate, although ample documentation exists in ministerial archives. Did a comparable situation of incipient stagnation trigger the decision after 1954 to sustain the rate of growth and levels of employment despite the dangers of domestic inflation and the inelasticity of demand for Brazil's traditional exports? Is Furtado's hypothesis accurate, namely, that the policy of massive state intervention of the past decade has liberated Brazil's economy from the bottleneck of terms of trade and capacity to import—in effect, placing Brazil at the level of self-sustained industrialization (Furtado 1961: Chap. VI)? How was this decision made? As a result of pressure-group politics, rather than via the political parties, if Lipson's hypothesis about the political process is correct (Lipson 1956)?

On reflection, it appears that the Vargas administration of 1930–45 was the great watershed in the history of modern Brazil. Wagley (1960: 177–230) has described the decades since 1930 as "the Brazilian revolu-

[12] On this subject see Normano (1935), Furtado (1963), Simonsen (1937), Prado (1942, 1945).

tion," and Bello (1956) and Werneck Sodré (1958) have also supplied provocative syntheses of the period. But these remain products of intelligent speculation until detailed monographic studies materialize. For example, unless the term "revolution" is employed only to indicate a more rapid rate of change within the existing structure, the historian must question its use to describe the Brazil's transformation since 1930. Unlike Mexico, where a massive redistribution of income was tried through agrarian reform, no similar phenomenon occurred in Brazil. Small and medium-sized holdings have increased, yet, as Sternberg (1955: 488–502) states, the traditional agricultural pattern of large estates and extensive agriculture has remained the dominant feature of the agrarian structure. How has the political influence of the 2 percent of the population active in agriculture, controlling 75 percent of total farm area, been preserved as the electorate expands? Since agricultural interests have resisted rising rural wage levels, how has there been created a larger domestic market for increased industrial output? Has the process of capital accumulation for the industrial investment of nineteenth-century Europe been repeated in Brazil, that is, by keeping to a minimum the rate of increase of real wages? In other words, the whole post-1930 period constitutes a serious lacuna of Brazilian historiography and a major field of inquiry for the economic historian.

Yet to be clarified is the ideology of the revolts in the decade preceding the October revolution, as well as that of the civilian and young military officers (*tenentes*) in 1930. Did the ideology of *tenentismo* only reflect interests and aspirations of the still small Brazilian petty bourgeoisie whence the *tenentes* were recruited?[13] Were the goals of 1930 a desire to democratize the political process inherited from the monarchy, to destroy the political power of regional oligarchies composed of rural magnates (the "colonels") (Leal 1948) who administered the politics of the monarchy and of the "old republic" of 1889, and to terminate the bipolar domination of the national government by the vested interests of São Paulo and Minas Gerais? To guarantee continuity of policy and orderly transmission of power, the Mexican revolutionaries engineered in the late 'twenties a remarkable instrument of political manipulation, a powerful one-party system, or what Cline has termed "single-party democracy." Why did Vargas' solution develop as a variety of creole corporativism (the New State) with legislation emanating from the executive office, with governmental censorship of communications media, with military support, and without elections (1937–45)? Via advanced codes of social legislation, however, the Vargas administration gave to the submerged masses of the interior and especially to the urban industrial laborers a sense of recognition and of participation that the old republican regime had failed to impart. Yet, while the Mexican single-party device survived with periodic adjustments, the apparatus of the New State collapsed when the military ousted Vargas in 1945. Was this a belated post-war liberal reaction to an authoritarian or creole fascist regime, or was its motivation the fear that Vargas' late flirtations with Communism foreshadowed radicalization of his regime? On the other hand, should the sustained and vigorous development of a multi-party political system since 1946, despite the suicide in office (1954) of a re-elected Vargas and the strain of an unexpected presidential resignation in 1961, lead historians to seek in the orderly constitutional processes of the slaveholding monarchy (in Oliveira Torres' nomenclature, the "crowned democracy") the roots of contemporary Brazilian political practice (Oliveira Torres 1957; Freyre 1959)? Or is the assumption of orderly constitutional processes the misinterpretation of a political process vacillating between authoritarian tradition and profound federalism? Should the origins of the present "prerevolutionary" political situation be sought in the tensions since 1946 between federalism and

[13] On this subject see Mello Franco (1931), Barbosa Lima (1933), Santa Rosa (1933), Lins de Barros (1953), Werneck Sodré (1958: 204–13).

the presidency, between electorate and political parties, and in the fact that pressure groups have forced decisions by direct action rather than via formal political parties lacking either ideology or program? Or is the present situation largely the product of an electorate that has mushroomed from 1.5 million (1933) to 15.5 million in 1954 (Lipson 1956)? Why has the Brazilian military establishment, unlike the Argentine military since 1945, apparently maintained the role of guardian rather than overlord of the political process (Johnson 1964)?

One final comment needs to be made about the related themes of economic growth through forced-draft industrialization, the appearance of many characteristics of an "open" or permeable social structure, and the seemingly peaceful evolution of modern Brazil. The industrial and agricultural heartland of south central Brazil, marked by relatively high indices of literacy, per capita income, and political participation, has indubitably widened the gulf separating it from the generally depressed areas of the north and northeast. Has the heartland functioned for at least a century as an internal frontier, a sector of opportunity, an escape valve of social discontent? At one time, planters of the north and northeast sold their slaves to south central planters when they recognized it was uneconomic to utilize their services; periodic droughts have sent waves of wretched and penniless *flagelados* formerly by river boats and coastal steamers, now by truckloads, to work in the fields and farms of south central Brazil. Has such internal migration, historians may hypothesize, averted until now serious social conflict in the depressed areas? It is evident, too, that the industrializing sectors have gained by tapping an apparently inexhaustible and highly elastic labor supply eager to work at low, i.e., near subsistence, wages (W. A. Lewis 1963: 406–10). Furtado (1962) has declared that industrial labor in the heartland constitutes a sort of Brazilian labor "aristocracy" resistant to revolutionary blandishments. Similarly, has the heartland generated enough economic opportunity so that the extended families of former agrarian and commercial elite groups have been able to participate in new enterprise, financial, distributive, industrial? With "room at the top," so to speak, has the elite accepted newcomers from the middle classes and presumably some middle-class values and aspirations? Is Lipson (1956) correct in his diagnosis that "instead of a transfer of power to the mass of the population" over the past century there have been in Brazil only periodic internal arrangements "and a relatively slight extension of the circle of privilege"? If so, this contrasts markedly with the situation in Colombia, according to Beals (1952–53). In Colombia, lack of economic opportunity at the elite level has forced many of its members down into the middle-class occupations, fastening their value orientation upon numerically weak middle groups and siring a rigid political system whose salient characteristic is violence. Indeed, is it plausible for diplomatic historians to assume that the current emergence of an independent, hence unpredictable, Brazilian foreign policy, as well as the unquestioned Brazilian paternity of the Alliance for Progress in Kubitschek's Operation Pan America, reflect the predictable pressures of a rapidly changing society and economy?

Argentina

In the post-1850 history of Mexico and Brazil, the historian finds a series of progressive surges either smashing or steadily eroding traditional institutions. In the post-1930 decades, moreover, and especially since the end of World War II, the major strains may be logically diagnosed as symptomatic of generalized growth, i.e., broad-scale industrialization, literacy campaigns, social mobility, and the search for and even the achievement of a measure of democratic political consensus. In Latin American diplomacy, he notes a new constellation of leadership, that of Brazil and only slightly behind, Mexico, replacing the once undisputed hegemony of Argentina from 1889 to 1936. But when the historian turns to post-1930 Argentina, he observes that its great twentieth-century watershed, the Peron era from 1945 to 1955, was a postwar phenomenon, a belated Argentine radicalism in a hemisphere consolidating rather than initiating revolutionary changes. In contrast with Mexican and Brazilian experimentation and modernization of the 1930's, Argentina offers what Whitaker (1954: 62–65) has called an era of "conservative restoration." As the historian maps the salient features of the contemporary Argentine landscape, he locates generalized stagnation, political fragmentation, and a society deeply divided against itself. While these symptoms are indisputable, the roots of the Argentine paradox have yet to be satisfactorily unraveled (Whitaker 1961b: 103–12).

Are the roots to be found in the nature of the revolt against Spanish colonial rule, as Acevedo (1957) and Barreiro (1955) believe, or in the unitary-federal schism that yawned in the decade of unitary experiment, the 1820's, associated with the figure of Bernardino Rivadavia? Or in the almost twenty-five years of authoritarian nationalist control of the right-wing federal, Rosas, whose career and action have always remained the subject of scholarly and not so scholarly debate? Rosas' ouster in 1852 seemed to have inaugurated a unitary-federal compromise, the mechanics of which have not been clarified. Was this compromise, reminiscent of the Brazilian era of reconciliation between liberals and conservatives (1850–68) and Mexican liberalism under the Porfiriato, an agreement between the rural and urban oligarchies that political fraticide dammed the flow of foreign capital and labor to a capital-scarce and labor-scarce Argentine economy? Alberdi's *Bases* (1852) and *Sistema económico y rentístico* (1954) would thus foreshadow the later appeal of positivism's order and progress. Such a compromise may have sired the patrician liberalism of the *Unicato* which dominated the Argentine polity and economy from 1880 to 1916 and, after Radicalism's brief interregnum under Irigoyen, was resurrected from 1930 to 1943. Both the republican revolution in Brazil (1889) and the Mexican revolution (1910) destroyed political systems unresponsive to the pressures of change. Why, the historian must ask, did violence in Argentina during 1890 (the *Noventa*) topple an administration but leave intact the political system of the Unicato and spawn parties of protest, Socialist and Radical (*Revista de Historia* 1957)?

Prior to the Peronist decade, Radicalism provided the Argentine masses with an ideology, a party, and a charismatic leader—none of which have historians carefully examined. Once in power, it was torn by corruption. As a form of Argentine progressivism with its emphasis upon political democracy, it seemed to aggregate a variety of interest groups, despite or perhaps because of the ambiguity of its ideology and the turgidity of its leader's oratory. Del Mazo has published a useful but far from impartial study of Radicalism. Historians should supply an objective balance-sheet of program and realizations, and critical biographies of Irigoyen and Alvear (Del Mazo 1952; Gálvez 1940). Equally superficial is our knowledge of anarcho-syndicalism and socialism in Argentina. Why, for example, has Argentine socialism failed to generate mass appeal?[14] Irigoyen's and Radicalism's fall have been attributed to Irigoyen's senility, the corruption of party hacks, and the great depression (Rennie 1945). Others have theorized that Irigoyen's attempts to barter Argentine foodstuffs for Soviet crude oil led conservatives to engineer with the military the revolution of 1930 (*Revista de Historia* 1958).

It was during the conservative restoration that there surfaced tendencies that Argentines had long thought moribund: militarism, clericalism, elitism, and overt manipulation of the political process. The historian may ask if the economic foundation of reaction in the 1930's was Argentine conser-

[14] Potash, who has been investigating the Argentine military after 1920, argues that "socialism as an imported ideology that stressed rationality, internationalism, and principle rather than romanticism, nationalism, and personalities seemed somewhat un-Argentine to the lower-class mind. A contributing factor was its deep-seated and doctrinaire anti-clericalism, which, outside Buenos Aires and a few other areas, was a self-imposed kiss of death" (Letter, Amherst, Mass., August 23, 1963).

vatives' faith in traditional dependence upon hitherto successful beef and grain export sectors on the assumption that Great Britain and other European customers would sustain the Argentine economy indefinitely. Or was it characteristic of a government run by and for agrarian and ranching interest groups to overlook the dangers of a massive rural exodus to the Buenos Aires megalopolis, to underestimate the pressures for diversification through industrialization, for unionism and social welfare legislation, and to defraud systematically the restless urban and rural masses at the polls (Weill 1944; Palacio 1955; Puiggrós 1956; Galletti 1961)? Was the political foundation of the restoration the conservatives' skill in wooing the collaboration of right-wing elements among the Radicals in the *concordancia* or, as some prefer to term it, the *contubernio*?

Obviously this is not the place to review the literature on the Peron era (see Barager 1959; Hoffmann 1956, 1959). However, two major questions may be appropriate. First, is it plausible to assume that between 1943 and 1945 segments of the Argentine middle classes joined urban labor and sectors of the military to overthrow an incompetent, reactionary conservative regime? If so, what were the promises of Peronism to the middle classes? This line of reasoning suggests that in 1955 the middle classes, fearing radicalization of the Peronist regime, chose to abandon it and joined sectors of the military and remnants of the still influential oligarchy to overthrow it. How, then, did that favorite target of Peronist vituperation, the oligarchy, preserve itself during the Peronist decade? Because, for all the rhetoric, Peronism never considered seriously agrarian reform? Given the mass appeal of Peronism's "social justice," why did the urban masses accept so docilely the ouster of Peron?

In the second place, what are the key factors in the long-term stagnation of the Argentine economy? During the last three years of the Peron regime, the rate of economic growth dropped, presumably through Peronist authoritarian ineptitude. Yet how is the historian to account for subsequent stagnation? By defects in the national character, as Fillol (1961) proposes? By an alliance of privileged landholding and industrial groups pursuing intransigently a policy of economic liberalism no longer adequate for Argentine conditions (Portnoy 1961)? By a large middle class unwilling to accept governmental controls, divided in its aspirations, ready to yield political decision-making to "military officers, and powerful business, banking and landowning groups" in order to stave off the political participation of the urban masses (New York *Times* 1963; Germani 1960, 1962)? Or does the trajectory of Argentine twentieth-century evolution imply that a large amorphous middle class in crisis will, as the European middle classes did in the interwar decades, turn to charismatic demogogues, clericalism, anti-Semitism, the parody of its former democratic traditions, and militarism?

Understandably modern Latin American militarism has drawn scholars' attention in recent years. Avoiding the problem of definition of varieties of militarism, it is obvious that militarism is no novel phenomenon in Latin American history.[15] However, its virulence in Argentina, presumably one of the most modernized republics, requires full-scale historical case study. There it cannot be dismissed as the product of nonprofessionalism; the Argentine military have not shown strong expansionist tendencies, and aggressive neighbors in recent times have not threatened Argentina's territorial integrity. How then does the historian explain the creation of a military caste in an "open" society? To generalize that militarism may follow "in the event of a serious political or economic crisis" in Argentina or anywhere, only begs the question: Why have Argentine civilian governments collapsed repeatedly since 1930 leaving to the military the role of constituting a "coalition government with groups of officers substituting for political parties? (McAlister 1961; Potash 1961)? Does the Argentine experience indicate that the military remain a bulwark in

[15] About this subject see Lieuwen (1960), McAlister (1960, 1961), Johnson (1962, 1964), Potash (1961), Wyckoff (1960).

Latin America for the existing structure of society, except where total defeat in revolutionary movements has reformed them as in Mexico after the revolution and Cuba since 1959?

Cuba

Until 1959, historians saw little in the development of Cuba to indicate that it would become the scene of Latin America's second major social upheaval of the twentieth century, and the first socialist republic of the western hemisphere. Its isolation, its military garrison, its role as refugees' haven during the anti-colonial upheaval against Spanish rule, and—the historian may speculate —the enjoyment of *de facto* free trade from 1808 onward, insulated it from the changes sweeping over Latin America, 1808 to 1824. With Puerto Rico, it remained a Spanish colony. With Brazil and the U.S. South, it formed part of "plantation America" (Wagley 1960b) in the nineteenth century, producing for export coffee, sugar, and tobacco with forced labor, African Negroes. On three occasions between 1868 and 1959 Cuban revolutionaries were embittered and disillusioned by their meager results, first during the Ten Years' War (1868–78), then in the struggle against Spain (1895–98) ending in the Platt Amendment, and finally the mass, bloody uprising that toppled Machado and led to the failure of the nationalist regime of Grau San Martín (Corbitt 1963). From the perspective of five years of Cuban revolution it may be argued that the lessons of these abortive movements as well, perhaps, as those of the Mexican and Guatemalan revolutions of the twentieth century made Castro and his collaborators—all historically minded and highly literate—intractable, unbending, and uncompromising where principle was involved.

Two major clusters of Cuban problems will engage the historian for some time. With that perverse insight historians generally obtain from hindsight rather than foresight, it can be seen that in the past half-century of Cuban history there have cropped up all the ingredients of a massive revolutionary explosion. The first major question for historians concerns, therefore, not the isolation of the factors contributing to the revolutionary explosion but rather the combination of factors, external and internal, that destroyed the Batista regime in 1958, entrusted the modernization of Cuba to the 26 of July movement and led to the tragic estrangement of Cuba and the United States. What forces led the Batista regime in the 1950's to what appears to have been the generalized alienation of almost all sectors of Cuban society? The idiosyncrasies of Batista and Castro? Or should the historian take a broader perspective and exhume the conflict suggested by Jenks (1928) in "the efforts of Cuba to reconcile nationality with the persistent penetration of alien enterprise and capital"? Much suggestive material will be found in the publications of Guerra y Sánchez (1927, 1935), Buell (1935), Thomason (1935–36), Portell Vilá (1938–41), Roig de Leuchsenring (1935, 1960), Nelson (1950), Hunter (1951), and Smith (1960) to name only a few, as well as in hitherto untouched manuscript materials in government and business archives in the United States and Cuba.

The second problem-cluster luring the historian—determination of the critical phases of the revolution since 1959, assessment of the factors involved in decision-making, evaluation of the consequences, domestic and foreign—will demand of the profession the maximum powers of source criticism, objectivity, perspective, and synthesis. For a long time to come the historian will have to learn to live cheek by jowl with the polemicist, for the crucible of modern social revolution is more conducive to the pyrotechnics of polemic than to the practice of the historian's craft. In Mexico and Bolivia the basic reform surge, agrarian reform, led to parcelization of large estates. In Cuba, on the contrary, there developed a rapid transition from the privately owned to the state-owned plantation, bypassing the phase of peasant agriculture. Is the historian to explain this phenomenon by a century of large-scale heavily capitalized agriculture which transformed large segments of the rural population into a plantion proletariat, gave Cuba one of Latin America's highest per capita income levels, and made it one of the most literate nations of the area (Sweezy and Huberman 1960: Chap. X; Seers 1964; Chap. I)? In the second place, given the presence of a powerful, modernized bourgeoisie, by Latin American standards at any rate, why did this social segment lose its influence over the revolutionary process, unlike the Mexican bourgeoisie after 1910? Because Castro resolved to betray his class, or because the revolutionary leadership in the spring of 1959 sensed in the Cuban bourgeoisie only another exploiting group, eager to nationalize foreign property and enterprise for their private use? Mexicans deny any clear ideological formulation in their revolution, and most observers of the Cuban scene argue that in January, 1959, the 26 of July movement had no well defined ideology, that it was then only a "national revolutionary" movement with only a common enemy to destroy, but no social and political program for the period of revolutionary reconstruction. Accepting this assumption, historians must then explain the rapid transition from revolutionary eclecticism of "liberty with bread and without terror" in January, 1959, to the proclamation of a socialist Cuba two years later. One school of interpretation argues that Castro arrived at this proclamation because he had to accept from Cuban Communists the elements he lacked, "disciplined and experienced cadres, the ideology and the international support to switch revolutions . . ." (Draper 1962: 57), while the opposing interpretation stresses external rather than internal pressures and contends that the revolutionaries "alienated from the West, in need of economic aid, and military and political support, . . . were to seek new friends" (Zeitlin and Scheer 1963: 142). Ultimately, of course, the historian of modern Latin America will have to address himself to the broader problem of the Cuban Revolution's contributions to the general theory of revolution in the twentieth century.

Some Broad Trends and Research Designs

The highly subjective review of lacunae in modern Latin American historiography should illustrate what is meant by the rich diversity and complexity of historical phenomena in that area. It should indicate that at specific epochs since roughly 1750 major foci of interest have drawn scholars' attention: the struggle for political independence and commercial liberty against Luso-Spanish overlordship, the search for new principles of authority and a viable economic base in neocolonial decades, the anticlerical crusades to eliminate the political role of ecclesiasticism, the integration of the Latin American and the world economy after 1850, the rise of the middle classes, the awakening of the masses, and in most recent times the quest for indigenous response to the problems of economic growth through industrialism. Above all, the survival of conservatism or traditionalism almost everywhere leads historians and social scientists to re-assess the taproots of its resilience.

After the United States it is Latin America that has had political independence longer than any once colonial area. By comparison with most areas of Asia and Africa, Latin America is not backward, although pockets of comparable human misery certainly exist in both rural and urban areas. Yet Latin America since the 1820's, and especially since 1850, has not achieved a large measure of economic autonomy; hence, many of its scholars and intellectual community refer to their colonial past *and* present, to the imperialist tradition of Great Britain and latterly of the United States. Historians must recall that newly emergent areas of Africa and the Near and Far East have not turned for guidance to Latin America. Is this because they discern in this area the institutions, values, and resistance to change that they desire ardently to abandon? In the quest for the foundations of conservative tradition, what should the historian examine? The hacienda and the plantation? The crossing of the elite groups from agriculture to distribution, banking, and heavy industry? The unexpected plasticity of the Church? The example of foreign corporations? The military? In short, is there a broad framework for the investigation of general and specific aspects of conservatism?

Ever since Bolton (1939) assayed a broad interpretation of the frontier as a unifying factor in the development of the western hemisphere, historians have been circumspect in floating new trial balloons of synthesis. Whitaker (1951: 73) has proposed as a "unifying idea" that Latin America's experience be viewed as part of the common experience of the Atlantic Triangle, of Europe, Anglo-, and Latin America. In the quest for methods of fusing "liberty with justice," the individual and society, and in common European roots Griffin (1951: 122–23) perceives a common hemispheric theme. An economist drawn to the historical origins of contemporary phenomena, Mosk (1948) points to the integration of the Latin American with the industrializing economy of Western Europe and the United States after 1850, to the outflow of raw materials in return for the inflow of consumer goods, capital goods, technology, investment, and skills.[16] By extrapolation students of the modern period may profit from the study of colonial demographic variations whose magnitude Borah, Cook, Simpson, and Kubler have been painstakingly documenting, but whose wide ramifications for Latin American history as a whole await fuller elucidation. What is common to all such approaches is their complementarity, not their exclusivism. They are scattered vantage points overlooking a vast canyon of unexplored or partially explored human experience.

It is perhaps through the prism of economic growth and related political and social aspects, i.e., via economic and political history, that historians may find the most satisfactory overview at this historical juncture. Have the principal instruments of modernization been technological innovations, the railroad, the steamship, and the electric generator, which have undermined isolation at both international and intranational levels? Or the secular trend in terms of trade, adversely affecting Latin America's capacity to import, and thereby impelling the area to abandon the international division of labor, to diversify rather than emphasize agricultural specialization, as Prebisch (1950) insists.[17]

The economic historian may hypothesize that there have been two principal stages in Latin American history since the late fifteenth century. Western Europeans brought commercial capitalism, but its effects were limited. Beside a Europe-oriented sector, there remained a large traditional precapitalist, or subsistence, sector creating a "dual economy" and, of course, two cultures, urban and rural (Mosk 1954: 3–26). Accelerated economic integration between 1850 and 1914 expanded the market-oriented agricultural sectors, encroaching upon the precapitalist sectors. With the movement toward industrialism, whose Latin American origins before World War I may be presumed in Mexico and Brazil, the second stage appears, the capitalist-industrial phase, which has had so varied an impact, political, social, cultural, and ideological, and which wars and depression have intensified. Modernization under the capitalist-industrial system is no reversible process, but it might well be argued that in historical perspective it has not severed Latin America from the principal social legacy of its colonial heritage, in Gibson's words (1963: 389), "the rigid class system, which neither the revolution for independence nor any of the subsequent revolutions successfully destroyed, and which is only now being partially modified."

Thus, the Latin American historian must undertake that reinterpretation every generation of historians faces, he must re-examine prejudices, premises, hypotheses, impli-

[16] Bolton's interpretation as well as the articles by Whitaker, Griffin, and Mosk may be found in Hanke, ed. (1964).

[17] See also the exposition of Prebisch's theory of Latin American underdevelopment in Baer (1963: 144–61). Prebisch's original manifesto should be compared with his recent reflections (1963) on the problems of Latin American development.

cit or explicit, in the light of unfolding reality. He may do this as an individual scholar, ready to turn to the resources of allied disciplines when necessary, or as participant in a research team. He must constantly review the broad issues and generalizations of Latin American history and test them at all levels, preferably at the local level—village, municipal, state, provincial, or departmental —searching for primary materials. In the study of hemispheric diplomacy, he must obtain a comprehensive background in the domestic foundations of the Latin American republics' foreign policy (Wood 1961). So closely related is the contemporary world that the historian examining relevant issues of the past is drawn inevitably to the main currents of his craft as practiced anywhere. But whatever his area of interest or specialization, the Latin American historian will sooner or later find that he must come to grips with the tenacity of conservatism— the persistent flexibility of traditionalism, whether his theme be hacienda, plantation, or mine, peddler, moneylender, or commercial or mortgage bank, factor or importer, enterprise of indigenous entrepreneurs or branch factory of foreign films, the problem of the domestic market and capital accumulation or international trade, capital flows and the amortization and servicing of public and private debt, the church as bulwark of the past or instrument of social change, the military as professional core, as modernizing agent, or as instrument of social and political immobility.

But enough of research opportunities and grand designs. Historians, to work!

BIBLIOGRAPHY

Acevedo, Edberto Oscar
  1957 El ciclo histórico de la revolución de mayo. Seville.
Alamán, Lucas
  1844–49 Disertaciones sobre la historia de la república mexicana. Mexico City. 3 vols.
  1849–52 Historia de Méjico. Mexico City. 5 vols.
Alberdi, Juan Bautista
  1852 Bases y puntos de partida para la organización politica de la republica argentina. Buenos Aires.

  1854 Sistema ecónomico y rentístico de la confederación argentina según su constitución de 1853. Valparaiso.
Amunátegui, Miguel Luís
  1862 Descubrimiento y conquista de Chile. Santiago, Chile.
Arcila Farías, E.
  1946 Economía colonial de Venezuela. Mexico City.
  1950 Comercio entre Mexico y Venezuela. Mexico City.
Armillas, Pedro
  1951 Tecnología, formaciones socioeconomicas y religión en Mesoamerica. In Civilizations of ancient America, selected papers of the International Congress of Americanists, Vol. I. Chicago.
  1962 The native period in the history of the New World. Mexico City.
Baer, W.
  1963 La economía de Prebisch y de la CEPAL. Trimestre Economico 30: 144–61.
Baltra Cortes, Alberto
  1961 Crecimiento económico de América Latina. Santiago, Chile.
Barager, J. R.
  1959 The historiography of the Rio de La Plata area since 1830. Hispanic American Historical Review 39: 588–642.
Barbosa Lima Sobrinho, A. J.
  1933 A verdade sobre a revolução de 1930. Rio de Janeiro.
Barreiro, José P.
  1955 El espíritu de mayo y el revisionismo histórico. Buenos Aires.
Barros Arana, D.
  1874 Los antiguos habitantes de Chile, Santiago, Chile.
  1844–1902 Historia general de Chile. Santiago, Chile. 16 vols.
Bastos, Abiguar
  1946 Prestes e a revolução social. Rio de Janeiro.
Bazant, J.
  1960 Tres revoluciones mexicanas. Historia Mexicana 10: 232.
Beals, Ralph
  1952–53 Social stratification in Latin America. American Journal of Sociology 58: 327–39.
Bello, J. M.
  1956 História de república (1889–1945). (Addenda, 1945–54.) São Paulo.

Bernstein, Harry
  1952   Modern and contemporary Latin Amer-
         ica. New York.
Bolton, Herbert E.
  1913   Guide to materials for the history of the
         United States in the principal archives of
         Mexico. Washington, D.C.
  1933   The epic of greater America. American
         Historical Review 38: 448–74.
  1939   Wider horizons of American history.
         New York.
Borah, W. W.
  1956   Representative institutions in the Spanish
         empire in the sixteenth century. III: The
         New World. The Americas 12: 246–57.
Borah, W. W., and S. F. Cook
  1963   The aboriginal population of Central
         Mexico on the eve of the Spanish con-
         quest. Ibero-Americana, Vol. 45.
Boxer, Charles R.
  1963   Race relations in the Portuguese colonial
         empire, 1415–1825. London.
Buarque de Holanda, Sergio (ed.)
  1960– Historia geral da civilização brasileira.
         São Paulo.
Buell, R. L.
  1935   Problems of the new Cuba. Report of the
         Commission on Cuban Affairs. New York.
Burgin, Miron
  1947   Research in Latin American economics
         and economic history. Inter-American
         Economic Affairs 1: 3–22.
Bustamante, Carlos María de
  1829   Historia del emperador Moctheuzoma,
         Xocoyotzín. Mexico City.
  1836–38   Notas y suplemento. In A. Cavo, Los
         tres siglos de México durante el gobierno
         español hasta las entrada del ejercito tri-
         garante. Mexico City. 4 vols.
Cardoso, Fernando Henrique
  1962   Capitalismo e escravidão no Brasil meri-
         dional. São Paulo. Chap. 6, pp. 299–305.
Castañeda, Jorge
  1963   Revolution and foreign policy: Mexico's
         experience. Political Science Quarterly
         78 (September): 391–417.
Céspedes del Castillo, G.
  1945   La avería en el comercio de Indias.
         Seville.
Chamberlain, Robert S.
  1954   Simpson's The encomienda in New Spain
         and recent encomienda studies. Hispanic
         American Historical Review 34 (May):
         238–40.

Chapman, C. C.
  1919   Catalogue of materials in the Archivo
         General de Indias for the history of the
         Pacific Coast and the American South-
         west. Berkeley, Calif.
Chaunu, Pierre, and Huguette Chaunu
  1955–60   Séville et l'Atlantique (1504–1650).
         Paris. 8 vols.
Chávez Orosco, Luís
  1938   Historia económica y social de México.
         Mexico City.
Chevalier, F.
  1952   La formation des grands domaines au
         Méxique. Paris.
  1961   Le soulèvement de Zapata. Annales.
         Economies. Sociétés. Civilizations. Vol.
         16: 66–82.
Cline, H. F.
  1949   Civil congregations of the Indians in New
         Spain, 1598–1606. Hispanic American
         Historical Review 29: 349–69.
  1953   The United States and Mexico. Cam-
         bridge, Mass.
  1962   Mexico: revolution to evolution, 1940–
         1960. London and New York.
Cline, H. F. (ed.)
  1959   Latin American studies in the United
         States. Washington, D.C.
Cook, S. F., and L. B. Simpson
  1948   The population of Central Mexico in the
         sixteenth century. Ibero-Americana, Vol.
         31.
Corbitt, D. C.
  1963   Cuban revisionist interpretation of Cuba's
         struggle for independence. Hispanic
         American Historical Review 43 (Au-
         gust): 395–404.
Cosío Villegas, Daniel (ed.)
  1955–63   Historia moderna de México. Mexico
         City. 6 vols. Vol. I (1955): La República
         restaurada. La vida política, pp. 45–107.
Cruz Costa, João
  1956   Contribuição à historia das idéias no
         Brasil. Rio de Janeiro.
Del Mazo, Gabriel
  1952   El radicalismo. Buenos Aires.
Diffie, B. W.
  1945   Latin American civilization: colonial pe-
         riod. Harrisburg, Pa.
Dore, Ronald P.
  1963   Some comparisons of Latin American
         studies and Asian studies with special
         reference to research on Japan. Social
         Science Research Council, Items 17
         (June): 13.

Draper, Theodore
1962 Castro's revolution: myths and realities. New York, p. 57.

Elkins, Stanley
1959 Slavery, a problem in American institutional and intellectual life. Chicago.

Fernandes, Florestan
1960 Mudanças sociais no Brasil. São Paulo.
1963 Reflexões sobre a mudança social no Brasil. Revista Brasileira de Estudos Políticos, No. 15 (January–July), pp. 31–71.

Fillol, T. R.
1961 Social factors in economic development. The Argentine case. Cambridge, Mass.

Flores Olea, Victor, et al.
1959 Tres interrogaciones sobre el presente y el futuro de México. Cuadernos Americanos, año XVIII, 102 (No. 1): 44–75.

Freyre, Gilberto
1945 Brazil: an interpretation. New York.
1949 República. In Manual bibliográfico de estudos brasileiros, Rubens Borba de Morais and William Berrien, eds. Rio de Janeiro, pp. 447–57.
1959 New World in the tropics. New York.

Frondizi, Silvio
1955–56 La realidad Argentina. Buenos Aires. 2 vols.

Furtado, Celso
1961 Desenvolvimento e subdesenvolvimento. Rio de Janeiro.
1962 Reflecciones sobre la pre-revolución brasileña. Trimestre Económico 29: 373–84. [Translated as Brazil: what kind of revolution? Foreign Affairs 41 (1963): 526–35.]
1963 The economic growth of Brazil. Berkeley, Calif.

Galletti, Alfredo
1961 La politica y los partidos. Buenos Aires.

Gálvez, Manuel
1940 Vida de Hipólito Yrigoyen. Buenos Aires.

García Icazbalceta, J.
1858–66 Colección de documentos para la historia de México. Mexico City.
1886 Bibliografía mexicana del siglo XVI. Mexico City.

Germani, Gino
1960 Política e massa. Revista brasileira de estudos políticos. Estudos sociais e políticos. Rio de Janeiro. No. 13.
1962 Politica y sociedad en una época de transición de la sociedad traditional a la sociedad de masas. Buenos Aires.

Gibson, Charles
1948 The Inca concept of sovereignty and the Spanish administration in Peru. Austin, Texas.
1952 Tlaxcala in the sixteenth century. New Haven.
1955 The transformation of the Indian community in New Spain. Cahiers d'histoire mondiale 2: 581–607.
1958 The colonial period in Latin American history. Washington, D.C.
1960 The Aztec aristocracy in colonial Mexico. Comparative Studies in Society and History 2 (January): 169–96.
1963 Colonial institutions and contemporary Latin America: Social and cultural life. Hispanic American Historical Review 43: 380–89.

Gibson, Charles, and B. Keen
1957 Trends of United States studies in Latin American history. American Historical Review 62 (July): 855–77.

Góngora, M.
1951 El estado en el derecho indiano. Época de fundación. Santiago, Chile.

Griffin, Charles C.
1949 Economic and social aspects of the era of Spanish-American independence. Hispanic American Historical Review 29: 170–87.
1951 Unidad y variedad en la historia americana. In Ensayos sobre la historia del nuevo mundo. E. McInnis, ed. Mexico City.
1961 The national period in the history of the New World. An outline and commentary. Mexico City.
1962 Los temas sociales y economicos en la época de la independencia. Caracas.

Griffith, W. J.
1960 The historiography of Central America since 1830. Hispanic American Historical Review 40: 548–69.

Guerra y Sánchez, R.
1927 Azúcar y población en las Antillas. Havana.
1935 La expansión territorial de los Estados Unidos a expensas de España y de los hispanoamericanos. Havana.

Guerra y Sánchez, R., et al.
1952 Historia de la nación cubana. Havana. 10 vols.

Hale, C.
1963 Liberalismo mexicano. Historia Mexicana 47: 457–63.

Hanke, Lewis
1949 The Spanish struggle for justice in the
      conquest of America. Philadelphia.
Hanke, Lewis (ed.)
1964 Do the Americas have a common history?
      A critique of the Bolton theory. New
      York.
Haring, C. H.
1947 The Spanish empire in America. New
      York.
Hill, R. R.
1916 Descriptive catalogue of the documents
      relating to the history of the United
      States in the Papeles Procedentes de
      Cuba. Washington, D. C.
Hoffmann, F.
1956 Peron and after. Hispanic American His-
      torical Review 36: 510–28.
1959 Peron and after: Part II. Hispanic Amer-
      ican Historical Review 39: 212–33.
Howe, Walter
1949 The mining guild of New Spain and its
      tribunal general, 1770–1821. Cambridge,
      Mass.
Humphreys, R. A.
1946 The evolution of modern Latin America.
      London and New York.
1950 Economic aspects of the fall of the Span-
      ish American empire. Revista de Historia
      de America, pp. 450–56.
1952 Liberation in South America, 1806–1827.
      London.
Hunter, J. M.
1951 Investment as a factor in the economic
      development of Cuba, 1899–1935. Inter-
      American Economic Affairs 5 (Winter):
      82–100.
Hussey, R. D.
1934 The Caracas company, 1728–1784. Cam-
      bridge, Mass.
Ianni, Octavio
1962 As metamorfoses do escravo: apogeu e
      crise de escravatura no Brasil meridional.
      São Paulo.
Jenks, Leland H.
1928 Our Cuban colony: a study in sugar. New
      York.
Johnson, John J.
1958 Political change in Latin America. Stan-
      ford, Calif.
1964 The military and society in Latin Amer-
      ica. Stanford, Calif.
Johnson, John J. (ed.)
1962 The role of the military in underdevel-

oped countries. Princeton, N.J., pp. 91–
129.
Jones, C. K.
1922 Hispanic American bibliographies. Balti-
      more.
Keniston, R. H.
1920 List of works for the study of Hispanic
      American history. New York.
Konetzke, R.
1946 El mestizaje y su importancia en el
      desarrollo de la población hispano-
      americana durante la época colonial. Re-
      vista de Indias 7: 7–44, 215–37.
Kubler, George
1946 The Quechua in the colonial world. In
      Handbook of South American Indians,
      Julian H. Steward, ed., Vol. 2: 331–410.
1952 The Indian caste of Peru, 1795–1940.
      Washington, D.C.
Lambert, Jacques
1953 Le Brésil, structure sociale et institutions
      politiques. Paris.
Lanning, J. T.
1940 Academic culture in the Spanish colonies.
      New York.
Leal, V. N.
1948 Coronelismo, enxada, e voto. Rio de Ja-
      neiro.
Leonard, I.
1949 Books of the brave. Cambridge, Mass.
Levene, Ricardo
1927 Investigaciones acerca de la historia eco-
      nómica del virreinato del Plata. La Plata.
Levene, Ricardo (ed.)
1936–50 Historia de la nación argentina.
      Buenos Aires. 10 vols.
Lewis, W. Arthur
1963 Economic development with unlimited
      supplies of labor. In The economics of un-
      derdevelopment, A. N. Agarwala and
      S. P. Singh, eds. New York.
Lewis, Oscar
1959 Five families: Mexican case studies in
      the culture of poverty. New York.
Lieuwen, E.
1960 Arms and politics in Latin America. New
      York.
Lins de Barros, João Alberto
1953 Memórias de um revolucionário. Rio de
      Janeiro.
Lipson, L.
1956 Government in contemporary Brazil.
      Canadian Journal of Economics and Po-
      litical Science 22: 183–98.

McAlister, Lyle
1960 The military in government. Hispanic American Historial Review 60: 582–90.
1961 Civil military relations in Latin America. Journal of Inter-American Studies 3: 341–49.
1963 Social structure and social change in New Spain. Hispanic American Historical Review 63: 349–70.

Marchant, Alexander
1942 From barter to slavery. Baltimore.
1951 The unity of Brazilian history. *In* Brazil: portrait of half a continent, A. Marchant and T. Lynn Smith, eds. New York.

Martínez Estrada, Ezequiel
1933 Radiografía de la pampa. Buenos Aires.

Mauro, Frederic
1961 México y Brasil: dos economías coloniales comparadas. Historia Mexicana 10 (April–June): 570–87.
1960 Le Portugal et l'Atlantique au XVIIè siècle. Paris.

Mello Franco, Virgilio
1931 Outubro, 1930. Rio de Janeiro.

Miguel Pereira, Lucia
1952 Cinquenta anos de literatura. Rio de Janeiro.

Miranda, J.
1952 Las ideas y las instituciones políticas mexicanas: primera parte, 1521–1820. Mexico City.

Morley, S. G.
1956 The ancient Maya. Stanford, Calif. 3rd ed.

Mörner, Magnus
1960 El mestizaje en la historia de Ibero-America. Stockholm.

Morse, Richard M.
1962 Some themes of Brazilian history. South Atlantic Journal 61: 159–82.

Mosk, Sanford A.
1948 Latin America and the world economy, 1850–1914. Inter-American Economic Affairs 2: 53–82.
1949 Latin American economics: the field and its problems. Inter-American Economic Affairs 3: 55–64.
1954 Indigenous economies in Latin America. Inter-American Economic Affairs 8: 3–26.

Naylor, R. A.
1962 Research opportunities in modern Latin America: I. Mexico and Central America. The Americas 18: 353–65.

Nelson, L.
1950 Rural Cuba. Minneapolis.

New York Times
1963 [Editorial.] July 5.

Normano, J. F.
1935 Brazil: a study of economic types. Chapel Hill, N.C.

Oliveira, Torres, J. C. de
1957 A democracia coroada (Teoria política do império). Rio de Janeiro.

Orozco y Berra, M.
1880 Historia antigua y de la conquista de Mexico. 4 vols.
1938 Historia de la dominación española en Mexico. Mexico City.

Palacio, E.
1955 Historia de la Argentina. Buenos Aires.

Palerm, A.
1955 The agriculture basis of urban civilization in Meso-America. *In* Irrigation civilization: a comparative study, Julian H. Steward *et al.*, eds. Washington, D.C., pp. 28–42.

Parry, J. H.
1957 The sale of public office in the Spanish Indies under the Hapsburgs. Ibero-Americana, Vol. 37.

Picón-Salas, M.
1944 De la conquista a la independencia. Mexico City.

Pinto Santa Cruz, Aníbal
1958 Chile: un caso de desarrollo frustrado. Santiago, Chile.

Portell Vilá, H.
1938–41 Historia de Cuba en sus relaciones con los Estados Unidos y España. Havana. 4 vols.

Portnoy, Leopóldo
1961 Análisis critico de la economía argentina. Buenos Aires.

Potash, Robert A.
1959 El banco de avío de Mexico. Mexico City.
1960 The historiography of Mexico since 1821. Hispanic American Historical Review 40: 383–424.
1961 The changing role of the military in Argentina. Journal of Inter-American Studies 3: 571–77.
1963 Personal communication. Amherst, Mass., August 23.

Prado Caio, Jr.
1942 Formação do Brasil contemporâneo. Colônia. São Paulo.
1945 Historia econômica do Brasil. São Paulo.

Prebisch, Raúl
1950 The economic development of Latin America and its principal problems. United Nations, Dept. of Economic Affairs (ECN 12/89 Rev. 1).
1963 Towards a dynamic development policy for Latin America (ECN 12/680 April 14, 1963); Política (Mexico) 4: No. 75 (June 1).

Puiggrós, Ricardo
1956 Historia crítica de les partidos políticos argentinos. Buenos Aires.

Ramos, Samuel
1934 El perfil del hombre y de la cultura en México. Mexico City.

Rennie, Ysabel F.
1945 The Argentine Republic. New York.

Revista de Historia [Argentina]
1957 La crisis del 90. Buenos Aires. No. 1
1958 La crisis de 1930. Buenos Aires. No. 3, pp. 3, 59, 70–71.

Robertson, J. A.
1910 List of documents in Spanish archives relating to the history of the United States. Washington, D.C.

Rodrigues, José Honório
1961 Africa e Brasil: outro horizonte. Rio de Janeiro.

Roig de Leuchsenring, E.
1935 Historia de la enmienda Platt: una interpretación de la realidad cubana. Havana. 2 vols.
1960 Cuba no debe su independencia a los Estados Unidos. Havana, 3rd edition.

Romanell, P.
1952 Making of the Mexican mind. Lincoln, Neb.

Romero, José Luís
1946 Las ideas políticas en Argentina. Mexico City.

Rosenzweig Hernandez, Fernando
1962 El proceso político y desarrollo económico de México. Trimestre Económico 29: 519–24.

Rowe, John Howland
1946 Inca culture at the time of the Spanish conquest. In Handbook of the South American Indians, Julian H. Steward, ed., Vol. 2: 183–330.
1957 The Inca under Spanish colonial institutions. Hispanic American Historical Review 38: 155–99.

Santa Rosa, Virginio
1933 O sentido do tenentismo. Rio de Janeiro.

Scholes, W. V.
1957 Mexican politics under the Juarez regime, 1855–1872. Columbia, Mo.

Seers, Dudley (ed.)
1964 Cuba, the economic and social revolution. Chapel Hill, N.C.

Shephard, W. R.
1907 Guide to the materials for the history of the United States in Spanish archives. Washington, D.C.

Simonsen, Roberto C.
1937 História econômica do Brasil, 1500–1820. São Paulo. 2 vols.

Simpson, Lesley B.
1949 Thirty years of the Hispanic American Historical Review. Hispanic American Historical Review 29: 188–204.

Smith, R. F.
1960 The United States and Cuba: business and diplomacy, 1917–1960. New York.

Smith, R. S.
1944 The institution of the consulado in New Spain. Hispanic American Historical Review 24: 61–83.
1948 Sales taxes in New Spain, 1575–1770. Hispanic American Historical Review 28: 2–37.

Stein, Stanley J.
1960 Historiography of Brazil. Hispanic American Historical Review 40: 234–78.

Sternberg, Hilgard O'R.
1955 Agriculture and industry in Brazil. Geographical Journal 121: 488–502.

Sweezy, P., and L. Huberman
1960 Cuba: anatomy of a revolution. New York.

Tannenbaum, Frank
1929 The Mexican agrarian revolution. New York.
1933 Peace by revolution. New York.
1947 Slave and citizen. The Negro in the Americas. New York.

Thompson, J. Eric
1954 The rise and fall of Maya civilization. Norman, Okla.

Thomson, C. A.
1935–36 The Cuban revolution. Foreign Policy Association, Reports, No. 11: 250–76.

Varnhagen, F. A. de
1854–57 História geral do Brasil. Rio de Janeiro. 2 vols.
1871 História das lutas com os holandezes no Brasil. Vienna.

Vernon, R.
1962 The dilemma of Mexico's development. Cambridge, Mass.

Wagley, Charles
1960a The Brazilian revolution: social change since 1930. *In* Social change in Latin America today, [by] Richard Adams *et al.* New York, pp. 177–230.
1960b Plantation America: a culture sphere. *In* Caribbean studies: a symposium, Vera D. Rubin, ed. Seattle, 2nd edition, pp. 3–12.

Wagley, Charles (ed.)
1952 Race and class in rural Brazil. Paris, UNESCO.

Weill, Felix
1944 The Argentine riddle. New York.

Werneck Sodré, Nelson
1958 Introdução à revolução brasileira. Rio de Janeiro.

Whitaker, Arthur P.
1941 The Huancavelica Mercury mine. Cambridge, Mass.
1951 The Americas in the Atlantic triangle. *In* Ensayos sobre la historia del nuevo mundo, E. McInnis, ed. Mexico City.
1954 The United States and Argentine. Cambridge, Mass.
1961a Latin American history since 1825. Washington, D.C.
1961b The Argentine paradox. Annals, American Academy of Social and Political Science 334: 103–12.

Whitaker, Arthur P. (ed.)
1942 Latin America and the enlightenment. New York and London.

Williams, M. W.
1930 The treatment of Negro slaves in the Brazilian empire: a comparison with the United States. Journal of Negro History 15: 313–36.

Wood, Bryce
1961 The making of the good neighbor policy. New York.

Worcester, D. E., and W. G. Schaeffer
1956 The growth and culture of Latin America. New York.

Wyckoff, T.
1960 The role of the military in contemporary Latin American politics. Western Political Quarterly 13: 745–62.

Zavala, Silvio
1943a New viewpoints on the Spanish colonization of America. Philadelphia.
1943b Orígenes coloniales del peonaje en México. Trimestre Económico 10: 711–48.
1962 The colonial period in the history of the New World. (Abridgment by Max Savelle.) Mexico City.

Zea, Leopoldo
1944 Apogeo y decadencia del positivismo en México. Mexico City.
1963 The Latin American mind. Translated by James H. Abbot and Lowell Dunham. Norman, Okla.

Zeitlin, M., and R. Scheer
1963 Cuba: tragedy in our hemisphere. New York.

72. The Colonial Period in Latin American History*

CHARLES GIBSON

This is a guide to recent research and recent changes in interpretation in the history of colonial Latin America. It is intended for the use of teachers in secondary schools, its purpose being to present a survey of modern development suitable for non-specialists and to call to their attention some of the major writings of the past twenty or twenty-five years. In its organization it proceeds from general works through certain principal subdivisions to additional bibliographical aids. Our emphasis will be on materials in English, though not to the exclusion of contributions in other languages.

Like many other topics of historical study, colonial Latin America is interpreted now in a manner rather different from that common only a generation or so ago. New primary and secondary sources have enlarged and refined the subject to such a degree that we can no longer regard it simply as one specialty but only as a multiplicity of specialties. Pushing back the frontier of knowledge has been an irregular process, with rapid advances at some points and much slower movement at others. Hence the distances separating the work of scholarship from the reading public have increased in differing amounts, and because few secondary school teachers teach the subject directly their immediate incentive for reducing these various distances, for catching up at one or at all points, is probably less in the history of Latin America than in the history of the

United States or Europe. On the other hand, though few United States schools offer courses in Latin America, it is frequently the case that materials pertinent at least to the colonial period are indirectly introduced, as aspects of the European Renaissance or as variant modes of imperialism or simply as instances of exotic historical behavior. In making comparisons with colonial Anglo-America a common practice is to emphasize conquest or the "inflexibility" of imperial institutions or the want of representative government as points of contrast. Undoubtedly Latin America continues to emerge from such comparisons in an unflattering aspect. Those who have been brought up to appreciate sanitation and punctuality and civil order are likely to adopt toward Latin America (where alternative values have sometimes been substituted for these) attitudes of amused or contemptuous superiority. Perhaps the most striking trait of modern scholarship on colonial Latin America, on the other hand, has been its rejection of the tone of disparagement, its insistence on impartiality, its sympathetic effort to understand. This, while it is not uniformly practiced, is much in accord with the trend of historical scholarship elsewhere and it implies a loss of emotionalism that has in its

* American Historical Association, Service Center for Teachers of History, *Pamphlet 7* (Washington, 1958). Reprinted by permission of the author and the original publisher.

turn contributed to the alienation of the scholar's audience. As emotionalism and a reading public have been lost, however, accuracy and historical sophistication have been gained—we believe and trust at least that such is the case—and these qualities have not failed to bring important consequences. One rarely sees now the bare statement that Spaniards were "bad colonizers." One finds instead scholarly investigations into particular aspects of their colonization and the conception that that colonization is neither bad nor good but instead an object of sober study.

General Works

The college textbook provides the serious modern reader with his most convenient ready access to a subject's content. In Latin American history there exists an abundance, perhaps a super-abundance, of textbooks, all of which provide more or less accurate information. It is probably true that each textbook writer benefits in some measure from the experience of his predecessors and it is certainly the case that textbook writers have achieved an over-all qualitative improvement from the 1920's to the 1950's. Hence, one who depends on textbooks for information (and everyone does to some extent) will normally find more satisfaction with the output of the later than with that of the earlier period. Such works as Hubert Herring, *A History of Latin America* (1955), and Donald E. Worcester and Wendell G. Schaeffer, *The Growth and Culture of Latin America* (1956), are demonstrable improvements over the equivalent works of a generation ago. As a group the more recent books are informative, unpretentious, clearly written, well indexed, attractive in appearance, and supplied with well chosen illustrations and maps. They reflect the advances of research scholarship and they invariably constitute aids to teaching.

Still for present purposes it is appropriate to note also certain covert tendencies of textbooks, generally and specifically. It must be said of them that they do not respond to innovating points of view so rapidly or affirmatively as they might; that they habitually imitate their predecessors as well as move beyond them; and that they rarely depend upon a thorough examination of sources. Moreover in some the colonial portion has suffered a relative decline. When C. E. Chapman published his two-volume text in the 1930's it was still possible to devote half of one's attention to the colonial period and half to the national. Textbook writers no longer do this. There is some tendency in modern textbook writing to understand the entire colonial period as a preparation for the nineteenth and twentieth centuries, where the more important material is believed to reside. The new Williams-Bartlett-Miller text advises that the time "should be approaching" when colonial studies will receive "less attention." These are, without question, legitimate and sincere views and it may be that they cast the subject in a revealing light, assisting thereby the process of understanding. But from the point of view of colonial Latin America *per se*, their message is one that subordinates the subject to other matters, and it is clear that the reader who seeks to enlarge his vision of the colonial period will receive only a special and limited assistance from works that approach it along these lines and will supplement his readings with other materials.

What these should be will depend, as is obvious, on particular requirements and preferences and all the complex factors involved in the process of evaluation. For the moment we wish to comment on several writings that undertake a more detailed and thorough task than does the usual textbook.

Since its appearance in 1947 C. H. Haring's *The Spanish Empire in America* has been the fundamental modern treatment of Spanish colonialism, widely recognized as such both in the United States and abroad. It is no doubt true, as the preface states, that the present condition of research is not conducive to an "adequate, systematic description" of Spanish American government and society. Adequacy, however, is measurable in relation to a criterion, and readers need fear no weakness in the scholarly standard of this volume. They may expect to find in it either the direct answers to their questions on the operation of the Spanish colonial system or bibliographical information leading them to the answers in other works. Its organization is such that it is additionally useful as a reference book, capable of any number of consultations after the first reading. It offers sections on race and environment, society, agriculture, and a wealth of other topics. Its tone is factual and sober. The author rejects the theoretical expansiveness that has so frequently characterized treatments of the subjects by Spaniards and Spanish Americans. It is probably the work that most often heads the lists of graduate students preparing for their examinations, and a student's common reaction is to wish that he had equally clear and comprehensive expositions in his other subjects.

A substantially different approach is found in a second work, B. W. Diffie's *Latin-American Civilization: Colonial Period*, though this embraces the same chronological period and is based on the same or similar sources. Diffie's work reflects the influence upon Latin American history of anthropology, especially of the anthropological concepts of culture and the relation of culture to physical environment. White, Indian, and Negro societies are examined in their original condition, and the transformations that each ethnic element underwent as a result of historical circumstances and group contacts are analyzed in detail. It is a readable and practical work, written without jargon. The concept of a series of cultural fusions, which underlies much of the presentation, does not distort the handling of more customary "historical" topics, such as viceregal organization and mining economy. Rather it enriches these topics in a way that ought to be of special interest to teachers seeking to enlist the attention and interest of their classes— for it is the experience of many teachers of Latin American history that a cultural presentation will restore a flagging interest, particularly one that has been surfeited with names and dates and the details of institutional form. The Diffie work is well designed to meet this need and is copiously supplied with maps and illustrative material.

Systematic expositions based on mono-graphs and factual research do not figure so prominently in the historical writing of Spaniards, Portuguese, or Latin Americans, for whom the meaning and utility of "history" are not the same as for people of the United States. Works of the type of those of Haring and Diffie are less frequent there than here, and the need for educational textbooks on the colonial period is not so keenly felt. In Latin American writing the colonial period is likely to be subdivided geographically and considered in connection with individual nationalistic histories. Comprehensive treatments of the colonial scene, when they occur at all in Spanish and Portuguese, are likely to be more theoretical or more lyrical, certainly less purely factual, than those in English, or to consist of sets of many volumes and of a more elaborate design than their English counterparts. An impressive example of the last is the *Historia de América y de los pueblos americanos*, edited by Antonio Ballesteros y Beretta, and consisting of separately published volumes on Indian cultures. Columbus, the conquests, the church, the viceroyalties, and similar subjects. The series, still incomplete, is notable for its illustrations, many of which are published nowhere else and are directly suitable for classroom use.

Included also in the category of General Works is the literature on hemispheric history, which continues to excite a strong interest among historians. It is argued that just as it is possible to conceive of a European history, international, diverse in its origin, yet manifesting some manner of internal "unity," so one can or should conceive of a hemispheric American history comprehending the dependencies and later the independent nations of English, Spanish, Portuguese, French, or other origin. The views expressed on the possibility, desirability, and value of such a conception have been of the most varied order. The subject is one of the more popular choices at historical conferences for it invariably provokes a lively discussion. Its implications are far-reaching; they include the philosophical meaning of "unity" and "diversity" in history and the Good Neighbor Policy of the twentieth century. The classic statement favoring the unitary hemisphere is that of Herbert E. Bolton, who identified among other features common to the various American areas their European origin, their adjustment to a new land, their resolution of Indian relations, their subjugation of a frontier, and their declarations of independence. Opponents of the unitary view note and stress differences of the Catholic versus Protestant, or authoritarian versus representative government, type, or assert that the unitary categories are fixed at too high a level of generalization to be meaningful. The Commission on History of the Pan American Institute of Geography and History has lately reopened the question and given it, in a rapid series of conferences, prospectuses, and publications, the most thorough treatment that it has yet received. A synthesis of the Commission's findings on the colonial period is being prepared by Silvio Zavala, and this when it becomes available will undoubtedly constitute a major item in hemispheric bibliography.

BACKGROUND

In Latin American history the term "background" has come to mean both (1) the relevant European, especially Iberian, history to the sixteenth century or beyond, and (2) the native societies of America considered archaeologically or ethnologically to the point of their contact with European civilization. Both aspects of "background" are very much in transition at the present time and the standard works have fallen or are falling rapidly out of date. This revision of knowledge is being accomplished in the case of the Iberian background by Spanish, Portuguese, and Latin American scholars systematically engaged in fresh investigations of the archives, and in the case of the Indian background by Latin American and United States ethnologists and archaeologists dedicated as never before to the investigation of Indian prehistory.

For the most part the Iberian "background" has been developed in recent years in the absence of contributions in English. Not since R. B. Merriman's *Rise of the Spanish Empire* has any comprehensive work on this subject in English appeared. Probably the foremost interpretative expression of recent years in Américo Castro's *La Realidad histórica de España* (a revision of his *España en su historia*), which is available in English translation as *The Structure of Spanish History*. This is the work of an intellectual historian who locates the "historical reality," the *essence*, of Spain in its tension of self-affirmation and self-destruction, its "enigmatic embrace of living and dying." Castro argues that the medieval centuries of association with Arabs and Jews fixed Spanish character positively and negatively and rendered it psychologically insecure in the Renaissance and modern worlds. Its collective will, incompletely integrated even before the seventeenth century, has been disintegrated since the seventeenth century. The conception is developed not after the manner of scientific history, but subjectively, existentially, and with sources drawn more from literature and art than from conventional historical documentation. His work provides at once an insight into the *avant-garde* historical philosophy of modern Spain and a series of brilliantly interpreted scenes of Spanish history. More prosaically the medieval precedents of American colonization and the problems of continuity from the Middle Ages to the Latin American colonial period have engaged the attention of Charles Verlinden, who identifies Italian economic practices as the major agencies of transmission, according these a much higher priority among "background" studies than most other students have been inclined to admit. Monographic writing in the Spanish "background" has been particularly productive in ecclesiastical history. Since the appearance of Marcel Bataillon's *Érasme et l'Espagne* in 1937 the great movements for religious reform in Spain, coinciding with the early overseas expansion, have come progressively to be identified, defined, and related to the early missionary movements in America. Equally significant has been a series of peninsular legal studies, which elaborate further a long Hispanic historiographical tradition and fill out the continuity toward imperial law pertaining to America. The an-

tecedents of conquest have been cultivated
with reference not so much to the Recon-
quista as to the Canary Islands, which have
been shown to exhibit many parallels with
later American experience. Other contributions have been made in economic and municipal history. But as C. J. Bishko has demonstrated in his well written and well informed article on progress and problems in
the study of the Iberian "background," the
number of topics still awaiting investigation
for their pertinence to Latin America remains large, and we are not yet able to explain in any convincing way why certain
elements were "selected" for transmission
to America while others never crossed the
ocean.

The Indian "background" presents teachers of Latin American history with serious
problems, for the disciplines within which
the subject is studied are ancillary to history
itself and they frequently entail an idiomatic
vocabulary and a set of alien concepts that
are at best difficult to master. Most teachers
of Latin American history will confront with
bewilderment the ever-increasing detailed
reports of archaeological excavations and
Carbon 14 reports and will feel the need for
some usable guide to maintain contact with
the elusive material, without at the same
time devoting a disproportionate attention to
its study. For South America the soundest
overall treatment is the six-volume *Handbook of South American Indians*, to which an
international body of authorities contributed,
each on his specialty. The *Handbook* is not
above criticism to be sure, but from an outsider's point of view the criticisms are likely
to appear technical and immaterial. Certainly nothing else approaches it for a balance of comprehension, reliability, and factual information, though even here discoveries have been made so rapidly that certain parts of the *Handbook* were already out
of date at the time of its publication. There
does not yet exist any comparable compendium on the Indians of Central America and
Mexico, although plans for a parallel work
are now being projected. S. G. Morley's *The
Ancient Maya* and J. E. Thompson's *The
Rise and Fall of Maya Civilization* head the

list of Maya studies, and G. C. Vaillant, *Aztecs of Mexico*, remains the foremost study
of the Indians of central Mexico. Of all Indian studies those on the "high" American
civilizations (Maya, Aztec, and Inca) elicit
the most immediate attention from classroom students, but it should be noted that
the current interest of many specialists is
directed rather toward the "middle" or
"early" cultures and toward the determination of absolute or relative chronologies from
the earliest occupations. The Indian migrations to America, only recently dated some
10,000 years ago, are now commonly dated
25,000 or more years ago, and intensive studies of documentary sources that were formerly rejected as "legendary" have yielded
genealogical, dynastic, and other data extending from the seventh and eighth centuries A.D. These new extensions and elab-
orations of the material of the American Indian "background" constitute some of the
most exciting new research developments in
the whole world of scholarship in the mid-
twentieth century.

DISCOVERY AND EXPLORATION

Discovery and exploration remain ever-
present subjects of Latin American colonial
historiography. They are subjects, however,
in which interpretation and factual knowledge—in contrast to that on backgrounds—
have undergone little basic modification for
a long time. The materials were examined
thoroughly and scrupulously in the late
nineteenth and early twentieth centuries,
when they formed one of the favorite early
objects of study in the new age of scientific
history. The major expeditions are now
known with an exactitude that is unlikely
to be appreciably amplified, and the minor
expeditions are, obviously, of less importance. Esoteric controversies continue to be
waged over certain dates and routes and
these frequently occasion a considerable
partisanship, as is the case with the Levillier
thesis relative to the authenticity of Ves-
pucci's letters (Levillier argues that Ves-
pucci did sail on four voyages and that all
letters attributed to him are authentic). But
for basic teaching purposes these and simi-

lar points of discussion appear fairly barren. The traditional students of discovery and exploration—Thacher, Harrisse, Bourne, and others—retain their very impressive authority; the explorers' narratives, published in the Hakluyt Society *Works* and the Cortés Society's *Documents and Narratives* and in a large number of independent editions, remain the foremost primary documents; and while respectable accounts of individual explorers continue to appear—as S. E. Morison on Columbus and Kathleen Romoli on Balboa—no revolutionary interpretations have been developed. The subject is always an appealing one and those who teach it naturally feel a temptation to linger over the circumstantial narratives in order to retain or foster the interest of students. But it is probably true that the readily available literature is more than enough to satisfy any such demand. Bibliographies of exploration are included in most textbooks of Latin American history. In Latin America the discovery literature has provided the material for an historiographical study by Edmundo O'Gorman, *La Idea del descubrimiento de América*, which, while its philological subtleties on the *idea* of discovery are hardly applicable to secondary teaching, presents brilliantly the history of discovery interpretation. With all this, however, it is probably still as true as it was fifty years ago that the single work on discovery and exploration most useful to teachers is E. G. Bourne's *Spain in America.*

Conquest and Colonization

Conquest has always been one of the celebrated topics of Latin American colonial history. No one who teaches the subject can afford to ignore it, and there are indications that in the popular mind conquest is the alpha and omega of the entire period, a pervasive and controlling theme. For this reason it may be that teachers will want to exercise more than ordinary care in dealing with conquest, in defining and limiting it, and in counteracting popular misapprehensions through a proper understanding of it. A point not always properly appreciated is that conquest was a short-lived and intro-

ductory aspect of colonial history in each area in which it occurred. The literature of the conquest narratives poses no problem, for it is nearly inexhaustible and the best of it is of excellent quality. The Prescott histories are still accurate, readable, and informative. Kirkpatrick's work embraces both the major and the minor conquistadores. Some of the classic first-hand reports—as Bernal Díaz on the conquest of Mexico and Francisco de Xérez on the conquest of Peru —are available in English. And the standard bibliographical aids contain references to the large literature on the subject. Save for certain of the minor conquests the literature in Spanish is not likely to be of material advantage over that in English. But it should be noted that the most impressive recent writings in all languages have abandoned the older concept of the conquests as a series of military episodes and have undertaken rather to examine their relation to their times as well as their contexts in intellectual and social life and the disputes over justification that they helped to engender. Thus many modern works whose titles contain references to conquest—such as Robert Ricard's *La "Conquête spirituelle" du Mexique* and Silvio Zavala's *The Political Philosophy of the Conquest of America*— understand conquest in relation to institutional or intellectual history. This development contributes to a most interesting trend and it is one that will receive further comment as we proceed.

The actual founding of colonies has played a lesser role in Latin American colonial studies than in Anglo-American colonial studies, probably because the process of settlement in Latin America has been regarded as a minor phase or consequence of conquest and because the conquests themselves have no counterpart in the English colonies of North America. Literature on settlement in a usable form for teaching is not easy to find. It occurs often in the form of local histories, written by patriotically inclined citizens of the town or region studied, and inclining toward an antiquarian view. No adequate synthesis of settlement as a whole has yet been written. Perhaps the best practical solution for teachers is to seek out appropriate principles from a few major examples, using such works as Manuel Toussaint *et al.*, *Planos de la ciudad de México*, or extracting materials on towns in general from Constantino Bayle, *Los Cabildos seculares*. The revealing royal ordinances for the establishment of new towns have been published in translation by Zelia Nuttall, and the important work of François Chevalier, *La Formation des grands domains au Mexique*, contains extraordinarily valuable data on rural settlement. Frontier settlement, especially that of northern New Spain, has been studied primarily by United States students, and of the literature on this subject the work of Philip Wayne Powell, *Soldiers, Indians & Silver; the Northward Advance of New Spain* is both exemplary in its scholarship and well adapted to classroom use.

THE SPANISH IMPERIAL STATE

The structure of Spanish imperialism is clearly and authoritatively set forth in the studies listed above under General Works, particularly in *The Spanish Empire in America* of C. H. Haring, which contains separate chapters or sections on the Council of the Indies, the viceroyalties, the audiencias, the institutions of local government, the church, and the economic organization. It remains to comment on a few particular features.

Encomienda, that ubiquitous sixteenth-century institution whose implications embraced economic, social, political, military, and religious affairs, has attracted the attention, directly or indirectly, of a large number of recent students of Spanish imperialism. Knowledge of it has accordingly increased markedly. Only a short time ago it was thought that encomienda carried with it title to landed property, that it was everywhere long-lived and highly exploitative, and that the continuity from encomienda to hacienda was straightforward and unbroken. No one has done more to upset these notions than the Mexican scholar Silvio Zavala, whose detailed studies of encomienda underlie most modern interpretations. It is now recognized that the trust relationship of encomienda involved no legal property ownership, that it entitled its holder principally to the exaction of labor and tribute from Indians, and that its development and duration were far from uniform throughout Spanish America. Studies of New Spain and Peru have suggested that the regulation of encomienda—the exercise of state control over its tendency toward private exploitation—was most effective precisely in the vice-regal centers, where the influential period of encomienda was largely confined to the sixteenth century. Studies of Chile and Paraguay demonstrate peripheral varieties of encomienda, the persistence of labor practices forbidden in New Spain and Peru, and closer forms of economic and cultural integration between Spaniards and Indians.

A general trend of modern historical thinking on the imperial state is illustrated by the declining prestige of the *Recopilación de Indias*. This great collection of colonial legislation has served in the past as the point of departure for a large number of historical investigations of Spanish imperialism, and it is even true that studies have been written depending upon it alone. But the exclusive or nearly exclusive authority of the *Recopilación* has lately become suspect, and the tendency now is to confine its application to its proper sphere, that of imperial legislation. The error lay in the assumption that imperial legislation was obeyed. It implied an unbalanced view of America taken from the vantage point of Seville or Madrid. Its effect was not only to misinterpret specific American practices but to exaggerate their uniformity. Students now much more generally recognize the limitations of that view and are alert to problems of diversity in the American scene. We are still far from being able to substitute a detailed analysis of regional variants and evasions of the law. But the example of encomienda suggests the possibilities for revised understanding on a variety of other subjects, among which urban economies, haciendas, and tribute collection may be mentioned as examples. It seems likely that future studies of the Spanish imperial system will probe more profoundly than those of the past the real historical application of the system in local colonial areas and at levels of historical experience well below the viceregal and audiencia administrations.

THE BLACK LEGEND

By the term "Black Legend" (*Leyenda Negra*) is meant the accumulated tradition of propaganda and Hispanophobia according to which Spanish imperialism is regarded as cruel, bigoted, exploitative, and self-righteous in excess of the reality. The teacher confronts a serious problem in dealing with the Black Legend, for he will normally find students already predisposed toward it and in combating it he runs the danger of pronouncing an unconvincing apologia. The difficulty lies in the fact that Spaniards *were* cruel, bigoted, exploitative, and self-righteous, though not consistently and not in any simple way. The subject has been over-argued, so that any factual statement concerning it likewise appears argumentative, and it may be that a direct attack upon the "legendary" exaggerations will prove less successful than an indirect approach that relates the Spanish achievement simply and affirmatively. Certainly each interpreter—and this means each teacher—should strive to achieve his own solution of the troublesome problem of the Black Legend.

The tendency of much modern scholarship has been through careful analysis of historical materials to reject the older provincialism ("The Spaniards were bad colonizers") and to see the Black Legend in a more comprehensive view. We may select three works for comment. Robert Ricard's *La "Conquête spirituelle" du Mexique* has in the relatively short time since its publication achieved the status of a near classic. With authority and insight Ricard analyzes the Mexican mission's Golden Age, the first post-conquest generations of conversion by Franciscans, Dominicans, and Augustinians in New Spain. Here Christian labor is presented as the peaceful counterpart to military conquest, the point being developed in detail and with subtlety and understanding. The result of Ricard's study has been to restore to modern usage the colonial phrase "spiritual conquest" and to encourage an awareness of this and related topics in other areas. Silvio Zavala's *The Political Philosophy of the Conquest of America* synthesizes a number of particular investigations published by the same author elsewhere. Zavala here considers the application of European theological, moral, and political doctrine to the problem of relations between Christians and pagans in the New World. A manifold tradition is identified, according to which Indians might be regarded as the objects either of proselytization or of enslavement, and it is shown that the winning philosophy, in the ideology and the law if not always in the practice, was one of civilizing trusteeship. Finally this branch of recent scholarship is notable for the contributions made to it by Lewis Hanke, particularly his summary work *The Spanish Struggle for Justice in the Conquest of America*. Hanke's writings afford a full introduction to an understanding of Bartolomé de Las Casas and the whole tradition of sympathy for the Indian, and they provide detailed information on the ideology of imperialist justification. All these writings have had a major influence in stressing Spanish imperialism's benevolent and legitimate side, frequently naive and impractical, but also profoundly Christian and humane—as in Las Casas' sixteenth-century assertion, brought to modern attention by Hanke, that "all the peoples of the world are men." The meaning here is that humanity establishes a uniform bond among the peoples of the world, all of whom are entitled to respect. That so far-reaching a humanistic dictum should have emerged from sixteenth-century America is remarkable enough, and the perspective induces a new appreciation of the paradoxes of the "Age of Conquest."

SPANISH COLONIAL CULTURAL HISTORY

Spanish American literature is customarily still classified as a distinct or nonhistorical subject in college and university curricula, being taught in departments of Romance Languages and generally ignored by historians to their own disadvantage. Its relation to standard historical topics remains undefined. Literary studies exist of course—

the *Spanish Colonial Literature in South America* of Bernard Moses is among the best known—but the concept of an "intellectual history" comparable to that that has become so familiar in writings on the United States remains almost wholly undeveloped. Of works in English Irving Leonard's *Books of the Brave*, a study of the romances of chivalry and their effect on the conquest, and John Tate Lanning's meticulous investigations of university life are major contributions. But with present materials in the history of colonial culture a far superior opportunity is offered to teachers by Latin American art, which lends itself to visual exemplification and does not depend—at least in the same way—on verbal translation. Some splendid recent studies are available—Manuel Toussaint, *Arte colonial en México*; George Kubler, *Mexican Architecture of the Sixteenth Century*; Elizabeth Wilder Weismann, *Mexico in Sculpture*; Harold E. Wethey, *Colonial Architecture and Sculpture in Peru*; Pál Kelemen, *Baroque and Rococo in Latin America*—not to mention a profusion of portfolios, photographs, and exhibition catalogues designed to foster the aesthetic recognition of colonial art. Much of this material lends itself admirably to the illustration of more strictly "historical" topics; in George Kubler's magnificent study of postconquest Mexican building the whole complex of Indian population, missionary instruction, and royal policy is made relevant to architectural quantity and quality. The teacher's opportunities for a graphic rendition of the transplantations, modifications, and convergences of cultures are abundant in the utilization of this material. Details of everyday life in the colony are depicted in the extraordinary Peruvian drawings of Felipe Huamán Poma de Ayala, and specimens of Indian and Spanish colonial cartography are contained in the *Relaciones geográficas* edited by Francisco del Paso y Troncoso and Marcos Jiménez de la Espada. Finally the codex literature of colonial Mexico provides many intriguing illustrations of colonial life, as in *Códice Kingsborough*, a pictorial encomienda record, or *Códice Sierra*, the illustrated history of the political and economic government of a Oaxaca town. All such pictorial texts are appropriate for visual modes of teaching and they demonstrate the material culture and the daily existence of the colony as no other sources can. Their utility appears to be more commonly recognized among historians now than was formerly the case, and this is consistent with the modern concern for the materials of colonial history itself as opposed to the schematic analysis of imperial legislation. The recognition of colonial Latin America as an environment favoring a rich artistic creativity is a striking development and it has occurred almost entirely within the past twenty-five years.

THE LATE SPANISH COLONY

Studies of the late eighteenth century and the prerevolutionary years have probably been most affected by the new appreciation of the Latin American "Enlightenment." A traditional view was focused rather narrowly on the political and economic reforms of Charles III, subjects that remain, to be sure, basic to an understanding of this period. No one could deny that the imperial reorganization and economic liberalization of the eighteenth century are vital prerevolutionary developments, though the connections between them and the revolutionary movements remain imprecise. It goes without saying that our knowledge of the antecedents of the revolutions for Latin American independence is meager in comparison with what has been studied of the Anglo-American and French revolutions. But the Enlightenment as a movement affording an innovating intellectual outlook has come to be recognized even in Latin American studies. The eighteenth-century scientific investigations, the literary publications, and the societies for the promotion of useful knowledge are seen as direct Latin American expressions of enlightened thought, and students are now aware, as they formerly were not, of the possibilities and pertinence of this topic. Many special studies of individuals, especially economic thinkers and scientists, have been published in Latin American historical journals of recent years.

In English the new recognition of the Enlightenment centers upon the brief but important collection of essays edited by Arthur P. Whitaker, *Latin America and the Enlightenment*, which is the only attempt to synthesize the subject in a single presentation.

Some basic contemporary travelers' views of the late colonial period, such as Humboldt and Ulloa, are available in English translation. There has occurred of course a steady accumulation of modern studies based on these and other materials, though it is probably too early to discover any major reinterpretations. Even so dominant a theme as the disharmony between creoles (whites born in the colony) and peninsulars (whites of Spanish birth) requires a far more intensive investigation if we are fully to understand its development and its significance. But it seems likely that the late colonial period will gradually be more firmly connected, point by point, with the revolutionary and post-revolutionary years. The concept of an abrupt transition at the time of the revolutions for independence appears to be yielding to a more meaningful concept of process, so that the period from 1770 to 1830, or even from 1750 to 1850, may take on an identifying characterization not previously perceived. The colonial student may learn much from the introductory chapters to the several parts of Harry Bernstein's *Modern and Contemporary Latin America*, where the late colonial antecedents of four Spanish centers — Mexico, New Granada, Argentina, and Chile—are summarized from the point of view of the revolutionary and early post-revolutionary years. For colonial studies the result is to place increasingly a burden of proof upon the earlier eighteenth century and behind that the seventeenth century, periods in which our knowledge is now weakest of all. The great void that all students recognize from the late sixteenth and early seventeenth centuries to the middle eighteenth century is not likely to be appreciably modified for some time, and this remains probably the most serious deficiency of our colonial scholarship in the mid-twentieth century.

THE INDEPENDENCE MOVEMENT

Like the conquests of the sixteenth century, the wars for independence of the early nineteenth century have received a large measure of historical attention. It is in the independence movements that the patriotic nationalism of Latin American historiography has found its fullest expression, and interpretations by United States historians —to be sure less fulsomely—have likewise tended to favor the revolutionary over the royalist cause. Students, especially those of Latin America itself, have traditionally been attracted to the heroic and military aspects of the independence movements, which have furnished the material for much adulatory biography and detailed reconstructions of battle scenes. Treatments of the period in English have been notable for their concentration on diplomatic and international topics, for this was the first occasion in three centuries for full expressions of British, French, and United States interest in the condition of Latin America. Major works in this category include Sir Charles Webster's on the British, W. S. Robertson's on the French, and A. P. Whitaker's on the United States. All students furthermore should know of the two leading biographies of figures in the independence movements, W. S. Robertson's life of Miranda, and Gerhard Masur's life of Simón Bolívar.

The possibilities for a revision in over-all interpretation of the revolutionary period are outlined in Charles Griffin's pioneering essay, "Economic and Social Aspects of the Era of Spanish-American Independence," published in 1949. This applies to Spanish America concepts comparable to those of J. F. Jameson's *The American Revolution Considered as a Social Movement* in United States history, and as the one effort to do this in any language it has attracted an attention beyond what would be expected of a single periodical article. It briefly analyzes the disruption brought about by military upheaval and the attendant weakening of social distinctions, the acceleration of external commercial contacts, and the appearance of a new economic liberalism as expressed particularly in the efforts to abolish slavery. The Griffin article is an introductory effort, and its results as a stimulant to major research along the lines proposed remain to be seen. But it may well be that it presages an important departure in Revolutionary studies, from overt military and political topics to less evident matters of social structure, economic groups, and class behavior. If so, it may be anticipated that these studies will pursue a course already outlined in the more productive scholarship on the Anglo-American revolution and not without certain analogies in other subdivisions of colonial Latin America. The fundamental writings on special topics of the Anglo-American revolution—Tyler on the literature, Schlesinger on the merchants, Jameson on the social classes, Elisha Douglass on political democracy, and a dozen or so more —all invite full and detailed comparable treatment by Latin Americanists.

BRAZIL

Save in Brazil itself, Brazilian colonial history has commonly been relegated to a second rank, a circumstance resulting from a widespread preference for the Spanish language and from the characteristic belief that the Brazilian colony was backward and neglected. From an older point of view Brazilian history did suffer from numerous disadvantages: it lacked a conquest and a conquistador tradition; its earliest colonies were "failures"; its intellectual life and its mining economy seemed rudimentary; the Portuguese imperial system appeared to depend on Far Eastern precedents or to be a diluted imitation of Spain's; and there was no revolution for independence. The main historical themes of the colonial period related, in other words, to Spanish America, and these were precisely the themes that were absent in Brazil.

Such attitudes are changing and there has emerged in recent years a creditable body of knowledge on colonial Brazil. Of the works mentioned above several deal with the Portuguese colony in conjunction with the Spanish. B. W. Diffie's *Latin American Civilization: Colonial Period* contains an ex-

cellent survey of Brazilian colonial history. The *Handbook of South American Indians* classifies and describes Brazil's native civilizations. The Portuguese Indian policy has been shown in a recent work of Mathias Kiemen to have confronted problems, reached solutions, and vacillated in ways similar to those already familiar in Spanish imperialism. A contribution by Alexander Marchant to *Latin America and the Enlightenment* demonstrates that though enlightened thinking found a less congenial atmosphere in Brazil than in Spanish America it resulted there too in the founding of literary and scientific academies and political clubs and in the collection of eighteenth-century literature in private libraries. And the important work of Harry Bernstein, *Modern and Contemporary Latin America*, approaches the late colonial period of Brazil, as it does that of the four Spanish regions, from the viewpoint of subsequent historical happenings. The generality that emerges from a survey of these several studies in English is that our knowledge of colonial Brazil has been broadened and deepened in certain ways equivalent to the new interpretations of Spanish America, but with fewer students engaged in monographic research and with a total accumulation of knowledge still deficient in comparison with the Spanish colony.

The masterpiece of Brazilian colonial interpretations remains *Casa grande e senzala* by Gilberto Freyre, first published in 1933 and translated in two United States editions (1946 and 1956) as *The Masters and the Slaves*. It is a bold and successful assertion of unconventional, non-academic history, to which sociology, anthropology, economics, literature, and all other relevant disciplines contribute. The title signifies two strata of Brazilian material and social culture: the "big house" (*casa grande*) of the slave master and the rude dwelling (*senzala*) of the slave, the recurrent theme of the work being the antagonisms and compromises of the relations between them. The work is not confined to the colonial period, but the consensus of many readers (eight Brazilian editions were published between 1933 and

1954) is that no other examination provides such suggestive insights into the basic social meaning of the colonial period as this. The Portuguese colonist is seen above all as "miscible," i.e. eager to mingle biologically and culturally with Indian and Negro, and not always on his own terms. The society that he created was hybrid, easy-going, ribald, and in disequilibrium, characteristics intriguingly reflected in the structure, style, and content of the book itself, which is specific on details of personal and family life lying well outside the scope of most histories. Freyre exalts and enthuses over the hybrid character of Brazilian society, interpreting as a positive virtue what had formerly been regarded, with shame, as a source of weakness. He has been criticized for his impressionism, his forthright candor, and his preoccupation with the subject of "miscibility," but these criticisms provoke the rejoinder that he is therefore profoundly and gloriously Brazilian.

Bibliographical Aids

Most of the books and articles mentioned contain notes or bibliographies that will lead the reader to still other sources. Attention may especially be called to four detailed surveys of recent research on particular topics: C. J. Bishko on the Iberian background; Pedro Armillas on the Indian background; R. S. Chamberlain on the encomienda; and R. E. Humphreys on the independence movements. There exist many general bibliographies on the history of Latin America, as well as special bibliographies on its law, its art, its economics, its folklore, its geographical regions, and other topics. A bibliography very useful for teachers is R. A. Humphreys' *Latin America: A Selective Guide to Publications in English*. For annotated commentary on current and future writing two continuing series may be profitably consulted: the *Handbook of Latin American Studies*, issued annually, and the *Indice histórico español*, issued every three months.

Bibliography

Armillas, Pedro. "Cronología y periodificación de la historia de la América precolombina," *Cahiers d'histoire mondiale*, III (1956), 463–503.

Ballesteros y Beretta, Antonio (ed.). *Historia de América y de los pueblos Americanos*. Barcelona, 1936——.

Bataillon, Marcel. *Érasme et l'Espagne; recherches sur l'histoire spirituelle du XVIe siècle*. Paris, 1937.

Bayle, Constantino. *Los cabildos seculares en la América española*. Madrid, 1952.

Bernstein, Harry. *Modern and Contemporary Latin America*. Philadelphia: J. B. Lippincott, 1952.

Bishko, Charles J. "The Iberian Background of Latin American History: Recent Progress and Continuing Problems," *The Hispanic American Historical Review*, XXXVI (February, 1956), 50–80.

Bolton, Herbert E. "The Epic of Greater America," *The American Historical Review*, XXXVIII (1932–1933), 448–474.

Bourne, Edward G. *Spain in America, 1450–1580*. (*The American Nation: A History*, III.) New York: Harper and Bros., 1904.

Castro, Américo. *The Structure of Spanish History*. Trans. by Edward L. King. Princeton: Princeton University Press, 1954.

Chamberlain, Robert S. "Simpson's *The Encomienda in New Spain* and Recent Encomienda Studies," *The Hispanic American Historical Review*, XXXIV (1954), 238–250.

Chapman, Charles E. *Colonial Hispanic America: A History*. New York: Macmillan, 1933.

——. *Republican Hispanic America: A History*. New York: Macmillan, 1937.

Chevalier, François. *La Formation des grands domaines au Mexique; terre et société aux XVIe–XVIIe siècles*. (*Université de Paris. Travaux et mémoires de l'Institut d'ethnologie*, 56.) Paris, 1952.

Códice Kingsborough. Memorial de los indios de Tepetlaoztoc, ed. Francisco del Paso y Troncoso. Madrid, 1912.

Códice Sierra. Traducción al español de su texto nahuatl y explicación de sus pinturas jeroglíficas. Trans. by Nicolás León. Mexico, 1933.

Cortés Society, *Documents and Narratives Concerning the Discovery and Conquest of Latin America*. (2 series, 9 vols.) Berkeley: University of California Press, 1917–1950.

Díaz del Castillo, Bernal. *The True History of the Conquest of Mexico*. Trans. by Maurice Keatinge. 2 vols. New York, 1927. Many other editions available.

Diffie, Bailey W. *Latin-American Civilization:*

Colonial Period. Harrisburg, Pa.: Stackpole Sons, 1945.

Freyre, Gilberto. The Masters and the Slaves; A Study in the Development of Brazilian Civilization. [Original title, Casa grande e senzala.] Trans. by Samuel Putnam. 2nd English language ed. rev. New York, 1956.

Griffin, Charles C. "Economic and Social Aspects of the Era of Spanish-American Independence," The Hispanic American Historical Review, XXIX (1949), 170–187.

Hakluyt Society. Works. (2 series, 206 vols.) London, 1847–1955.

Handbook of Latin American Studies. 19 vols. Cambridge: Harvard University Press and Gainesville: University of Florida Press, 1936–1957.

Hanke, Lewis. The Spanish Struggle for Justice in the Conquest of America. Philadelphia: University of Pennsylvania Press, 1949.

Haring, Clarence H. The Spanish Empire in America. New York: Oxford University Press, 1947.

Harrisse, Henry. Christophe Colomb; son origine, sa vie, ses voyages, sa famille et ses descendants. 2 vols. Paris, 1884–1885.

Herring, Hubert C. A History of Latin America from the Beginnings to the Present. New York: Alfred A. Knopf, 1955.

Humboldt, Alexander de. Political Essay on the Kingdom of New Spain. 4 vols. Trans. by John Black. London, 1811.

Humphreys, Robert A. Latin America: A Selective Guide to Publications in English. London and New York: Royal Institute of International Affairs, 1949.

———. "The Historiography of the Spanish American Revolutions," The Hispanic American Historical Review, XXXVI (February, 1956), 81–93.

Índice Histórico Español. Barcelona, 1953.———.

Jiménez de la Espada, Marcos (ed.). Relaciones geográficos de Indias: Perú. 4 vols. Madrid, 1881–1897.

Kelemen, Pál. Baroque and Rococo in Latin America. New York: Macmillan, 1951.

Kiemen, Mathias C. The Indian Policy of Portugal in the Amazon Region, 1614–1693. Washington, D.C.: Catholic University of America Press, 1954.

Kirkpatrick, Frederick A. The Spanish Conquistadores. 2nd ed. London, 1946.

Kubler, George. Mexican Architecture of the Sixteenth Century. (Yale Historical Publications, History of Art, V.) 2 vols. New Haven: Yale University Press, 1948.

Lanning, John Tate. Academic Culture in the Spanish Colonies. New York: Oxford University Press, 1940.

Leonard, Irving A. Books of the Brave, Being an Account of Books and of Men in the Spanish Conquest and Settlement of the Sixteenth-Century New World. Cambridge: Harvard University Press, 1949.

Levillier, Roberto. América la bien llamada. 2 vols. Buenos Aires, 1948.

Masur, Gerhard. Simón Bolívar. Albuquerque: University of New Mexico Press, 1948.

Merriman, Roger B. The Rise of the Spanish Empire in the Old World and the New. 4 vols. New York: Macmillan, 1918–1934.

Morison, Samuel E. Admiral of the Ocean Sea; a Life of Christopher Columbus. 2 vols. Boston: Little, Brown and Co., 1942.

Morley, Sylvanus G. The Ancient Maya. 3rd ed. Stanford: Stanford University Press, 1956.

Moses, Bernard. Spanish Colonial Literature in South America. New York: Hispanic Society of America, 1922.

Nuttall, Zelia (trans.). "Royal Ordinances Concerning the Laying Out of New Towns," The Hispanic American Historical Review, IV (1921), 743–753; V (1922), 249–254.

O'Gorman, Edmundo. La Idea del descubrimiento de América; historia de esa interpretación y crítica de sus fundamentos. Mexico, 1951.

Paso y Troncoso, Francisco del (ed.). Papeles de Nueva España. 9 vols. Madrid and Mexico, 1905–1948.

Poma de Ayala, Felipe Huamán. Nueva corónica y buen gobierno (codex péruvien illustré) (Université de Paris. Travaux et mémoires de l'Institut d'ethnologie, XXIII.) Paris, 1936.

Powell, Philip W. Soldiers, Indians and Silver; the Northward Advance of New Spain, 1550–1600. Berkeley: University of California Press, 1952.

Prescott, William H. History of the Conquest of Mexico, with a Preliminary View of the Ancient Mexican Civilization, and the Life of the Conqueror, Hernando Cortés. 3 vols. New York, 1843. Many other editions available.

———. History of the Conquest of Peru, with a Preliminary View of the Civilization of the Incas. 2 vols. New York, 1847. Many other editions available.

Recopilación de leyes de los reynos de las Indias. 4 vols. Madrid, 1681. Many other editions available.

Ricard, Robert. La "Conquête spirituelle" du Mexique. (Université de Paris. Travaux et *mémoires de l'Institut d'ethnologie, XX.*) Paris, 1933.

Robertson, William S. *France and Latin-American Independence.* Baltimore: Johns Hopkins University Press, 1939.

——. *The Life of Miranda.* 2 vols. Chapel Hill: University of North Carolina Press, 1929.

Romoli, Kathleen. *Balboa of Darién, Discoverer of the Pacific.* Garden City: Doubleday, 1953.

Steward, Julian H. (ed.). *Handbook of South American Indians.* 6 vols. (*Smithsonian Institution, Bureau of American Ethnology Bulletin 143.*) Washington, D.C.: U.S. Printing Office, 1946–1950.

Thacher, John Boyd. *Christopher Columbus: His Life, His Work, His Remains, as Revealed by Original Printed and Manuscript Records,* 3 vols. New York: G. P. Putnam's Sons, 1903–1904.

Thompson, John Eric. *The Rise and Fall of Maya Civilization.* Norman: University of Oklahoma Press, 1954.

Toussaint, Manuel. *Arte colonial en México.* Mexico, 1948.

Toussaint, Manuel, Federico Gómez de Orozco, and Justino Fernández. *Planos de la ciudad de México, siglos XVI y XVII; estudio histórico, urbanístico y bibliográfico.* Mexico, 1938.

Ulloa, Antonio de. *A Voyage to South America.* 5th ed. Trans. by John Adams. London, 1807.

Vaillant, George C. *Aztecs of Mexico; Origin, Rise and Fall of the Aztec Nation.* New York: Doubleday, Doran and Co., 1941.

Verlinden, Charles. *Précédents mediévaux de la colonie en Amérique.* (*Instituto Panamericano de Geografía e Historia, Publicación núm. 177.*) Mexico, 1954.

Webster, Sir Charles K. *Britain and the Independence of Latin America, 1812–1830.* 2 vols. New York: Oxford University Press, 1938.

Weismann, Elizabeth Wilder. *Mexico in Sculpture, 1521–1821.* Cambridge: Harvard University Press, 1950.

Wethey, Harold E. *Colonial Architecture and Sculpture in Peru.* Cambridge: Harvard University Press. 1949.

Whitaker, Arthur P. (ed.). *Latin America and the Enlightenment.* New York: D. Appleton-Century Co., 1942.

Whitaker, Arthur P. *The United States and the Independence of Latin America, 1800–1830.* Baltimore: Johns Hopkins University Press, 1941.

Williams, Mary W., Ruhl J. Bartlett, and Russell E. Miller. *The People and Politics of Latin America.* 4th ed. Boston: Ginn, 1955.

Worcester, Donald E., and Wendell G. Schaeffer. *The Growth and Culture of Latin America.* New York: Oxford University Press, 1956.

Xérez, Francisco de. "Narrative of the Conquest of Peru," *Reports on the Discovery of Peru.* Trans. by Clements R. Markham. London, 1872, pp. 1–109.

Zavala, Silvio A. *De encomiendas y propiedad territorial en algunas regiones de la América española.* Mexico, 1940.

——. *The Political Philosophy of the Conquest of America.* Trans. by Teener Hall. Mexico, 1953.

73. Latin American History Since 1825*

Arthur P. Whitaker

Although few secondary schools are able to devote an entire course to Latin America, many draw upon that area for purposes of illustration and comparison in courses of broader scope, such as those labelled "Social Studies" or "World Affairs."[1] Consequently, it should be pointed out at the beginning that the history of Latin America in the national period is rich in materials suitable for courses of the latter kind.[2]

Latin America provides prime illustrations of two of the most frequently discussed worldwide phenomena of the present era, the "revolution of rising expectations" and the "population explosion." These phenomena are of relatively recent origin, but from the beginning of its political independence about 1825 Latin America has illustrated other themes of broad interest, such as the conflict between democracy and dictatorship, the struggle for economic development, and the spread of modern technology, capital investments, and various kinds of ideas—literary, philosophical, educational, scientific—from Western Europe and the United States to other parts of the world.

On these and other important themes, materials suitable for use in secondary schools are now available in English on most aspects of Latin American history in the national period, though, as indicated below, there are still some important gaps. Taking up where the companion essay in this series[3] left off—the completion of the main struggle for Latin American independence—the following account presents one historian's view of the main trends in the historical writing of the last generation about the national states of Latin America. Individual works (books in most cases, articles in a very few) are cited below for illustrative purposes, but lack of space has made it necessary to omit many others of high quality. Heavy stress will be laid on works in English because they are so much more easily available; although the great majority of these have been produced in the United States, some notable contributions have been made by British writers. Stress will also be laid on the problem approach and on the broadening effect of the growing impact of the humanities and social sciences on historical writing during the period under consideration. In the latter connection, it should be noted that Latin American historians were among the first to use the "area studies" approach in the 1930's. Unlike some other scholars, they have continued to work as individuals rather than as members of interdisciplinary teams, but they have nevertheless made increasing use of the findings of other disciplines.

General Accounts—Problems of Organization

Latin America in the national period has had sufficient cohesion to justify treating it

---

* American Historical Association, Service Center for Teachers of History, *Publication*, 42 (Washington: 1961. 2nd ed. 1965). Reprinted by permission of the author and the original publisher.

[1] *Latin America in School and College Teaching Materials*, published in 1944 by the American Council on Education and edited by H. E. Wilson, brings together the results of a careful study of the subject. In view of the extensive subsequent changes, both in Latin America and in our schools and colleges, it might be well to make a similar inquiry today.

[2] For aid in this revision the author makes grateful acknowledgement to Howard F. Cline, John J. Johnson, Lyle McAlister, Richard M. Morse, and Stanley J. Stein.

[3] Charles Gibson, *The Colonial Period in Latin American History*, 1958. See also Charles Gibson and Benjamin Keen, "Trends of United States Studies in Latin American History," *American Historical Review*, LXII (July 1957), 855–77, which deals with both the colonial and national periods.

as a unit of history. Yet satisfactory treatment of it in a general account is rendered extraordinarily difficult by the facts that it is made up of twenty independent and highly diverse states, that some of the most important foreign ties of each of the twenty have bound it not to its neighbors but to Europe or the United States, and that many of the forces shaping Latin American development in the national period have been generated in those two areas rather than in Latin America itself. The historian of modern Europe faces a somewhat similar problem, but it is easier to solve because Europe has been much more autonomous in shaping its history.

Two main types of solution to this problem have been employed in the general histories of Latin America in this period. All of these have been primarily textbooks and almost all cover the colonial as well as the national period. Among the books now widely used, the encyclopedic, national-history type was the first to appear and is still favored. It is characterized by separate treatment of each country and by strong emphasis on political and military history; in its extreme form, the whole national history of each country is narrated continuously in one chapter, and all the chapters are approximately equal in length. In addition, all books of this type have a few general chapters on such themes as "Arts, Letters, and Education" and "International Relations." Recent variations have included the chronological division and regrouping of national histories (e.g., 1900 has become a popular dividing line) and greater concentration on leading countries; but the treatment is still essentially national. The oldest work of this type still widely used is by the late M. W. Williams (revised to 1955 by others); the most recent, by John E. Fagg (1963).[4] In between have appeared those of H. M. Bailey and A. P. Nasatir (1960), J. F. Bannon and P. M. Dunne (1963), Hubert Herring (1961), T. B. Jones and W. D. Beatty (1950), D. G. Munro (1960), J. F. Rippy (1958), A. B. Thomas (1956), and A. C. Wilgus (1963), as well as the most extreme variant, Harry Bernstein's (1952), which begins with the late colonial period and concentrates almost exclusively on five leading countries.

The second main type departs more or less widely from the national narrative pattern in favor of topical or regional grouping, or both together. This type is more analytical, more explicitly interpretative, and much less preponderantly political. In widely different ways it is represented by the books of Robin Humphreys (1946), J. F. Rippy (1945), W. L. Schurz (1954), and (jointly) D. E. Worcester and W. G. Shaeffer (1956).

Each type has its own merits and defects. The first and older type is still more widely used, mainly on the grounds that students prefer continuous national narrative and that encyclopedic treatment provides wider coverage. On the other hand, many feel that the second type brings out more clearly both general trends and national differences, and is more stimulating to thoughtful students. The trend towards concentration on a few leading countries, found in both types, offers obvious advantages but is exposed to the hazard that a minor country scanted or omitted may suddenly become a major problem, as has happened recently in the case of Cuba. The reader who is not a specialist should consult accounts of different types, such as Lewis Hanke's *Modern Latin America*, and Preston James's *Latin America*, a human geography. For the problem approach based on selected readings, all students should consult the volume edited by Benjamin Keen and the Knopf Latin American series edited by Lewis Hanke.

WIDER HORIZONS

Probably the most important of the major trends of the past generation in the writing of Latin American history has been towards widening its horizon. The term "widening its horizon" is not used here in the sense given it more than two decades ago by that outstanding Latin Americanist, Herbert Eugene Bolton, in his volume of collected es-

[4] Dates in parentheses are for the most recent edition.

says, *Wider Horizons of American History*. In that case the term had a strong geographical-political connotation, and the feature essay, "The Epic of America," first published in 1933, seems to mark the end of one period of historical writing rather than the beginning of another, and to express the political mood of romantic Pan Americanism associated with Franklin Roosevelt's Good Neighbor policy. Since the publication of his essay, a substantial change (reflected in Lewis Hanke, ed., *Do the Americas Have a Common History?*) has taken place in the conception of Latin American history, both in its relation to the history of the rest of America, as will be explained below, and also in itself.

The latter change has consisted in a broadening both of the subject matter of Latin American history and of the means used by the historian for writing it. Concretely, the early preoccupation with political, military, and diplomatic history has been greatly reduced; interest in social, cultural, and economic history has quickened; and in place of the compartmentalization that formerly separated these various aspects of history, a stress on their inter-relationships with one another has reflected a more integrated view of the historical process. Accordingly, an essential feature of the change has been that increase in the Latin American historians' use of the findings of the other humanities and social sciences to which reference has already been made. It is in this sense that the term "wider horizons" is used here.

Specific instances of this process of expansion and integration will be given below, but first a brief explanation of how it came about is in order. It is often attributed mainly to the continuing influence—on Latin American historians as well as on scholars in other fields—of extensive and fruitful interdisciplinary co-operation during World War II, mainly under the auspices of the United States government. This was, indeed, an important factor, but it was not the only one, and it was all but the last to come into play. The first was the contagion of ideas from other fields; one result

was the development of the "area approach" mentioned above. These ideas are represented in various ways by such books as J. H. Robinson's *The New History* and the multivolume work on the non-political aspects of the history of the United States, *A History of American Life*, published in the 1920's and '30's and widely read. The second factor, which may be described as contagion from the public sector, resulted from the double impact of the economic depression of the 1930's and the rise of the totalitarian threat. The result was, in general, to shake confidence in accepted ideas and, in particular, to give thoughtful historians a greater awareness of the complexity of the historical process. And finally, since World War II, another factor has been the compilation and publication of important new sources of information on many aspects of Latin American life. Most of these are official publications (particularly of departments or affiliates of the United States government, the Organization of American States, and the United Nations); they are easily accessible, and many of them contain data of historical as well as current interest.

For the most part, the direct influence of the above factors has been confined to the study of the recent and contemporary period, but the new viewpoints established by them have been carried back more and more into the earlier national period, as far as the beginning of Latin American independence. How early the change began is shown by the first three works, all published between 1929 and 1934, of Frank Tannenbaum, now an outstanding member of the older generation of Latin Ameican historians: *The Mexican Agrarian Revolution*, which covers the hundred-year period ending in the 1920's; *Peace by Revolution: An Interpretation of Mexico*, which takes a sociological approach; and *Whither Latin America?*, which projects the area's future from its past in mainly social and economic terms. Subsequently, although numerous substantial works of the once conventional kind have continued to appear, their rate of incidence has diminished as most of the younger historians and some of their elders have chosen the newer approaches. The many single works that illustrate the change include C. H. Haring's *The Brazilian Empire* and the works of two of his former students, David Bushnell's on Colombia in the 1820's and T. F. McGann's on Argentina from 1880 to 1914. But the most striking example is provided by the groups of works described in the next section.

THE MEXICAN REVOLUTION OF 1910

No aspect of Latin American history has attracted more attention from English-speaking historians during the past generation than the revolution that began in Mexico in 1910, completed its principal fighting phase by 1920, and its principal constructive phase by 1940, though the latter is, at least theoretically, still going on. It deserved this attention, for it was the most genuine of the many Latin American revolutions up to that time and had far-reaching effects, not only in Mexico itself but in Latin America at large.

H. I. Priestley's *The Mexican Nation: A History* will serve as the starting point for measuring recent changes in interpretation. No reflection on this very able scholar is intended, for the changes in question were due not only to a new conception of history, which he came to share later, but also to the light reflected on the first or "fighting" phase of the revolution, which he described, by its second or constructive phase, which had hardly begun when he wrote. Yet the fact remains that his account of the revolution is essentially a political and military narrative and shows little appreciation of the depth and complexity of the movement underlying the surface events he recounted.

The exploration of these depths and complexities was begun almost at once by Frank Tannenbaum in the first of his books on Mexico cited above. It has been continued in various ways by Nathan L. Whetten, Oscar Lewis, Frank Brandenburg, Raymond Vernon, and others, at many levels ranging from Indian village communities to the national government and international relations. The results to 1953 are reflected in H. F. Cline's *The United States and Mexico*, which, despite its title, deals mainly with the internal development of Mexico, above all since 1910. His account of this period, the best of its kind, shows what the historian can accomplish with the aid of anthropology, sociology, economics, and political science. If it leaves lacunae in the history of ideas and art, the reader can fill these by consulting such works as Patrick Romanell's *Making of the Mexican Mind* and any one of a dozen good books published in the last twenty-five years on Mexican painting, architecture, and music. And works on political history, broadly conceived, continue to appear; notable among these are *Mexican Revolution: Genesis under Madero* (the first of a proposed trilogy), by C. C. Cumberland; *Francisco I. Madero*, by S. R. Ross; Robert Quirk's monograph on the Convention of Aguascalientes; and Robert E. Scott's *Mexican Government in Transition*. A new synthesis of Mexican history from 1940 to 1960, also by H. F. Cline, has recently [1962] appeared.

ECONOMIC HISTORY

One of the principal achievements of the historians of the past generation has been to lay the foundations for a serious study of the economic history of modern Latin America. Most of the task still remains to be done, but up to 1930 almost nothing has been done in English and very little more in any other language; even Latin America's own pioneers in this field, such as Roberto Simonsen of Brazil and A. E. Bunge of Argentina, did their major work after this date. Whatever the reasons—want of guides, sources, and trained scholars, or sheer lack of interest—the few good studies of the national period that appeared before then were too restricted in scope for wide application. As a result, even the main outlines of Latin American economic history since independence remained unclear. Although a handful of specialists knew better, most historians wrote as if the winning of political independence had also opened a new era in the economic history of the area. They failed to realize the continuing strength of the old colonial economy. Likewise, for a later period, they failed to appreciate the tremendous impact of foreign capital, business enterprise, and modern technology when these at last reached the several Latin American countries on a large scale at various times after about 1870, producing what many Latin Americans resentfully describe as a "new colonial system."

Awareness of these phases—and also of the latest phase, the industrialization of a large part of Latin America—has now been generalized among historians of the area. There is still no one-volume economic history of Latin America; the two general works on its economy, by W. C. Gordon and S. G. Hanson, deal mainly with recent and contemporary developments. Nevertheless, enough first-rate studies of crucial aspects have now been published to establish most of the outlines of the historical process as well as many of its details.

The studies of J. F. Normano and C. H. Haring, published in the mid-1930's, were among the first to give an impulse to the exploration of this field. Relative ease of access to sources has led to the concentration of most subsequent investigation on the late nineteenth and twentieth centuries, but Miron Burgin's *The Economic Aspects of Argentine Federalism, 1820–1852* showed that, with field work, a first-rate scholar could produce a first-rate study of the early nineteenth century as well.

Representative works of the past generation on various aspects of the economic history of Latin America include the following: on industry, studies of broad scope by George Wythe and J. F. Rippy, and more limited but significant studies by Sanford Mosk, *Industrial Revolution in Mexico,* Celso Furtado, *The Economic Growth of Brazil,* and S. J. Stein, *The Brazilian Cotton Manufacture;* on agriculture and agrarian reform, C. C. Taylor's *Rural Life in Argentina,* N. L. Whetten's *Rural Mexico* and *Guatemala,* Lowry Nelson's *Rural Cuba,* James Scobie's *Revolution on the Pampas,* and T. Lynn Smith's *Agrarian Reform in Latin America.* Parts of two neglected fields of history, transportation and urban development, have been opened by D. M. Pletch-

er and R. M. Morse in several articles on railroads in nineteenth-century Mexico and the rise of São Paulo, Brazil, in the nineteenth and twentieth centuries, respectively. In the well-developed field of trade and investments, most readers in the United States will be especially interested in histories of United States business enterprises in Latin America, such as *Petroleum in Venezuela* by Edwin Lieuwen. Economic policy-making in Latin America is examined by Albert O. Hirschman in *Journeys Toward Progress.*

These historical studies show, among other things, how at least some of the Latin American states began long ago to grapple with problems such as industrialization and agrarian reform that are in the forefront today. At the same time that they record some progress toward solution, they also point out at complex of tenacious features—social and political as well as economic—that explain why progress has not been more rapid.

CLASS AND CASTE

The twentieth-century "population explosion" in Latin America, first fully reported by Kingsley Davis in the 1940's, has intensified—though it alone did not create—a social storm that has as its center problems of class and caste. Partly by inheritance from colonial times, and partly as a result of subsequent economic and other developments, Latin American society in the national period has been characterized by great and growing disparities of wealth and opportunity for advancement. These have produced an increasing tension among social classes, which has not been greatly alleviated by the rise of a new middle class since the turn of the century. They have also brought to the fore again the perennial problem of the large numbers of Indians and Negroes who, in most Latin American countries, have constituted virtually separate castes and have been, at best, peripheral to the dominant society.

Historians did not need the news of the "population explosion" to alert them to this situation, for their own studies had already familiarized them with its deeper roots in the nineteenth century that ranged from the frustration of liberal and humanitarian reforms in the early years of independence to the advent of organized socialism in Latin America toward the century's close. In addition, by the 1930's historians had found further proof of the importance of problems of this type in the growing body of anthropological studies of Latin America, on which they were beginning to draw. Consequently, with the added impetus given by the current population crisis, the theme of social conflict and social change is now well established among them. Although it is true that, with a few exceptions, they have left it to anthropologists and sociologists to produce most of the works noted below, the latter are now so widely recognized as an essential part of the historian's armory that note must be taken of them even in this brief survey.

Prominent among the exceptions referred to is J. J. Johnson's stimulating recent study of the role of the "middle sectors" or middle class in selected Latin American countries, mainly since 1900, though with some attention to the nineteenth century. As indicated by its main title, *Political Change in Latin America*, even this book has a predominantly political orientation. Morever some of the best spade work on this subject has been done by Latin Americans such as Gino Germani (Argentina) and Oscar Fals Borda (Colombia). They have continued to lead in the study of social history; unfortunately, few of their works are available in English translation. The same is true of many of the uneven but generally illuminating essays in the pioneering work on Latin American middle groups edited by T. R. Crevenna in 1950–51. Likewise, historical writing in English on organized labor has been confined to a handful of works such as those of Marjorie Clark on Mexico and of R. J. Alexander and Moises Poblete Troncoso on Latin America at large.

Other notable exceptions are the general histories of the Negro in the New World, including Latin America, by J. H. Franklin and Frank Tannenbaum. But special studies of this subject continue to be the work of non-historians, as represented by those of the Negro in Brazil by Donald Pierson and Arthur Ramos. The same is true as regards the Indians of Latin America. An important trend of the past generation has been toward carrying the study of this subject forward from pre-Colombian and colonial times into the national period. This trend, too, has been almost entirely the work of anthropologists and sociologists, as in the six-volume *Handbook of South American Indians* and its one-volume summary by J. H. Steward and L. C. Faron; in the *Handbook of Middle American Indians*, vol. 1 of which appeared in 1965; and in *Economic Anthropology*, by M. J. Herskovits. Other relevant studies range from those by T. R. Ford and George Kubler on Peru, by John Gillin on Guatemala, and by Oscar Lewis on Mexico to Charles Wagley's *An Introduction to Brazil*, Samuel Ramos' *Profile of Man and Culture in Mexico*, and the volume on urbanization edited by Philip Hauser. And finally, a wealth of data on all these aspects of social history has recently been assembled and analyzed by R. N. Adams and others in *Social Change in Latin America Today*.

CHURCH AND STATE

Although now nearly three decades old, J. L. Mecham's *Church and State in Latin America* still stands without a rival in its important field. This fact is a tribute to the quality of his work, but it is also explained by the wide variations in the status and role of the Roman Catholic Church from one Latin American country to another and the consequent difficulty of giving coherence to a general account of the subject. Far from abandoning the theme, historians have explored it more actively than before, but they have done so on a country-by-country basis and have stressed the Church's functional role in society, rather than, as in Mecham's book, its juridical status. A recent sampling of the literature is provided by *The Conflict between Church and State in Latin America*, edited by F. B. Pike.

The works dealing with this subject fall into two main groups: those concerned largely or exclusively with the church, and those that discuss it as one element in a broad context. To the first group belong studies of the church in Argentina by J. J. Kennedy, in Guatemala by M. P. Holleran, and in Venezuela by Mary Watters. The second group is far more numerous, for the church-state theme has been a prominent one throughout the history of Latin America since the beginning of independence. There have, however, been wide variations from country to country in its character and in the amount of attention devoted to it by historians. In the case of Mexico, for example, where the tension over relations between church and state has been relatively high most of the time, hardly any political study or biography of a public figure fails to devote a substantial amount of space to it. On the other hand, it plays a small part in similar works on Brazil, where in most of the national period the tension has been much lower.

In addition to the trends already mentioned, historical writing on this theme in the past generation has been marked by a limited but perhaps significant modification of the prevailingly anticlerical temper of the earlier period. Examples include Richard Pattee's sympathetic biography in Spanish of Gabriel García Moreno, a nineteenth-century dictator who converted Ecuador into a kind of theocratic state; Kennedy's objective study of Argentina, referred to above; and the less-detached study of Mexico by F. C. Kelley, *Blood-Drenched Altars*. Yet the mounting influence of Marxism still keeps anticlericalism very much alive, while also provoking the defensive reaction of Christian Democracy.

Given its predominantly national character, the historical writing of this period has understandably not produced comprehensive estimates of changes from time to time in the relative strength of the Roman Catholic Church in Latin America. Some well informed observers tell us that the Latin American is still "Catholic or nothing." In so far as historical studies throw any light on the validity of this statement, they tend to confirm it, provided the "nothing" is understood to include two categories that have been shown—by anthropological studies and opinion polls, respectively—to be

rather large: paganism among the Indians and indifference in other sectors of society. At any rate, the few recent histories of Protestant churches in Latin America do not indicate a rate of growth that is likely to challenge the primacy of the Roman Catholic Church in that area, at least in the near future.

LITERARY AND INTELLECTUAL HISTORY

Both of these closely related fields have long been cultivated with considerably more élan by Latin America's native historians than by Latin Americanists writing in English. Nevertheless, important contributions in English have been made in both fields, and nearly all of these have been made since 1930.

Of the two, literary history has made by far the greater progress. Given a head start by the labors of such scholars as Alfred Coester and Isaac Goldberg before 1930, literary history was a special beneficiary of the Good Neighbor enthusiasm after that date. This not only stimulated the study of the Spanish and Portuguese languages and literatures in general but also directed special attention to their branches in Spanish America and Brazil. As a result, the reader has at his disposal today a substantial number of both special and general studies in English. The latter include general surveys of Spanish American literature by Pedro Henríquez-Ureña and E. H. Hespelt and others, of Latin American literature by Arturo Torres-Ríoseco, and of Brazilian literature by Samuel Putnam. Representative special studies are those of Spanish American and Brazilian fiction by J. R. Spell and F. P. Ellison, respectively. Also, particular literary themes have been investigated. Such themes include the Brazilian Indians and Negroes (studied by D. M. Driver and R. S. Sayers, respectively), the Argentine *gaucho* (by M. W. Nichols), and horsemen of the Americas generally (by E. L. Tinker). Progress in this field is also evidenced by the numerous anthologies and translations now available in English; it even has its own special journal, published in the United States, but this is in Spanish.

The more esoteric subject of the history of ideas in Latin America has been developed rapidly in the last two decades by Latin American writers. Unfortunately, the great bulk of their works remains untranslated. Exceptions are João Cruz Costa on Bazil, José Luis Romero on Argentina, and Leopoldo Zea on Latin America at large. English-speaking scholars have been somewhat tardy in matching the Latin Americans' interest in the field, although two good introductions to the subject in English appeared nearly twenty years ago: the book by Henríquez-Ureña referred to above, which, with admirable conciseness, combines literary and cultural with intellectual history, and W. R. Crawford's volume of valuable sketches of leading exponents of Latin American thought in the national period. Subsequently, Patrick Romanell has made an important contribution, also noted above, to the history of Mexican thought. Most recently, attention has been directed to the theme of nationalism. This is discussed, for example, in the course of T. F. McGann's book on Argentina; it is the theme of a collection of essays on Latin America published in 1961 under the editorship of R. N. Burr; K. H. Silvert and others analyze it in *Expectant Peoples*; and *Nationalism in Contemporary Latin America*, by A. P. Whitaker and David Jordan, is about to be published.

Democracy and Dictatorship

The diversification resulting from increasing use of the social sciences and humanities in the past generation has ended the near-monopoly of interest that the political and ancillary military aspects of Latin American history formerly enjoyed among English-speaking writers. Yet political history, now better based, still retains first place in the affections of most of them. The new disciplines, which at first weakened its hold, have in the end strengthened it by providing political history with a firmer underpinning that has helped renew its prestige. In the main, however, publication on the subject has been diffused over a wide variety of discrete problems and situations. In most cases these have involved only one country or a small group of countries and they have seldom been considered in relation to each other. Some of the more notable exceptions have been produced by political scientists with a sense of history, such as R. H. Fitzgibbon, F. G. Gil, Harry Kantor, K. H. Silvert, W. S. Stokes, and P. B. Taylor; but these are focussed on recent and contemporary developments.

Of the few major themes that run through the historical writing of the past generation in this field, the most important is the conflict between democracy and dictatorship. As used here, the term comprises all the diverse phases of a conflict that has gone on throughout the national history of Latin America, from the struggle between liberal leaders and *caudillos*, or local tyrants, in the earliest years of the new states to that of the present era between the forces of democracy on the one hand and those of fascist or communist dictatorship on the other.

The problem has been discussed many times before 1930—most recently and most comprehensively in Cecil Jane's *Liberty and Despotism in Spanish America* (1929), which a leading authority has described as "misleading" but also as "stimulating." Since then there has been at various times much discussion of the major aspects of the problem. First, inthe 1930's, the early *caudillo* type was analyzed in an article by C. E. Chapman, a biography of a Paraguayan representative of the type of R. B. Cunninghame Graham, and several biographical sketches in a volume edited by A. C. Wilgus; years later, Robin Humphreys subjected them to a penetrating re-examination in a chapter of his *Modern Latin America*. Outstanding studies of the persistence of the *caudillo* type have been made by G. I. Blanksten and Robert Gilmore. In 1950 another aspect of the problem was appraised by a political scientist, an economist, a sociologist, and a historian in a symposium, "The Pathology of Democracy in Latin America," edited by W. W. Pierson; this was reprinted the next year in the useful collection of essays, *The Evolution of Latin American Government*, edited by A. N. Christensen. Of still a third aspect, the emergence of the

modern type of Latin American dictatorship, no comprehensive study has yet appeared, but three case studies of the first full-
fledged example of this type, the Perón regime in Argentina, are contained in books
by R. J. Alexander, G. I. Blanksten, and A.
P. Whitaker. The latest aspect, communism,
is discussed comprehensively by R. J. Alexander and Rollie Poppino; both cover it
since its Latin American beginnings about
1920. Notable among the recent books that
stress the historical approach to current authoritarian trends in Latin America are a
collection of essays edited by F. B. Pike and
one of extracts edited by Hugh M. Hamill,
Jr.

An obviously related theme is military
history. While often a prominent minor
character, this theme has seldom been given
the leading role in works by English-speaking historians of Latin America. As a rule,
they have made it the handmaiden to political and diplomatic history and have
treated it episodically. Even in the rare cases
in which wars have provided the main focus
for major studies, these have almost always
been confined to their diplomatic aspects.
Exceptions are the Chaco War of the 1930's,
as studied in a recent monograph by D. H.
Zook, Jr., and the war of 1846–48 between
Mexico and the United States. Although the
military aspects of the latter conflict have
continued to be discussed in English, a book
published in 1919, Justin Smith's *The War
with Mexico*, still remains the classic account of the subject.

The appearance of Edwin Lieuwen's
Arms and Politics in Latin America in 1960
aroused widespread interest by its central
theme, the evolving role of the military in
Latin American public life. Subsequent
studies of it include the same author's *Generals vs. Presidents*, John J. Johnson's *The
Military and Society in Latin America*, and
a meaty article by Lyle N. McAlister in
Continuity and Change in Latin America,
edited by Johnson.

INTERNATIONAL RELATIONS

Some teachers of courses dealing with the
international relations of Latin America
prefer S. G. Inman's *Latin America: Its
Place in World Life*, but J. F. Rippy's *Latin
America in World Politics*, last revised in
1938, remains the only comprehensive history of the subject. In the light of subsequent
developments both in world politics and the
study of them, a work written under the
same title today could hardly fail to shift the
emphasis from Latin America's passive role
as a pawn in the great-power chess game to
its active role as a participant in world affairs, and from formal diplomacy to the dynamics of international relations. Rippy's
own subsequent probings of the subject, for
example, his books on the history of British
investments and on the industrial age in
Latin America, have helped to bring about
the change. So have other works noted in preceding sections, particularly those on Wider
Horizons, Economic History, and Democracy and Dictatorship, as well as still others
to be noted below in the discussion of relations between Latin America and the United
States.

Since most historical writing in English
about Latin America is produced in the
United States, it is not surprising that a
large part of the total deals with relations
between this country and Latin America.
Since 1930 the proportion has remained
high, though with fluctuations, and most of
the works have continued to be distributed
in much the same proportion as before
among three major categories: United
States policy, direct relations, and multilateral, inter-American relations.

There have, however, been significant
new approaches as well as important contributions along more familiar lines. The
outstanding example of the former is S. F.
Bemis' excellent historical study (1943) of
the Latin American policy of the United
States. In contrast to all previous accounts,
this is a ringing defense of that policy at almost every stage of its development, links it
firmly throughout to the problem of national
security, and, in the part relating to the
twentieth century, makes extensive use of
economic and financial data. Unfortunately,

this book has not been brought up to date. Other examples are A. P. Whitaker's *The Western Hemisphere Idea*, which is a tentative effort, but the first of its kind, to identify a basic idea in inter-American relations and trace its history; *The United States as Seen by Spanish American Writers, 1776–1890*, by José de Onís, which is another contribution to the history of ideas; and Harry Bernstein's recent study of inter-American cultural relations in the nineteenth century.

The outstanding example of the second type is provided by Dexter Perkins' continuation of his illuminating studies of the history of the Monroe Doctrine, which he finally summed up in a magisterial synthesis (1955). Other examples of this kind are the histories of direct relations with individual countries; studies of the Latin American policies of Herbert Hoover and Franklin Roosevelt, of the Calvo Clause, and of the diplomatic struggle for the Panama Canal; and J. A. Logan, Jr.'s *No Transfer: An American Security Principle*, in which that familiar principle is submitted to a fresh and rewarding scrutiny. The most recent major works are Bryce Wood's on the Good Neighbor Policy to 1943, D. G. Munro's on U. S. intervention and dollar diplomacy in the Caribbean to 1921, and J. L. Mecham's on the U. S. and inter-American security to 1960.

Various aspects of multilateral relations are brought into many of the works mentioned above. The only comprehensive historical account of the inter-American system, J. T. P. Humphrey's, stops with 1940.

Writers in English have as a rule continued to avoid the history of the Latin Americans' relations with each other and with the Old World. Most of the exceptions have to do with wars and diplomatic disputes, though one of the most notable, *Britain and Argentina in the Nineteenth Century*, by H. S. Ferns, has an economic focus. An English translation of *Brazil and Africa*, by José Honório Rodrigues, is scheduled for early publication by the University of California Press.

Much-needed source materials were published during this period. Two of the most useful are *The Evolution of Our Latin American Policy: A Documentary Record* and *Documents on Inter-American Cooperation*, edited by J. W. Gantenbein and by R. N. Burr and R. D. Hussey, respectively. A mine of information on the history of territorial and boundary disputes in the Americas was brought together in two volumes by Gordon Ireland.

BIOGRAPHIES

The production of Latin American biographies in English since 1930 has been small in volume and has reflected, not the broadening interest characteristic of other fields of historical writing about that area, but rather the persistence of the formerly general political-military bias. Even in this category only Mexico is well provided for with biographies in English, which include those of Iturbide, Santa Anna, Juárez, Porfirio Díaz, and Francisco Madero by W. S. Robertson, W. H. Callcott, Ralph Roeder, Carleton Beals, and S. R. Ross, respectively. In the same category are the biographical studies of dictators referred to in an earlier section and the biographies of José Martí of Cuba by Félix Lizaso; of Pedro II of Brazil by M. W. Williams; and of two other Brazilian leaders, Joaquim Nabuco and Ruy Barbosa, by Carolina Nabuco and C. W. Turner, respectively. Watt Stewart's *Henry Meiggs* is about a man who won fame as a railroad builder in Chile and Peru, but he was a Yankee. A. W. Bunkley's *Sarmiento* is a borderline case since Sarmiento was President of Argentina as well as a great writer. Women, scientists, and apolitical intellectuals have been almost completely ignored. Some of the gaps can be filled with the aid of articles tucked away in periodicals, if one has the means to consult them. H. E. Davis has produced two useful volumes of biographical sketches of Latin American "leaders" and "makers of democracy." Works by or about American citizens prominently connected with Latin America at various stages of its national history, through diplomacy or otherwise, can be located through the guides listed below. An important new biography is the first of a projected two-volume work on the Uruguayan José Batlle y Ordóñez, by M. I. Vanger.

MISCELLANEOUS

Although space does not permit a description of them here, interesting but isolated contributions have been made to legal and constitutional history and to the history of science, medicine, and the arts; and several comprehensive and very useful histories of individual countries have appeared. In the last-named group, special mention should be made of the series of "country" studies recently published by the Royal Institute of International Affairs (London), to which additions are still being made. Concise, generally well-written, and scholarly, these are particularly useful to non-specialists. Finally, there is now available in English a spotty but useful sampling of the important category of works on Latin American history by Latin American writers. These range from selections in *The Green Continent*, edited by Germán Arciniegas, to Gilberto Freyre's *New World in the Tropics: The Culture of Modern Brazil*. Guides to these and other materials are indicated below.

In view of the lively interest in national histories, it should be noted that two such series are in course of publication. One is "Latin American Histories," edited by James R. Scobie (Oxford). The other is the Latin American sub-series in "Modern Nations in Historical Perspective," edited by Robin Winks (Prentice-Hall). A topical series is being edited by John J. Johnson (Free Press of Glencoe, Macmillan).

Bibliographical Aids

The three most useful aids in the field covered by this essay are *Latin American History: A Guide to the Literature in English* (London: Oxford University Press, 1958), by R. A. Humphreys; the section "Latin America," prepared by L. D. Hefner, H. F. Cline and others of the Library of Congress, in *A Select Bibliography: Asia, Africa, Eastern Europe, Latin America* (New York: American Universities Field Staff, Inc.,

1960), supplements to which were issued in 1962 and 1963, and 1965; and the Latin American and Inter-American sections of the *Guide to Historical Literature* (Washington: American Historical Association, 1961). All were most helpful in the preparation of this essay. Teachers will find the second work particularly useful for its topical lists of teaching aids, including readings. In preparation is a *Guide to the Historical Literature of Latin America*, under the editorship of Charles Griffin, to be issued by the University of Texas Press for the Conference on Latin American History.

Current guides are the annual *Handbook of Latin American Studies* and these periodicals: *Hispanic American Historical Review, The Americas, Hispania, Inter-American Economic Affairs, Inter-American Review of Bibliography*, and *Journal of Inter-American Studies*. Primarily a news digest, *Hispanic American Report* (publication suspended, December 1964) also contained a brief section of notes on new books.

Readers with an interest in a particular area should consult the series of regional articles on the history of historical writing about the national period of Latin American history in course of publication in the *Hispanic American Historical Review*. Those published to date are by J. R. Barager on the River Plate countries (Argentina, Uruguay, Paraguay) in the number for November 1959; S. J. Stein on Brazil, May 1960; R. A. Potash on Mexico, August 1960; W. J. Griffith on Central America, November 1960; Charles W. Arnade on Bolivia, August 1962; Robert F. Smith on Cuba, February 1964; and Adam Szásdi on Ecuador, November 1964. Also see S. J. Stein on history in Charles Wagley (ed.), *Social Science Research on Latin America*.

REFERENCES

Adams, Richard N., and others, *Social Change in Latin America Today*. New York: Harper, 1960.

Alexander, Robert J., *Organized Labor in Latin America*. New York: Free Press, 1965.

——, *Communism in Latin America*. New Brunswick: Rutgers, 1957.

Anderson-Imbert, Enrique, *Spanish American*

Literature, A History. Detroit: Wayne State Univ., 1963.

Bannon, John F. (ed.), *Bolton and the Spanish Borderlands*. Norman: Univ. of Oklahoma, 1964.

Beals, Carleton, *Porfirio Díaz*. Philadelphia: Lippincott, 1932.

Bemis, Samuel F., *The Latin American Policy of the United States*. New York: Harcourt, Brace, 1943.

Bernstein, Harry, *Making an Inter-American Mind*. Gainesville: Univ. of Florida, 1961.

———, *Colombia and Venezuela*. Englewood Cliffs, N.J.: Prentice-Hall, 1964.

Blanksten, George I., *Ecuador: Constitutions and Caudillos*. Berkeley: Univ. of California, 1951.

Bolton, Herbert E., *Wider Horizons of American History*. New York: Appleton, 1939.

Brandenburg, Frank R., *The Making of Modern Mexico*. Englewood Cliffs, N.J.: Prentice-Hall, 1964.

Bunkley, Allison W., *The Life of Sarmiento*. Princeton Univ. Press, 1952.

Burgin, Miron, *The Economic Aspects of Argentine Federalism, 1820–1852*. Cambridge: Harvard, 1946.

Burr, Robert N. (ed.), *Latin America's Nationalistic Revolutions*, in *The Annals*. American Academy of Political and Social Science, March 1961.

Bushnell, David, *The Santander Regime in Gran Colombia*. Newark: Univ. of Delaware, 1954.

Callcott, Wilfrid H., *Santa Anna*. Norman: Univ. of Oklahoma, 1936.

Carey, James C., *Peru and the United States, 1900–1962*. Univ. of Notre Dame, 1964.

Christensen, Asher N. (ed.), *The Evolution of Latin American Government*. New York: Holt, 1951.

Cline, Howard F., *The United States and Mexico*. Cambridge: Harvard, 1953.

———, *Mexico, 1940–1960: Revolution to Evolution*. London: Royal Institute of International Affairs, 1962.

Cochran, T. R., and Ruben Reina, *Entrepreneurship in Argentine Culture: Torcuato di Tella and S.I.A.M.* Philadelphia: Univ. of Pennsylvania, 1962.

Crawford, William R., *A Century of Latin American Thought*. 2nd ed. Cambridge: Harvard, 1961.

Cruz Costa, João, *History of Ideas in Brazil*. Stanford Univ., 1963.

Cumberland, Charles C., *Mexican Revolution: Genesis under Madero*. Austin: Univ. of Texas, 1952.

D'Antonio, William V., and F. B. Pike (eds.), *Religion, Revolution, and Reform: New Forces for Change in Latin America*. New York: Praeger, 1964.

Davis, Harold E., *Latin American Leaders*. Washington: Inter-American Bibliographical and Library Association, 1949.

——— (ed.), *Latin American Social Thought since Independence*. Univ. Press of Washington, D.C., 1961.

Davis, Kingsley, "Population Trends and Policies in Latin America," in *Some Economic Aspects of Post-War Inter-American Relations*. Austin: Univ. of Texas, 1946.

Dozer, Donald M., *Are We Good Neighbors?* Gainesville: Univ. of Florida, 1959.

Fals Borda, Oscar, *Peasant Society in the Colombian Andes*. Gainesville: Univ. of Florida, 1955.

Ferns, H. S., *Britain and Argentina in the Nineteenth Century*. Oxford: Clarendon, 1960.

Ford, Thomas R., *Man and Land in Peru*. Gainesville: Univ. of Florida, 1955.

Franklin, John H., *From Slavery to Freedom: A History of American Negroes*. 2nd ed. New York: Knopf, 1956.

Freyre, Gilberto, *New World in the Tropics: The Culture of Modern Brazil*. New York: Knopf, 1960.

Furtado, Celso, *The Economic Growth of Brazil*. Berkeley: Univ. of California, 1963.

Hamill, Hugh M., Jr. (ed.), *Dictatorship in Spanish America*. New York: Knopf, 1965.

Hanke, Lewis, *Modern Latin America*. 2 v., Princeton: Van Nostrand, 1959.

———, (ed.), *Do the Americas Have a Common History?* New York: Knopf, 1964.

Hanson, Simon G., *Economic Development in Latin America*. Washington: Inter-American Affairs Press, 1951.

Haring, Clarence H., *Empire in Brazil: A New World Experiment with Monarchy*. Cambridge: Harvard, 1958.

Hauser, Philip (ed.), *Urbanization in Latin America*. New York: Columbia, 1961.

Henríquez-Ureña, Pedro, *Literary Currents in Hispanic America*. Cambridge: Harvard, 1945.

Hespelt, Ernest H., and others, *An Outline History of Spanish American Literature*. New York: Crofts, 1942.

Hirschman, Albert O., *Journeys Toward Progress. Studies of Economic Policy-Making in Latin America*. New York: Twentieth Century Fund, 1963.

——— (ed.), *Latin American Issues*. New York: Twentieth Century Fund, 1961.

Holleran, Mary P., *Church and State in Guatemala*. New York: Columbia, 1949.

Humphreys, Robin A., *The Evolution of Modern Latin America*. Oxford: Clarendon, 1946.

Inman, Samuel G., *Latin America: Its Place in World Life*. Rev. ed. New York: Harcourt, Brace, 1942.

Johnson, John J., *Political Change in Latin America: The Emergence of the Middle Sectors*. Stanford Univ., 1958.

—— (ed.), *Continuity and Change in Latin America*. Stanford Univ., 1964.

——, *The Military and Society in Latin America*. Stanford Univ., 1964.

Keen, Benjamin (ed.), *Readings in Latin American Civilization* . . . Boston: Houghton Mifflin, 1955.

Kennedy, John J., *Catholicism, Nationalism, and Democracy in Argentina*. Univ. of Notre Dame, 1958.

Kubler, George, *The Indian Caste of Peru, 1745–1940*. Washington: Smithsonian, 1952.

Lewis, Oscar, *Tepoztlán, Village in Mexico*. New York: Holt, 1960.

Lieuwen, Edwin, *Petroleum in Venezuela: A History*. Berkeley: Univ. of California, 1954.

——, *Arms and Politics in Latin America*. Rev. ed. New York: Praeger, 1961.

Lizaso, Félix, *Martí, Martyr of Cuban Independence*, tr. by Esther E. Shuler. Albuquerque: Univ. of New Mexico, 1953.

McGann, Thomas F., *Argentina, the United States and the Inter-American System, 1880–1914*. Cambridge: Harvard, 1957.

Maier, Joseph, and R. W. Weatherhead (eds.), *Politics of Change in Latin America*. New York: Praeger, 1964.

Marchant, Anyda, *Viscount Mauá and the Empire of Brazil*. Berkeley: Univ. of California, 1965.

Mecham, J. Lloyd, *Church and State in Latin America*. Chapel Hill: Univ. of North Carolina, 1934.

——, *The United States and Inter-American Security, 1889–1960*. Austin: Univ. of Texas, 1961.

Mosk, Sanford A., *Industrial Revolution in Mexico*. Berkeley: Univ. of California, 1950.

Munro, Dana G., *Intervention and Dollar Diplomacy in the Caribbean, 1900–1921*. Princeton Univ., 1964.

Nelson, Lowry, *Rural Cuba*. Minneapolis: Univ. of Minnesota, 1950.

Nichols, Madaline W., *The Gaucho: Cattle Hunter, Cavalryman, Ideal of Romance*. Durham: Duke Univ., 1942.

Onís, José de, *The United States as Seen by Spanish American Writers, 1776–1890*. New York: Hispanic Institute, 1952.

Pike, Frederick B. (ed.), *Freedom and Reform in Latin America*. Univ. of Notre Dame, 1959.

—— (ed.), *The Conflict Between Church and State in Latin America*. New York: Knopf, 1964.

——, *Chile and the United States, 1880–1960*. Univ. of Notre Dame, 1963.

Perkins, Dexter, *A History of the Monroe Doctrine*. Rev. ed. Boston: Little, Brown, 1955.

Peterson, Harold F., *Argentina and the United States, 1810–1960*. State University of New York, 1964.

Poblete Troncoso, Moises, and Ben G. Burnett, *The Rise of the Latin American Labor Movement*. New York: Bookman Associates, 1960.

Poppino, Rollie, *International Communism in Latin America . . . 1917–1963*. New York: Free Press, 1964.

Priestley, Herbert I., *The Mexican Nation: A History*. New York: Macmillan, 1923.

Putnam, Samuel, *Marvelous Journey: A Survey of Four Centuries of Brazilian Writing*. New York: Knopf, 1948.

Quirk, Robert, *The Mexican Revolution, 1914–1915*. Bloomington: Indiana Univ., 1960.

Rippy, J. Fred, *Latin America in World Politics*. 3rd ed. New York: Crofts, 1938.

——, *Latin America and the Industrial Age*. 2nd ed. New York: Putnam, 1947.

Roeder, Ralph, *Juárez and His Mexico*. New York: Viking, 1947.

Rojas, Ricardo, *San Martín, Knight of the Andes*, tr. by Herschel Brickell and Carlos Videla. Garden City: Doubleday, 1945.

Romanell, Patrick, *Making of the Mexican Mind: A Study in Recent Mexican Thought*. Lincoln: Univ. of Nebraska, 1952.

Romero, José Luis, *A History of Argentine Political Thought*. Stanford Univ., 1963.

Ross, Stanley R., *Francisco I. Madero: Apostle of Mexican Democracy*. New York: Columbia, 1955.

Scobie, James, *Revolution on the Pampas*. Austin: Univ. of Texas, 1965.

Scott, Robert E., *Mexican Government in Transition*. Urbana: Univ. of Illinois, 1959.

Silvert, K. H. (ed.), *Expectant Peoples. Nationalism and Development*. New York: Random House, 1963.

Smith, Robert F., *The United States and Cuba. Business and Diplomacy, 1917–1960*. New York: Bookman Associates, 1960.

Smith, T. Lynn (ed.), *Agrarian Reform in Latin America*. New York: Knopf, 1965.

Stein, Stanley J., *The Brazilian Cotton Manufacture: Textile Enterprise in an Underdeveloped Area, 1850–1950*. Cambridge: Harvard, 1957.

——, *Vassouras. A Brazilian Coffee County, 1850–1900*. Cambridge: Harvard, 1957.

Steward, Julian H., and Louis C. Faron, *Native Peoples of South America*. New York: McGraw-Hill, 1959.

Stewart, Watt, *Henry Meiggs: Yankee Pizarro*. Durham: Duke Univ., 1946.

Tannenbaum, Frank, *Peace by Revolution: An Interpretation of Mexico*. New York: Columbia, 1933.

——, *Seven Keys to Latin America*. New York: Knopf, 1962.

——, *Slave and Citizen: The Negro in the Americas*. New York: Knopf, 1947.

——, *Mexico: The Struggle for Peace and Bread*. New York: Knopf, 1950.

Taylor, Carl C., *Rural Life in Argentina*. Baton Rouge: Louisiana State Univ., 1948.

Torres-Ríoseco, Arturo, *The Epic of Latin American Literature*. Rev. ed. New York: Oxford, 1946.

Vanger, Milton I., *José Batlle y Ordóñez . . . 1902–1907*. Cambridge: Harvard, 1963.

Vernon, Raymond, *The Dilemma of Mexico's Development*. Cambridge: Harvard, 1963.

Wagley, Charles, *An Introduction to Brazil*. New York: Columbia, 1963.

—— (ed.), *Social Science Research on Latin America*. New York: Columbia, 1964.

Watters, Mary, *A History of the Church in Venezuela, 1810–1930*. Chapel Hill: Univ. of North Carolina, 1933.

Whitaker, Arthur P., *The Western Hemisphere Idea: Its Rise and Decline*. Ithaca: Cornell, 1965.

——, *The United States and Argentina*. Cambridge: Harvard, 1954.

——, and David Jordan, *Nationalism in Contemporary Latin America*. New York: Free Press (in press).

Wilgus, A. Curtis (ed.), *South American Dictators during the First Century of Independence*, Washington: George Washington Univ., 1937.

Williams, Mary W., *Dom Pedro the Magnanimous*. Chapel Hill: Univ. of North Carolina, 1937.

Wood, Bryce M., *The Making of the Good Neighbor Policy*. New York: Columbia, 1961.

Wythe, George, *Industry in Latin America*. 2nd ed. New York: Columbia, 1949.

Zea, Leopoldo, *The Latin American Mind*. Norman: Univ. of Oklahoma, 1963.

Zavala, Silvio, *History of the New World*. Mexico City: Pan American Institute of Geography and History, Commission on History, 1961.

Zook, David H., Jr., *The Conduct of the Chaco War*. New York: Bookman Associates, 1960.

74. Four Bibliographical Tools Needed for Latin American History*

Robin A. Humphreys

There are four bibliographical tools which, in my opinion, are urgently needed. I put them in ascending order of magnitude. (i) "A Guide to the Materials for Latin American History in the Official Publications of the United Kingdom"; (ii) "A Guide to the Materials for Latin American History in the Official Publications of the United States"; (iii) "A Guide to the Sources for Latin American History in the Libraries and Archives of Great Britain"; and (iv) "A Guide to Latin American History."

(i) and (ii) "The Guides to Latin American History in the Official Publications of the United Kingdom and the United States."

The bulk of the material is in the *Parliamentary Papers*, House and Command Papers, that is, the Reports of Committees, and the Returns to Parliament made by Departments, e.g., the trade and customs returns in *Accounts and Papers*. But there is also Hansard to be considered, the *British and Foreign State Papers* and, in the twentieth century, the separate publications of the various Departments.

The Guide, I think, should be annotated. Possibly it could be issued in successive installments in the *Review*, and published separately later. This was the method followed by C. K. Jones with his *Bibliography of Latin American Bibliographies*, and it has the advantage of allowing for comment and revision. Dr. A. J. Walford, a Latin American historian by training and a librarian by profession, now in the government service, has agreed to undertake the preparation of this guide, though he cannot begin immediately.

Obviously, however, if American scholars are of the opinion that a "Guide to the Materials for Latin American History in the Official Publications of the United States" should also be undertaken, it is desirable that the two guides should follow the same general method and be as uniform as possible. If they could be published together, so much the better.

* *HAHR*, 38:260–262 (May 1958). Reprinted by permission of the author and the original publisher. These proposals were drawn up by Professor Humphreys after discussions last summer in London, in which Howard F. Cline and the managing editor participated. They were then presented for informal consideration at the 1957 annual meeting of the Board of Editors in New York. A lively discussion ensued. In general all present voiced interest in the projects, though there was some difference of opinion in the order of priorities, and everyone recognized that the successful completion of the four guides would require much time and effort as well as financial support. It was also felt that more detailed statements on the projects need to be drawn up. Professor Humphrey's statement is now printed in the hope that *HAHR* readers will become interested in the projects and work toward their accomplishment. [Ed. *HAHR*]

(iii) "A Guide to the Sources for Latin American History in the Libraries and Archives of Great Britain"

Important as the first two projects are, a "Guide to the Sources for Latin American History in the Libraries and Archives of Great Britain" is more fundamental. What I have in mind is a volume on the lines of the old Carnegie guides, which would analyse the manuscript resources of the British Museum and of the Public Record Office, together with the manuscript materials in other depositories, e.g. the National Maritime Museum, the University Libraries, the Companies Registration Office, and so on.

Such a guide would need to be financed by one of the foundations. I would hope that it might be sponsored by the Hispanic Foundation of the Library of Congress, that a young historian could be appointed to give his full time to the enterprise over a period of two or three years, and that a small advisory committee would be set up with representatives both in the United Kingdom and in the United States. I should hope also that facilities for administering the project in England could be provided by the Institute of Historical Research.

(iv) "A Guide to Latin American History."

The last of these projects, though I would put it first in order of importance, is the production of a "Guide to Latin American History" embracing all languages and all periods and attempting not only to select and list but also to describe and/or evaluate.

I do not know why the proposal made in 1927 for a critical bibliography of Latin American history failed to be carried out. But whatever the arguments adduced in its favor then they are much stronger now. The volume of production in the last thirty years has enormously increased. The range of Latin American historical studies has been broadened. New horizons have been opened up. But there has been no manual to provide for students of Latin American history the service which Channing, Hart and Turner performed for past generations of students of American history and which the *Harvard Guide* aims to supply now. And I can think of no instrument of scholarship likely, on the one hand, to give a greater impetus to Latin American studies and, on the other, more calculated to assist in breaking down the barriers which still exist between those historians who write in Spanish and Portuguese and those who write in English.

It may be thought that a project such as this is one which an international organization might properly sponsor. The main objection to such a proposal and, in my view, the decisive one, is the difficulty of maintaining uniform standards of judgment and criticism in an enterprise conducted by nationals of various countries. The Guide, I believe, can best be run from the Library of Congress. Its sectional editors ought to all be within easy reach of the Library, where the editor-in-chief would, I assume, most properly be found. And though the sectional editors would, as I also assume, each have consultants in various fields and various countries, the enterprise itself would be a national, not an international enterprise.

I ought, perhaps, at this point, to confess that I have myself recently compiled a guide to the literature in English on Latin American history and that this guide is now in the press. But its compilation has merely served to convince me still more of the urgent need of the project which I have here outlined.

75. Ethnohistory: A Progress Report on the Handbook
of Middle American Indians*

Howard F. Cline

Since the appearance of the invaluable *Handbook of South American Indians*, edited by Julian Steward and published by the Smithsonian Institution (1941–1946; Index, 1959), hope that a comparable coverage of the Central American and Mexican areas would sometime be forthcoming was often expressed by individual scholars and various groups of investigators. It is pleasing to report that such hopes are nearer being realized. The *Handbook of Middle American Indians* is currently being prepared, and its several volumes are scheduled to appear in the latter part of the 1960's. It should have special interest for historians, as a substantial allocation of space has been given to ethnohistory.

The enterprise is sponsored by the Committee on Latin American Anthropology of the National Research Council, headed by Professor Gordon Willey (Harvard).[1] This group met in New York on October 20, 1956, to discuss the general problems involved in outlining a *Handbook* and securing the necessary scholarly and financial support. A small sub-committee was successful in securing such interest, and the National Science Foundation provided an initial grant that has permitted further detailed planning and actual preparation of the *Handbook*. The grant was made to Tulane University, and the Committee enlisted the services of Robert Wauchope, Director of the Middle American Research Institute at Tulane, as General Editor. He was also named to the National Research Council Committee. From its membership, he selected a group of specialists, each to act as Editor for a particular field, and as a body to act as Advisory Board to him. The Editorial Advisory Board has also met as a group on one occasion, and meetings of the several Editors

with the General Editor have been convened to solve particular problems. In January 1960 more than 238 articles had been solicited of leading authorities, with 184 acceptances. On advice of the Editorial Advisory Board, Dr. Wauchope has not made final commitments for publication although negotiations are in progress with several interested presses.† Mrs. Margaret A. L. Harrison will be Associate Editor, and is already planning format and style, and is assembling a master bibliography of anticipated references cited.

So much for the administrative side of the *Handbook*. Its contents are perhaps of greater interest. In the first place, plans have been made on the basis that there will be approximately the same number of words, about two million, as in the *Handbook of South American Indians*. However, profiting from experience with that work, it was decided to divide the *Handbook of Middle American Indians* into eleven volumes (rather than the six fat tomes of the South American *Handbook*) to facilitate editorial handling and continuing reference use. The area included in the *Handbook of Middle American Indians* is Mexico plus Central America. Thus it covers the area south of the old but still usable Hodge, *Handbook of*

---

* *HAHR*, 40:224–229 (May 1960). Reprinted by permission of the author and the original publisher.

[1] Other members of the Committee include H. E. D. Pollock; Clyde Kluckhohn, *ex oficio;* Norman McQuown; T. D. Steward; M. W. Stirling; J. B. Griffin; G. M. Foster; E. Z. Vogt; G. F. Ekholm; Angel Palerm; Howard F. Cline; Glenn Finch.

† The University of Texas Press was selected. It issued Volume 1 of the *Handbook* in February 1965. The current order of volume numbers differ slightly from those used in this article. [Ed. note]

North American Indians, and will up-date recent developments in the southern Central American area also described in the Steward *Handbook of South American Indians*. Beause of the nature of the area thus covered, contents of the eleven Middle American volumes are organized somewhat differently from either of the other two major *Handbooks*.

An initial volume of Introduction will treat briefly of the history of studies, as well as covering developments in the area through the origins of agriculture and the incipient patterns of farming life and earliest signs of native civilizations. The second volume deals with the natural environment. Robert Wauchope will edit Vol. I, and Robert C. West Vol. II. Vols. III-V summarize the archaeology and ethnohistory of the area, basically sub-divided into southern Mesoamerica (Maya, Oaxaca), Central and Western Mexico, with Northern Mexico and the various relationships of the area with other parts of America and the world treated in Vol. V; Gordon Willey and Gordon F. Ekholm are the Editors of the archeological volumes, which bring developments to Spanish contact. Howard F. Cline, with Charles Gibson and H. B. Nicholson as Co-Editors, is in charge of Vols. VI and VII, which provide a guide to sources and materials for ethnohistory, stressing post-contact materials, to the point where the first ethnological and ethnographic reports on living peoples began to appear in the nineteenth and twentieth centuries. The contents of these volumes are discussed below. Vol. VIII and IX, under editorship of Evon Vogt and Manning Nash deal with ethnology and social anthropology of recent and contemporary groups. Vol. X, under the direction of T. D. Steward, synthesizes physical anthropology. Language and linguistics, edited by Norman McQuown, terminates the substantive volumes of the *Handbook of Middle American Indians* with Vol. XI. Still open for discussion by the Editorial Advisory Board is the problem of indexing and the further consideration of an additional volume of essays on topics not otherwise covered in the previous eleven volumes.

Although nearly all the contents of the *Handbook* will be of some interest to historians, two parts of it should have special appeal. Substantial essays on the development and history of native societies before the coming of the Spaniards appear in the volumes on archeology (III–V). As mentioned, Vols. VI and VII are exclusively devoted to providing aids and tools for ethnohistorical work.

For each of the major cultural areas of Middle America there is planned a summary article in Vols. III–V on "The native society at Spanish contact." Thus for Highland and Lowland Maya, Zapotec and Mixtec, groups in southern Veracruz and Tabasco, Central Mexico, the Huasteca, Central Veracruz, Guerrero, and Western Mexico will appear general ethnohistorical syntheses, as will also be the case for the northern areas, generally considered to be outside Mesoamerica. In addition, there are a number of special articles in the archeological volumes of historical interest. For instance, for Central Mexico essays on social organization, structure of the Aztec empire, and Native History review and synthesize much modern research which has carried knowledge considerably beyond that summarized in the pioneering work of Vaillant, still widely used for teaching and research purposes by non-specialists.[2]

Pioneering in a different sense are Vols. VI and VII of the *Handbook of Middle American Indians* devoted exclusively to ethnohistory. Together these will amount to about 1,000 pages, or half a million words, approximately a quarter of the total content of the *Handbook*. After consultation and discussion with the Advisory Board, the General Editor, and interested specialists, the Co-Editors felt that the major contribution which could be made at this time was to provide the means by which ethnohistory could be written rather than attempt syntheses for the various culture groups of the area following Spanish domination of their areas. It was readily apparent that neither the methodology for ethnohistory was suffi-

[2] George C. Vaillant, *The Aztecs of Mexico*, N. Y., Doubleday, 1941, 340 p.

ciently advanced, nor was the monographic base sufficient, to provide anything but the most superficial coverage if attempts were made to provide essays surveying the developments between the time the Spanish first saw the groups and the point at which modern scientists had described the recent or contemporary descendants. Therefore, the emphasis is heavily bibliographical in the two volumes, hence its general title, "Guide to Sources and Materials for Ethnohistory."

Vol. VI attempts to place the general and chronological materials together, while Vol. VII is devoted to regional and topical matters. The scope and nature of ethnohistory, as well as its methodology, both from the point of view of the anthropologists and that of the historians initiates the Guide. This is followed by a listing of institutional and related resources for archival and documentary research; the institutions of an international nature, as well as those in the Middle American area, United States and Canada, Europe, and elsewhere in the world which have materials of interest for writing native history, either in the form of documents, or in periodical publications, are thus surveyed and an annotated handlist of them is being developed. Derivative from this effort is a selected annotated listing of the major periodicals. As often anthropologists and others are not fully aware of the timing and nature of the development of European and national administration, institutions, and imported traditions into Middle America, one rather substantial general essay is being presented to summarize matters which are generally more familiar to historians. Its analogue, however, is a pioneering essay which attempts to sketch the adjustment and development of post-contact native institutions and traditions in Middle America to the changed environment caused by European colonizations.

One of the more baffling aspects of ethnohistory is the scattered and unreliable bibliographical information about the great corpus of material, almost unique to Middle America, of works primarily in the native tradition, often written by natives themselves in the immediate post-contact era. The

Guide will provide discussions, as well as a rather extended set of handlists, first of such works in codex form, generally meaning those productions which have pictorial content (often prose as well), as distinct from the non-pictorial or prose material: annals, native chronicles, and the like. The handlists will include even the known falsifications and dubious documents, and will provide as extended a description of each document as space will allow.

Works primarily in the European tradition form a large part of Vol. VI. Here, the materials are or should be more familiar to historians, but are often neglected by the anthropologists and archeologists attempting historical reconstructions. In the section devoted to these materials, there is scheduled a sub-section in which certain key figures in the development of ethnohistory will be treated in critical, bio-bibliographical form: Sahagún, Torquemada, Herrera, Clavigero, Orozco y Berra, and H. H. Bancroft. Included too is a small section that will systematically provide notes on major published collections, with an annotated bibliography of them and the finding aids related to them. The final and most important sub-section deals with colonial treatments to about 1800, preceded by a brief discussion of the types and trends of source material created by European-type hands. Among these, the Co-Editors have singled out the *Relaciones Geográficas*, principally of the 1579–1581 series, as being extremely important and relevant to detailed knowledge of native societies; an annotated handlist of all the known *Relaciones*, both published and unpublished is included in treatment of them, together with maps showing areas for which such materials are known to exist. More orthodox in treatment will be summary essays on the historians and chroniclers, both religious and secular, on which most of us rely for similar data.

Though equal in space and possibly importance, Vol. VII of the *Handbook*, the second of the *Guide*, is rather simple to outline. It consists of specialized, annotated bibliographies, preceded by brief introductory essays touching on the status of problems in the bibliography for each of the major cultural areas of Middle America and for the principal topics on which there exists specialized or source materials. It is expected that some 10,000–15,000 bibliographical entries will be thus made available, including in special cases, important manuscript items. The areas for which such bibliographies are well advanced include Central Mexico, Maya (Lowlands and Highlands), Oaxaca and its neighbors, the west, the north, and the frontier and border zones at the northern extremities of Middle America and at the south. The Co-Editors have already accumulated in the order of 9,000 or 10,000 of these entries, and have begun to subdivide them not only into area categories, but also subjects and topics. The final determination of the latter will rest on completion of bibliographical research.

The *Guide to sources and materials for ethnohistory* should be of some assistance to students and scholars working along more established lines of historiography for this important Latin American area. The Co-Editors welcome suggestions which would improve the utility of the *Guide*. To that end, at the 34th Americanist Congress, scheduled for Vienna, July 18–25, 1960, Paul Kirchhoff and Howard F. Cline are organizing a Symposium on problems of ethnohistory at which a number of European views of the proposed coverage in the *Handbook of Middle American Indians* will be given, not only in short papers on various topics, but in a general discussion. Suggestions and inquiries from the readers of the *HAHR* would also be most welcome, and can be addressed to the Director of the Hispanic Foundation, Library of Congress, Washington 25, D. C.

76. Ethnohistory: Mesoamerica*

Henry B. Nicholson

Since this section appears in the *HLAS* for the first time, a brief statement is in order explaining its nature and the criteria employed for inclusion of items in it.

There has been increasing recognition recently of a distinct branch of New World anthropology and history, for which the label "ethnohistory," has come into common use. Although definitions differ, its core is clearly the utilization of written records to reconstruct the culture and history of the American Indian. Within anthropology, it bridges the gap between excavational archaeology and ethnography. Within history, it constitutes a distinct sub-field, with intimate ties with anthropology. What best earns ethnohistory the right to be considered an area of research in its own right is the specialized nature of the evidence with which the ethnohistorian deals, necessitating special techniques of research and interpretation that combine the skills of the documentary historian and the cultural anthropologist. In the U. S., ethnohistory has flowered rapidly since World War II, greatly stimulated by the research required in connection with litigation resulting from the *Indian Claims Commission Act of 1946*, and has developed its own professional organization (American Indian Ethnohistoric Conference) and journal (*Ethnohistory*). In the

* Introduction, *Handbook of Latin American Studies*, 22:30–32 (Gainesville, 1960). Reprinted by permission of the author.

aboriginal high culture area of Middle America (Mesoamerica), ethnohistoric research, although only recently tagged with this label, has had a long and honorable history. Here, for example, it was a well-developed branch of study long before scientific archaeology made its appearance in the area.

Mesoamerican ethnohistory can be conveniently divided into two major divisions: (1) that focusing on the pre-Hispanic and Conquest periods; and (2) that chiefly concerned with the colonial and independence periods (up to the era of modern ethnographic investigations, although even in this most recent period ethnohistoric techniques can often be profitably employed). The present section, at least in its début, will be confined to the first period. Any items which contain significant information concerning pre-Hispanic and Conquest-period native Mesoamerican cultures and which are derived, not from archaeological excavation or analysis of ancient architectural features and artifacts and monuments, but from documentary sources, are eligible for inclusion in this section. Many studies, of course, are concerned with both; when a significantly large proportion of the information is based on written documents, the study would qualify for this section. "Written documents" includes those uniquely valuable pictorial records in the native tradition, pre- or post-Hispanic, the so-called "codices." Most studies of the codices and the native systems of writing, therefore, will qualify, except those concerned with highly specialized astronomical-mathematical matters or confined to analyses of texts on the monuments or other archaeological pieces. With one exception, no items which have appeared in former numbers of the *HLAS* are included. A few items go back as far as 1956, but the vast majority date from the past two years.

Certain recent developments in Mesoamerican ethnohistorical studies deserve special mention. A number of important document publication projects, initiated some time before, were continued during this period. One of the foremost of these is the *Quellenwerke zur alten Geschichte Amer-*

ikas series of the *Ibero-Amerikanische Bibliothek* of Berlin, which published in 1958 one of the most important Nahuatl sources on pre-Hispanic central Mexican history, the *Memorial breve* of Chimalpahín. The great Dibble and Anderson, Sahagún *Florentine codex* translation project moved well past the half-way mark with the publication of Book IX in 1959. In Mexico, the Seminario de Cultura Náhuatl, led by Ángel M. Garibay K. and Miguel León-Portilla, continued to spark a growing major movement of Nahuatl linguistic and cultural studies. The Seminario launched an ambitious publishing program during this period, with three series now underway: (1) *Fuentes indígenas de la cultura náhuatl,* concentrating so far on the publishing of paleographs of the Nahuatl texts and direct Spanish translations of the Sahagún-compiled *Códices matritenses;* (2) *Monografías,* with a recent second edition of León-Portilla's *La Filosofía náhuatl* and, in preparation, a Spanish version of Friedrich Katz' recent study of Aztec socio-economic structure, and (3) *Estudios de cultura náhuatl,* the first volume appearing in 1959. The Seminario, particularly its director, Ángel M. Garibay K., has provided much of the stimulus for the growing interest in the Nahuatl poetic-literary achievement, which was reflected during this period by the appearance of a considerable number of articles and books on this theme. Two other new series of considerable importance to Mesoamerican ethnohistoric studies were recently launched in Mexico: *Colección "Siglo XVI,"* under the general editorship of Ernesto Ramos, concentrating on the Jalisco-Michoacan region of the West and *Documentos para la historia del México colonial,* published by Porrúa and edited by France Scholes and Eleanor Adams. *Tlalocan,* the only journal devoted exclusively to the publication of Mesoamerican ethnohistoric and linguistic sources, continues to appear occasionally, always with important material. Significant individual source publications during this period include: the Relación de Michoacan, Recinos' edition of some lesser-known, but important, highland Guatemala native chronicles, Eulalia Guzman's edition of the Vienna codex version of the first two Cortesian *Cartas de relación*, the new Porrúa edition of Landa, León-Portilla and Garibay's collection of excerpts from the native accounts of the Conquest of Mexico, and Garibay's collection of Nahuatl poems, from the *Cantares mexicanos* and the *Romances de los señores de la Nueva España*. Mention should also be made of Schultze Jena's partial translation of the *Cantares mexicanos* in an earlier number of the *Quellenwerke*.

Research specifically directed to the elucidation of problems of pre-Hispanic political and cultural history, based on the documentary *corpus*, resulted in some important contributions, although the number of competent students working in this area seems disproportionately small; this theme received considerable attention during the seventh (1957) and eighth (1959) Mesas Redondas of the Sociedad Mexicana de Antropología devoted to the anthropological problems of Oaxaca and Chiapas-Guatemala, respectively. The pictorial manuscripts, the codices, continued to receive their share of attention, evidenced particularly by the continuance by Dark and, especially, Caso, with their important studies of the Mixtec group; by Burland and Mengin with studies covering a wider field; by the appearance of Robertson's pioneer work of central Mexican colonial styles, which also deals extensively with the pre-Hispanic background; and by the preparation of a number of accurate facsimiles, of which the forthcoming editions of the *Codex Bodley*, the *Codex Borbonicus*, and the *Codex Becker II* are particularly noteworthy. Interest in Mesoamerican writing and calendric systems was unflagging, with Caso continuing his basic researches in the Mexican field and Thompson still outstanding in the Maya field. Knorozov's claims continued to stir up controversy; Thompson and Barthel both published withering critiques of his system during this period.

Lastly, a major development of the past two years is the launching of the great, long-awaited "Handbook of Middle American Indians" (Robert Wauchope, Editor-in-Chief), of which two volumes have been assigned to ethnohistory, under the editorship of Howard F. Cline, assisted by Charles Gibson and the Contributing Editor. It is planned that these two volumes will be largely of a bibliographic nature, at least partially answering the long recognized need for greater system in the organization of Mesoamerican ethnohistoric materials.

77. Latin America*

HOWARD F. CLINE

In the quarter century since I. J. Cox summarized Latin American materials for the original *Guide*, there has been a notable development in the scope, depth, and quantity of historical writing in the United States, in Latin America itself, and to a lesser degree in European centers, especially Spain. Many of these trends are summarized in the Gibson-Keen article, and are evident in the selections below.

The bibliographical apparatus supporting studies is by no means fully adequate, but

* Introduction to Section Z, American Historical Association, *Guide to Historical Literature* (New York, 1961), pp. 656–657. Reprinted by permission of the original publisher.

basic summaries like those of Jones and Haring, as well as that of Humphreys for those restricted to the English language, represent highly useful tools at the student's ready disposal. Absolutely indispensable for following current production is the *Handbook of Latin American studies*, annually reporting substantial items in the social sciences and humanities. Stress is placed on these and other helpful publications because the restriction of space and the enormous output on Latin American history in the past quarter century make the listings below highly selective.

The entries cover twenty countries for the nearly half a millennium since America entered history in the written word. Innumerable worthy monographs, significant older books, and important articles and source materials simply could not be squeezed into the space of this bibliographical panorama. Hence emphasis has been placed on specialized bibliographical listings within area, period, or topical subdivisions. In general, chronicles, travel accounts, and other writings have reluctantly been omitted; many of those listed by Cox are equally important today.

The predilection of Latin Americanists to mass their interests in the 16th century or the late 18th and early 19th century period of independence movements and to eschew narrative or analysis of the recent past are still dominant traits. Similarly, preferences for the biographical approach, the publication of documents rather than documented syntheses, and strong urges toward antiquarianism still plague a great deal of their historical writings. Strong currents of nationalism have inhibited any general syntheses of consequence, to which has been added the growing realization of the complexity of the area. Monograph after monograph has shown that many of the easy generalizations concerning uniformities common to earlier generations rested on insubstantial bases, often legal codes that were normative rather than illustrative of actual practices. With mounting data have come changed interpretations. The major one is that rather than one specialty, Latin American history is now breaking into a multiplicity of specialities. Equally striking is the steady drift toward mundane establishment of fact and a reduction in the moral fervor and apologetics that enlivened earlier treatments. The exotic, the romantic, the crusade has by no means entirely disappeared, but the earlier cool superiority of the Anglo-Saxon treatments of Latin American phenomena and the heated polemic tones of writers in the latter republics treating their own past have been increasingly displaced by sympathetic attempts at understanding and impartiality.

78. History*

Charles Gibson

Year after year the section on history remains one of the largest and most important of the *Handbook*. The remarks made are designed to introduce the entire section through a preliminary essay. We initiate here a series of annual statements analyzing and evaluating historical writing as a whole.

It is, of course, no longer the case that historical work is dominated by the colonial period. The materials reviewed this year demonstrate a strong interest in all periods. The point may be made most convincingly in the major countries—Mexico, Argentina,

* Introduction, *Handbook of Latin American Studies*, 25:195–197 (Gainesville, 1963). Reprinted by permission of the author.

and Brazil show it clearly—and it is especially notable in the work of United States students and in the large general compendia. Russian writings, of which there is an increasing quantity, also concentrate upon recent times. But a reasonable balance between national and colonial periods pervades the whole bibliography, and in an over-all sense this reflects one principal transition in the historical outlook of the present generation.

The broadening of historical subject matter is another long-term process in recent Latin American historiography, and this also is reflected in the offerings of the present year. We have important new studies in economic and intellectual history to supplement and inform the traditional emphases.

Works such as Sergio Villalobos' on the trade monopoly or Wilcomb E. Washburn's on the meaning of words in the period of exploration, or Eduardo Arcila Farías' two studies, one on 18th-century economy in Mexico and the other on Venezuela engineering, are in different degrees representative of a wider vision and understanding. The broadening process is still incomplete (histories of society and culture are notably weak), but it will surely follow the lead set in European and United States historical writing, and we may be confident of its continued development.

A third trend, the professionalization of the discipline and an increasing sophistication in the treatment of historical materials, is likewise manifest. The quality of "intellectualism" has never been lacking in the writing of Latin American historians themselves. But it becomes less personal now and more scientific. History in Latin America can no longer be so uniformly classed as a branch of literature, for it requires much more than literary expression and literary quality is yielding to other standards. In the publications reviewed this year, we have an important professional achievement in the new volume edited by Sérgio Buarque de Holanda, a cooperative, systematic exposition of Brazilian history in the early 19th century. Other events of professional import, such as the First Symposium of University Professors of History in São Paulo, are indicated by George Boehrer in his introduction to the section on Brazil. Many similar remarks for other countries might be made.

The tendencies are not uniform, of course. There are clear regional emphases in quality and quantity. Mexico, Argentina, and Brazil continue to produce well; Central America, Ecuador, and Chile far less so. In Mexico, publication on the Revolution of 1910 steadily increases, and it includes both primary documentation and re-evaluation. The more recent Cuban revolution likewise yields a large literaure, but it is more ephemeral, less restrained, and less disciplined by an historical frame.

Chronological emphases also persist. We may note especially how much of colonial writing falls in the first 75 years and how little is being done to fill the void between the late 16th and the mid-18th centuries. In the national period all nations preserve their interest in the independence movement. But the focus of attention varies sharply after independence, each nation possessing its standard emphases. Only occasionally do individual historians break through these traditions.

Mature professional historical writing in Latin America is now an expectable feature of every year. Thus Ricardo Krebs Wilckens' analysis of the thought of Campomanes and Pedro Borges' discussion of missionary methods are major contributions to knowledge of the colonial period and should be included in scholarly bibliographies for many years. Villalobos' *Tradición y reforma de 1810* is a sound study of the early independence years. In the national period such works as *La caída de Rosas* by José María Rosa and Angelina Lemmo's examination of Venezuelan education demonstrate the continuing production of good monographic work. Two first-rate biographies are Manuel Giménez' life of Las Casas and Caracciolo Parra-Pérez' life of Mariño. As usual United States students contribute substantially. Studies by William Shiels on the *patronato*, Lowell Blaisdell on the 1911 movement in Lower California, and Robert Burr on the Panama Congress are representative of a large number of offerings. In the very recent period the monumental analysis of Mexico, 1940–1960, by Howard F. Cline demonstrates that objective, comprehensive treatment is not impossible even for the very recent past.

As would be expected, deliberate revisionism or innovation is most often suggested in short papers or expressed in works dealing with limited subjects. Thus, Richard M. Morse's study of cities outlines an entire "theory" of Latin American urbanism, and though only 20 pages in length stands as one of the significant contributions of the year. Examples of writings on more limited subjects but with a similar quality of conceptual reordering are those of Juan A. Ortega y Medina on Humboldt, Mario Góngora on "Galicanismo," and Moysés Vellinho on the Spanish and Portuguese gaucho.

In the large-scale undertakings innovation of this sort is rare. Continuing works, such as the history of the viceroys of New Spain by J. Ignacio Mañé, tend to be conventional in their outlook and method. The statement should not be taken in a pejorative sense, for the value of such writing lies in their fullness and scope and in the documentation and proof provided for what was only superficially familiar. The best example of what we mean here is the work of Pedro Leturia on relations between Latin America and the papacy, which is traditional in method and conception but also exhaustive and definitive in its content.

Local studies, often antiquarian, may nevertheless open surprising new vistas to the historian or present to him known propositions in unsuspected and revealing ways. Even the publication of local documents may contribute dramatically to this end, especially if, as in the Mexican *Boletín del Archivo General de la Nación*, they are well selected and edited and introduced with appropriate commentary. Charles Arnade's studies of St. Augustine, Ernesto Lemoine's of Baja California, and Cline's work on the Patiño maps all fall in this category. A work such as Antonio de Béthencourt's examination of wood cutting in 18-century Tehuantepec is fascinating in its detail and wonderfully revealing on the life that people actually led.

It need hardly be pointed out that works of the type cited above are of more importance than the anniversary writings that occur so plentifully in this as in other years. Commemorative writing tends to be conservative and the stimulus that gives rise to it tends to be artificial. Only in a special sense does an historical event gain in importance for having occurred exactly 100 or 150 years ago. In the selections included this year, we are confronted with many titles that depend on sesquicentennials of the independence movement or on the centennials of events of the 1860's. The writings commonly recapitulate known facts and they do so in a ritual or patriotic way. Only rarely does this holiday writing yield substantial results. Yet it must be said that the Sarmiento materials that have appeared in Argentina comprise a respectable, as well as an extensive, corpus.

That historians are not yet prepared to capitalize upon their resources and produce large-scale reinterpretations of the whole receives striking affirmation this year in the Program for the History of the Americas. The Program has come to an end now with the publication of the final products, by Silvio Zavala for the colonial period, and by Charles Griffin for the national period. Both are sound summaries, and no one could argue that the authors have failed to work valiantly within the project's terms. But the result is far from the clarion call that the supporters of the Program in past times exuberantly predicted. In preliminary planning, in conference and committee, in time and expense, and in fanfare, the Program has been one of the continuing focal points of Latin America historiography for a long time. Its real accomplishment is incommensurate with these efforts, and it seems most unlikely that future historical study will be so influenced by it as was once expected. Many factors contribute to this result, not the least being the "cooperative" basis of an enterprise undertaken in a time of historical transition, and in the absence of any clear agreement on the topics and methods of the future.

In the fundamental areas of documentation and bibliography the year is a good one. Documentary publications of importance include the series on the Mexican Indian nobility by Guillermo Fernández de Recas and on the Mexican Revolution of 1910 by Isidro Fabela, the British naval papers edited by Gerald Graham and Robert A. Humphreys and the 19th-century Venezuelan text edited by Pedro Grases and Manuel Pérez Vila. In bibliography the major works are Lino Gómez Canedo's account of colonial archives, Agustín Millares Carlo on municipal archives, and the materials of modern Mexico listed by Luis González and others. The documentary index or summary is represented in Castro Seoane's continuing catalog of 16-century missionaries and Vicenta Cortés catalog of manuscripts in the Library of Congress. Many other bibliographical and documentary works listed below are valuable and durable contributions.

. . . .

The general introduction to the section on History, initiated in the preceding number of the *Handbook*, is continued this year with the following remarks on historical writing as a whole.* We anticipate that general introductions of this type will become a regular feature of the History Section.

History continues to be an extremely large and important subject in Latin America. In sheer volume the output indicates an active group of researchers and a wide public following. Partly because history in Latin America is not yet thoroughly professionalized its popularity remains high. More so than our own historical writing in the United States, it serves patriotic, partisan, literary, and other ends, quite apart from its scholarly function. There appear many indications that the role of history in Latin America is undergoing change, but it does not seem to be diminishing in any degree.

A consequence of increasing size and complication of Latin American history is that it becomes progressively more difficult for any one historian to be conversant with the whole in any detailed or authoritative way. Even the individual sections listed below represent bibliographical areas of huge complexity. The traditional subdivisions themselves become subdivided. For the first time this year the national period in Mexico becomes two sections, one on the period to 1910 and the other on the Revolution and post-Revolution; similar reorganizations in other areas will undoubtedly appear in the future.

As always, writings in Spanish and Portuguese predominate. Relatively few historians in Latin America study other areas than their own. Within Latin America they write for an expanding and increasingly literate population. Universities and institutes sponsor new studies, and publishing houses look with favor upon works in history. The typical work in this bibliography is still that written by an historian who feels himself close to the historical event itself by way of national or regional ties. Argentines rarely study Ecuador. Brazilians rarely study Guatemala.

Externally, on the other hand, the subject becomes steadily more international. Spanish historians are extremely active in studying Spanish American history. Contributions from the United States, France, England, and Germany make a very respectable showing. It is abroad rather than in the Hispanic world that the twentieth-century techniques of historical inquiry have reached their highest degree of refinement, and the impact of European and United States contributions on the field of Latin American studies has been far reaching. It is significant that Germany, which has not been a large-scale contributor to Latin American studies, has inaugurated one of the few journals of Latin American history outside of Latin America itself.

Writings by United States students comprise the largest and most important body of historical works by foreigners. The *Handbook* itself is indicative of this United States

* *Handbook of Latin American Studies*, 26:38–42 (Gainesville, 1964).

interest, and it may be noted in passing that nothing of the size or scope or thoroughness of the *Handbook* is published anywhere else in the world. The United States writings of the present year relating to Mexico alone include the biography of Antonio María Bucareli by Bernard E. Bobb, the biography of Bernal Díaz by Herbert Cerwin, the history of the Mexican *mesta* by William H. Dusenberry, the study of the French army in Mexico by Jack Autrey Dabbs, and the reinterpretation of the United States occupation of Veracruz by Robert E. Quirk. For Central America, David Burks observes that the only bright spots on the list are two articles that appeared in the United States. For Cuba, United States writings appear among the most important and durable, e.g., Richard B. Gray's book on Martí and David F. Healy's analysis of United States-Cuban relations. Many other books and articles attest to an undiminished United States activity in this subject.

Translation is another aspect of internationalization, and while publications in translation rarely constitute true contributions to knowledge they ordinarily reflect a widening interest among non-specialists. Foundation funds have been devoted to translation programs in the United States, to the point that one can now become quite broadly educated in Latin American history exclusively through works published in English. It is an event of some significance that François Chevalier's *La formation des grands domaines au Mexique* (1952) should now appear in English, for the fact that translators are alert to the major writings in non-Hispanic languages as well and they are systematically searching for key works to translate. Indeed it would appear that publishers are prepared to issue more writings in English than are available for, or merit, translation.

Outside of western Europe and the United States, Russian works continue to appear. Though undoubtedly the Russian interest in Latin American history is to a degree an aspect of a more pragmatic international concern, Soviet research has reached a point where a Latin Americanist who cannot read Russian finds himself at a disadvantage. This marks a sharp change from only a few years ago. The present reviewer (who cannot read Russian) is not the best person to comment on this literature. But it is obvious that the topics of Russian historiography, even when handled with the standard Russian formulae of interpretation, are worthy of our western attention. Incidentally, a few items of past *Handbooks*, and item 401 of this one, suggest that the complete Latin Americanist may soon be obliged to add Japanese as well as Russian to his linguistic repertory.

Relations between Latin American history and the history of other parts of the world receive increasing attention as we learn more about Latin America itself and as the concept of world history gains a new respectability among historians. As C. J. Bishko pointed out some years ago, the traditional understanding of Iberian history in relation to Latin America is seriously inadequate. Signs are beginning to indicate that Bishko's message is being acted upon. Cases in point are the work of Vicenta Cortés on slavery in Valencia and of Ruth Pike on Genoese influence in Seville. Here traditional Spanish "background" is carried into the colonial period and its content is enriched—the topic is not the limited political one of conventional studies of the *reyes católicos*—and the works illustrate the important theme of American influence upon the Old World, a theme that historians are now beginning to recognize in its complexity and manifold dimensions.

The colonial period offers numerous other opportunities for studies of relations between Latin America and Europe, and if we assemble the various writings completed and in progress on this subject we see the result to be an impressive one. The relevant work includes further studies of the origins and distribution of Hispanic colonists, relations between the American colonial Church and the Vatican, themes of Indian-white contact, and international rivalries over American colonies. This year's survey provides data on all these subjects, and one may predict that important contributions of the future will lie not only in the detailed local areas of colonial history but in the broader field of relations between the colony and the Old World.*

Internationalism in the period after 1810 is reflected primarily in studies of diplomacy and foreign affairs. It receives a special impetus at the present time when Latin America appears as a battleground, actual or potential, in the larger rivalries of the twentieth century. Crucial contemporary subjects relevant to Latin American communism tend to be explored and explained through a rather shallow historical past. Latin Americans themselves struggle with the problem —frequently seen as a half-historical, half-philosophical problem—of the identity of their nation or of all America as related to other nations or to the rest of the world.

Within the Latin American area, regional emphases remain. Major historical writing is taking place in Mexico, while the showing for Central America is sparse and poor. Continually the Mexican Revolution of 1910 emerges as one of the truly important events of the twentieth century, and the amount of writing devoted to it exceeds that of any other single topic. Nearly all historical writing dealing with modern Mexico recognizes the revolution of 1910 as the critical event. The only comparable subject in the bibliography is the Castro revolution in Cuba; however abundant the output may be, it is still in the main unscholarly and polemical.

Regional emphases in South America preserve the already established patterns. Argentina, Peru, Colombia, and Venezuela are represented by some basic contributions for all periods. Mario Góngora, from whose pen have come some of the most acute reinterpretations of recent years on early colonial society, extends his researches on conquest groups to the Panamanian isthmus. Fundamental works of documentary compilation appear in the biographical compendium of Tunja "corregidores" by Ulises Rojas, in Ildefonso Leal's history of the University of Caracas, and in José María Vargas' large-scale examination of the colonial Church in Ecuador. The missionary movement in Chile has been examined in detail for the first time by Olivares Molina. A work

of exceptional merit for the Independence period is Rafael Gómez Hoyos' extensive analysis of the revolutionary ideology in Colombia. Materials on Paraguay and Bolivia on the other hand are thin. And Brazil, normally a strong contender, is relatively weak this year.

One exception to the tendencies in the direction of professionalism relates to the old subject of the Las Casas criticism. The exact shading that historians should assign to the Black Legend continues to be a matter of dispute. The kind of work represented by Ramón Menéndez Pidal indicates the persisting emotionalism of this subject, which major historians can still treat in vituperative and essentially non-historical terms. As Lucien Febvre and others in the twentieth century have demonstrated, effective progress in historical writing is made when we begin by revising not the answers but the questions. A work such as Menéndez Pidal's leaves the question where it was and makes an impact through the violence with which it asserts one of the conventional answers. It is hard to believe that the cause of historical truth is properly served by methods such as these. Menéndez Pidal's writings leave us no better informed than before, save perhaps with respect to the degree to which patriotic preconceptions can prevail over historical judgments.

On the whole the materials of this year maintain and reinforce a tendency to shift the balance of attention from the colonial to the national period. Works of value on the nineteenth and twentieth centuries appear, as would be expected, principally for those regions that have responded most to the economic and social revolutions of the past 100 or 150 years. The more interesting of them escape from a narrow political conception and deal directly with culture or society or economic history, either in conjunction with or in separation from polit-

* Professor Gibson's modesty has led him to omit direct mention of his own major contribution to Mexican colonial history, *The Aztecs under Spanish rule: a history of the Indians of the Valley of Mexico, 1519–1810* (Stanford Univ. Press, 1964), item 4412. *HLAS* [Ed. note]

ical affairs. It is quite evident that students are increasingly prepared to examine the national period at more fundamental levels than those of sequential political administrations. The outstanding large-scale example for Mexico, of course, is Daniel Cosío Villegas' *Historia moderna de México*, the sixth volume of which appeared this year, while to a lesser degree the point is illustrated for Peru by Jorge Basadre's revised *Historia de la República del Perú*.

With the expansion of professionalism, it is no longer so true as it was only a few years ago that history in Latin America is a branch of literature. The reprinting of "classic" historical works from the nineteenth century is declining, and these works no longer hold the place in the historical world that they once did. The publication of primary sources is increasing. Each year we encounter fewer treatises on the precise dates of foundation of small towns, fewer panegyric biographies of military heroes, fewer personal genealogies, and in general fewer evidences of immaturity. To be sure, these, like all changes in this field, are quite unevenly distributed and there are large areas in which they hardly make their appearance at all. Moreover, it should be remembered that the works listed in the *Handbook* are selective and that the listing favors works that make substantial contributions. Though writings of pseudo-history in a traditionally literary form continue to be published, a more representative association of literary and historical interests of the present time is Martha Hildebrandt's study of word usage in the writings of Bolívar, which furnishes some acute insights into the mind of the Liberator and into the spirit of his age in Venezuela.

That there are new avenues into which strict professional techniques can be profitably extended is particularly illustrated in the Mexican demographic work of Woodrow Borah and Sherburne F. Cook. This is with-

out doubt the single most far-reaching historical reappraisal of recent years. Demographic studies have expanded further than anyone could have predicted in 1948 when they were intiated in this present sense by Lesley Byrd Simpson. This year's writings indicate that the techniques are now being applied to later colonial times, and it surely will not be long before similar work is conducted for Central and South America. From every point of view, this research represents a commendable expenditure of effort, one that results in important new knowledge and utilizes to the full the methods of inquiry appropriate to our own time.

Finally we may note the many works of the section that deal with "contemporary history." The pervasive implications of colonialism in the modern world, and the appearance of formerly secondary nations at the forefront of the world's stage, have inspired a new interest in Latin America's present situation and in its future. It is interesting, and probably to be expected, that historians have not contributed to these analyses of present and future to the degree that they might have. The works are written by journalists or travelers or persons untrained in Latin American studies. Most professional historians beg the question of connection between past and future and deny any predictive value to their studies. This represents a natural and commendable caution, and the pitfalls of prediction are of course very evident. But in a sense the failure of historians to contribute meaningfully to analyses of the present represents an abdication of responsibility, for the present is a dangerous time and the vacuum that historians fail to fill attracts others less competent to deal with it. Latin America is one of the areas of the world that very explicitly challenges historians to a reconsideration of the meaning and limits and purpose of historical study.

79. The Hispanist in the American Historical Association*

JOHN TATE LANNING

Before you bombard with the china and charge with the cutlery, know that I have taken counsel with my peers. My topic I put to them with a plea that they give me a judgment of my theme, or some notion of the tack I should take. "Singularly barren, your theme," came the first response. Said the next: "You ask for a tack; I suggest a sledge hammer." Awesome, though, was this: "If you say what ought to be said, you will be crucified; and if you don't, can you be pleased with that?" "If you can do it undetected, slide off the subject," advised a wily one. Another, though he discounted them, had heard rumbles, womblings I take to spring from the viscera, not the head. The secretaries of our academy assure me, however, that these infirmities, already affecting the skin, often break out in a rash upon their records.

One chairman, still smarting after four years, thinks, ". . . so far as the AHA is concerned, we [. . . are] at the bottom of the totem pole: . . . too peripheral for inclusion in a crowded annual meeting. The meager space devoted to things Latin American in the AHR and their invariable position at the very end of each number reinforce a longstanding impression. I do not accept that we are that unimportant." Well I remember how, having read proof of a review for the *American Historical Review*, and having sought promptly but in vain for my handiwork in the next neat blue issue, and,

being younger than I now am, at long, long last, with the timely succor of the editor, I located it. Publishers, who lack our experience and forbearance, are puzzled and irritated at the way reviews of Hispanic works of importance are compressed and hidden away. Unfortunately, something or some field has to be at the end; the most we can hope for, if we are always placed at the tail end, is that this location have no symbolic meaning. *The American Historical Review* could not give us adequate coverage in 1915, as Altamira noticed; how can we expect it now? The *Review* is already too thick, the print too small. On account of its prestige and high technical standards, however, good Hispanists will consent to write the over-compressed reviews, giving an author a chance at a sound, if not devitalized appraisal outside the two or three he might expect in the journals of his own field.

The vortex of the rumbles we hear, if we consult the files of the Conference, swirls around the number of sessions at the annual meetings. These are intermittent and, like malaria, should be avoidable. True, three or four sessions would enable us to bring young scholars onto the stage to be seen more in proportion to our numerical growth, but so many sessions are patently too many for the space the Association has available

* *Americas*, 20: 393–406 (Apr. 1964). Reprinted by permission of the author and the original publisher.

and for the constitution of the listeners. The last two sessions will always find me in a semi-recumbent position in the cocktail lounge. Truth to tell, we do not instruct one another very much here. A program, then, to be truly useful, must eventuate in publication, as ours often have.

So, as I see it, the stalemate has been reached upon occasion because of human failings.

One of these is a misunderstanding by our chairman and program committee about their functions. Our constitution plainly states that, so far as *our* committee is concerned, its "purpose" is "to assist the Program Committee of the American Historical Association in preparing the program for the Latin American session." The chairman of the Conference and his program committee, I suspect, have upon occasion felt free to sign, seal, and deliver a program, marked *sin réplica*. On the other side, each new general chairman of the Program Committee of the American Historical Association has just discovered how hard it is to get hundreds of professorial prima donnas to answer his letters. In the midst of his exertions, which he at first merely planned to take on as a side task, he even despairs of getting a program together at all. He grows testy—asserts his authority. He may also, to allow for all the possibilities, regard us as pedestrian, troublesome fellows. Everything converges with the powder dry and the spark glowing. A little more balsam, a little less touchiness from us, and a little catholicity from him should stay the count-down. Having served on the program committee of both the Association and the Conference, I can say, from these vantage points, there is no disposition on the part of the AHA program committee to slight the Hispanists. We have fared all right, given the "size and complexity" of the Association and "what we have to offer." If committees were standing, and not liable to repeat mistakes every year, the risk of quarreling might be overcome for decades at a time.

We have, it is true, too few programs on Spain; in this country, to come to the point, we are all but bereft of historians of Spain.

Now that African history, in the blink of an eye, has beamed upon our sight in such resplendent dress, we can no longer dismiss Spain with the flippancy: Africa begins at the Pyrenees. When I lamented to a Portuguese student that there were no Portuguese historians in the United States, he replied: "Neither are there in Portugal." These shortcomings are more a defect of ours than of the Association.

Do the honorary elections to the American Historical Association reflect the fame or ill-fame of the Hispanist? These have been sporadic because, perhaps, to stage them at all, we had to imitate the French— against our traditions as well as against our grain. When honorary memberships, first begun in 1885, were suspended in 1906, the accolade had fallen upon the shoulders of three Englishmen and two Germans— Bishop Stubbs, Samuel Rawson Gardiner, Lord Bryce, Von Ranke, and Mommsen. Since the resumption in 1943, Spain has rung the bell once with Rafael Altamira, Portugal not at all, and Latin America four times from a total of thirty for all the rest of the world. This is fully as good a showing as the merits of the individuals and some recognition of geographical distribution warrant.

Before I draw blood and mutilate member, may I don priestly robes and grant absolution to the American Historical Association in its constituent and formal capacity? Any supercilious disposition to bias will have to be sought in the petty professionalism of academic people. A professor has something to kick and a soul to be damned, but not so this Association.

I, myself, have heard rumbles, but never uttered them before, that we are secondary, even second rate. Yet, in any pair, one will be second to the other—between Shakespeare and Goethe, or, more appropriate for us, between Beelzebub and Huitzilopochtli. The longer the comparative list, the more iniquitous is comparison. Take the most learned man in the Duke University faculty, withal articulate, neat, and kindly disposed toward the young and sophomoric of mankind. Where did he come out as a teacher in the undergraduate-ranking list? No. 346!

As individuals, we should fear no generic damnation. Each man among us has it in his power, if he has the talent, to make his own showing by truly self-sacrificing application to scholarship and to the development of a style good enough to make him heard outside his own guild and the courage— even the foolhardiness—to use it there.

We cannot say we had a bad start. No branch of learning could have had a more dignified beginning in the historical literature of this country than the Hispanic. A century, perhaps a century and a quarter ago, men of culture, tempted to write in the Spanish field, had a ready-made public, willing to cap anything Iberian with a romantic aura. Did Washington Irving labor under a disadvantage when he turned from the Devil and Tom Walker to Granada and the Alhambra? Was George Ticknor second rate when his lectures on Spanish literature inflamed Prescott's sensitive imagination and started him toward immortality? Did Prescott, as a consequence, lose ground around Boston? Around Cambridge even? Did Archer Huntington lose prestige among contemporary millionaires for feeling the same fascination? Such toleration was still alive "in the schools" when I betook myself from college to university. Poised to go to Yale, the academic Valhalla of Southerners, to work on English colonial history under Charles McLean Andrews, I followed a brother to California. There was not one of my professors in Trinity College, though there was not a Hispanist among them, but advised me to take the bent in California that I did take.

Half a century ago our men made their reputations as American historians through the vehicles of American history. When the Carnegie Foundation began financing guides to materials in foreign archives on American history, Spain and Spanish America were not omitted. If Shepherd's work on Spanish archives was slighter than that of Bolton on those of Mexico, this was because the papers were so overwhelmingly abundant that they made his assignment impossi-

ble. William R. Manning published his model monograph on the Nootka Sound Controversy in the Annual Report of the American Historical Association for 1904. In 1918, Bolton gave us his influential essay on the missions as a frontier institution in the pages of the *American Historical Review*, an avenue to respectability now closed more and more. The Spaniards might be the monsters of Thomas Churchyard, Richard Hakluyt, and Justin Winsor, but they were still entrancing monsters.

So, when *The Hispanic American Historical Review* was conceived, Spain was still a land of enchantment, and we were still American historians. As the Panama Canal opened California and the Pacific for a second time to the world, the American Historical Association met in 1915 with the Panama Pacific Exposition in a mood of exhilaration. The subject of the Iberian world, naturally, blew into white heat. Rafael Altamira, there in person, suggested a journal to keep the increasing numbers of Hispanists who "came forward," as Dr. Jameson put it, informed of publishing and professional activities. Historians outside the Hispanic field, such as M. L. Burr, J. Franklin Jameson, Victor H. Paltsits, and Frederick Jackson Turner joined a phalanx of eminent businessmen at the dinner that founded the *Hispanic* at the Cincinnati meeting of the Association in 1916. Well, if the outstanding historians of the century—even the statesmen—saw us off with deep concern, with a respect and esteem we no longer enjoy, what is wrong?

When we founded our own journal, we entered into competition with the local boys —most of them campus-wide celebrities; we got into the pen with them and began to root for their acorns. With this act, the death knell tolled for the exclusive tradition. Inevitably, we would now spread throughout the whole country as a pedestrian species, let us say *homo insapiens hispanicus*. Hispanic culture could no longer remain in a single spot in the East, cultivated by a brilliant literatus like Prescott here and an occasional classically grounded academic like Merriman there.

The price of getting our own marbles to go and play with we first paid in the fate of the *Hispanic*. Brought forth in 1918, it lay in state, neither buried nor resurrected, from 1922 to 1926, not for want of articles, but for want of financing—financing furnished ever since by Duke University, representing the inevitable spread of universities as our arrival represented the inevitable spread of a branch of culture and learning. These ancestors of ours devoted the 1926 program of this Association in Rochester to a plaintive, purely pedagogical cry for an increase of courses, an increase in students, and incidentally, I suppose, an increase in subscribers. What more pathetic proof of our new, mundane status!

The Conference, as we understand it, came into formal being after this long *ad hoc* period at the 1938 meeting of the Association in the Stevens Hotel in Chicago, where I quaveringly read the luncheon paper. Professor Chapman alone of the Committeemen drafting the constitution that year refused to sign the document labeling the Conference "Latin American" and not "Hispanic American," though willing to accept *"Ibero-American Historical Review,"* the label agreed upon at Cincinnati in 1916. Professor Chapman under the persuasion of Mr. Juan C. Cebrián, first guarantor of the *Review*, had become the advocate of "Hispanic American," and as late as World War II he was still hounding the *Encyclopaedia Britannica* and the dictionary companies to substitute *Hispanic* for *Latin* with the meaning "pertaining to things Spanish and Portuguese." In fact, at the beginning of this campaign of his, such statesmen as Woodrow Wilson, Robert Lansing, William G. McAdoo, and Charles Evans Hughes wrote letters of endorsement. When he published these, Professor Chapman suppressed that of Charles Evans Hughes—not because Hughes had just lost a famous presidential election, but because he had written: "My dear Professor Chapman: I heartily endorse the idea of a Latin American Historical Review . . ." The rest of this generous letter makes no difference.

But I must not flounce by the murmurings of the Young Turks in this Conference a decade or so ago. The visions of these anonymous illuminati I now see through a glass darkly. They never intended—in justice I say it—to increase their weight by their numbers. One of them, in fact, expiated all our sins when he wrote: "No organization can supply essential scholarship . . . still an individual matter."

Now, the ordinary history professors in universities, whom we have come to live among, have been accustomed to ascendancy. Their unconscious, massive "contentment," with respect to the Hispanic field, yields here and there to conscious parochialism. Some time ago, an estimable woman historian sat down at a dinner honoring Ricardo Donoso. Turning to her side, she asked: "Tell me, Mr. Hamill, are there any Latin Americanists doing *anything* worth while . . .?" In my own beloved Tarheelia, the North Carolina Literary and Historical Society each year gives a prize for the best historical work by a native son, solicits works in competition from all fields, announces them as in the competition without the consent of the author, and then obligingly docks those on Latin America and other transmontane fields a flat thirty per cent. There you would begin with a grade of 70, something that troubles you if you are young enough to aspire to Phi Beta Kappa. But no worry! The judges would not know how to evaluate you if you started at 110 per cent. What can they do with you, then? They can ignore you.

A name may be sullied because of a lack of quality, but this ostrich type of exclusiveness has no relation to sound standards of criticism; it is, in truth, a worldwide academic phenomenon. When, in 1931, I gave a lecture in the University of Córdoba, Argentina, on a theme of South American history, the celebrated Michigan-educated architect, Ing. Jaime Roca, used his over-generous introduction of a quaking youth to pound this into his fellow countrymen: "We ought, in turn," he urged, "to be able to send to the 'North Americans' young men willing to risk talking to them in their language about the history of the United States. We ought to have chairs in *some* of our universities on their history as they have in *all* of theirs on ours." When I puzzled, in the presence of Dr. Richard Konetzke, that the Germans had no chairs of American history in their universities, despite the two points where the collision of their history with ours should have afforded them some instruction, he thus enlightened me: "Mein Herr: To get a chair on Persian antiquities has the blessing of academic convention; neither American nor Hispanic American history does." Thus the orthodox academic—comfortable, complacent, and imperturbable throughout the world! Throughout history, I might add.

We have rarely had the proper help at all times in any of the universities and never in some of those that esteem themselves most highly. None of us has been able to see why Yale University, with its enviable literary and documentary resources, with the enlightened beginning that it gave us in Edward Gaylord Bourne, and continued in the Yale Peruvian expedition—none of us, I repeat, can see why Yale never gave the Hispanic historians the help they deserved and the conditional respect which, at least, they needed there. If the field was not respectable, why not make it so? If not well served, why not serve it better? If you are occult, you can train yourself. Look south! It winds round the desert trails of Atacama to us that we have never produced a man fit to grace a chair at The Johns Hopkins. Is it at all impossible that such a man might not have been recognized should he have appeared?

Nor have we had the sustained help of European and American historians we began with. If Henry Morse Stephens, an Englishman and an authority on British constitutional history—not a Hispanist—had made the same mistake, think what a gap that might have left in the story of historical education in the West, even in the country at large! Has a pure Hispanist ever received an honorary degree from an American university as have many historians of modest attainments in other fields? Salvador de Madariaga, wishing to show the delicacy of the Spanish boatman alongside his loveable bravado, quotes this:

> I do not say that my boat
> Is the best in all the bay;
> But that it has the best movements
> Of the harbour, I do say.

To run on with his lilt:

> That no Southerner can
> Be president of the USA
> I no longer say;
> But that a Hispanist has never
> Been president of the AHA
> I do say.

Except in his outlook, the reputation of Herbert Eugene Bolton lay in Western history—the borderlands border the United States first. Passed over were Roger Bigelow Merriman and Clarence H. Haring, straightforward Hispanists, also in the best traditions and sound in scholarship.

Looking inward, does the quality of our scholarship justify a high reputation? During the shadowy months of the war the national figures of our first generation went on to their reward in heaven or, at least, to that of a slackened pace on earth. Were there among us worthy new hands to take the tiller from them?, Lewis Hanke put it then. I put it now. One of my peers, in his *consulta*, does not equivocate; scholarship in the Hispanic field, he holds, is low and unimaginative. It even shows a distinct lack of quality alongside the European and American fields—putting us at a marked disadvantage in this Association.

Are there more than vague, subjective grounds for this comparison? As chairman of the Conference Committee in the Bolton competition and as chairman of the Beveridge Committee to select prize books in all American fields, I find myself obliged to say that the work of the Hispanist, judged in these two limited areas, is at no disadvantage. However, the works in the Bolton contest had already been screened by publication and were often by established scholars, while the Beveridge competition depended almost entirely on manuscript Ph.D. theses, many never to appear in print. We have certainly given the American Historical Association the highest type of delegate to historical congresses abroad. If I must judge, then, I say this: We have as many eminent scholars among us as we had in the generation that preceded us as an organization, but we are too far from having the same proportion.

But we do not stand at the bar defenseless. Never before has any field of history been so ensnared in time of crisis and overlooked in time of peace as has ours. An uncontrollable rise in academic, public, and political interest accompanies each oscillation of the world's shifty affairs. An unmerciful wane follows. As in the unnecessary Castro catastrophe, the state ends with no policy—save the mark!—and we end minus nearly everything we need. The sources of money, looking for some singular slant, decide we must have "programs." Do you know what a "program" can be? It can be something to keep you from doing what you know in your bones should be done first of all. You might be publishing books, turning out a couple of excellent Ph.D.'s a year, but what is that without a "program?" Too, we must turn history upside down and write it backwards—Castro before Cortés. The pressure to talk to women's clubs of the latest pustule to erupt and to vaccinate the undergraduate with the same surface stuff often brings us the graduate student who has no feeling for history, no idea of the rigor of research; he merely wants to take the whole area into his brotherly loving arms. The professor must produce special committees and institutes—which he obligingly supplies by putting the Hispanists already on the faculty into another paper combination. He must plan *noches veladas* for the visiting poet. If this is not enough, you can make him edit a magazine, for which he is not decorated with purple hearts, in defiance of all logic and justice.

Now come the calls from an infinity of colleges and universities, the formula staccato, telegraphic: "Going into Latin American history. Need a young man right away —brilliant teacher, promising scholar, certain to publish. Must teach Latin American history, a section in Western Civ., and another in diplomatic history, counsel Freshmen, direct little Latin American group we

plan. Rank: instructor. Wire recommendations." Perhaps we hearken back five years when this paragon should have started his graduate education. Then we had to find private financing for candidates to study in foreign archives or let them fail. Perhaps we recall the highly instructive, unpublished thesis on Cuban guerilla techniques— still unpublished when we slosh into the Bay of Pigs. In this mood I recently sat me down to indite these words: "Dear Dean Doe: I suggest that you watch the Ed Sullivan show; he has the only Hispanic magicians in this country." I hate to admit I never mailed the missive.

If there ever was a need for convincing writing in a profession, it is among us now. Think what half a dozen essays, based on a lifetime of erudition, yet written with lucidity, grace, and force, would have meant to the public at large in the last decade! But alas! Our craft has fallen from the plane of literature where it was in the days of the enchantment. We have gone, perforce, farther and farther away from the fall of Granada and the massacre at Cholula. We have come to the price of indigo, the foibles of a university cloister, the make-up of the royal *protomedicato*, subjects upon which we cannot reduce our readers to a state of panting anticipation. We toil with a difficult paleography in mountains of sources. Mastering other men's languages instead of polishing our own, we dull our yen, perhaps our very capacity, to clothe the resulting story in artistic dress.

It is also most damaging to style among us that every flurry of wave and wind that sweeps over us leaves us under a dune of jargon. With stereotypes a writer does not think; he puts pieces he never shaped into wholes he cannot manage. The historian— thank heaven!—has aesthetic sense left, but I ask you if this awful language has not invaded the groves of Academe, captured our students lolling there, and many of our colleagues as well—in other departments, of course—and sometimes deployed between our own jaws? Could any sensitive man use the now shopworn "colonialism" without making a speech for our enemies? As envenomed anti-American phrases appeared and congealed, we stood back and thereby failed our colleagues and this Association.

Under our very noses the grey legend became the New Black Legend. Everybody knows that forty years ago, the most successful writers in South America were precisely those who could reach the loftiest pitch in denouncing the United States. Whoever could pluck the feathers of the American eagle with the hardest jerk was the most influential writer. In the essay and in poetry we became materialists—energetic and invincible, making the spine of the Andes tremble—while the writer soared in high Andean spirituality. Our elections became fradulent, our Roosevelts palavering. As a character in a Spanish American novel, if you were an American male, the odds were two to one that you would come out a heel; if a married female, six to one that you would abandon your children and tread the primrose path.

In a sheep-nibble mood, we read this dog-bite humor to our students. "Ha, ha," they laughed. They recognized the ludricrous when they heard it. We had to laugh, too.

We endured this exalted jargon for a generation. Charged with bumptiousness, we did not wish to begin by being bumptious. We would not review a Latin American book unless we could commend it or, at least, toe-dance a tight rope. It jolted me, as an editor, to receive this succinct review of a Chilean book, postmarked in the United States: "This book is not worth the [poor grade of] paper it is printed on." In a state of semi-shock, I turned to the signature of the writer. "Arturo Torres-Rioseco," I read. Condemned as the least courteous, we at last found ourselves impotent from courtesy. Convert this neurotic anxiety to please into policy—we fail to recognize the point of no return for our security.

We approach this hour. The international forces of distortion take over this historic cant—never effectively contested by us or by any class of historians. In Havana, they do not think it funny—merely appropriate —to plan a new statue of liberty with the torch lifted from the hand held aloft and a money bag placed in its stead. When a picket of Casavubu troops shoots a demagogue in the fastnesses of the Congo, before whose embassy do the claques howl "Imperialist! Colonialist!" Before yours!

When the vice-president of the United States is rocked at San Marcos, rocked and rolled at Caracas, with one voice our query goes up in the United States, "What have we neglected—what have *we* been doing wrong in Latin America?" Said they: "Indeed, what *have you* been doing wrong?" Reverse the tape: Imagine a vice-president from Peru heckled at Harvard and waylaid in Washington! Who in Lima would ask: "What have *we* been doing wrong?"

Having waited too long to start this paper, at this stage I dozed off, despite the stimulating effect of my mounting irritation. As I did so, I felt myself seized as if under arrest and hurried through space toward a Hudsonian Trapalanda, catching glimpses of the opal ocean below, suggesting the "keys" of the Flowered Land. Suddenly descending through the atmosphere, still unincinerated, I found myself hustled up to a great, gray building with rows of uniform windows, all covered with iron bars. Over the portal I read: "Castle Cliché." Here two old men took my right arm in their palsied grasp, seeming to abhor my left. By their measured, decrepit tread, their *ex cathedra* conversation, the dropping of such words as "Ariel," "Caliban," "spirituality," and "materialism," I judged them to be José Rodó and Rufino Blanco-Fombona. Clamping down on my left were two young men, one wearing an armband marked FPFC, who swore that before they would touch my right arm, they would pull the other from its socket. They repeated the phrases of the old men, to whom they would not speak, in a patois I was startled to hear them allude to as Españolski. As they stepped me with funereal pace by the barred cells lining the cloister, I noticed that over each such words as "Cruel Spaniards," "Gold Chasers," "Inquisitorial Fiends," had been imperfectly erased and the following substituted:

Dollar Diplomats
Big Sticks
Colonialists
Images, projected ugly *and* pretty
Materialists, all levels
Imperialists, old and new dimensions

In my consternation, as I trudged along, a strange calm took hold of me. I could reflect that I had spent much of my life correcting the iniquity that prejudicial clichés can do to the history of a people. I braced myself to be thrown into a cell set aside and labeled by Blanco-Fombona for American university professors who write about the affairs of Hispanic America: To wit, "Supine Ignoramuses." They hustled me past, though, and flung me into a cell marked "Bigots, Haters, and Violencers." (To avoid detection as a professor, I kept my silence about the etymology and diction involved in that last word.) When I protested the classification, they replied: "You are a Yankee *gusano*, and a Southern worm at that, are you not?" Though the spirits of my grandfathers might turn over in their gray uniforms, I proudly answered yes to both implications. Still brash, I protested the injustice to my cellmates, professors from Cambridge, New Haven, New York, and Chicago. "The juxtaposition is unnatural," I said. "These men I know personally; they are genteel, learned, and humane; they don't even qualify geographically as 'bigots and haters'." "Listen, generous camarada," said the youngest guard. "Don't let it disturb you; we plan to dump all of you together anyway."

The last I saw of this factotum, he snapped on an electronic device called "permissible-phrase machine," arranged to pass only the stereotypes that, in my anger, I had the bad taste to let fall from my lips, and to scramble all the rest.

To come back from Erewhon, our failure to make our erudition instructive left this country on trial without advocates. If, perchance, a professor cut unflinchingly to the line, even if it did favor the United States, what did he get for his undeviating course? If his middle name happened to be Flagg, his students, with easy undergraduate lev-

ity, substituted "flag-waving." If, twenty years ago another professor, entitled to authority if any of us was, wrote that "our fiat" should be law if it were necessary to "keep powerful enemies from establishing dangerous bases in the Western Hemisphere that might be used against us"—what happened to him? He failed of publication. Fidelito's Forty perceived, where we did not, that the American public would not demand authentic scholarship and integrity. It got neither—in time, at least. That no one drove home where the interests of this country truly lay puzzles me as much as it does Fulgencio Batista. A lawyer I know, a perceptive student of Hispanic America, thinks we were afraid of the label, "Jingo"; that, though it is too late, the old men among us might still speak up. Controversy cannot stay their advancement.

When too few of the old men appear, the cliché boys take over. These roving, dynamic fellows startle our laymen by rehashing as fresh discoveries all the hoary distortions of us. Against them we have no influence. Upon our initial failure three decades ago, the first of this pack frisked joyously upon the field and gave cry. Waldo Frank, said *La Prensa* of Buenos Aires, has a great reputation in Argentina because of the reputation the Argentines imagine he has in the United States where his reputation is owing exclusively to his prestige in Argentina. In our generation, C. Wright Mills and Herbert Matthews re-sold our laymen the abominations of the New Black Legend. Last year, at the doors of the venerable San Marcos de Lima, students who had never heard of a solitary one of us begged a colleague of mine to answer C. Wright Mills' *Power Elite* and the screeches of his *Listen, Yankee!* Why should Raúl Roa not agree to pay $25,000— as I have rumbles he did pay—for a book like this—out of our own mouths, as out of the mouth of the Bishop of Chiapa.

But do we have to eat our own offal as the bamboozled sociologist and depraved popularizers have had us do? A successful trick of theirs was to call upon us to stand up for democracy as if we had turned against it; another to renounce dictatorship, as if dictators were, somehow, our responsibility; that they are there because of us. After the San José Conference, when we voted sanctions against Trujillo, the veriest novice waited for the pay-off. It never came. Secretary Herter explained to the press that Trujillo "conducts a vicious government." What, I submit, was Cuba conducting? A May Court, with Fidel as Queen of the May?

There is no one among you, I assume, but holds open the prospect for democracy throughout Latin America as he holds open the possibility of Extra-Sensory Perception. But who is there among you naive enough to base a policy upon our ability to get democracy in a twinkling or to impose it in a millennium? Who would hold up the Alliance for Progress while, in a few casual weeks, somebody solved Latin America's complex land question? Whose sympathy does not lie with the bewildered statesman, facing problems of such unbelievable difficulty, complexity, and fluidity?

In this hemisphere, I conclude, inestimable damage has been done because spiteful and impassioned men there have interpreted us to Latin Americans and pretentious and superficial opportunists here have interpreted them to us. How different if Silvio Zavala, Germán Arciniegas, and Ricardo Donoso had spoken for them; Carl Becker, Samuel Eliot Morison, and Allan Nevis for us!

American historians, who know United States history better than we do, cannot imagine that falsification about us, in an area about which they have scarcely reflected, could be of world-wide and lasting harm to this country. Can they, can any of us, go on tranquilly browsing, with our blinds on, in our own narrow fields, while the vitiating forces of history sweep over the country and over us without our having essayed or accomplished any noteworthy deflection of them? It is time—past time—that our nominal union in this Association should once again become a real one. May our finest hours not include our eleventh! *He dicho.*

80. The Conference: A Fecund Decade, 1954–1964*

Howard F. Cline

Historians look at the past. In the case of the Conference on Latin American History we do have a history, dating from at least 1928. Briefly I should like to highlight some important developments of the past decade. During that span the Conference has moved from a determined but underdeveloped group to a position of dignity and significance within the historical guild, and especially within the American Historical Association, with which we meet concurrently.

The names of previous Conference Chairmen since 1954 attest to the qualities of leadership and competence which we are able to bring to this responsible post year after year.[1] During the same period, we have

* HAHR. 45:434–438 (Aug. 1965). Reprinted by permission of the author and the original publisher. These remarks were delivered on December 28, 1964, at the annual luncheon meeting of the Conference on Latin American History, Washington, D.C.

[1] Conference Chairmen: Bailey W. Diffie (1954); John F. Bannon (1955); Engel Sluiter

seen the *Hispanic American Historical Review* grow and develop under two successive editors; we expect its quality to be maintained and its coverage expanded under yet another who will be taking responsibility this coming year.

The institutional framework within which the Conference operates has been stabilized. Exactly ten years ago, in December, 1954, this body ratified the present Constitution, itself a revision of a document adopted in 1938 on the eve of the Second World War when most other area studies were still far over the academic horizon. The Conference could be counted among the more stable governments of Latin America, in view of the fact that we have required only one amendment to our constitution, adopted in 1960 to provide for a Vice-Chairman.

In 1964 the Conference took an important step. It became an incorporated organization under the laws of the District of Columbia, thus a legal body. This advance in our evolution, taken after consideration of many issues, resolved one old question that especially disturbed the Conference members during the 1920's and 1930's: relations of the Conference with the American Historical Association. Unilaterally the Conference frequently claimed to be an organic part of the larger, parent Association. From time to time Conference meetings even sent diplomatic missions to the Association to see if we could obtain funds to cover postage and other secretarial costs. The membership was quite disturbed when these overtures were uniformly rebuffed. As an incorporated, affiliated but autonomous body, the Conference now treats with the Association on friendly but equal terms. Each has its special missions, but both are engaged in numerous common enterprises for the improvement of the teaching and study of history. As our Mexican friends say, we are "Juntos

pero no revueltos"—close but not mixed together.

Another noteworthy institutional step was taken during 1964. At a meeting in November the General Committee recommended that the Hispanic Foundation in the Library of Congress be the secretariat for the Conference. Among the several implications of this recommendation, which was approved by the Librarian of Congress, was the end of the era of the black suitcase. For those who have not been the Secretary-Treasurer, let me explain. Perhaps fifteen years or so ago, each Secretary-Treasurer received from his predecessor a black fibre suitcase jammed with earlier papers, all presumably pertaining to the Conference. The suitcase in its travels lost its lock and usually arrived very thoroughly wrapped in clothesline. Apparently each succeeding Secretary added his bulk to the unexamined previous records. Among the duties which the Secretariat has undertaken is to organize a set of files and the Archives of the Conference. We have donated the black suitcase to the Salvation Army.

Significant among developments during the past ten years has been the establishment of a series of prizes offered by the Conference for excellence in historiographical work. The first of these prizes more or less was founded by accident, through administrative error on the part of your speaker. In 1953 he offered to have the Hispanic Foundation give a prize of $100 per year for the best article on Latin American History; upon returning from the annual meeting, he learned that to his dismay the Library of Congress, by order of Congress, could not offer prizes. Apparently our national legislators had disapproved of the Library's bestowing a prize on a poet who later was institutionalized and around whom suspicions of disloyalty to the United States had swirled. In any event, loyal Conference members donated from their own pockets sufficient funds to found and continue the James A. Robertson Prize. When articles have merited it, this oldest of our prizes has been given annually for the past ten years.

Shortly thereafter, in 1956, the Herbert

_____

(1956); Walter V. Scholes (1957); John Tate Lanning (1958); Charles C. Griffin (1959); Irving A. Leonard (1960); John J. Johnson (1961); James F. King (1962); Charles Gibson (1963); Howard F. Cline (1964).

E. Bolton Prize was established. It has been consistently funded by the Pan American Foundation, largely through the generosity and good will of our colleague, A. Curtis Wilgus. We hope this happy relationship between the Conference and the Pan American Foundation will continue for many years to come.

The General Committee of the Conference itself founded the Conference Prize in 1961. Although not administered directly by the Conference, its members were instrumental in establishing the Clarence H. Haring Prize, the first award of which will be made in December, 1965. The American Historical Association and the Conference cooperate in its administration, the membership of the AHA Prize Committee being drawn from our own constituency.

During the past few months, the growing complexity of the Conference and its evolving maturity have brought into being a number of committees to carry on work of interest to the Conference as a whole. In 1963 a Committee on Activities and Projects was established; its life has been extended and now renewed for at least the next three years.[2] As we shall see in a moment, I believe that the establishment of this Committee marks the beginning of a new phase in the life of the Conference.

Also in 1963, the Conference entered into a cooperative arrangement with the Library of Congress to produce a guide to the historical literature of Latin America, a major project of interest to each of the two sponsoring organizations. Its Advisory Editorial Board is considered a Committee of the Conference; the Editor, Charles Griffin, was jointly appointed by the Conference and the Library of Congress. We all expect this Guide to be a monumental and lasting contribution of the Conference.

Yet another relatively permanent Committee was created by the General Committee during 1964. Looking forward to various works of importance for the improvement of teaching and investigation of Latin American history, the Conference now has authorized a Publications Committee. The General Committee at the same time estab-

lished a series, the Conference on Latin American History Publications, among which the Guide will be included. There will be included in the series, which will be issued by a university press yet to be selected, other similar "tool" volumes.[3] The General Committee named Charles Gibson as Chairman of the Publications Committee for three years, with professional responsibility for the series.

All these developments within the last decade indicate the growing importance and vitality of the Conference. The capstone to this clear line of development came recently. The Ford Foundation permitted your Chairman to announce publicly now for the first time that its International Training and Research Program has granted the American Historical Association the sum of $125,000, which AHA will administer but the purpose of which grant is to permit the Conference to expand and improve its own programs over a 36-month period. The Conference is grateful both to the Foundation and the Association for their efforts on our behalf.

This important development is an outcome of work done by the Conference Committee on Activities and Projects. They drafted the proposal which the Conference and the Association jointly presented to the Ford Foundation during July, 1964. More than 40 plans, projects, and proposals from Conference members were reviewed by the Committee, were given priority ratings, and were placed in a series of programs, for which the grant funds will be disbursed through the Committee on Activities and Projects.

At a meeting in November, 1964, the General Committee reviewed the particular projects, and took appropriate action for the administration of funds. It prolonged the life of the Committee on Activities and Projects

[2] Howard F. Cline, Chairman; Woodrow W. Borah, Charles Gibson, John P. Harrison, Lyle N. McAlister, John L. Phelan, Stanley J. Stein, members.

[3] The Publication Committee announced that on May 28, 1965, a contract was signed with the University of Texas Press to publish the series.

and authorized it to be the administrative body to grant funds, the principal authority as approving and authorizing officer for the Conference to be lodged in the Chairman of that Committee.

Without getting into great detail, as these matters will be reported at further length in the Conference Newsletter, let me summarize for you the proposed programs.

The largest program is to obtain bibliographical control, then selection and filming of newspapers of historical importance in Latin America. Another program is aimed at seeing what can be done to fill the crying need for historical statistics, the absolute backbone of any comparative work. Control of certain bodies of colonial sources, and their publication is yet another group of proposed activities.

Attention will be given to the development of certain graduate teaching aids. Among these we hope will be an atlas.

There are a group of service functions which support the bibliographical and other investigations. Money for the publications series mentioned above is included among these, as are budgeted items permitting the Conference to join with other learned bodies in sponsoring small professional meetings. A small sum has been set aside for secretariat services, which include regular publication of the Newsletter, a matter also discussed by the General Committee in November.

Finally, included is a project that is controversial but interesting. It is the discussion and perhaps planning of a summary work on Latin American history, which for the field of history would do what the *Handbook of South American Indians*, and now the *Handbook of Middle American Indians* have done for anthropology: put in a series of volumes agreed and significant historical information on Latin America for use by the public, librarians, graduate students, and others, and provide the specialists with a frame of reference and a point of departure for further monographic studies. The Committee on Activities and Projects wishes to discuss some of the innumerable problems of the multivolume history before presenting recommendations to the Conference for its own debates. I might add, for the record, that the Ford Foundation has indicated in the grant letter to the American Historical Association that funding for such a multivolume history would necessarily have to be sought apart from the Ford Foundation.

In summary I believe that the past decade for the Conference has been a fecund one. I would hazard a guess that we are on the threshold of even more impressive contributions to the study and teaching of the history of Latin America. As an historian I am reluctant to predict Conference history of the future, but certainly the Conference has within its grasp a magnificent opportunity to demonstrate concretely that historians have something meaningful to say about Latin America—ancient, colonial, modern, recent.

81. The Ford Foundation Grant Program of the Conference:
A Special Report*

HOWARD F. CLINE

At the annual luncheon meeting of the Conference on Latin American History in the Shoreham Hotel, Washington, on December 28, 1964, the Chairman of the Conference, Howard F. Cline, announced that the Ford Foundation had granted the American Historical Association $125,000 to permit the Conference to expand its activities over a 36-month period. The General Committee of the Conference recommended that this special issue of the NEWSLETTER be sent to CLAH members to outline the scope of the grant and its proposed administration.

BACKGROUND

In 1963, under the chairmanship of Charles Gibson, a special CLAH Committee on Activities and Projects was named to advise the General Committee on a number of proposals that had come before it. Dr. Carl Spaeth, then a consultant to the Ford Foundation, also requested that the Conference provide him information on needs to improve the research and teaching of Latin American history in the United States. In response to the Spaeth inquiry, the Committee on Activities and Projects, consisting of Stanley J. Stein and Howard F. Cline, Co-Chairmen, and Woodrow Borah, Lyle N. McAlister, John L. Phelan, members, developed a list of about 40 projects of varying magnitude and significance, all related to improvement of Latin American historical studies.

In December 1964 the General Committee prolonged the life of the Committee on Activities and Projects for one year, with a mandate to place the suggested activities and projects in order of priority and to seek means to implement the resulting programs. Early in February 1964 the Committee met and divided the proposals into five groups, ranging from "Highly essential" (Priority

I) to "Reject" (Priority V), using an array of criteria that had been earlier developed. The General Committee accepted the report and recommendations of the Committee on Activities and Projects, which was then authorized to enter into negotiations to implement the program. The Committee was also then enlarged to include John P. Harrison.

Discussions among the officials of the American Historical Association, the International Training and Research Program of Ford Foundation, and the Chairman of the Conference (Howard Cline) led to formulation of a joint memorandum from the Association and the Conference to the Ford Foundation, forwarded in July 1964. On December 16, 1964, the Ford Foundation generously granted the requested funds.

ADMINISTRATION

On November 21, 1964, eight of the nine members of the General Committee met in Washington to lay down guide-lines for administration of the grant. It extended the life of the Committee on Activities and Projects and its current membership for a 36-month period, and named Howard F. Cline its Chairman for that period. The Committee was authorized to administer the grant funds for the Conference. The General Committee also reviewed the budgets and priorities. At its meeting on December 28, 1964, the General Committee added one additional activity, secretariat services, which the Hispanic Foundation had on November 21 agreed to undertake on behalf of the Conference, subject to approval by the Librarian of Con-

* Conference on Latin American History, Newsletter, n.s., 1/1:2–5 (Jan. 1965). Reprinted by permission of the author.

gress, who subsequently authorized this further cooperation with CLAH.

The American Historical Association agreed to receive and disburse grant funds for the Conference, such disbursements to be made on recommendation of the Chairman of the Committee on Activities and Projects. For these and other administrative services, the Conference and the Ford Foundation agreed to allow the Association 10 percent overhead costs on the grant funds, amounting to $11,300, leaving $113,700 for Conference programs over a three year period. The Conference will receive interest on unspent grant funds, applicable to its programs and secretariat services.

PROGRAMS

The general purpose of the grant funds and the Conference program of activities and projects is to strengthen the national infrastructure of historical work by providing necessary tools, scholarly resources, and communication among teachers and investigators of Latin American history in the United States. Purposely there are no provisions for travel grants, training scholarships, or similar activities now normally channeled via the ACLS-SSRC Joint Committee on Latin American Studies, the Ford Foundation Area Fellowship Program, and similar programs. The Committee on Activities and Projects recommended strongly that no funds be regranted to individual members of the Conference for personal research or graduate fellowships, on which the General Committee unanimously concurred, in view of the existence of these several other grant programs to cover such needs. Thus the Conference programs are for the general national advancement of the study and teaching of Latin American history rather than to support particular research or teaching by individuals or institutions.

The activities and projects have been divided into eight main Programs, the general headings indicating the range of matters for which varying grant funds have been allocated, to cover various related activities. The Programs are herewith summarized.

Program 1. *Historical Newspapers*

It is expected that bibliographical research will provide a current guide to nineteenth and twentieth century newspapers in U.S. repositories (in original or filmed copies). On the basis of that inventory, Conference committees, working with librarians and others, will indicate among missing newspapers or years those most desirable for filming. As funds are available photoreproductions of these will be obtained and deposited in the Library of Congress. The long-term goal of this Program is to have for each Latin American country a set of its newspaper files spanning the years from about 1825 through 1938, starting with major missing runs such as *La Prensa* (Buenos Aires). Suggestions from Conference members of titles of historical significance would be much welcomed by the Committee on Activities and Projects.

Program 2. *Historical Statistics*

The object of this Program is to develop doctrines for proper collection and publication of the historical statistics of Latin America, by selecting one country as a pilot project. For various reasons, Colombia has been chosen for the test case. The long-term goal is to develop comparable arrays of historical statistics for major Latin American countries since about 1825, to provide an adequate quantitative base for comparative work. Again, CLAH members who have interest in specific categories of historical statistics are urged to communicate with the Committee on Activities and Projects.

Program 3. *Cooperative History of Latin America*

The purpose of this Program is discussion and possible planning of a single work, undoubtedly multi-volume, which for Latin American history would provide data comparable to that for anthropology in the *Handbook of South American Indians* of the 1940's, and the *Handbook of Middle American Indians,* in progress. The Ford Foundation has specifically stated that funds for the preparation and publication of such an ambitious work, if found feasible, will necessarily be financed apart from Ford Foundation funds. The Conference will have opportunity to discuss and debate these issues, once preliminary work has been done by the Committee on Activities and Projects.

Program 4. Teaching Aids

Within the specific scope of this Program is the development of an historical atlas for graduate teaching purposes. Included similarly is preparation of an anthology of articles written since 1898 on the development of the study of Latin American history in the United States, primarily for graduate instruction.*

Program 5. Conferences and Consultations

This Program provides funding for various small conferences on specific topics and to assist the Conference in joining with other professional bodies to sponsor small conferences of joint or mutual interest. The Program also permits the Conference to bring to its annual meetings one or two foreign scholars whose presence would strengthen these annual gatherings.

Program 6. Colonial Sources

Funds have been specifically earmarked to aid in the preparation and scholarly editing of two bodies of colonial sources of general importance. These include the 1577–1585 corpus of *Relaciones Geográficas*, and the Instructions which New World viceroys left to their successors.

Program 7. Publications Series

On November 21, 1964 the General Com-

mittee established the *Conference on Latin American History Publications* series. It also named a Publications Committee, of which Charles Gibson is Chairman, to issue various titles prepared by and for the Conference. The *Guide to the Historical Literature of Latin America*, co-sponsored by the Hispanic Foundation and CLAH, under the editorship of Charles Griffin, for example, will appear in this series. Other publications resulting from activities under the grant funds will also have this Conference imprint. It is not envisaged that at the outset the Publications will issue monographic studies by individual CLAH members, but will rather be confined to general and particular guides, indices, directories, and other "tool" publications, including sources.

Program 8. Secretariat

The Hispanic Foundation has agreed to house the CLAH archives, and to perform certain centralized secretariat services. Among the latter will be publications of the *Bio-Bibliographical Directory of U.S. Historians with Latin American Specializations*, as well as a general *Handbook of the Conference on Latin American History*, which will include its constitutions, prizes, committees, officers since 1928, and related reference data. The secretariat will also aid the Secretary-Treasurer to prepare and issue future NEWSLETTERS. It is hoped also that the secretariat can provide limited but specialized reference assistance to members of the Conference. It is planned that after July 1, 1965, a full-time staff member of the Hispanic Foundation will carry these various responsibilities for the Conference.

* This volume. [Ed. note]

82. Language as a Key to Latin American Historiography*

RICHARD M. MORSE

Latin Americanists have in recent years become increasingly concerned with constructing the basis for a unified history of Latin America. Frequently this enterprise leads them to contemplate the even larger design of a history of the Americas. While the New World may still be, in Hegel's words, "a land of desire for all those who are weary of the historical lumber-room of old Europe," it is now recognized as having an independent heritage; its history is no longer experienced as "only an echo of the Old World."[1]

Two general approaches toward the writing of Latin American and, more broadly, "American" history have been used: the analytic and the synthetic. The analytic is illustrated by the average textbook in Latin American history, or by the activities of the *Comisión de Historia* of the *Instituto Panamericano de Geografía e Historia*. The *Comisión* disseminates research aids and monographs relating, for the most part, to individual American nations. With but few exceptions the publications that it sponsors avoid the act of integration and interpretation; and, since interpretation is something other than the mere collating of national histories, the most relevant materials are not always made available for it.

The synthetic approach, which does not lend itself to bureaucratic enterprise, has been used by such authors as Edmundo O'Gorman[2] and Juan Larrea.[3] Writers of this order often rely upon a high degree of philosophic abstraction or poetic intuition—and in the case of Larrea upon mysticism and numerology. Though greatly illuminating within a certain realm, their insights are frequently of too cryptic a nature to inform the practical labors of historiography.

Working needs of the Latin Americanist have thus far been best served by studies which effect a compromise between the two approaches. Such studies are synthetic in that they have unified perspectives and criteria for selecting data which cut across the designless mosaic of self-contained national histories. They are analytic in that their scope is carefully delimited; their themes are explored with an eye to the diversities and necessary qualifications of an "American" perspective; their conclusions are merely suggestive of, or ancillary to, "Americanism" in its broadest meaning. Studies of this sort, to name only a few, are: Jane's inter-

---

* *Americas*, 11:517–538 (Apr. 1955). Reprinted by permission of the author and the original publisher. This article received second prize in the James Alexander Robertson Prize Essay Contest conducted by the Conference on Latin American History of the American Historical Association during the year 1954. [*Americas* Ed. note]

[1] G. W. F. Hegel, *Lectures on the Philosophy of History*, tr. by J. Sibree (London, 1894), p. 90.

[2] In his *La idea del descubrimiento de América* (Mexico City, 1951) Edmundo O'Gorman lays the groundwork for an integral history of the Americas; see especially pp. 9–24, 361–367.

[3] Juan Larrea, *Rendición de espiritu* (2 vols.; Mexico City, 1943).

pretation of Spanish American political history;[4] histories of the Negro in the Americas by Herkovits[5] and Tannenbaum;[6] analyses of Latin American economics by Gordon[7] and Hanson;[8] and Beals' study of Latin American social stratification.[9] (Institutional history confined to the colonial period is of course more amenable to broad, interregional treatment.)

The present essay is of the third, or hybrid, type. Its concern is with the characteristic ways in which European languages are spoken in Latin America, and with suggesting the implications of speech habits for the study of Latin American history. In emphasis of certain points supplementary references will be made to the English spoken in British America.

Language—its rhythm and timbre, its idiom and imagery—ought to provide the historian with his richest insights. For language responds to the full round of a people's activities and attitudes; it enshrines their traditions and reflects their affairs of the moment; it is employed and molded by all, by plebe and aristocrat, ignoramus and scholar; it transcribes a society in its diffuse panorama and its angular detail. If Latin American historiography has hitherto made little use of linguistic analysis, this is largely because the historian distrusts his own impressionistic sense of speech habits and because the philologists' conclusions are couched in too formidably specialized terms. Since neither of these limitations can be disregarded, the sources of this essay are largely confined to the works of a few language scholars who have presented their findings in a way that suggests their broader relevance.[10]

Another difficulty is the objection that there are no standard speech habits within any of the sprawling New World language areas and, further, that regional variants in America are more different from one another than an American archetype would be from its European counterpart. Navarro Tomás once pointed out, for example, that consonantal pronunciations generally cited as distinguishing American Spanish (s, j, z, ll and rr) are not uniform in the New World and also occur in regions of Spain.[11] The reasons for denying typically Latin American speech habits, however, could be extended into a denial of distinctive Latin American history, social patterns or art. The objection of Navarro Tomás is legitimate only when the Panamerican context is treated as an exclusive one. This essay advances a New World perspective to complement and sharpen rather than to displace the many other possible perspectives. It is concerned not with American languages that are *sui generis*, but with European languages as they are spoken in America. And it will be found that the New World characteristics most significant for the historian are not dialectal innovations, but archaic survivals and shifts in the frequency and emphasis of European usages.

It is often held that Latin American customs and institutions, especially those of the colonial period, exhibit many "medieval" traits. One obvious explanation is that the New World was colonized shortly after the Middle Ages, an era from which the Iberian mother countries were somewhat tardily emerging. This, however, accounts merely for the *transplantation* of certain formal elements of *high* medieval society. From another point of view, New World colonization entailed a *re-creation* of certain conditions that had ushered in Europe's *early* Middle Ages. In post-Roman Europe, as in

[4] Lionel Cecil Jane, *Liberty and Despotism in Spanish America* (Oxford, 1929).

[5] Melville J. Herskovits, *The Myth of the Negro Past* (New York, 1941).

[6] Frank Tannenbaum, *Slave and Citizen, the Negro in the Americas* (New York, 1947).

[7] Wendell C. Gordon, *The Economy of Latin America* (New York, 1950).

[8] Simon G. Hanson, *Economic Development in Latin America* (Washington, 1951).

[9] Ralph L. Beals, "Social Stratification in Latin America," *The American Journal of Sociology*, LVIII, 4 (January, 1953), 327–339.

[10] A good handbook of studies on American Spanish is Madaline W. Nichols, *A Bibliographical Guide to Materials on American Spanish* (Cambridge, 1941).

[11] Tomás Navarro Tomás, "El idioma español en el 'cine' parlante—español o hispanoamericano?" *Revista de las Españas*, V, 48–49 (August-September, 1930), 418–427.

post-Columbian Latin America, norms of the imperial metropolis were of limited effect. Organizations for defense and for economic production were local, pragmatic arrangements, informed by a morality born of "frontier" conditions. Anthropologists claim, for instance, that the co-parenthood, or *compadrazgo*, system, which afforded a "horizontal" cementing of relationships in early Europe, was freshly evoked by American conditions of life at the very time when it was giving way to more impersonal modes of organization in the mother countries.[12]

Karl Vossler suggested that the disintegration of imperial Roman Europe into a network of agrarian communities was reflected in the transition from classical to Vulgar Latin—that is, to the "peasant dialects." Classical Latin had been forced toward articulation and suppleness by sophisticated, forensic city-dwellers who preferred the "visually more objective" and used language as a "gesture of thought." Vulgar Latin evinced a new phonetic structure, partly determined by the speaking or shouting of Latin "in still air and at great distances." The peasant, preferring the "acoustically more objective," forced Latin toward greater volume of sound, toward sonority rather than articulation.[13]

By the time of the discovery of America, certain of the "peasant dialects" of which Vossler speaks had become legitimized within the new nation-states. They, like classical Latin of old, were used by an educated, courtly élite. And, just as Latin had in the post-Roman world to accommodate to agrarian Europe, so in the sixteenth century these citified languages had to accommodate to the uses of the American wilderness.

This analogy, of course, cannot be pressed to the ultimate, for post-Columbian America—as will later be discussed—never lost contact with Europe's metropolitan norms. Furthermore, the New World, notably Spanish America, soon produced its own urban centers, which acted against the legitimizing of any "peasant dialects" of the hinterland. Yet, even if one grants these qualifications, the settlement of America can, like

post-Roman Europe, be taken to represent a "telluric" experience—or a reassertion of the claims of physical environment upon human culture. The European in America, though often more bedouin than peasant, became earthbound—that is, less tradition- and culture-bound. While it is difficult to substantiate the kind of conjecture which Vossler makes as to the effect of natural environment upon the quality of speech, the vast new setting of forest, plain and cordillera to which European tongues were transplanted should not be lost sight of.[14]

In the imagery of speech environmental influences are more easily identified than in its aural quality. The ocean, for instance, which any European emigrant came intimately to know, was for America not an outer limit but the arterial connection with the matrices of civilization. Because of the importance of ocean commerce, and doubtless because of the landman's admiration of the sailor, nautical expressions passed into general currency; and, for those who penetrated the boundless, undulating pampas, *llanos* and Great Plains, nautical images re-

[12] Sidney W. Mintz and Eric R. Wolf, "An Analysis of Ritual Co-parenthood (Compadrazgo)," *Southwestern Journal of Anthropology*, VI, 4 (Winter, 1950), 341–368. The importance of studying Latin American institutional history both as *transplantation* and as *independent formation* is stressed by Richard Konetzke in "Las ordenanzas de gremios como documentos para la historia social de Hispano-américa durante la época colonial," *Estudios de historia social de España*, ed. by the Instituto "Balmes" de Sociología (Madrid, 1949), I, 483 ff.

[13] "Hence the phonetic manifestations of Vulgar Latin are concerned more with consonants than with vowels, and consonantal changes are usually induced by the expansion of neighboring vowel sounds." Karl Vossler, *The Spirit of Language in Civilization* (London, 1932), pp. 109–110.

[14] It is suggestive that, just as certain consonantal groupings of Latin were smoothed out in medieval French (in such words as *esprit*, *étude*, *épée*), so in turn the spoken French of Canada planes down in its own mother tongue. (Pierre Daviault, "La langue française au Canada," *Royal Commission Studies* [Ottawa, 1951], pp. 31–32.) As will later be brought out, however, such linguistic trends cannot wholly be attributed to the effect of "wide open spaces."

tained especial pertinence.[15] In New World Spanish *amarrar* (to moor) took the broader meaning of "to tie," while *flete* (cargo) was extended to mean "horse."[16] In French Canada—administered, significantly, by the *Ministére de la Marine*—the same trend occurred: "Le Canadien *traverse* d'un *bord* de la rue á l'autre. Il *aborde* quelqu'un pour lui parler, quand cette personne est *accostable*. Ou bien, il *vire de bord*. *Bordée* (*de neige*) est de même origine, ainsi que *embardée*, *amarrer* (*un cheval*) et *touer* (une auto)."[17] And in the British West Indies, according to Bryan Edwards:

. . . they say, *hand such a thing*, instead of bring or give it. A plantation well stocked with Negroes, is said to be *well handed*: an office or employment is called *a birth* [*sic*]; the kitchen is denominated the *cook-room*; a warehouse is called a *store*, or *store-room*; a sopha is called *a cot*; a waistcoat is termed *a jacket*; and in speaking of the East and West, they say to *windward* and *leeward*. This language has probably prevailed since the days of the bucaniers.[18]

The novelty of the American environment and of the patterns of human effort which it evoked, affected more than pronunciation, idiom and vocabulary. For much of New World experience, being unprecedented for Europeans, did not answer to the larger structures of expression inherited from their past. As Cortés wrote to his emperor: ". . . querer de todas las cosas destas partes y nuevos reinos de vuestra alteza decir todas las particularidades y cosas que en ellas hay y decir se debían sería casi proceder a infinito."[19] The early American diaries, chronicles and natural and human histories are enumerative and analytic in character. They record a childlike vision for which each occurrence is fresh and unique, for which the synthetic, recurrently applicable generality of the adult is useless even when available.[20] Nor was the discursive, expository mode abandoned in later centuries, as any reader of Fernández de Lizardi, Sarmiento, Euclides da Cunha, Martín Luis Guzmán, José Vasconcelos or Freyre well knows.

The analytic uses of colloquial, as of written, languages were emphasized in the New World. The pragmatic, denotative services

which were exacted of it prejudiced its connotative attributes. Used instrumentally for "expression," language lost in "expressiveness." Brazilians, for example, show a tendency to avoid cultivated pronominal intricacies of the mother country and to employ a basic subject-pronoun form.[21] In Brazil the idiomatic preposition *a* gives way to connectives or idioms that are more functional.[22] Brazilian Portuguese tends to replace conditional and future verbs with the more manageable imperfect and present, and to negate imperatives directly without first turning them into the subjunctive.[23] Similarly,

[15] The analogy of the sea came easily to Domingo Faustino Sarmiento when he described transportation on the pampas: "Nuestras carretas viajeras son una especie de escuadra de pequeños bajeles, cuya gente tiene costumbres, idioma y vestido peculiares que la distinguen de los otros habitantes, como el marino se distingue de los hombres de tierra." (*Facundo* [Buenos Aires, 1942], p. 32.)

[16] William J. Entwistle, *The Spanish Language together with Portuguese, Catalan and Basque* (London, 1936), p. 256.

[17] Daviault, *loc. cit.*, p. 29.

[18] Bryan Edwards, *The History, Civil and Commercial, of the British Colonies in the West Indies* (2nd ed.; 2 vols.; London, 1794), II, 9.

[19] Hernán Cortés, *Cartas de relación de la conquista de Méjico* (5th ed.; 2 vols.; Madrid, 1942), I, 37.

[20] An illustration will perhaps make this analogy more clear. During a country walk I once met a little girl and exchanged greetings as we passed. Later, on the return, I encountered her once more. "We meet again," I said, and she simultaneously observed, "First you were going this way and I was going that way and now I'm going this way and you're going that way." One of us, that is, called up a cliché which related the incident to many others of his experience; the other could only describe the meeting discursively, since she could supply for it no context.

[21] A Brazilian is inclined to say *o artista que a voz dele me agrada* rather than *o artista cuja voz me agrada*, *o livro que te falei nele* rather than *o livro de que te falei*. (Clóvis Monteiro, *Português da Europa e português da América* [Rio de Janeiro, 1931], pp. 93–95.) It is of interest that this construction is a peninsular archaism.

[22] *Medo a pobreza* becomes *medo da pobreza*; *trabalhar a preceito* becomes *trabalhar com preceito*; *estou a correr* becomes *estou correndo*. (Renato Mendonça, *O português do Brasil* [Rio de Janeiro, 1936], pp. 257–261.)

[23] *Ibid.*, p. 266.

New World Spanish shies from puristic verb forms. The *voy a, vas a, . . .* construction is a greater threat to the future tense in the Americas than in Spain; verb forms are falsely correlated in independent and dependent clauses; and in using impersonal verbs the Spanish American more frequently prefers to construct according to sense instead of according to the logic of syntax (*hubieron temores de guerra* rather than *hubo . . .*).[24]

Latin American speech habits, however, must be related to a social as well as to a natural environment if they are to achieve their full relevance for the historian. When this is done, they recall to him that the colonization of Latin America was a "plebeianizing" process—that is, one of cultural democratization. It is true that Spain and Portugal swiftly extended traditional hierarchies into the New World—social, political and ecclesiastical. But the Latin American historian, more than the British American, needs the reminder that the vastness and strangeness of the New World inevitably induced social leavening, and bred new intimacies and criteria for leadership. Menéndez Pidal stresses that large numbers of Spanish American colonists were persons of lower-class origin, for the first time cast forth and dispersed from proximity to urban, intellectual life. "El habla de estas clases bajas había de producirse con mucha menor presión del elemento culto que en España." This leads the writer to an important distinction between the *popularismo* of peninsular language and the *vulgarismo* of Spanish American:

Ya en la Península el *popularismo* es uno de los caracteres propios de la literatura y de la lengua, savia que produce florecimientos maravillosos como el romancero, el teatro clásico, la prosa de Santa Teresa o del mismo Cervantes; y ese carácter, en las nuevas condiciones de vida de América, se matiza de *vulgarismo*. La diferencia del matiz es evidente: lo popular supone la compenetración del elemento culto con el pueblo en general; lo vulgar supone la mayor iniciativa del pueblo inculto. Ahora bien; este matiz de vulgarismo no es sólo propio de la lengua, sino de la literatura y de la vida entera.

Menéndez Pidal goes on to state that "al reconocer el vulgarismo como un rasgo del hispanoamericano, no podemos menos de insistir en la comparación con el latín vulgar.[25] He introduces a social dimension, that is, to the analogy between America and post-Roman Europe which was earlier suggested.

That the social leavening of the New World did not go unacknowledged by Spaniards of the time is proven in two quotations culled by Amado Alonso. In 1568 Juan de Mal Lara wrote: "Preguntado uno que era caballero, y que fué a Indias y vino rico: '¿Cómo ganaste de comer?,' respondía: 'Quitándome el *don*'." And the better known Juan López de Velazco, speculating on certain transformations of body and soul exhibited by New World Spaniards, wrote: ". . . por haber pasado a aquellas provincias tantos espíritus inquietos y perdidos, el trato y conversación ordinaria se ha depravado, y toca mas presto, a lo que menos fuerza de virtud tienen; y así en aquellas partes ha habido siempre y hay muchas calumnias y desasosiegos entre unos hombres con otros."[26]

In the light of the foregoing Tocqueville's contrast between England and the United States in the nineteenth century has no little validity for Spain and Spanish America in the sixteenth and thereafter. Language in an aristocratic European society, he observed, partakes of "that state of repose in which everything remains." The mutation has a narrow radius of contagion, for a given language comprises norms that distinguish poor from rich, commoner from noble, tradesman from scholar. "When, on the contrary, men, being no longer restrained by ranks, meets on terms of constant inter-

[24] Entwistle, *op. cit.*, p. 262; Avelino Herrero Mayor, *Presente y futuro de la lengua española en América* (Buenos Aires, 1944), pp. 156–157. For the evasion of the niceties of future conjugations in American English see H. L. Mencken, *The American Language, Supplement I* (New York, 1945), pp. 402–404.

[25] Ramón Menéndez Pidal, *La lengua de Cristóbal Colón* (3rd ed.; Madrid, 1947), pp. 113–115.

[26] Both citations given in Amado Alonso, *El problema de la lengua en América* (Madrid, 1935), pp. 130–136.

course, . . . all the words of a language are mingled."[27]

The theories of Menéndez Pidal and Tocqueville can be illustrated by the most widely recognized characteristic of New World Spanish: the *seseo* (pronunciation of *z* or of *c* before *e* or *i* as an *s* rather than, as in most of Spain, a voiceless *th*). It has in some quarters been maintained that, since the *seseo* is native to southern Spain, its prevalence in the New World merely reflects a high ratio of Andalusians among the conquistadores. As the late Amado Alonso pointed out, however, Andalusians did not preponderate on the conquest; in 1500, furthermore, the *seseo* was not yet widespread in Andalusia and appeared in Spain merely as a sporadic, plebian variant. Within a century or two its use was more common, but the *seseo* in Spain has never transcended its popular, regional origin. Only in the New World could it slip its bonds—profiting by the discomposure of a transplanted society—and attain legitimacy. As early as the sixteenth century occasional rimes in the verses of the Spanish-born Mexican poet González de Eslava document the *seseo's* eventually successful bid for supremacy.[28]

Comparable to the *seseo* is the *voseo*, that is, use of *vos* instead of the Castilian *tú* as the second person singular (intimate) pronoun. In medieval Spain *vos* was a respectful form of address, while *tú* was used familiarly or with persons of inferior station. Later, however, *usted* (*vuestra merced*) dislodged *vos* as the polite form. At the time of the conquest *vos* was used familiarly but was less well received than *tú* and might denote a master-servant relationship or a speaker's wrath. In Spain the *voseo* was obsolescent by the seventeenth century, but in America it widely persists as evidence of New World *vulgarismo*. Significantly, it is strongest in the historically outlying areas (La Plata region, Andean highlands, Central America) and weakest or non-existent in places that maintained closer contact with metropolitan Spain (the circum-Caribbean region and the viceregal centers of Mexico and Peru).[29]

Many characteristics of language in the New World are therefore to be understood not as neologisms but as a natural fulfillment of certain tendencies which Europe's equilibrated systems had held in check. The shuffling of classes and of regional groups during colonization removed the stigma from many plebeianisms and provincialisms whose applicability to new conditions of life recommended their universal usage. The seventeenth-century French colonists who went to Canada, for example, were largely provincials and *petites gens*. They did not speak the Francien dialect of Ile-de-France and Orléans which in the thirteenth century had come into prestige as the language of the court. Indeed, even as late as the French Revolution only ten or fifteen per cent of France's citizenry spoke Francien, or "French," with complete fluency. In Canada dialectal groups therefore intermingled with little guidance from the courtly norm. A modern Parisian who visits Canada hears a relatively homogeneous French yet one which coincides neither with any of the contributory dialects nor with official modern French, and one which exhibits archaisms no longer current in Europe.[30]

[27] Alexis de Tocqueville, *Democracy in America* (2 vols.; New York, 1945), II, 67–68.

[28] Amado Alonso, "Primeros problemas históricos del castellano en América," *IIº Congreso Internacional de Historia de América* (Buenos Aires, 1938), pp. 607–621. See also Pedro Henríquez-Ureña, *Sobre el problema del andalucismo dialectal de América* (Buenos Aires, 1952).

[29] Bertil Malmberg, "L'espagnol dans le nouveau monde—problème de linguistique générale," *Studia linguistica*, I, 2 (1947), 97–99; Arturo Capdevila, *Babel y el castellano* (Madrid, n. d.), pp. 85–129.

[30] Daviault, *loc. cit.*, pp. 26–30. Entwistle (*op. cit.*, p. 264), Carlos Martínez Vigil (*Arcaísmos españoles usados en América* [Montevideo, 1939]) and Mendonça (*op. cit.*, pp. 119–121, 240–245, 252–256) point out archaisms in American Spanish and Portuguese, while H. L. Mencken does so for American English in *The American Language* (4th ed.; New York, 1936), pp. 124–129, and in *Supplement I*, pp. 224–226. Research which would specify to what extent such archaisms are passive survivals, to what extent they have actively served specifically American functions and to what extent they are independent recreations of medieval usage might illuminate much cultural and institutional history of the New World.

From the discussion thus far it can be deduced that the transatlantic migration effected a certain impoverishment of language —a conclusion perhaps relevant to other realms of cultural history. In the first place, the linguistic heritage was thinned out to the degree that emigrants fell short of fully representing the human spectra of their respective colonizing countries. Secondly, the intermingling of these emigrants in America consigned to oblivion those regional or dialectal ways of speech which failed to pass into general currency. Languages became standardized in the New World; and in this connection it is significant that Navarro Tomás, who was previously cited as being unwilling to recognize an "American Spanish," once affirmed that "el oído español puede confundir a un mejicano o antillano y hasta a un argentino o chileno con un extremeño o andaluz, per no, por ejemplo, con un asturiano, castellano o aragonés."[31] Malmberg points out that the speech of an Argentine gaucho, despite its many idiosyncracies, is much closer to standard Castilian than is the speech of an Aragonese or Leonese peasant. He then generalizes as follows: "Ce phénomène revient en d'autres territoires oú une langue européene a été répandue à l'époque moderne par suite d'une conquète d'une colonisation. C'est aussi le cas du portugais au Brésil, de l'anglais en Amérique du Nord et du Russe en Sibérie."[32]

The thinning-out and uniformalizing of American Spanish (which have other aspects to be taken up shortly) led the poetess Gabriela Mistral to remonstrate:

El vocabulario hispanoamericano corriente es de una miseria que puede llamarse desértica. La lectura de las obras de muchos pedagogos criollos prueba de sobra lo que aquí afirmamos, pues son generalmente unos libros jadeados, tiesos, chatos y grieses. . . . ¡Qué linda sería una mocedad sudamericana que hablase, a lo menos, como el campesino de Córdoba, de Toledo o de Salamanca! Yo querría volver a vivir para oírla. Tendría gracia, donaire, calor y sabor, agilidad y jocundidad en cada decir, en el preguntar y en el responder; en el describir y el narrar, hasta en el enamorar y el pelear![33]

This is not of course to say that the New World was unproductive of fresh words and expressions. The earliest chronicles bristle with terms lifted from Arawak, Nahuatl, Quechua and Tupí-Guaraní, in Spanish such words as *bohío, piragua, henequén, chocolate, cacao, alpaca, pampa, jaguar*, and in Portuguese such ones as *samba, caatinga, abacaxi, caipira*.[34] To Indianisms must be added contributions from African dialects, especially prominent in Brazilian Portuguese (*quitanda, cachimbo, quilombo, batuque, senzala*).[35] Moreover, European languages in the New World borrowed *inter se* across loosely defined frontiers, within settlements of mixed provenience or in colonies which changed ownership in forced or peaceful transactions. Finally, one finds tropes, such as the nautical expressions discussed earlier, and coined or adapted words pointing new activities or shifted centers of experience—indicating, for example, new political arrangements or economic pursuits.[36]

When Gabriela Mistral, however, spoke of the impoverishment of American Spanish, she was not tabulating its neologisms against Old World expressions which did not survive the ocean crossing. She referred not so much to a quantitative abridgment of vocabulary as to a diminution of its incisiveness and of the levels of references across

[31] Tomás Navarro Tomás, cited in Herrero Mayor, *op. cit.*, p. 174.

[32] Malmberg, *loc. cit.*, p. 87. This point is elaborated for the United States in Mencken, *American Language*, pp. 354–356, and for English-speaking Canada in Henry Alexander, "The English Language in Canada," *Royal Commission Studies*, p. 13.

[33] Gabriela Mistral, cited in Herrero Mayor, *op. cit.*, p. 172.

[34] Entwistle, *op. cit.*, pp. 239–247; Mendonça, *op. cit.*, pp. 142–172.

[35] Jacques Raimundo, *O elemento afro-negro na lingua portuguesa* (Rio de Janeiro, 1933); Renato Mendonça, *A influência africano no português do Brasil* (2nd ed.; São Paulo, 1935).

[36] Neologisms have been less abundant in the Spanish and Portuguese than in the English of the New World. The Iberian languages, or the attitudes which they reflect, do not lend themselves to extremities of neologistic contortion and invention. Moreover, the protean socio-economic effects of the United States' mercantile and later industrial capitalism have, until the twentieth-century, been only mildly paralleled to the south.

which it ranges. What I have called the "thinning-out" of American languages implies that they were uprooted from rich "substrata" identified with the regional traditions of Europe. Some Latin American philologists of the late nineteenth century claimed that new and equally fertile substrata were provided by Indian tongues as soon as racial miscegenation took place. Such claims, however, now appear to reflect more of nationalism than of scientific method. According to Entwistle:

Far from conserving their own mental habits while adopting a new vocabulary, the American Mestizos have abandoned their ancient speech-habits but passed on a number of words needed to describe new things and customs. There is not even any syntactical influence of any of these tongues on Spanish, apart from the dubious instance of the Quechua suffix-*y* in the Argentine district of Tucumán. . . . The influence of the American substrata, in short, has done no more than provide the names for exotic things, not all of which have a wide circulation, and many of which stand liable to replacement by newer European terms.[37]

That the Americas have no rich and fanciful vernacular literature that compares with Europe's is evidence of the point that is being made. Regarding this lack Walt Whitman fulminated:

The Scotch have their born ballads, subtly expressing their past and present, and expressing character. The Irish have theirs. England, Italy, France, Spain, theirs. What has America? With exhaustless mines of the richest ore of epic, lyric, tale, tune, picture, etc., in the Four Years' War; with, indeed, I sometimes think, the richest masses of material ever afforded a nation, more variegated, and on a larger scale—the first sign of proportionate, native, imaginative Soul, the first-class works to match, is (I cannot too often repeat) so far wanting.[38]

The poet Martínez Estrada advances the following explanation for the poverty of Argentina's popular balladry. Spanish migrants to the pampas, he contends, created a progeny, the gaucho-type, whose mothers—upon whom cultural transmission largely depended—could as Indians neither perpetuate the Spanish legacy nor instil that of their own race. The mestizo offspring were

without roots or history. Their culture was a function of the day-to-day claims of environment; it gave off no resonances of the past. Their speech, dried out, flat and without mystery, was "el habla de mercar y mandar, como simple instrumento verbal, subsidiario del arma y la herramienta, sin sustancia étnica"; it appeared to be "un idioma artificial, creado exprofeso para la conquista." Language was transmitted by teaching how things are named and sentences formed, not through repetition of tales and verses. Such balladry as existed was the oral, spontaneous, highly personal song of the *payador*, which preserved the stripped-down weft and modulation of common speech. "Pues la poesía gauchesca no es sentimental ni afectiva: es apasionada y al mismo tiempo cuidadosa de no extralimitarse en lo confidencial."[39]

Translated into broader terms, Martínez Estrada's remarks suggest two complementary qualities of the "creole" temperament. One is the practical-mindedness and impatience with ancient customs that characterize men whose energies are released within an untamed natural environment. The other is the chariness of the backwoodsman who knows that to overcome nature entails acquiescence and adaptation as well as strenuous assertion. Both attitudes are reflected in language.

During his stay in the United States Tocqueville was impressed by the effect which the supremacy of practical affairs had upon language. To a large extent his remarks are germane both to sixteenth-century Latin America and to the Latin American "Caesarist" democracies of his own time. In such societies the majority, which sets the linguistic and other norms:

. . . is more engaged in business than in study, in political and commercial interests than in philosophical speculation or literary pursuits. Most of

[37] Entwistle, *op. cit.*, pp. 237–238. See also Malmberg, *loc. cit.*, pp. 79–86.
[38] Walt Whitman, *Democratic Vistas* (New York, 1949), p. 55.
[39] Ezequiel Martínez Estrada, *Muerte y transfiguración de Martín Fierro* (2 vols.; Mexico City, 1948), II, 442–443.

the words coined or adapted for its use will bear the mark of these habits, they will mainly serve to express the wants of business, the passions of party, or the details of public administration. In these departments the language will constantly grow, while it will gradually lose ground in metaphysics and theology.

The supremacy of the norms of the majority and of its practical affairs, Tocqueville observed, blunts the cutting-edge of language. It becomes prompt and convenient to extend the received meaning of an expression, to render it ambiguous. The abstract or generic term is preferred—not, obviously, because interests have become less concrete but because such a note of speech assists the mind in practical fashion by "enabling it to include many objects in a small compass."[40] Complementary to the release of practical energies in the New World is a creole passivity, or lassitude, which testifies that colonization was not only exploitation but adaptation. Adaptation cannot be forced. It demands native shrewdness, patience, receptivity. It is a casting of one's lot with forces that are sensed but not defined. It is malleability in the face of whatever gods are more efficacious. It is biting skepticism toward those who purport to embody the systems and decorum of Europe—the traditional attitude of "creole malice." It entails lack of certainty in the outcome of enterprises or human relationships, and hence refuge in democratic courtesies, negligent speech and the loose or evasive response. D. H. Lawrence found that citizens of the New World: ". . . refuse everything explicit and always put up a sort of double meaning. They revel in subterfuge. They prefer their truth safely swaddled in an ark of bulrushes, and deposited among the reeds until some friendly Egyptian princess comes to rescue the babe." Spanish Americans and Yankees alike resist post-Renaissance humanism and "hated the flowing ease of humor in Europe. At the bottom of the American soul was always a dark suspense, at the bottom of the Spanish-American soul the same."[41]

These two phases of New World life, the *assault upon* nature and the shrewd *acquiescence* in natural forces, therefore exert-ed correlative influences upon language. They each represented a shift in man's primary interests, one which occasioned indifference to, even distrust of, inherited lore and culture of regional communities and intellectual assurances of the metropolis. Human associations in America were less a celebration of ancestral ways of life than a practical measure for projecting a new pattern of society across new continents. Consequently, human communication became more functional, more responsive to needs of the moment, more cautious of conclusive assertions.

These qualities are clearly exhibited in the Portuguese of Brazil, where nature was vast, colonists were few, and life unfolded in relative isolation from the indigent mother country. It is often called Portuguese spoken with sugar in the mouth. "A energia da fala portuguesa, rápida e áspera," writes Mendonça, "forma um contraste perfeito com a elocução brasileira, arrastada e branda."[42] The Brazilian softens the characteristic nasal endings of his language; he slurs over diphthongs; he mollifies certain consonants by palatalizing them; he does not, as the Portuguese does, drop out vowels that separate harsh consonants. His desires are phrased as requests rather than commands (*me diga* instead of *diga-me*). His superfluous negatives—*não vou não, não tem nada não*—act less to point up than to attenuate a denial (as does perhaps the double negative common in the United States.) Portugal's explosive interrogative *que?* is preceded by the article (*o que?*). A frequent Brazilianism is to preface a statement with *diz que* . . ., signifying the vagueness of a rumor or the wily provision of a loophole.[43]

[40] Tocqueville, *op. cit.*, II, 65–69. George Santayana wrote of the North American: ". . . the urgency of his novel attack upon matter, his zeal in gathering its fruits, precludes meanderings in primrose paths; devices must be short cuts, and symbols must be mere symbols." (*Character and Opinion in the United States* [New York, n. d.], p. 174.)

[41] David Herbert Lawrence, *Studies in Classic American Literature* (New York, 1923), pp. ix, 8.

[42] Mendonça, *op. cit.*, p. 218.

[43] *Ibid.*, pp. 216–229, 266–267.

Still another Brazilian characteristic is the generous use of diminutive endings, which are applied not only to nouns and adjectives but to pronouns and verbal forms.[44] Buarque de Holanda attributes this to the Brazilian's "aversão ao ritualismo social." In his more loosely structured society human relations are less predetermined by convention. Coexistence with one's fellows depends less upon a skilful control of social formulae and "masks" than upon allowing natural rapport to govern each relation individually. The diminutive is a request for reciprocal benevolence which: ". . . serve para nos familiarizar mais com as pessoas ou os objetos e, ao mesmo tempo, para lhes dar relevo. E' a maneira de fazê-los mais accessíveis aos sentidos também de aproximá-los do coração."[45] Similarly, Spanish Americans are more free with the diminutive than Spaniards. The frequent *ahorita, cerquita, pronito, en seguidita* or *adiosito* is a courtesy, a "toning down" of language, that operates as insurance against unpredictable behavior in a restless society.[46]

The Chilean Torres-Ríoseco makes the following observations about New World Spanish:

The Spaniard is dogmatic, simple, severe, sober, impassioned, carved of a single block; the Spanish American is less decisive, less assured, more flexible, elegant, pliant, superficial, sensitive. . . . Our manner of speaking is less declamatory, less emphatic than that of the Spaniard; rather it is softer, more intimate; the Spaniard is more dramatic, we are more lyrical. Hardly can our expression convey the violence of Spanish emphasis. We soften the consonants where the Spaniard intensifies or suppresses them with harsh effect. For example, our final "s" is at times almost completely lost, or at most becomes a very fine sibilant; in Spain, on the other hand, it is almost sonorous. In the past participles of the first conjugation the intervocalic "d" is among us a vague, undecided sound, whereas in the pronunciation of Madrid it disappears entirely, leaving two strong vowels in vigorous contrast. The same phenomenon may be observed also in the final "d": the Spaniard omits it, ending the word with a stressed vowel, while the Spanish American forms at least the beginning of the sound.[47]

Amado Alonso pointed out a tendency of

Spanish Americans to give the wrong stress to such words as *caído, país, maestro* and *créia*. This habit (less observable today than during the last century) is a form of the hesitancy which Torres-Ríoseco describes and reflects the inclination to distribute rather than to consolidate the natural emphases of speech.[48]

The popular speech of Buenos Aires has prototypically American qualities. Throughout the colonial period the La Plata region was isolated and provincial. Only during the past century did its metropolis mushroom forth, untempered by the rote and custom of a hierarchical society. The received idiom was that of the mestizo hinterland, and Ar-

[44] *Ibid.*, pp. 98–100.

[45] Sérgio Buarque de Holanda, *Raízes do Brasil* (2nd ed.; Rio de Janeiro, 1948), pp. 215–218.

[46] J. B. Trend, *The Language and History of Spain* (London, 1953), pp. 173–174.

[47] Arturo Torres-Ríoseco, *New World Literature* (Berkeley and Los Angeles, 1949), p. 117. Canadian French has traits comparable to those of American Portuguese and Spanish. Harsh or decisive sounds are mollified by vowel shifts and consonantal palatalization. The speech tone is "monocorde, lourd et nasalisé," the "pronunciation est gutturale, l'articulation insuffisante." (Daviault, *loc. cit.*, pp. 31–32.)

Of language in the United States Marryat remarked in 1839: "The Americans dwell on their words when they speak—a custom arising, I presume, from their cautious, calculating habits; and they have always more or less of a nasal twang. I once said to a lady, "Why do you drawl out your words in that way?' 'Well,' replied she, 'I'd drawl all the way from Maine to Georgia, rather than *clip* my words as you English people do.' " (Frederick Marryat, *A Dairy in America* [3 vols.; London, 1839], II, 222.) The verbs *reckon, believe, calculate, expect, guess* and such qualifiers as *pretty, sort of, kind of* and *couple of* have been heavily worked in the United States as a form of wary noncommitment. (Mencken, *American Language*, pp. 319 ff., 471–473.) And Canadian English, according to Alexander (*loc. cit.*, p. 15), has a monotony and even articulation which deprive it of "light and shade."

[48] Alonso, *op. cit.*, p. 78. Similarly, when American English throws the accent forward(*inquiry, résearch, céntenary*) or back (*mischíevous, exquísite, primárily*), the effect is to even out irregularities of stress. Mencken suggests that indecisive, evenly distributed accentuation betrays the social parvenu who is apprehensive that his speech may disclose his vulgar origin. (*American Language*, pp. 323–327.)

gentine plebeianism has been compounded by waves of immigrants, notably Italians, who shift only vegetatively into language of ill-defined and unenforced norms.[49] Of his countrymen's speech the novelist Eduardo Mallea writes:

Si asistimos al modo de hablar de un inglés, de un francés, de un español, advertimos cómo en cada palabra pronunciada cae, con efectivo peso de acento y entonación, la persona todo del sujeto. . . . Si asistimos, en cambio, al modo de hablar de los argentinos metropolitanos veremos, ante todo, una gran igualdad en las formas de no expresarse, una inseguridad recaída en el momento de tener que ir a escoger las palabras, inseguridad que se resuelve en recurrir a los modismos más primarios y socorridos.[50]

Martínez Estrada attributes this "inseguridad" and the laconic, unimaginative sentences of Argentine speech to present-day psychological needs which keep alive (and perhaps partly stem from) inherited plebian modes. He remarks that when a writer or speaker comes to the threshold of an explicit, clearly elaborated turn of speech, he cuts himself off, or else switches to an exclamation or to a hasty, evasive conclusion.

La claridad en la elocución, entregarse inerme, es tan extraña a nuestra habla como la idea categórica, apodíctica. La forma toma así un sesgo dubitativo, de imprecisión, aun cuando el locutor esté bien seguro de lo que sabe y de lo que quiere decir. El circunloquio, la vaguedad son formas psicológicas más que gramaticales, un modo de ser nosotros.[51]

So far this study of language has not led to any generalizations about Latin American history which were not common knowledge to the historian. It has merely attempted to suggest, using the evidence of language, the type of proposition which affords a working hypothesis—and sets a fruitful perspective —for approaching "Latin America" as an integral subject. The generalization advanced, to summarize them, are: that an analogy exists between post-Roman Europe and post-Columbian America; that emigrants to America represented narrower and differently distributed human spectra than those

of the mother countries; that the American physical environment, the interspersion of emigrants from diverse regions of Europe, and miscegenation with Indian and Negro all had important effects on transplanted cultures; that relations among men in the New World—owing to these factors and their historical sequels—were of a different quality than those in the Old World. This essay neither initiates nor conclusively proves these generalizations. It has been aimed, rather, at objectifying them in token illustrations selected from a particular realm of culture. And it will by now have been observed that, in most cases, language manifests historical circumstances only in their complex interaction—which for the historian is both an advantage and a drawback.

There remains, however, a critical dimension of Latin America's history still to be examined, namely, its continuing relations, through its own cities, with metropolitan Europe. New World history, indeed, may largely be construed as a counterpoint between, on one hand, the fresh experiences and spontaneous, pragmatic solutions of the hinterland and, on the other, the continuing influence of European institutions, imperatives and patterns of thought. Americans have lived under an historic compulsion to resist, imitate or adapt European norms.

[49] Américo Castro, *La peculiaridad lingüística rioplatense y su sentido histórico* (Buenos Aires, 1941), *passim*.
[50] Eduardo Mallea, cited in Herrero Mayor, *op. cit.*, pp. 169–170.
[51] Martínez Estrada, *op. cit.*, II, 459–460.
It it worthwhile to note that the linguistic *vulgarismo* of the New World, which smoothes out words and phrases, freeing them of layered connotations, has disclosed literary possibilities. The *modernistas* of Rubén Darío's generation and the imagists of Amy Lowell's were led to inspect the pure tactility of words, to array them as counters for inducing a play of sensations. Gertrude Stein found that the colloquial flow of speech, although semantically thin, is fresh and evocative when one heeds its rhythmic patterns. Human utterance, she wrote, is never repetitious "because the essence of that expression is insistence, and if you insist you must each time use emphasis and if you use emphasis it is not possible while anybody is alive that they should use exactly the same emphasis." (Gertrude Stein, *Selected Writings* [New York, 1946], p. xiii.)

An example of how the tension between hinterland and metropolis affects human relations and language itself can be found in the "comedy ballet" *El Güegüence* of eighteenth-century Nicaragua, which still receives annual productions in that country.[52] The dialogue of the piece, a slipshod hybrid of Nahuatl and Spanish, flows colloquially and repetitiously, unrelieved by monologues or scenic divisions. The stage business, moving strictly within the interests of a provincial audience, hinges upon the impudence and cunning of the creole hero, El Güegüence. The often obscene complications arising from the disreputable hero's deafness afford comic devices and a crude vitality. El Güegüence's sly and ribald *malentendus* continually undercut the pomposity of the Spanish colonial officials who must cope with him, paralleling the linguistic effect of a fluid, earthy idiom which has mockingly absorbed the grandiloquent salutations of imperial bureaucracy.

On other occasions the creole mind assumes a more ingenuous attitude toward the metropolis. European travelers in the New World are perennially shocked upon exposure to the latinized bombast of its legislatures and newspaper columns. They are startled, that is, at the cosmopolitan norm, uncritically accepted because the hinterland mind invests it with magic civilizing powers or because to employ it assuages a colonial inferiority complex. Euphemism, like bombast, is a veneer for earthy provincialism. In Buenos Aires, for example, such straightforward words as *coger* and *acabar* are decommissioned by secondary meanings; girls must *descender* rather than *bajar la escalera*; newspapers prudishly prefer *guardar cama* to *dar a luz*.[53] The city's linguistic *vulgarismo* has evoked an overcompensating *cultismo* from its pedagogues and would-be sophisticates. Florid circumlocutions, often given currency by the newspapers, occur in speech; and, in the last century, Sarmiento was surprised to learn that Castilian Spanish did not make the distinction between *b* and *v* which the misinformed purism of Argentine schools were inculcating.[54] In Argentina, as in the many regions of America

characterized by fast-growing cities and scattered, shifting rural populations, the artificial language of the printed page usurped the normative function from the living speech of an élite.[55]

Language in the Americas therefore exhibits two important characteristics which might be called the "adaptive" and the "mediative." The former is evinced in accommodations to environment and to social leavening; in spite of new expressive tones and occasional picturesqueness, it represents an impoverishment of traditional linguistic resources. The latter reflects the need for mediation between the hinterland and the metropolis, between the freshly experienced and the historical or conventional and, by extension, between sense and intellect. Sometimes this mediation, or counterpoint, shows itself merely as random interspersion of provincial and citified expressions. But fuller achievement of the mediative function, particularly at the hands of literary masters, imparts a range and vigor to language which recall the possibilities afforded by the commingling of Anglo-Saxon and Latin components in English.

Since the many patterns of regional and urbane speech in Spanish and Portuguese America shade into and influence each other —without, as a rule, showing differences of dialect—it is difficult systematically to discriminate in them the hinterland and cosmopolitan elements. In the Franco-Caribbean lands, however, one finds the counterpoint schematized in the sharp dualism of patois and salon French.

The various Franco-Caribbean patois reveal African influences more clearly than,

[52] Daniel G. Brinton, *The Güegüence* (Philadelphia, 1883).

[53] Castro, *op. cit.*, pp. 125–128. For the bowdlerization of American English see Mencken, *American Language*, pp. 284–311, and *Supplement I*, pp. 565–661.

[54] Alonso, *op. cit.*, pp. 69–72, 138.

[55] One is reminded of the conversation of Mr. Scully in Stephen Crane's "The Blue Hotel": ". . . a combination of Irish brogue and idiom, Western twang and idiom, and scraps of curiously formal diction taken from the story books and newspapers." (*Selected Prose and Poetry* [New York, 1950], p. 197.)

say, the speech of coastal Brazil or the southern United States. This is so for a number of reasons, having to do with the ratio of Negroes to whites; the imported patterns of settlement and of landholding (and the effects upon them of New World geography and climate); and the degree to which slaves, licitly or illicitly, preserved tribal associations.[56] Even in the French colonies, however, African vocabulary was largely lost, partly because it contained no expressions for French systems and artifacts, partly because African language groups, mutually unintelligible, were intermingled during the forced migration. With the principal exception of terms relating to vodun and its tutelary genii, patois (or creole) drew its vocabulary from sixteenth- and seventeenth-century dialects of Picardy, Anjou, Poitu, Ile-de-France, and, above all, Normandy.[57]

French vocabulary, however, forthwith received a syntax and mode of utterance which had been common to the slaves' native dialects: "L'influence de l'africain fut plutôt occulte et d'ordre psychologique. Forcé d'apprendre la langue imposée par ses maîtres, il y mit cependant du sien, en y apportant son accent propre, cette douceur, ce rhythme harmonieux, cette musicalité qui en sont la plus belle parure."[58] The French was pared down, dis-inflected, syncopated. Its subtleties and concise abstractions became blurred. Elaborate, interlacing structures of speech were melted down into a single melodic line.

Thus for example the *r*-sound—which suffers mutation in all New World languages—was suppressed, exchanged for a vowel sound, or sometimes interchanged with an adjacent letter. Delicate French vowels became broad and rich. Gender was dispensed with. So too were articles, except when absorbed into the noun, as in *quat'nomme* (*quatre un homme,* "four men") or *ein jolie labouche* (*une jolie la bouche,* "a pretty mouth"). Verbs were omitted wherever feasible; if used, they were uninflected. Tenses, limited in number, were formed by adding suffixes to the personal pronouns. Superlatives of adjectives and adverbs, and emphasis for other parts of speech, were rendered by simple repetition of the words in question.[59]

Caribbean patois therefore exemplifies—one might say caricatures—the fluid, smoothed-down, plebeian component of American speech. Along with its Africanism, it clearly discloses the quality of New World adaptivity. These two traits are, in fact, sides of the same coin, for of the three New World races it was the Negroes who in many ways showed the greatest malleability. The tribal interspersion which occurred during his migration deprived the Negro—with certain local exceptions—of the bulk of his cultural heritage. In his forced acculturation he could preserve only those culture fragments and "motor habits" which were a common denominator to many African tribes. European patterns that were imposed upon the Negro, therefore, instead of striking roots in the rich "substratum" of a peasant culture, were imbued with a "coloration" which tended to disintegrate and render them flexible. So characteristically "American" is the Negro's adjustment that when one examines language and folk music in predominantly white areas, distant from the Caribbean, it is difficult to distinguish African influences from mutations independently occurring in other cultures.[60]

The counterpart to Caribbean patois is the standard French spoken by a citified élite, notably the Haitian, that is socially, if not always biologically, mulatto rather than Negro. For sociological reasons salon French and patois have preserved strict identities, and travelers are wont to remark on the near-classic purity of the speech of the Haitian upper class.[61]

[56] Herskovits, *op. cit.,* pp. 111 ff.
[57] Jules Faine, *Philologie créole* (2nd ed.; Port-au-Prince, 1957), pp. 1–3.
[58] *Ibid.,* p. 4.
[59] Lafcadio Hearn, *Gombo Zhèbes* (New York, 1885), pp. 4–5; Edward Larocque Tinker, *Gombo—the Creole Dialect of Louisiana* (1936), pp. 8–10.
[60] See Herskovits, *op. cit.,* pp. 276–291 and *passim.* Hermann Keyserling quotes some interesting speculations of C. G. Jung on this point in *America Set Free* (New York, 1929), pp. 34–36.
[61] James G. Leyburn, *The Haitian People* (New Haven, 1941), pp. 297–304.

Even under these circumstances, however, the European language does not wholly evade the mark of New World plebeianism. The salon French of Haiti, however pure its vocabulary and grammar, has been colored by the *ton significatif*. This is a characteristic common to the Bantu languages which allows control of meaning through modulation of the tonal register, and is a companion to the complex of African motor habits. The Haitian élite have resisted creole syntax, but not the *ton significatif*. Their speech as well as the common man's, according to Dr. Price-Mars, is "coloré par la musicalité de l'accent, par des réticences, des sous entendus, des apostrophes, des exclamations, des gestes qui renforcent ou minimisent les vocables exprimés."[62]

The pervasiveness of the *ton significatif* in the speech of the Caribbean area is the third of the broad reminders which this essay purports to hold for the Latin American historian. The first is that the New World in-duced initial and recurrent mutations in European culture and institutions that were extended to it. The second is that the new patterns and tone of life in the Americas have been in constant counterpoint with Europe's continuing influence. The third is that this counterpoint is not a mere juxtaposition of disparate elements. For as soon as an element of European culture acts upon Latin America, it partakes of the New World culture continuum. An "influence," that is, cannot be "pure." Just as the melodic lines of musical counterpoint cannot be considered individually, but only relationally, so the Latin American historian cannot render historical processes by enumerating discrete circumstances. It is his commitment to be ever alive to the nature of the continuum within which they interact.

[62] C. F. Price-Mars, *Formation ethnique, folklore et culture du peuple haitien* (Port-au-Prince, 1939), pp. 118–121.

83. Latin American Economics: Needs and Prospects*

SANFORD A. MOSK

The Latin American countries, along with other "under-developed areas," have in recent years become strongly interested in economic development. Of course, not everyone in Latin America wants economic development to take place. This view is often shared by outside observers who fear that fundamental cultural and social values will be sacrificed for purely material gains, and thus they believe that these countries would be better advised to avoid seeking material progress. Nevertheless, it is a fact that the aspiration for a higher standard of living is widespread nowadays, and that statesmen in Latin American countries have set their sights on bringing about improvement in material well-being in the foreseeable future.

The broad goal has been set. There will be no turning back. Economic development is, therefore, not a fad of the moment, but

* *Latin American Studies in the United States: Proceedings of a Meeting Held in Chicago, November 6–8, 1958, Sponsored by the American Council of Learned Societies and the Newberry Library (assisted by the Hispanic Foundation)*, edited by Howard F. Cline. Hispanic Foundation, *Survey Reports*, 8:52–55 (Washington, 1958).

rather a subject which is going to occupy attention for a long time to come, and it is to be expected that the problems associated with development will be the main stimulus to research in Latin American economics in the years that lie ahead.

Thus far the problems most effectively dealt with are certain short-run questions which can be handled by contemporary economic analysis. There is a cluster of such problems around the balance of payments of every Latin American country, involving foreign trade and foreign investment; in many cases exchange control is also an important issue. A second cluster is found in monetary policy and the related question of inflation. All these questions, it will be observed, have been much studied by advisory missions of the International Bank and other agencies. They are important issues, and they need to be looked at continually. But such studies, even though they give useful guides to immediate policy in a Latin American country, have little bearing on the process of long-run institutional change which is fundamental in economic development.

As this last remark suggests, there is a whole range of Latin American economic problems which have been comparatively neglected. They are problems which arise because new and relatively large developments are being attempted by deliberate action while the older ways of thinking and behaving run counter to the new developments, or at any rate do not facilitate them. This condition is found in different degree among the Latin American nations, but it is found in all of them. We need, therefore, a full understanding of the institutions—social, cultural and political, as well as economic—which impinge on development, and of the rate and direction of change in such institutions. Basic to such understanding is the study of the economic history of Latin American countries. Much has been done in this field for the colonial period, but the economic history of virtually every country in Latin America since independence still remains to be written. A major task, then, is to encourage systematic study of the economic history of Latin America in the national pe-

riod, such studies to be carried out by Latin American scholars, and others as well.

A somewhat related question, but one which merits special attention, is the study of indigenous economies in the Indian countries of Latin America, where the incorporation of the Indian in the national economy is a major aspect of economic development—possibly the most important aspect. We need knowledge of the degree to which indigenous groups are already tied into national ("commercial") economies. What articles do they buy from, or through, the national economy? Are transactions in local products affected by prosperity and depression in the national economy? And, finally, with respect to all such matters, is there evidence that changes have been taking place in, say, the last 25 or 50 years? It is not easy to find answers to such questions, but they make up an important field of investigation in which economists, anthropologists, and other social scientists as well, can do fruitful work if they direct their attention to it.

The two fields I have referred to above—namely, economic history and the study of indigenous economies—are the ones in which I believe a major scholarly effort needs to be made. They are also fields in which international and other official agencies are likely to do very little, if anything at all. These are fields for the academic scholar, whether Latin American or North American. I hope that the foundations will encourage research along the lines I have suggested.

In emphasizing these two fields, I do not intend to imply that they are the only ones deserving of support. Of the many other kinds of study that need to be done, special attention might be made of fiscal systems, and of the nature of "economic planning" in Latin American countries. United States' economic policy towards Latin America offers another fruitful field of inquiry. True, there is an abundant literature on this subject, but much of what has been written has been wanting in balance and impartiality. These last three topics I have mentioned, with the possible exception of the one on fiscal systems, cannot be adequately treated by official agencies. And this leads me in conclusion to strengthen the view, implied above, that there is an appropriate division of labor between official agencies and academic scholars, and that the foundations should concentrate their support on research that neither international nor governmental agencies are able to undertake.

84. Some Characteristics of Latin American Urban History*

RICHARD M. MORSE

The important and integrative role that the study of urban development has played in the historical analysis of European institutions suggests a similar approach to the history of Latin America, an approach that has not received adequate consideration. We may assume that the quest for a theory of town origins will not dominate Latin American urban historiography as it has European, for the New World it is relative easy to determine when and why a given town was founded. Towns created formally and *ex nihilo* in a moment of time, such as Santo Domingo, Lima, or, to take a contemporary example, Brasília, are distinct from those which grew out of the soil, around garrisons, transportation break points, centers of production, and places of religious pilgrimage. In the Indian areas, one can classify towns or villages having a pre-Columbian origin and those formed by the resettlement of Indians by the Spaniards.

This essay is not an inquiry into origins, which would entail description and quantification, but it is rather a search for hypotheses toward a theory that will have special explanatory value for Latin America. This theory would be functional rather than genetic in its emphasis, clarifying the relation of the Latin American city to the settlement of the land and to the forms of economic production. The striking incongruity of the institutional history of Latin America is that the most important job of production has been that of extracting commodities from the soil and subsoil, though the persons who settled the area, as well as the immigrants of later centuries, crossed the ocean with the idea of the city in their minds. The number of European small farming communities transplanted to Latin America was almost negligible, nor was such transplantation crowned with success. By and large, the rural emigrant to the New World was sufficiently exposed to city life, at the two terminal points of the crossing if nowhere else, to change whatever peasant outlook he may have had. To find anything resembling peasant communities in Latin America one must look principally among the non-European groups: among the highland Indians in some regions, where lines of pre-Columbian tradition have been maintained, or among the descendants of African slaves in the Caribbean, whose forbears were happy to escape the conditions of plantation life.

Still another incongruity accompanied this development of a vast agricultural and mining economy by an urban-minded people. In 1500 the rulers of Renaissance Europe, prompted by their architects and city planners, were just approaching the idea of

* *American Historical Review*, 67:317–338 (Jan. 1962). Reprinted by permission of the author and original publisher.

the city as a symbol of imperium, set apart from the countryside by its pageantry and geometric design, rather than being incorporated into it by natural arteries and exchange. Yet the older cities of Europe could be remodeled only slightly in this Renaissance image, and only rarely could new ones be built. Happily, or ironically, the city builders found free rein in the wilderness of the New World.

The picture should not be oversimplified. The late medieval towns of Western Europe, excepting perhaps those of the Moors in Spain, were not characterized by haphazard growth and jumbled street plans. Although the plans were often irregular, they might show ". . . a close relation in form between rural and urban settlements in the same countryside. This relation is due, not to the gradual topographic and functional transformation of a village, but rather to the adoption of the same principles of lay-out for the town as for the village, modified to suit the needs of an urban community."[1] In many cases a geometric design was observable: either a radial concentric system centered on the town nucleus, frequently a fortification, of the rectangular or grid system similar to that of the Roman *civitates*. The grid plan, a natural form of linear and lateral growth for towns expanding along a single route axis, is seen particularly in towns founded north of the Alps in the later Middle Ages.

The point is not that geometric planning was unknown to the Middle Ages, but that the rationalistically conceived master plan, reflecting more of imperial or even an assumed universal order than of local need and function, was a Renaissance product. Not until after 1500 were European cities built, rebuilt, or extended in conformity with such master plans. By then the modern network of towns was almost wholly in existence in Western, Central, and Southern Europe. The Renaissance and later baroque planners were resricted to laying out a mere handful of new towns and to enlarging the capitals, the courts, and some of the seaports.

It would be another oversimplification to say that the conquistadors traveled to the New World with town plans fresh from Italian drafting boards. Whether the Spanish American gridiron city represented spontaneous planning that comes naturally to city builders in any time and place; whether it was influenced by pre-existing Indian cities, particularly in Mexico and Peru; whether it stood directly in the tradition of the ancient Roman city; or whether it was indeed inspired by the revived classicism of the Italian Renaissance model is controversial.[2]

Perhaps there is foundation for all of these theories. During the early years of Spanish colonization the crown established no strict control over the form of new towns. The first plans seem to have flowed from medieval practice and to have showed, in Mexico at any rate, occasional Indian influences. Little is known about the towns founded on Hispaniola in the 1490's, except for Isabela, the ruins of which show no traces of rectangularity. The first checkerboard plan was probably given to Santo Domingo when Governor Nicolás de Ovando transferred it to the right bank of the Ozama River in 1502 and intervened personally to establish the plan and distribute the town lots. In 1526 the historian Gonzalo Fernández de Oviedo compared the city favorably to Barcelona: "The streets are much more level and much broader and incomparably more straight; for as the town was founded in our time . . . it was laid out by rule and compass with the streets all of the same size, in which respect it is far ahead of all the towns I have seen."[3] The model for this layout was provided by the rectangular city plans used by the Catholic monarchs on recaptured land at the end of the Moorish campaign, most notably the one for Santa Fe, at the gates of Granada.

[1] Robert E. Dickinson, *The West European City: A Geographical Interpretation* (London, 1951, 272–73.

[2] Erwin Walter Palm, "Los orígenes del urbanismo imperial en América," in *Contribuciones a la historia municipal de América*, ed. Rafael Altamira y Crevea *et al.* (México, D.F., 1951), 246.

[3] Gonzalo Fernández de Oviedo, *Sumario de la natural historia de las Indias* (México, D.F., 1950), 88–89.

The first Spaniard to arrive in America with precise royal orders regarding the setting out of cities was Pedrarias Dávila in 1514. His instructions, applied to Panama City in 1519, read in part:

. . . let the city lots be regular from the start, so that once they are marked out the town will appear well ordered as to the place which is left for a plaza, the site for the church and the sequence of the streets; for in places newly established, proper order can be given from the start, and thus they remain ordered with no extra labor or cost; otherwise order will never be introduced.[4]

The inspiration for this directive may have been a memory of Roman practices kept alive through the later Middle Ages by the survival of such works as the *Rei Militaris Instituta* of Vegetius. Only later in the sixteenth century did the revival of Vitruvius and the work of the Italian Renaissance planners affect city building in the New World.

The conquest of Mexico was carried out "during a decade of humanist ascendancy in Spain."[5] A dialogue by Francisco Cervantes de Salazar printed in 1554 describes Mexico City a generation after its reconstruction by the Spaniards. He speaks of houses "built so regularly and evenly that none varies a finger's breadth from another." In a reference to humanist doctrines, one of the residents exclaims: "The columns are round and smooth, since Vitruvius did not recommend square columns and those that are grooved in the middle." Wide streets allowed the winds to blow off "pestilential vapors" from the nearby swamp. As for the plaza: "Look carefully, please, and note if you have ever seen another equal to it in size and grandeur." "Indeed, none that I remember," says the guest. 'What order: What beauty! . . . Truly, if those colonnades that we are now facing were removed, it could hold an entire army."[6]

When this dialogue was written, Mexico City had already become the largest city in the Spanish world, and it was unique among great cities of its time "in that it was an unfortified metropolis, occupying a plan that shows close affinities to the ideal town plan of Italian architectural theory."[7] George Kubler reminds us, however, that many Mexican towns, whether founded under secular or missionary auspices, bore no traces of rational planning. The vast outskirts of Mexico City itself, which served as a reservoir of Indian labor, were formed by "casual, dense agglomerations of huts and shelters."[8] It was not until 1573 that the body of statutes governing the layout of towns in the New World was promulgated by the crown.[9]

For purposes of this inquiry the extent of Roman or of Italian humanist influence upon Spanish American architecture and city planning has a largely symbolic value. Whether or not the Renaissance left its clear mark upon the disposition and construction of the civic center, the decisive feature of the master grid was the subordination of the streets to a central will. "That is, the streets cease to be lines of centripetal forces which create the plaza by their confluence; on the contrary, they radiate to the limit of the motive power of the organism of the city, now become aggressive in space."[10] To anyone steeped in the history of European cities, their organic growth and their slow sedimentation of function, the act of founding a town in a New World wilderness and in a

[4] "Ynstrucion para el Governador de Tierra Firme, la qual se le entregó 4 de Agosto DXIII" in *Orígenes de la dominación española en América*, ed. Manuel Serrano y Sanz (Madrid, 1918), I, cclxxxi.

[5] George Kubler, *Mexican Architecture of the Sixteenth Century* (2 vols., New Haven, Conn., 1948), I, 69.

[6] Francisco Cervantes de Salazar, *Life in the Imperial and Loyal City of Mexico in New Spain and the Royal and Pontifical University of Mexico* (Austin, 1953), 39–42.

[7] Kubler, *Mexican Architecture*, I, 77.

[8] *Ibid.*, I, 74.

[9] "Ordenanzas de Su Majestad hechas para los nuevos descubrimientos, conquistas y pacificaciones" (July 13, 1573) in *Colección de documentos inéditos, relatives al descubrimiento, conquista y organización de las antiguas posesiones españolas de América y Oceanía, sacados de los archivos del reino, y muy especialmente del de Indias* (42 vols., Madrid, 1864–84), VIII, 484–537.

[10] Palm, "Orígenes del urbanismo imperial," 258.

moment of time will seem almost gratuitous.

Juan Terán once observed that the Spanish American city was laid out in a moment of repose from march or combat by persons dreaming of distant cities and of the power for which they stood. The European city "grew like an organism, from within," while the American ones grew "like mechanisms, from without, as when the headquarters of a lieutenant became those of a governor, or were erected into an *audiencia* or a bishopric." The New World city is provisional; it has "no penates or prytaneum, for it does not live in the memory of its sons." It does not commemorate its founder, nor keep alive such legends as those of the Roman wolf, the stones of Deucalion, or Cecrops of Athens.[11]

Sites, of course, were not chosen arbitrarily for New World cities. The royal instructions to Pedrarias Dávila, drawn up in 1513, contained many specifics in this respect. Settlements were to be well located for protecting and provisioning ships and for defending the land. Seaports were to be established with regard for the expeditious handling of cargoes. Where pack animals were unavailable, inland settlements were to be near rivers. All towns were to be close to a water supply and the mountains, swept by favorable winds, and adjacent to rich soil.[12] The founding of Lima, Peru, is a classic example of careful site selection. The preliminary capital had been Jauja, at 3,300 meters altitude and 40 leagues from the coast. In 1534 the Jauja town council decided to transplant the capital near the coast. The site for Lima was chosen for its good lands, its water supply and firewood, and the commercial and military advantages of its proximity to the ocean. The region had a prosperous Indian population and was a natural missionary center. Finally, the mild climate and low altitude permitted the breeding of European livestock, which had been virtually impossible in the highlands.[13]

In spite of these careful calculations and in spite of the experiment at Jauja, which gave an empirical basis to the founding of Lima, the Peruvian capital has been called an artificial city. Jorge Basadre writes:

Lima was a natural capital for reasons deriving from the circumstances of the moment and later, as the centuries passed, for reasons of a cultural, intellectual and historical order. But it was an artificial capital in the sense that the political structure here came before the economic structure. . . . The main center of population and wealth was in the mountains, and Lima lacked the contact which Cuzco had had with all regions of the country.[14]

The key observation here is that the political structure preceded the economic. In the case of medieval Europe, of course, not every town nucleus was of commercial origin. Many were historic centers of defense, or of civil or ecclesiastical administration; there were even cases of agricultural villages which received their liberties. But the transformation of such nuclei into full-fledged towns, particularly during the thirteenth and fourteenth centuries, is frequently attributable to a strategic location at the intersection of two or more routes of reawakened commerce. They become natural points of crystallization for an immediate region and for far-reaching arteries of trade. Their expansion, as suggested by the *faubourg* theory of Henri Pirenne, was centripetal. That is, the town's increments of population and of economic activity in some measure obeyed regional and commercial determinants that were external to itself. In the light of European urban history, the Latin American town appears "artificial," to use Basadre's word, in so far as it aspired to be something more than a military, administrative, or missionary outpost. For a New World town was established in a vast continent where regional trade routes and regional economies were not to achieve per-

[11] Juan B. Terán, *El nacimiento de la América Española* (Tucumán, 1927), 303–305.

[12] "Ynstrucion . . . 4 de Agosto DXIII," cclxxx-xi.

[13] Juan Bromley, *La fundación de la Ciudad de los Reyes* (Lima, 1935), 37–39, 43, 62–64; Carlos Monge, *Acclimatization in the Andes* (Baltimore, 1948), 34–35.

[14] Jorge Basadre, *La multitud, la ciudad y el campo en la historia del Perú* (Lima, 1929), 35.

manent features for generations, even centuries.

A measure of the uncertainties of town settlement in the New World is the frequency with which town sites were abandoned or towns themselves transplanted. These occurrences were rare in Western Europe after 1500, by which time the modern network of towns was patterned. Though the function of a European town may change, or it may suffer decline, it generally adjusts to new social and economic conditions.[15]

Throughout colonial Latin America the short-lived or ambulatory town is a predictable feature. In the Río de la Plata region, Buenos Aires was founded, abandoned, and refounded forty years later. Many sixteenth-century towns of the Tucumán district lived only briefly.[16] In Peru, the towns of Arequipa, Huamanga, and Trujillo were all moved to new sites, and San Miguel de Piura was transplanted three times.[17] Guayaquil was rebuilt on a new site by Francisco de Orellana and transplanted again in 1693.[18] Panama City, Cali, Guatemala City, San Salvador, Havana, and León (Nicaragua) were all moved from the original sites. The first location of Puebla, in New Spain, proved to be cold and subject to frost, and its settlers were disputatious; a transfer of the town was arranged to a site some leagues distant, where the original allocation of municipal lands was maintained.[19] In New Granada as late as the eighteenth century there frequently occurred "transplantations *en masse* of existing settlements to new sites, brought about either voluntarily or by order of the authorities, and obeying considerations of a fiscal or economic nature."[20] Of Brazilian towns a geographer concludes: "The urban network is not so much the result of natural development as it is the expression of the whim of man, of the *plantadores de cidades*. The very instability of the towns is the cause of their multiplicity."[21]

Such urban transfers are often individually explainable by Indian attacks, earthquakes, or faulty initial judgments of soil and climate. But taken together, and seen over a period of three or more centuries, they reflect the unstable equilibrium of a continent not internally knit by exchange and commerce. Spanish American cities were separately linked with Seville overseas, which served both as market and as source of imports. If a region had no produce for the mother country, its economy centered almost exclusively upon the market of the local town. "The city of Havana, for example, is in the sixteenth century merely the symbol and center of a certain area of land inhabited by isolated settlers, who have trouble communicating with one another and have no relations at all with the rest of the cities of the island."[22]

In Paraguay, the farms and ranches around Asunción were so productive that the local market became saturated. It was felt that the founding of new towns would create markets and afford relief. But as new towns appeared, each developed its own economic interests. Disputes with the mother city arose over boundaries, ownership of cattle, and access to Indian labor. Asunción soon returned to its original isolation.[23]

The region that is now the department of Norte de Santander, Colombia, has experienced sudden economic and population shifts for four centuries. When cacao is king,

[15] Dickinson, *West European City*, 266–67, 279.

[16] "La Hispano-América del siglo xvi: Colombia—Venezuela—Puerto Rico—República Argentina," in *Relaciones geográficas de Indias*, ed. Germán Latorre (Seville, 1919), 136–37.

[17] Bromley, *Ciudad de los Reyes*, 66.

[18] George Juan and Antonio de Ulloa, *A Voyage to South America* (4th ed., 2 vols., London, 1806), I, 152.

[19] François Chevalier, "Signification sociale de la fondation de Puebla de los Angeles," *Revista de historia de América*, XXIII (June 1947), 115 ff.

[20] José María Ots Capdequí, *Nuevos aspectos del siglo xviii español en América* (Bogotá, 1946), 283.

[21] Pierre Deffontaines, "The Origin and Growth of the Brazilian Network of Towns," *Geographical Review*, XXVIII (July 1938), 399.

[22] Francisco Domínguez y Compañy, "Funciones económicas del cabildo colonial hispano-americano" in *Contribuciones a la historia municipal de América*, 143–44.

[23] Fulgencio R. Moreno, *La ciudad de Asunción* (Buenos Aires, 1926), 126, 151–54.

the uplands are abandoned, and valley towns are founded; when coffee is king, the reverse occurs. Until the nineteenth century the three main cities were mere way stations and supply centers for the surrounding agricultural holdings. "Among these three points there was no unifying net of settlement."[24]

Charles Gibson has described the "uncontrolled disunity" and the "evershifting emphases" of the Peruvian economy after the Spanish conquest. The magnificent Inca highway system centering on Cuzco was soon fragmented, not simply because the Spaniards abused and badly maintained it, but because: "In contrast to the directional emphasis of the Inca state, Spanish economy emphasized the lateral connecting roads, as outlets from mining areas to the sea."[25] Even when the main flow of exchange with the mother country passed along overland routes in the New World, the location of the routes and their economic importance were strongly influenced by antecedent decisions of the crown.

The interplay of Spanish mercantilist restrictions, local economic possibilities, and the economic aspirations of New World cities has been analyzed in a study of Lima and Buenos Aires. After the second founding of Buenos Aires in 1580, its penurious inhabitants often went without salt, oil, vinegar and even wine for the Mass. In 1588 they sent their first representative (*procurador*) to Madrid. "In one form or another, [the city] would always have one, for being represented at the Court is so essential a means toward the progress of the city that it will stop at no sacrifices to maintain one."[26] At times the townsmen even petitioned the king that their city be abandoned. This, however, could not be done because of political and religious reasons. The strategic river mouth could be seized by the English or French, while the Indians would revert to paganism.

What was the remedy? It was to authorize regional commerce for Buenos Aires since trade with Spain, itself a cattle-raising country, would have been inadmissible. To use Basadre's terms again, an economic or commercial structure had to be created as under-

pinning for a design of colonization already decided upon. Trade with Upper Peru would have been difficult for many reasons. The only alternative was to authorize trade with Brazil, then under the Spanish crown, which offered possibilities for commercial reciprocity. In 1602 the Brazil-Plata economic system was created. Buenos Aires immediately emerged from poverty. It had a market for its hides, meat, and tallow. It imported slaves to tend cattle and work in the fields. Portuguese merchants settled in the city to teach new skills to the creoles. At length the regulations were so abused that the Brazilian trade was suspended, officially at least, in 1622, and Buenos Aires was limited to a yearly traffic with Spain of two one-hundred-ton ships.

For the time being Lima made good her pretensions to be the commercial queen of the continent. She had in her favor the merchant groups of Peru and Spain, whose interest it was to preserve the galleon route via Panama and to carve out for the city as vast a commercial hinterland as possible. Buenos Aires' contraband activities were irrepressible, however, and by the late seventeenth century that city showed signs of renewed prosperity. In 1676 the custom house at Córdoba was moved north to Salta and Jujuy, signalizing Buenos Aires' capture of the whole Platine market. By the mid-eighteenth century the city was vying with Lima for the markets of Chile and Upper Peru.[27]

The case of Lima and Buenos Aires is an example of how New World cities had to strive, not merely for commercial advantage, but for what might be called their very legitimation by commerce. It shows also the economic energies of the New World work-

[24] *Geografía histórica y económica del Norte de Santander*, ed. Miguel Marciales (Bogotá, 1948), I, 231.

[25] Charles Gibson, *The Inca Concept of Sovereignty and the Spanish Administration in Peru* (Austin, 1948), 94–96.

[26] Guillermo Céspedes del Castillo, *Lima y Buenos Aires—Repercusiones económicas y políticas de la creación del Virreinato de la Plata* (Seville, 1947), 16.

[27] *Ibid.*, 5–45.

ing at cross purposes with a preconceived design for urban distribution. Finally, it illustrates an early phase of the typically American phenomenon of the metropolis which comes to dominate the economic life of an extensive hinterland that is sparsely or unevenly settled and badly articulated for internal exchange.

When we narrow our focus to the lands adjacent to the city, we soon perceive that the city is the point of departure for the settlement of the soil. The municipality is in fact "the juridical agent authorized by the crown to effect concessions and allotments of land, whether rural or urban."[28] In other words, while the city of Western Europe represented a movement of economic energies away from extractive pursuits toward those of processing and distribution, the Latin American city was the source of energy and organization for the exploitation of natural resources.

The settlement of the Americas came at a time when the revival of Roman law had established juridical principles of separation between the public and private orders and, specifically, between land held by persons who were in feudal relation to the king as a lord and land granted by royal grace or concession by the king as head of the state. In Spain these principles were in process of application to the different types of crown lands. In America the Roman tradition became exclusive, and all lands were conceived to be the property of the king as monarch, not as a private person. All land titles, then, whether for European settlers or for the Indians themselves, had to flow from royal concessions. Initially the concessions were granted in the name of the king by conquerors, viceroys, governors, or other agents. But as soon as a city was established, this power became an attribute of its town council. Although the *Leyes de Indias* stipulated that such municipal awards be confirmed by the viceroy or the president of the *audiencia*,[29] one historian asserts that "in spite of these requirements, which seem to limit the power of the cabildo, the latter was the body in America which most widely exercised that power and which definitely controlled

the distribution of lands."[30] It was the power to distribute encomiendas,[31] not the power to grant lands, that the centralizing power of the crown reserved exclusively to the highest royal officials.

The policy of Governor Ovando on Hispaniola was to use the town from the beginning as an instrument of colonization. It was the action of Ovando's captains, rather than spontaneous compacts among groups of settlers, that was responsible for the network of towns which sprang up over the island as subcenters of political control.[32] Thereafter, and until the exhaustion of the treasury under Philip II, the town's political function of settling the land and the economic function of cultivating it were given more weight than the fiscal one of providing crown revenues. There even existed special authorization for creating towns *por vía de colonia*—the founding of new towns by the town council of an already established one— in contrast to the various types of settlement *por vía de capitulación*—by authority of a designated official. The crown's concern for the permanency of the settlements is revealed in an order of 1526 which forbade the inclusion in colonizing expeditions of persons who had already become settlers in the New World, "except for one or two persons in each expedition and no more, as interpreters and for other purposes necessary to such voyages."[33]

[28] Domínguez y Compañy, "Funciones económicas," 166.

[29] *Recopilación de Leyes de los Reynos de las Indias* (3 vols., Madrid, 1943), II, Libro IV, Título 12, Leyes xx, xxi.

[30] Domínguez y Compañy, "Funciones económicas," 172.

[31] The encomienda conferred a right to collect various forms of tribute from the Indians. The recipient had only limited rights to acquire land holdings within his encomienda. See Silvio Zavala's essay "De encomiendas y propiedad territorial en algunas regiones de la América Española" in his *Estudios indianos* (México, D.F., 1948), 205–307.

[32] Ursula Lamb, *Frey Nicolás de Ovando, Gobernador de las Indias (1501–1509)* (Madrid, 1956), 153, 160, 183.

[33] "Las ordenanzas sobre el buen tratamiento de los indios" (Nov. 17, 1526) in *Colección de documentos para la historia de la formación social*

The process of land distribution on a new site has often been described. In the famous case of Lima, the first city plan contained 117 blocks, 450 feet on a side, each subdivided into 4 lots or *solares* and bounded by streets 40 feet wide. The lots were allocated on the day of the city's founding, and each recipient's name was written in the appropriate square on the master plan. Beyond this urban center came the city commons and pasture lands (partly intended as a safety valve for future city growth), then the lands that might be rented to or distributed among the townsmen. The distributed lands went to persons who had received urban *solares*.[34] All land was under municipal jurisdiction, and theoretically there were no interstices between jurisdictions. This meant that in less settled territory the municipal radius might extend for hundreds of miles. The *cabildo* of Havana made land grants on both the northern and southern coasts of Cuba, sometimes thirty-five or forty leagues distant from the city.[35] Since agriculture and stock raising remained under the supervision of the town council, municipal representatives might be sent long distances to inspect the state of production, and, in time of shortage, to requisition supplies wanted for the town.

As has been implied, a spirit of collectivism was carried to the New World in a distinction between private and communal lands. Even private lands were not to be given in perpetuity until four to eight years of effective possession could be shown. Many factors, however, militated against the communitarian spirit and against an organic pattern of settlement. Among these, importance is often given to the increased fiscal demands of the crown under Philip II, which prejudiced the functions of the town as an agent for settling the land and for appropriating its resources. More and more, lands were auctioned off to the highest bidder, without regard for the nature of their subsequent utilization. But to dwell upon this trend would divert us from our func-

tional examination of the city in its New World setting.

Since lands in America were deemed the possession of the crown rather than a feudal holding, it was natural for the attribute of outright ownership to be assumed by settlers who received land in concession. In the vast spaces and shifting communities of America, status was defined by the control of land, rather than, as in a traditional society, the relation to the land being a function of status. The urgency with which land was pre-empted was therefore heightened by the process of social leveling that attended the settlement. In 1509 King Ferdinand reported that in the distribution of urban lots "no distinction is made in giving to and favoring some persons more than others, but the farmer and common people are given just as much as other leading persons."[36] It was the crown's initial policy that the artisan and agricultural colonist should replace the soldier and adventurer. This was difficult to carry out. Spain had few colonists to export, and the adventurers, those at least who had luck, prowess, or ingenuity, were soon entrenched. The sequel, therefore, to the leveling process is the entrenchment of the privileged few, the conquerors, at the expense of the latecomers and the unprivileged many, who often found their rallying point in the municipality. Throughout the colonial period a struggle persisted between, on one hand, those early colonizers and their descendants "who had become *latifundistas* with the support of real or assumed privileges" and, on the other, a series of needy people who desired land for farming and lacked it, in districts where the land was available in prodigious quantity."[37] This clash of interests was sharply articulated

---

[34] Juan Bromley and José Barbagelata, *Evolución urbana de la ciudad de Lima* (Lima, 1945), 51–53.

[35] Domínguez y Compañy, "Funciones económicas," 176–77.

[36] "Real Cédula a Don Diego Colón" (Nov. 14, 1509) in *Colección de documentos inéditos*, XXXI, 501.

[37] José María Ots Capdequí, *El régimen de la tierra en la América Española durante el período colonial* (Ciudad Trujillo, 1946), 40.

---

de Hispanoamérica 1493–1810, ed. Richard Konetzke (2 vols., Madrid, 1953–58), I, 89–96.

when the crown at length attempted to regularize the system of land titles.

In short, the town which gave the thrust for utilizing both land and rural Indian labor, might soon be encircled by private holdings, with opportunities for further settlement closed off and perhaps the municipal common lands distributed. In 1541 the council of Mexico City complained of private cattle and sheep *estancias* on municipal lands; later it reproached the landowners who were holding grain off the market and creating a food shortage.[38] The acts of the Havana council record that as early as 1552 private farms in the commons, or *ejido*, impeded the leading of cattle to pasturage, for landowners had the right to kill animals that damaged their crops. Twenty-five years later the commons had wholly disappeared, and "neither in this town nor near to it does there exist an *ejido*."[39]

In Buenos Aires twenty-six persons soon took possession of all the arable land that could be worked easily from the city and was readily accessible to the consuming market. "The band of iron was thus created which would hold back the economic development of the city for many years."[40] The latecomer had the choice of usurping common lands; becoming a tenant, with the knowledge that his landlord might confiscate a good crop; or pushing to the frontier where, working under the threat of Indian attack, he could expect his holding to be awarded to a person of influence with the governor as soon as he had improved it.

From what has gone before, it is clear that a significant of municipal society was composed not of townsmen, but of mere cohabitants whose horizons of hope or endeavor the city failed to contain. The city distributed status- and fortune-seekers out to unexploited areas of economic promise with a centrifugal effect that contrasts with the centripetalism of the late medieval town.

New World settlers brought with them, to be sure, traditions of the medieval Iberian community. These were standardized in Spanish and Portuguese legislation for the Indies on such matters as the municipal control of common lands, the corporate or guild structure of urban crafts, professions, and commerce, the election of town officials by property owners, and price control and regulation of commerce. It can even be argued that municipal autonomy showed renewed life in America at the very time it was being stifled on the peninsula.[41] Much of this original vigor, however, was externally induced by the threat of Indian attack, by threats of foreign attack upon the coastal cities, by deprivation from famine or drought, and by geographical isolation. Occasionally, an earthquake would kindle the guilt feelings of a city and quite literally shake its citizenry into a sense of civic responsibility. But as the external threats to survival were lifted, the disintegrative attraction of plain, mine, and forest was asserted. This attraction was more damaging to the cohesion of urban society than was the surrender of municipal liberties to the nation-state, which occurred throughout the Western world. To elucidate this point, one may take from a study of New World immigrants the generalization that, whereas in Europe territorial vicinity is the foundation of community life and of social organization, in the New World a rational calculation of life chances becomes the main factor of territorial concentration.[42]

Occasionally in America the European blueprint of municipal nucleation was defeated from the start by the dissolvent effect of the hinterland. The captain-general of São Paulo despaired of implanting the Portuguese system of village settlements in Brazil. In 1768 he wrote:

There is nothing so useful, and necessary, as villages. . . . I do not speak of the difficulties of trans-

---

[38] *Actas de Cabildo de la Ciudad de México* (15 vols., México, D.F., 1889–1900), IV, 258 (Nov. 4, 1541), and V, 44–45 (May 15, 1544).

[39] Domínguez y Compañy, "Funciones económicas," 168–69.

[40] Juan Agustín García, *La ciudad indiana* (Buenos Aires, 1937), 57–58.

[41] See José María Ots Capdequí, *Manual de historia del derecho español en las Indias* (Buenos Aires, 1945), 368.

[42] William I. Thomas and Florian Znaniecki, *The Polish Peasant in Europe and America* (2d ed., 2 vols., New York, 1927), II, 1546–47.

planting the new settlers, those who do not want to go, others who ask the impossible, others who cry, and others who hide, for all of this is overcome; I refer to the many desires that it is necessary to conciliate for a thing so just, and necessary, and which I am unable to do with my forces, and neither is it possible for me to compel them.

The captain-general described the wasteful methods of agriculture and wrote, "Men seeking virgin forest ever are separating themselves further from Civil Society." Newly arrived Portuguese were almost the only persons of means in the towns, for well-to-do landowners maintained only secondary residences in them. People of humble station objected to community life "because they want to live in liberty, in dissoluteness, in their vices, free from every kind of justice; and the great ones because they want to exploit the former, . . . and from this are born or thought up all the ways possible to impede the establishment of the villages."[43]

The frustrations of this official had their counterpart in the Spanish realm. In 1750 the viceroy of New Granada wrote to the governor of Santa Marta telling him first to take advice from the most practical householders and then to order that: ". . . all persons having no estate or occupation from which to live to be invited, and if necessary *compelled*, to group together and reside in those places to be designated, obliging them to assist each other to build their houses and allotting among them, in common and privately, the lands they will need."[44]

Not only was it difficult to nucleate the settlement process, but the smaller nuclei, once created, were difficult to maintain. In northern Mexico by 1600 many municipalities were on the brink of dissolution. Their chief inhabitants lived on distant estates, and regulations had to be passed obliging every person of property to maintain a house in the town and to reside in it at least during the important ceremonial periods.[45] The little towns of eighteenth-century Puerto Rico were generally deserted during the week except for the priest, and even he was frequently visiting the farms. On Sundays and feast days the people rode into town on horseback, made themselves comfortable in their houses—or in other houses, as doors were not locked—then heard Mass and returned directly to the country.[46] Colonial Buenos Aires was left without any government on occasions when the whole town council rode out to make war against the Indians or to conduct a cattle roundup.[47] During the last years of the Mexican regime, San Francisco, California, still had no jail. When a criminal was seized, the inhabitants asked that he be sent to prison in San José, for they themselves each had "agricultural and stock interests at a great distance from the town, so that there were very few remaining to guard the criminal, and these could not spare the time from their personal business."[48] The streets of colonial Salvador, Brazil, were lively only from April to June. For the rest of the time the owners of sugar estates lived in the country with their retinues, where they could hear Mass and celebrate feast days in their private chapels. This dislocation of the proprietors drew off from the city a swarm of peddlers, middlemen, and urban officials.[49]

In the São Paulo region of Brazil, outlying sugar plantations exerted such attraction for town fathers that often they could not be bothered with the long journey into town to conduct municipal business. Town government might be paralyzed for months, even years at a time, as the able-bodied men,

[43] Letters of Morgado de Mateus quoted by Carlos Borges Schmidt, "Rural Life in Brazil," in *Brazil, Portrait of Half a Continent*, ed. T. Lynn Smith and Alexander Marchant (New York, 1951), 169–71.

[44] Quoted in Ots Capdequí, *Nuevos aspectos*, 284–85.

[45] François Chevalier, *La formation des grandes domaines au Méxique: Terre et société aux xvie–xviiie siècles* (Paris, 1952), 293.

[46] Íñigo Abbad y Lasierra, *Historia geográfica, civil y natural de la Isla de San Juan Bautista de Puerto Rico* (new ed., San Juan, 1866), 407.

[47] Adolfo Garretón, *La municipalidad colonial—Buenos Aires desde su fundación, hasta el gobierno de Lariz* (Buenos Aires, 1933), 81–82, 107–108.

[48] Bernard Moses, *The Establishment of Municipal Government in San Francisco* (Baltimore, 1889), 22.

[49] Thales de Azevedo, *Povoamento de cidade do Salvador* (2d ed., São Paulo, 1955), 152.

organized into *bandeiras*, roamed the hinterland in search of Indian slaves or precious metals. The *bandeira* was a significant institution. For if, in their formal aspects, the Spanish American city and the Spanish Jesuit mission were projections upon America of idealized European communities, the *bandeira* appears as the ideal version of a community obeying the imperatives of the New World. It was a community become completely mobile. When far from home, a *bandeira* might settle in the wilderness, clearing the ground, planting and harvesting a crop, then continuing its quest. Its human spectrum included Europeans (Portuguese with a scattering of Spaniards, Italians, Flemings, and others), Indians, mestizos, and sometimes Negroes, accompanied by one or more priests. The group was tightly knit and hierarchically organized. Extended, patriarchal family systems pointed its structure; ability to dominate the wilderness determined its leadership; and the morality and trust born of the frontier were its binding force. The *bandeira* adapted to the ways of the Indian, taking over his crops, his implements, his hammocks, and utilizing his Tupi Guarani language as a lingua franca.[50]

Despite its appearance of nomadic tribalism, the *bandeira* was of municipal, not of agrarian or pastoral origin. It was organized in the towns, and town councilors were its leaders. It has been called a "city on the march." "Only the city could furnish the 'social impetus,' the political organization, the element of command, the cultural requisites . . . and the other conditions indispensable for constituting the *bandeira*. The language of its documents (acts, inventories and testaments) leaves no doubt on this score."[51] When the *bandeira* left permanent settlements behind it, they took the form of municipalities.

Qualification is needed of distinction frequently made between the towns of Spanish America and those of Brazil. It has been pointed out that whereas the Spaniards implanted their proud, geometric cities boldly inland, on carefully chosen and strategic plateau sites, the modest Brazilian towns grew up haphazardly, straggling along the coast like crabs, in subordination to the great rural estates and to the magnetic attraction of the backlands.[52] Now it is true that Brazilian society was more agrarian than Spanish American and that the Brazilian city before the eighteenth century was a center neither of prestige nor of power. But we are interested here in the relation of city and backland, not in the distribution of social power between them. It has been said that the first Brazilian towns were, like the Spanish, "products of the metropolitan will. Nothing spontaneous or natural attends their birth. For some, even the site is preselected from Lisbon."[53] The founding of a town was marked by the erection of the *pelourinho*, a column with an iron shackle representing administration of justice. Soon, a council house, jail, and church were built, and grants of land (*sesmarias*) were made to the settlers. In the case of the first capital, Salvador, the site was specified by the crown, as was the need for proper winds, a good water supply, and a deep port. To be sure, none of the early towns boasted elaborate public buildings, and although some had the beginnings of a geometric plan, grid-planning came into systematic use only in the nineteenth century.[54] As was said, however, the towns' physical appearances are partly of symbolic value for our purposes. One can still make the case that the more important Brazilian towns represented, no less than the Spanish, the intrusion of formal, metropolitan bureaucracy into an empty continent.

Salvador may have seemed little more than a village to the eye. Yet it was founded in 1549 with "a complete judiciary, financial,

---

[50] See José de Alcantara Machado, *Vida e morte do bandeirante* (2d. ed., São Paulo, 1930).

[51] Cassiano Ricardo, *Marcha para oeste* (2d ed., 2 vols., Rio de Janeiro, 1942), II, 191–93.

[52] See Sérgio Buarque de Holanda, *Raízes do Brasil* (2d ed., Rio de Janeiro, 1948), 130 ff., and Roger Bastide, *Brésil, terre des contrastes* (Paris, 1957), 25–26.

[53] Edmundo Zenha, *O município no Brasil (1532–1700)* (São Paulo, 1948), 24.

[54] Aroldo de Azevedo, *Vilas e cidades do Brasil colonial* (São Paulo, 1956), 72.

administrative and military organization."[55] Before long the city's streets were filled with students, clerics, magistrates, lawyers, and other urban types who were virtually parasitic in this small outpost on the rim of an ocean of untamed land. Those human elements having functional and productive potential were drawn off to extractive pursuits in the backlands or on plantations, or in the case of clerics, to the Indian missions. For those remaining in the city, temptations of parasitism and vagrancy were great. The vagabond became a familiar type. By 1775 the Lisbon government had learned that a good proportion of the city's 45,000 inhabitants were "robust youths who, abandoned to a lazy and licentious life, serve the republic only by stirring up disorders.[56] At about this time the first Brazilian viceroy wrote of Rio de Janeiro that it was necessary "to rehabilitate this city a little, which had only friars, clerics, soldiers and beggars. The noblemen live in the country and are the ones which serve me. They are good vassals."[57]

In the Spanish realm the king learned as early as 1509 that "many of them who go to those *Indies* were accustomed before going there to earn their own living with their hands, and after arriving there they do not wish to do so."[58] The vagrant or parasite was soon prominent in New Spain.[59] Forty years after the conquest it was calculated that more than one Spaniard in six there had no fixed domicile.[60] In 1608 a crown official in Guadalajara urged forced employment for the many vagabonds, such as the ". . . Spaniards who come from other parts and, from being officials, turn into idlers and either travel around as small traders with little capital . . . or else shift from job to job. And if a magistrate visits the land or a judge acts severely, they give him the slip and wander elsewhere without appearing where they can be brought to reckoning."[61]

The fluidity and uncertainties alluded to suggest the unleashing of an individualistic, almost predatory spirit in New World life, and a highly unstable element in the hierarchical society which soon took shape. As in the United States of Tocqueville's time, so in colonial Latin America there occurred

a traumatic process of cultural and, at moments, social democratization. To this process the nature of the rural-urban complex in the New World clearly contributed. The city was an outpost of metropolitan bureaucracy, imperial and ecclesiastical, in which status and function were determined by royal appointment. On lands surrounding the city, and in the smaller towns, they were controlled by persons who soon pre-empted the soil and Indian labor. Those who were not favored by privilege or bound to the land in servitude faced the choice of living parasitically off the vested interests or of scattering from the centers of settlement centrifugally in search of windfalls and unpreempted productive lands.

We have noted the dissolvent effect of the new continents both upon the communitarian traditions of rural, seignorial Europe, and upon the metropolitan institutions of urban, imperial Europe. As compensation for this effect, it has been suggested that the *compadrazgo* and other extended family systems took a new lease on life in the Americas at the very moment when they were giving way in early modern Europe to the "more impersonal modes of organization" of the nation-state and of industrial society.[62]

In the case of Salvador, the partial atrophy of the metropolitan bureaucracy was compensated by a strengthening of familial ties. Among the upper class these might take the form of coparenthood relations, among the slaves and poor Negroes, that of a ma-

---

[55] Thales de Azevedo, *Povoamento da cidade do Salvador*, 131.

[56] *Ibid.*, 429 n.

[57] Quoted in Vivaldo Coaracy, *Memórias da cidade do Rio de Janeiro* (Rio de Janeiro, 1955), 567.

[58] "Real Cédula a Don Diego Colón" (Nov. 4, 1509), 494.

[59] Norman F. Martin, *Los vagabundos en la Nueva España, siglo xvi* (México, D.F., 1957).

[60] Chevalier, *Formation des grandes domaines au Méxique*, 29.

[61] "Como se remediará el exceso de muchos bagabundos . . ." (Feb. 28, 1608), *Ibid.*, 432.

[62] Sidney W. Mintz and Eric R. Wolf, "An Analysis of Ritual Co-parenthood (Compadrazgo)," *Southwestern Journal of Anthropology*, VI (Winter, 1950), 341–68.

triarchal organization showing African influence. The substrata of urban and rural society, indeed, appeared not to be highly differentiated.[63] In Mexico the *compadre* system fortified and extended the guarantees of mutual aid and protection determined by ties of blood. Leaders or officials made their power effective by attracting bands of retainers reminiscent of the extended Mediterranean families, the Roman gens or the Corsican vendetta. The crown frequently acknowledged and sought to eliminate the threat to its power created by this new feudalism.[64] In Buenos Aires a patriarchal and authoritarian extended family system "counteracted the dissolvent germs, the evil results of an unhealthy social situation."[65] In the Cauca region of New Grandada the strong family units were tied to the municipality by the weakest bonds. The municipality, in turn, was hostile toward the natural region, and the regions were cut off from each other. The family was therefore the innermost of a series of units—including the *municipio*, the region, and the central political unit— which were in the relation of concentric, rather than interlocking rings.[66]

The importance of family ties in Latin America's urban social organization continues into the modern period. The prominent institutions of the modern metropolis, the factory system, the political party, the labor union, have had to accommodate to familial or primary group types of association, which have limited spheres of effectiveness and which may not be brought to extremes of rational organization. The city, therefore, which has contributed an individualistic, exploitative spirit to the settling of the land, exhibits internally the traces of agrarian, familial social structure.

A second aspect of the modern urban history of Latin America which the colonial centuries help to explain is the tumultuous growth of certain large cities and the intensification of the metropolis-hinterland complex. The principal causes of the phenomenon are the extension of modern transportation systems, generally centered upon capital cities, into areas where there exist no tightly woven networks of economically vigorous towns; and the existence of impoverished rural proletariats living in weakly organized communities and easily drawn off by the attraction of city life. The economic activity which made the metropolis possible was not manufacturing and internal trade, which would have multiplied and decentralized the growth of cities, but plantation agriculture, cattle raising, and mining. Profits went abroad or to middlemen in a few cities, and they brought little benefits to the centers of production. Even the landowners were often heavily mortgaged; in any case they lived more and more in the capital city or outside the country. That is, just as in earlier centuries the encomienda drained the leadership and vitality of the town, so in the nineteenth century the city drained those of the hacienda.

Western Europe, of course, knows the metropolis, but not the vast metropolitan hinterland. For there the close spacing of many cities, each with its own economic vigor and traditions of civic independence, constricts the radii of influence. The marketing territory for a given city or port is often not clearly defined.[67] Moreover, the rural migration to European cities, heavy though it has been since the Industrial Revolution, still shows traces of the organic process posited for the late Middle Ages.[68] The Latin American migration to cities has a diluvial character, and the abrupt change of occupation from unskilled agricultural labor to factory work is not uncommon. This may be attributed in part to large wage differentials and to the rapidity with which recent industrialization has occurred. But we can also say

[63] Thales de Azevedo, *Povoamento de cidade do Salvador*, 209–13.

[64] Chevalier, *Formation des grandes domaines au Méxique*, 28–38, 193, 214, 431–32.

[65] García, *Ciudad indiana*, 81–91.

[66] Raymond E. Crist, *The Cauca Valley, Colombia, Land Tenure and Land Use* (Baltimore, 1952), 40.

[67] Robert E. Dickinson, *City, Region and Regionalism: A Geographical Contribution to Human Ecology* (London, 1947), 232 ff.

[68] *Villes et campagnes: Civilisation urbaine et civilisation rurale en France*, ed. Georges Friedmann (Paris, 1953), 159–61.

that the exploitation of the land, which was settled from the town during the latter's centrifugal phase, created forms of rural social organization which largely lacked inner coherence and roots in the soil. Now that the city has become centripetal, it attracts massively and unselectively from the rural zone. As the Latin American city once sowed, so now does it reap.

It may be that exception will be taken to the emphasis which this exposition places upon New World environment, and to the silence in which the Iberian municipal backgrounds are passed over. For, it will be argued, the Iberians became a municipal people during the Reconquest of Spain from the Moors, which was necessarily a process of colonization by towns rather than by unprotected rural settlement. It has even been said that chronic instability throughout the Mediterranean area was responsible for historic patterns of municipal settlement which contrast with the villages and landed feudalism of northwestern Europe.[69] On this view, the conquest of America is an overseas continuation of the conquest of Moorish Spain, and the colonizing pattern has medieval origins in the peninsula. This argument is reasonable, and it is precisely in recognition of it that the city of northwestern Europe has been taken as a purer type for contrast with the city of the New World. It is by intention that historical innovation has been stressed, rather than historical continuity.

Even so, there are grounds for contrasting the Reconquest of the peninsula and the conquest of America. In Spain and Portugal the weight of Christian-Visigothic usage, the traditions of a slowly evolved social hierarchy, the long-standing pressures of religious faiths and regional cultures, and the limited horizons of economic possibility combined to endow regional societies of the peninsula with a certain coherence and organicity. The medieval Reconquest of Spain lasted seven centuries and resulted in the retaking of some 200,000 square miles of land. The conquest of America occurred under the impetus of the commercial revolution; within fifty years of the landing of Hernando

Cortes in Mexico a territory that could contain thirty or forty Iberian peninsulas had been claimed, and much of it settled, by a few thousand men. To stress only the similarity of Iberian institutions in these two settings is to run the risk of formalism. This is repeatedly done by the historian who finds "no essential difference between the colonizing technique of the high Middle Ages in the Mediterranean and that of modern times in the Atlantic area, that is, particularly in America."[70]

Since our theory of town and land in Latin America has been elaborated with particular reference to New World environment, even a cursory comparison with the settlement patterns of North America would serve to check its usefulness. It will be remembered that both at Plymouth and in Virginia the initial experiments in corporate production and trade were failures. The colonial promoters soon "introduced private ownership of land, economic inequality, and the profit motive."[71] In British North America as in Latin America the first yields of the land worked their centrifugal effect upon the nuclei of settlement once the initial hardships had been surmounted. Twelve years after the founding of Plymouth, its people were "flowing into the country" to grow crops and raise cattle, wrote Governor William Bradford. The economic benefits therefrom "turned to their hurt," he observed: "For now as their stocks increased and the increase vendible, there was no longer any holding them together. . . . [They] were scattered all over the Bay quickly and the town in which they lived till now was left very thin and in a short time almost desolate."[72] In South Carolina the crown attempted to achieve the ideal of "compact settlement" in the laying out of townships. "In course of time, however, the rural town sys-

[69] Pierre George, *La ville: Le fait urbain à travers le monde* (Paris, 1952), 42–43.

[70] Charles Verlinden, *Précédents médiévaux de la colonie en Amérique* (México, D.F., 1954), 10.

[71] Curtis P. Nettels, *The Roots of American Civilization* (New York, 1938), 222.

[72] William Bradford, *Of Plymouth Plantation 1620–1647* (New York, 1952), 252–53.

tem . . . was largely absorbed by the plantation."[73] In French Canada, the "ribboning" of the seignories along riverbanks made nucleation an infrequent occurrence, much to the distress of French officials. "Village life, a characteristic of the feudal system in France, was thus eliminated."[74]

Checkerboard town planning is generally not associated with British North America until the nineteenth century. The streets of early Connecticut towns, however, were often symmetrically arranged.[75] Two important colonial cities, Charleston and Philadelphia, were laid out on gridiron plans, and Philadelphia's became the model for the subsequent frontier cities. The plan for New Haven is of interest for the Latin American comparison because it was inspired by the maxims of Vitruvius. Making allowance for the magnetic declination from true north at New Haven in 1638, one finds that the orientation of the city's streets almost exactly followed the directions given by Vitruvius for counteracting the force of prevailing winds.[76]

As the settlement of the trans-Appalachian West got under way, "the establishment of towns preceded the breaking of soil. The towns were the spearheads of the frontier."[77] Public lands were always set aside and almost always alienated as the town grew. Population figures for St. Louis during the early years "are unsatisfactory because a large number of its residents spend most of their time in the mountains or mines."[78] Each town had its quota of "traders and transients who had no stake in its development"; of seasonally employed boatmen, wagoners, and prospectors; and of vagabonds leading "the aimless and uncertain life of floaters."[79] Even when a town was established at the confluence of two navigable rivers, it was a gamble whether the choice of site would be legitimized by the subsequent development of regional production and trade. The most successful cities followed the earlier example of Boston, which by 1680 had subjugated and become the commercial agent for a broad hinterland stretching from Newfoundland to the Connecticut River towns.[80]

In North as in South America we come upon this paradox, that the town, distinguished in Europe for its commercial radius and its manufacturing activity, served in the New World as the point of departure for contact with the soil, in territories where no internal trade routes were defined and where manufacturing was restricted by the policies of mercantilism. A disproportionate number of the European emigrants were of urban origin, and a great many of them had been, for social, economic, or religious reasons, marginal types in the Old World. Inevitably, the acquisitive and speculative spirit found new avenues of release. Generous possibilities for exploiting soil and subsoil pulled newcomers across the face of the land, dimming the memories of feudal restraint. Environment and opportunity rather than usage and ceremony dictated social organization. Space rather than time became the leading factor of the American experience.

The preceding analysis of the settlement of Latin America is set forth with a view to its relevance for all the Americas. It hinges neither upon the national culture and traditions of the settlers nor upon a localized and culture-bound definition of a given New World "frontier." What is stressed is the process of change and innovation that affects any migration of people, whatever their

[73] Lewis Cecil Gray, *History of Agriculture in the Southern United States* (2 vols., New York, 1941), I, 378–79.

[74] Ralph H. Brown, *Historical Geography of the United States* (New York, 1948), 48–49.

[75] Anthony N. B. Garvan, *Archecture and Town Planning in Colonial Connecticut* (New Haven, Conn., 1951), 42–43; see also Granville Sharp, *A General Plan for Laying Out Towns and Townships, on the New-acquired Lands in the East Indies, America, or Elsewhere* (London, 1794), 3–4.

[76] Garvan, *Architecture and Town Planning*, 44–49.

[77] Richard C. Wade, *The Urban Frontier: The Rise of Western Cities, 1790–1830* (Cambridge, Mass., 1959), I.

[78] *Ibid.*, 201 n.

[79] *Ibid.*, II, 123, 219.

[80] Carl Bridenbaugh, *Cities in the Wilderness: The First Century of Urban Life in America, 1625–1742* (New York, 1938), 32–33.

cultural heritage and motivations, who venture forth from a mature society into an empty continent. Such a stress, it is felt, is the one most likely to yield fruitful hypotheses for a comparative history of the Americas.

85. An Essay on Regionalism and Nationalism in Latin American Historiography*

Charles C. Griffin

The paramount problem for those concerned with the interpretation of the history of our time is to see it whole, for there can be no doubt that in the twentieth century the historic civilizations of both East and West, to say nothing of many other cultures which are marginal to them, are being transformed into a world civilization. The history of no nation, of no region, of no continent in the twentieth century can be fully understood in isolation from this ecumenical tendency. The major task for historians of the contemporary world, therefore, is to recognize, analyze, and define the forces which have revolutionized the world within the lifetime of those here assembled.

The whole can not be understood without a comprehension of its parts and of their relation to each other. It should, therefore, contribute to the larger task to consider the place of national and regional history in the interpretation of contemporary world history, and in this instance to evaluate their significance for the understanding of contemporary Latin America.

National history needs no definition; we are all familiar with it; we were born and brought up in its atmosphere. So fundamental has been its influence that it is with difficulty that we are able to free ourselves from its limiting influence. Regional history, however, is not so clear a concept, and it will be necessary to explain the term as it is used here.

The definitions of the word "region" in standard dictionaries do not help us very much. It is clear that the word can be applied to areas of greater or lesser extent determined by natural characteristics, ethnic composition, political or administrative organization, etc.[1] There is a good deal of historical justification for using the term "region" for geographical or ethnic provinces within countries or nations. Thus, in my

* *Journal of World History*, 8/2:371–378 (1964). Reprinted by permission of the author.

[1] The vagueness of the term "region" is extraordinary. *Webster's New International Dictionary* (2nd ed., Cambridge, Mass., 1949) gives as the third of ten meanings listed the following definition: "A large tract of land: one of the large districts or quarters into which any space or surface is conceived of as divided; hence in general an indefinite area; a country, province, district, tract." *The New Oxford Dictionary*, somewhat similarly, refers to a region as "a large tract of land, a country; a more or less defined portion of the earth's surface, now especially distinguished by certain natural features, climatic conditions, a special fauna or flora, or the like." Nothing could be more imprecise than these attempts at definition. The *Diccionario de la lengua española* of the Real Academia Española (15th ed., Madrid, 1925) is more concise, but equally inconclusive: REGION, "Porción de territorio determinado por carácteres étnicos o circunstancias especiales de clima, producción, topografía, administración, gobierno, etc."

country we refer to New England, or the South, or the Middle West as regions.[2] Similarly, it is customary for Spaniards to refer to the Basque provinces or to Catalonia as regions of Spain. I shall use the term, however, in another way, applying it to groups of countries and nations of related history and culture forming larger supra-national entities.

Even after making this distinction, it must be noted that nations can be placed in regional groupings at various levels. At the first level we find such groupings as Central America, or in Europe, the Balkans; at a somewhat more extended level such terms as the Caribbean or the Mediterranean region appear. At the most extended level we find such terms as Latin America or the Middle East. Any discussion of regional history must take into account these varying, sometimes concentric, and at other times overlapping groupings of countries or nations.

To give a concrete example taken from Latin America, the Republic of Cuba is a part of the Caribbean region, which can be narrowly defined as consisting of the greater and the lesser Antilles, or more broadly to include also countries bordering on the Caribbean sea. This group of countries includes several which are English speaking and it consequently can not be thought of as exclusively Latin. But Cuba also belongs to a larger regional group—that which is composed of the Latin American nations, Geographically, also, Cuba can be said to belong to the American continent, and until recently it even had political affiliations of continental scope in which the United States was also included.

Though for certain purposes there is utility for the historians in regional groupings of continental extent or even of some which surpass such limits, I shall consider here only the less extensive ones: Latin America as a whole and its major subdivisions.

It may properly be assumed, I believe, that there are aspects of the history of any country that can best be explained in a national framework. This is true unquestionably, for such subjects as the American Civil War or the Mexican Revolution. This does not mean,

however, that such events or movements did not have repercussions outside the nations in which they appeared. It is possible, therefore, to consider a subject as having both national and regional significance. There are other subjects in the history of any country which can not be understood without bringing into consideration a larger part of the world. Examples of such topics are the achievement of independence by the American republics or their relation to such international organizations as the United Nations or the Organization of American States. The problem, then, becomes one of discovering which aspects of a country's history can best be dealt with in these different contexts. If this question can be answered, it may be possible to go on to weigh the relative importance of national and regional history in a given period.

At first consideration it seems possible to make a distinction based on the categories of politics, economics, society and culture. Political history, because it concerns the activities of the State, might be considered suitable for treatment on a national basis. Economic history, depending so much on the character of natural resources might well be considered suitable for regional consideration. Social history, involving as it does the structure and dynamics of ethnic and class groups might also be said to relate more to a region than to individual nations. Cultural history, though it undoubtedly has national and regional aspects, may be considered to depend very largely on movements in the arts, literature, philosophy, and science, etc., which, if they are not universal, are broadly derived from outside the Latin American region.

Analysis, however, soon shows that this hypothesis is inadequate. Political history includes the interactions of states—their conflicts and their efforts towards co-operation— and can not, therefore, be dealt with wholly on a national basis. Even the domestic poli-

[2] In the United States there is a large literature on the subject of regionalism and on a variant term—sectionalism. See Merrill Jensen, ed., *Regionalism in America* (Madison, University of Wisconsin Press, 1951).

tics of a single nation frequently center on ideological conflicts which may be worldwide. One might point by way of example to such broad political influences as the Christian democratic movement or the ideology of anti-imperialism.

What of the suggestion that economic history should be studied by using a regional approach? This does, indeed, have a rational justification. As the Economic Commission for Latin America has discovered, there are a great many common elements among the economic problems of Latin American states, in spite of the wide variations among them in the degree of development achieved. There are, nevertheless, important aspects of economic history which transcend the region. The international trade of Latin America, in spite of the growth of its regional, inter-Latin American dimensions, is largely carried on with other parts of the world. Capital investment, too, both public and private, depends on circumstances and conditions in the United States and in Europe. The whole field of technology, so important for the study of economic change, can only be studied on a worldwide basis.

Latin American economics, then, has a character of its own, but in order to deal adequately with its history, extra-regional factors, such as the role of the USA, of the EEC, and even of the USSR, must be taken into account. The development of atomic energy, of electronic communications, air transport, the automation of industrial processes, and many other topics can not be studied in one region by itself. The participation of Latin American governments in such organizations as ILO, FAO and WHO bears witness to the universal aspect of many Latin American economic problems.

Social history fits the regional frame somewhat better. Though nations in Latin America differ, racial and class relationships are easily distinguishable from those which obtain in Europe, or Asia, or in the United States. However, the study of changing mores, folkways, and group situations and relations can perhaps be understood better by a less extensive kind of regional grouping than Latin America as a whole. Social history may perhaps fit best such regions as Brazil, the Andean countries, the Caribbean area.

And what shall we say about culture? Is its history something that can be related most properly to a universal base, to national ones, or to an intermediate regional one? Here, as in the case of economic history, there are certain obvious points to be made as well as some qualifications of the obvious.

The culture of Latin America is fundamentally Hispanic, i.e., derived from Spain and Portugal, with modifying influences derived from aboriginal America and from non-Hispanic areas such as Western Europe and the United States.[3] Latin American culture, therefore, must be recognized to have a territorial base broader than the American continent. But in some ways, in spite of the cultural bonds which relate Hispanic American peoples to those of the Iberian peninsula, the former have come to be sufficiently differentiated from the latter in certain ways to justify us in speaking of Hispanic American or Latin American culture. This is particularly true of popular culture which in the course of centuries has deviated from the original European base and absorbed local American and other exotic elements. To the extent that modern mass communications make possible an intermediate middle culture in Latin America, this tends to be Latin American rather than Hispanic. This is also true of aspects of culture which depend on governments such as education at its various levels. On the other hand, language and literature are examples of aspects of culture which remain Hispanic in their essentials. Religion and law, however, belong to a still more universal base in Western civilization. In many of the arts the possibility of expressing national or regional ideas, themes or modes of feeling are limited. Universal tendencies, such as functionalism

[3] If the new independent states now appearing in the Caribbean area such as Jamaica, Guyana, Trinidad, etc., are to be included in Latin America the above statement will not be as true as it was at one time. The region will have a more cosmopolitan culture.

in architecture, or abstraction in painting may be as important as the local component in contemporary Latin American cultivation of those arts.[4]

The attempt to discuss the national vs. the regional approach to contemporary history in Latin America in terms of the categories of politics, economics, society, and culture thus seems to break down. It is to be noted, however, that so far in our discussion it has not been so much a question of how much in contemporary history is national and how much regional, but rather how much is regional and how much transcends the regional basis of treatment.

For the Latin America of our time national history of the conventional type has a limited role. It is true that every sovereign state, no matter how small, has its own political annals. Within its frontiers a struggle for power is carried on; elections and coups d'etat occur; legislation is adopted; politicians exercise their powers of leadership. History as chronicle can clearly be developed on a national basis. As soon as we go beyond narrative and attempt to explain how and why changes have taken place, the national basis for history seems insufficient. It must be recognized of course that, in addition to history written for the purpose of explaining historical change, there is also a didactic type of history written for partisan, ideological, or patriotic purposes rather than for the extension of knowledge. Such history, frequently inculcated in official texts and programs, may well find the national basis ideal.

Some reservations must be made to the foregoing statement. There are countries like Brazil, for example, which are not only very large in terms of territory and population, but also rather sharply differentiated from their neighbors. Brazil provides a better base for a meaningful national history than some other countries. It is also necessary to recognize that there are particular periods in which the national history of a single country takes on special historical significance. This is true of Mexico in its revolutionary era, of Chile in its period of expansion during the nineteenth century. Other examples

of this could be added. It does seem, however, that even Brazil is now less self-contained, and more immersed in the same stream of history in which her sister nations are being carried along, than she was in the nineteenth century. The case for a regional approach to the history of our times in Latin America is strong.

But what kind of regional approach shall this be? Should Latin America as a whole be selected as the most meaningful subject for the historical study of this century? Is it possible that other smaller regions should be taken into account?

The importance of the smaller regional subdivisions of Latin America seems to be on the decline. In the nineteenth century historical events occurred to a very large extent within the confines of such sub-regions as the Rio de la Plata, the Andean countries, or Central America, or the Caribbean islands. Today this is no longer true to the same extent. Juan Manuel de Rosas, for example, was of concern not only to Argentina but also to such neighboring countries as Uruguay, Paraguay, Bolivia, and Brazil. The regime of Juan Perón, a century later, had repercussions which were much more extensive and affected the whole of South America. In the nineteenth century the economic growth of Brazil, or of Argentina and Chile, took place without much relation to the course of history in northern South America. As a matter of fact, what happened in Great Britain, France, Spain, or Italy was of much greater concern to Argentina at that time than what might be going on in Colombia or Venezuela. This is no longer true.

But, in spite of the trend towards closer ties among all the Latin American nations, there is still some validity in the use of sub-regions for historical study and analysis. The Caribbean area, for example, has to a certain extent been polarized by the power and influence of the United States, which has been

[4] There have been periods in history, of course, in which the expression of the local and the national spirit in the arts have been given great emphasis, perhaps outstandingly in the romantic era and in all countries when nationalism is powerful.

exerted so strongly in this sub-region in the twentieth century. Though countries like Mexico and Cuba at various times have resisted American influence with varying degrees of success, the United States influence has been an important factor in their history. Further south, Venezuela and Colombia, little influenced by the United States in the nineteenth century, have felt the North American impact strongly in this century. In addition, the gradual emancipation of European colonies and their increasing autonomy is another force working for the coherence and meaningfulness of the Caribbean region broadly defined to include almost all of northern Latin America. South of the Caribbean, Brazil still stands as a region in its own right. The rest of South America can for certain purposes be divided into the Platine sub-region and the Andean one. Such a division is useful in discussing agrarian reform or Indian problems, but these boundary lines are less important than they were at one time.

It may be that the lesser value of the national approach to history in Latin America in comparison with its use in countries like the USA or the USSR, or even in comparison with Germany or Italy, may be due to the fact that nationalism here has tended to be a divisive force. Within national boundaries nationalism in Latin America has been integrative, but not in the region as a whole. Latin American nationalisms have attached themselves to the successor states of the Spanish empire as part of a disintegrating tendency. Nationalism in the United States or Germany, or Italy, has involved the bringing together of previously disunited territories and peoples. Only in Brazil has Latin American nationalism escaped being a dividing force.

It is probably the recognition of this fact that has animated a long succession of efforts to constitute fewer and larger political units in Spanish America or to bring about a confederation of the whole. Of the former tendency Central American federation, the shortlived union of Peru and Bolivia under Andrés Santa Cruz, and the republic of Gran Colombia serve as examples. Of the latter we

see a beginning in the Bolivian tradition and a continuation in José Martí and his "Nuestra América." According to one recent observer of nationalism in Latin America, it is possible to speak of a continental nationalism that coexists with and competes with the conventional nationalisms of the separate republics.[5] The more that this sentiment grows the more the significance of the individual histories of twenty separate republics declines.

It may be that the recently completed project of the Commission on History of the Pan American Institute of Geography and History on the history of the Americas may have some relevance to our present problem.[6] The task faced by that project, i.e., to investigate the extent to which the whole of the New World has a common history, was a very different one. However, in that case too it was necessary to evaluate the significance of regional history. In dealing with the recent period the study to which I have just referred distinguished between broad extra-continental influences, continental developments, and regional developments. It did not attempt to include strictly national history. To the present speaker, who had the honor of participating in this co-operative enterprise, it was a surprise to see how much of American history could be dealt with regionally. Even when large topics of world wide significance had to be dealt with, it seemed to be between regions, rather than among nations that the most significant comparisons and distinctions could be made as to impact, reception, and consequences. I have in mind the impact on America of such events as the world economic depression of the 1930's, or the Second World War, and even certain intellectual currents such as existentialist philosophy or Marxist ideology. Occasionally the differen-

[5] Arthur P. Whitaker, *Nationalism in Latin America* (Gainesville, University of Florida Press, 1962).

[6] For a description of the project see *Programa de Historia de América, Introducciones y comentarios* (Mexico City, 1955), Publication No. 79 of the Pan American Institute of Geography and History. See also by the present writer, *The National Period in the History of the New World: An Outline and Commentary* (Mexico City, 1961).

ces between sub-regions seemed to be important: Brazil, the Caribbean, Andean South America could not always be dealt with *en masse*, but more frequently, the significant point was the contrast between Latin America and other parts of the New World.

In conclusion, I would contend that the major changes which have taken place in Latin America in our times can best be explained in a regional organization of contemporary history. The extent and timing of changes noted may vary enormously from country to country, but it would be hard to maintain that parts of the region have been subject to qualitatively distinct influences, though certain major sub-regions have sufficiently greater common ties to make it necessary to take these fully into account.

Latin American regionalism, therefore, as a basis for the study of contemporary history, is not a simple homogeneous regionalism, but a very complex one, composed of sub-regions which vary in importance according to the time span under consideration and the nature of the particular historical topic being studied. The closer contacts and the increasing solidarity of the peoples of Latin America during the course of the last generation leads us on to ask whether we are not now witnessing the gradual evolution of a larger Latin American nationality. Whether that will prove to be the case, or whether the centripetal forces at work in the region will bring about important but less spectacular results only the future can tell.[7]

[7] It will at once appear to the reader that the conclusions of this paper are sharply at variance with the practice of Latin American historians. Though in the United States and in Europe there have been efforts to deal with the history of contemporary Latin America as a whole (See, for example, R. A. Humphreys, *Latin American History: A Guide to the Literature in English* (London, 1958), pp. 14–15), Latin Americans themselves have tended to avoid and distrust such efforts. This may be an indication of the general conservatism of historians, for in the discussion of contemporary public affairs, or even of culture, Latin Americans hardly ever hesitate to take for granted the reality of the regional group to which they belong. The author regrets that lack of time and space prevents the documentation of this statement here.

86. The Unity of Brazilian History*

ALEXANDER MARCHANT

The unity of Brazilian history is a striking thing even to the casual observer. Here is a vast country—one of the vastest in the world —that emerged from a colony into an independent empire and finally into a republic without having become broken up into smaller, separate states. It has regions that are well marked off by distinctive characteristics, and yet regionalism was never successfully carried to the point of separatism. In it the conflict of native, European, and African peoples has at times been bitter, but from diverse components a recognizably Brazilian culture appears to be emerging.

It may well be that such an impression of unity is but a reflection of a certain uniformity in Brazilian life. Language and religion, for example, are, with regional variations, demonstrably the same wherever studied in the huge territory of Brazil. Perhaps uniformity in the structure of the property-owning class, with a community of attitude and a uniform effect in political action, underlies other social characteristics that appear the same in all parts of the country. Or, to take an effect rather than a cause, the impression of unity may come from the relatively little change among social and economic classes that has occurred over decades and centuries. Traditionally, and with the rise of an industrialized urban group as a recent exception, the people of Brazil have been overgeneralized into those who were the possessors and those who were the unfree or the servile and the dependent.

On the other hand, the possibility ought not be excluded that the sense of unity may come not from the matter of Brazilian history but from the treatments and interpretations that have been given it. What may be called the standard periodization is political, and this does not make for any feeling of fussy detail, for it consists of the large, simple headings of colony, kingdom, empire, and republic. Perhaps, also, Brazil is a country that has no history, in the classic meaning that its past has been little marked by foreign and civil wars, invasions, illustrious captains, rebellious nobles, and parliamentary struggles. It has had its share of such events, but they give the impression of having been put passing incidents in a broad landscape of peace and plenty.

Even when Brazilian historians turn to their economic history, an engaging simplicity prevails. The whole diversified life of over four centuries is often fitted into a few great cycles of sugar, gold, and coffee, and into lesser and more regional ones of leather, diamonds, rubber, and even cacao. Should such categories be insufficient to explain social history, then the history of Brazil may be seen as growing from the interrelations of the White, the Red, and the Black—the

* Brazil: A Portrait of Half a Continent, edited york, 1951), pp. 37–51. Reprinted by permission of the original publisher.

usual metaphor for the three racial strains on which Brazil is based.

The reasons for the existence of these attitudes in Brazilian historiography may perhaps be found in the way in which the discipline of history exists in Brazil. There, the writing of history remains largely in the Renaissance vein of politics and biography, with more emphasis on literary presentation than is usual in the United States, although some works of value have appeared in this century with economic, sociological, and other interpretations. Brazilian historiography is much less than in the United States the work of professional historians, but rather that of gifted amateurs, intellectuals, political figures, and others who exemplify in the facility with which they woo Clio the versatility of intellectual accomplishment that Brazilians prize highly. Indeed, the Brazilian historian is usually self-taught in the technique and aims of his craft. If he enjoys the strength of greater individualistic expression, he also suffers from the weakness of lack of formal acquaintance with the history and history writing of other countries, and in any large work he is apt to have to do an unnecessary amount of bibliographic research before he can properly place his work in the context of the problem he studies. There are few schools in Brazil where much of the formal background of the study of history may be obtained, and in none of them[1] is there any work in the methods and craft of history.

What may be called the institutionalization of history writing even today leaves the Brazilian historian at a disadvantage. Bibliographies, libraries, and archives are still not well developed or too readily accesssible. The most striking feature of such institutions is the number of historical societies, beginning with the more than century-old *Instituto histórico e geográfico brasileiro* and supplemented by those of many of the states. They reflect the intellectual history of their country and their regions as places where historical documents could accumulate, and such of them as publish or have published their journals have thus provided a good source of printed documentary material.

The writing and teaching of history, however, do not as a rule form a full-time occupation, or one that provides the bulk of the scholar's income. The historian there does not have open to him, as does his colleague in the United States, a relatively large number of schools and colleges in which to earn a living by the pursuit of his interest. Often the Brazilian historian is distracted from his research by the need for having to seek additional employment in the government, the professions, or business. Too seldom does he have the time or the money to explore any but the archives most nearly at hand. As a consequence, all but the most original of Brazilian historians have tended to concentrate their attention on a few periods and a few aspects of the past, and all too few of them have been able to base their work on fresh exploration of archives.[2]

With these all-too-general considerations in mind, it will be seen that no more is intended here than to suggest some other themes which run throughout Brazilian history and which, like some of the interpretations mentioned above, may also have a bear-

---

[1] So far (April 1949) as I have been able to determine. There was some prospect in the reorganization of the University of Brazil in 1946 that the study of method would receive attention, but I have seen nothing that indicates that the idea was put into practice. The University of São Paulo, however, has produced some excellent doctoral dissertations in history, one of which (Alice Canabrava's *O Comércio Português no Rio da Prata, 1580–1640*) is referred to below.

[2] These comments should be taken in relation to the general neglect of Brazilian history in the United States, which, with the exception of Portugal, is today perhaps the foreign country most actively cultivating Brazilian studies. But such neglect is now being to some extent remedied, because, to take but a single index and one of quantity if not always of quality, the number of doctoral dissertations on Brizilian history being written in universities in the United States has been steadily increasing. There is, of course, and for a number of sound reasons, no comparison between the attention given Brazil here and that paid to the history of the Spanish empire and the Spanish American republics. In that field, as is evidenced by C. H. Haring (*The Spanish Empire in America*, New York: Oxford University Press, 1947), scholarship is now mature and sets a standard for the emulation of Brazilianists.

ing on the making of a Brazilian unity.[3] For one thing, Brazil was a colony of Portugal for over three centuries. For another, it is a country that has been slowly and consistently expanding its frontiers. And, lastly, it is among the countries of the world in which great families have characteristically perpetuated themselves as economic and political leaders. Because too little work has been done to test the following hypotheses, conclusions in this short space will be left implicit in the discussion, and the reader may choose those that he wishes as points of departure for further study.

To suggest where these hypotheses occur in time, the reader may be reminded of the main lines of the development of Brazil. Discovered by Cabral in 1500, neglected at first in favor of more attractive India, Brazil was colonized by the Portuguese only when the threat of French capture became real. In 1532, the land was given out to proprietary landlords (*donatários*), and when all but two had failed, a royal government was established in Bahia in 1549. In the successful proprietary lands of Pernambuco, and elsewhere under royal encouragement, sugar became widely established as an export crop and created a society of patriarchal families, great landholdings, and slaves. São Vicente (later São Paulo), the other proprietary grant, was too far south for sugar, and its people later became the *bandeirantes* who explored the interior of the continent in search of gold and slaves. Aside from landlords, African slaves, government officials, and merchants, the population consisted of a small but increasing number of freedmen and free squatters who occupied small pieces of land left among unsurveyed land grants. Indians had been assimilated or, in both north and south, had fled before the raiding of the planters and their suppliers of slaves. The ephemeral Dutch conquest of the sugar northeast in the first half of the seventeenth century left little impress on Brazilian life there, and even the transient glory of gold and diamonds found in Minas in the next century did not depopulate the coast, though it attracted people to the interior.

Brazil continued more and more remote from the rest of the world until the Portuguese royal family took refuge there during the Napoleonic wars. That event turned the attention of the small literate urban class toward Europe, but Brazil became an independent empire in 1822 under Pedro I with no alteration of its patriarchal, slave-owning, landholding character.

The second Pedro did not alter that character, because he recognized it as the basis of his regime. In politics, though himself conservative and jealous of the imperial prerogatives, he encouraged the development of parliamentary forms and insisted on the orderly application of laws above men. But he was content to leave the country as a one-crop economy, dependent as it was on the fluctuations of world markets, while power shifted from the declining sugar northeast to the rising coffee planters of São Paulo. He permitted such industrialization as was useful to that shift, but in this, as in his eventual abolition of slavery, he insisted on only very gradual evolution.

The removal of his austere personal control by the founding of the Republic in 1889 permitted the appearance of elements that indicated how much Brazil had nevertheless changed. To the population was now added an incipient urban working class, living on wages and without the privileges of dependents in the old paternalistic society. And the whole population had commenced its enormous increase in numbers that today gives it 45,000,000, with every prospect of 90,-000,000 in another quarter-century. Politics did not display a like flexibility to match. The army became a political force, to the dismay of civilianist republicans. In the name of federalism, the states, led by Minas Gerais and wealthy São Paulo, passed into the hands of regional bosses and oligarchies, who, no longer restrained by the Emperor,

[3] For systematic general treatment in English, the reader is referred to J. P. Calógeras, *History of Brazil* (English translation, with additional material by P. A. Martin, of *Formação Histórica do Brasil*, São Paulo: Companhia Editora Nacional, 1938), Chapel Hill: University of North Carolina Press, 1939; and Lawrence F. Hill, ed., *Brazil*, Berkeley: University of California Press, 1947.

excluded the bulk of the population from participation in politics and struggled among themselves to possess the federal government. Finances became chronically disordered, especially when the one-crop coffee economy failed in a series of crises in world markets, while the executive increasingly assumed emergency powers. The importance of popular representation progressively declined but, as industrialization continued through the 1920's and 1930's, a small urban proletariat became a potential political power, to which a series of leaders, culminating in Getúlio Vargas in 1930, more and more appealed.

With great skill Vargas ruled until 1945 by playing the army, big business, workingmen, and the regions of Brazil against one another. The workingmen he conciliated with enough of a social program to give them the impression that something was being done for them, but his various new constitutions kept control over them ultimately in the hands of the state and left big business undisturbed as it rapidly proceeded with industrialization. Attention was distracted from the problems of the littoral by a "march to the West," but this, like so many other programs, lost its sense of direction in the competition among expensive and predatory bureaucratic agencies directly responsible to the executive. Constitutional experiments concerning the basis of suffrage remained on paper, while a police state functioned through an active and privileged civil and military police.

Following his overthrow by the army, an election between an army-conservative group and nineteenth-century political liberals produced a government with a new constitution, in which a strong executive ("presidentialism") remains paramount. In practical politics, however, regional oligarchies regained the power taken from them by Vargas, and the general tone is conservative, with the attitude of the army constantly kept in view. The constitution of 1946 and the existence of a congress allow some scope for popular representation, though not on a scale proportionate to the increase in, and diversification of the interests of, the population. Lower-class participation is not welcomed, and no great readiness has been shown to provide a government program to take the place of that of the suppressed Communist Party.

Colonial Brazil has been assiduously studied by Brazilian scholars—but usually as a subject in itself and not as a part of the Portuguese empire. Indeed, a glance at bibliographies indicates that in no language are there works on the Portuguese empire, including Brazil, comparable in number or quality with those on the Spanish empire. The principal characteristics of the Portuguese empire are sufficiently well known, so that here only certain phases affecting Brazil will be brought into sharper relief by contrast with the Spanish empire.

The first difference, and an obvious one, is between the native populations of the two empires at the time of European conquest. It is trite but nevertheless useful to point out that the most important centers of the Spanish empire grew up in those two large regions where some of the Indians of the New World were concentrated in a city culture. Implicit in the existence of such cities was the holding of land by a numerically small class that used military strength to enforce its political and ecclesiastical domination over the population. Whatever the degree of personal or economic freedom, most people among the Indians neither participated in nor expected to participate in government, and few, it seems, did little more than pay tribute of goods and services and otherwise acquiesce in the wishes of those who governed. About 1500, some peoples seem to have tended to retreat as the empires of the Incas and the Aztecs, for example, expanded.

In this perspective, the Spanish conquest of the city cultures was the replacement of the native ruling class by a Spanish ruling class. On the one hand, the Spaniards certainly seem to have been willing enough to assume autocratic rule; and, on the other, most of the native population seems to have accepted the new kings, priests, and warriors with as much resignation as they had the Incas or others. Such a change in the nature of those who ruled could not have meant much to most natives. They had had to labor for or pay tribute to Indian chieftains who may or may not have spoken their language. The Spaniards introduced new crops, stimulated mining, and so altered to some extent the methods and purposes for which the natives were put to work.

The lack of city culture among the Indians of Brazil deprived the Portuguese of what for the Spaniards had been the relatively rapid and easy taking over of an existing system of organizing and dominating people. The generally nomadic or, at least, migratory nature of the life of the Brazilian Indians made their flight from contact with the Portuguese easy. The Portuguese, consequently, instead of having their Indians and precious metals ready at hand for conquest, so to speak, were forced to diffuse themselves over a vast area in search of both.

In comparison with that of the Spanish empire, the administrative machinery by which Portugal governed Brazil and the rest of its empire seems almost insignficantly slight. Here again, the reasons are obvious. In their first conquest of the Indian trade routes, the Portuguese seemed to have found the way to inexhaustible wealth in an empire with a vast population. Had Portugal been a larger country with more people, it might have stood the strain of having a large number of its men depart overseas as soldiers, sailors, merchants, imperial officials, workmen, and servants. But it was not large, the loss of such men was irreparable, and it soon found itself with an empire that earned less than it cost to run and defend. In time, the Indian venture was in effect abandoned, and Portugal concentrated its strength on holding and developing its two other principal colonies—Angola and Brazil. These were both productive regions. Angola, with its slave trade, was large, and Brazil, with its sugar, was slowly expanding in area. But in each of these, despite their size and the value of their commerce, the number of people was, in comparison with the Spanish empire, negligible. This does not mean to say that Portugal had no imperial administration. It did promulgate and codify its legislation for overseas, and it had an imperial council, with the usual apparatus of viceroys, captains, judges of various categories, royal examiners, and the indispensable fiscal officials. But all this did not need to be on so large a scale as in Spain.

It seems unsound, however, to conclude that, because this administration was more modest, it was for that reason less effective. Two instances from the last century of the Portuguese empire in Brazil come to mind readily, both of them affecting the gold country of Minas Gerais. When gold had been found, the government exercised great care in seeing that the *quinto*, or the king's fifth, was conveyed to the royal treasury as a right on all subsoil treasure. Royal smelters, guards, licenses, and fiscal officials were put together in a relatively elaborate system of protection, and special attention was paid to preventing losses through contraband, though it was tacitly recognized that some such loss was inevitable. In addition to such fiscal supervision, the government acted with some degree of promptness to put down the Conspiracy of Minas when that protorepublican movement began to take shape; and, after prosecuting the suspects for three years, it exacted sentences that, even when commuted, were not light. It seems fair to conclude that, small though their number was, the government officials played much the same role in Brazil as their counterparts did in the Spanish empire, and *empleomania* seems to have been characteristic in both that in both empires government officials were able to recognize that some decrees promulgated by their monarchs in Europe were impracticable in America, and that they obeyed but did not execute.

A glance at the basic attitudes and policies of the two empires, however, shows some differences. The Spanish empire has long been thought of as a mercantilist monster that robbed its colonies of their gold and other wealth and allowed them no freedom to develop their own industries and commerce. Now we perceive that the fines, licenses, taxes, supervision, and fees of all kinds were not abnormal for the period, despite the eloquence with which Spanish American patriots complained against them. Further, the Spanish empire is now beginning to appear as almost a model of the wise and tolerant encourager of local industry and commerce in the colonies. Quite early Spain recognized that so many people in so large a land could not be supplied from the metropolis and that as a consequence the colonies should themselves make the goods they needed. Only those things were restricted that might injure Spanish industry and commerce, or interfere with the production of gold and silver or other activities of unquestioned importance. For the rest, the colonies could and did mix Indian and European handicrafts to attain self-sufficiency. Indeed, more than subsistence was attainable, as is evidenced by the growth of such a luxury business as silk making in Mexico.

The usual understanding is that in economic affairs Portugal did not allow such latitude to Brazil and its other colonies. Manufactures and industries were all restricted or prohibited. At times, a specific end was sought, as, for example, the prohibition of industries in or near the gold fields in the eighteenth century for fear that labor might be attracted away to the detriment of the production of gold. In this, the Portuguese Government of Brazil seems much more like that of the British in North America than like that of the Spanish empire. And it also seems that government officials and their troops saw to it that restrictive decrees were enforced.

Nor was a restrictive attitude confined to these matters alone. In its limitation of the means of intellectual life, the Portuguese empire differed markedly from the Spanish. Whereas in Spanish America schools, seminaries, even universities of a sort increased in number, in Brazil none were permitted. If the upper-class Brazilian wished an education, he had to go to Europe for it; and if on his return to Brazil he wished to publish his ideas, he found that no printing press was allowed to exist.

Closely connected with the restriction of economic diversification was the attitude of Portugal toward the participation of the Brazilians in their own government. In this, Portugal was like Spain, so far as existing studies indicate. In both empires, offices of responsibility were reserved to the Portuguese and Spanish, and in both the number of creoles who held important posts seems to have been small. On this point, studies of the composition of the imperial administration of the Spanish empire are far more detailed and search than anything existing on Brazil. It would be a matter of considerable interest to know how many of the men who governed Brazil were Brazilians by birth. Some Brazilians did study law in Portugal during the colonial period and were appointed *juizes de fora*, for example, but their identity and their number have yet to be determined.

Local government in Brazil meant municipal government, at a time when the town or city was more like a city-state, with its built-up center and outlying lands. Its business was conducted by the *câmara*, or chamber, a body whose history and functions closely parallel those of the *cabildo* of the Spanish empire. Like the *cabildos*, the *câmaras* occupied themselves with municipal administration, and a fair amount concerning their functions may be learned from even a cursory reading of such minutes of the meetings of the more important ones as have already been published. Certainly the government of towns or cities was an important function, especially when the control of *câmaras* over the distribution of the lands of the city-state, as it may be called, is taken into account.

But what the practice of the *câmaras* was in various regions and periods in Brazil still remains an insufficiently studied subject. Certainly, there have been no studies of *câmaras* comparable to those of *cabildos*. Perhaps the reason for their failure to arouse the interest of Brazilian historians lies in what seems to be the essential difference between the *câmaras* and the *cabildos*. Spain was itself a country in which municipalities had attained an unusual importance because of the assistance given by townsmen to those monarchs who were imposing centralized royal rule on regionally important military Spanish nobility. In time, even though the kings of Spain had to check the powers and privileges of the towns and cities, Spanish civilization acquired a distinctly urban cast, which was reflected by the towns and cities established in Spanish America. The city Spaniards of the New World withstood the efforts of the great rural landlords and the Indians to reduce their importance, and, indeed, gave prestige to city life and urban mores. To think of Spanish America is to think as much of great and lesser cities as of vast stretches of plains, deserts, jungles, and mountains.

Cities and towns in Brazil never attained a similar importance. The members of the *câmara* were elected on a basis of property qualification. If the premise is sound that the wealthiest and most powerful men were the rural landlords who maintained houses, business, and other interests that gave them a voice in municipal government, then it appears that they could bring about the election of those persons most congenial to them. On the basis of Gilberto Freyre's studies of the sugar northeast, the part of Brazil that had earliest established and longest maintained any considerable density of population, the impression may be gained much more of the overriding prestige and power of the *senhores de engenho* than of the municipal officials. It may not be going too far to say that the *senhores de engenho* gave the orders and that the *câmara* obeyed or was influenced. The *senhores de engenho,* who proverbially believed that even the king's law stopped at the gates of their *fazendas,* welcomed no authority, royal or municipal, that tended in any way to affect their own freedom of action. What the situation was in Minas, after the gold rush had attracted and concentrated a population and created cities, still remains obscure, and it is possible that municipal authority had more substance there. In the more remote parts of the country, such as the cattle region of the south, the bandeirante bases for the explora-

tion of the center, or the municipalities created later along the Amazon, the vestige of townsmen and *câmaras* seems not to have been great.

If, then, the towns and *câmaras* seem to have been dominated or overawed by the physical power and the social prestige of the rural landlords, it does not follow that they were always acquiescent. Lacking the relatively more numerous commercial and professional classes of the Spanish American cities, it was more difficult for the Brazilian townsmen to embody and assert successfully an urban point of view. But instances are not few of disputes between town and country, carried in some instances to the point of actual fighting.

The desire of some *câmaras* to act on occasion independently of and perhaps in opposition to the surrounding rural society appears to find a parallel in the attitude of some municipalities toward the imperial government. There is reason to believe that in some of the wealthier towns as well as in some of the remote ones the *câmaras* did at times refuse to obey imperial orders or did assume powers and responsibilities without royal sanction. On this point more study is needed to determine whether such resistance to royal government was offered by a group in the *câmara* asserting municipal interests or a group reflecting rural interests. Until these instances of resistance receive fuller treatment, it will be difficult to decide what the role of the *câmaras* in the movement for independence was in comparison with that of the *cabildos* in Spanish America. But to test this hypothesis, study of individual towns and *câmaras* is needed to determine who were the electors and who the elected, what policies the *càmaras* sought to apply, and the degree of success. Only then will it be possible to evaluate the place of the *câmara* in Brazilian history. Heretofore, it has generally been regarded from two points of view. Some students of Brazilian history and political development, such as, for example, the advocates of increasing the power of the central government, find it valuable only insofar as it acted as the acquiescent agent of Lisbon or, later, Rio de Janeiro. Others, such as Capistrano de Abreu, sought those elements in the past that might have contributed to the growth of a Brazilian liberalism, and they were inclined to search for evidence of independent action by *câmaras* that appeared to be representing and defending local interests. But, generally speaking, Capistrano, for example, thought their contribution to liberalism slight and was inclined to disregard them. In any discussion, however the fact should not be lost sight of that the *câmaras*, like the *cabildos*, provided the only place in Brazilian politics in the colonial period in which the creoles could participate as a class.

It may thus appear that whereas the Portuguese did have an imperial system, of which Brazil was a part, they lacked the rigor, the elaborate development, and the all-pervading thoroughness of the Spanish counterpart. They did affect the life of the Brazilians, usually in a restrictive way, but at the same time, and perhaps because of the difficulties of communication, they left the Brazilians considerable latitude to develop as they wished. In Brazil, for example, partly for reasons inherent in Brazilian society and partly because of the difference in temper of Portuguese rule, there never grew up the belief in and yearning for *limpieza de sangre* that so colored the relations of the Spanish Americans with one another and their government. Perhaps the symbol of the administrative difference between the two empires is the *Recopilación de las leyes de las Indias* of the Spaniards, expressing the very spirit of exhaustive regulation down to the finest details. The physical symbol certainly seems to be the difference between the Spanish American cities and the Brazilian cities, as Sr. José Arthur Rios has pointed out elsewhere in this volume. In both, the center of town was the square, with the principal church and government edifices, surrounded in the nearby streets by shops and by the dwellings, sometimes magnificent, of the leading citizens. But there the resemblance ends. The Spaniards specified in the *Recopilación* exactly how the rest of the town was to be laid out, and missed no detail of street widths, secondary squares, paving, and upkeep of buildings. As a consequence, one Spanish American city, despite differences of terrain, soil, water, and climate, is, with relatively minor differences in architectural style, very apt to look like another. But no two Brazilian cities may be superimposed on each other. The Brazilians let their streets follow the slope or the level of the ground, jumbled three or four colossal churches together cater-cornered, interspersed built-up streets with open grounds, and otherwise allowed their towns to reflect a greater independence of spirit on the part of the Brazilians, who built where and how they wished.

If a feeling subsists that the Portuguese policy toward Brazil was one of almost capriciously benevolent paternalism, of lack of sternness, and even in some instances of smiling grace (so far as these figures may be applied to governmental institutions to suggest the contrast with Spain), it must not be supposed that the Portuguese empire and, later, independent Brazil were lacking in a general policy of obtaining resources and opportunities for their population and making them secure against other claimants. The temptation is to create an uninterrupted succession of Portuguese and Brazilian statesmen who handed down to one another a four-century-long master plan in which every detail of expansion in time and space was consciously worked out. In fact, the expansion of the people of Brazil, at times on a scale of mass migration, seems to have been as undirected and as amorphous as that of any other people. Individuals or groups, acting singly or in concert, unaware of their effect and implications, entered unexplored territory in search of real or imaginary attractions. To this vast territory into which they went, with the exception of the region toward the River Plate, Preston James' term of "hollow frontier" may well be applied. The boundaries on the periphery were formed by the farthest reaching out of the Brazilians, but, in some instances partly because of inhospitable terrain, later population never filled in the space between them and the older inhabitants of the coast.

But such an unguided action and such a hollowness of frontier must not be allowed to obscure the fact of the readiness and decision with which the governments took advantage of and obtained legal title to land that Brazilians had occupied.

Trite though it may seem, reference should be made to the Tordesillas line by which the Portuguese Government in 1494 pushed its boundary with Spanish America far enough to the west to gain possession of the South Atlantic seaway to India and, eventually, of Brazil. By agreement rather than by exact determination of longitude, the line seems to have been marked at its ends and served formally as the terminus for the land grants of the Portuguese crown to the *donatários*. It probably may be assumed that the Portuguese had at first every intention of not crossing the line into Spanish lands, but the difficulty of determining longitude at that time would have prevented most people lost in the interior of Brazil from knowing in which empire they were, even had they wished. It would be a matter of considerable interest, then, to ascertain how long the Portuguese clung to the idea of respecting the Tordesillas line and how soon the Brazilians lost all awareness of it as a possible restraint on their westward exploration. How completely the Tordesillas line came to be disregarded is shown by the treaty of Madrid of 1750, in which the line was abandoned as the basis of delimitation of the boundary between the two empires in South America and its place taken by the principle of *uti possidetis*.

The obvious instance of Portuguese expansion within the continent is the *bandeirantes*, whose prodigious explorations of the west, principally in the seventeenth and eighteenth centuries, have been extensively studied, especially by their Paulista descendants of today. And yet the very extent of their forays and the volume of the literature on them tend to throw out of perspective what had been going on at other times and in other regions. It is here suggested that the initial expansion of the Brazilians into the Spanish empire began with a Brazilian

contraband trade into the Plate, as Alice Canabrava has amply demonstrated.[4] In addition to adding a sphere of commerce for a time to the agricultural Brazil of the sugar northeast, the persistence of the Portuguese and Brazilians there gave them a notion of the relation between even partial control of the estuary and the use of the upriver country for development and as a way to possible wealth in the interior.

This theme of interest in the far south may profitably be pursued much further and in detail. In 1680, the Brazilians again pushed down to the River Plate and established their colony of Sacramento on the north shore. The threat of their presence was so obvious that the Spaniards mustered strength to expel them, but, though once expelled, they remained on the northern shore and kept returning to Sacramento and to other points. In the treaties of Madrid and San Ildefonso, Spain seemed able in this sector of the boundary to move the Portuguese northward and make both shores of the estuary its own, but it seems unlikely that all Brazilians left the disputed area or that the Portuguese Government abandoned the notion of at least sharing control of the river.

And this notion certainly persisted in Brazil as a kingdom and as an independent empire. Both John VI and his vexatious queen, Carlota Joaquina, continued to press government support for Brazilian settlers and occupants of the zone, and their son, Pedro I, carried forward their efforts. From this point of view, the final creation of an independent Uruguay in 1830 counts as a repetition of the settlements of Madrid and San Ildefonso. Ostensibly, imperial Brazil was barred by a buffer state from physical occupation of the north shore, but by then the empire felt that it could not view with equanimity any policy of other governments around the River Plate that might harm Brazilian subjects and their interest. The involvement of the empire in the Paraguayan war beyond the point of expelling the invader from Bra-

[4] Alice Canabrava, *O Comércio Português no Rio da Prata, 1580–1640*, São Paulo: Universidade de São Paulo, 1944.

zilian soil was therefore a foregone conclusion, as is the inheritance by republican Brazil of the attitude of holding at least a watching brief for the interest of Brazilian citizens south of its borders.

If the Portuguese and Brazilians failed to keep physical possession of part of the southern river mouths, in the north they succeeded amply. Commencing with the destruction of the attempted French colony in Rio de Janeiro, they next expelled the French from Maranhão and followed them well beyond the Amazon to the region of what is today French Guiana. That such pursuit carried them beyond the Tordesillas line seems for a time to have escaped the attention of the Spanish, who in the eighteenth century were themselves pushing eastward from New Granada against the English and the Dutch. John VI in the period of the kingdom and Rio Branco in the period of the republic finally obtained definitive international agreement for that portion of the northern boundary.

The advance of the *bandeirantes* of São Paulo into the lands of the Spanish king is too well known to need recital here. Starting from a number of settlements on the *planalto* near the Atlantic, they established outposts in the interior from which to provision and send forth more expeditions. Everywhere they looked for gold and other riches and, aided by native allies, captured Indians as slaves for use in São Paulo and for export to other parts of Brazil. Their drive carried them not only well into the quasi-state of the Jesuit missions but, in effect, to approximately the present boundaries of Brazil with Paraguay, Bolivia, and Peru. To consolidate the effect of their expansion, and taking advantage of relatively easier travel by water, the Portuguese Government later established forts at a number of the most remote of the *bandeirante* outposts in the Amazon basin. By the time of the treaties of Madrid and San Ildefonso, the region of Tabatinga, today on the borders of Colombia, was acknowledged by Spain to be Portuguese by occupation.

The empire and the republic continued the work of obtaining formal government possession of all these occupied points. In the republic, the final phase was reached in the magnificent series of arbitrations by which Rio Branco made good the Brazilian *uti possidetis* claim to even the most remote of the present boundaries of Brazil.

To turn to the family after a discussion of expansion of peoples and affairs of state may seem to someone from the United States to reduce the object of study to the personal and the sentimental. But the family in the history of Brazil, as in most countries whose society and codified custom descend from the Roman rather than from the Anglo-American law, possesses certain legal characteristics that add to it a great deal more than connection by blood, allusive humor, and four-generation reunions. Certainly, it seems different if only because of the way in which relatives of even distant degree, clients, dependents, and servants may claim the recognition and protection of the paterfamilias. The most notable characteristic is its permanence over many generations as an upper-class means of possessing and transmitting property, and, in this sense, it displays a uniformity in all Brazil that is relatively little affected by regional variations.

The foreign student, influenced by the work of Gilberto Freyre, is apt to form an impression of that family, especially in the colonial period, as indistinguishable from the *casa grande*, rich in overtones of slave quarters, African traits, family religion, and other connotations of the sugar northeast. It should be noted, however, that Brazilians from other sections are not universally willing to generalize his concepts and illustrations as true for all Brazil. Because, for example, African influence is not powerful in the south, some feel that Freyre's imagery cannot be reconciled with conditions there, and yet others point out that a regional characteristic of small farming or some industry other than his "patriarchial slavocratic latifundiary monoculture" makes his economic corollaries inapplicable. Despite criticism, *Casa grande e senzala* is a unique work and needs no defense beyond setting the boundaries of the part of the country in which his conclusions are valid. If the regional and the specific are cleared away, his idea of a Brazilian patriarchalism and familism emerges as a basic interpretation of Brazilian history.

The vigor with which this concept has been debated has led some to set aside the family of the sugar northeast as a particular type that finds no counterpart elsewhere in Brazil. The corollary then appears reasonable that each of the regions of Brazil imposes a special character on the families within its boundaries. That this is so is amply shown by regional differences in houses, dress, urban-rural relations, even familiar language.

While escaping any undue legalism, an attempt should be made to see what features the family has in common in the regions of Brazil. The first is the system of inheritance. For its historical development and present status, the reader may consult the legislation and codes of Portugal and Brazil and the standard works of commentators and jurisconsults. In essence, the greatest difference between the civil law and the Anglo-American law is that the testator in the civil law is less free to dispose of his property as he wishes. A certain proportion of the estate normally must go to the immediate family, and the customs preserved in the law require that descendants, ascendants, collaterals, and other connections of the family may not be neglected. This is especially true in the case of intestate death, when the distribution of property follows rules *per capita* and *per stirpes.*

The second feature is the family council. This further heritage of the Roman law has over centuries acquired a concreteness that in the United States would probably be meaningless except to residents of Louisiana. Its function is to embody the interests of the immediate family, ascendants, descendants, collaterals, and any other interested or affected members. The principal occasion for its meeting is the death of the paterfamilias, though it often convenes to arrange marriages, property settlements, transfer of property, and other matters of common concern. By providing for consultation and the expression of the interests of all, it tends to prevent, for example, in the alienation of property, damage to the welfare of the group and of the individuals or branches represented.

Intimately connected with succession and the structure and operation of the family is the legal position of adoption and legitimation. Because of the perpetuation in Brazil of yet another process of Roman law and family custom, the testator seldom need lack an heir. With greater facility in the legal arrangements and with a long series of historical precedents in Rome and Portugal, he could adopt as his heir a person not closely related, sometimes not even a blood relative. And in the civil law the position of the natural child is more readily made regular than in the Anglo-American system, and in many cases may be formalized by the later marriage of the parents. Even if not legitimated, the natural child has rights of inheritance that cannot formally be denied, and, once legitimated, he takes an unexceptionable legal place in the family. It was thus possible for the paterfamilias, if predeceased by his presumptive heirs and wishing to prevent the dying out of the direct line, to bring into the family someone to discharge those duties required by the civil law of the necessary heir.

It would be unwisely bookish to take what is provided for in legal codes and sanctioned by custom as proof of what happened in Brazil, except possibly in settled parts in times of peace, when households were in order and drowsy amity ruled among all the members of a family. More instances come to mind of rebellious sons, avaricious widows, predatory uncles, and law-defying sons-in-law. The caprices of the *senhor de engenho* were often the law of the *fazenda,* and the history of the north is shadowed by *lutas de famílias,* when generations of families fought among themselves and with each other in vendettas of more than Mediterranean malignancy. Without going into the political influence of great families through *compa-*

drismo and their economic power through the accumulation of lands linked by marriage, enough has been said to suggest that the legal precepts applicable to the family could be uniform for the whole country and make for the increased strength and permanence of the family.

87. Some Themes of Brazilian History*

RICHARD M. MORSE

In examining modern interpretations of Brazilian history and civilization one is struck by the recurrent preoccupation with the theme of diversity and unity. The French sociologist Roger Bastide has written a book called *Brazil, Land of Contrasts*, the final chapter of which is "The Unity of Brazilian Problems." In it he says:

> All these contrasts of landscape and vegetation, of races and cultures, of customs and styles of life, remain Brazilian contrasts. . . . Let us not speak of the harmonization of opposites, of water and fire, of sugar and coffee, of the coast and the backlands. Let us say only that these antagonistic civilizations, that of the southern gaucho and that of the northern cowpuncher, that of the planter and that of the industrialist, that of the Negro and that of the immigrant, are rather complementary than antagonistic. They everywhere confront the same basic problems, imposed by the geographical environment or inherited from history.[1]

Earlier, the author had qualified the meaning of "contrasts" by saying that, "Brazil, land of contrasts, is also and at the same time the land of nuances, such that one no longer knows which dominates, the rules or the exceptions to the rule."[2]

The high priest of Brazilian pluralism is Gilberto Freyre, whose recent *Brazils, Brazil and Brasília* is a series of essays on the theme. Now, as in its history, Brazil is a collection of "Brazils" having social, cultural, ethnic, economic, and political meaning only "in the form of a vast and single Brazil which, for being plural, does not cease to be unitary." Only modern Russia, claims Freyre, exhibits a similar interplay of unity and diversity in a large space continuum. China has not the "ethnic multiplicity" of Brazil. In the United States the "mystique of Americanization" devours devours cultural idiosyncrasies. Brazil's own "mystique of Brazilianization" allows for pluralistic accommodation of many cultures to tropical America, from Europe, Africa, the Near East, and the Orient. The continuing diversity of these subcultures, Freyre maintains, is acclaimed rather than deplored by the average Brazilian as well as by the intellectual.[3]

Freyre's historical works have the quality of a lush tropical symphony that celebrates the confused jostling of natural and human landscapes, of ethnic types, of social groups, of historical moments, in an exuberant Brazilian subcontinent. He is attentive to even the most unlikely human elements. We might expect, for instance, that within the

---

* *South Atlantic Quarterly*, 61:159–182 (1962). Reprinted by permission of the author and the original publisher.

[1] Rogert Bastide, *Brésil—terre des contrastes* (Paris, 1957), p. 290.

[2] *Ibid.*, p. 85.

[3] Gilberto Freyre, *Brasis, Brasil e Brasília* (Lisbon, 1960), pp. 13–14.

"Luso-tropical" continuum a personage so jarring as the sober, frock-coated English engineer or commercial consul of the last century would receive cool or frankly derisive treatment. How else could he be woven into the rich tapestry of Indian and Negro slaves, mulatto concubines, lethargic grand ladies in their hammocks, authoritarian plantation-owners, magniloquent politicians, and the latter-day streams of immigrants from Italy, from Spain, from Japan? Yet Freyre gives us a lengthy volume entitled *Englishmen in Brazil*,[4] the first page of which promises two more books on the same theme. It is an affectionate chronicle of the outlandish contributions of the English to tropical Brazil (railroads, streetcars, gas lighting, steamboats, sewage systems), and of their unpronounceable additions to the mellifluous Portuguese of the country in such words as *yacht, knickerbocker, bungalow, goalkeeper,* and *high-life.* Whatever criticisms he may hold in reserve about commercialism, racial intolerance, and emotional inhibitions in the society from which the Englishman comes, Freyre describes Brazil as a charmed land where even the dour figure of the British consular agent becomes humanized and responsive.

Writers who take such a point of departure strive not so much toward uttering a "thesis" about Brazilian history as toward defining the *mise en scène,* or the manifold, within which the nation's historical development has occurred. The orchestration of the Brazilian symphony is of concern, rather than its melodic line.

Quite evidently, the notion of contrast and unity needs historical elucidation for it to serve as a threshold to the understanding of Brazilian civilization. For there is scarcely any national history which has not at some time been construed in dialectical fashion, if we except those monolithic societies of the imminent future of which Orwell, Huxley, and Zamiatin have been the prophets. European philosophies of history, most notably the Hegelian, have in fact long been available to provide the guidelines for such speculation. A consideration of Brazil will therefore flow more easily after a preliminary comparison. The one with Mexico, Latin America's largest country save for Brazil, comes readily to mind.

Using the title of Simpson's *Many Mexicos*[5] as a chapter heading, Howard Cline has drawn a concise picture of Mexico's regional diversity.[6] He distinguishes between the *patria chica* (the family or village grouping outside of which the average Mexican is "a stranger in a puzzling world"), the larger region (each with its characteristic ethos and human geography), and finally the Republic as a whole. The principal outlying regions are the south of Mexico (semitropical, "overwhelmingly Indian and agricultural," relatively free in its history from agrarian unrest); the west (Catholic, nationalistic, more creole than Indian, conservative yet susceptible of integration into the national scene); and the north (long a frontier area of hostile Indians and large haciendas; scene of lively economic development). The hub of these regions is the great Mexican plateau. Since long before the Conquest this "Core" has contained half the people of Mexico. Its metropolis, Mexico City, built on the ruins of Tenochtitlán, has a continuous history dating from at least 1325. The massive core—which is both highly modern and, outside of the cities, still primitive and traditional—has mediated between the other regions and the Western World. It thus dominates Mexican history and, even more so, Mexican historiography.

Throughout Brazilian historiography, on the other hand, regional differences receive consistent notice, even though they are in some respects less dramatic than those of Mexico. Southey's classic history of Brazil[7] and the modern history of the Jesuits in Brazil by Serafim Leite[8] are simply two exam-

---

[4] Gilberto Freyre, *Ingleses no Brasil* (Rio de Janeiro, 1948).

[5] Leslie B. Simpson, *Many Mexicos* (3rd ed.; Berkeley, 1952).

[6] Howard F. Cline, *The United States and Mexico* (Cambridge, 1953), pp. 88–111.

[7] Robert Southey, *History of Brazil* (3 vols.; London, 1810–1819).

[8] Serafim Leite, *História da Companhia de Jesus no Brasil* (10 vols.; Lisbon and Rio de Janeiro, 1938–1950).

ples of an exclusively region-by-region treatment. In considering Brazilian regionalism, of course, we should remember the difference in scale. Brazil could contain four Mexicos, with room left over for Chile. The Amazon region alone has space for two Mexicos. It is the immensity of Brazil and, to a large degree, its vegetation (the rain forests and the spiny *caatinga* of the backlands) which have hindered the knitting together of the nation—not, as with Mexico, the volcanic thrusting up of the land itself.

For summary purposes, the regions of Brazil can be described as seven.[9] First, the vast Amazon basin—kingdom of the rain forests and the rubber tapper, last holdout of the forest Indians, sometimes called the steaming land of the seventh day of creation. Second, the "polygon of drought," lying athwart the eastern bulge of Brazil, cutting from Ceará south and inland into Bahia— the famous *sertão* or backlands, a sunbroiled land of stone, sand, and spiny shrubs, a civilization of beef and hides, of strait-laced families, of messianic and penitential religion. Third, the historic sugar coast, stretching around the eastern promontory and south to Rio de Janeiro—the cradle of settlement, government, and civilization, domain of the plantation and its "big house," the *casa grande*, semitropical, African Brazil as well as cosmopolitan, seaboard Brazil.

Fourth, inland from the southern sugar coast, the mountainous mining area, scene of conflict after the first gold strikes, source of fleeting splendor for eighteenth-century Portugal. Amoroso Lima calls Minas Gerais a kind of Brazilian Switzerland, a point of compensation and equilibrium in the nation, a social and psychological resting-point. Social, because historically it has been a focus of attraction for migrations, not a center of radiation like Ceará in the north and São Paulo in the south. Psychological, because the inhabitant, the *mineiro*, is turned in upon himself, spiritually concentrated; his will conquers his imagination; his revolutionary spirit is easily snuffed out by good sense or good humor; he opposes fanaticism with passive resistance and, in the Chestertonian spirit, resorts to "boycott by epigram." The key to the history of Minas is the centripetalism and concentration which the activity of mining aptly symbolizes.[10]

A fifth region is the modern frontier, site of the new national capital, the just-awakening states of Goiás and Mato Grosso, heartland of the whole South American continent. Sometimes called the Brazilian Far West, this zone contains almost one quarter of Brazil's area but only 4 per cent of the population. It has a comfortable climate and and open plateaus, in spite of the name "Mato Grosso" (dense forest.) Sixth is the rich *paulista* coffee region, centering on the metropolis of São Paulo, largest city in the nation. In colonial times this zone was little more than a subsistence economy which sent roaming bands (*bandeiras*) of Europeans, mestizos, and Indians throughout the whole of modern Brazil in search of gold, emeralds, and Indian slaves. It was in effect almost autonomous of the sugar coast. A century ago São Paulo began to prosper from coffee, and soon thereafter to attract immigration from southern and central Europe, later from the Slavic countries and the Near East, finally from Japan. If Minas is the balance wheel of Brazil, it has been said, industrial São Paulo is the motor. Finally, there is the southernmost region, and in particular the sweeping pampas with their horse and cattle culture, colonized much later than the coastal area. Although Brazil borders on all but two of the other South American countries, Rio Grande do Sul is the only social and cultural frontier with any of them.

Picking up the comparison, it would be idle to speculate whether Mexico or Brazil is more highly differentiated, although one point deserves mention. It is that the cultural spectrum of Mexico still offers sharp discontinuities between the Occidental or creole culture and the vestiges of autochthonous culture. As late as 1940, one Mexican in eight spoke an Indian tongue, a ratio which

[9] See Manuel Diégues Júnior, *Regiões culturais do Brasil* (Rio de Janeiro, 1960).

[10] Alceu Amoroso Lima, *Voz de Minas* (2nd ed.; Rio de Janeiro, 1946).

increased to one in three in the southern region. In Brazil, the Indians have been wholly absorbed, except for the relatively few forest Indians who still live outside civilization. The population as a whole, despite its great heterogeneity of origin, dwells more nearly within a single culture continuum than Mexico's.

For an understanding of Brazilian history, however, to determine the scale of regional diversity is less important than to recognize the configuration and interplay of the regions. Remembering the case of Mexico, we observe that Brazil has had no monolithic core, no dominant metropolis. So true is this that Rio de Janeiro, the capital from 1763 till 1960, could with equal justification be said to lie in any of three regions. It can be considered the southern terminus of the coastal sugar plain, the seaboard outlet for the central mining area, or the northern limit of the coffee-industrial complex centering on São Paulo state. In 1827, when Brazil's first two law academies were created, soon to become its foremost intellectual centers, one was established in São Paulo and one in Recife—neither one in the capital. The recent transfer of the national capital to the interior, in some ways an extravagant piece of showmanship, was not wholly a fancy of the moment but the fruition of a scheme which had been in the air for at least seventy years. Freyre has criticized the "messianic" building of Brasília not on principle but with respect to its execution. The work is too much that of urbanists and architects. Geographers, sociologists, anthropologists, and biologists have not had their say. Brasília should be a work of "tropical ecology"; it should enlarge "the perspective of a Brazil truly interregional in its manner of being a Nation."[11]

It might not be farfetched to develop our point by applying, on a national scale, the sociological notions of mechanical and organic solidarity. The typical Spanish-American county is centrally dominated and controlled by a single city, to which other cities and regions stand in direct and subordinate relation. Peru, for example, has been called an immense spider, with Lima its overgrown body and the rest of the country its cold and shriveled legs. Montevideo is often called a suction pump that mercilessly draws off the vital energies of Uruguay. In Brazil there exists more in the way of a shifting equilibrium of regions, signalized by the two transfers of the national capital. Many a Spanish-American historian has thought that he has written a national history by chronicling events in Buenos Aires, Lima, Havana, or Mexico City. It is difficult to name a historian of Brazil who has been similarly misguided. In short, the regionalism of Brazil has been more to the historian than a subterranean presence. And while it may not offer such sharp contrasts as in Mexico or Peru, the alternative to recognizing it has been found less plausible. For example, a standard method of setting forth Brazilian economic history is to construe it as a function of the country's regional economic cycles: first, in the early sixteenth century, the cutting of dyewood along the coast; soon afterward, the planting of sugar along the same coast, followed in the eighteenth century by the rush on the mines in the central inland section. The nineteenth century brought the coffee boom on the São Paulo plateau, south of Minas; the late nineteenth and early twentieth brought the spectacular but less important Amazon rubber boom. In the contemporary period this, like most other unilinear schemes of history, broadens from a river into a delta—although the industrial development of the Rio-São Paulo area is certainly one of its main channels.

This view of Brazilian history reminds us that the principal economic epochs, except for the industrial boom, hinge upon commodities sold on the world market. Production of these commodities has done little to integrate the nation, and its internal economic development has proceeded as a series of passive and geographically scattered responses to possibilities of the world market. This is one reason why the North-American version of the frontier has no counterpart in Brazil as a whole, but only within certain local

[11] "Brasília" in Freyre's *Brasis, Brasil e Brasília*, pp. 151–172.

areas of productivity, most notably the coffee region. Even these local frontiers have been called "hollow," for they often advance swiftly without leaving behind balanced and prosperous patterns of settlement. It has never been easy to envision a "Brazilian system" comparable to the "American system" which John Calhoun described in 1817 as making "the parts adhere more closely" and forming "a new and most powerful cement."

Having examined aspects of Brazilian regionalism, we may pose the question of Brazilian national unity. Why did Portuguese America—roughly a third of modern Latin America in size and population—remain single while Spanish America split into what are now eighteen republics? This is a final-examination sort of question which can lead to an indiscriminate listing of factors and circumstances. Only three points will be made here, in an effort to suggest the complexion of Brazilian unity rather than to set forth an exhaustive causal analysis.

First, as the historian Sérgio Buarque de Holanda points out, and as the eighteenth-century French Jesuit Lafitau had observed before him, the Spanish conquest was a single epic of imperial design, elaborated in a variety of local episodes from Mexico to the River Plata.[12] Yet that very epic was produced by a country which, even after the conquest of Granada, could itself scarcely have been called unitary. The Spaniards' passion for uniformity and symmetry—revealed in the shape of their New World cities, their restrictions upon emigration of foreigners and non-believers to America, the elaborate casuistry of their great law code for the Indies, which sought to foresee and prescribe for all contingencies—did not this very passion compensate for the separatism of a people whose nationhood rested as much upon fiat as upon fact? The Portuguese in Brazil, says the historian, acted "through quite unconnected interventions, in a large number of diverse regions, obeying different leaders who often held conflicting ideas and displayed neither coherence nor perserverance: a kind of chaos, in short, in which no unity exists, beyond the circumstance that

these actions, ideas and leaders come from the same nation."[13] Portugal, which basked in a national unity achieved in the thirteenth century, imparted no such imperial design as did Spain to New World colonization. Whereas, for example, the Spanish crown maintained permanent inquisitorial tribunals, in Lima, Mexico City, and Cartagena, the Holy Office made only two brief visits to Brazil, both of them during the sixty years when the kings of Spain ruled Portugal as well.

The point is not that the settlers of Brazil harbored a sense of national unity, inherited from the mother country, but rather that their collective life was less dominated by the emblems, codifications, and hierarchical officialdom of imperial, metropolitan Europe. Brazilian institutions developed more freely in response to their New World setting—and interacted more freely with each other. It has become a commonplace in Brazilian history and sociology to say that until well into the nineteenth century the dominant institution was the self-sufficient extended family of rural Brazil, sometimes called the clan. This was much less true of Spanish America, where, except in outlying regions, one feels the paramount institution to have been the Spanish crown, and the various lines of civil and ecclesiastical offices through which its powers were somewhat hesitantly delegated. Upon the crown, ultimately, depended the cohesion of the realm. Here again, the Durkheimian analogue of mechanical and organic solidarity is illuminating. In Spanish America, the parts of society—the *encomiendas*, town governments, Indian villages, merchant gilds, religious orders—depended more clearly and continuously upon the favor of the crown and its deputies. Those very deputies, in fact—the viceroys, captains-general, intendants and, since the church was virtually a national one, the high prelates—had recourse to the crown for definition of their sometimes conflicting prerogatives. In Bra-

[12] UNESCO, *El Viejo y el Nuevo Mundo—sus relaciones culturales y espirituales* (Paris, 1956), pp. 201–218.

[13] *Ibid.*, pp. 209–210.

zil, certainly, this medieval tradition of the protective, arbitrating crown lingered on, but the machinery which might have given it effect worked only fitfully. For example, conflicts between municipal councils and Jesuit missionaries were a constant theme of colonial history, and often took their course without bureaucratic intervention. In both northern and southern Brazil the townsmen of certain communities banished the Jesuit order for years at a time. The status of the Indian in Brazilian society was worked out in different places and at different times under relatively little influence from royal decrees and scholastic controversy in the mother country. Finally, one can mention the *bandeiras*, which, as well as playing an exploring and colonizing role, served as a kind of autonomous striking force, subject to local control, that went into action against Jesuit missions in Paraguay, against the Dutch invaders, and against Palmares, the so-called republic of runaway Negroes.

A second source of national cohesion lies in the economy of the New World rather than the institutional inheritance from the Old. We have said that the axis of the colonial Brazilian economy was the export to Europe of tropical agricultural products and, in the eighteenth century, precious minerals —these in return for manufactures and African slaves. Complementing and making possible this commerce, however, was an internal movement of jerked beef and other foodstuffs, hides, and cash commodities in transhipment which has only a modest place in colonial statistics, yet which inconspicuously served to articulate those very regions which production for export appeared to isolate one from another. Here again, the point is not that internal trade was wholly lacking in Spanish America, but that in Brazil it did not center, cartwheel fashion, upon a principal city, nor was it funneled through a few principal ports.

Internal Brazilian trade was contained within four main systems. In the north, the vast Amazon river system. In the northeast, a system of routes, often making use of riverbanks, which spread out from the modern state of Piauí. Essentially, this system made possible overland transit between Maranhão and Ceará, north of the "bulge," and Bahia, under the shoulder of it. The component routes brought cattle from scattered backlands areas to the coastal markets. Their more historic function was to articulate the backlands and interconnect their settlements.

They permitted those mass displacements and migrations, so common during the periodic droughts. . . . The routes of communication described contributed to melt and intermix all the disparate elements which make up the composition of the backlands population, who, coming from diverse and greatly distant points, were little by little entering into communication and contact.[14]

In the south-central area there were a number of subsystems leading inland to Minas Gerais, Goiás, and Mato Grosso. And finally, there were the southern routes, which had as their axis the highroad from São Paulo south to Rio Grande do Sul. Because of the difficult access to Rio Grande by sea, it was in large measure this highroad that made possible the colonization of southernmost Brazil in the second half of the eighteenth century and its eventual absorption into Portuguese America.

It is not to be forgotten that the spinal column of the Brazilian transportation system was coastal shipping along the Atlantic seaboard. This became less important, however, as the overland routes penetrated inland, ramified, and became interconnected. Furthermore, the northwest trade winds made sea traffic around the "bulge" extremely difficult, a condition which led to the establishment of a separate state of Maranhão on the northern coast in 1621. By the end of the eighteenth century, the elaboration of a system of internal land and river routes promised to knit together most of the settled areas of the country. The introduction of steam navigation in the next century, however, gave new impetus to maritime shipping, interrupting the process of internal consolidation.

[14] Caio Prado Júnior, *Formação do Brasil contemporâneo—colônia* (2nd ed.; São Paulo, 1945), p. 241.

The inland routes described were by no means highroads paved for rapid travel by stagecoach or pony express. Many were barely passable by man or beast even during the dry season. Bridges were almost unknown. Oxcarts were in general use only on the flat plains of Rio Grande do Sul. Elsewhere wheeled transportation was impossible save in limited areas. The principal means of conveyance were mule teams of twenty to fifty animals which adhered to surprisingly regular schedules and charged fixed prices; trains of several hundred oxen; and convoys of slaves traveling on foot. Although the government established a few posthouses along the main routes for travelers, most of the shelters were built by local landowners, who charged nothing for lodging but did a brisk business in the corn which sustained their masters. Until well into the nineteenth century, mules were the most important pack animal. Their breeding and sale helped to create a network of traffic covering southern and central Brazil as far as Bahia. Each year as many as 30,000 mules would be herded from Rio Grande to the great fair at Sorocaba in São Paulo for distribution to all points except the far north.

Without further details, the point may be made that by the time of its independence in 1822, Brazil's principal regions of settlement—the coast, the backlands, the mining area, and the cattle plains in the south—were achieving complementariness in the exchange of the products of farm, ranch, and mine, an exchange made possible by a growing tissue of land and river routes. The primitive nature of these routes was compensated by their adequacy to the means of transportation available, the insignificant cost of their maintenance, and the advantages gained from their decentralization and from the ease with which they could be extended to new or bypassed settlements. The introduction of railroads after the mid-nineteenth century had something of the same rigidifying effect upon Brazilian transportation as did steam navigation. The creation of a limited number of rail arteries, which had to be fed by shipment in large bulk, not only interrupted the tissue-like growth of more primitive transportation, but often caused commercial stagnation in the interstitial areas. By then, however, Brazilian unity could rest upon other foundations.

A third factor contributing to the cohesion of the nation, the last to be discussed, was the nature of the leadership under which Brazil made the transition to independence and eventually to republican government. At the risk of a severely narrowed focus, we shift from the plane of institutions to that of persons, where the fate of emergent Latin-American nations so often balances precariously. On this score it does not suffice to dwell upon the historical accident that Prince John, later John VI, escaped the Napoleonic invasion and fled overseas. For had a member of the Spanish Bourbon family established him or herself in Spanish America, it is problematical whether a smoother transition and a milder degree of territorial fragmentation would, in the long run, have been achieved in those lands. This I think is so, even had the claimant been a more plausible figure than Ferdinand VII, and even if we limit consideration to a single more manageable region, such as the Platine region, the Andean region, or Mexico and the isthmus.

In the case of Brazil, what is important is that the king and later the emperor were not imbued with the kind of mystique—that is, with the sanction of ancient tradition, of royal prerogative, of the Christian faith itself—which many claim could have been the only binding force for the anarchy and separatism of nineteenth-century Spanish America. Brazil under the Braganças has been called a "crowned republic," and one Brazilian historian has written:

Really, we never shared the belief in the divine right of kings. . . . The principle of monarchy reached us when it was already losing its aura of sacredness. The king was not, when we became a nation, the "anointed of the Lord" . . .; he was, on the contrary, a privileged person, whose privilege was discussed, combatted, denied.[15]

[15] F. J. de Oliveira Vianna, *O occaso do imperio* (2nd ed.; São Paulo, n.d.), p. 203.

When the Brazilian empire was finally abolished in 1889, the then president of Venezuela remarked, "The only republic that existed in America has been done away with: the Empire of Brazil."[16]

The first of the Braganças in Brazil, who became John VI in 1816, was described as follows by Euclides da Cunha:

Dom John VI, a mediocrity, was predestined. Averse to acts of bravery, an ingenuous and accommodating soul, endowed with bourgeois placability, dejected by the disorders of an unhappy home, saddened by the figure of the old queen mother, Dona Maria I, who had gone mad— inertia and narrow vision were his leading characteristics. They allowed him to act with single purpose upon the spirit and will of a few superior men who fortunately surrounded him.[17]

For all of the muddleheadedness and procrastination which historians attribute to King John, he managed, during the dozen or so years of his Brazilian sojourn, to expand the nation's territory by conquest; to open Brazilian ports to trade of friendly countries; to create the nation's first bank; to sponsor the first attempts at industrialization and at colonization by non-Iberians; to establish a royal printing press; to invite a mission of French artists to the country; to found military and medical schools and a botanical garden. As the time was not yet ripe for economic development and immigration, it was probably those measures for urbanizing and sophisticating Rio da Janeiro —and, by contagion, the other cities of Brazil—which had the strongest catalytic effect. John even went so far as to abolish the jalousies of Rio house-fronts, traditional symbol of patriarchal seclusion and of the agrarian foundations of the culture. At the very moment, therefore, when the fragmented Spanish-American countries were getting rid of vice-regal pomp and panoply, and falling, many of them, under caudillo leadership of popular origin, Brazil received those endowments of urban civilization and courtly life which it had so far lacked.

Indecisive and apprehensive till the last, King John returned to Portugal in 1821, and his son, Pedro, declared Brazilian independence the following year. Unlike most or all of the other American nations, Brazil produced no outstanding national hero at the time of independence. One can of course write it off as an accident of history that no Washington or Bolívar or Toussaint L'Ouverture was waiting in the wings. Or, one may speculate that because there was no all-out war against the mother country, and because the ruling dynasty was transferred to Brazil, there existed no crucible of violence and nationalism to forge a leader symbolizing the personality and freedom and aspirations of the newborn country. I cannot help but draw from this fact, however, the homespun moral that Brazil has never had all of her eggs in one basket. Nor can I help but regard the lack of a national hero as symptomatic of a rather elusive quality of Brazilian history itself. For nineteenth-century Brazil turned out to be a Catholic country which had as its regent for a while a priest who opposed clerical celibacy; a country whose Catholic emperor would have preferred being president of a republic, and who acquiesced in the imprisonment of two honorable but zealous bishops; an empire which was turned into a republic by an army coup d'etat; and a slavocracy whose slaveholders formed abolitionist societies. There are tonalities to Brazilian national life which are neither caught up in fixed symbols nor properly encompassed in stereotyped notions about such institutions as the church, the army, the government, and the plantation in Latin America.

The two protagonists of Brazilian independence each had important qualities for leadership. Pedro I, who was twenty-four when he declared the country's freedom, had the dash, handsomeness, and physical prowess of Venezuela's Simón Bolívar; he was a natural, highly personalistic leader of much native intelligence; his sentimental life was impetuous; he moved as easily among the commonest people as among those of his station. In declaring Brazil an empire rather than a kingdom, he did so to acknowledge a

[16] José Maria dos Santos, A política geral do Brasil (São Paulo, 1930), p. 11 n.
[17] Euclydes da Cunha, A marjem da historia (Oporto, 1909), p. 262.

popular base of political support and not merely to enhance his own public image.

José Bonifácio de Andrada, Pedro's principal counselor at the at the moment of independence, was a scientist, schooled in the Enlightenment. He had been director of mines in Norway, established the chair of mineralogy at the University of Coimbra, and served as lieutenant-colonel against the Napoleonic troops in Portugal. He was a man of outstanding intellect, a leader and organizer, and a constitutionalist in politics with fundamentally conservative leanings—although progressive in his plans for social and economic improvement. Like the emperor whom he briefly served, he could be vindictive and intolerant of criticism.

One might say that these men exhibited two sets of traits which, in the case of Simón Bolívar, were combined. Pedro had physique, bravado, and personal charm. José Bonifácio had a superior intellectual sense of political purpose and a mature vision of national institutions. Bonifácio was the architect and Pedro the agent of Brazilian independence. In 1823, shortly after this fruitful collaboration, José Bonifácio and his brothers resigned from the government and were exiled. As Oliveira Lima once wrote, ". . . the personal relations between Dom Pedro and José Bonifácio . . . had consisted rather in the conjunction of two energies that in the sympathy of two personalities."[18] With the constituent assembly dissolved and the reins in his own hands, Pedro named a commission of ten to draw up the Constitution, famous for the so-called Moderating Power accorded to the emperor, which he imposed on the nation in 1824.

We are addressing, let me emphasize, only the question of leadership at the time of independence, and how that leadership successfully mediated between the practical requirements of the moment, the articulated aspirations of the few, and the shapeless desires of the larger multitude. In Brazil, as in any Latin-American country after independence, a government had to meet four specifications if the society were not to fall upon the rocks of despotic or oligarchical caudillismo, or the shoals of disintegrated

authority and anarchic factionalism. These specifications were legitimacy, constitutionalism, nationalism, and personalism. That is, a new government, coming on the heels of three centuries of Catholic monarchical rule, the ultimate authority of which had never been questioned, needed that very aura of legitimacy which Metternich was then preaching in Europe. Second, it had to be constitutional, given the example set by the United States, and given a penetration of Enlightenment ideas that was deeper than in many corners of Europe. Third, it had to embody a popular aspiration toward democratic national sovereignty. And finally, given a situation of political inexperience and incipient social chaos, a new government could be institutionalized only by the astute intervention of strong personalist leadership.

Needless to say, these four elements were difficult to orchestrate. Legitimacy generally meant a European prince (except to those who envisioned a restoration of the Incas), yet this was hard to square with nationalism, or with the need for shrewd personalistic leadership. Personalism and constitutionalism were of course uneasy bedfellows—for, as Machiavelli long ago observed in his *Discourses on Livy*, the charismatic leader who establishes a constitutional regime must, like the old soldier, be willing to fade away.

In Brazil all of the four requirements were met. To the legitimacy of his Bragança lineage Dom Pedro gave popular, nationalist sanction by consulting with local leaders on the eve of independence; by acting under the advice of José Bonifácio, who was rabidly anti-Portuguese; and by declaring Brazil an empire in something of Napoleon's spirit. Then, at the critical moment, when factionalism threatened to impede the process of constitutionmaking, Pedro packed the Andrada brothers off to Portugal and—in personalistic style that would have pleased Machiavelli—promulgated a constitution. From then on his leadership faltered. His demo-

---

[18] M. Oliveira Lima, *Formación histórica de la nacionlidad brasileña* (Madrid, 1918), p. 190.

cratic convictions could never be reconciled with his authoritarian temperament, and in 1831 he abdicated in obedience to pressure for responsible government from the soldiery and the populace. Luckily, exile was made palatable by the fact that there awaited him in Portugal the task of rescuing the crown from his usurping brother. As his successor, Pedro left in Brazil his five-year-old son, who came under the tutelage of José Bonifácio, now returned. The decade of the regency which followed placed the fate of the nation, the further elaboration of its constitution, and the handling of separatist revolts squarely in Brazilian hands. When Pedro II assumed power in 1840, he did so as an eminently Brazilian monarch. This retelling of Brazilian independence is neither fresh nor complete. Its object is simply to draw attention to the complex and delicate balance of elements that was necessary to produce, stable, constitutional government in nineteenth-cenury Latin America, and to suggest that the transplantation of the Bragança line to Rio de Janeiro was but one of these ingredients.

That the political system devised in Brazil during the 1820's and 1830's was workable could by no means be taken for granted when Pedro II reached his majority in 1840. The classic analysis of just how order, stability, and progress *were* achieved during the half century of his reign was made by Joaquim Nabuco in his biography of his father,[19] one of the leading nineteenth-century statesmen. The picture is a more intricate one than emerges if we classify Dom Pedro simply as a benevolent and enlightened despot. Benevolent he was, enlightened also, and, if not despotic, he was certainly paternalistic and made full use of the moderating power allowed him by the constitution. It was he personally who decided the ascendancy of each political party and of each leader. "To oppose him, his plans, his policy, was to renounce power. . . . As the cabinets were short-lived and he was permanent, only he could make long-term policy; only he could wait, temporize, continue, delay, and plant seeds to be harvested later, at the proper time."[20]

Under such circumstances, what then marked Dom Pedro as something more, or something less, than an enlightened despot, making free and arbitrary use of his power? It was, said Nabuco, "the sacrament of form."[21] Never did he step from his role as constitutional monarch; never did he violate the usages and fictions of the English parliamentary system. Furthermore, the policy lines worked out under his aegis were not his own creation. "He was merely the clock, the regulator; he told the time or set the rhythm." He determined the limits within which policy would be formulated; he took the sounding on either side of the channel which was being navigated. He was not the inspiration but the conscience of governmental action. He examined each appointment, each decree, each word of his ministers. But he left responsibility to them. He almost never intervened in the political parties, and maintained direct, personal relations only with their leaders, who would some day be ministers. As one Brazilian summed it up, "The Emperor spent fifty years pretending that he governed a free people."

If Brazilian elections were not really free, if there was no electoral force capable of supporting ministers in the event of an appeal to the people, this was the fault of the parties themselves, not of the emperor. The parties were little more than alliances of the great clans jockeying to capture the central power. Platforms and expressed opinion borrowed the rhetoric formulated in Europe and North America, which gave them an artificial, derivative character. Underlying such rhetoric there did not exist the native foundations for ideological conflict, even in so rudimentary a form as the antagonism between rural and urban interests. Far from being arbitrary in using his power of dismissal, Dom Pedro kept one ear open to popular opinion—such as it was—and the other to the logical necessities of each situation. In meetings with his ministers he played devil's

[19] Joaquim Nabuco, *Um estadista do império* (4 vols.; São Paulo, 1949).
[20] *Ibid.*, IV, 103.
[21] *Ibid.*, IV, 108 ff.

advocate, clarifying issues, citing precedents, furnishing information from his wide experience. He was careful to leave his ministers free to dispense patronage and to carry out the ideas which they had supported while in the opposition. In some areas, such as finances or legal questions, he rarely if ever intervened.

Nabuco's interpretation of Dom Pedro's methods appears to have every virtue but that of credibility. For the skeptic will ask, wasn't this simply another South American caudillo, garbed in imperial robes and managing the country with unusual tact and decorum? And those who accept Dom Pedro as a kind of national conscience, who applaud his unimpeachable public and private morality, who congratulate him for an intellect which ranged widely if it did not soar to heights—such devotees will be hard put to explain why it was that the emperor was not thrown out bag and baggage years ago, decades before the republican coup of 1889. For the question is, if a South American ruler has moral fiber and the courage of his convictions, if he is innocent of political chicanery, if he is broadly informed as to the scientific and material progress of the Western world and is anxious for his own country to share that progress—if we grant him these attributes and interests, how can we imagine his not coming to grief within a quasi-feudal setting where the familial organization of society and its systems of privilege would offer continuing resistance to rationalistic schemes of reform and institutional rearrangement? In short, we posit a man of high principles, moral courage, and an up-to-date knowledge of the drift of the Western world. How can such a man have the *patience* not to devise and attempt to impose sweeping reforms of the political, social, and economic orders, reforms which might well have cost him his throne years earlier? How, psychologically, did he keep to his role as a national conscience, and never assume that of social engineer?

What I take to be the answer to this question is suggested in the letters of Dom Pedro to the Countess of Barral.[22] The Countess had been the governess of the emperor's children and was twenty years older than he. Although Pedro's letters to her are always correct and there is little reason to believe that there existed any improper relation between them, one detects as the years pass a surge of yearning, indeed of sentimentality, that permeates the recital of daily thoughts and doings. We receive the impression that this elderly and accomplished lady was the symbol of both maternity and romance to an aging monarch who had enjoyed neither the tender comfort of a mother nor the comforting tendernesses of sentimental adventures. To the emotional life of Dom Pedro there had been no center and no fulfillment. His mother had died when he was an infant, and his gorgeous stepmother, Amelia of Leuchtenberg, left Brazil with his father in 1831. The sober statesmen and the Swiss governess who brought him up—and who warned him against emulating the erotic improperties of his father—were a pale substitute for maternal understanding. While he was still a youth, his marriage was arranged with Princess Teresa Cristina of Naples, to whom he was always a devoted husband. But she did little to kindle in him those flames of romantic passion which had nearly consumed his father. When Pedro went to greet the princess aboard the frigate which brought her to Brazil and found her to be short, lame, and four years older than he, he sank into nervous collapse. "I don't like her!" he sobbed. "Send her away!"[23]

Although conscientious to a fault in performing his public duties and in improving his mind, Dom Pedro lived as though the mainspring of his affective life had snapped. What more romantic career can we imagine than the emperorship of a tropical Latin country? Yet Pedro seemed rather bored with the possibilities. He remarked that he would gladly have given up his crown and scepter for the frock coat of the president of a constitutional republic. In the letters to the Countess Barral, indeed, one senses that Pedro very nearly bored himself to death. He attended endless oral examinations at

[22] Alcindo Sodré, *Abrindo um cofre* (Rio de Janeiro, 1956).
[23] *Ibid.*, p. 11.

the famous secondary school in Rio which bore his name, at the Polytechnic School, at the military schools. He went to fortnightly meetings of the Historical and Geographical Institute. He studied such forbidding languages as Hebrew, Arabic, and Sanskrit.

The strain of apathy and fatalism in Pedro's character intensified during the last years of his reign. His eventual exile was by no means imposed by the ardent will of the people. Until the very end of his reign, it was generally assumed that he would die in office. But when the military overthrow came, Pedro acquiesced as though it were an event long before decreed by fate. We have the image of Pedro at the moment of exile as an octogenarian patriarch, a kind of equatorial King Lear, leaving the shores of a silent and ungrateful realm. There has even appeared a Freudian analysis of the event which purports to detect a complex of guilt shared by Brazilian leaders of the 1890's.[24]

In appearance, certainly, Dom Pedro was a patriarch, and that was the public role which he played. But he was not an octogenarian; he was only sixty-four when he left Brazil. He had grown old before his time—had never perhaps been young. Nor did he have the inner character of a patriarch. For, we imagine as a patriarch someone who has lived through the full round of a strenuous and emotionally forceful life and who continues to dominate his world with charismatic leadership and Mosaic utterances. In this sense Pedro was a patriarch *manqué*. He looked and moved and was accepted as a patriarch. But he lacked the primordial zest, the craggy nobility, the eternal slyness which the role when fully played demands. Dom Pedro was more an image than a presence on the Brazilian scene more a conscience than a will—or, to use the Freudian terms into which we inevitably lapse nowadays, more a superego than an ego.

If these reflections do anything to elucidate the character of Pedro II, they perhaps help to explain by implication his remarkable achievement in giving Brazil a stable, orderly, yet adaptable government during

the span of half a century. By the 1880's, however, the tempo of national life was accelerating; contacts of every order with the outside world were multiplying; the technology of the nineteenth century was making its impact; the national spectrum of political ideology was expanding. The dignified ballet of parliamentary cabinets, alternating at the cautious command of an aging emperor, was not sufficiently responsive to the rhythms and imperatives of the century soon to be born. The social and material progress for which the Brazilian positivists clamored was not developing at the proper pace. If the exiling of Pedro was somewhat fortuitous, the demise of the empire was not.

Let us now recapitulate the rather disparate lines of our perspective on Brazilian history. We began with the frequently made assertion that Brazil is a land of contrasts, stressing the aspect of human and economic geography—though importance should also be given to the range and diversity of the social structure and substructures, to forces of political separatism which recurrently rise to the surface, to glaring disparities of economic and technological development, and to the varieties of religious life. The fact of Brazilian unity needed no elaboration. Portuguese America remained one country while Spanish America became eighteen. Brazil's political development has been peaceful. The transitions to independence, to the republic, even in and out of dictatorship, have been relatively bloodless. There is no counterpart in Brazil to either the American Revolution or the American Civil War.

Some commentators, having stated this thesis, leave the antinomy planted on its back, its two feet waving in the air. Others describe the tone of human relations in Brazil as the factor of reconciliation. Referring to antecedents in Portuguese national character, they speak of the warmth and intimacy of Brazilian religion; the tendency of Brazilians to resolve the cold ideology of politics into the give-and-take of personal relations; the ready wit of the Brazilian, ever

[24] Luis Martins, *O patriarca e o bacharel* (São Paulo, 1953).

alert to prick the balloons of arrogance and pomposity; the tolerance of Brazilians in race relations. The explanation by national character, however, will be left for the novelist at the end of this essay.

In our highly selective treatment we have stressed institutional history and, within it, the accident of leadership. We have said that the Portuguese colonial system was less layered than the Spanish, that it allowed for more grass-roots adjustment to the New World. We have said that the intensive production of certain export crops did not preclude the tissue-like growth of primitive transportation networks inland from the coast. This allowed the interregional circulation of persons and commodities, and a gradual dispersive pattern of settlement. We have examined the independence period and concluded that, beyond the transference of the Bragança dynasty to Brazil, it was specifically the interaction between Portuguese rulers and Brazilian ministers that was responsible for the smoothness of the transition. A number of players was needed for the success of the drama, and when the presence of any one of them encumbered the movement of the plot, the possibility existed for his temporary or permanent exit. Finally, and continuing our theatrical analogy, we have applauded Dom Pedro II for being an excellent stage manager. Much like the stage manager of Thornton Wilder's play, he created the mood, called the scenes, clarified the action, but never usurped the stage.

Although the word has been used, we are not, then, arguing so much the *unity* of Brazil. We make no claim for a powerful sense of national identity, or an achieved social, political, or economic integration in the face of dramatic contrasts. What *is* suggested is that circumstance and happenstance here combine to create the institutions, the precedents, and the psychological setting for mediating the prodigious contrast and diversity which Brazil, like any Latin-American country, exhibits. And therefore it is the modulation rather than the reconciliation of contrast to which our attention is drawn.

Those secrets of national life which the historian toils so painfully to disclose are often placed within easy reach by the novelist. There is one Brazilian novel, *Esau and Jacob* by Machado de Assis, which appears to be a complex allegory of significance for the political history of Brazil. Rather than undertaking here the delicate task of exegesis, let us single out one episode.[25] Typically Brazilian in its ironic humor, it suggests that the rhetoric, the platforms, the turbulent crosscurrents of public life are ever verging upon an ultimate distillation in human terms.

It seems that the wise and sardonic Ayres, a retired diplomat, was one day savoring his postprandial cigar when Custodio, proprietor of the sweetshop across the street, made a sudden appearance, worried and out of breath. It was in November, 1889, the month of the republican coup d'état.

"What's the matter, Sr. Custodio?" said Ayres. "Are you stirring up revolutions?"

"Me senhor? Ah, senhor, if Your Excellency only knew..."

"If I knew what?"

Custodio explained. He was having a new sign painted for his shop, the "Sweetshop of the Empire." The day before, the painter had already lettered the words "Sweetshop of..." This morning a battalion had marched down the street and there were rumors of a republic. He had rushed a note to the painter: "Stop with 'of'." But it was too late. The sign was already finished: "Sweetshop of the Empire."

Custodio tried to cancel the order, but the painter threatened to display the sign with Custodio's name and address. The revolutionaries would then break his windows. Custodio had to give in. "Devil take the revolution! What name would he use now?" Then he remembered his neighbor Ayres and ran to get his advice.

"Does Your Excellency think," he asked Ayres, "that if I keep the name 'Empire' they'll come break my windows?"

"That I don't know."

"Really, there's no reason; it's been the

[25] José Joaquim Maria Machado de Assis, *Esaú e Jacob* (Rio de Janeiro, 1940), pp. 233–242.

name of the shop for thirty years; nobody knows it by any other name . . ."

"But couldn't you call it 'Sweetshop of the Republic'?"

"I thought of that on my way here, but I also remembered that if there's another turnover in a month or two, I'll be where I am today, and I lose my money again."

Ayres proposed a noncommittal solution: "Sweetshop of the Government." It would serve for either regime.

"I won't say no—except for the extra expense. But there's one thing against it. Your Excellency knows that there is no government without an opposition. When opposition groups come down the street they might take offense, imagine that I'm challenging them and smash my sign. Whereas what I really want is everyone's respect."

Well understanding the terror that accompanied avarice, Ayres produced another idea. "Why not leave the sign painted as it is and, in the righthand corner, under the name 'Sweetshop of the Empire,' have them add 'Founded in 1860'? . . . Or you could leave 'Sweetshop of the Empire' and add beneath it, in the center, the two words 'Of Laws'."

Both ideas were attractive. But then Custodio realized that either addition would have to be in smaller letters. It might go unnoticed by a politician or a personal enemy.

Undaunted, Ayres tried another tack. Why not name it after the street: "The Catete Sweetshop"? But then there was another sweetshop on the same street; customers attracted by Custodio's publicity would enter the first sweetshop they encountered. With heightened respect for a man who reasoned so clearly amid such tribulation, Ayres made his final suggestion. Why not simply call it the "Sweetshop of Custodio"? That was what most people knew it as, anyhow. "A name, the proper name of the owner, had no political meaning or historical significance; it showed neither hate nor love, nothing which would attract the attention of the two regimes, and thus nothing to place in danger the sweet pastries, still less the life of the owner and employees. Why not take that solution? He would spend a little more to change one word for another, Custodio instead of Empire, but revolutions always cause expenditures."

"Yes, I'll think about it, Your Excellency. Perhaps I should wait a day or two, to see what the fashion becomes," said Custodio gratefully.

He bowed, withdrew, and made his exit. Ayres watched him from the window, imagining that Custodio might carry from his house a ray of joy. Life is not all expenditure, and the aura of friendship may soften the bitterness of the world. But this time he made a wrong guess. Custodio crossed the street without stopping or looking behind, and he headed for the sweetshop, immersed in his desperation.

88. New Demographic Research on the Sixteenth Century in Mexico*

WOODROW BORAH AND SHERBURNE F. COOK

The soldiers and missionaries who took part in the conquest of Mexico, or were active shortly after the Conquest, reported that they found a very large aboriginal population in central Mexico. The veracity of their reports has been a hotly debated historical question. Accepting the accuracy of the testimony, some writers have declared that central Mexico; that is, the area from the Isthmus of Tehuantepec to the northern limit of sedentary settlement in 1520, had a pre Conquest population larger than the present rural population. Others have declared that such a population never existed and could not have existed. In a rather strange way, the controversy has become complicated by the attachment of some writers to an idea of progress which requires that at every stage of history there be more people than there were previously.

In recent years attempts have been made to resolve the question by estimating native population in central Mexico during the first century of Spanish rule. Such estimates are possible because the Spanish not only continued the Indian system of levying tribute, but continued it with unusual meticulousness, using written assessments based upon actual counts of the number of adult males or of families. For the earlier half of the sixteenth century such tribute assessments did not normally state the number of people counted. For the second half of the sixteenth century, when the system was overhauled and greatly revised, the tribute assessments increasingly stated the exact number of tribute-payers based upon an explicit definition of tributary. Furthermore, we have runs of assessments for specific towns since there were re-examinations and re-assessments. These materials are supplemented further by careful reporting by missionaries of the numbers of communicants. For the period 1558–1578 the tribute counts and missionary reports for central Mexico probably approach the accuracy of many modern censuses.

In 1948 Cook and Simpson used a large mass of tribute assessments and missionary reports for estimates of the native population of central Mexico during the sixteenth century. They converted tributary males to total population by using a factor of 4.0; that is, husband, wife, and the two children necessary to carry the family forward into the next generation. Their calculation gave them a relatively well authenticated figure for approximately the year 1565. From that, by examination of samples they were able to calculate population at other points in

* Presented at XIth International Congress of Historical Sciences, Stockholm, 1960. A Spanish translation is "La despoblación del México Central en el siglo XVI," *Historia Mexicana*, 12:1–12 (jul.– set. 1960). Reprinted by permission of the author.

the sixteenth and early seventeenth centuries. The population of central Mexico on the eve of the Spanish Conquest, they estimated through examination of reports by missionaries, statements of numbers of warriors, and extrapolation of their figures for the middle of the sixteenth century. For the sake of completeness, they also added calculations for the later colonial period based on the report of the viceregal census of 1793 in Alexander von Humboldt, and upon extrapolation. Their figures are as follows:

1519 . . . . app.	11,000,000
1540	6,427,466
1565	4,409,180
1597 . . . . app.	2,500,000
1607	2,014,000
ca. 1650	1,500,000
1700 . . . . app.	2,000,000
1793	3,700,000

The calculations for 1650, 1700, and 1793 are for total population rather than merely Indians. For the sixteenth century, of course, non-Indian population was virtually negligible.

Publication of the Cook-Simpson estimates, which upheld the reliability of sixteenth-century soldiers and missionaries, evoked a storm of protest. For several years, few meetings could be held by anthropologists and historians on pre-Conquest or colonial Mexico without heated debate on these figures. At one such meeting, an eminent historian declared flatly that, regardless of evidence, he would never accept the view that the brilliance of the Mexican eighteenth century was supported by a smaller population than there had been in the sixteenth century. With the passage of time, however, a number of scholars in Mexico began independent assessments of the data, with curious results. For the Mixteca, one scholar actually arrived at an estimate of pre-Conquest population double the Cook-Simpson figure.

In the meantime, Cook and Simpson continued a series of independent studies on the exploitation of land, soil erosion, and density of settlement, all of which contributed additional and extraordinarily interesting material. Through a study of the records of land grants in the Mexican National Archive for the years 1536 to 1620, Simpson was able to demonstrate that there had occurred in Mexico during those years a massive replacement of human beings by livestock. In an even more intricate series of studies Cook examined the deposition of soil in valley bottoms, tracing the eroded material back to the parent strata on hillsides and determining, by the presence of potsherds, other artifacts, and bones, whether or not the erosion was associated with agriculture. He thus was able to demonstrate that erosion due to agriculture has been going on in central Mexico for at least 3,000 to 5,000 years. In one study, of the historical ecology of the Teotlalpan region, the heart of the Toltec Empire, Cook uncovered evidence of three cycles of increase in population to excessive numbers, destruction of soil with sharp population decline, and eventual increase in population again. Only the last cycle has been associated with European methods of cultivation. According to Cook's studies, therefore, most of the very striking erosion in central Mexico has been due to digging-stick cultivation and demonstrably took place before the Spanish Conquest; erosion due to cultivation by the plow and pasturing of livestock has been secondary and has reached serious proportions only in the past four decades. These studies gave massive support to the theory of an enormous pre-Conquest population, but also began to indicate that the Cook-Simpson estimates for pre-Conquest population might be too low.

In most recent years, Sherburne Cook and Woodrow Borah have collaborated in a new examination of fiscal and missionary materials, using substantial new masses of tribute assessments, including a very large mass of assessments for the 1530's, which have recently become available. In addition, studies of the development of the Spanish system, particularly the brilliant one by José Miranda of the University of Mexico, have made it possible to determine much more precisely the relation of assessment to population.

Our new approach to the problem has involved: (1) the analysis of much larger masses of material containing far more information on numbers of tributaries and enough counts of persons other than tributaries to enable us to set ratios for the relation to total population of tributaries, married men, and other categories; (2) the examination of population counts for the same towns at various times during the sixteenth century, which has made possible a tentative study of rate of decline; (3) the study of wholesale prices of tribute commodities and rates of assessment per tributary in monetary equivalents, so that it has been possible to estimate tributary population from earlier tribute assessments which do not state explicitly the number of peoples involved; and (4) the application to all these materials of much wider knowledge of the development of the system of tribute assessments, especially in regard to the existence of the nontributary classes, who were prominent in pre-Conquest society and for the first forty years after the Spanish Conquest.

The results to date of our studies have been to establish the ratio to total population of tributaries, as that term was defined after 1558, with provision for assessment of widows and bachelors as half-tributaries, at 2.8. That is the factor by which one must multiply the number of tributaries in a post-1558 count to arrive at total population. This factor is the lowest reached in any study. Previous studies or suggestions have proposed ratios ranging from 5.0 to 2.9. For married males, our factor is 3.3. Married males should be equated with tributaries before the reforms of the 1550's.

Our estimates of population, using these factors, and applying as well the factors arrived at in our study of wholesale prices and rates of tribute assessment are as follows:

1523	16,800,000
1548	6,300,000
1568	2,650,000
1580	1,900,000
1595	1,375,000
1605	1,075,000

A very provisional study, based on rate of population decline during the sixteenth century and applying that rate to the estimate for 1568, suggests for central Mexico a probable pre-Conquest population of approximately 25,000,000. Our studies thus indicate a much higher pre-Conquest population than that postulated by Cook and Simpson in 1948 and indicate further a much steeper decline. According to our estimates, under the impact of war, economic and social dislocation and new diseases, a remarkably dense pre-Conquest population shrank by over 90% between 1519 and 1607. The demographic catastrophe which followed the Spanish Conquest of Mexico must be declared one of the worst in the history of mankind.

What happened during this precipitous shrinkage of population that lasted for well over a century? Our estimates and series of allied studies shed much light upon the social and economic affects. They also suggest an interpretation of the history of Mexico from aboriginal times to perhaps the end of the eighteenth century. Before the coming of the white man, cultivation by the digging stick of maize, beans, and other crops encouraged the development of a remarkably dense population in central Mexico. The Indians, living upon approximately two pounds of corn a day per adult male, multiplied to an extent only paralleled among the peasantry of rice and of the potato. There were no domestic animals of consequence to use land so that virtually all tillable area was devoted to the maintenance of human beings. It seems likely that the inhabitants of the highlands, especially those in the Valley of Mexico with its unusual urban concentrations, were unable to feed and clothe themselves from theier own production. The meaning of the successive empires centered in the highlands was that the highlands made up deficits of foodstuffs, cotton, and other items by exacting them as tribute from the densely populated and highly productive coastal areas. The coasts were then free from disease and, with their tropical climate, were able to produce several crops a year.

During the fifteenth century the population of central Mexico probably passed the long-term carrying capacity of land at the then current level of technology. The vast areas of land either destroyed or seriously eroded by relatively benign digging stick methods of cultivation support this view. Such frightful erosion as that at Yanhuitlán is due to the density of semi-urban settlement —to clearings for houses and courtyards and the steady beat of human feet upon the slopes. Our view is further attested by the holocausts of Aztec human sacrifices and the prevalence of human sacrifice throughout central Mexico. Human lives were plentiful and cheap. By the close of the fifteenth century the Indian population of central Mexico was doomed even had there been no European conquest.

The coming of the Spaniards brought vastly disruptive factors into play in a situation already ripe for catastrophe. To erosion of soil were added European diseases of immensely destructive power in a population with little or no resistance, and severe dislocations of the economic and social systems, including arrangements for distributing and storing foodstuffs. In addition, there was the simple physical destruction of conquest, for the Indians did not submit without resistance. In the coastal areas the coming of malaria, which could be spread by an insect vector, meant within a generation the virtual depopulation of once densely settled and highly productive areas.

It was against the fact of this steady shrinkage of population that the adjustments and changes of the Spanish sixteenth and seventeenth centuries took place. One may distinguish three periods in these centuries: (1) an initial phase of relatively little change in social forms and systems of production; (2) a second period in which the declining ability of Indian production to meet the charges upon it was largely met by curtailing the charges but by retaining the traditional village forms of production; and (3) a third period in which continued decline in Indian production was met by drastic revision of the organization of production in order to increase the output directly available to the white upper stratum. In both the second and third of these periods, the lowest Indian strata probably gained substantially better conditions of work and diet as labor became scarcer.

During the first three decades after the Conquest, that is, from approximately 1520 to 1550, the Spaniards attempted relatively little change in the organization of native society. Christianity was substituted for the heathen cults and some temple revenues were devoted to church use. Aztec overlordship was replaced by Spanish overlordship, tributes being sent as before to the imperial center in the Valley of Mexico. The bulk of the tributes continued to consist of foodstuffs, clothing, other items for household consumption, and service. There was some change in the tributes since the Spaniards were not interested in ceremonial warriors' costumes and feather-work, and were interested in gold dust and certain products which could be sold for cash; but the change was fairly small. Native population and production under the traditional system were sufficient to meet almost all demands both old and new.

By the middle of the sixteenth century the native population and attendant production fell off so much that it was no longer possible to meet all demands within the tradiional organization. The deficit showed up especially in sharply rising prices and an increasing inability of Indian towns to fulfill their tribute assessments. Between 1547 and 1570, therefore, there took place a series of careful inquiries into the organization of Indian society, the charges upon production within it, and the charges upon production by the Spanish upper stratum. After 1558 the inquiry was complicated by the bankruptcy of the Spanish Crown in Europe, which led Philip II to insist that the reform of the tribute system provide him with far greater revenue. The result was a sweeping reorganization. Thenceforth each tributary family was held to a reasonable and carefully stated quota; the total assessment of each Indian town was set on the basis of a careful count, and this count was re-examined at fairly frequent intervals to make allowance for further decline in population; but the shares of most groups in Indian production were drastically curtailed and almost all Indians became tribute-payers. The shares of the Church, as the heir of heathen temples and priesthood, was sharply reduced, and the exemption from tribute of the large numbers of Indians working for the church and embellishing church services was abolished. The exemption from tribute of the old Indian nobility was ended, except for insignificant exceptions. Even Indian slaves were freed and made tribute-payers. The large class of serfs cultivating the lands of the nobility without rights to communal lands, and therefore without obligation to pay tribute, was declared subject to tribute. One result was to free them from serfdom and entitle them to allocations of communal land on the same basis as other members of the community. With the shrinkage of population there was plenty of land available for this purpose. The further result was either to deprive the Indian nobles of all or part of their lands, or to leave them with unusable and untilled holdings. In addition, payments by the community to the old Indian nobility, the allocation of members of the community to them for service in payment for administration, and indeed all payments within the community for administration, were sharply curtailed or abolished. The old Indian nobility thus was shorn of its prerequisites and virtually eliminated, to be replaced by a newer and far smaller group dependent on Spanish favor. The reforms of the mid-century, which adjusted the burden of tributes to the carrying capacity of the Indian population, thus meant the virtual end of the old Indian society and its organization on a European basis.

During the mid-century a series of other interesting developments came about because of the almost complete depopulation of the coasts. The highlands were forced to trade as far afield as Central America to procure the prized cacao, paying for it with Spanish silver, which could be secured only by working for the European upper stratum. The disappearance of coastal production of cotton and weaving of cloth, furthermore, favored development in the highlands areas of sheep raising, and the weaving of woolen cloth. Within a few years the province of Tlaxcala, for example, became a vast sheep range and the town a series of weaving establishments. The coasts themselves became malaria-ridden wastelands inhabited, except at the ports, by a scanty mixed-blood population. The major coastal industry became a sparse stockraising, to remain so until the recovery of the coast lands in recent decades for a new and immensely productive irrigated farming.

The continuing decline of native population during the remainder of the sixteenth century and the first decades of the seventeenth century led to even more drastic reorganization of native society and even of European society in Mexico. During this period the European population steadily increased so that there was a rising demand from it for products and services. Since these could no longer be derived as tribute or by direct levy upon the Indian towns, production and supply for the Europeans had to be organized on a different basis. The Indian communities continued to supply the cities of the Europeans to some extent, but in exchange for cash payment which enabled them in turn to pay their tribute and taxes to the Crown and to buy certain products such as cacao and European wares. The Europeans developed great semi-feudal estates for their own supply of wheat and livestock. The vast tracts of land left vacant by the disappearance of natives provided land for such estates and provided land further for the remarkable expansion of livestock—essentially a replacement of man by cattle, sheep, and goats. Labor for the great estates and for other European industries was derived by a new system of debt peonage, instead of the earlier system of direct labor drafts upon the Indian towns. The new system, which bound the workers to the employer by a permanent bond of debt and settled them on the employer's estate or in his workshop, drew natives permanently from their original towns. The Indian towns thus lost a substantial number of their members. At the same time the new peons were moved into European urban centers or European estates where they mingled freely with people drawn from other areas and rapidly became Hispanized. They thus entered into the new mestizo culture that became the basis of present day Mexico. The sharp decline in population of the sixteenth and seventeenth centuries thus brought about the replacement of the Indians by a mestizo, Europeanized population and vastly favored the formation of large estates with labor forces of debt peons. The recovery of the Indian population which began in the late seventeenth century came too late to arrest massive Europeanization. Mexico today is a predominantly mestizo and Europeanized country because of the demographic catastrophe touched off by the Spanish Conquest.

BIBLIOGRAPHICAL NOTE

This essay is based upon the works listed below. The research is primarily that carried on at the University of California, Berkeley, and reported in the Ibero-Americana Series.

Works in the Ibero-Americana Series:

No. 29.   Sauer, Carl. *Colima of New Spain in the Sixteenth Century* (1948).

No. 31.   Cook, Sherburne F., and Simpson, Lesley Byrd. *The Population of Central Mexico in the Sixteenth Century* (1948).

No. 33.   Cook, Sherburne F. *The Historical Demography and Ecology of the Teotlalpan* (1949).

No. 34.   Cook, Sherburne F. *Soil Erosion and Population in Central Mexico* (1949).

No. 35.   Borah, Woodrow. *New Spain's Century of Depression* (1951).

No. 36.   Simpson, Lesley Byrd. *Exploitation of Land in Central Mexico in the Sixteenth Century* (1952).

No. 40.   Borah, Woodrow, and Cook, Sherburne F. *Price Trends of Some Basic Commodities in Central Mexico, 1531–1570* (1958).

No. 43.   Borah, Woodrow, and Cook, S. F. *The*

Population of Central Mexico in 1548: An Analysis of the Suma de visitas de pueblos (1960).

No. 44.   Cook, Sherburne F., and Borah, Woodrow. *The Indian Population of Central Mexico, 1531–1610* (1960).

Other Works:

Borah, Woodrow. "The Scientific Congress at Mexico City," *The Hispanic American Historical Review*, XXXII, 153–156 (February, 1952).

————. "The Séptima Mesa Redonda of the Sociedad Mexicana de Anthropología," *The Hispanic American Historical Review*, XXXVIII, 48–50 (February, 1954).

Caso, Alfonso. "Land Tenure among the Ancient Mexicans," an address to the American Anthropological Association, Mexico City, December, 1959. (This is an excellent summary of present-day knowledge.)

Cook, Sherburne F., and Borah, Woodrow. "The Rate of Population Change in Central Mexico, 1550–1570," *The Hispanic American Historical Review*, XXXVII, 463–470 (November, 1957).

Jordan, Barbro Dahlgren de. *La Mixteca. Su cultura e historia prehispanicas* (Mexico City, 1954).

Mexico. Instituto Nacional Indígenista. *Metodos y resultados de la politica indigenista en México.* By Alfonso Caso, Silvio Zavala, José Miranda, Moisés Gonzáles Navarro, Gonzalo Aguirre Beltrán, and Ricardo Pozas A. *Memorias*, VI (Mexico City, 1954).

Miranda, José. *El tributo indigena en la Nueva España durante el siglo XVI* (Mexico City, 1952).

N.B.   Especially important is the discussion of the non-tributaries in Chapter IV of Ibero-Americana: 43, and the references cited there. They are essentially the same as those used by Dr. Alfonso Caso, as are the conclusions.

89. The Intellectual History of Eighteenth-Century Spanish America*

ARTHUR P. WHITAKER

I. INTRODUCTION

The focus of this necessarily brief historiographical essay is the eighteenth-century Enlightenment. It was the central theme of the most significant thought of that period both in and about Spanish America, and since then changing attitudes towards it have been a major factor in the interpretation of the intellectual history of Spanish America in that century.

No informed person would claim that the whole of that history is embraced in the Enlightenment. Indeed, there is some reason to suspect that the importance of the latter's role may be found to diminish rather than increase as the problem is subjected to the more systematic and discriminating study which it still sorely needs.

Some of the limitations of its role have already been suggested even in scholarly works of a rather general character published in the past two decades. To give only three random examples, it has been pointed out by C. H. Haring that "the impact of foreign ideas [on eighteenth-century Spanish America] was more discernible in the realms of philosophy and science," whereas "literary production in the colonies seems to have suffered a decline"; by Pedro Henríquez Ureña, that the baroque tradition persisted in Spanish America to the end of the colonial period, long after it had died out in Spain, and that while Hispanic America's "most distinguished men of the 'age of enlightenment' were scientists and scholars of a truly modern type," they very seldom attempted comprehensive theoretical generalizations and confined themselves to making "contributions to descriptive science"; and by Luis-Alberto Sánchez, that one of the most striking phenomena of the latter half of the eighteenth century was one which had no necessary connection with the Enlightenment, namely, the *insurgencia del criollo* as manifested in the rise of the theatre, journalism, and picaresque poetry. Other limitations are suggested by some of the more detailed studies discussed below. Yet even works of this kind belong to the historiography of the Enlightenment and give added warrant for choosing it as the touchstone of this essay.

The reader is invited to take note that this paper deals only with trends in historical writing, and that since the space allotted for it is limited, it stresses the historical writing of the past generation in the three areas that have produced most of the significant works on the subject, namely, Spanish America, Spain, and the United States.

On the negative side, this paper is in no sense bibliographical—individual works will be mentioned sparingly and only in order to illustrate trends. Moreover, it either omits entirely or at most mentions briefly two groups of topics: (1) those aspects of the Enlightenment relating to the Bourbon reforms and the independence movement, which are discussed in the sections of this report prepared by Messrs. Ots Capdequí and Humphreys; and (2) peripheral subjects, such as the history of art and medicine, on which much important historical writing has been done in the past generation, but which cannot be properly discussed in the space at my disposal.

* *Relazioni del X Congresso Internazionale di Scienze Storiche* (7 v., Firenze and Rome, 1955–1957), 1:187–206. Reprinted by permission of the author. A slightly revised and augmented version also appears as "La Historia Intelectual de Hispano-América en el Siglo XVIII," *Revista de Historia de América*, 40:553–573 (dic. 1955).

II. General Considerations

The reader is entitled at this point to a statement of the general considerations about the historiography of the Enlightenment at large which form the framework of the more detailed account of its Spanish American aspect given below. The following sketch is perforce extremely brief, but I trust it is sufficiently explicit to discharge my obligation to the reader in this matter.

As all historiography is a branch of the history of thought, the development of historical writing about the Enlightenment or any of its phases, including the Spanish American, has followed more or less closely the successive changes in the intellectual climate of the Atlantic World—Western Europe and America—since the eighteenth century. Each stage has been characterized by a widely accepted set of value judgments and conceptions or definitions of the Enlightenment. Yet also at each stage there have been wide deviations from the norm, whether for national, religious, or other reasons.

There have been three main stages in the history of historical writing about the Enlightenment. For convenience, we refer to these as the eighteenth, nineteenth, and twentieth centuries. These terms are not to be taken literally, however, since for at least Spain and Spanish America the eighteenth century extended to about 1810, and for most of the Atlantic world the nineteenth century ended in 1914.

Though the age of the Enlightenment established ideas and value judgments that profoundly influenced subsequent generations of historians, it produced little in the way of finished historical writing about itself. A very rare exception was the brief but vivid description of the Bourbon reforms in Spain contained in the influential *History of America* by one of the two founders of the modern school of Spanish American history, William Robertson (the other being the Spaniard Juan Bautista Muñoz.) Save among his Spanish contemporaries, Robertson was also a *rara avis* in rejecting the fiction of the "noble savage" and with it a large part of the *leyenda negra* of Spanish

injustice and cruelty. For the rest, before time had provided the perspective desired by most historians, the outbreak of the French Revolution and the long wars arising out of it shifted interest and sympathy to other topics, or else perverted the Enlightenment to the teleological function described below.

The nineteenth century early developed a lasting dislike for the Enlightenment. Historians fell in with the spirit of the times to the extent that this century produced no study of the Enlightenment remotely comparable to Jakob Burckhardt's great studies of the 1860's on the Italian Renaissance. In so far as they were interested in the Enlightenment, they were generally sympathetic towards it, though there were some notable exceptions, such as the distinguished Spanish scholar, Marcelino Menéndez y Pelayo; but unfortunately the direction of their interest was determined by the hypnotic effect of the French Revolution and, where historians of Spanish America were concerned, by that of the Spanish American wars of independence as well. In the latter case the pattern was reinforced by the vogue which these wars gave to the *leyenda negra*.

As a result, nineteenth-century historians on both sides of the Atlantic accorded the Enlightenment what may be called a teleological treatment, picturing it merely as a preparation for the political revolutions in question. That this produced a narrow and distorted view of the richly varied Enlightenment need not be argued here, what should be stressed is the fact that the error was not corrected until the past century, first by historians of the European phase of the Enlightenment and then by historians of its Spanish American phase. So far as the latter is concerned, the work of rectification is not yet complete.

The twentieth century has been marked by a far-reaching change in the historical interpretation of the Enlightenment on both sides of the Atlantic. The change was due to a complex combination of factors which were sometimes mutually contradictory. One of these was another alteration of the general intellectual climate in the direction of what

Crane Brinton has described as the "badly but probably irretrievably named" cult of "anti-intellectualism." The new cult represented a reaction against nineteenth-century ideas, such as the theories of Evolution and Progress, and thereby tended to rescue the Enlightenment from the disparagement which it had suffered in the nineteenth century and to encourage the study of it on its own account and not merely as a preparation for the political revolutions of the late eighteenth and early nineteenth century.

Yet the new anti-intellectualism did not exalt the Enlightenment, which was as "intellectualist" as the nineteenth century, though in a different way; so that while twentieth-century historians studied the Enlightenment more broadly than their predecessors had done, they also studied it more critically and in the light of less favorable value judgments. So far as its Spanish American phase was concerned this trend was fortified by the cultural reconciliation between Spain and Spanish America which got under way about the turn of the century and which has greatly weakened the hold of the *leyenda negra* over historians in the latter area. It has also correspondingly made them more hospitable to that critical attitude towards important phases of the Enlightenment which has been strongly rooted in Spain ever since the eighteenth century. A somewhat vehement but nevertheless representative expression of the new attitude in Spanish America is the Mexican José Vasconcelos's characterization of the "enlightened despot" Charles III as "*un traidor*" and his admirers as "*bastardos*."[1]

The broader and deeper study of the Enlightenment for its own sake has produced three exegeses of its European phase which, though they have little or nothing to say about the Spanish American phase, are indispensable to its proper study. By a remarkable coincidence two of these, though written independently, appeared in the same year, 1932. These are Ernst Cassirer's *Die Philosophie der Aufklärung* and Carl Becker's *The Heavenly City of the Eighteenth-Century Philosophers*. The third is Paul Hazard's *La pensée européene au XVIIIème siécle* (1946).

In their specific aids to the student of the Spanish American phase, these three books differ rather widely because of their different approaches to the problem of the Enlightenment.

Becker's is full of pregnant suggestions, particularly regarding the stress of the later Enlightenment on the promotion of useful knowledge, which are valid for Spanish America as well as for the United States and Europe. Cassirer's more systematic and thorough analysis of the Enlightenment emancipates it from its servitude to the political revolutions and provides that authoritative statement of criteria so much needed by students of the history of its Spanish American phase. Of the three parts of Hazard's book, those most useful for the Spanish American phase are the first, in which he argues, contrary to the trend of much previous historical exegesis, that the Enlightenment was not merely anti-clerical but anti-Christian, and the third, which provides the means for correcting the widespread tendency of historians of the Spanish American phase to lump all the thinkers and thought of the Enlightenment together in one harmonious and continuous whole.

III. Trends in Spain, Spanish America, and the United States

Subsequent investigators of the Enlightenment's Spanish American periphery have made some use of the invaluable guides provided by Cassirer, Becker, and Hazard, but much of the work in this field still remains to be done—or to be done over again. What progress has been made can best be shown by an examination based upon the differentiations that the all-pervasive nationalism of the nineteenth and twentieth centuries has brought about even in the historiography of so international a subject as the Enlightenment. In this necessarily brief examination the stress will be laid on the historical writing of the past quarter century.

Spain

The Spanish historiography of the En-

[1] J. Vasconcelos, *Breve historia de México*, Mexico City, 1937[1], pp. 261–263.

lightenment has continued to reflect the division of opinion on that subject which existed in Spain during the eighteenth century. As is well known, certain aspects of the movement were strongly supported at that time by such writers as Benito Feijóo, Antonio de Ulloa, and Melchor Gaspar de Jovellanos, and those aspects of it connected with the promotion of useful knowledge were encouraged by the crown and its ministers, such as Counts Aranda, Floridablanca, and Gálvez, particularly during the reign of Charles III.

On the other hand, certain aspects of the Enlightenment encountered determined resistance in Spain. Perhaps the most striking example is the cult of the "good" or even "noble" savage. To most eighteenth-century Spaniards, this was a most dangerous cult, for praise of the savage was frequent coupled with an attack on Spain's alleged maltreatment of the "noble" savages of America ever since the discovery and conquest, thus greatly fortifying the *leyenda negra*. Understandably, most good Spaniards rejected the cult. And as so often happens in such cases, they broadened their counteroffensive to include any public criticism of Spain's record in America. Accordingly, as Benito Sánchez Alonso has recently pointed out, even Juan Bautista Muñoz's scholarly as well as official *Historia del Nuevo Mundo*, published towards the close of the century, gave rise to "*vehementes polémicas*" because of its critical comments on the early conquistadores, which were attributed to the influence of the eighteenth-century Philosophers upon him.[2]

Spanish reservations about the Enlightenment were strengthened by its identification in the minds of many Spaniards with the regime of the "intruder king," Joseph Bonaparte, and the Spanish *afrancesados* who supported him. This experience also helps to explain why subsequent Spanish historical writing has interpreted the Enlightenment very largely in the narrow terms of a French phenomenon and until quite recently has failed to appreciate its breadth and depth as an international movement, which has been so well brought out in the German historian

Cassirer's book mentioned above. In varying degrees, this interpretation characterizes a long line of Spanish works which differ widely in their value judgments of the Enlightenment. Examples are the unfavorable account in Marcelino Menéndez y Pelayo's *Heterodoxos españoles*, in which he significantly identifies the Enlightenment as *Enciclopedismo* and its Spanish supporters as "heterodox" and therefore not true Spaniards; the favorable account in Rafael Altamira's *Historia de la civilización española*, whose most notable contribution on this subject—its discussion of the learned societies of the *Amigos del País* type—represents these societies as constituting an extension of French influence; and the rather neutral account in Antonio Ballesteros y Beretta's *Historia de España*. More recently, the same interpretation was applied from a different angle in Salvador de Madariaga's *The Rise of the Spanish Empire* (1947), mentioned above, in which he said: "Intellectualistic, the [eighteenth] century gradually loses touch with the rich human soil of the [Spanish] nation. . . . Spain was no longer relying on her own substance, as in the days of old. She was confident and she felt strong; but because she felt able to learn all these new arts and forms of living which came from abroad" (pp. 216–8).

There are still many gaps in the Spanish historiography of the Enlightenment even in its Spanish phase. Not only is there as yet no comprehensive and thorough study of it; important details as well have been left to foreigners to fill in, as was done, for example, by a French historian, G. Delpy, in his *L'Espagne et l'esprit européen: L'oeuvre de Feijóo, 1725–1760* (1936).

On the Spanish American phase the gaps are still wider; whatever the reasons may have been, this phase has seldom attracted Spanish historians. Nevertheless, indirectly they have illuminated it in a number of ways. For one thing, they have done so by their studies of the Spanish phase, since Spain was one of the chief channels

---

[2] B. Sánchez Alonso, *Historia de la histografía española*, vol. III, Madrid, 1950, p. 258.

through which the Enlightenment reached Spanish America, often with a Spanish coloration. One might cites as examples a long line of books and articles stretching from Novo y Colson's now seventy-year-old book on the Malaspina mission, through the account of the *Sociedades de Amigos del País* by Altamira and others, to the recent edition of Viceroy Amat's *Memoria de Gobierno*, with a historical introduction by Vicente Rodríguez Casado and Florentino Pérez Embid.

Spanish historians have also contributed to the still far from complete task of identifying the distinctive features of the Enlightenment in Spain. In one of very recent date, Vicente Rodríguez Casado and Vicente Palacio Atard differentiate between enlightened despotism in Spain and that in other countries. "Si el Monarca del despotismo ilustrado está lleno de la Filosofía de la Ilustración . . . , hay que declarar sin rodeos que en España no hay despotismo ilustrado," they maintain, because, among other things, Charles III encouraged the worship of the Virgin Mary, which the Philosophers regarded as a gross superstition.[3] Whatever one may think of this proposition, such refinement of the analysis is at any rate a step in the right direction.

It has remained for a French writer, Marcel Bataillon, however, to take another step by pointing out that a kind of Humanism grew up in Spain in the eighteenth century, though it was a "profoundly modern humanism, based upon French thought." Here again we note the tendency to picture France as the sole source of the Enlightenment in the Spanish Empire. There were, of course, other sources as well, including in the later years Germany and other North European countries. That the latter have received so little attention is surprising when one remembers Alexander von Humboldt and the enormous prestige that he enjoyed throughout the European-American world in the first half of the nineteenth century and which he gained primarily as a result of his labors in Spanish America, under Spanish auspices and in the spirit of the Enlightenment.

Spanish America

While the historiography of each of the Spanish-American countries has its own individuality, in most cases certain common features have been shared at any given time in the period since independence. Again, though still with no pretense to precision in dating, we may divide this period into the nineteenth and twentieth centuries.

As regards the Enlightenment, nineteenth-century historical writing in Spanish American was characterized by two features. In the first place, for the reason already suggested, the *leyenda negra* aspect of the Enlightenment enjoyed a great and almost universal vogue here until the close of the century. Secondly, with a few rare exceptions, such as José Toribio Medina, Spanish American historians confined themselves very largely to the histories of their respective nations even when they were dealing with the colonial period, and to political and military themes, particularly with reference to the independence movement and the formation of the new states.

The combination of these two characteristics made their accounts of the Enlightenment not only fragmentary, local, episodic, and biased against Spain, but above all teleological, with political independence as its goal. These traits were prominent even in the *Historia jeneral de Chile* by Diego Barros Arana, one of the best and least parochial of all the Spanish American historians of that period. For example, his whole attitude in his 90-page chapter on the "Desarrollo de la ilustración y de enseñanza" (Tomo VII, 1886) is summed up in the title of one of its sections: "Ignorancia jeneral creada i mantenida a la sombra del réjimen colonial." It apparently never occurred to Barros Arana to determine whether his authorities were reliable or to compare the Spanish American universities with those of Europe in the same period.

In the twentieth century there has been a far-reaching revision of Spanish American

[3] V. Rodríguez Casado, *La política interior de Carlos III*, in *Simancas: Estudios de Historia Moderna*, Valladolid (1950), pp. 123–186, citing an article by V. Palacio Atard.

accounts of the Enlightenment. While the results have varied greatly from country to country, and even from author to author in the same country, four common traits characterize most of them. First, the hold of the *leyenda negra* has been broken by a reaction in favor of Spain. Secondly, some progress has been made towards the emancipation of the Enlightenment from its teleological servitude to the movement for political independence, and towards the exploration of its non-political aspects. In the third place, Spanish American historians have shared in the general re-evaluation of the Enlightenment, whether in response to the anti-intellectualism of the past half century or for some other reason. Finally, a broader outlook has to a considerable extent supplanted the nationalism or parochialism of the nineteenth century.

A particularly striking example of the change is provided by the contrast between Barros Arana and his twentieth-century fellow-Chilean, Francisco A. Encina, who has likewise produced a multi-volume history of his country. Encina's long account of the Enlightenment is diametrically opposite to Barros Arana's at crucial points, such as the *leyenda negra* and the influence of the Enlightenment in Spanish America. Thus, on the former point, Encina tells us that: "Cumpliendo los mandatos del despotismo ilustrado, los reyes, a partir de Carlos III, pusieron gran empeño en fomentar la ilustración en sus colonias de América. La mas honrosa página del gobierno de Godoy es su empeño en difundir la cultura de España en sus posesiones." On the latter point, speaking of "la Enciclopedia y . . . las obras de los filósofos franceses del siglo XVIII," he asserts that "las personas capaces de leer y asimilar estas obras se contaban con los dedos de las manos en los paises americanos; y la influencia que podían ejercer sobre la gestación de la idea de la independencia era nula, delante de los factores que realmente venían incubando el proceso revolucionario."[4]

Although no comprehensive study of the Enlightenment in Spanish America has yet been produced in that part of the world, its historians have done much both to widen the treatment of particular problems of the Enlightenment from local to continental scope and to relate the local phases to their European antecedents. The former point is illustrated by several works of the prolific Carlos Pereyra and by José Torre Revello's invaluable monograph, *El libro, la imprenta y el periodismo en América durante la dominación española*, Buenos Aires, 1940, which, though not focused on the Enlightenment, nevertheless contains important information about it. Illustrations of the second point are the study of José Celestino Mutis now in progress by Guillermo Hernández de Alba on the basis of extensive research in Spain, and *La evolución de las ideas argentinas* (1937), by José Ingenieros. The latter is notable for its analysis of those elements in the European background of the Enlightenment that were of special significance in Argentina. The author's conclusions on this point provide an instance of the broadening Spanish American conception of the Enlightenment, for of the three European works which he found to be most important in the Argentine phase of it (Rousseau's *Social Contract*, Quesnay's *General Maxims of Political Economy*, and Condillac's *Treatise on the Sensations*) only the first was primarily political, and the other two were, respectively, economic and philosophical.

The political aspect of the Enlightenment has, nevertheless, continued to excite great interest among Spanish American historians, as the following sampling of significant contributions of recent years will show.

To begin with, we may note that despite its excellence in other respects, even Torre Revello's *El libro, la imprenta*, mentioned above, adheres to the traditional treatment of the Enlightenment as a mere antechamber to the struggle for independence. This is apparent in almost all his references to the subject, as when he quotes with approval José de la Riva Agüero's description of Jose Baquíjano y Carrillo's famous *Elogio* of

[4] F. A. Encina, *Historia de Chile desde la prehistoria hasta 1891*, Santiago, 1946, vol. V, pp. 545, 547.

Viceroy Jáuregui as "el remoto anuncio de la Independencia" (p. 113), or when he links "las obras de los filósofos y enciclopediastas franceses" to "las ansias de independencia" (p. 126), or when, in his concluding chapter, he speaks of these same *obras* as having been read by "los precursores de la independencia ... con ansias de construir nuevos moldes gubernativos, para regir con independencia el destino de sus pueblos" (p. 233).

Other recent writers, however, have taken a very different view of this problem. By an interesting coincidence, there appeared in 1947 three independent studies—one by an Argentine, Ricardo Levene; another by a Mexican, Silvio Zavala; and the third by a Spaniard, Manuel Giménez Fernández—all of which developed the same theme, namely, the importance of traditional Spanish-Catholic ideas, as compared with those of the *philosophes*, in the growth of the independence movement in Spanish America.[5] Since the latter topic belongs to Professor Humphrey's section of the present report, I shall only point out that Levene identifies as "scholastic" the theory of reversion of sovereignty to the people during an interregnum and as quintessentially Spanish the application of this idea through the convocation of the *cabildo abierto*; that Zavala likewise notes an affinity between eighteenth-century Spanish American ideas and "scholastic principles," though he by no means excludes "the rationalism of the epoch"; and that Giménez Fernández holds that the doctrinal basis of American insurgency was provided, not by Rousseau's *Social Contract*, but by Suárez's doctrine of popular sovereignty, which in turn derived from St. Thomas Aquinas's theory of the civil power.

The net result of these and other studies has been to diminish considerably the importance of the European Enlightenment as an ideological factor in the independence of Spanish America. This result should be welcomed as an aid to the proper study of the Enlightenment for what it was.

In 1954 a Colombian historian, Leopoldo Uprimny, developed this same theme with special reference to his own country, but in different terms and with different results.

His study can best be considered for the sharp contrast which it offers with the one published hardly a decade ago by his fellow countryman, the late Nicolás García Samudio.[6] While the latter follows Altamira and others in describing the Enlightenment (a term which he uses interchangeably with *despotismo ilustrado*) as a multiform and complex movement made up of conservative as well as revolutionary tendencies, and while he points out that its influence varied greatly from one Spanish American country to another, nevertheless the aspect of it which he develops most fully is its contribution to the independence movement.

Uprimny takes a view diametrically opposite to that of García Samudio. Confining his study to Colombia, the former argues that "*el pensamiento enciclopedista*" and "*las ideas de 1789*" contributed to the independence movement in that country only in the sense that they provoked among its creole aristocracy a conservative reaction against the "three-fold revolution"—political, religious, and moral—which that thought and those ideas had brought about in Spain in the late eighteenth and early nineteenth century.

In thus turning upside down the generally accepted view of the role of the Enlightenment in the Spanish American independence movement, Uprimny's study marks the culmination of a trend in historical writing which had begun a good many years earlier. For example, in Colombia itself, he points out, he had been anticipated, insofar as the influence of scholastic thought is concerned, by a work by Monseñor Rafael N. Casquilla published in 1907; and the same influence had been developed more broadly in the three studies of 1947 mentioned above. Nevertheless, Casquilla's

[5] R. Levene, *Historia de las ideas sociales argentinas*; S. Zavala, *La filosofía política en la conquista de América*; M. Giménez Fernández, *Las doctrinas populistas en la independencia de Hispano-América*.

[6] L. Uprimny, *Capitalismo calvinista o romanticismo semiscolastico de los próceres de la independencia colombiana?*, in *Universitas*, Bogotá, N. 6 (1954), pp. 87–148; N. García Samudio, *Independencia de Hispanomérica*, México, 1945.

thesis had not been widely accepted and in fact another Colombian, Alfonso López Michelsen, had quite recently published a book which traced the ideological origins of the independence movements in both Spanish America and the United States back through the thought of the Enlightenment to its origin in "capitalistic Calvinism."

Whether Uprimny's reinterpretation is valid for Colombia, and whether it could be extended to Spanish America in general, are questions which obviously cannot be taken up here. We may properly point out, however, that it at least renders more understandable one of the major problems in the intellectual history of Spanish America in the eighteenth century—the twin problem of the role of the Jesuits in Spanish America and the Spanish American reaction to their expulsion in 1767.[7]

Further light has been thrown on the Jesuit problem by some of the numerous and important contributions to the history of eighteenth-century thought which have been made in the past decade by Mexican historians, especially by those connected with the seminars on history and philosophy in the Colegio de México. Two such studies appeared almost simultaneously in 1948: Barnabé Navarro's *La introducción de la filosofía moderna en México*, and Pablo González Casanova's *El misoneísmo y la modernidad cristiana en el siglo XVIII*. The latter does not feature the role of the Jesuits, but merely discusses them along with other participants in the Mexican conflict between *misoneísmo*, or hatred of novelty, and the *modernidad cristiana* of the moderate reformers. Navarro, on the other hand, focused his study on the Jesuits, whom he credits with the systematic introduction of "modern philosophy" into Mexico. A notable feature of this book was its use of a new type of source—the *cursus philosophicus*, a kind of textbook prepared by the teacher for his students.

The historiographical significance of these two books has been ably discussed by other Mexican historians. Reviewing the one by Navarro, Antonio Alatorre made a distinction that students of the history of the Enlightenment too often overlook. The *hombres ilustrados* of eighteenth-century Mexico, objects Alatorre, were not really philosophers at all, but merelyy exponents of *enciclopedismo ilustrado*. As for their philosophy, he continues, they took this ready-made and it was an essentially scholastic philosophy, which stood midway between the traditional scholasticism of the Middle Ages and present-day neo-scholasticism, which is still essentially Aristotelian and Thomistic.

A question of fundamental importance for the subject of the present paper was raised by Leopoldo Zea in a review of Gonzáles Casanova's books, which he compares with Monelisa Lina Pérez-Marchand's *Dos etapas ideológicas del siglo XVIII en México a través de los papeles de la Inquisición* (1945), likewise a product of the Colegio de México. The latter work, Zea points out, represents eighteenth-century Mexico as merely continuing the long-standing European conflict between Christianity and modernity, whereas González Casanova defines the Mexican struggle in quite different terms, as one between *misoneísmo* and modern Christianity. Endorsing the latter view, Zea maintains that it is valid as regards not only Mexico but the rest of Spanish America as well and that eighteenth-century Spanish America differed fundamentally from Europe in this respect. One may (as the present writer does) have reservations on this point, believing that the difference between Spanish American and Europe (or between Spanish America and the United States, for that matter) was one of degree rather than of kind. However that may be, the joint result of González Casanova's study and Zea's gloss on it, together with Navarro's study and Alatorre's critique of it, has been to promote one of the most essential tasks in the field of the present paper—that of refin-

---

[7] An important monograph received after the completion of the present essay is Miguel Batllori, S. J., *El abate Viscardo: Historia y mito de la intervención de los Jesuitas en la independencia de Hispanoamérica*, Caracas, 1953.

ing the analysis of the Enlightenment in Spanish America.

The United States

Only in the past generation has systematic study of the Spanish American phase of the Enlightenment developed in the United States. Even today the results are not impressive for their volume, though perhaps a little more might be said for their quality.

Ninteenth-century historians in this country were primarily concerned with the age of Discovery and Conquest and took little interest in any phase of eighteenth-century Spanish American history. The chief exception, Henry C. Lea's *The Inquisition in the Spanish Dependencies* (a typical product of the nineteenth century, though it appeared after 1900), is not an important one. Primarily a medievalist, Lea derived a large part of his information on this subject from the works of José Toribio Medina and many of his guiding ideas from the *leyenda negra*. As a result, his book does little to illuminate those questions about the role of the Inquisition in relation to the Enlightenment which interest the present generation of historians.

In the first three decades of the present century Latin American history gained a firm foothold in the universities of the United States and a large part of the growing scholarly output in this field was devoted to colonial Spanish America and was characterized by the more understanding attitude towards Spain represented by Edward Gaylord Bourne's influential book, *Spain in America* (1904). Nevertheless, for reasons that cannot be given here, this period produced only a single book focussed on the Enlightenment in Spanish America—Bernard Moses' little volume, *The Intellectual Background of the Independence Movement in Hispanic America*, which was admittedly incomplete because of the author's failing eyesight.

Perhaps by contagion from the older fields of history, in which there had been for some time past an increasing concern with cultural and intellectual problems, since about 1930 these aspects of Latin American history

have received attention from a small but growing group in the United States. Several of this group have occupied themselves with various phases of the Enlightenment in Spanish America, particularly those relating to education, science, and the promotion of useful knowledge. The chief contributions in this field have been made by John Tate Lanning, partly in connection with his study of the universities of colonial Spanish America on the basis of his use of a new type of source—the manuscript masters' theses which are preserved in large numbers in the archives of various Spanish American universities, but which had not been consulted by previous historians. He now (1954) has in press one volume on the history of the University of San Carlos de Guatemala in the colonial period and another on the Enlightenment in Guatemala. It was my privilege to read these volumes in manuscript and I am confident that they will at once take their place as classics in the field of history covered by the present paper.

In 1942 Lanning joined with several other historians, including myself, as editor, in producing a volume of essays entitled *Latin America and the Enlightenment*.[8] So far as I am aware, this was the first, and still remains the only broad survey of that subject. Except for one essay on Brazil, it relates very largely to Spanish America. The consensus of the contributors was summed up in Lanning's "tentative conclusion" that "almost every aspect of the conventional attitude toward Latin American Enlightenment should be subjected to careful scrutiny and, in most respects, sharp revision."

Conclusion

Although, as the preceding pages have

---

[8] The other contributors were R. D. Hussey, Harry Bernstein, Alexander Marchant, and A. S. Aiton. Federico de Onís provided the introduction. Arthur P. Whitaker, and Others, Latin America and the Enlightenment (New York, 1942); in the second edition (Ithaca, N. Y., 1961) the article by A. S. Aiton, "The Spanish Government and the Enlightenment in America," has been replaced by Charles C. Griffin, "The Enlightenment and Latin American Independence"; there is also a

shown, sharp revision sustained by careful scrutiny is now well under way, much still remains to be done. Historians of the Spanish American phase of the Enlightenment still lag well behind those of its European phase and still have not availed themselves sufficiently of the aids to a balanced and discriminating account of the subject produced by such members of the latter group as Cassirer, Becker, and Hazard. Thus Antonello Gerbi's interesting *Viejas polémicas sobre el Nuevo Mundo* (Lima, 1946, 3rd ed.) seems to have been regarded in some quarters as a significant contribution to this subject, whereas in fact the chief significance of the polemics to which it relates lies in the field of political rather than intellectual history and the leading European polemist, De Pauw, was a very minor figure in the Enlightenment. Yet Gerbi's book seems to show that the controversy aroused great interest in Spanish America—much more than in Europe: and this fact raises a whole series of questions about the degree of resemblance between the European and Spanish American phases of the Enlightenment to which we have not yet been given a firm answer.

Also, while we have been told a good deal in recent years about the way in which the Enlightenment in its various aspects was transmitted to Spanish America, we still need to know much more on this subject, as well as about its reception there, whether friendly or hostile—a problem the complexity of which has been increased rather than diminished by some of the principal con-

tributions of recent years discussed earlier in this paper. Finally, while progress has been made towards the emancipation of the Spanish American phase of the Enlightenment from its teleological servitude to the wars of independence, even this indispensable prerequisite to its proper study has not yet been completed.

* * *

A. P. Whitaker.* I am grateful for this opportunity to preface the discussion of my report with three additions to the illustrative works cited in it. One of the three, Luis Sánchez Agesta's *El pensamiento político del despotismo ilustrado,* though published in 1953, did not come to my attention until after the completion of my report. The author is a Spanish scholar, now Rector of the University of Granada. His book deals with Spain, which played an important role in the transmission of the Enlightenment to Spanish America, and it contributes notably to that refinement of the analysis of the Enlightenment, the need for which is stressed in my report. The other two additional items were published after the completion of my report. The first is an article by Peter Gay of Columbia University, *"The Enlightenment in the History of Political Theory,"* published in the *Political Science Quarterly* for September 1954. It does not discuss Spanish America but, like the preceding item, it makes a notable contribution to the analysis of the Enlightenment. Finally, there is the substantial book by Jean Sarrailh, Rector of the University of Paris, *L'Espagne éclairée de la seconde moitié du XVIII siècle* (Paris, 1954), which has little to say about Spanish America but gives an extremely useful account of the Enlightenment in Spain itself.

---

selected bibliography of books and articles published since 1941 on the Enlightenment. [Ed. note]

* "Seduta Antimeridiana dell '8–9–1955," *Atti del X Congresso Internazionale, Roma, 4–11 Settembre 1955* (Rome, 1957), p. 64.

90. The Clergy and the Enlightenment in Latin America: An Analysis*

KARL SCHMITT

Several currents of "enlightened" doctrine ran swiftly and strongly through Latin America by the end of the eighteenth century. Scholarly work of the past two decades obviates the need to prove that the new philosophy, the new science, and the new politics found acceptance in the Spanish world. Forbidden books made their way into Latin America with relative ease, the Inquisition proved ineffective in preventing the spread of new ideas, and the Spanish crown itself not only promoted useful knowledge but encouraged "modern" philosophical studies. Aside from special studies on the Enlightenment, however, the more general histories of Latin America too frequently take the position, implicit if not explicit, that the Catholic clergy, monolithic in their obscurantism, constituted the primary obstacle to the complete victory of "enlightened" ideas. It appears to me that this point of view is somewhat inaccurate. This paper holds as a thesis, rather, that the clergy were seriously split on practically all aspects of the Enlightenment. Some supported, some opposed, and many were indifferent to or ignorant of "enlightened" notions. The degree of support or opposition varied, and not all who opposed or supported the movement, supported or opposed it *in toto*.

Before launching into my subject, let me set some limitations to this paper. First, I shall concentrate my inquiry primarily in three areas of Latin America: Mexico, Colombia, and Argentina. Each of these in the late colonial period constituted the heart of a viceregal administration, but each in a different stage of development. Secondly, I intend to center attention on the period between 1750 and 1820. And thirdly, I shall discuss "enlightened" ideas in their four primary aspects: the philosophical, the scientific, the economic, and the political in that order. One more word of introduction is necessary. Both in Spain and in Latin America the anticlerical and antireligious character of the Enlightenment, prevalent elsewhere, was muted, and political agitation for constitutional government, insignificant until the 1790's.[1] Furthermore, Latin American independence movements failed dismally prior to the overthrow of Ferdinand VII and the assumption of the throne by Joseph Bonaparte in 1808. The Jesuits with their doctrine of "probabilism" and their teaching of Suárez and Mariana on the limitations of authority caused some stir in the early and middle years of the eighteenth century. These teachings were outlawed with the expulsion of the Society in 1767, but were revived, in Argentina at least, after 1808.

PHILOSOPHY

In previous discussions of the new philosophy in Latin America, emphasis has been placed upon the book trade, upon the prevalence of forbidden books in libraries, upon Inquisitorial records which indicate the possession and reading of forbidden literature. That a considerable number of the clergy possessed and read such books need not be labored. Let us rather consider how some of them reacted to the new philosophy.

It appears that the introduction and ac-

* *Americas*, 15:381–391 (Apr. 1959). This article was originally presented as a paper at the annual meeting of the American Historical Association, in a joint session with the Catholic Historical Association, December 30, 1958. Reprinted by permission of the author and the original publisher.

[1] Jean Sarrailh, *La España Ilustrada de la Segunda Mitad del Siglo XVIII* (México, 1957), pp. 573–579, 605–612, and 660–661.

ceptance of the "modern" philosophers into Latin America resulted not so much from the attractiveness of their philosophy as of their methodology. In their adoption of new philosophical concepts, the Latin Americans tended to be eclectic. Descartes' methodical doubt, and Bacon's and Newton's emphasis upon experimentation both in philosophy and in science found a ready audience among a number of Latin American scholars surfeited with a sterile and decadent scholasticism. The Jesuit, Francisco Clavigero, best known for his *History of Ancient Mexico*, "embraced with youthful fervor modern or experimental philosophy," and among his works is listed the "Dialogue between Filaletes and Paleófilo against the argument of authority in Physics."[2] And a canon of the Cathedral of Mexico persisted in a life-long opposition to scholasticism as a result of the obsolete theories taught him in the physics section of his philosophy course.[3]

By the last quarter of the eighteenth century some Mexican priest philosophers had begun to adopt some of the new concepts into their own writings. One of the earliest and perhaps the most important of these was Father Juan Gamarra's *Elements of Modern Philosophy*, first published in 1774, and received with general and even glowing approval by its reviewers. These included a professor of mathematics at the university, a professor of Sacred Theology at the College of St. Michael, and a committee composed of the doctors of the university and the priest professors of Sacred Theology in the city of Mexico. In the purely philosophical sections of the work, hardly original, Gamarra does not break fully with the scholastics, although he accepts with some limitations the Cartesian theory of innate ideas. It is in the section on physics, however, that he directly attacks the scholastics for their reliance on authority rather than on experiment. The reviewing committee in an apparent reference to this section noted that Gamarra's teaching could not " 'be ignored or controverted without dishonor or ignominy'."[4] Scholasticism, of course, was not overthrown by this single blast, but it is revealing that

of some forty known authors of philosophical treatises in eighteenth-century New Spain, about ten may be considered members of the new school, and of these all were of the second half of the century.[5]

In Buenos Aires and Bogotá the Jesuits played a leading role in introducing the new philosophical concepts, with the Franciscans continuing their work after 1767. Like Gamarra in Mexico, both Jesuits and Franciscans tended to be eclectics in their adaptation of the "moderns" to the scholastics.[6] What they rejected of modern philosophy was what they considered to be in opposition to Catholic doctrine. Major changes in philosophical studies were introduced into New Granada by Viceroy Manuel Guirior in the mid-1770's when he ordered the *Institutes of Moral Philosophy* by Gregorio Mayáns to be used in the courses on Moral Philosophy at the colleges of St. Bartholomew and the Rosary. Mayáns' work, characterized as "secularized moral theology," omits all reference to the scholastics and contains brief, though favorable, references to Bacon and Descartes.[7] Although the bishops appear to have played a small part in the introduction of the new philosophy, their passive assent may be assumed; and in 1786 the Archbishop-Viceroy of Mexico did introduce the *Institutes* of François Jacquier, the modernist French priest, philosopher, and mathematician into the philosophy course in the pontifical seminary.[8]

SCIENCE

Closely related to the purely philosophical

[2] Emeterio Valverde Téllez, *Bibliografía Filosófica Mexicana* (2nd ed.; León, 1913), I, 130.

[3] *Ibid.*, I, 143.

[4] Quoted in Emeterio Valverde Téllez, *Apuntaciones Históricas sobre la Filosofía en México* (México, 1896), pp. 41–43.

[5] *Ibid.*

[6] Guillermo Furlong, S. J., *Nacimiento y Desarrollo de la Filosofía en el Río de la Plata, 1538–1810* (Buenos Aires, 1952), pp. 69 and 159 ff. and 246 ff.

[7] Juan David García Bacca, *Antología del Pensamiento Filosófico en Colombia* (Bogotá, 1955), p. 35.

[8] José Antonio Alzate, *Gacetas de Literatura de México* (Puebla, 1831), I, 12–13.

controversies of the age was the dispute over the relative merits of experimentation vs. authority in the natural sciences, then a section of the philosophy course. Both within and without the schools the clergy were foremost in the ranks of the combatants. A running battle was fought throughout much of the eighteenth century, and despite all the evidence, a goodly number of the philosophy professors continued to teach physics on the basis of Aristotle. By the latter part of the century, however, leading proponents of the new approach to science were largely concerned wih experimentation and study of nature rather than controversy.

In both New Granada and New Spain the outstanding scientific investigaors were priests: José Celestino Mutis and José Antonio Alzate. The Plata region produced no such luminaries either lay or clerical. Mutis, best known for his organization and leadership of the great botanical expedition in New Granada, was also an astronomer, mathematician, and physician. Though not a university professor, he trained a number of young men in the sciences, and though not a politician, his foremost student, Francisoo Caldas, became a hero in the wars of independence. Alzate worked largely through the press, founding several newspapers, some of prime importance, between 1768 and 1794. His interests ranged from his own studies on the migratory habits of swallows to Benjamin Franklin's studies on optics and heat waves which he published in his newspaper.

Nor were these two priests lone clergymen crying in the wilderness. Mustis had the direct encouragement and assistance of his archbishop and Alzate had at least the tacit approval of his superiors in his scientific work. Furthermore, Mutis' subdirector on the botanical expedition was a priest, and of the six original assistants, one was a Franciscan friar. When later Caldas established his newspaper, the *Semanario del Nuevo Reino de Granada*, at least six priests contributed articles on scientific topics.[9] In Mexico the Jesuits had early shown an interest in science, and among Alzate's contemporaries, one secular priest left in manu-

script a *Compendium of Algebra* and published a study on the major rivers of the world,[10] while another composed the non-Euclidian geometry section for Father Gamarra's philosophy course.[11] In the Plata area the Jesuits appear to have been the first to introduce the study of Newton and the experimental sciences. With their expulsion, scientific interests were taken up by the Franciscans, notably by Friar Cayetano Rodríguez who composed a treatise on physics in 1796.[12] However, there appear to have been few scientific experiments or investigations carried out in the area, certainly nothing to compare with the botanical expedition of New Granada.

ECONOMICS

The promotion of useful knowledge was largely non-academic. Private economic societies were organized to this end, usually with some official support, in eighteenth-century Spain and Spanish America. Primarily interested in agriculture, they also promoted education and the dissemination of a wide range of practical knowledge. About ten such societies were founded in Spanish America, but few were of major importance. None ever existed in Mexico City or Buenos Aires. One was founded in Mompox, New Granada, of which Father Mutis was a corresponding member, and a short-lived one was founded in Bogotá by Mutis himself. Where these organizations did exist, the clergy formed an important element of the membership, including an occasional bishop as well as curates and friars.[13]

---

[9] Jesús María Fernández, S. J. and Rafael Granados, S. J., *Obra Civilizadora de la Iglesia en Colombia* (Bogotá, 1936), pp. 81–84; Francisco José de Caldas, *Semanario del Nuevo Reino de Granada* (Bogotá, 1942), I, 229–231 and III, 6–7.

[10] Valverde Téllez, *Bibliografía*, I, 109 on Diego Abad.

[11] *Ibid.*, I, 128 on Agustín de Rotea.

[12] Rómulo D. Carbia, *La Revolución de Mayo y la Iglesia* (Buenos Aires, 1945), pp. 20–22; Juan Carlos Zuretti, *Historia Eclesiástica Argentina* (Buenos Aires, 1945), p. 190.

[13] Robert J. Shafer, "Ideas and Work of the Colonial Economic Societies, 1781–1820," *Revista*

Outside the societies the program was pursued by individual reformers. Archbishop Caballero y Góngora of Bogotá with his plans for university reform, Alzate with his *Gaceta,* and Bishop José Antonio de San Alberto of Córdoba with his advocacy of manual training and the education of women are well known. Many others were interested, but some were ill-prepared to contribute to the spread of truth. The work of an obscure priest in New Granada contains an amusing potpourri of fact and fancy. His books, composed for the entertainment and edification of his fellow priests, show his acquaintance with Father Feijoó, the great popularizer of the Enlightenment in the Spanish world, as well as with the standard classical commentators on natural phenomena. For example, he recommends Father Feijóo's remedy for killing moths (tobacco smoke) and cites some of the latest authorities in his discussion on the length of the Spanish league. However, in his section on meteorology he repeats some of the erroneous opinions of the ancients. He classifies air as one of the elements and comets as signs of impending catastrophe.[14]

POLITICS

The political role of the clergy is far more complex than their participation in "enlightened" economic, scientific, or philosophical affairs. A contributing factor was the emergence in the eighteenth century of two distinct and divergent currents of "enlightened" political thinking. Although both advocated increased national authority, one branch supported "enlightened despotism," while the other demanded some form of constitutionalism. In the first two decades of the nineteenth century the political situation in Latin America was further complicated by a widespread drive for independence from the mother country, a drive resulting in large part from "enlightened" political ideas on rights and freedoms.

Prior to 1808 there was little disloyalty to the crown among either priests or laymen. Miranda and Nariño are exceptions, and their clerical support was insignificant. True, a youthful seminarian in minor orders was involved with Nariño in Bogotá in 1794, and the Viceroy of New Granada accused other unnamed ecclesiastics of complicity.[15] Miranda, it appears, received some help from Jesuits exiled from Latin America. However, there is no evidence of widespread dissatisfaction, desire for independence, or advocacy of constitutional government among the clergy. The clergy obviously were loyal to Spain, but does this mean that they were out of tune with "enlightened" politics in all respects? The facts will not support such a contention.

Two important issues divided the clergy in the eighteenth century: regalism vs. ultramontanism and divine-right monarchy vs. constitutionalism. The Jesuits and the hierarchy were at odds on both. Since one of the goals of "enlightened despotism" was the extension of national authority over autonomous or semi-autonomous bodies within the state, the crown broadened its sphere of control over Church affairs beyond the limits of papal grants. With the notable exception of the Jesuits, however, the clergy of Latin America, including the bishops, acquiesced without serious protest. Furthermore, the hierarchy accepted the expulsion of the Jesuits in 1767, and some heartily approved it, banning the use of books by Jesuit authors in the schools and seminars. In a pastoral letter of April 1769, the archbishop of Mexico bitterly attacked the Jesuits for their methods of operation, their philosophical doctrines, and their educational system. The following year the bishop of Oaxaca issued the following order when certain Jesuit papers were discovered in New Spain.

We order under pain of greater Excommunication *latae sententiae* . . . *ipso facto incurrenda* and other penalties . . . that this and any other paper,

_____
de Historia de América, XLIV (December, 1957), 331–368.

[14] Basilio V. de Oviedo, *Cualidades y Riquezas del Nuevo Reino de Granada,* ed. by Luis Augusto Cuervo (Bogotá, 1930), pp. 57 and 71–74.

[15] José M. Pérez Sarmiento (ed.), *Causas Célebres a los Precursors* (Bogotá, 1939), I, 163 and II, 183–185.

printed or manuscript, even a private letter, which proclaims as unjust the expulsion of the Jesuits from any monarchy throughout the world . . . [be placed in our hands within three hours of being discovered].

The bishop of Puebla justified the expulsion on the grounds that the king had the right to protect himself from subversion which the Jesuits were teaching.[16]

From this resumé, it might be concluded that until 1767 the Jesuits, admitted ultramontanists, were the bulwark of "unenlightened" politics. But not quite—the clue lies in the accusation of subversion made against them by the bishop of Puebla. This subversion consisted in the fact that the Jesuits held and taught the doctrine of "probabilism" and the constitutionalism of the Spanish Jesuit theologians, Suárez and Mariana. The bishop maintained that the Jesuits were thereby undermining all authority, civil and ecclesiastical. It appears, therefore, that Jesuit political theories which favored liberty over authority, advocated the right of revolution, and insisted upon limitations to royal power should be considered in harmony with "enlightened" political thinking. So too, the regalist views of the hierarchy should be considered. Conversely, both Jesuits and bishops should be classified as "unenlightened" in their respective positions and divine-right monarchists.

With the replacement of the Spanish Bourbons by the French Bonapartes in 1808, the political climate began to change rapidly in Latin America. Creole leaders in many parts of Spanish America succeeded in establishing regimes which were independent of the mother country but which still proclaimed loyalty to the dethroned monarch, Ferdinand VII. In many areas great numbers of the lower clergy supported these movements even after they became frankly separatist and republican. There were loyalists, to be sure, and many, perhaps a majority, who played no active role on either side. The bishops and the upper clergy, with some exceptions, opposed separation and independence.

Few of these clergymen can be categorized as "enlightened" or "unenlightened." Dean Gregorio Funes of the Cathedral of Córdoba was unquestionably a devotee of the Enlightenment. Interested in modern philosophy, the new science, and the spread of useful knowledge, he was also among the first to rally to the Revolution of May despite the opposition of his own bishop, and consistently supported the exercise of the civil power, whether monarchical or republican, in ecclesiastical affairs.[17] Also "enlightened" were Father Servando de Mier of Mexico and Father Juan Azuero of New Granada who supported not only the independence movement but the new government's desire to obtain the patronate over the Church. So too, apparently, was Bishop Cuero y Calcedo of Quito who not only advocated the spread of useful knowledge but joined the fight for independence. Captured by royalist forces, he died in Lima on his way to exile. Conversely, the best example of politically "unenlightened" clergy are the bishops of Mexico who bitterly opposed the independence movement until it was taken over by the conservative Iturbide who promised to establish a Catholic conservative regime in place of the liberal Spanish monarchy of 1821. In renouncing their loyalty to the king, the Mexican bishops also renounced their regalism; although they supported a strong native monarchy, they opposed its attempt to control the Church.

Now for some complications. The Dominican friar, Isidoro Guerra of Buenos Aires, an "unenlightened" scholastic and anti-Cartesian, supported the independence movement.[18] Father Mariano Medrano of Buenos Aires, an eclectic in philosophy, an admirer of Newton, a supporter of independence, took an anti-regalist position toward ecclesiastical reform in 1822. Medrano, then vicar-general of Buenos Aires, argued that the proposals invaded the rights of the Church in threatening institutions which owed their origin to the independent power of the

[16] The three pastoral letters cited are included in *Papeles Diversos* of the García collection of the University of Texas.

[17] Roberto I. Peña, *El Pensamiento Político del Deán Funes* (Córdoba, 1953), pp. 174–175.

[18] Furlong, *op. cit.*, pp. 313–316.

Church.[19] The clergy of Bogotá seriously differed among themselves on this same question in 1820 when the new government requested their opinions. Father Azuero, as noted above, held that the government had an absolute right to exercise the patronato, while Father Garnica, a Dominican, insisted that it could be exercised only by papal grant. The government, dissatisfied with the variety of opinions which it received, put the question to the capitular vicar, Father Nicolás Cuervo, who refused to commit himself, suggesting that the government request the opinion of the Holy See.[20]

Similar problems arise with the opponents of independence. In Yucatán several loyalist priests advocated limited constitutional monarchy, and strongly supported the Constitution of 1812 and the liberal revolt of 1820 in Spain. To reconcile Catholic doctrine and the new political philosophy, one of these priests founded the Association of St. John. Originally established as a discussion club for priests and laymen, the association soon evolved into a political organization. Despite persecution and imprisonment, they remained loyal to Spain to the end of the colonial regime.[21] Another loyalist, a canon of the Cathedral of Mexico, supported political absolutism, but at the same time was an advocate of education, an admirer of Humboldt, and a promoter of useful knowledge.[22] Somewhat similar is the case of Manuel Abad y Queipo, bishop-elect of Michoacán. An advocate of social, economic, and even political reform, Abad was no democrat. Loyal to Spain and to the king, he felt that reform should come from above. When Hidalgo began his revolt, no prelate in New Spain more bitterly denounced the patriots.[23] My last example, Archbishop Fonte of Mexico, presents the most interesting reactions to conflicting drives. Politically conservative, he alone among the upper clergy of Mexico remained loyal to liberal Spain in 1820 and 1821. His *Edict* of July 1820 contains a queer combination of regalism, loyalty to the mother country, and defense of liberal doctrines. Obedience to the constitution is a civil duty and a religious obligation, said the archbishop; the person of the king is sacred and inviolable, and citizens must not disturb public order. Surprisingly, he offered no criticism of the decree suppressing the Inquisition, pointing out that not by such institutions alone does the "preservation and triumph of our holy religion . . . depend." The archbishop also commented that the press law was a grant of liberty not license, significantly adding: "But above all, let us not judge the goodness of the justness of the law by the evil use which is made of it, in the same way that it would be absurd to attribute imperfections to the divine law because of the frequent violations of its precepts." On political liberty and equality he said:

In the Spanish Constitution [these terms] mean civil liberty and political equality; in that these citizens are free of all arbitrary acts and unjust injury, but subordinate to the law. Therefore it would be absurd to confuse this rational and honest liberty with license to do whatever caprice or the impetus of the passions might suggest. . . . In the same way, with the grant of political equality in rights and obligations, an absolute is not established; therefore, the possessions of the rich are not to be taken from them to make them equal to the poor; however, neither the one nor the other will enjoy any preference or any advantage before the law; their conduct will receive equally, reward or punishment, for their only difference . . . will be in their own vices and virtues.[24]

It must be concluded, obviously, that the role of the clergy in the Latin American Enlightenment was a major one with differ-

[19] Carbia, *op. cit.*, pp. 101–102.

[20] José Restrepo Posada, "El Doctor Nicolás Cuervo y nuestras primeras relaciones con la Santa Sede," *Boletín de Ristoria y Antigüedades*, XXVIII (January–February, 1941), 290–291.

[21] Eligio Ancona, *Historia de Yucatán desde la época más remota hasta nuestros días* (Barcelona, 1889), III, 20–21, 37–38, 114–121, and 188–189.

[22] José Toribio Medina, *D. José Mariano Beristain de Souza Estudio Bio-Bibliográfico* (Santiago, 1897), pp. xv–xvi; Joseph Mariano Beristain, *Discurso Político Moral y Cristiano* (México, 1809), pp. 17 and 31–32.

[23] Lillian E. Fisher, *Champion of Reform Manuel Abad y Queipo* (New York, 1955), pp. 65–96.

[24] *Edict* of Archbishop Fonte of Mexico, July 18, 1820, in F. H. Vera, *Documentos eclesiásticos de México* (Amecameca, 1887), II, 341–347.

ences from area to area being of degree and emphasis rather than of kind. Secondly, the evidence is clear that the clergy were seriously divided in their response to the movement. Books and ideas condemned in Rome and Madrid were read and absorbed by numerous clergymen in Latin America, but not all reacted similarly. The bishops excoriated the independence movement, but their anathemas went unheeded by many of the lower clergy. The Jesuits taught a doctrine of constitutionalism and ultramontanism, the bishops were regalists and absolutists. The Franciscans in Buenos Aires taught the experimental method in the sciences, the Dominicans in Bogotá adhered more to authority. Mutis advocated the observation of nature, the Bishop of Cuenca wanted to destroy the tower of his own cathedral, then being used for astronomical observations, to make way for a new cathedral.[25] Finally, strict classification of most of the clerical participants as "enlightened" or "unenlightened" is inaccurate. Although many opposed the new philosophy, fewer objected to the use of the experimental method in science, and hardly any murmured against improved economic well-being. Various political views could be held by the same person, some of which could be considered "enlightened" and some not. Furthermore, certain clergymen could be "unenlightened" in one field, while wholeheartedly supporting "enlightened" ideas in one or more other fields. I have attempted no head count of the clergy in Latin America to determine their sentiments; it appears an almost impossible task. A careful study of the bishops, heads of religious communities, and the faculties of universities may indeed prove rewarding, and would probably turn up similar complexities. Professor Lanning's recent observation strikes me as coming close to the mark: "Of forty-nine hardworking bishops, at any one moment, I would guess forty went about their business, while seven actively promoted the aims of the Enlightenment and two grew sour."[26]

[25] *Archivo Epistolar del Sabio Naturalista José Celestino Mutis* (Bogotá, 1941), II, 154.
[26] John T. Lanning, "The Enlightenment in Relation to the Church," *The Americas*, XIV, no. 4 (April, 1958), 493.

91. Authority and Flexibility in the Spanish Imperial Bureaucracy*

JOHN LEDDY PHELAN

The approach to the Spanish colonial bureaucracy is that of the "conflicting standards analysis," first suggested by Andrew Gunder Frank. Given the ambiguity of goals and the frequent conflict among the standards, all the laws could not be enforced simultaneously. The prevalence of mutually conflicting standards, which prevented a subordinate from meeting all the standards at once, gave subordinates a voice in decision making without jeopardizing the centralized control of their superiors. Historians have traditionally assumed that the Spanish administration had a nonambiguous set of goals and that standards of conduct for its admin-

* *Administrative Science Quarterly*, 5: 47–65 (June 1960). Reprinted by permission of the author and the original publisher.

*istrative agents were not mutually conflict-
ing. The conflicting-standards hypothesis,
however, provides a more satisfactory explanation of the wide gap between the law and
its observance in the Spanish empire. Particular emphasis is given to an analysis of
elements of centralization (the* residencia
and the visita*) and those of decentralization
("I obey but do not execute" formula). This
approach not only applies to the Spanish-
American administrator; it may also throw
some light on the structure and nature of
several kinds of bureaucratic organizations.*
[Ed. note, *Administrative Science Quarterly.*]

Societal and political stability was a predominant feature of Spain's vast overseas
empire. In an age of slow communications
Spain was able to preserve her widely scattered colonial dominions in both America
and Asia against frequent foreign threats
and occasional internal revolts without
heavy reliance on military coercion.[1]

Two institutions were primarily responsible for the maintenance of a social status
quo that endured for three centuries. They
were the Spanish Catholic Church—and it
was more Spanish than Roman—and the imperial bureaucracy. The effectiveness of
these two institutions became apparent in
the period following the wars of independence. Political emancipation swept away the
imperial bureaucracy, and the Church
emerged from the struggle with its traditional sources of power considerably undermined. Political instability resulted. The
new republican ideology inspired by the
American and the French revolutions did
not fill the vacuum created by the abolition
of the colonial bureaucracy and the weakening of the Church. Actually the military
organization seized control after independence, and the various ideologies were
scarcely more than a façade for masking this
control.

In view of the predominate role of the colonial bureaucracy in creating conditions of
durable social stability, the dynamics of this
system merit some scrutiny. The aim of this
essay is to examine the Spanish bureaucracy

in terms of a thought-provoking hypothesis
recently advanced by Andrew Gunder
Frank. Although Frank's hypothesis was inspired by his study of the operation of the
industrial system in the Soviet Union, his
model illuminates the functioning of other
bureaucratic systems as well.

THE HYPOTHESIS

Mr. Frank outlined his model as follows:

More than one hierarchal channel of communication is maintained. Multiple and, at least, in part
conflicting standards are set by superiors for subordinates. Conflict may arise among standards set
within each hierarchy as well as among those set
by different hierarchies. Subordinates are free to
decide which of the conflicting standards to meet,
if any. However, subordinates are responsible to
superiors for their performance with respect to all
standards; and subordinates may be held responsible for failure to meet any standard. The relative importance of standards is neither well, nor
completely defined, nor is it entirely undefined.
The priority among standards is ambiguous. Subordinates make their assessment of priority to
guide their decision making and task performance.
Each subordinate appeals to those standards which
are most in accord with his incentives and the circumstances of the moment and to those which are
most likely to be invoked by superiors in evaluating his performance. Superiors in turn make their
assessment of priority to guide their necessarily
selective evaluation of subordinates' performance
and enforcement of standards. The entire process
is continuous: superiors modify the set of standards
to comply with their changing objectives; subordinates adapt their decisions to changing standards and to changing circumstances; superiors enforce standards in accordance with the changing
priority.[2]

In this model two outstanding features
are flexibility and authority. Flexibility en-
compasses (1) the response of subordinates

[1] We would like to take this opportunity to express our appreciation to James D. Thompson, director of the Administrative Science Center at the
University of Pittsburgh. This paper was discussed
at a meeting of the Center May, 1959.

[2] Andrew Gunder Frank, "Goal Ambiguity and
Conflicting Standards: An Approach to the Study
of Organization," *Human Organization*, published
by the Society for Applied Anthropology, 17
(1958–1959), 11.

to changing objectives of their superiors, (2) the adaptability of subordinates to adjust to changing circumstances, and (3) the initiative of subordinates in sponsoring innovations. In this context of the term, authority means sensitivity of subordinates to their superiors' objectives rather than mere adherence to their rules. The Weberian distinction between formal rationality and substantive rationality is pertinent. Formal rationality refers to rational calculation and predictability based on adherence to specified procedures, which result in task performance; substantive rationality refers to the achievement of task performance itself regardless of the means employed. The bureaucratic systems under discussion exhibit substantive rather than formal rationality.

The multiplicity of standards permit superiors to make their ever-changing wishes felt by adding new standards or shifting the emphasis among existing ones. By their very incompatibility, multiple standards allow a wide latitude of discretion to subordinates, resulting in the decentralizing of decision making. Selective evaluation of performance and selective enforcement of standards makes the incompatibility among the standards operationally feasible.

This system also generates authority. Superiors can invoke, if they wish, one of the many standards that has not been met. Selective enforcement permits superiors to convert potential authority into real authority at any given time. Hence subordinates remain sensitive to the wishes, both formal and "real" of their superiors. The existence of multiple hierarchies and alternative channels of communications prevent subordinates from obstructing the upward movement of information about their own malperformance. By providing superiors with a wide fund of knowledge about conditions, subordinates are made more responsible to their superiors.

In applying this hypothesis to the Spanish imperial bureaucracy, the structural features of the colonial administration must first be outlined. Then the kinds of standards imposed on the colonial magistrates by their superiors in Spain must be classified before

the nature of the magistrates' response to the superiors can be assessed. Finally superiors' evaluation and enforcement of their subordinates' conduct in the colonies will be considered.

The illustrative data will be chosen from events connected with the Indian policy of the Crown during those decades spanning the end of the sixteenth and the beginning of the seventeenth century. The illustrative material could equally well have been selected from the eighteenth century. The essential organizational features of the bureaucratic system created by the Habsburg monarchs were not appreciably altered after the advent of the Bourbon dynasty in 1700. In the eighteenth century, however, the change of emphasis was the effort to make the system more efficient to increase the Crown's revenues. This study offers few new data. Its primary purpose is to outline a working hypothesis which may provide a new conceptual framework for fresh research.

THE STRUCTURE OF THE COLONIAL ADMINISTRATION

At the summit of the Spanish colonial bureaucracy was the king. Directly under the monarch was the Council of the Indies, exercising by royal delegation supreme jurisdiction over all phases of the colonial administration: legisative, financial, judicial, military, ecclesiastical, and commercial. Only at the top was the imperial bureaucracy highly centralized in the persons of the king and his Council. The Crown's agents in America and in the Philippines were the viceroys, the governors, and the Audiencia. The viceroys and the governors ostensibly held supreme sway in both civil and military matters;[3] in

[3] Before the eighteenth century there were two viceroyalties in the New World. That of New Spain embraced all of Spanish North America, and that of Peru included all Spanish South America. The viceroyalties were divided into Audiencia districts headed by a governor, a captain general, or a president. In the viceroyalty of New Spain there were Audiencia districts for Mexico City, Guadalajara, the Antilles, Central America, and the Philippines. Although the viceroy enjoyed greater social prestige than the chief magistrates

their territories they were the immediate representatives of the king. Command of the military establishment and the secular aspects of church government were under their jurisdiction. They nominated most of the lesser colonial officials subject to the eventual confirmation of the Council in Spain.

The centralization of authority in the viceroys and the governors was, however, more apparent than real. In various spheres the jurisdiction of those magistrates was rigidly limited. Many of the viceroy's subordinates as well as the judges of the Audiencia and the exchequer officials, who were his quasi peers, were appointees of the Crown. They corresponded directly with the Council. Under these circumstances the control of the viceroy over some of his subordinates and his quasi peers was frequently nominal. Although the viceroys had virtually unchallenged freedom in matters of routine administration, even in this their powers were limited; for every aspect of colonial life down to the most minute and insignificant details was regulated by a voluminous body of paternalistically inspired legislation issued by the Council. Viceroys and governors were under standing orders to enforce these mandates. These regulations were codified by 1681 in the celebrated *Recopilación de leyes de las reynos de las Indias*. In matters of policy the viceroys were supposed to refer all decisions to Spain.

The viceroy shared many of his powers with the Audiencia, the second hierarchy in the system. Those bodies were the highest court of appeal in their respective districts. The Audencia also served as an advisory council to the viceroy or governor and exercised certain legislative functions. In any clash between the two, ultimate authority usually rested with the viceroy. Yet a vacillating presiding officer or a refractory Audiencia could easily upset this rather delicate balance of jurisdictions.

In addition to the viceroys and the Au-

diencia the two other administrative hierarchies were the ecclesiastical and fiscal. Under the system of the *real patronato de las Indias* the king, as patron of the Church of the Indies, acted as the Pope's vicar in ecclesiastical administration. Royal agents administered ecclesiastical taxation, and they nominated all church dignitaries from archbishop to parish priest. Discipline and doctrinal matters were the only significant spheres beyond the immediate control of the Crown. Although the viceroy acted as vicepatron of the Church in his district, the ecclesiastical hierarchy enjoyed a wide degree of quasi-independent action. The prelates could appeal directly to the Council in Spain. They often played the viceroy off against the Council and vice versa.

In ecclesiastical administration the bishops were responsible to the king as patron of the Church of the Indies. In matters of faith, morals, and sacerdotal discipline, however, the episcopacy was accountable to the Pope, and under him the sacred congregations in Rome. There were no substantive conflicts between the Spanish Crown and the Holy See in the area of dogma and doctrine. Jurisdictional clashes, on the other hand, were endless and violent.

Nor was the authority of the bishops over all the priesthood unchallenged. The regular clergy, who initially bore most of the responsibility for converting the Indians, exercised powers often at variance with episcopal prerogatives.[4] This brief survey is meant only to suggest that the government of the Church in the Indies was of such character as to constitute a partly independent and a partly interdependent hierarchy.

The officers of the royal exchequer, while of lower rank than the viceroys and the gov-

___

of the Audiencia districts, the latter in their districts exercised substantially the same powers as the former did in their. For purposes of discussion the viceroys and the governors may therefore be included in the same classification.

[4] For a survey of the *Patronato* see Clarence Haring, *The Spanish Empire in America* (New York: Oxford University Press, 1947), ch. x. For a discussion of the jurisdictional conflict between the episcopacy and the regular clergy in the Philippines see the author's book, *The Hispanization of the Philippines, Spanish Aims and Filipino Responses, 1565–1700* (Madison, Wis., 1959), pp. 32–35. The Inquisition, which did not have jurisdiction over the Indians, formed another semi-autonomous administrative hierarchy inside the Church.

ernors, were of co-ordinate authority in their sphere of administering royal revenue.

The viceroy, in reality, was the co-ordinator of the various administrative hierarchies. He served as the presiding officer of the Audiencia in its role as a Council of State, as vice-patron of the Church, and as president of the *junta superior de la real hacienda* (the exchequer office). Furthermore, the functions of each hierarchy were sometimes exercised by members of another. In the event of the sudden death of the viceroy, the Audiencia assumed supreme command of the government until a successor arrived from Spain. Archbishops sometimes served as viceroys. In spite of these occasional mergers of offices and the nominal centralization of power in the viceroy, the three other hierarchies retained a substantial amount of autonomous power, and each one was responsible directly to the Council of the Indies in Spain.

The Crown deliberately maintained several channels of communication with its colonial agents. The purpose was to ensure that superiors in Spain would have multiple sources of information as to actual conditions. As Clarence Haring has put it:

The only real centralization was in the king and his Council in Spain. Spanish imperial government was one of checks and balances; not secured as in many constitutional states by a division of powers, legislative, judicial, executive, but by a division of authority among different individuals or tribunals exercising the same powers. There never was a clear-cut line of demarcation between the functions of various governmental agencies dealing with colonial problems. On the contrary, a great deal of overlapping was deliberately fostered to prevent officials from unduly building up personal prestige or engaging in corrupt or fraudulent practices.[5]

Motivated by an abiding distrust of its agents overseas, the Crown gradually fashioned during the course of the sixteenth century a complex bureaucratic pyramid with multiple, partly independent and partly interdependent hierarchies. Under this system the conflicts between the various bureaucracies were continuous and acrimonious, since their jurisdictions often overlapped. Internal conflicts within the bureaucracies themselves were perhaps somewhat less frequent, but did occur. In the ecclesiastical bureaucracy the tensions were particularly severe. The bishops and the secular clergy were pitted against the regular clergy, and conflict between the various orders of the regular clergy was not uncommon. The bishops and the Crown often clashed over jurisdictions.

THE NATURE OF THE STANDARDS IN THE SPANISH ADMINISTRATION

Standards refer to that multiplicity of pressures to which all colonial administrators had to adjust in order to survive in office. The most apparent standards were those interminable directives issued by the Council of the Indies. These mandates were often mutually contradictory. The incompatibility of the Council's directives in regard to the Indians stemmed in part from the Crown's desire to reconcile the needs of the natives and those of the colonists. The Spanish monarchs partially justified their sovereignty over the Indies from the missionary obligation to convert the Indians to Christianity. Both as infidels and even more so as "new Christians," their property rights and personal liberty merited some protection.[6] Furthermore the Church threw its considerable weight toward the protection of native rights. The spirit and intent of the Indian legislation of the Crown reflected the conviction that the Indians constituted an inferior group in society whose rights and

[5] Haring, *op. cit.*, p. 122. This study is an authoritative account of the structural features of the colonial bureaucracy. See especially chs. vi, vii. Also, see Enrique Ruíz Guiñazú, *La magistratura indiana* (Buenos Aires, 1916); José María Ots Capdepuí, *El estado español en las Indias* (Mexico, 1941); Ernesto Schäfer, *El consejo real y supremo de las Indias* (2 vols.; Seville, 1935).

[6] For a discussion of the missionary justification of Spanish sovereignty in the Indies see the author's *The Millennial Kingdom of the Franciscans in the New World: A Study of the Writings of Gerónimo de Mendieta, 1525–1604* (University of California Publications in History, No. 52; Berkeley and Los Angeles, 1956), ch. i; also "Some Ideological Aspects of the Spanish Conquest of the Philippines," *The Americas*, 13 (1957), 221–239.

obligations, however, deserved paternalistic protection. The conditions under which the Indians might render labor services to the colonists were minutely regulated in a voluminous body of legislation eventually codified in the *Recopilación*, but these edicts were more frequently honored in their breach than in their observance.

This wide gap between the law and its enforcement resulted partially from another source of pressure. Colonizing had to be made profitable for the Spanish colonists, and that meant some form of exploitation of native labor. The Crown usually sought to reconcile the welfare of the Indians and the general well-being of the colonial economy. Harmonized they sometimes were, but there were striking cases when the two objectives stood in naked conflict with each other. The economic crisis created by the diminution of the Indian population in Mexico after 1576 is one notable case in point; another one was the crisis in the Philippines (1609–1648) precipitated by the Hispano-Dutch war in the Orient.[7] There were also countless other cases in which magistrates in the Indies had to cope with mutually incompatible directives handed down by the Council in Spain.

The prevalence of mutually conflicting standards was further compounded by the ignorance of the central authorities as to actual conditions in the colonies. These local conditions could make the directives of the Council either impracticable or even impossible to enforce. In many cases the Council deliberately defied local conditions. The tendency of the central authorities was to eliminate regional differences, as the Council's aim was to standardize practices throughout the empire. Hence circular cedulas were often dispatched to all the Audiencias of the empire. Such a practice reflected the supreme indifference, if not the active hostility of the central authorities, to local conditions. The Philippines, for example, would be treated on occasion as if they were another Mexico.

In view of the Spanish procedure of assigning the same functions of government to different agencies, bureaucrats had to cultivate a sensitivity to the aims and the procedures of their peers in the other administrative hierarchies. In the sphere of Indian legislation, for example, the viceroys had to take into account the views of the clergy. The Bishops in their ex officio role as protectors of the Indians could intervene in those cases where the economic demands of the state or the colonists encroached upon the religious welfare of the neophytes. Given their countless missions among the natives, the regular clergy also had a vested interest in all matters pertaining to the welfare of the Indians. The officers of the exchequer were concerned with the fiscal aspects of Indian administration. A special responsibility of the Audiencia was the legal defense of the natives. In the administration of Indian affairs a viceroy or governor would be ill-advised not to take into account the viewpoints of his judicial, ecclesiastical, and fiscal peers. Decisions were often the result of tension and conflict, the consequence of the fact that the jurisdictions of these partly independent and partly interdependent hierarchies overlapped. Nor could the governors or viceroys ignore their subordinates. The middle-echelon officials, by virtue of their long tenures in office covering many administrations, were not without the means to influence the conduct of their superiors, the viceroys.

Although there was no organized and articulate press to serve as a vehicle of protest against bureaucratic incompetence, colonial subjects did not lack means for voicing their grievances. The wealthy and the educated often corresponded directly with the Council of the Indies. The Archivo General de Indias in Seville contains countless petitions and protests of corporate groups like town councils or class groups like encomenderos as well as memoranda from private citizens.

A system of incentives and penalties further encouraged colonial magistrates to adjust to the multiplicity of pressures. The offices in the colonial bureaucracy were in effect monopolized by peninsular Spaniards. They formed a class of career bureaucrats.

---

[7] For the Philippine crisis see *Hispanization of the Philippines*, pp. 98–102.

They were likely to be sent to any region of the empire. Promotion and spoil were their incentives, as was assignment to a favored geographical location. Posts in an isolated and economically underdeveloped colony like the Philippines were considered far less desirable than stations in Mexico or Peru, where a more agreeable climate and more lucrative emoluments of office attracted ambitious royal servants. Notwithstanding severe and widespread clashes of interests and values among the members of the system, colonial bureaucrats appeared to share an underlying esprit de corps that they belonged to a common body whose existence ought to be perpetuated. Most of the members seem to have been motivated to some significant degree by a feeling of personal involvement in the system's ultimate welfare. In addition to the incentives of advancement there was also a whole series of penalties. They ranged from reprimands, demotions, loss of office, fines, and criminal prosecution for those who miscalculated the pressures of a given situation.

All of these pressures—orders from Spain, local conditions, the peers and subordinates of bureaucrats, public opinion, incentives, and penalties—served to create a whole complex of standards, which guided and conditioned the conduct of colonial officialdom.

The very multiplicity and the often mutually contradictory character of the standards contributed both to maintaining authority and to providing flexibility. The issuing of new directives by superiors made those objectives known to their subordinates and hence contributed to the maintenance of authority, whose two components are knowledge by subordinates of the wishes of their superiors and compliance by subordinates. Multiplicity of standards also increased flexibility. Superiors had the opportunity to change directives and standards as the occasion demanded. In view of their contradictory nature, subordinates necessarily had a certain latitude in their choice of what standards to enforce.

FLEXIBILITY

There were a variety of ways in which co-lonial administrators responded to those manifold pressures created by mutually incompatible standards.

A well-documented example occurred in Mexico. New Spain's century of depression originated in the great epidemic of 1576–1579, in which the Indian population was massively diminished by the spread of contagious diseases against which they had no acquired immunity. The crisis was hastened by the accompanying rapid decline in available native labor, the increase of the non-Indian population (Spaniards and mestizos), and the extensive use of native labor by the regular and secular clergy for their many architectural enterprises. Another factor complicating the plight of the Indians was a change in land use, in which a large portion of the land of central Mexico was removed from the production of maize and given over to the raising of livestock. The landscape of Mexico was radically altered by the advance of herds of cattle, sheep, and goats. The non-Indian population was determined to maintain its customary standard of living, with the result that the pressure on the rapidly diminishing Indians for increased grain production became almost intolerable. Stopgap measures such as the establishment of public granaries and a crude system of price fixing did not succeed in guaranteeing an adequate flow of foodstuffs to the cities.

The *repartimiento* (a system of compulsory draft labor) and the rise of a latifundia system based on Indian debt peonage by the middle of the seventeenth century arrested the contracting economy. Earlier, during the first administration of Velasco the Younger (1590–1595), the *repartimiento* was failing to draft enough labor from the steadily diminishing Indian population to meet even those demands which crown officials recognized as having a prior demand on what labor was available.

As the labor market was tightening, new orders arrived from Spain. The reform projects contained in the cedulas of November 24, 1601, and May 26, 1609, envisaged a drastic lightening of the labor burdens of the Indians. Motivating the crown's policy were a variety of considerations, ideological as well as humanitarian and economic. The Indians as recent converts to Christianity merited the Crown's special protection. Compassion for the plight of the Indians who were being decimated by famine, disease, and overwork was another factor. Thirdly, enlightened self-interest advocated measures of relief. The Indians must be preserved, for they were the colony's principal labor force. The viceroys, the Audiencia, and even the clergy did not discount the pertinence of these arguments. Yet the same officials realized that the implementation of the cedulas of 1601 and 1609 would only aggravate an already desperate crisis. Famine in the cities of New Spain instead of the threat of famine might ensue. In the face of conflicting standards, the responsible authorities in New Spain gave priority to the overall economic crisis rather than the specific plight of the Indians. Invoking a traditional formula of Spanish administrative procedure, the viceroys and the Audiencia obeyed but did not execute the orders of the Council.[8]

The actual operation of this formula merits closer examination. Geographical isolation of the colonies, wide divergence in regional conditions, and only partial awareness of these conditions on the part of the central authorities made some such institutional device desirable. The formula's origins go back to the Roman law concept that the prince can will no injustice. The "I obey" clause signifies the recognition by subordinates of the legitimacy of the sovereign power who, if properly informed of all circumstances, would will no wrong. The "I do not execute" clause is the subordinate's assumption of the responsibility of postponing the execution of an order until the sovereign is informed of those conditions of which he may be ignorant and without a knowledge of which an injustice may be committed.

Presiding magistrates in the Indies were permitted by law to postpone the execution of royal orders whose implementation might create an injustice or undesirable social conflicts. Colonial administrators were required

to justify immediately their conduct to the Council. The central authorities in return might reissue the orders in their original form, or they might modify them in accordance with the suggestions of the local authorities. The latter in turn might invoke the formula again in the hopes that by procrastination the unwanted proposals might be buried by bureaucratic inertia.[9]

Colonial administrators had to apply with discretion the "I obey but do not execute" formula. A reckless use of this power might arouse the ire of the Council. Offenders might incur any number of penalties, ranging from reprimands to demotions, to loss of office or imprisonment. The colonial bureaucrat constantly needed to strike a delicate balance between the orders of his superiors in Spain and the dictates of local pressures. Many a bureaucratic career ended in disgrace that could be traced back to a miscalculation of the relative importance of the pressures in a given situation. The Spanish colonial bureaucrat like his modern Russian counterpart had to orient himself to his superiors' "real" objectives, which were often not reflected in the actual instructions emanating from Spain.

Thus, the "I obey but do not execute" formula appears as an institutional device for decentralizing decision making. Its frequent use enabled colonial officials to postpone indefinitely the execution of royal wishes. Furthermore, its operation reveals the more positive role of subordinates as policy makers. By postponing the execution of royal mandates and presenting fresh proposals, viceroys, Audiencia, and archbishops could influence the reformulation of their super-

[8] For the demographic crisis see Lesley Byrd Simpson and Sherburne F. Cook, *The Population of Central Mexico in the Sixteenth Century* (*Ibero-Americana*, 31; Berkeley and Los Angeles, 1948); for the change in land use, Lesley B. Simpson, *The Exploitation of Land in Central Mexico in the Sixteenth Century* (*Ibero-Americana*, 36; Berkeley and Los Angeles, 1952); for the economic crisis Woodrow Wilson Borah, *New Spain's Century of Depression* (*Ibero-Americana*, 35; Berkeley and Los Angeles, 1951).

[9] Haring, *op. cit.*, pp. 122–123.

iors' directives. New instructions from Spain often reflected to some extent, at least, the viewpoint of officials in the Indies.

The dialectic of the Spanish administrative system may be clarified by Hegelian formula. The thesis is the wishes of the Council embodied in its directives dispatched to the colonies. The antithesis is that complex of pressures or standards to which colonial administrators had to adapt, pressures often in conflict with the Council's instructions. The synthesis is what actually emerged. That was not always a satisfactory but usually a workable compromise between what the central authorities intended and what local pressures would permit.[10]

The Spanish colonial administration was, in effect, a dynamic balance between the principles of authority and flexibility, in which the highly centralized decision making vested in the king and the Council was counterbalanced by some substantial measure of decentralized decision making exercised by bureaucratic subordinates in the colonies.

INSTRUMENTS OF CONTROL

If the "I obey but do not execute" formula gave colonial magistrates some measure of freedom in which to maneuver, other institutional devices made officers in the colonies sensitive to the wishes of their superiors in Spain. There were two institutional procedures by which superiors in Spain enforced standards and reviewed the performance of subordinates in the Indies. They were the *residencia* and the *visita*.

The *residencia* was a judicial review of the conduct of a magistrate at the end of his term of office. All appointees of the Crown with the notable exception of the clergy were required by law to submit to a *residencia* at the termination of their tenure. A specially designated *juez de residencia* conducted a public court of inquiry in which he heard all charges of malfeasance against the former incumbent. After receiving the latter's defense, the judge passed sentence and remitted his findings to the Council of the Indies for final review. Heavy fines, con-

fiscation of property, imprisonment, or all three, were customary sentences in cases of grave misconduct in office. The fact that sentences in the Indies were often reversed or altered in Spain does suggest that decisions sometimes reflected the personal bias of the judges or that the official under investigation was able to bring to bear commanding influence at Court. Thus there was a Spanish counterpart to the Russian *blat*.[11]

The *visita* differed from the *residencia* in respect to procedure. Both devices, however, shared a common purpose, that is, to serve as agencies of royal control over subordinates in the colonies. The *residencia* was public and statutory. It took place at the end of a magistrate's term of office. The *visita*, on the other hand, was a secret inquiry which could be made at any time during a magistrate's incumbency. Generally applied as a crisis measure, it usually reflected the discontent of the central authorities with a specific situation in the colonies. The aim of the *visita* was to prod apathetic subordinates into taking a more vigorous action, whereas the *residencia*'s objective was to expose and punish illegal practices. There were restricted *visitas* applying to a single official or to a single province, and there were general *visitas* in which an entire viceroyalty or an Audiencia district came under investigation. The visitor general could examine all aspects of administration. He might interrogate any magistrate from the viceroy or the archbishop downward. It is indeed a moot question as to whose authority was supreme during the term of the visitation—that of the viceroy or that of the visitor.[12]

[10] If local conditions gave officials in the Indies a comfortable freedom of action in enforcing mutually incompatible directives from Spain, these same conditions allowed the natives to be selective in their responses to the settled governmental policy of hispanizing indigenous culture. See *Hispanization of the Philippines*, pp. 153 ff.

[11] *Blat* in the Russian productive setup represents the element of personal influence which oils the wheels of the informal procurement system. See Frank, *op. cit.*, p. 9.

[12] Haring has an evaluation of both the *residencia* and the *visita*, *op. cit.*, pp. 148–157. Also see *Recopilación*, Bk. V, tit. xv (1681).

The opinion of the Marquis of Montesclaros, viceroy of Peru (1607–1615) has often been quoted. He likened the *residencia* and the *visita* to gusts of wind which one frequently encounters in the streets and in the public squares and which accomplish nothing but to raise the dust and refuse and cause everyone to cover his head. This bon mot may be an apt contemporary evaluation of the institution from the viewpoint of subordinates subject to investigation. Yet the perspective of the investigators, the Council of the Indies, was a different one. These twin procedures enabled superiors in Spain to enforce standards in the colonies and to review periodically the performance of subordinates. The *visita* functioned as a means of enforcing old standards, establishing new ones, or enunciating a new priority among existing standards. The *residencia* became an instrument for reviewing the past performance of subordinates. Both procedures were highly selective. Some standards were violated in order to enforce others, as the wide gap between the law and its observance in the colonies amply attests. Magistrates in the Indies, however, never for a moment forgot the existence of this highly institutionalized system of enforcement and review, however selective its application may have been in practice. Its operation certainly encouraged them to keep in harmony with their superiors' "real" wishes.

The key to this hypothesis about social organization lies in selective evaluation and selective enforcement. Selectivity makes a system with conflicts among the standards operationally feasible.

Conclusions

In summary, the operation of the Spanish colonial system apparently has some features common to the Soviet industrial system.

1. The members of both organizations were motivated to some significant degree by personal involvement in the system and its welfare.

2. Looking at the Spanish administration as a whole, one can see no single guiding goal or objective save that tendency common to all bureaucracies—the tendency toward self-perpetuation. Nor are there several goals commensurate with each other. Hence the goals are difficult to rank. The standards to which individual agents were subject often clashed with one another, and no clear-cut priority among these standards was available for the agents. A notable exception to the over-all goal ambiguity of the Spanish system is the case of the Church. The spiritual welfare of the natives and the colonists was a clear-cut goal from which the Church could scarcely deviate, although various branches of the clergy clashed over the means of reaching that goal.

3. The Spanish system like the Russian was task-performance oriented.

4. Both systems are hierarchal and bureaucratic organizations.

5. In short, both administrations constitute multiple, partly interdependent and partly independent, hierarchies with mutually incompatible standards, selective enforcement of standards, and selective review of performance.

The fact that the Soviet productive system is undergoing intensive change while the Spanish administration was not does not seriously impair the over-all validity of the analogy between the two systems. The Spanish system was not static. Change there was, although it was slow in comparison to the quick tempo of change in the Russian industrial system. The Spanish administration possessed a feature lacking in the Soviet industrial organization, that of geographical distance. A one-to-two-year period ensued in the exchange of correspondence between the Council of the Indies and the colonial bureaucrats. This temporal hiatus contributed markedly to slowing down the pace of change in the colonies. As a consequence colonial magistrates had greater freedom in selecting their responses to orders from Spain than do officials in the Soviet productive system, dominated as it is by fast-moving change. More procrastination and a greater degree of venality probably prevailed in the Spanish system than in the Russian one, although unfamiliarity with the Russian sources makes it impossible to make a clear affirmation. A basic issue, which merits more attention, is how essential the element of change is to the hypothesis of conflicting standards and selective enforcement. The fact of geographical distance and its corollary of slow communications seems in the case of the Spanish colonial administration to replace rapid change as an assumption.

Historians have assumed that the Spanish bureaucracy like other bureaucratic organizations had only one goal or a set of commensurate goals and that standards of conduct for members were not mutually conflicting. If this assumption is cast aside in favor of goal ambiguity and conflicting standards, new light is thrown on the chasm between the law and its observance in the Spanish empire. The wide gap between the two was not a flaw, as has been traditionally assumed. On the contrary, the distance between observance and nonobservance was a necessary component of the system. Given the ambiguity of the goals and the conflict among the standards, all the laws could not be enforced simultaneously. The very conflict among the standards, which prevented a subordinate from meeting all the standards at once, gave subordinates a voice in decision making without jeopardizing the control of their superiors over the whole system.

This hypothesis, I suggest, can serve as a point of departure for monographic research that may provide us with a new and richer perspective on the working of the Spanish bureaucracy. Here only a few suggestions for future research will be outlined. In this essay the "downward" communication from superior to subordinate rather than the "upward" or "lateral" communication from subordinate to superior has been stressed. One aspect of this has already been touched upon. Subordinates did play a role in formulating the directives of their superiors through the advice and information they transmitted upward. It would be equally desirable to explore at greater depth the "hori-zontal" relations of the members of the various administrative hierarchies.

Since the standards set by the Council of the Indies were often mutually incompatible as well as in conflict with local conditions, the task of the historian is to evaluate the priority among those standards in any given situation. Which ones were enforced at the expense of others? In many cases a compromise emerged with token or partial enforcement of some standards. In this essay I have stressed some of the conflicts inherent in the Crown's Indian policy. Equally significant incompatibilities prevailed in other spheres of colonial administration.

In a sense this essay has been a "shakedown cruise." If this preliminary investigation proves anything at all, it justifies making further efforts. The various components of Frank's hypothesis now must be tested against a mass of documentary evidence in a concrete historical setting. The historian tries to preserve the flavor and uniqueness of individual human experience. My primary concern is not with bureaucracies as such, but with a particular bureaucracy during a specific time span. In a study of the dynamics of the Spanish imperial bureaucracy in which we are currently engaged, we have little doubt that Frank's hypothesis will provide a useful set of questions with which to interrogate the documents.[13] That the answers which will emerge from this interrogation may result in significant revisions of the original hypothesis is highly probable, but this net result ought not to obscure the creative role that such hypotheses play in stimulating fresh research.

---

[13] The specific topic of the book will be a study of the dynamics of the Spanish imperial bureaucracy as reflected in the career of a representative figure of that system. Antonio de Morga (1559–1636) was a vigorous, versatile, and articulate bureaucrat, who achieved distinction as a historian, a jurist, and a specialist in finance. The fact that he served in the Audiencias of Manila, Mexico, and Quito lends to this study something of an empire-wide dimension.

92. Social Structure and Social Change in New Spain*

Lyle N. McAlister

The purpose of this paper is to examine the social structure of New Spain using a conceptual framework somewhat different from those commonly employed and one which may be more useful for the explanation of certain historical phenomena. It does not purport to be a piece of "basic research." It is more properly a theory of social structure. The principal concepts employed are abstracted from infinitely complex historical situations. A number of observations made cannot be precisely documented; they are hypotheses which seem to "make sense" in the light of the author's reading and research. Hypotheses and substantiated observations, however, appear to fit together and to accommodate the known "facts." The concept of society is arbitrarily separated from that of the state and the latter treated only incidentally, although Spanish political thinkers did not regard such boundary establishment as either real or desirable, and the political role of estates and corporations is factored out. This procedure can be justified by regarding the state as "nothing more than the organization of all social forces that have a political significance . . . as that part of society which performs the political function."[1] Conceptually, therefore, state and society may be distinguished one from the other and the problem of the relationship between the two, while real and important, is somewhat different from the one to be examined here.[2]

A word is in order about terminology. Such expressions as social structure, social organization, social system, class, caste, and the like are used rather loosely by historians, so that confusion in terminology often produces confusion in ideas. On the other hand, sociologists and social anthropologists in attempting to define such concepts more rigorously have come up with so many conflicting "scientific" definitions that they have simply created terminological confusion at another level. The term "social structure" is here used in a non-technical sense. It presumes that a society is made up of individuals grouped according to the possession of common interests, attributes, and qualities; that these groups are definable, and that they are related to each other in some definable, non-random order.[3] Other terms commonly used in social analysis are either explicitly defined or, it is hoped, their usage is implicit in the context.

On the eve of the conquest of America, the constituent elements of Spanish society were groups and associations identifiable in terms of (1) ascribed functions and/or statuses, (2) systems of shared values, attitudes, and activities associated with the latter, (3) distinct and unequal juridical personalities expressed in general legal codes or special *fueros*, *ordenanzas*, and *reglamentos*, and involving some degree of autonomous jurisdiction. This society was conceived of in organic terms; that is, like the human body, its several parts were structurally and functionally interrelated and interdependent. The health of the body social depended on the vigor and proper functioning of the constituent organs.

* *HAHR*, 43: 349–370 (Aug. 1963). Reprinted by permission of the author and the publisher.
[1] Gaetano Mosca, *The Ruling Class* (New York, 1939), pp. 158–159.
[2] The treatment of some quite similar concepts in this paper and in Richard M. Morse, "Toward a Theory of Spanish American Government," *Journal of the History of Ideas*, XV (1954), 71–93, might be compared.
[3] See the remarks on social structure in Julian Pitt-Rivers, *The People of the Sierra* (London, 1955), pp. xiii–xiv.

The constituent elements of Spanish society fell into two logical categories:[4] the vestiges of the medieval estates and functional corporations. The primary estates, noble, clerical, and common, had a functional derivation. Thus, in the High Middle Ages they were identified as *defensores*, *oratores*, and *laboratores*. Leaving aside the church for the moment, as between the two secular estates the function of warrior was assigned a higher social value and initially was completely identified with the nobility. Despite isolated voices upholding the dignity and value of production, it was commonly held that without the defensores, the other estates would fall victim to predatory forces and the social order would disintegrate. Function and its assigned social value conveyed social quality and status and conferred or withheld honor. Thus the bearing of arms was honorable while productive occupations—agriculture, trade, manufacturing—were dishonorable. Quality and honor, moreover, came to be conceived of not as individual attributes which could be acquired but as deriving from lineage. The military function of the nobility and derivative social quality and status were juridically recognized in the *fuero de hidalguía* whereby the noble was exempted from personal taxes and tributes (*pechos*); he could not be imprisoned for debt nor could his residence, horse, or arms be attached for debts, and he could not be subjected to judicial torture or to base punishment.[5]

Within the primary estates, hierarchies of social rank existed. Thus the highest level of the nobility consisted of the grandees who were the social equals of the king. Below them ranked the rest of the titled nobility—marquises, counts, etc.—and at the bottom of the pyramid of nobility was the mass of knights or hidalgos.

Coincidentally with the evolution of a hierarchy of estates and substates, countertrends were deforming its structural purity. These had their origin in the growth of towns, trade, and a money economy. They assumed the form of increased diversification of function and the modification of the functional base of the secular estates. Within the common estate, an emerging group of merchants, bankers, and legalists (*letrados*) performed functions so indispensable to society and the state that they could not be denied social honor and status. In the case of mercantile elements, wealth could literally buy many of the attributes of social quality. Moreover, when city dwellers organized urban militia and the *Santa Hermandad* for their defense, and as the nucleus of a mercenary army developed in the fifteenth century, the nobility lost its monopoly on the role of defensor. At the same time, the pressures of a money economy reduced many of the lower strata of the nobility to indigency or compelled them into money-making activities. Hidalguía, furthermore, acquired an economic value. The hidalgo as distinct from the commoner (in this case identical with the *pechero*) was exempt from personal taxes or tributes, and pretensions to hidalguía came to be based not so much on aspirations to honor or status but on financial advantage. Conversely, the emergent bourgeoisie were anxious to acquire a social quality and status which could not be validated completely by wealth alone. Juan Huarte de San Juan describes these attitudes in his *Examen de ingenios*: "To be well born and of famous lineage is a very highly esteemed jewel but it has one very great fault; by itself it has little benefit . . . but linked to wealth there is no point of honor that can equal it . . ." "Some," he adds, "compare nobility to the zero of the decimal system; by itself it is nothing but joined with a digit it acquires great value."[6]

As a consequence of these complementary trends, the traditional hierarchy of estates and substates became blurred at the point

[4] The following discussion of Spanish social structure, except where otherwise indicated, is based on Juan Beneyto, *Historia social de España y de Hispanoamérica* (Madrid, 1961) and Jaime Vicens Vives, dir. and contr., *Historia social y Económica de España y América* (4 vols. Barcelona, 1957–59), vol. II.

[5] *Novísima recopilación de las leyes de España*, Lib. V, tit. ii, ley xv.

[6] As quoted in Beneyto, p. 215.

of contact between the lower nobility and the upper strata of the common order and a new sector emerged which combined the values and functions of the nobility and the bourgeoisie. Nevertheless the image of a society ordered on the basis of functionally derived social quality remained virtually unimpaired in the minds of Spaniards. Jurists and theologians might challenge the system on philosophical, religious, or logical grounds, but any popular opposition to it that existed arose from dissatisfaction of individuals and groups with their place in it rather than from a realization of its inequity.

Examined on another plane, the constituent elements of Spanish society were a multitude of functional corporations which included the army, merchant's guilds (*consulados*), artisan's guilds (*gremios*), municipal organs, the *mesta*, and the like, each with a special juridical status. The relationship between the estates and the corporations raises a number of conceptual problems, the most fundamental being whether they actually represented two distinct systems of social organization. Beneyto observes that the corporate theory supported the stability of social stratification in that "the status of the corporation has to correspond to the status of the individuals who enter into it," implying that the corporations were actually suborders within a stratified society of estates.[7] However, a case for the coexistence of two social systems can be made on the following grounds: (1) Within the estates, the ordering came to be on the basis of social quality and status divorced from their original functional bases whereas the corporations were specifically functional in fact and by virtue of their formal ordenanzas and reglamentos. (2) The boundaries between corporations in contrast to those separating social classes were sharp and absolutely definable in functional and legal terms. (3) Although there was some general correspondence between the status of corporations and the individuals who composed them, it was often blurred. Thus, as suggested above, within the merchant guilds, the noble-commoner dichotomy tended to disappear, and the standing army which

emerged in the fifteenth century contained men from all ranks of society although recognition of social quality was maintained in the wide gap that existed between the statuses of officer and enlisted man. (4) The corporations maintained a higher degree of internal discipline. (5) Among the several functional corporations there was no explicit hierarchical ordering. The social structure deriving from estates was stratified; that based on corporations was conglomerate. Although two systems existed, there was a significant intersection or interpenetration between them.

The church cannot be accommodated in either of the categories established above. Historically it was one of the primary medieval estates. It was also a functioning corporation. Its position in the social order, however, transcended both. It was, in fact, a society in itself providing for all the needs of its personnel. It possessed its own social stratification grading downward from the prelates—archbishops, bishops, and abbots who were identifiable with the secular nobility—to the parish priests identifiable with the commoners. It also had a conglomerate structure whose components were "subcorporations" such as the regular and secular clergy, the military orders, the Inquisition and the universities, each enjoying a particular fuero or jurisdiction. Moreover, although in terms of historical experience, self-identification, and certain aspects of its juridical status, it was a Spanish institution, it was also but a branch of the church universal. In view of these difficulties, within the conceptual framework of this paper, the church can be more properly considered in terms of its constituent groups rather than as a social estate or as a unitary corporation.

At a time that was particularly significant for social formation in America, agitation against and eventual expulsion of Moors and Jews from Spain activated a latent element in peninsular social organization. The status-seeking Spaniard became almost pathologically concerned not only with establishing his hidalguía but also his purity of blood

[7] *Ibid.*, p. 117.

(*limpieza de sangre*). Indeed the two qualities became almost coextensive. The latter is overtly ethnic, but its basic derivation was religious. It signified a lineage of impeccable orthodoxy. Thus Pedro de la Caballería, a member of Ferdinand the Catholic's entourage and a well-known Jew, forged an *expediente* supported by testimony from eminent nobles, according to which his progenitors had been "*verdaderos cristianos viejos de limpísima sangre.*"[8] The possession of such qualities or the lack of them influenced not only social status but corporate membership. Purity of blood was a condition of membership in artisan guids, religious and military orders, municipal *consejos*, and for the award of university degrees.

The concepts of estate and corps were integral parts of the cultural baggage which Spaniards carried with them to the Indies. Social structure there, however, developed a character that differed from its peninsular prototype. This divergence derived from two powerful influences: first, the deliberate intervention of the crown in the process of social formation, a phenomenon which will be considered later in this paper;[9] second, the survival of large portions of the indigenous population, the importation of substantial numbers of Negro slaves, and miscegenation involving the three races. The ethnic factor produced what colonial writers called a system of castes. The latter word, however, should be taken as the equivalent of the Spanish term *casta*. It did not denote a rigid, closed social system such as that associated with India.[10] Various classifications of the castes appeared. In the early nineteenth century amateur anthropologists constructed elaborate taxonomies such as the following:[11]

1. Spaniard with an Indian woman, *mestizo*
2. *Mestiza* with a Spaniard, *castizo*
3. *Castizo* with a Spanish woman, Spaniard
4. Spaniard with a Negro woman, *mulato*
5. *Mulata* with a Spaniard, *morisco*
6. *Morisco* with a Spanish woman, *chino*
7. *Chino* with an Indian woman, *salta atrás*
8. *Salta atrás* with a *mulata*, *lobo*
9. *Lobo* with a *china*, *gíbaro*
10. *Gíbaro* with a *mulata*, *albarazado*

11. *Albarazado* with a Negro woman, *cambujo*
12. *Cambujo* with an Indian woman, *zambaigo*
13. *Zambaigo* with a *loba*, *Calpa mulato*
14. *Calpa mulato* with a *cambuja*, *tente en el aire*
15. *Tente en el aire* with a *mulata*, *no te entiendo*
16. *No te entiendo* with an Indian woman, *torna atrás*

A simpler classification was commonly used which appears to be the basis of descriptions of "colonial society" in modern textbooks. The elements were:

Spaniard or white (European or American)
mestizo: various mixtures of Indian and Spaniard
mulatto: various mixtures of Negro and Spaniard
zambo or zambaigo: Indian and Negro
Indian
Negro

For official purposes, particularly the assessment of tribute and military service, three primary groups were identified: Spaniard (European and American); castes (castas), that is, persons of mixed blood; and Indians.[12]

Although such classifications were overtly ethnic they were strongly influenced by cultural factors. Thus, in fact and in law, "white" or "Spaniard" was practically coextensive with *gente de casta limpia*, a category which included not only persons of pure Spanish origin but mestizos and castizos who were of legitimate descent, free from the taint of Negro blood, and who

[8] *Ibid.*, p. 223.
[9] The role of the state in social formation is examined in Richard Konetzke, "Estado y sociedad en las Indias," *Estudios americanos*, III (1951), 33–58.
[10] See the remarks on the use of the word "caste" in Joaquín Roncal, "The Negro Race in Mexico," *HAHR*, XXIV (1944), 531, note 2.
[11] These are described in Nicolás León, *Las castas del México colonial o Nueva España* (México, 1924). See also Gonzalo Aguirre Beltrán, *La población negro de México, 1519–1810* (México, 1946), pp. 175–179.
[12] *Instrucción reservada que el conde de Revilla Gigedo dió a su sucesor en el mando* . . . (México, 1831), pars. 579–580; Aguirre Beltrán, p. 226; Fernando Navarro y Noriega, *Memoria sobre la población del Reino de Nueva España escrita en el año de 1814* (México, 1954), Table and pp. 21, 24.

"lived like Spaniards."[13] The distinguishing feature of the castes were illegitimate descent or the suspicion of it and the possession of Negro blood or the suspicion of such a taint because of illegitimacy.[14] The taint associated with the Negro derived from his supposed physical and psychological characteristics and his juridical status. His pigmentation and features were regarded as repellent; early colonial officials and chroniclers regarded Negroes and mulattos as *"viles, traidores, ocisos, borrachos,"* etc. They were the people most *"mastreros, pérfidos e inmorales de la humanidad."*[15] As slaves or the descendants of slaves they were *infames por derecho.* As such they were forbidden to bear arms or to enter military service, they were excluded from the clergy and public office, and they were forbidden to intermarry with Indians or whites.[16] In regard to the Indian group, it was composed of ethnic Indians and mestizos who were culturally Indian. In a curiously reverse

sort of way, a Spaniard or white might be most accurately defined as a person who culturally and legally was neither an Indian nor a caste; an Indian was a person who was neither a Spaniard nor a caste; and a caste was an individual who was neither Spaniard nor Indian.

Aguirre Beltrán has developed the following method of classifying castes which explicitly recognizes cultural factors in their formation:[17]

European: persons of pure European descent

Indians: ethnic Inndians

Negroes: ethnic Negroes

Euromestizos: persons of mixed European and Indian orgin but with predominantly European ethnic and cultural characteristics

Indomestizos: European-Indian mixtures but ethnically and culturally predominantly Indian

Afromestizos: Mixed bloods with a Negro strain

The several systems of classification described above may be correlated as follows:

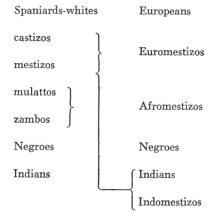

[13] Juan de Solórzano Pereira, *Política indiana,* Lib. II, cap. xxx núms. 1, 20–28; Aguirre Beltrán, pp. 174–175; Angel Rosenblat, *La población indígena de América desde 1492 hasta la actualidad* (Buenos Aires, 1945), pp. 264–65, 271–272.

[14] Aguirre Beltrán, pp. 248–254; Solórzano, Lib. II, cap. xxx núms. 2, 20–28, 55; Salvador de Madariaga, *The Rise of the Spanish American Empire* (London, 1947), p. 21.

[15] Aguirre Beltrán, pp. 187–190.

[16] The legal status of the castes is examined in William H. Dusenberry, "Discriminatory Aspects of Legislation in Colonial Mexico," *Journal of Negro History,* XXXIII (1948), 284–302.

[17] Aguirre Beltrán, pp. 270–271.

The questions arises as to whether these ethnic cultural groups constituted elements in a definable social structure. The system of castes was certainly a contemporary reality and its component elements were identified in the contemporary mind in a loose reputational way. It is a useful framework for descriptive purposes but it has a limited value for structural analysis. In the case of the elaborate constructions of the early nineteenth-century taxonomists, the types are too numerous to be manageable; they are difficult to identify with any degree of precision, and status distinctions among them are by no means clear. The same criticism is true to a lesser extent of simpler traditional systems and the typology of Aguirre Beltrán. Or perhaps it would be more accurate to say that there are not enough data available in a usable form to enable such groups to be identified and ordered in a scientific system. The trichotomy Spaniard—caste—Indian, however, presents fewer problems. It does constitute a social structure. Its elements are identifiable; they possess definable social and juridical statuses, and they exist in an ordered relation to each other. They represent an American system of estates which evolved in an *ad hoc* fashion out of New World circumstances without the support of any fundamental social theory.

The Spanish sectors of the population, although of diverse social and ethnic origin, possessed a certain homogeneity deriving from its position as a conquering race and its assumed superior culture. Its identity was supported, moreover, by the possession of or pretension to limpieza de sangre and descent from cristianos viejos, qualities which were identified with legitimate lineage. Its superior status was also expressed in almost universal claims to nobility or hidalguía. Theoretically, this quality derived from two sources: lineage and royal concession, both subject to documentary substantiation. In fact, many Spanish families could claim hidalguía on one of these grounds. Some of the conquerors, first settlers, and later arrivals came from peninsular families of substantiated nobility. The crown also made concessions of hidalguía to Mexican families, although rather sparingly.[18] From the outset, however, the conquerors exhibited a sharp consciousness of nobility deriving not from lineage or royal concession but from a sense of personal excellence, from glory in deeds of valor done during the Conquest, and from a pride in noble action. It was such sentiments that moved Pizarro to claim that the Conquest created a new nobility. These feelings became diffused through the entire Spanish population and led the Council of the Indies to declare: "It is undeniable that

in those kingdoms [in America] any Spaniard who comes to them, who acquires some wealth, and who is not engaged in a dishonorable occupation, is regarded as a noble." Alexander von Humboldt went even farther. "Any white person," he wrote, "although he rides his horse barefoot, imagines himself to be of the nobility of the country."[19] Nobility, in fact, became largely an officially recognized individual and social state of mind. The concepts of Spanishness, whiteness, limpieza de sangre, vieja cristianidad, and hidalguía tended to become coextensive and together formed a system of values and status determinants clearly identifiable with a major social sector. These qualities were recognized in law, particularly in exemption from tribute, and the hidalgo-pechero dichotomy was thus preserved in the New World.[20] The white or Spanish component of society was the American counterpart of the noble estate of Spain.

The place of the castes in the Spanish concept of a hierarchically organized society is rather difficult to define. Their existence was deplored. They really were not supposed to exist. In the eyes of most of the white population they were lazy, vicious, irresponsible, and a threat to social and political stability.[21] Yet they formed a large proportion of the artisan and laboring population of the viceroyalty. As infames por derecho and as payers of tribute they possessed a juridical status or personality and a social status universally recognized and defined by reputation.[22] They constituted a common estate deformed by New World circumstances.

In regard to the Indian, universally minded jurists and theologians argued for the equality of the Spaniards and the indigenous population, but from the outset of colonization a wide chasm yawned between the two races. The Indians existed as conquered

[18] Richard Konetzke, "La formación de la nobleza en Indias," *Estudios americanos,* III (1951), 330, 341–346.

[19] Both quoted in *ibid.,* p. 356.

[20] Vicens Vives, III, 430; Mario Góngora, *El estado en el derecho indiano* (Santiago de Chile, 1951), pp. 186–187.

[21] Aguirre Beltrán, pp. 187–190.

[22] Solórzano, Lib. II, cap. xxx, núms. 20–28.

people, the Spanish as conquerors. The Spanish became the employers and exploiters of labor, the Indians the hewers of wood and the drawers of water. Profound cultural differences existed between the two peoples; the Indians refused to live like civilized people, that is, like Spaniards, and were regarded by the latter as *rústicas* or *miserables*. Thus, the indigenous population acquired a dependent if not an inferior status which was juridically recognized. In the Laws of the Indies, the Indians were regarded as perpetual minors and wards of the crown and were placed under the tutelage of royal officials in *corregimientos*, of individuals and corporations in *encomiendas*, and of the regular ecclesiastical orders in missions. In recognition of their vassalage, they were required to pay tribute; they were forbidden to dress like Spaniards, to ride horses, or to bear arms. On the other hand, they were conceded privileges and immunities which in effect constituted a fuero. Official lay and clerical protectors oversaw their welfare; they had access to special tribunals such as the *Juzgado de Indios*; they were exempt from the direct jurisdiction of the Holy Office and from various taxes such as the *alcabala* and *diezmos*. Although functionally they were commoners, they were juridically distinct from the castes and constituted a peculiarly American estate.[23]

The three primary estates contained internal stratifications based partly on ascribed status deriving from lineage, degree of whiteness, and nobility, and in part from status acquired through wealth or royal favor. Within the Indian component, the upper stratum consisted of a nobility whose rank was inherited from the preconquest *caciques* and confirmed by the Spanish crown. This group was juridically identified with the white nobility in that it was exempt from tribute and from legal inhibitions imposed on the general Indian population but it remained culturally Indian.[24] At a lower level were the notables who occupied posts of distinction in Indian communities, while the base of the pyramid consisted of the mass of the indigenous population.

Within the white estate there existed a group which might be described as an upper nobility. Initially this was comprised of the conquerors who by virtue of their feats of arms regarded themselves as a new nobility. Immediately below them came the first settlers whose excellence derived not from martial exploits but from merits acquired in the initiation of colonization, the occupation of new territory for the king, and the founding of towns and cities. These two groups were rewarded for their eminent services by encomiendas: that is, grants of Indians from which they were privileged to extract labor and/or tribute. During the seventeenth century they tended to fuse and together were called by jurists, *beneméritos de Indias*.[25] Initially the encomendero class gave indications of evolving into a military nobility along lines reminiscent of the emergence of the Spanish nobility in the Middle Ages. The encomienda initially displayed distinctly feudal features, particularly in its military aspects. In effect the crown and the encomenderos were parties to a feudal contract. The former granted the encomienda as a benefice, while the latter acknwledged vassalage, swore fealty, and were obligated to be ready with arms, horses, and retainers to fight the enemies of their lord. In order to fulfill this obligation, they were required to reside in the province in which they held their encomienda; in case of absence—for which permission was required—they had to appoint a champion (*escudero*); if a minor inherited, his guardian or tutor appointed a champion; if an encomienda passed to a woman, she was required to marry within a year so that her husband could fulfill the military obligations entailed.[26] The army of encomenderos resem-

[23] The principal legislation affecting the juridicial status of the Indian in Spanish America is brought together in *Recopilación de leyes de los reinos de las Indias,* Lib. VI. Extensive commentary on Indian legislation is found in Solórzano, Lib. II. It is analyzed in Góngora, pp. 198–221.

[24] Lesley B. Simpson, *The Encomienda in New Spain* (Berkeley, 1950), p. 120.

[25] Góngora, pp. 186–190.

[26] Solórzano, Lib. III, cap. xxv; José Miranda, *Las ideas y las instituciones politicas mexicanas, 1521–1820* (México, 1952), pp. 33–34, 46; J. H.

bled the feudal host and was the principal reliance of the crown for defense of the viceroyalty up to the last quarter of the sixteenth century. Thus operations against the Chichemecas in New Galicia in 1541–1542 were conducted largely by encomenderos.[27] Some ten years later when Viceroy Velasco requested assistance from the crown for operations against rebellious Indians, he was told that the responsibility lay with the encomenderos because "the encomiendas are rents which His Majesty gives to the encomenderos because they defend the land."[28]

The emergence of a military nobility from the encomienda system, however, was prevented by several factors. In the first place, the encomienda proved to be unsatisfactory as a military institution. The encomenderos were a restless lot and, despite repeated prohibitions, abandoned their provinces for the lure of new conquests. Moreover, they displayed a marked reluctance to engage in organized campaigns, particularly if these were distant from their city and of long duration.[29] As a result, during the last part of the sixteenth century the burden of defense was shifted to regular troops and to a citizen militia drawn from the white population in general.[30] The sons and grandsons of the conquerors failed to perpetuate the martial spirit of their ancestors. Although the trappings of military service—titles of rank, uniforms, and military honors—were eagerly sought after, they were honorific in character and were not associated with attraction to a military way of life. At the end of the sixteenth century, old soldier Bernardo de Vargas Machuca lamented that although the military profession was the most honorable and sublime of all the arts, it had fallen into disfavor and there were few citizens who would not smile at the thought of a career of arms.[31] A century later, Viceroy the Marquis of Mancera complained about the disinclination of the Mexican nobility for military service.[32]

A second factor which inhibited the development of a powerful upper nobility in the Indies was the opposition of the crown. The encomenderos, whose mentality was essentially medieval, aspired to combine encomiendas with possession of land and jurisdiction to create seignorial estates, but the crown insisted on keeping grants of land and grants of Indians separate; it refused to grant Indians in perpetuity and, except in rare cases such as the Marquisate of the Valley of Oaxaca and the Dukedom of Atrisco, it denied seignorial jurisdiction to encomenderos. In the reforms of the 1540's, the latter were prohibited from extracting personal services from their charges and allowed to collect only tribute.[33]

Thus the beneméritos became pensioners of the crown, a tamed nobility without any real vitality. Essentially they were dilettantes. They adopted the dignified mien and deportment of the noble estate. Among themselves and in their intercourse with other social sectors they insisted on being addressed as hidalgo or caballero. They eagerly sought titles of Castile and habits in the military orders of Spain. Their reading consisted of books of noble deeds and pious works and they displayed an extreme religiosity. They were vain, sensitive, disdainful of the mechanical and commercial arts, and addicted to luxury and ostentation. Perhaps their most distinguishing characteristic was an exaggerated sense of honor, a term not translatable in bourgeois concepts of recti-

---

[27] Góngora, pp. 175–176; Simpson, *Encomienda,* p. 121.

[28] Góngora, pp. 176.

[29] Góngora, pp. 175–177; Silvio Zavala, *New Viewpoints on the Spanish Colonization of America* (Philadelphia, 1943), p. 73.

[30] Konetzke, "Estado y sociedad," pp. 38–39; Philip W. Powell, *Soldiers Indians and Silver* (Berkeley and Los Angeles, 1952), pp. 111–112, 115, 119, 130.

[31] *Milicia y descripción de las Indias* (2 vols., Madrid, 1892), I, 60–61; II, 61–62.

[32] "Instrucción del marqués de Mancera al duque de Veragua," 1673, *Instrucciones que los vireyes de Nueva España dejaron a sus sucesores* (México, 1867), p. 275.

[33] Konetzke, "La formación de la nobleza," pp. 350–352; Góngora, pp. 179, 340.

Parry, *The Audiencia of New Galicia in the Sixteenth Century* (Cambridge, 1948), p. 9. Góngora presents a thoughtful essay on feudal elements in the conquest and settlement of America (pp. 181–185).

tude, strict accounting for responsibility, moral conduct, and the like, but as self-esteem based on status. The meaning is more precisely conveyed by the Spanish word *pundonor*.[34]

The formation of an American structure of estates was accompanied by the transference and florescence of the functional corporation along with its legally defined responsibilities, privileges, and immunities. The church came with the Conquest and during the sixteenth century most of its major subcorporations, the university community, the Holy Office, the secular and regular orders, the cathedral chapters, and the like became constituent parts of Mexican society. The municipal corporations likewise followed the Conquest. A permanent army appeared in the latter part of the century. The consulado of Mexico City was chartered in 1592,[35] and most of the artisan guilds made their appearance in the late sixteenth and early seventeenth centuries.[36]

As in Europe the relation between the estates and corporate structure was complex. On the one hand, following the medieval prescription, there was some correspondence between the two. Theoretically, *casta limpia* was a requirement for admission to all the corporations, and in practice the white element monopolized the consulado, the miner's guild, the officer corps of the army, the university community, and the higher levels of the ecclesiastical corporations. However, the reluctance of whites to engage in dishonorable occupations complemented by the economic aspirations of the more enterprising castes and Indians led to the admission of large numbers of non-whites into the craft guilds.[37] They were also enlisted in the army and found their way into the lower levels of the church, particularly the secular clergy. Following the peninsular pattern there was an interlocking of class and corporate organization.

The preceding analysis of social structure employs a reputational or subjective method. That is, it is based on the way people of the time conceived of and defined their own and others' role and status. Colonial Mexican society may also be examined objectively; that is by assuming the position of an outside observer and by means of objective criteria dividing a society into groups, classes, or strata. Thus, a modern class system—upper, middle, and lower groups—based on the ownership and use of property may be discerned. The upper class consisted of the owners of haciendas and estancias, mines, textile factories, and mercantile establishments, and the upper levels of the bureaucracy and the clergy. At a point not clearly definable, this sector graded into a middle class composed of retail merchants and shopkeepers, the more substantial artisans, professionals, owners of small and middle-sized ranchos and mines, managers and salaried employees of rural properties, mines, and workshops, and lower ranked ecclesiastics and bureaucrats. The lower class comprised less affluent shopkeepers, peddlers, and artisans operating outside the guilds; servants, laborers, and a mass of landless, propertyless, and jobless idlers and vagabonds.[38] Such a classification presents serious difficulties. Given adequate data on distribution of wealth, income, occupation and the like, it might be practicable to analyze colonial social structure in terms of economic classes. The value systems commonly associated with such sectors, however, were lacking or at best rudimentary. Miners, merchants, and artisans might be functionally bourgeois but their mentality was not. Until the very end of the colonial period at least, they continued to think of social role and status in terms of nobility, titles, honor, and corporate mem-

---

[34] Vicens Vives, III, 427.

[35] Robert S. Smith, "The Institution of the Consulado in New Spain," *HAHR*, XXIV (1944), 61–62.

[36] The best account of the guilds in New Spain is Manuel Carrera Stampa, *Los gremios mexicanos* (México, 1954). A collection of their ordinances may be found in *Legislación del trabajo en los siglos XVI, XVII y XVIII. Breve ensayo crítico* (México, 1938).

[37] Carrera Stampa, pp. 223–243.

[38] The best discussion of colonial social structure in terms of economic class is Sergio Bagú, *Estructura social de la colonia* (Buenos Aires, 1952).

bership, although in the case of the Spanish upper classes wealth reinforced nobility and vice versa.[39]

The lower classes can be roughly identified with castes and Indians. Functionally they formed a proletariat. No class consciousness, however, existed within either element or linked the two together. A wide gap separated the rural Indian peon and the urban mulatto shoemaker. Their placement in society did not derive ultimately from economic function but from ethnic and cultural qualities recognized in law. Economic classes can probably be best regarded as an incipient situation and as a concept which can best be used for studying social development over a period extending beyond the colonial era rather than for the colonial period itself.

The social organization of New Spain was complicated by a peculiarly American cleavage which cut across the white estate and the corporate structure in general. This was the sharp status distinction between the European-born and American-born Spaniard, between criollo and *gachupín*. This schism originated within the first generations of Spaniards in the New World. The conquerors, first settlers, and their descendants deeply resented latecomers, both private citizens and crown appointees, who competed for the royal favors which they regarded as rightfully theirs. The new arrivals, on their part, resented the arrogance and privileges of the beneméritos. Original resentments were deepened and elaborated in subsequent generations. The peninsular Spaniard in common with his northern European contemporaries deprecated colonials as culturally and even biologically inferior. They were unenterprising, unreliable, and frivolous. The creole regarded the gachupín as common, pushing and, except for the higher levels of the church, army, and bureaucracy, as socially inferior. He resented the preemption of the choicest benefices in church and state by the European Spaniard despite the strict legal equality of the two groups. But he was embittered above all by the fact that the status conveyed by "born in

Spain" was forever beyond his reach. Yet there was a certain ambivalence in the creole attitude. While he maligned and contemned the gachupín, he envied him because his lack of extended contact with Indian or Negro gave him a better claim to limpieza de sangre, and he eagerly sought marriage alliances with the European, even the most common, to reinforce his family lineage.[40]

Some observations may now be made on the related problems of social cohesion, social control, and social change. The hierarchical society continued to be thought of in organic terms. Its component parts were supposed to be mutually interdependent, interacting and together forming the functioning body social. In fact, however, the parts exhibited a strong compulsion toward autarchy. Juridically, each to some extent was a separate entity, a state within a state. Each was wrapped up in its own affairs and interested only in its own welfare, its privileges, and its immunities, all of which had to be defended jealously against similar aims of other segments. There existed no common values, interests, or objectives. There were Indians, castes, nobles, soldiers, priests, merchants, and lawyers but there were no citizens.[41] In the

[39] The last statement is probably debatable. M. Hernández Sánchez-Barba in describing colonial society in the eighteenth century postulates a "bourgeois mentality" (in Vicens Vives, IV, pp. 422–427). The research of Stanley Stein on Mexican merchant groups may throw some light on this subject.

[40] On the subject of gachupín-creole rivalry the observations of Jorge Juan and Antonio de Ulloa in their *Noticias secretas de América* (2 vols., Madrid, 1918), II, Chap. V, are particularly revealing. Among modern studies of specific aspects of the problem is Antonio Tibesar, "The *Alternativa:* A Study of Spanish-Creole Relations in Seventeenth-Century Peru," *The Americas, XI* (1955), 229–283. A more theoretical approach is Richard Konetzke, "La condición legal de los criollos y las causas de la independencia," *Estudios americanos*, II (1950), 31–54.

[41] Pablo de Olivides' description, written in 1769, of the highly compartmentalized character of Spanish society (quoted in Beneyto, p. 290) is equally applicable to New Spain.

terms of Ortega y Gasset, it was an invertebrate society.[42]

This society was held together by a combination of a number of circumstances. Among them was inertia. A society of estates and corporations was in the natural order of things and until the latter part of the eighteenth century there was no serious protest against a social system based on juridical and social inequality. Social unrest took the form of drives to improve the status of the individual and the group, not efforts to change the system. The hierarchical order was supported through the virtual monopoly of arms, wealth, prestige, and authority by the white nobility. Until the very end of the colonial period, its existence was encouraged by the crown as a means of social and political control. In an opinion of 1806, the Council of the Indies stated:

It is undeniable that the existence of various hierarchies and classes is of the greatest importance to the existence and stability of a monarchical state, since a graduated system of dependence and subordination sustains and insures the obedience and respect of the last vassal to the authority of the sovereign. With much more reason such a system is necessary in America, not only because of its greater distance from the throne, but also because of the number of that class of people who, because of their vicious origin and nature, are not comparable to the commoners of Spain and constitute a very inferior species.[43]

The crown contributed to the creation and maintenance of the system in various ways. It was the "head" of the body social. It was the ultimate author of legislation defining the status of each estate and corporation. It had at its disposal the means of compulsion: the bureaucracy, the ordinary courts, the military, and the police. It was also the ultimate source of privileges and favors; it conceded land, monopolies, titles, honors, and offices. It reconciled class and group conflicts; it was the supreme court of appeal. As the final arbiter it checked and balanced the powerful centrifugal forces which were a constant threat to social stability. Perhaps most fundamental was the crown as a mystique and a symbol. Américo Castro observed that the people of Spain and Spanish America were united by a principle external to them, a mystical faith in and loyalty to the symbol of the crown. This faith was "an anchor of salvation, as was religious faith . . . ."[44] "The monarchy . . ., especially from Ferdinand and Isabella on, appears surrounded by Messianic prestige."[45] Bad legislation was not the fault of the king; he was inadequately informed. Wrong decisions could not be attributed to him; he was improperly advised. The hostility of creoles was directed against Spaniards, not the crown. Revolts and riots were not against the king but against his servants. The monarch might be a weakling or an imbecile; his servants might be ridiculed or even defied; his laws could be evaded, but the crown as a symbol was sacrosanct.[46]

The church was an active partner of the crown in maintaining social control. It wholeheartedly supported a society of hierarchies and privileged classes both on doctrinaire grounds and as a beneficiary of the system. It employed directly to this end its control over education, its vast resources of moral suasion, and its temporal wealth. It upheld, moreover, the role of the crown as the ultimate temporal authority and as a symbol of Spanish Christianity.

Mexican colonial society has traditionally been viewed as static and ponderously stable, an interpretation epitomized in the expression, *la siesta colonial*. Traditional history has it that this structure was abruptly fractured by the Wars of Independence producing a half century, more or less, of anarchy. In fact, from the moment of the Conquest it was characterized by continous although unspectacular change.[47] The formation of the

[42] The theme of his book *Invertebrate Spain* (New York, 1937).

[43] Quoted in Konetzke, "Estado y sociedad," p. 58.

[44] *The Structure of Spanish History* (Princeton, 1954), p. 51, note 15.

[45] *Ibid.*, pp. 187–188.

[46] Antonio Domínguez Ortiz, *La sociedad española en el siglo XVIII* (Madrid, 1955), pp. 29–30; Morse, p. 78; Vicens Vives, IV, 416.

[47] The evolutionary character of Mexican society is clearly brought out in Lesley B. Simpson, "Mexico's Forgotten Century," *Pacific Historical Review*, XXII (1953), 113–121.

castes and the creation of an American system of estates was certainly an evolutionary if not a dynamic process. In the preceding pages reference has been made to qualities of flexibility and openness which characterized social stratification. Within certain limits upward and downward mobility existed. Castes with luck, enterprise, or official favor might and did become whites, while whites through misfortune or mismanagement might sink into the lower estates. A similar mobility appears to have existed between castes and Indians. Bagú emphasizes the miscibility of the colonial social system and particularly stresses the instability of the "middle classes." Adverse regulation, misfortune, lack of enterprise, or alcoholism constantly submerged artisans and shopkeepers into the mass of the indigent poor.[48] Substantial changes in the character of the upper nobility also took place in the seventeenth and eighteenth centuries. In rural areas the nucleus of a new elite appeared, the masters of the great haciendas and estancias. Some of its members derived from the old encomendero nobility but others were American and European Spaniards who were rewarded for services to the crown by grants of land. Although some of the beneficiaries came from titled families and others subsequently acquired titles, the new upper nobility was primarily a nobility *de hecho* rather than *de derecho*. Titles simply confirmed a status derived from the ownership of latifundia. In contrast to its attitude toward the encomienda, the crown permitted and encouraged the growth of the hacienda as an instrument of economic development and social control. The strength of the hacendado group was consolidated by the entailment of its estates. By preserving indivisible family patrimonies, entailment established a family lineage through which status could be transmitted.[49]

The growth of a landed aristocracy was paralleled by the development of a mercantile patriciate in the cities of the viceroyalty. This element derived in part from the old *morador* class; that is householders (*vecinos*) of the sixteenth century towns who were not among the privileged few receiving

encomiendas and who generally lived by trade or manufacturing.[59] It was augmented by second sons of encomenderos and new arrivals from Spain who entered commerce. The concentration of trade in a few cities, and monopolistic privileges conceded to merchant groups encouraged the accumulation of mercantile fortunes by a relatively small number of families. The mineowners who accumulated great wealth through the exploitation of Mexico's silver resources constituted a related group. The possession of great wealth conferred influence and status, much to the disgust of the old encomenderos. "Those who yesterday operated shops and taverns and engaged in other base occupations," wrote one disgruntled benemérito, "are today placed in the best and most prized positions."[51] Mercantile and mining fortunes were recognized or perhaps it would be better to say exploited by the crown through the concession of titles of nobility. These were granted with increasing frequency in the latter half of the eighteenth century.[52]

At the same time that new elite elements were emerging, the economic base of the encomenderos was deteriorating. In the seventeenth century there was a strong trend toward reversion of encomiendas to the crown while those remaining in private hands were subjected to new fiscal exactions. The lot of the bulk of the encomenderos is described by Guillermo Céspedes:

With such a small sustenance, the more tenacious of the beneméritos—converted into social parasites—composed accounts of the merits and services rendered by their distinguished ancestors, and swarmed the antechambers of the viceroys to beg

[48] Chap. II and particularly pp. 87, 92, 104–105. See also Vicens Vives, III, 526.

[49] François Chevalier summarizes the formation of this class in his *La formación de los grandes latifundios en México* (México, 1956), pp. 233–240. See also Vicens Vives, III, 520–524.

[50] Góngora, p. 185.

[51] Quoted in Vicens Vives, III, 524–525.

[52] *Ibid.*, III, 529–530; IV, 423; José Bravo Ugarte, "Títulos nobilarios hispanoamericanos," *Memorias de la Academia Mexicana de la Historia*, XV (no. 3, julio–septiembre, 1956), 258–264.

corregimientos, tenientazgos, alcaldías, or any other bureaucratic post befitting the glory of their lineage. Their pride of caste, exacerbated by their economic difficulties would not countenance any occupation nor employment other than waiting patiently for a shower of royal favors. They looked down on the newly rich, emerged from the "ashes and soot of the stewpots," and particularly on the hateful and wealthy merchants and on the *chapetones* who came from Spain to enjoy benefices in the governmental bureaucracy. They continued their addiction to pious works which revealed to them a God by whose inscrutable designs the grandsons of the conquerors lived on the verge of starvation. Some even reached the point of asking if they were suffering punishment and penance for the blood which their heroic ancestors shed during the conquest.[53] With the abolition of the encomienda system in the early eighteenth century they finally disappeared as a class.

A certain coalescence took place in at least a peripheral way among the various elements of the colonial elite. The more enterprising encomenderos managed to escape the general decadence of their class. Some managed to retain or acquire landed estates. Others, forgetting their class pride, married into the aristocracy of wealth or entered commerce themselves. Such concessions although distasteful were not degrading since commerce at the wholesale level had become officially and socially honorable.[54] Among the other groups, wealthy merchants and miners employed excess capital for the purchase of rural estates, and needy hacendados contracted marriage alliances with willing merchants and mining families.[55]

During the eighteenth century and particularly its later four decades social change was accelerated by the interaction of multiple influences including population growth and progressive miscegnation, expansion of areas of settlement, economic development and the increase of wealth, fiscal, administrative, and military reforms, and infiltration of egalitarian doctrines from abroad. Among the whites, new opportunities appeared to acquire wealth and improve social status. Creoles found additional avenues for social advancement in the officer corps of newly organized regular and militia regi-

ments while the castes through enlistment in the army achieved exemption from tribute and acquired status through the possession of the *fuero militar*.[56] In general there appears to have been a further blurring of the line between white and caste. Official documents and legal formulae of the last half of the eighteenth century frequently employ expressions such as *que se tenga por español* or *recibido por español*[57] when referring to mixed bloods, and euphemisms such as *pardo* and *moreno* were increasingly used in place of Negro and mulatto. Aguirre Beltrán quotes contemporary sources to the effect that all those who were not clearly Indians or of *color achocolatado* were said to be and were considered as Spaniards.[58] Indeed, identifications based on place of birth and ethnic origins tended to be replaced by others expressing only social quality. In the service records of militia and regular officers in the 1770's, under *calidad* are found the terms mestizo, castizo, pardo, *español europeo* and *español americano*. By 1806 these were largely replaced by such identifications as *noble, ilustre, conocida, distinguida, honrada,* and *buena*.[59] Without renouncing its support of a stratified society, the crown attempted to ameliorate some of the more obvious—and more troublesome—inequities The new army had an explicitly stated secondary aim of providing honorable and status-conferring careers for creoles in the

[53] In Vicens Vives, III, 518–519.

[54] Beneyto, p. 226.

[55] Vicens Vives, III, 526; Chevalier, p. 240.

[56] Konetzke, "Estado y sociedad." pp. 40–41; L. N. McAlister, *The "Fuero Militar" in New Spain* (Gainesville, 1957), *passim* and particularly Chap. IV.

[57] Rosenblat, pp. 264–265, 271–291; "Diversas solicitudes," AGN (México), Indiferente de Guerra, vol. 194, *passim*.

[58] Pp. 174–175, 273.

[59] For example, compare the *hojas de servicios* of the Legion of the Prince for 1771 (AGN, Indiferente de Guerra, vol. 138A) with those of the Battalion of Provincial Infantry of Guanajuato and the Regiment of Provincial Dragoons of the Prince for 1804 and 1806 respectively (AGN, Indiferente de Guerra, vols. 121A and 278A). The latter two units were formed from the Legion of the late 1790's.

officer corps and castes in the ranks.[60] Titles were conceded with greater frequency to creoles, and the castes could achieve legal whiteness by the purchase of cedulas called *gracias al sacar*.[61] Moreover, a cedula of February 1, 1795 dispensed pardos and *quinterones* from the status of *infame*, authorized them to contract matrimony with whites, and permitted them to hold public office and enter Holy Orders.[62] The castes also found advocates among the whites. Viceroy Croix believed that their superior physiques, amenability to disciplines, and inclination toward military service made them better soldiers than the effete and prideful whites.[63] Lucas Alamán, who was certainly no egalitarian, rated them as the most useful part of the population and reported that the only time that Matías Martín de Aguirre, a European Spaniard and deputy to the Cortes of Madrid in 1821, rose to speak was to deliver a eulogy of the mulattoes who had served in the royalist armies.[64]

There appears also to have been some erosion of the bases of the corporate social structure. During the reign of Charles III, direct and indirect efforts were made to restrict or to level or to rebalance the power and status of traditional corporate groups. The principal device was the limitation of privileged fueros and the renovation and extension of the royal or ordinary jurisdiction. Crown policy was most striking in the case of ecclesiastical corporations. The royal patronage was extended, the ordinary ecclesiastical fuero was restricted, rights to church asylum were limited, the power of the Holy Office was circumscribed, the Society of Jesus was expelled from Spain and the empire and the famous *amortización* of 1804 struck at the pious foundations. In New Spain there appears to have been both an absolute and relative decline in the power and prestige of the ecclesiastical establishment as a whole.[65] The reglamento of free trade of 1778 was a blow to the power of the consulados and at the same time the state loosened the restrictive practices of the artisan guilds. In New Spain an increasing volume of trade and manufacturing was conducted outside the guild system.[66] One striking and consequen-

tial exception to these trends must be noted. At the same time that the status and power of other corporate groups were being subverted, the metropolitan and colonial armies were not only strengthened and reorganized, but their fueros were extended, their prestige enhanced and their morale cultivated.[67]

In summary, three general and interrelated observations may be made. First, a close look at New Spain on the eve of independence reveals a gradual erosion of a social structure based on estates, corporations, and juridical inequality, and outlines, at least, of a new system based on economic class. Perhaps the most apparent manifestation of the latter phenomenon was the growing strength of the mercantile "bourgeoisie" and the emergence of an entrepreneurial sector among the textile manufacturers of Val-

[60] *Instrucción del virrey marqués de Croix que deja a su sucesor Antonio María Bucareli* (México, 1960), par. 138 (pp. 111–112); "Dictamen del Coronel D.n Fran.co Antonio Crespo, Inspector interino de las tropas . . . de N.a Esp.a sobre su mejor arreglo y extablecim.to," México, July 31, 1784, MS 173, Biblioteca Nacional de México, pars. 227–235; 238–254.

[61] Rosenblat, p. 291.

[62] Peneyto, p. 276.

[63] "Memoria conserniente à la expedición q.e bajo las ordenes del Exm.o Sr. D. Juan de Villalba se hizo à la América," August 20, 1764–April 30, 1769, MS in the Edward E. Tyer Collection, the Newberry Library, pp. 156, 159; Croix to Minister of the Indies, Julián de Arriaga, México, October 26, 1767, AGN, Correspondencia de los Virreyes, vol. 1/11, no. 289, fol. 456.

[64] *Historia de México* (5 vols. México, 1942), I, 33.

[65] Mariano Otero makes some penetrating observations on the state of the Mexican church on the eve of independence (*Ensayo sobre el verdadero estado de la cuestión social y política que se agita en la república mexicana* (México, 1842), pp. 54–59.

[66] Agustín Cue Cánovas, *Historia social y económica de México* (2 vols., México, 1946–1947), I, 115.

[67] Manuel Giménez Fernández, "Las doctrinas populistas en la independencia de Hispano-América," *Anuario de estudios americanos*, III (1946), 615; Félix Colón de Larriátegui, *Juzgados militares de España y sus Indias*. 2nd ed. (4 vols., Madrid, 1786–1796), I, lxv–lix. See particularly the royal decree of February 9, 1793, reproduced in McAlister, pp. 76–77.

ladolid, Guadalajara, and the Bajío.[68] Second, the velocity of change was insufficient to accommodate severe tensions within the social order, principally the stored-up resentments of the lower estates and the frustrations of the white creoles. The former exploded in 1810, the latter boiled over in 1821, and the two combined fleetingly in the latter year to produce political independence. Third, the hierarchical colonial society survived the break from Spain with some reordering of its components, but with the disappearance ofthe symbol of the crown as an instrument of social control, its invertebrate character became fully emergent. It required nearly one hundred years for the formation of a juridically egalitarian society and the creation of a new social myth as an instrument of cohesion.

[68] In connection with the textile manufacturers see Robert A. Potash, *El Banco de Avío de México* (México, 1959), Chap. I.

93. Whither the Latin American Middle Sectors?*

JOHN J. JOHNSON

Fidel Castro's conduct in Cuba has tended to obscure the fact that a major part of Latin America is in the throes of a painful transformation. The entire fabric of the region's social structure is being torn apart. The republics are turning their backs on traditional values and ancient obligations. Old and time-honored but recalcitrant institutions are being replaced by totally new economic, social, and political models that transcend existing societies. The masses, who have historically lacked the power of sustained indignation and who have accepted ignorance, poverty, and disease as their lot, are now aroused. They can no longer be dissuaded from seeking self expression.

As if the present crisis created by adjusting to enforced adaptations were not disturbing enough, the twenty nations are confronted with a population explosion that will probably increase their numbers from the present 190 million to 300 million by 1975 and to 500 million by 2000. The leaders of the area believe that industrialization, by revolutionary means if necessary, is their only hope of escaping the pressure of their expanding millions against their limited agricultural resources. Industrialization thus becomes the mainspring of a promethean urge towards modernity and the economic problem becomes the fundamental political problem.

The leavening that produced the current social, economic, and political upheavals was provided originally by imaginative and, for their day, radical political leaders heading the parties of the dominant elements within the urban middle sectors. These groups were comprised of members of the liberal professions, writers, publishers, artists, professors, bureaucrats, the secular clergy, the lower and middle echelons of the armed forces, and the owners, managers, and technicians of industry and commerce.

With the passage of time the original middle-sector leaders and their successors have tended to assume a centrist position and now face the prospect of being overwhelmed by the forces they fathered in the not too distant past. The fate of these leaders and their parties will be decided in most cases in this decade. An assessment of their strengths and weaknesses in their struggles for survival may provide a basis for understanding Latin America better during the tense years ahead. It may also suggest the very narrow range of choices that are open to President Kennedy and his administration in making major policy decisions affecting the Latin American area.

I

A party led by the urban middle sector—the Colorados—came to power as early as

* *The Virginia Quarterly Review*, 37: 508–521 (Autumn 1961). Reprinted by permission of the author and the original publisher.

1903 in Uruguay, and another—Acción Democrática—as late as 1958 in Venezuela. In between those dates middle-sector parties established their sway over Argentina (1916), Chile (1920), Mexico (1940), and Brazil (1946). These six republics contain over two thirds of the total area of Latin America, boast over two thirds of its total population, and produce over three fourths of its gross income. Argentina, Brazil, Chile, Mexico, and Uruguay, along with Costa Rica, which is controlled by a land-holding rural middle sector, are the most progressive, democratically mature countries in Latin America. Their ascendancy seems to be unchallengeable proof that in the present century the current of public opinion has run strongly in favor of the middle-sector political leadership.

In each of the republics a middle-sector party first achieved pre-eminence when the middle sectors comprised between ten and twenty per cent of the total population. These groups have grown under the leadership of their own members, yet today they constitute less than forty-five per cent of the population in each of the republics. In Brazil, Mexico, and Venezuela, they are minorities of less than twenty per cent. Thus, on the basis of numerical strength alone they could never have won elections, even if they had been politically monolithic, which certainly they have not been. Historically, the middle sectors have ranged the political spectrum. Many of them have viewed representative government and political democracy as luxuries that can readily be priced out of the ideological market. There is every reason to believe that the middle sectors are becoming more rather than less independent in their thinking as new choices among competing political systems become available to them.

The hard core of the middle sector's electoral support came originally from organized urban industrial labor. In the second phase the mass vote came from both organized and unorganized urban labor. In the present era—the third—the popular base of the parties has been extended to include many adherents from newly emerging rural labor.

Their constituencies have dictated that the middle-sector parties be pragmatic and reformist. Their leaders have been content to win the voter's sanction without asking him to accept an ideology. In this respect their political approach has been markedly different from that of the Communists and now of the *fidelistas* (inspired by Fidel Castro of Cuba).

Long before the Russians staked out a claim to the moon by planting a red flag on it, the middle-sector leaders in Latin America were promising it to their followers. They demagogically made direct appeals— larger loaves of bread, shoes for unshod feet —to the formerly forgotten worker. They became masters at the art of repetition as again and again they offered simple answers to complex problems. They proposed to add social guarantees to individual guarantees by protecting labor and promoting the expansion of social welfare. They attacked the secular power of the Catholic Church and promised to reduce that power by creating great public-school systems that would drive the Church school out of business. They promised more industry and made the integrated iron and steel plant the symbol of progress. When local manufacturers were unable to compete in the open market and domestic capital did not accumulate rapidly enough to maintain an acceptable rate of industrial expansion, the promise of more industry irresistibly led the middle-sector parties to champion nationalism and state interventionism. Nationalism soon was raised to the level of a political ideology. It was made synonymous with national progress and as such it was used to aggregate a wide range of special interests. State interventionism often was substituted for economic orthodoxy.

The platforms of the middle-sector leaders seemingly were unbeatable. They weaned labor away from its early anarchist leadership and brought it into the political arena under "respectable auspices." Even when achievements fell far short of expectations and progressive social legislation proved to be statements of aspirations rather than binding regulations, the labor elements of the parties could not revolt because politically there was no place for them to go. Beyond the leftism of the middle sectors lay a great political void into which only the Communists occasionally intruded. Communist successes were short-lived, their failures monumental. They were prestigeless and distrusted because of their international orientation.

Although the programs of the middle sectors were radical, they always kept to the framework of Western representative democracy. Also, they always reserved greater areas for private initiative and domestic private capital than the interested parties could fill. This served a twofold purpose. The embattled landed élites were largely isolated from the urban propertied elements. And foreign capital, which tended to supplant domestic capital in industry but had no direct voice in government, could simultaneously be made to bear the brunt of financing "social justice" and to serve as a massive target at which to discharge anxieties and frustrations.

For reasons quite apart from the content of their programs, the middle sectors' leaders in general have had the support of the commisioned officers of the military establishments and, thus far, through them the backing of the armies, navies, and air forces. In this century senior officers, with very few exceptions, have come from middle-sector backgrounds, and with equally few exceptions they, for opportunistic rather than ideological reasons, associated themselves with the old élites as long as those groups retained power. Thus, when the middle sectors gained in political and social stature vis-à-vis the old élites as long as those groups retained power. Thus, when the middle sectors gained in political and social stature vis-à-vis the old élites, it was easy for officers to shift their allegiance and to work out arrangements with the new leadership that seldom refused to pay handsomely for military support of consitutional norms.

II

The middle-sector leadership is now being seriously threatened by the upheavals that are taking place in Latin America, and an examination of its position as it enters the five most crucial years of its existence is in order.

One of the major assets of the middle-sector leaders is the solid background of cultural and political experiences they possess. Their cultural background gives them access to the great avenues looking to the past and also a faith in the future that helps to keep them from becoming slaves of antecedent circumstances. They have had valuable lessons in practical politics. They have learned that it is easier to stimulate demands than to satisfy them. They know some of the problems of telescoping the economic processes and the dangers of dealing in absolute postulates. Increasingly often this experience should help them from becoming confused by the economic fictions they formulate for political purposes. Included in the body of political experience that they have accumulated is the art of compromise. In a region where for a hundred years after the winning of independence between 1810 and 1825 differences were commonly resolved by the breaking of heads rather than the counting of them, the middle-sector leaders have elevated to a high level the art of achieving some equilibrium by balancing political antagonisms. In the process they have become the great stabilizers and harmonizers of Latin America. These are all worthwhile experiences and lessons, provided that they are not substituted for imagination in the politicians' repertoire.

Governments under the middle-sector leadership are stronger than at any time in Latin American history. Except in Brazil, where the central authority exercises only a tenuous hold over large parts of the North and the great Amazon Valley, they can for the first time make themselves felt in every part of the nations they control.

This new sense of strength and assurance that the states currently enjoy has been one of the important factors in bringing about an

era of better understanding and co-operation between the middle-sector leadership
and the Catholic Church. When the middle
sectors were bidding for power, they successfully exploited the always potentially
explosive anticlerical issue. Once they consolidated their position and found new
scapegoats—for example "economc imperialists"—they could afford to be more tolerant of the Church which for its part was simultaneously becoming more socially conscious. At the moment there is no major
anti-Church movement, except in Cuba, and
in some countries the clergy have become the
champions of social change within the
Christian context. As such, churchmen can
work with the middle-sector leadership or
alternatively their programs and those of the
middle sectors may pursue parallel courses.

On those occasions when the middle sectors formulate operative ideas they have the
right to expect a sympathetic response from
the United States and western European
countries in a position to export skills and
give financial assistance. More than any
other groups in the republics, the middle
sectors are spokesmen for the Latin American version of the political and economic
systems that the United States and western
Europe believe provide the best climate for
the growth of moral values, public liberties,
and private initiative. The middle-sector-led
governments of Latin America have generally supported the Western bloc in international organizations. In return they have
asked that the United States lead them, not
in a crusade against Communism but in an
attack on the real and pressing problems
with which they are confronted.

After 1957 the forces building up against
the middle-sector leadership came to out-
weigh those operating in its favor. The unfavorable forces have reached the point
where they threaten to overwhelm the
middle sectors. This is another way of saying that the current leadership is now on the
defensive. The shift of the balance came as
the result of a number of circumstances that
cost the middle-sector leadership support
among labor, its own social groups, and the
military.

Urban labor has paid heavily for the industrialization of its countries. Industrial
entrepreneurship has failed largely to realize the relation between mass production
and consumption and has continued to operate on a nineteenth-century high-unit-
profit concept of business. Industry has also
been unwilling to assume capital risks. Capital for industry is also obtained through in-
flationary borrowing, often by interests already possessing great wealth but reluctant
to risk it. Workers are often not paid enough
to buy the things they produce, and chase
after the cost of living through politically
directed pressure tactics, sometimes winning
across-the-board wage arbitrations that have
little regard for production objectives. These
factors have contributed to a persistent inflation that has eroded the real wage position of workers and limited the growth of
the industrial market.

But despite the sizable investment in industry, factories do not provide jobs for the
hundreds of thousands that enter the labor
markets each year. As the lines of workers
waiting for jobs in factories grow longer, the
patience of the workers grows shorter. Translated into political terms, the discontent of
the urban laborers has meant a declining
enthusiasm for the middle-sector leadership
and a greater tendency on the part of the
workers to search out those who offer the
most radical solutions and who promise that
welfare programs will not be curtailed. Thus
in Chile the strongest labor unions are Com-
munist-controlled. In Argentina urban
workers generate bitter opposition to the
Frondizi government.

The threat to the middle sectors of discon-
tented urban labor is compounded by the
fact that the labor movement is basically
immature. For this the middle sectors can
thank themselves. Middle-sector-led governments early assumed control of the labor
movement in most of the countries, and the
worker was placed in a position of being
forced to seek his objectives by political action, in marked contrast with the approach
of labor in the United States. Labor did not
develop independence of action but rather
was conditioned to look to politicians for sup-

port. Now that labor is beginning to reject middle-sector leaders, it lacks the equipment to make rational decisions and tends to give enthusiastic assent to the promises and slogans of the radical opposition.

Rural labor is probably about to prove itself a greater obstacle to continued middle-sector domination than urban labor has been up to now. Rural laborers are numerically much larger and politically less sophisticated. Millions of them were only recently brought into the political arena following a widespread discarding of literacy tests and property qualifications for voting. But once they were enfranchised no entrenched group was quite ready to receive them. Organized labor, "the aristocracy of the worker class," was reluctant to see the position of rural labor improved at its expense. The middle sectors solicited the rural worker's vote but their commitment to industrialization discouraged them from evolving imaginative rural developmental programs of the scope and pace that would help close the technological gap between city and county. Nowhere have the middle sectors shown a disposition to satisfy the growing clamor for land through large-scale redistribution of excessively large holdings. All this has served to clothe the rural voter with the respectability of first-class citizenship while in fact keeping him a second-class citizen with only faintly heard demands upon local and national governments.

The middle-sector is also being challenged by many disenchanted intellectuals, including students and civilian bureaucrats. These restless, aspiring elements come from the same social groups that produced the middle-sector leadership and like it they are emotionally and intellectually committed to modernizing their entire societies. But the enchanted feel a greater sense of underdeveloped and thus a greater sense of urgency. Also, they have little or no prospect of gaining great wealth or great power so long as the present systems obtain and therefore are in no way pledged to the existing basic political framework. Many of them, particularly among the students, dedicate all their energies to agitation because they

feel that were they to suffer total political defeat they would have no place to turn. But they are also disruptive because they know from their history books that it has been from ranks such as their own that revolutions have been born in Latin America. The skills and talents of the malcontent intellectuals are particularly appropriate for providing leadership during periods of uncertainty and excitement but the malcontents may be peculiarly lacking in the skills necessary for leadership during less dramatic phases of trying to create stable egalitarian societies. Were they to seize power, the gap between the rich and the poor would at best be filled with people unsure of their social identity.

Finally, the middle-sector leadership faces the very real prospect of soon losing the backing of the armed forces. This possibility arises from two sets of circumstances, one affecting the commissioned officers, the other the non-commissioned officers.

Since World War II commissioned officers have undergone two basic changes that make their continued support of the middle sectors questionable. First, they have become more professional and bureaucratic and in the process less ready to jeopardize their own professional standing or to weaken the military as a respected national institution by meddling unduly in politics. Second, in much larger numbers than ever before they have been drawn from the lower-middle groups and the working class. The generation of officers now reaching decision-making positions has, as a consequence, closer affinity than their predecessors had with the popular masses. It appears that the day is rapidly approaching when they will be reluctant to support unpopular civilian regimes by sending their troops against rioters, especially when they and the rioters have common social backgrounds. If this is true, then it follows that increasingly often commissioned military officers will permit the swearing in of elected political officers, including those from the extreme left, who may use their seats in Congress and elsewhere to disrupt normal constitutional processes.

The new revolutionary potential of the non-commissioned officers stems on the one hand from conditions resulting from the modernization of the armed forces and on the other from the rising level of competence and political awareness of the non-commissioned officers from the privileged commissioned officers of middle and senior rank. In the small forces of the past this condition was in part offset by a close personal comradeship between officers and their men. But in the modern military establishments there are almost no permanent line officers and as a consequence the climate for officers and non-coms to develop personal relationships is not favorable. This situation has encouraged the latter to turn to civilians, who are often from the political opposition, to fill the vacuum of representation between them, their superiors, and the public.

The relatively high academic and technical standards required of the modern non-commissioned officers open to them at least two avenues that may lead to trouble for the middle sectors. They can insist on the right to become commissioned officers, and certainly many of them possess the ability to learn all that is demanded of the average commissioned officer. If their requests are refused for any reason—for example, because they are too old, because they and their wives cannot hope to adjust to the new social status, or simply because good sergeants do not necessarily make good commissioned officers—the rebuked non-com officer becomes a prospective revolutionary. The other avenue leads directly to involvement in politics. In such cases the non-commissioned officer has a built-in constituency among the enlisted men and recruits whose respect he commands because of his military position, because they know him personally, and because of his superior education. In Brazil and Venezuela in particular, non-commissioned officers are being urged by the doctrinaire opposition to engage in politics.

III

As few as five years ago the malcontents of both city and country could still be expected to dissipate their energies against the solid wall of middle-sector values that had been erected during the period between the two world wars. The scattered and limited successes of the restless workers and disillusioned intellectuals were pricks that surprised and shocked more than they hurt. The middle sectors, meanwhile, actually appeared to be entrenching themselves still further as the people of Argentina recalled them to power and the people of Venezuela called them to power after expelling military dictators. All this has now changed, or is changing, not so much because the middle sectors moved to the right, although in some instances they have, but because those in Latin America who are in the greatest hurry in many cases turned sharply to the left. Here they have found sympathy and assistance from the Soviet bloc. Thus the U.S.S.R. and international Communism have become the principal catalysts that are keeping the Latin American political caldron boiling.

Communists were already active in Latin America when the middle-sector leadership made its first bids for recognition. But they were premature, and the middle sectors, without regard for them, grew strong by winning over the working groups to which the Communists appealed. After World War II the Communists were unable to fill the power vacuum created when the middle-sector leadership shifted to the center of the political spectrum, although their attacks upon the United States won them some followers among the xenophobic nationalists and urban labor. The Communists failed at this time because their international showpiece, the U.S.S.R., despite an unexpectedly large contribution to the defeat of the Axis, was still largely an unknown quantity. This is no longer the case. The U.S.S.R. has demonstrated its economic and scientific capabilities, and they are impressive by any standard. Its prestige is at an all time high. These developments have made it much easier for the disenchanted and the cautious to accept the Communist claims that the U.S.S.R. and now Red China have found the way to modernize and grow strong rapidly. In so doing, the U.S.S.R. and Communist China also made known to the malcontents the fact that the capitalistic, free-enterprise system is not the only one. Furthermore, the Communists have willingly provided funds and given leadership to the outburst of strongly felt but formerly unorganized interests. Under Communist strategy and tactics vague demands have become the demands of organized groups. It is the combination of Communist organization and anomy that is so dangerous to established systems in Latin America today.

Also, the Communists quickly came to the aid of the *fidelista* movement in Cuba and are probably prepared to make that nation a showcase of a successful "national liberation" movement which can survive and get assistance from the Soviet bloc in the face of United States opposition. Despite its growing association with international Communism, *fidelismo* is still considered by many in Latin America to be an indigenous movement. It can consequently appeal to certain intellectual elements who have been reluctant to accept Communism because of its international connections but who in common with the Communists have an unrestrained hatred for the United States. Students in general have been highly susceptible to the appeals of *fidelismo* and in December, 1960, the *fidelistas* won control of the student University federation of San Marcos University of Lima, the second oldest university in the hemisphere. Over the short range the importance to Latin America of the *fidelista* movement is twofold. It has shown the middle-sector intellectuals and bureaucrats that a determined group of such people can take over a government and achieve power, at least the power to make what they regard as vital decisions about the direction and pace of social and economic change. And it has taught the malcontents a quick way to end "economic imperialism."

Communism and *fidelismo*, and for that matter the more radical Maoism, which in some of the more agriculturally depressed areas receives a more enthusiastic reception than does either Communism or *fidelismo*, will win added support before they decline in favor in Latin America, if such is their destiny. There is no assurance that they are

so destined. This is particularly true if the middle sectors are left to their own resources.

IV

In the present political climate of all the major countries of Latin America—and most of the others as well—the middle sectors have for all intents and purposes become the spokesmen for a type of moderation that tends towards conservatism. There are no groups to the political right of them that can reasonably hope to achieve power legally. The middle sectors have surrendered the championship of nationalism to the more radical left and to a lunatic fringe on the extreme right. Except for the Christian Democrats, who have made gains in several countries since 1957, the middle-sector parties have given priority to economic values more or less to the exclusion of moral values and the dignity of the individual. This not only puts them in a position of staking their entire future on their ability to create viable economies but it also places them in direct competition with the Communists and *fidelistas*. No non-Communist political group in the rising nations of Asia and Africa could expect to gain or retain power with a program so narrowly based or so long range in its projection. It is doubtful that the middle sectors in Latin America can hope to outbid the Communists and *fidelistas* in the economic areas. If they do, it will be because funds for capital investment are forthcoming in massive amounts. A vast share of that capital would have to flow from the United States, in the form of public loans.

The United States can hope that middle-sector elements with a social conscience and hope for the future will gain the initiative so that their countries can escape the radical upheavals of Communism and *fidelismo*, but it must be expected that under the best of circumstances the present leadership will suffer some defeats, electoral or otherwise. Every country in Latin America is today a potential candidate for a Communist-*fidelista* takeover. In many of them a façade of modernity in the capital city masks feudalism on the land and nineteenth-century robber barons in the urban centers. Five years hence

Communist or *fidelista*-like groups will have taken over these countries, or will still be trying desperately hard to do so.

It would behoove the United States and its allies to realize that for the first time the Latin American radical left has what are to it acceptable alternatives to United States approval. From time to time they will demand and get, if not from the United States then from the U.S.S.R. or Red China, the right to be judged by standards derived from their own experience. Also, they will demand and get the right to work out a new set of social-economic requirements within the framework of that experience.

94. Civil-Military Relations in Latin America*

Lyle N. McAlister

It is hardly necessary to assert that the armed forces have been important factors in the historical development of the nations of Latin America. By bringing into association men from all parts of the national territory, by posing as the incarnation of the national spirit, and by teaching patriotism and exalting national virtues, they have been a significant influence in overcoming regionalism and localism. By providing an avenue for advancement for members of lower social strata, they have encouraged social mobility. In many countries they have contributed to the transition from traditional to modern societies through their work in constructing communications systems, their emphasis on general and technical education within their ranks, and by their demands for industrialization. In the political sphere they have repeatedly overthrown the governments that created them; generals have employed the forces entrusted to them to make themselves heads of state; military factions have intervened in the political process in support of specific economic objectives or of broader ideologies. In a less spectacular fashion, the armed forces acting through political parties as in Mexico, or through officers occupying cabinet posts have exerted powerful influences on public policy.

These facts are generally recognized and a great deal has been written about Latin-American "militarism." Existing literature, however, raises some serious conceptual and methodological problems. These may be defined by posing and commenting on a series of questions. In the first place, do the interrelations between the military and society at large constitute a discrete sociological and historical problem susceptible to systematic description and analysis? Some scholars concerned with general principles of social organization and with the history of sociology of regions other than Latin America have conceived of them in this fashion. Max Weber and later Gaetano Mosca recognized the importance of military factors in shaping societies and developed concepts and methods for dealing with the problem. Subsequently historians and social scientists have refined and expanded the ideas of Weber and Mosca and produced a substantial body of literature dealing with these interrelationships in general and with their manifestations in the United States, Germany, Japan, the Middle East, and Southeast Asia.

Perhaps because of their more obvious and

* *Journal of Inter-American Studies*, 3: 341–350 (July 1961). Reprinted by permission of the author and the original publisher.

immediate nature, the political and administrative aspects of this problem have been stressed; that is, the distribution of power within the state between civil and military elements. This area of study is commonly called "civil-military relations." The range of civil-military relations extends from situations in which civil authority is supreme to the direct and forcible usurpation of power by the military for nonmilitary ends.

The political role of the armed forces has likewise been stressed in Latin America. In general, however, Latin Americanists have been unwilling or unable to face up to the nature of interrelations between the military and civil elements of the state. The recent publications of Edwin Lieuwen, Victor Alba, and Theodore Wyckoff are exceptions to this generalization. Much of Latin-American history has been written in terms of "Progress toward Democracy" or "The Struggle for Democracy." Within this teleological system the armed forces are regarded as "Obstacles to the Achievement of Democracy." Now no right-thinking person would deny that democracy is a desirable goal and it would be mean-spirited indeed not to wish the Latin-Americans success in their struggle toward it. Yet, this conceptual framework encourages simplistic interpretations and explanations. The military is conceived of as a force external to and interfering with "normal" historical processes rather than as an integral element in them. In this position it can conveniently be regarded as a constant whose importance is recognized and accepted but which need not be described or analyzed systematically.

Second, if the importance of the military as a power factor in Latin America is accepted and the nature of its relations with the civil elements of the state can be regarded as a discrete historical and sociological problem, what is the scope of the problem and how may it be defined? The most commonly used term to describe the role of the armed forces in Latin America is "militarism." In the sense that it means the use of military force or threat of force to achieve nonmilitary ends, it is adequate. It has, however, two disadvantages. To many scholars it has a more specific usage; that is, a system or way of life which glorifies war, in which the military is a high-status profession, in which an entire nation is oriented toward military virtues and mores, and which has strong imperialist overtones. Such a system may have existed in Paraguay during the dictatorship of Francisco Solano López, and the G. O. U. in Argentina may have aspired to it. It has, however, been atypical of Latin America. Also, it does not cover instances in which armed forces have been nonpolitical and, if the problem is to be viewed broadly, such instances also require description and analysis. Another commonly-used expression is "the army in politics," but this term also excludes situations where the military has been nonpolitical. Moreover, it seems rather too mild an expression with which to describe the praetorian excesses of some Latin-American armies in the nineteenth century. "Civil-military relations" is also open to the latter criticism. It is, however, comprehensive enough to cover the range of phenomena involved in the problem and its accepted usage elsewhere in an argument for its adoption by Latin Americanists.

Third, what is the structure of the problem? As H. Stuart Hughes remarks, historians are reluctant to make distinctions and tend to view their problems as all of one piece. Thus *pronunciamientos, cuartelazos, golpes de estado, machetismo,* militarism, praetorianism, and all other instances where armed forces transcend their purely military functions tend to be viewed as phenomena of the same order and explainable with more or less the same formula. Sometimes these phenomena are even confused with military history. This is equivalent to regarding the Assumption of Mary and the exercise of the ecclesiastical patronage as belonging to the same order of things or of teaching surgery and medical sociology in the same course. In fact a diversity of patterns or systems of civil-military relations has existed in Latin America and each pattern consists of complex interactions involving the structure, status, and power of groups, both civil and military, and the motivations of individuals, as these several elements are influenced by the political, social, and economic environment. Thus the role of the Brazilian officer corps in the overthrow of the Empire, the institutionalized gangsterism prevailing in the contemporary Dominican Republic and the *pronunciamientos* of Antonio López de Santa Anna are sharply different examples of civil-military relations involving different types of civil and military elements interacting in different environmental situations.

At a schematic level several types of civil-military relations in Latin America may be defined. The first might be called the "Praetorian State." It is characterized by the frequent overthrow of governments by military revolutions or *coups d'état* for nonmilitary purposes. It tends to be associated with a high degree of social and political disorganization and a low degree of professionalism within the armed forces. Examples are Mexico during the first thirty years of the republic and Venezuela before and after the dictatorship of Juan Vicente Gómez. The second might be described as the "Gendarmist State." It emerges when a single individual, generally but not always a military man, uses a mercenary army to make himself master of the state, imposes social and political order, tames the army and uses it as a gendarmery to maintain himself in power. The dictatorships of Gómez in Venezuela, and Anastacio Somoza in Nicaragua are examples. The third type, after Harold Lasswell, is the "Garrison State." In it the military not only dominates or strongly influences the political system but it attempts to militarize the state and society at large. It occurs in connection with deep fears of aggression from the outside or strong aggressive tendencies within and is associated with a relatively high degree of political and social stability and a professionalized military establishment. Paraguay under Francisco Solano López might be taken as an example of this type. As noted above, it is atypical of Latin America. Fourth, is the "Civilist State." It is characterized by civil supremacy over the military and exists in relatively stable societies with professionalized armed forces. Examples are Argentina between 1861 and 1930 and Uruguay since the turn of this century. A fifth type may be emerging in Cuba but it is as yet difficult to identify.

It should be added that these are ideal types in the Weberian sense. They do not exist in pure form and may shade or metamorphose into one another. Thus a strong *caudillo* may in certain circumstances transform a praetorian state into a gendarmist state as in the case of Porfirio Díaz and Rafael Trujillo, or the weakening or death of a leader or pressures within a society may turn a gendarmist state into a praetorian state as, for example, Mexico after 1910. Changes in the social or economic structure within praetorian or gendarmist states may result in the emergence of a civilist pattern as in contemporary Mexico, while conversely political, social or economic strains within a civilist state may result in the emergence of praetorian or gendarmist patterns as in the case of Argentina after 1930 or Colombia after 1949. These paradigms, it should be added, are not intended to present conclusions. They are devices to illustrate a point and to encourage the asking of pertinent questions.

The emphasis in the preceding paragraphs on the diversity of systems of civil-military relations in Latin America raises another question. Does Latin America itself constitute an adequate conceptual framework for the study of civil-military relations? Is it simply a convenient geographical and cultural delimitation or have civil-military relations in this region exhibited characteristic features or patterns? It is rather suggestive that Spain and Spanish America have had many similar experiences with their armed force. It might, therefore, be assumed that the Hispanic world is distinguished by typical patterns of civil-military relations. This assumption, however, is challenged by the fact that there seem to be greater structural and functional similarities between the Nasser regime in Egypt and the Perón regime in Argentina than between the latter and the dictatorships of Santa Anna in Mexico. It was recently suggested to the writer that there are certain "built-in" features of instability in the social and political organization of Moslem society which encourage military intervention in politics and that Hispanic civilization absorbed these features through its long contact and intermingling with the world of Islam. The idea is challenging. Yet it does not account for the fact that armies in Burma and Thailand appear to have acted in much the same way in much the same circumstances as armies in Spain, Latin America, and the Moslem world. This leads to the hypothesis that in general the patterns of civil-military relations in Latin America are typical of "developing areas." This might test out for the last decade when Latin America has undoubtedly shared many problems and aspirations with the emerging nations of the Middle East, Africa, and South and Southeast Asia. For earlier periods, however, it is not applicable. At the outbreak of World War Two, most of the latter nations were still dependencies or colonies of western powers while Latin America had enjoyed independence for over a century. Thus the argument comes full circle. It is quite possible that historically, Latin America or at least the Hispanic world provides a functional as well as a convenient unit for the study of civil-military relations.

If civil-military relations in Latin America can be conceived as a discrete problem of considerable diversity and complexity and if it is accepted that these relationships have been important factors in the historical development of the region, historians are confronted with a challenge and an opportunity. The problem, or perhaps it would be better to say, the complex problems, may be redefined as follows: What are and what have been the patterns or systems of civil-military relations historically present in Latin America, why has one pattern prevailed at a particular time and place rather than another, and how and why have patterns changed, These questions pose others that are still more fundamental: What are the elements or ingredients whose interaction has produced patterns of civil-military relations in Latin America in general or in particular instances? How do these elements interact to produce a particular patterns and how do they and their interactions change in time to produce different patterns?

The statement of the problem in this fashion raises a final query: What methods will be most fruitful in providing answers to the preceding questions? It is not the purpose of this paper to lecture historians on their methods. We all know what they do and how they go about it. Without committing themselves to explicit assumptions and without explicit hypothesizing they begin with empirical data and develop conclusions, interpretations, or generalizations in terms of how the data arrange themselves or are arranged. Their normal procedure is, moreover, to work from the particular to the general, first the monograph, then the synthesis. Therefore it would seem that in view of the diverse character of civil-military relations in Latin America, a number of "case studies" dealing with particular countries and periods are needed before any convincing generalizations can be made. In undertaking such projects, the historian may use any one of several approaches: (1) he may describe and analyze a system or pattern of civil-military relations as it existed at a particular time and place in the past; (2) from this base he may "trace" and explain the process whereby this system changed to another; (3) without initially defining a system he may identify its elements and show how over a period of time they combined to form a system; (4) he may define a pattern as it existed at a particular time and place and then explain the process whereby it came to be what it was. In each case, if the method is narrative rather than analytical, patterns may remain implicit. These approaches and methods have and will, yield sophisticated explanations and interpretations of civil-military relations as, for example, Gordon A. Craig's, *The Politics of the Prussian Army, 1640–1945* and Yale C. Maxon's *Control of Japanese Foreign Policy: A Study of Civil-Military Rivalry, 1930–1945*. Without abandoning their humanistic and literary traditions, however, historians can profit from a selective and cautious use of the theory and methods of the social sciences. The potentials and dangers of this kind of borrowing have been explored at length by Social Science Research Council, *Bulletin 64* and by H. Stuart Hughes, Richard Hofstadter, Sir Isaiah Berlin, and others and it is unnecessary to review the argument and conclusions here. Instead certain general approaches and several specific methods will be discussed.

First, the sheer volume of sources now available and a growing awareness of the complexity of historical processes suggest that in many situations a more explicit definition of problems and assumptions would be a valuable aid to research. This entire paper is, in fact, an argument for such a procedure. Second, Lord Acton notwithstanding,[1] it would be useful for research purposes to regard Latin-American armed forces "scientifically," that is, as social phenomena rather than as disasters and their relationships to civil society as a problem properly belonging to history and the social sciences rather than to demonology. It would, of course, be inhumane and illiberal not to deplore military excesses, but if "militarism" is to be regarded as a social disease, some knowledge of its pathology is necessary before remedies can be prescribed.

Third, the functional approach to political systems evolved by that new hybrid, the political sociologist, helps put the military in proper perspective. James S. Coleman, et al. in their search for "a genuinely comparative and analytical approach" to comparative politics (The Politics of the Developing Areas) postulate that all societies from the primitive tribe to the modern nation state have political systems which perform the same set of functions although in different ways and through different structures; that is, associational and nonassociational interest groups, parliaments, bureaucracies and the like. These functions are: political recruitment and socialization; interest articulation, interest aggregation, political communication, rule-making, rule application, and rule adjudication. In this system, when armed forces cease to be neutral instruments of policy, they may be regarded as actively performing one or more of these functions, and civil-military relations involve how and to what extent they do so.

The trend of this discussion leads to an examination of the possible value to the historian of theoretical frameworks and models. Social scientists concerned with Latin America have by and large been of a traditional turn of mind and cannot provide us with models of political systems or of civil-military relations in that region. There are, however, some general models available for examination. Samuel P. Huntington in his The Soldier and the State identifies six elements that in various triangular combinations shape universal patterns of civil-military relations. These are: antimilitary ideology (within the society at large), promilitary ideology, low military political power, high military political power, high military professionalism, and low military professionalism. He states that the pattern most common to the Near East, Asia, and Latin America combines antimilitary ideology, high military political power, and low military professionalism. The systems of civil-military relations in Latin America which were constructed earlier in this paper are based extensively on Huntington's work and might themselves be regarded as primitive models. Stanislaw Andrzejewsky (Military Organization and Society) builds much more complex systems. He postulates various types of military organization deriving from triangular combinations of six elements: high military participation ratio (the ratio of the number of men under arms to the total population), low military participation ratio, high military subordination, low military subordination, high military cohesion, and low military cohesion. The several combinations are identified by neologisms. These models are then related to types or social organization. Although none of the examples given is drawn from Latin America, the type of military organization which appears to most closely fit that region is the Ritterian which is based on low M. P. R., low cohesion, and low subordination. The society in which such a type exists is characterized by steep

[1] Reference is to Acton's complaint that von Ranke sometimes spoke of "transactions and occurrences" when he should have spoken of "turpitude and crime."

stratification and egalitarianism within the élite. The accompanying political form is a decentralized nobiliary republic.

This kind of conceptualization is uncongenial to most historians. It violates their highly particularistic and humanistic view of the social universe, and evokes among them emotions ranging from hilarity to deep hostility. These reactions derive in part, at least, from a misunderstanding of the use of models. They are intended not as the conclusions of prolonged and painstaking research but, as remarked above, are devices to facilitate the asking of pertinent questions and the ordering of data. It is not suggested that historians become model builders but those constructed by social scientists can be stimulating if employed with caution. For example, by pointing out the significance of military professionalism and ideology in any system of civil-military relations, Huntington's theoretical frameworks suggest lines of research that might illuminate this relationship in Latin America.

Finally, traditional historical methods are inadequate to eliminate the greatest single obstacle to the systematic of civil-military relations in Latin America. As Huntington points out, the principal focus of any system of civil-military relations is the relation of the officer corps to the state. Without commenting on the adequacy of our knowledge of the structure of Latin-American states in general or particular, we have little except impressions based on random samples about those military groups in Latin America loosely and often interchangeably referred to as the 'officer corps,' the 'officer class,' and the 'officer caste.' Until more precise information is available about these elements, even the sociological validity of terms such as corps, class, and caste is doubtful. The techniques of group and élite analysis developed by social scientists can be of assistance in solving this problem. Morris Janowitz's careful study of the social origins, career motivations, career development, style of life, ideology and self-image of the armed forces of the United States is an example of what can be done. If similar studies of Latin-American officer corps in several countries at different periods were available it would no longer be necessary to rely on vague generalities.

It would be convenient if Janowitz or others would do the job for us, but inasmuch as social scientists are concerned primarily with contemporary phenomena, it is likely that historians will have to strike out for themselves. It will be a difficult task. The successful use of social science methods depends to a large extent on the availability of large masses of quantitative data systematically arranged (such as censuses) and the use of interviews, questionnaires, field work, and the like. The historian has nothing but his documents written by persons who mischievously neglected to collect and systematize the data needed and which at best have been randomly collected and stored. His task, however, is not impossible, as Woodrow Borah and S. F. Cook, Sir Lewis Namier and Marc Bloch have demonstrated in their research on other types of historical problems.

BIBLIOGRAPHY

Alba, Víctor. "Armas, poder y libertad," *Combate,* I (No. 1–No. 6).

Andrzejewsky, Stanislaw. *Military Organization and Society.* London, 1954.

Berlin, Isaiah. "The Concept of Scientific History," *History and Theory,* (1960), 1–31.

Bloch, Marc L. B. *Les caractères originaux de l'histoire rurale française.* Oslo, 1931.

Borah, Woodrow and Cook, S. F. *The Population of Central Mexico in 1548* [Ibero-Americana: 43]. Berkeley and Los Angeles, 1960.

Coleman, James S. *et al. The Politics of the Developing Areas.* Princeton, 1960.

Craig, Gordon A. *The Politics of the Prussian Army, 1640–1945.* Oxford, 1955.

Hofstadter, Richard. "History and the Social Sciences," in Fritz Stern, ed., *The Varieties of History.* New York: Meridian Books, 1956.

Howard, Michael, ed. *Soldiers and Governments.* London, 1957.

Hughes, H. Stuart. "The Historian and the Social Scientist," *The American Historical Review,* LXVI (1960), 20–48.

Huntington, Samuel P. *The Soldier and the State. The Theory and Politics of Civil-Military Relations.* Cambridge, Mass., 1959.

Janowitz, Morris. *The Professional Soldier: A Social and Political Portrait.* Glencoe, 1960.

Khadduri, Majid. "The Role of the Military in Middle East Politics," *American Political Science Review,* XLVII (1953), 511–524.

Lasswell, Harold D. "The Garrison State," *American Journal of Sociology,* XLVI (1941), 455–468.

Lieuwen, Edwin. *Arms and Politics in Latin America.* New York, 1960.

Maxon, Yale C. *Control of Japanese Foreign Policy: A Study of Civil-Military Rivalry, 1930–1945.* Berkeley, 1957.

Mead, Margaret and Métraux, Rhoda, eds. *The Study of Culture at a Distance.* Chicago, 1953.

Mörner, Magnus. "Caudillos y militares en la evolución hispanoamericana," *Journal of Inter-American Studies,* II (1960), 295–310.

Mosca, Gaetano. *The Ruling Class (Elementi di scienze politica).* New York, 1939.

Namier, Lewis. *The Structure of Politics at the Accession of George III.* London, 1929.

Rustow, Dankwart A. "The Army and the Founding of the Turkish Republic," *World Politics,* XI (1959), 513–552.

Social Science Research Council. *The Social Sciences in Historical Study* [Bulletin 64]. New York, 1954.

Vagts, Alfred. *A History of Militarism.* New York, 1960.

Weber, Max. *Wirtschaft und Gesellschaft.* Tubingen, 1922.

Wyckoff, Theodore. "The Role of the Military in Contemporary Latin American Politics, *The Western Political Quarterly,* XIII (1960), 745–763.

95. The Changing Role of the Military in Latin America*

EDWIN LIEUWEN

"A new Latin America is rapidly emerging" —This has been the message of many Hispanic-American social scientists. The traditional order, under which a landed aristocracy, a praetorian military caste, and a Catholic church hierarchy monopolized power, wealth, prestige, and influence, is crumbling. Society is in a state of upheaval; politics is being revolutionized; the economy is undergoing a fundamental transformation; new institutional forms are reshaping the environment.

The extent and intensity of change among the various Latin-American countries has been uneven. At one extreme is Mexico whose "new look" strikes nearly all contemporary observers. Meanwhile, neighboring Nicaragua still lives in the nineteenth century. Despite their distinct identities, however, all the Latin-American states have felt the impact of fundamental shifts in the recent world environment.

World War One marked the beginning of the end of the old system under which Latin America's well-established economic and social organization was firmly tied to a stable old-world order. The fractures in the neat international system of trade and diplomacy precipitated by the 1914–1918 upheaval were compounded by such subsequent crises as the Great Depression, World War Two, and the Cold War. Added to this was the ideological impact of Socialism, Fascism, Communism, and New Dealism, all of which helped hasten the breakdown of the old order.

The sense of insecurity resulting from the collapse of a colonial-type economic system

* *Journal of Inter-American Studies,* 3: 559–569 (Oct. 1961). Reprinted by permission of the author and the original publisher.

under which Latin America exchanged her raw materials for manufactured goods stimulated industrialization and diversification. Social change became a by-product of the economic, for as rural labor migrated to city factories and offices there arose a new white-collar class and an organized labor force. And as these latter groups grew and become conscious of their growing political strength, they began to displace the traditional groups as the governing class.

The modest business of this brief paper is to attempt to shed light on the role the military have been playing in Latin America's socio-political metamorphosis. Focus upon the armed forces is especially important since in most of the twenty republics this key institution has been—and still is—the arbiter of politics. As such, its voice carries great weight in social and economic matters as well.

I

The collapse of Spanish authority in the early nineteenth century ushered in an era of predatory militarism in Latin America. The leaders of the revolutionary armies who secured independence and claimed the credit for creation and consolidation of the new republics emerged as the new rulers. Within each nation, undisciplined, ambitious, local chieftains vied for supreme power. Politics became the plaything of the military. For more than a generation, nation after nation was subjected to the whims of army-officer politicians who ruled by the sword, perverted justice, pillaged the treasury. Through the first half of the nineteenth century, these *caudillos* and their followers lived, with some exceptions, as parasites upon the society they were supposed to protect.

A common assumption has been that this militarism represented the rankest kind of class exploitation. Who is not familiar with the story of how the typical landed oligarch provides for his three sons: the first-born inherits the *hacienda*; the brilliant second son becomes a clergyman; the imbecillic third is fit only for an army career. Yet nothing could be farther from the truth. The scions of the propertied elite simply had no taste

for the hard life of the barracks. Neither did they relish risking their lives in the crude jungle of politics. Such tasks were left to the clever, ambitious sons of the unstable, amorphous middle groups. For the latter, an army career provided the opportunity to break through the arbitrary restrictions of the old order.

Armed forces in the early national period were mainly undisciplined armed hordes of men, whose allegiance went to the best officer-politician in a given locality. There was little or no concept of a military career as a profession. Rather it was an opportunity to shoot one's way into a share of the power, wealth, and social prestige enjoyed by the oligarchy.

Military caudillos were not all predatory nor equally bad. A Ramón Castilla or a José Antonio Páez might even be termed a progressive when compared with a Juan Manuel de Rosas or an Antonio López de Santa Anna. However, the general pattern of political rule until about 1860 in most Latin-American republics was military, and more often than not these military politicians were inclined to be predatory types.

The worst excesses of militarism began to die out in the major countries during the latter half of the nineteenth century, and governments became progressively more civilian in character. F. García Calderón, influenced by the theories of Spencer, interpreted this transition as an inevitable, evolutionary law of history. On the eve of World War One he wrote:[1]

... Invariably we find the sequence to two periods, one military and one industrial or civil. The independence realized, the rule of militarism sets in throughout the republics. After a period of uncertain duration the military caste is hurled from power, or abdicates without violence, and economic interests become supreme. Politics is then ruled by "civilism."

Whether militarism had primarily consumed itself through its own outrageous excesses, or whether rising civilian political forces had developed the capacity to over-

[1] F. Garcia Calderón, *Latin America: Its Rise and Progress* (London, 1913), p. 86.

come it, cannot be vouchsafed with certainty. What is certain, however, is that much of Latin America began to enter a new epoch in the latter half of the nineteenth century. The chaotic after-effects of the long wars for independence began to subside. Political experience began to be accumulated, culture diffused, illiteracy reduced. Immigrants began to arrive. A heavy influx of foreign capital financed construction of telegraph lines and railroads. And along with the people, capital, and technology came ideas, as Latin America was increasingly Westernized.

A concomitant development was the decline of military caudillism—in Chile by mid-century, in Argentina after 1880, in Uruguay and Colombia at the turn of the century. Even in those countries where militarism remained dominant, like Ecuador, Peru, and Venezuela, less irresponsible types tended to gain control. And in Mexico, Díaz crushed the military anarchists, disciplined —for the first time—the armed forces, brought about order (though at the expense of liberty), and paved the way for economic development.

It was inevitable, as militarism declined, as governments became more stable, as economic development progressed, that Latin America's armed forces would become more professional bodies, that the officer corps would concentrate its energies more and more on the development of the military function (as opposed to the political), that armies would tend to become the tools rather than the masters of the state.

And rising professionalism in the Latin-American officer corps received great impetus from Europe. It was part of the general Occidental impact upon the area. At the end of the nineteenth century, French and German missions began introducing their modern military methods. They also helped inculcate a professional pride and *esprit*. In the vanguard of professionalism was the Chilean Army, which invited a German mission in 1885, and Argentina soon followed her neighbor's lead. By early in the twentieth century, most Latin-American countries were being serviced by European military missions. German influence was predominant in southern South America, French in the center (particularly in Brazil and Peru), and a mixed European influence prevailed in northern South America, the Caribbean, and Central America. Of course, the degree of increasing professionalism and declining militarism was closely related, not only to European mission influence, but also to the relative stage of economic development and political stability of a given country.

Indices for measuring the phenomenon of increasing professionalism in Latin America's armed forces in the early twentieth century are legion. Objective academic requirements for entry into the various military academies were revised steadily upward, and the military educational system itself underwent periodic improvements in most countries. Also military staff systems, hitherto unknown in Latin America, began to be organized. New laws and regulations requiring professional *expertise* and merit as criteria for promotion had signal effects in bringing the best professionals to the top in some countries. This legislation also reveals determined efforts on the part of civilian politicos to convert the armed forces into apolitical professional bodies excluded from exercising any function aside from their two legitimate military duties of preserving internal order and defending the nation against external threats.

With the gradual elevation of the career in arms into a respectable profession, better types went into it. As in the past, the new cadets were drawn from the middle groups, but increasingly the rewards were now for technical *expertise* and devoted, patriotic service rather than for political opportunism and institutional adventurism. Increasingly, the military academies in the more advanced countries were filled with the serious, responsible sons of growing urban professional and commercial groups.

II

With militarism thus definitely on the wane, with professionalism on the rise, it is small wonder that the writers of García Calderón's generation believed Latin America to be on the verge of ending the curse of the military in politics. At the time of World War One, a declining fraction of the total area and population was military dominated, and by 1928, only six Latin-American countries containing but 15 per cent of the total population were ruled by military presidents. Then abruptly, following the onset of the world depression in 1930, the trend was reversed. There occurred a striking relapse into militarism. By 1936, more than half the countries and nearly half the total population were under the heels of the military caste once more. Such regimes were frozen in power during most of World War Two. Then towards the end of the war and the years immediately following, the discrediting of military fascism and all forms of totalitarianism helped bring on a noticeable thaw in Latin America. By 1947, for example, only seven out of twenty governments (but with about half the total population) were ruled by military presidents. Then following the outbreak of the Korean War, there occurred a new upsurge in military rule. The twentieth-century high was reached in 1954, when 13 out of the 20 republics were ruled by military presidents, all except one of whom originally came to power by armed revolt.

What is the reason for this sudden resurgence of militarism in Latin-American politics during the past generation? Why were such definite trends away from it suddenly reversed? The basic explanation must be sought in the area's developing social crisis, in the turmoil and upheaval resulting from the progressive twentieth-century crumbling of the old traditional order. In the resulting political chaos, the armed forces were provoked to intervene. The devoted professionals did so in the name of their legitimate duty to preserve internal order; the latent militarists did so for motives of political opportunism. Still a third group of military idealists—men determined to secure social justice by force—competed with the other two.

Over the past five years, a strong anti-militaristic trend has been running in Latin America, for in this period nine countries have changed from military to civilian rule, and many optimistic, liberal, democratically-inclined souls believe it only a matter of a brief time before Latin America will be forever free of the curse of militarism.

It behooves objective scholars and historians to take a more cautious view of contemporary political realities in Latin America. First of all, it must be appreciated that the recent pronounced trend away from presidents in uniform does not mean that the socio-political role of the armed forces has been correspondingly reduced. On the contrary, armed forces of Latin America continue to play key political roles in fourteen of the twenty republics. Also, an examination of history reveals the current ebb in military dictatorship is but a cyclical phenomenon, though there are some indications of a long-term secular trend towards civilian rule.

To understand fully the significance of the role the armed forces are playing in contemporary Latin America, historical analysis must proceed on two planes—the political and the social—which are not always closely correlated. For example, an ostensible shift of political power to a civilian from a military regime, or vice versa, does not inevitably means a change in political philosophy or orientation. Also, the issue of military rule versus democracy, particularly since 1930, cuts across the issue of traditional order versus social reform.

III

It is dangerous to generalize about the Latin-American area as a whole, or any regional part of it, for the contemporary role of the military is not identical in any two countries. At the one extreme is Costa Rica, which abolished its army; at the other is the Dominican Republic with its absolutist military dictatorship. In between there are eighteen gradations.

It is possible, however, to group the countries into political categories. The twenty republics can be broken down into three groups, each of which includes about one-third of the total number.[2] In one group

[2] I am unable to include in my classification the present Cuban army.

the armed forces dominate politics; in the second they stand aside from political activity; the third is transitional. In the political and non-political groups, the role of the armed forces is well defined and stable. In the transitional group a struggle is going on between the officers who want to run the government and those who want to keep hands off. In both the political and transitional groups, the military exercise a profound influence upon the problem of social change and reform; in the non-political group the armed forces affect the social problem very little, if at all.

Countries in which the armed forces, traditionally and in the last analysis, dominate politics include the Dominican Republic, Nicaragua, Paraguay, El Salvador, Haiti, Honduras, and perhaps Panama. These seven countries are all small; combined they possess only 8 per cent of Latin America's population and only 4 per cent of its area.

All seven have tropical climates, racially heterogeneous populations, high rate of illiteracy, low *per capita* incomes, and primitive agricultural economies. They are the most backward, the most underdeveloped countries in Latin America. Their social structures are characterized by a high degree of stratification. Land and other forms of wealth are concentrated in the hands of the few; the middle group is relatively small, and the great politically inert mass of the population exists at a bare subsistence level. The twentieth-century popular revolutionary stirrings by which the rest of Latin America has been deeply affected have hardly been felt at all in these seven countries. Such are the environmental conditions in which irresponsible militarism thrives, and militarism, by its predatory activities, in turn exaggerates the depressing features of the economic and social milieu in which it operates.

In two of the seven countries of this group old-fashioned *caudillismo* still flourishes. The most primitive type is found in the Dominican Republic, but the operations of the Somoza family in Nicaragua are not far removed from it. The other five countries in this group are only slightly less primitive

politically. They are more sophisticated only in the sense that their military regimes are not so exclusively personal. The countries they run are not family estates. The presidents have to rely for their survival on the solid institutional backing of the armed forces. Only two of the five (Paraguay and El Salvador) have military governments today, but all five are essentially soldier republics. Military regimes came to an end in Honduras as recently as 1957, and in Panama in 1955, while in Haiti military control of political provinces has been nearly exclusive since 1950, despite the 1957 election of a civilian president. The armed forces of all five nations are like the Roman Imperial Guard. They intermittently and openly take power for the sake of their institution. These modern praetorians, like their forbears, identify themselves with no particular class and are devoid of any discernible social philosophy. Yet they are a conservative force because they insist upon order, preventing reform-minded elements from creating political instability. Invariably they react negatively when their vested institutional interests are threatened or their role as political arbiter. They are sometimes willing to allow a civilian to occupy the presidential palace, provided he makes no disturbing changes.

The second group of countries, those in which the armed forces are in transition from political to non-political bodies, include Guatemala, Venezuela, Peru, Ecuador, Argentina, and Brazil. These six countries contain over 60 per cent of Latin America's population, more than 70 per cent of its area, and the great bulk of its natural resources.

In this group of countries a most serious crisis exists. In every one the revolutionary stirrings of this century, the demands from below for political, economic, and social emancipation have been deeply felt. In all these countries, except Peru, reform-minded military elements at one time or another after 1930, allied with rising popular forces, launched successful revolutions, and backed programs of fundamental reform. In response to rightist alarms and counter-pressures, however, the armed forces have veered politically to the right in recent years and accordingly halted labor-leftist political evolution in Ecuador in 1947, in Peru and Venezuela in 1948, in Brazil and Guatemala in 1954, and in Argentina in 1955. In all cases, the armed forces have subsequently withdrawn from overt political activities, but in all six countries the role of the military still looms large in the background. This is because the social revolution, still uncompleted, threatens to break out again. The result is that the armed forces are torn in three directions. One group of officers wants to intervene in politics to conduct a holding action to resist further labor-leftist evolution, or at least slow it down. A second group wants to leave politics to the civilians. Some members of this group are devoted professionals; others, disillusioned over the failure of men in uniform to resolve the social crisis, simply want at this time to eschew politics entirely. The third group, now everywhere in eclipse, is made up of young officers biding their time to identify themselves with the social revolution, to lead it to victory and completion.

The armed forces in these six countries are in different stages of advancement in their evolution from a highly political institution to one that is politically neutral. Brazil and Ecuador appear to be in the middle to advanced stages; in Argentina, Guatemala, Peru, and Venezuela, the process is only beginning, the old habits of predatory militarism being merely dormant at present. In the latter four countries, also, the armed forces are inclined to lag farther behind the popular revolution, and when they do intervene to promote it, the reaction is apt to come more quickly than in Ecuador or Brazil. In these four countries, the officers who avoid political activities are more nearly equal in strength to those who are politically-inclined. And even among the latter in Brazil and Ecuador, there appears to be more of a sense of national and social responsibility than in Venezuela, Guatemala, Peru, and Argentina.

The final group includes six countries in which the armed forces have completed, or virtually so, their transition from dominant factors in government to a profession status, politically neutral. These countries contain about a third of Latin America's population, a quarter of its area. They range from big Mexico to tiny Costa Rica. Included in the group are white countries (Uruguay, Chile, and Costa Rica), Indian countries (Bolivia and Mexico), and a mestizo country (Colombia). These six countries are of particular importance, because they are among the most democratic politically, which is both a cause and a result of the absence of militarism. They set an example; they point the way for other Latin-American nations to follow towards orderly solutions of grave national problems.

In the two countries in this group where the social crisis still awaits resolution (Chile and Colombia), the armed forces occupy a unique position, politically. They are autonomous bodies, dominated and controlled by devoted professional officers. The latter do not espouse the cause of any class nor do they express any social or political philosophy. The armed forces of Chile and Colombia are not under the control of the civilian governments. The military's representative in the government, the Defense Minister, makes it understood that the armed forces' customary 20–25 per cent of the budget must not be revised downward. A sort of gentleman's agreement exists. If the government allows the armed forces to function unmolested and to look after their own affairs, it need have no fear they will seize control.

In four of these countries the basic problem of bringing the masses into the body politic has been largely resolved, in Mexico and Bolivia by violent revolution, in Costa Rica and Uruguay by peaceful evolution. Only in these four Latin-American countries can it be said that the armed forces are under the control of the civilian authorities. Only in Mexico, Bolivia, Costa Rica, and Uruguay can presidents call erring officers to order. Here the professionals are dominant in the armed forces, and militarism is rendered further impotent by strong, loyal police forces plus an effective labor counterpoise. The most revealing indication of civilian political dominance is to be found in the budget figures. In these countries the armed forces get appreciably less than the customary 20–25 per cent of the national revenue. In Bolivia they get only 15 per cent, in Mexico 12, in Uruguay 11, and in Costa Rica nothing.

What has been the role of Latin America's armies over the past thirty years? On balance, they have been a conservative force which has resisted political change and which has conducted a holding action against social transformation. Despite the notoriety of such army-officer revolutionaries like Perón in Argentina, Arbenz in Guatemala, and the "*tenentes*" in Brazil, military reformers in Latin-American politics have been the exception rather than the rule since 1930. Of the 56 career officers who have held presidential office in the various Latin-American countries over the past thirty years, only about one-quarter can be classed as active proponents of social change and fundamental reform. Military reformers, like any other reformers, can thrive only in propitious local and world environments. In the 1930's, during the world economic crisis, they were especially active. Then the trend moderated noticeably with World War Two, following which there was a brief flurry of military-backed liberal and reform activity. But since Korea, the trend in Latin America in the armed forces has been away from any sort of social radicalism. There are no military reform regimes—unless one counts Fidel Castro's revolutionary army in Cuba as such—on the Latin American political scene today.

Selected Bibliography

Amaya, Gen. Laureano Orcencio, *El ejército: factor ponderable en el desenvolvimiento económico, social, y político de la nación* (Buenos Aires: 1949).

Bazán Pérez, Javier, *El ejército en la constitución y en la política* (Mexico City: 1952).

Betancourt, Rómulo, *Venezuela: política y petróleo* (Mexico City: Fondo de Cultura Económica, 1956).

Bielsa, Rafael, *Caracteres jurídicos y políticos del ejército: su misión esencial* (Santa Fe: Instituto Social, Universidad Nacional del Litoral, 1937).

Blanksten, George I., *Constitutions and Caudillos* Berkeley: University of California Press, 1951).

Blasco Ibáñez, Vicente, *El militarismo mejicano* (Valencia: Prometeo, 1920).

Bustamante Maceo, Col. Gregorio, *Historia militar de El Salvador* (San Salvador: Imprenta Nacional, 1951).

Cavero Bendzú, José, *El ejército en las democracias hispanoamericana* (Chorillos, Peru: Escuela Militar, 1944).

Chiriboga, Gen. Angel I., *Fuerzas morales en el ejército* (Quito: Imprenta Nacional, 1932).

Coutinho, Lourival, *O general Góes depõe* (Rio de Janeiro: Coelho Branco, 1956).

Delgado, Luis Humberto, *El militarismo en el Perú, 1821–1930* (Lima: American Express, 1930).

Díaz Arguedas, Col. Julio, *Historia del ejército de Bolivia, 1825–1932* (La Paz: Instituto Central del Ejército, 1940).

Dutra, Gen. Eurico Gaspar, *O exército em dez, anos de govêrno do presidente Vargas* (Rio de Janeiro: D. I. P., 1914).

Epstein, Fritz T., *European Military Influences in Latin America* (unpublished manuscript in possession of the author in the U. S. Library of Congress, 1941).

Figueiredo, José de Lima, *Brasil militar* (Rio de Janeiro: 1944).

Fluharty, Vernon Lee, *Dance of the Millions: Military Rule and the Social Revolutions in Colombia, 1930–1956* (Pittsburgh: University of Pittsburgh Press, 1957).

Freyre, Gilberto, *Nação e exército* (Rio de Janeiro: J. Olympio, 1949).

García, Leonidas, *El militarismo en Sud América* (Quito: La Prensa, 1912).

Hidalgo, Daniel, *El militarismo, sus causas y remedios* (Quito: R. Racines, 1913).

Jane, Cecil, *Liberty and Despotism in Latin America* (London: Clarendon Press, 1829).

Johnson, John J., *Political Change in Latin America* (Stanford: Stanford University Press, 1958).

Lemus, Lt. Col. José María, *Pueblo, ejército, y doctrina revolucionaria* (San Salvador: Imprenta Nacional, 1952).

Lieuwen, Edwin, *Arms and Politics in Latin America* (New York, Praeger, 1960).

McAlister, Lyle N., *The "Fuero Militar" in New Spain* (Gainesville: University of Florida Press, 1957).

Navarro, Pedro Juan, *Dictadores de América* (Bogotá: Mundoaldía, 1936).

Pinto, Heráclito Sobral, *Os forças armadas em face de momento político* (Rio de Janeiro: Editorial Ercilla, 1945).

Prado Vásquez, Col. Guillermo, *La carrera del oficial* (Santiago: 1952).

Saez Morales, Gen. Carlos, *Recuerdos de un soldado* (Santiago: Editorial Ercilla, 1933–1934; 3 v.).

Santander, Silvano, *Nazismo en Argentina: la conquista del ejército* (Montevideo: Pueblos Unidos, 1945).

Simonsen, Roberto C., *A construcção dos quarteis para o exército* (São Paulo: 1931).

Torrea, Gen. Juan Manuel, *La lealtad en el ejército mejicano* (Mexico City: Ediciones Joloco, 1934).

96. The Changing Role of the Military in Colombia*

J. León Helguera

The role of the Colombian military in politics is a recent development in that republic's history. It is also basically ephemeral, with few historical or traditional antecedents, such as those, for example, of Mexico or Venezuela.

Most of the successful battles which freed Colombia from Spanish domination were fought by non-Colombian armies led by Venezuelans. The end of the independence period (1830), found Colombia throwing off a Venezuelan army officers' government (that of General Rafael Urdaneta) imposed by force, and destined to be short-lived because it violated the unwritten Colombian constitution, as well as its written charter. The paucity of Colombian military men available to joust in the lists of political debate was heightened by three factors: one, many lesser officers went off into exile after 1830, with the fall of the Bolivarian Urdaneta; two, the failure of the abortive *coup* against the Santander regime led by General José María Sardá in 1833, and the brutal fashion in which it was suppressed; three, the defeat of the military followers of General Santander in the 1839–41 civil war and their subsequent exile or exclusion from political leadership. This goes to explain the collapse of the military dictatorship headed by General José María Melo during eight months in 1854.

But the main fact of almost all Colombian history in the post-Independence or National Period is that the power élite was civilian. It exercised sovereignty by means of legal or para-legal devices. It was (and still is) a government of civilian *caudillos*, whose prestige rested not upon how many divisions would follow them, but on their administrative record and on their ability to retain support within their respective party directorates.

The nineteenth century was for Colombia, as it was for the majority of the other Latin-American nations, a period of severe civil struggles: those of 1839–41; 1860–61; 1875; 1885; 1895; and, finally, the so-called Thousand Days' War of 1899–1903 which left the country a shambles. The violence of these conflicts in Colombia was heightened by the lack of trained military personnel. The 1899–1903 war, one which cost Colombia about 100,000 dead, was directed by men untrained in the soldiers' arts of tactics and strategy, and consequently in large part consisted of head-on, point-blank range battles between two opposing conglomerations of peasants led by lawyers turned generals. They were as profligate in their wastage of their men's lives as they might be of words

* *Journal of Inter-American Studies*, 3: 351–558 (July 1961). Reprinted by permission of the author and the original publisher.

in a Bogotá café dispute. The battle of Palo-
negro, in 1900, is an excellent case in point.

The administration of Rafael Reyes, whose
draconian rule of five years from 1903–1909,
while dictatorial and arbitrary, did much to
rebuild his shattered country's self-confidence and economic stability. Reyes was
quick to see that Colombia should bend
every effort to the establishment of a for-
mally-trained military officer cadre. To this
end, Reyes called on the services of the
Chilean Army which sent a training mission
to Bogotá in 1907. The result of Chilean pre-
cept was the beginning of a truly regular
army officer class, trained in its own military
college at Bogotá.

The restoration of constitutional government and electoral process which followed
the overthrow of Reyes in 1909, brought in
its train the resumption of the basically civil-
oriented direction of national affairs. The
Colombian army languished. The *Colegio
Militar* became for all practical purposes, a
junior college where one year out of a total
of five was devoted to military subjects, and
where a young man with suitable political
connections could acquire a free education
at government expense.

Some progress (on a small scale) was made
toward the training of an educated soldiery,
when in 1912, all army recruits were obliged
to learn reading and writing. Reflecting the
penury of the Colombian treasury during
the 1909–1919 period was the revival of the
nineteenth-century practice of using military units for road-building and for various
colonization schemes, especially in the
Chocó on the Eastern slopes of the Andes.

1919 saw the passage in the Colombian
congress, of a law (Ley 91 de 1919) designed
to enlarge the strength of the army to three
battalions and to raise officers' pay. An indication of the status of the military in Colombian society is given by the relatively modest salaries they received even after the 1919
raise. Generals (of whom there were usually
two and rarely more than six or seven on
active duty) received but 200 *pesos* a month,
and *subtenientes* (second-lieutenants) but
65 pesos. This condition caused the Minister
of War, in 1920, as usual a civilian, Jorge

Roa, to point out to the congress that the low
salaries paid officers worked great hardship
on them and served as an effective deterrent
to their remaining in the service.

In making his appeal for higher pay for
the army, Minister Roa revealed the salient
difference between Colombia and most of
her sister Latin nations in the new world
when he stated:

. . . De las épocas en que imperaba el caudillaje
en los coarteles y en que los pronunciamientos
militares (hoy a la órden de día en otras naciones),
imponían gobiernos y decidían de la suerte de la
República, hemos evolucionado notablemente al
punto de que *ni por pienso* se atribuye al ejército
participación en asuntos políticos. (Italics added.)

The response of the Congress to Roa's plea
was negative. The Congress, in its attitude,
reflected the traditional Colombian viewpoint that the army was barely worth maintaining, and then only for the purpose of pa-
rading before the citizenry on national holidays. Indeed, its officers totalled 139, and its
enlisted men no more than 1,500, in 1922.

The prosperity that came to Colombia because of foreign loans and increased world
demand for its coffee and petroleum between
1922 and 1929 saw little reflection in the
condition of her army. Although the number
of troops had risen to about six thousand by
1932, the ratio of soldiers to civilians in the
total population was three quarters of one to
one thousand (¾: 1,000), making it proportionately the smallest army in the New
World. Its cost, four million pesos, was nine
per cent of the national budget in 1932.
These statistics took on added significance
by revealing the unpreparedness of Colombia on the eve of her conflict with Peru over
Leticia. The Peruvians had at their disposal
more than twice that number of men and
more than twice the annual Colombian military budget.

The clashes between Colombian and Peruvian forces at Leticia during 1932–1933
awakened Colombian public opinion to the
sad state of the army and resulted in bud-
getary increases for the military amounting
to more than eight million pesos yearly. Colombia's role as an ally of the United States

during World War Two, made implicit a considerable enlarging of the military establishment. By 1943, the army budget had risen to nearly sixteen million pesos. By the end of the war, it was to reach almost twenty-five million pesos.

Heightened political and social conflicts began tearing at the Colombian body politic during the second presidency of Alfonso López, 1942–1945, and, on October 10, 1944, an *opéra bouffe* attempt was made on the person of President López by some dissident army officers near Pasto, which collapsed largely because some of their subordinates disputed the legality of certain vital orders issued by the plotters. While the *coup* was a total fiasco, and its leaders were caught and imprisoned or forcibly retired from the army, it did reveal that at least a segment of the enlarged Colombian military establishment was not averse to imitating Venezuelan or Peruvian military-political *modi operandi*. As disturbing as this was to many civilian politicians in Colombia, it was soon overshadowed by the deepening political crisis of the last months of the López presidency, which resulted in his resignation in 1945, and the caretaker regime of Alberto Lleras Camargo who served as chief executive until 1948.

The split of the dominant Liberal Party into two irreconcilable factions in the 1946 presidential campaign saw the election of Colombia's first Conservative president in sixteen years, Mariano Ospina Pérez, and the beginnings of small-scale violence in rural areas—violence which was to have such dreadful consequences for Colombia.

The lamentable assassination of the popular leader, Jorge Eliécer Gaitán, on the streets of Bogotá on April 9th, 1948, brought to a head the smouldering social crises which the upper-class leadership of both historic political parties had refused to recognize, and very nearly destroyed them and Colombia's capital, Bogotá.

Within minutes after news of Gaitán's murder reached the masses in the city, the presidential palace of Nariño was surrounded by large, armed, and infuriated mobs. President Ospina Pérez, taken as much by surprise as the rest of the country by Gaitán's death, was determined not to give up power to the mobs destroying the capital and howling for his blood. Thanks to the determined gallantry of the small force of soldiers stationed at the palace, the mobs were kept at bay, and the chief executive was saved. It was during the height of this crisis that Ospina Pérez attempted to form a compromise coalition regime with the more moderate elements of the Liberal Party. The leader of the Conservative Right, Laureano Gómez, (whom many consider the guiding hand behind the Ospina regime) suggested the formation of a military *Junta* until order could be restored. This, however, was a solution unacceptable even to the right-wing Liberals, and was scrapped. Riots and similar acts of mob violence broke out in other Colombian cities and towns, and only the determined action of army and police prevented complete chaos. Within a week, order was restored in most urban areas, but the half-hearted coalition between the Liberals and the dominant Conservatives was ended, and political violence against the Liberals became the rule, rather than the exception, especially in rural Colombia.

Civil war, in fact, characterized the condition of much of the country's hinterland, from 1948 to 1953, and from 1954 to 1958. Smouldering ruins marked the sites of former Liberal and Conservative peasant towns and villages, and thousands of armed individuals roamed the mountains and plains, at first seeking revenge against the Conservative-directed soldiers and police who had destroyed their homes, and later, as violence blurred political lines, becoming bandits in fact as well as in name. The army became the rock upon which the state clung for survival.

The policy of violence which the Conservatives had initiated in early 1948, grew in intensity and was effective in keeping Liberals from the polls in the farce of an election which brought the most violent of Colombian Conservatives, Laureano Gómez, to the presidency. For the next three years (1950–1953), Gómez was to continue the policy of physical and political extermination of the Liberals. This resulted in a greatly-expanded military establishment (official figures list about 15,000 soldiers in the army by 1956), the cost of which was largely defrayed by increasingly-valuable coffee crops. Gómez continued to stimulate Colombian industrial development, securing foreign loans for the building of the country's first steel mill, Paz del Río, most of whose construction took place during his rule. The military were not, however, willing to remain mere instruments of power for an increasingly ailing Laureano Gómez.

Politically unknown, but professionally influential, Lt. General Gustavo Rojas Pinilla was able to depose Laureano Gómez in a bloodless coup on June 13, 1953. Gómez was forced into exile, and army leaders occupied cabinet posts and most governorships. There is little question that Rojas Pinilla was, for a time, the most popular man in Colombia. He managed to bring some semblance of a cease-fire to the eastern *llanos* and the Department of Tolima, the most war-torn areas of the country. Rojas also permitted the Liberal press to function (it had been muzzled since 1948). By June, 1954, however, the peaceful era of bi-partisan collaboration with the military regime came to an end. So did the truce in the countryside. So did freedom of the press.

The Rojas Pinilla regime has been classified as a "Third Force" type of military government, one concerned with the social problems of an increasingly industrialized society. Much of the Rojas Third Force boiled down to government subsidy of the military as a class. Post Exchanges, wholesale commodity price rebates, and bank loans on doubtful security for the purchase of country estates and urban property converted many of the higher-ranking officers into a newly-rich class. To be sure, direct taxation of the upper class was increased, housing projects for low-income families (mostly government employees and military personnel) were projected, and many official pronouncements emphasizing a new social justice were made.

Economic set-backs (a drop in coffee prices in 1954, a temporary rise in 1955, and a bad crop in 1956) exposed the basic insta-bility of the Rojas Pinilla regime—and Colombia's economy. The peso fell badly in relation to the dollar from 1953 to 1956, and in the latter year, 1956, a number of short-term foreign loans fell due, causing an acute foreign currency shortage. Thus, by the end of 1956, trade arrears totalled more than 200 million dollars—sixty million dollars more than Colombia's gold and foreign exchange holdings. These set-backs badly weakened the regime's ambitious public works program, and also probably cost it the support of large segments of the business community, who, by 1955, had come to resent the favored economic position of the military.

To make matters worse, the civil war continued to swallow huge sums of the national budget precisely when export income declined, and a too-rapid increase in government bank credits caused an over-abundance of currency. Until the end of 1955, consumer prices remained relatively moderate. In 1956, however, with the decline in foreign consumer imports, prices soared, adding further fuel to mass discontent. As if these reasons were not enough to give pause to the Rojas regime's prospects, an historic bi-partisan agreement was negotiated (July, 1956) in Sitges, Spain, between the aged but still vocal leader of the Conservatives, Laureano Gómez, and the generally-accepted chief of the Liberals, Alberto Lleras Camargo. Both men agreed to pool forces in a combined effort to unseat the Rojas dictatorship.

An unexplained explosion of seven military vehicles in Cali a few weeks later resulted in the death of an estimated twelve hundred persons, and the destruction of two thousand buildings. National indignation grew as the Rojas regime blamed the disaster on rising civilian opposition and as rumors circulated that members of the regime were enriching themselves from voluntary contributions raised to aid survivors of the blast. To crown Rojas' problems, the Church began to implement the Sitges agreement by permitting meetings of men of both traditional parties on Church grounds and by condemning the Third Force openly from the pulpit.

Early in May, 1957, a carefully-organized coup, supported by a number of prominent businessmen, wrote finis to the Rojas interlude. The military dictator went into exile, and a temporary military junta occupied the seats of power in trusteeship for the reestablishment of constitutional government via free election. Most of the following year posed severe strain on the bi-partisan civilian alliance, since Laureano Gómez succeeded in discarding the all-union candidacy of Guillermo León Valencia, and in securing Lleras Camargo's acceptance of the candidacy. The strain was made worse by the discovery of a military police plot to assassinate Lleras Camargo and the five-man junta on May 2nd, 1958. It was squelched.

As a curious postscript to the golden age of the Colombian military, the former dictator, Rojas Pinilla, returned to Colombia on October 11, 1958, ostensibly to "defend" the armed forces from what he termed vile slander and to uphold his honor. Little doubt exists that Rojas' return was not motivated by altruistic or private reasons but was, indeed a new bid for power. It was probably the worst mistake of his life. A few weeks after his return, he was charged with conduct unbecoming a President of Colombia and many other serious offenses and was put on trial before the Senate.

After many weeks, the trial ended and sixty-one senators found him guilty (one voted not guilty) of *lesé majesté* and peculation in office, and in April, 1959, took away his rights as a citizen, his rank, titles, honors, and pension. The convict (formerly Generalíssimo) Gustavo Rojas Pinilla faced further trial by the Supreme Court.

The trial of Rojas Pinilla, which was initiated in January, 1959, with some natural feelings of trepidation by the civilian Lleras Camargo administration, passed further and further into the rear sections of the newspapers as its slow, eminently legal—but ponderous—process continued over the space of nearly three months, thus subtly indicating better than anything else, the increasing oblivion of a self-styled soldier liberator and the eclipse of his fellow officers in Colombian politics.

This eclipse may prove temporary or final, depending upon the ability of the civilian politicians to compromise their differences and to meet the pressing economic and social challenges facing their country, so that the Colombian army may once again serve only to parade on national holidays.

BIBLIOGRAPHY

I. Books & Public Documents

Azula Barrera, Rafael. *De la revolución al órden nuevo* (Bogotá: Editorial Kelly, 1956).

Bushnell, David. *The Santander Regime in Gran Colombia* (Newark: University of Delaware Press, 1954).

Colombia. *El gobierno, el ejército y las medidas del estado de sitio* (Bogotá: Imprenta Nacional, 1944).

——. Ministro de Gobierno. *Orientación política de la actual administración* (Bogotá: Imprenta Nacional, 1954).

——. Ministerio de Guerra. *Memoria . . . del Ministro de Guerra . . . al Congreso . . . 1920* (Bogotá: Imprenta del Estado Mayor, 1920).

——. ——. *Memoria . . . 1922* (Bogotá: Imprenta del Estado Mayor, 1922).

——. ——. *Memoria . . . 1937* (Bogotá: Imprenta del Estado Mayor, 1937).

——. ——. *Memoria . . . 1944* (Bogotá: Imprenta del Estado Mayor, 1944).

——. ——. *Memoria . . . 1945* Bogotá: Imprenta del Estado Mayor, 1945).

——. Presidencia. *Seis meses de gobierno* (Bogotá: Imprenta Nacional, 1953).

——. Senado de la República. *En defensa de la democracia colombiana. Las históricas jornadas del 10 y 11 de julio* (Bogotá: Imprenta Nacional, 1944).

Currie, Lauchlin. *The Basis of a Development Program for Colombia* (Baltimore: Johns Hopkins Press, 1952).

Fluharty, Vernon L. *Dance of the Millions. Military Rule and the Social Revolution in Colombia, 1930–1956* (Pittsburgh: University of Pittsburgh Press, 1957).

Hudson, Manley O. (Ed.). *The Verdict of the League: Colombia and Peru at Leticia* (Boston: World Peace Foundation, 1933).

Lleras Camargo, Alberto, *Un año de gobierno, 1945–1946* (Bogotá: Imprenta Nacional, 1946).

López de Mesa, Luis. *Escrutino sociológico de la historia colombiana.* 2nd. Edition (Bogotá: Editorial ABC, 1956).

Osorio Lizarazo, J. A. *Colombia-dónde los Andes se disuelven* (Santiago de Chile: Editorial Universitaria, 1955).

Peñuela, Cayo Leonidas. *El doctor y general Próspero Pinzón* (Bogotá: Editorial Centro, 1941).

Riascos Gruesco, Eduardo. *Geografía guerrera colombiana* (Cali: Imprenta Bolívariana, 1950).

Rueda Vargas, Tomás. *El ejército nacional* (Bogotá: Editorial Minerva, 1940).

Sanín Cano, Baldomero. *Administración Reyes. (1904–1909)* (Lausanne: Imprenta de Bridel, 1909).

Urbia Gavira, Carlos. *La verdad sobre la guerra.* 2 volumes (Bogotá: Editorial Cromos, 1935).

II. Periodicals

El País (Cali) 1958–1959.
El Tiempo (Bogotá) 1953–1959.
Hispanic-American Report (Stanford, California) 1956–1959.
The *New York Times* 1950–1959.
Semana (Bogotá) 1953–1959.

97. The Changing Role of the Military in Argentina*

Robert A. Potash

The Argentine military emerged as a major political force with its overthrow of the Irigoyen government in September, 1930. It remains an active political force to this day. The role of the military has played during this period has varied in terms of the specific objectives sought, the methods used, and the intensity of its action, but at no time did it cease to be a political force, at no time have the governing authorities whether military or civilian been able to discount its desires or demands. The purpose of this paper is to analyze the nature of the role the military played between 1930 and 1958 and to attempt an assessment of its more recent activities. As used in this paper, the term "military" will refer to the officers, active and retired, of the three armed services. The one-year conscripts who have comprised the bulk of the enlisted men in the army and a substantial part of those of the navy and air force have never been initiators of political action. The non-commissioned officers have also played an insignificant role save in the Perón era when beneficial treatment accorded them created special ties of loyalty to the dictator that paid off during the abortive 1951 revolt led by General Menéndez. Pro-

Peronist non-commissioned officers also took an active part in the numerous conspiracies that plagued the existence of the Provisional Government in the first year after Perón's ouster, but most of these were weeded out in 1956–57. Today there is little evidence of organized political activity at this level. With this exception, then, we shall be concerned with the role of the officers.

The military uprising of September, 1930, the first attempt at forcible overthrow of an Argentine government since 1905, and the first to suceed since 1862, was the work of a small group of high-ranking army officers aided and abetted by anti-Irigoyen civilian political elements. The actual ouster was executed by a small force whose nucleus was the entire personnel, cadets and teachers, of the Military College. Tacit support for the uprising was provided, however, by the inaction of the rest of the armed forces who in the Buenos Aires area alone outnumbered the revolutionaries several-fold. Their failure to act in defense of the threatened regime demonstrated that it had in fact lost the

* *Journal of Inter-American Studies* 3: 571–578 (Oct. 1961). Reprinted by permission of the author and the original publisher.

confidence of the armed forces, as the rebel military leaders confidently claimed in their original proclamation.

While the ouster of the Irigoyen regime proved to be ridiculously easy, subsequent events demonstrated that the military had no common program and that the problem of what to do with the power it had seized was much more difficult of solution than that of planning and executing the revolt itself. A basic difficulty lay in the divergence of objectives sought by the revolutionary officers themselves. Dissident groups of varying orientation had joined in the anti-Irigoyen conspiracy, but once its goal was accomplished the unity of the movement broke down.

The more extreme elements within the ranks of the revolutionaries looked for leadership to General Uriburu himself, at least until his assumption of presidential powers. Uriburu shared the views advocated by these anti-Liberal, Fascist-influenced, nationalist groups (that had grown up in the late 1920's) to the effect that the Army should be the instrument for effecting basic reforms in existing political institutions. Universal suffrage, the secret ballot, and the Sáenz Peña electoral law, in their view, had led only to demagoguery, corruption, and a loss of moral values. In their view, the solution lay in abandoning institutions copied from the United States and in introducing a political system based on corporate representation, a restricted electorate, and the rule of an élite.

While this program had the support of a number of officers, the bulk of the military, including the navy, were not prepared to accept so radical a break with tradition, or the indefinite dictatorship its implementation would require. Particularly opposed to it were the officers aligned with Alvear's former War Minister, General Justo, who had played an ambiguous role in the anti-Irigoyen revolution, but whose primary objective once that government was ousted was to have himself elected to the presidency through the support of the former opposition political parties. General Uriburu, unable to implement his own program but determined to prevent the return of the Radicals to power, reluctantly agreed to liquidate the revolution in a fraudulent election that enabled General Justo to fulfill his presidential ambitions. The irony was that the military, having left its barracks professedly to restore a national dignity threatened by the political excesses and ineptitudes of the Irigoyen administration had succeeded only in becoming the accessory to a lowering of political morality and a reintroduction of the worst political practices of the past.

The role of the Argentine military between 1932 and 1943 is at once more obscure and less dramatic than it was before and after those dates. As constitutional president, General Justo sought to emphasize the civilian character of his administration and his remoteness from those who had given him power. Nevertheless, in his first two years in office he had to cope with a series of Radical-inspired *coups*, mostly of minor importance although that of December, 1933, extended into several provinces, but all of which were readily suppressed. Justo's prestige as an officer and the loyalty of his personal clique within the army also enabled him to maintain effective control over the centers of Fascist and Nazi influence that were growing among its officers in the mid-1930's. The exact extent and significance of this ideological penetration among the officer class is a subject that requires study; but there can be little doubt that it grew to substantial proportions under the impact of European events and that it played an influential role in shaping the policies of the Castillo administration and in the decision of the military to resume direct political control of the nation in June, 1943.

The ouster of the Castillo government was the product of an Argentine militarism more mature and more naked than that which overthrew Irigoyen thirteen years before. Organized by the Minister of War himself, General Ramírez, and agreed upon by the major unit commanders meeting at the Campo de Mayo garrison, the movement was neither disguised nor accompanied by civilian participation. The army had decided that the corrupt and, from their viewpoint, because of the failure to obtain armaments, ineffectual, Castillo administration had outlived its usefulness and now proposed to govern in its own right.

The decision to act, however, was not an expression of general agreement to a specific program for the future military government, but the intersecting point at which the ambitions and plans of various officers and factions came together. The inevitable result was that from the moment the Casa Rosada was occupied there ensued an internal struggle for power, a struggle that was to continue intermittently for over two years until, through the creation of an effective counterpoise to military power in the form of labor unions loyal to himself, Juan Perón assumed complete control.

This control, however, rested on more than the adherence of captive labor unions; it reflected the active support given to Colonel Perón and his policies by substantial elements in the army and certain sectors of the navy. Responsibility for the social and economic revolution that took place in Argentina during the nearly three years between Castillo's ouster and Perón's election to the presidency thus rests in no small degree with the military. The fact that conservative officers opposed the trend and sought unsuccessfully in September and October, 1945, to reverse it, merely serves to emphasize the positive role of collaboration and support which other sectors of the military provided. Their intent, to be sure, was not to elevate labor into an independent political force, but rather through a program of material benefits and social security to create a contented laboring mass willing to cooperate with their plans for an industrialized and militarily more powerful Argentina.

While Perón's election in 1946, like that of General Justo in 1931, served as a guarantee of continued influence for the Argentine military, it should be emphasized that the Justo election was a response to the weight of conservative forces within the military and without, whereas Perón's election represented a victory for the more radical elements both in and out of uniform. In both instances, the Argentine armed forces had overthrown a civilian government and in both the power acquired through revolution was transferred via elections to a president from their own ranks. But whereas the Justo election was engineered through fraud and contempt for the popular will, the election of Perón was secured by a military government catering demagogically to the discontent of the masses. A pattern for the future Nassers and Kassems was being worked out here.

The Perón regime, it is generally agreed, rested basically on the twin supports of organized labor and the armed forces. For the military this partnership in power was never a comfortable one even for those officers who had earlier encouraged the program of social reform. For what they had apparently failed to see was that even a captive labor movement can generate political power. The growth of this power under the deliberate sponsorship of Eva Perón, the unrestrained political ambitions of this remarkable woman, and the ill-disguised corruption of some of Perón's closest collaborators, were the principal causes of the disaffection that spread among the officer class and which culminated in the abortive coup of September, 1951. Despite the extensive purge of officers that followed and the death of Evita ten months later, Perón never really regained the wholehearted support of the army leadership. Through such devices as periodic purges, the appointment of personal followers to positions of command, the distribution of automobile import permits and other perquisites to supplement military salaries, and the opening of officer ranks to enlisted men, Perón managed to maintain control over the military establishment until 1955; but elements of discontent persisted and new elements appeared awaiting the appropriate moment to unite and burst into action.

That moment came in September, 1955, and for the third time in 25 years the Argentine military overturned the constituted government. In so doing it acted neither as the instrument of discredited minority political groups as in 1930, nor as the essentially self-centered, nationalist and totalitarian-oriented force of 1943. Rather it acted in harmony with broad but heterogeneous sectors of civilian opinion that for various reasons had come to oppose Perón and whose common aspiration was the destruction of his dictatorship. In resorting to force the military to be sure was responding also to its own grievances against the regime. These included its basic longstanding resentment of labor's influential role; the widespread corruption; the use of espionage and intimidation by the regime; the belief that Perón was leading Argentina to economic ruin and the belief that by his undignified personal behavior as well as by his policies, Perón was discrediting Argentina in the eyes of the world. However, in its decision to act in September, 1955, the military was sharing to a greater degree than ever before civilian attitudes of outrage and resentment against the regime. For Perón by his anti-Church measures and his petroleum policy had provided issues, religious and nationalistic, of such emotional intensity as to arouse civilians and military in a common reaction and make possible a united effort on the part of politically disparate groups.

The 1955 Revolution differed from its predecessors in still other ways. It was not a swift and relatively bloodless military coup, but a geographically widespread movement in which all three services as well as small civilian groups took part, and in which the destruction of life and property resembled that of civil war. Another difference was the role of the navy, previously a minor force in Argentine politics. In 1955, it went over *en masse* to the Revolution and made a decisive contribution to its success.

Although the leaders of the September, 1955, Revolution had proclaimed that it was "carried out not for the benefit of parties, classes or trends, but to re-establish the power of law," the direct result was the creation of a provisional government dominated by the armed forces. To be sure, civilian collaboration was sought, in the cabinet and through a special consultative body in which the anti-Peronist parties could express their views; but ultimate responsibility for policy rested with a military *junta* representing the military services.

Under the weight of this responsibility, the Argentine armed forces became increasingly politicized. Officers were assigned to direct the provincial governments and various state agencies, and to serve as interventors in a wide range of organizations including the labor unions. More significant, the orientation of the government and the adoption of specific policies became matters of debate not only for the ruling military junta but for more or less organized groups of junior officers who sought to exert pressure on their superiors. With various shades of political opinion reflected within the services, especially the Army, and with the inevitable inter-service rivalries, the military junta took on the attributes of a coalition government with groups of officers substituting for political parties.

The danger in this situation for the long-run stability of Argentine political life and for the future of the military institutions themselves was recognized by a considerable group in all three services. These officers, headed by the Provisional President General Aramburu, were determined to restore both constitutional government and civilian control. Accordingly, in the early months of the regime, they committed it to a policy of holding free and impartial elections in which no officer of the armed forces could present his candidacy. Despite the pressures from sectors that would have preferred the indefinite continuation of military rule, it was this policy that ultimately prevailed. Thus, in sharp contrast to the two previous occasions when the armed forces had seized power, the political succession went to a civilian and moreover to a civilian who had been a bitter critic of the provisional regime.

The acceptance by the military of the Frondizi presidency despite the apprehensions aroused in its circles by his political orientation and campaign tactics, can and perhaps ought to be interpreted as evidence of the military's increased commitment to constitutionalism. Certainly there can be no doubt of the sincerity and dedication with which Provisional President General Aramburu rejected alternative courses and insisted on fulfilling the pledges he had solemnly given on behalf of the armed forces. But the realization of this constitutionalist and civilianist solution to the power transfer problem was also fostered by shifts in the military balance of power. This refers to the growth in physical power of the Argentine Navy that took place in the two years after the 1955 Revolution and to its unwillingness to accept either the prolongation of military rule, which would have necessitated the ouster of Aramburu and the creation of an army dictatorship, or the election of a general to the presidency as happened in 1931 and 1946. The institutional interests of the navy thus favored the course which constitutionalist-minded officers of all three services preferred.

The Frondizi administration inherited the legacy of a military establishment accustomed to participating in political decisions. The adjustment of the military to the new status created by the resumption of civilian rule would probably have been difficult under any circumstances. But the fact that the President had come to power with support from Peronists, Nationalists, and Communists, all of whom had been in opposition to the Provisional Government, encouraged the military to assume the role of guardian of the Liberating Revolution. In this capacity, the military has not hesitated to exert pressure on the President while at the same time seeking to maintain a maximum of independence from political control.

Since the key officials linking the administration to the armed forces are the respective military ministers, it is not accidental that the major military crises since May, 1958, have involved the appointment or retention of these ministers. For despite the constitutional provision which makes the appointment and removal of cabinet ministers a prerogative of the President, the military has enforced a *de facto* amendment which subordinates this prerogative to the consent of the ranking officers and stipulates, moreover, that in order for an incumbent to retain his position he must reflect their views and avoid subservience to the President.

The Argentine military thus continues to play a political role despite its acceptance of a civilian president. It may be argued that such a role is forced upon it by the failure of the Argentine political system to develop effective checks on the powers of the President. The extreme centralization of authority in his hands and the inability of either the Congress or the provincial governments, whether under Irigoyen, Perón, or Frondizi, to exercise real independence have led the armed forces to assume a self-appointed role as the balance in the political system. For the present, that role seems to consist of watchful waiting and intermittent intervention in political decisions, but the dangers in such a situation for maintenance of political stability are obvious. Moreover, in view of the factionalism and divisions that exist within the military services, especially the army, their insistence that the military minister be responsible to his subordinates permits intra-institutional differences to be magnified into national crises.

BIBLIOGRAPHICAL NOTE

This paper embodies tentative conclusions arrived at through reading of selected Argentine newspapers, memoirs, chronicles, and secondary works, and of the standard English-language and other non-Argentine works on recent political history. Among the most useful Argentine sources were: General José María Sarobe, *Memorias sobre la revolución de 6 de septiembre de 1930* (Buenos Aires, 1957); Rear Admiral Guillermo D. Plater, *Una gran lección* (La Plata, 1956); Ernesto Palacio, *Historia de la Argentina (1515–1938)* (Buenos Aires, 1954); José Luis Romero, *Las ideas políticas en Argentina* (Mexico, 1946); and Manuel Goldstraj, *Años y errores* (Buenos Aires, 1957), the memoirs of a former Radical Party leader and secretary to ex-President Alvear. Of the non-Argentine sources consulted, *Nuestros vecinos justicialistas* (10th ed., Santiago, 1955) by the Chilean, Alejandro Magnet, contributed helpful data as did Ysabel Rennie, *The Argentine Republic* (New York, 1945); Robert J. Alexander, *The Perón Era* (New York, 1951); Arthur P. Whitaker, *The United States and Argentina* (Cambridge, 1954); and George Pendle, *Argentina* (London and New York, 1955).

GENERAL

98. History in British Studies of Latin America: The Importance of Latin American Studies*

JOHN H. PARRY AND OTHERS

Latin America, in the geographical sense of the term, contains nearly eight million square miles, about one-seventh of the world's total land area. Its population, estimated in 1963 at about 225 million, is increasing faster than that of any other major area of the world; by the end of this century, if present trends continue, it is likely to be double the population of the United States and Canada combined and younger in composition. The great natural resources of the area are as yet comparatively little exploited, and so, consequently, are its potentialities as a market. Even in the most developed centres, industrialization, though proceeding rapidly, is still in a relatively early stage. Economically, Latin America still depends chiefly upon the production and sale abroad of primary commodities. Many Latin American countries, nevertheless, possess large and highly sophisticated urban concentrations, strong and long-established cultural traditions of European type, and considerable stores of trained skill and intelligence. These characteristics of Latin America distinguish it clearly from some other major areas of the world commonly described as "under-developed." They make it a particularly promising field for projects of technical co-operation and economic development, despite a reputation for political instability which, in some countries, has tended to discourage investment capital.

Frontier and other disputes have from time to time led to conflict between Latin American states; but in international dealings outside their own area the twenty republics, or a majority of them, tend to find common ground. Whatever the differences between them, their interests are broadly similar. Led by two or three major states, they form a powerful concentration of votes and voices in international gatherings. To Great Britain, with its world-wide interests and obligations, the importance of understanding such a grouping of countries needs no emphasis.

The cultures of Latin America are mostly European in character, modified in varying degrees in some countries by Amerindian influences on the one hand and by North American influences on the other. The basic European cultures were, of course, Iberian; but among educated people throughout the area the cultural influence of France has been powerful for at least two hundred years. More recently, immigration from other parts of Europe, particularly Italy and Germany, has strongly affected some Latin American countries. The commercial dealings of Latin America, however, have been

* University Grants Committee, *Report of the Committee on Latin American Studies* (London, 1965), pp. 6–8, 40–46. This is a survey by a distinguished English group, looking toward development of such studies in Great Britain. [Ed. note]

chiefly with English-speaking countries; with Great Britain in the nineteenth century and predominantly with the United States in the twentieth. Technical practice and technological ideas have come, for the most part, from these two countries in succession; and today considerable numbers of young Latin Americans go to United States institutions for technical education. As one result, English has become in the last half-century the usual second language for those Latin Americans who can speak a second language. This is an obvious convenience for Englishmen having any kind of dealings there, though it would be a great mistake to conclude from it that Englishmen can make much contact with any aspect of Latin American life unless they have some knowledge of Spanish, or Portuguese. Further, Britain is not regarded with the suspicion which the United States, as a near and over-whelmingly powerful neighbour, inevitably incurs. On the contrary, old ties with England, the attitude of Great Britain towards Latin American independence and the part played by individual Englishmen, Scotsmen and Irishmen in the wars of independence are well remembered, and many aspects of English life, notably education, are regarded with respect, and even with admiration. We have been much impressed by the interest shown in our work by Latin Americans themselves and by their evident hope that closer relations, particularly closer academic relations, would result from it.

These advantages of good-will and respect, however, are largely outweighted by the prevailing ignorance of Latin American affairs in Britain; an ignorance which Latin Americans attribute, with some justice, to indifference, and understandably resent. We have heard many complaints of this indifference and ignorance. We have been told of senior members of British firms in business in Latin America who speak neither Spanish nor Portuguese and so are excessively dependent upon their local representative; of the relatively small British participation in Latin American projects sponsored by United Nations organizations, by reason of the small number of Englishmen who combine the

relevant scientific knowledge or technical skill with the appropriate languages; of the apparent indifference of British universities to proposals for scholarly exchange; of the complexity and rigidity of the entrance requirements of British universities, which make the admission of Latin American students peculiarly difficult; and of the small scale of the activities of the British Council, whose scholarships in particular, though valuable and much sought-after, are available only in small numbers to Latin Americans. There are, no doubt, reasonable answers to some of these complaints; differences between British and Latin American educational organization and tradition; shortage of university places; lack of funds; and heavy British commitments to colonial or former colonial territories. But, behind these practical difficulties, there are also others less easy to explain. In this country, both among university people and the general public, a wholly out-of-date nineteenth-century image of Latin America often still lives on, and the desultory and sometimes inexpert coverage of Latin American affairs in much of the press does little to correct it. Among the business community generally there are still many who are more aware of past losses than of present opportunities. It is often held that, since Latin America is within the sphere of influence of the United States, there is not much point in the British interesting themselves in the area. This is a view which is not shared by other European countries, nor is it held in the United States itself. Probably, too, something of the curiously irrational suspicion, with which many British intellectuals sometimes approach the cultures of Spain and Portugal, colours their attitude to the culture of Latin America. If British contact with Latin America is to be closer and more fruitful, it is a matter of urgency that the prevailing prejudice and ignorance should be dispelled and the appearance of indifference corrected. This, in our opinion, is a proper task for universities.

The importance of the serious study of Latin America on practical economic and political grounds is clear enough. From the point of view of people working in universities, even more compelling reasons are to be found in the intrinsic interest of the area. In Chapter IX* we discuss in some detail particular aspects of Latin America which have been neglected and to which academic attention should be drawn. Here it is sufficient to say that to students of the descriptive sciences Latin America offers an immense wealth of material, much of it as yet imperfectly studied; that the human communities of the area possess rich and diverse cultural traditions and a long and complex history, all deserving of study; that contemporary Latin American societies present problems and object-lessons of urgent importance and interest to the economist, the sociologist and the student of politics; and that in archaeology and anthropology Latin America is an area of unique significance, since its Amerindian societies grew up for many millenia in virtual isolation from the much larger range of cultures in the Old World, and so are of vital interest to the student of independent cultural origins. On intellectual grounds, therefore, both in research and in formal education—quite apart from the practical importance of the area, to which allusion has been made—Latin American studies demand a much larger place in the curricula of our universities.

In view of what has been said of prevailing ignorance, it is curious to reflect that there has long been a distinguished tradition of Latin American studies in Great Britain. It is only necessary to recall the names of Robertson and Southey among the historians, of Sir Clements Markham among the geographers, of A. P. Maudslay and T. A. Joyce among the archaeologists, and of Bates, Wallace and Spruce among the naturalists. But this tradition has existed almost entirely outside the universities. It was only in the nineteen-twenties that the first courses in Latin American history were given in our universities (Chapter IX), and few of the scientists and scholars who had been interested in Latin America in the hundred and fifty years before 1918 were university teachers.

What was true of Latin American studies, however, was equally true of North American studies. In 1866 the University of Cambridge refused to accept an endowment for a lectureship in the history of the United States on the ground, apparently, that it might lead to the spread of unitarianism,[1] and it is salutary to recall that seventy-five years later there were only two chairs of American history in the United Kingdom, at Oxford and London, the one dating from 1922 and the other from 1930. To-day North American studies are firmly entrenched in the university curricula and no one denies their right to be there. The present neglected state of Latin American studies need not be cause for despair. Until comparatively recently these studies were no less neglected in Europe than they were here, but the present great expansion of interest in them in continental European universities, particularly in France, Germany and Spain—as well as in a number of centres in eastern Europe—shows what can be done if the will, and adequate government backing, are available.

THE BALANCE OF DISCIPLINES†

We have attempted in earlier chapters to give some account of the present position of Latin American studies in our universities and to suggest how their further development can best be organized, but we are conscious that the acceptance of our general recommendations, coupled with more teaching of Spanish and Portuguese in schools and universities, will not in themselves ensure a balanced development. As we have recorded, a considerable number of universities provide some teaching in some aspects of Latin American studies. Many of them are anxious to extend their work. Other universities would like to introduce the teaching of Latin American subjects, but as yet have not been able to do so. The subject range both of existing and of proposed studies is, however, relatively narrow and some fields are almost entirely neglected. The establishment of Centres of Latin American studies

* Reproduced below. [Ed. note]
[1] F. W. Maitland—*The Life and Letters of Leslie Stephen* (London, Duckworth, 1906), p. 175.
†This is Chapter IX of the *Report*. [Ed. note]

should in due course stimulate diversification, but not, we think, as quickly and as extensively as we deem desirable without positive and concerted effort within the universities and some measure of consultation and planning among them. It may be useful, therefore, to indicate the fields of study in which it appears to us that foundations for further development already exist and those in which particular effort will have to be made if deficiencies are to be made good.

Language and Literature

Though it is well over thirty years since the late W. J. Entwistle, first at Glasgow, then at Oxford, pioneered the inclusion of Latin American studies in the curricula of university departments of Spanish, so far very little research leading to publication has emerged from British universities in connection with either the linguistic or the literary aspects of Latin American studies. This contrasts strikingly with the not inconsiderable amount of undergraduate teaching in these same subjects. Two main factors probably account for the present situation of research. One is certainly the difficulty of financing visits to Latin America for research purposes. Perhaps an even more important factor inhibiting formal research in the Latin American field so far as Spanish and Portuguese departments are concerned has been the peripheral status of the subject within most departments. Awareness of this has inevitably persuaded both established teachers and postgraduate students—who have to consider their promotion prospects— to confine their formal research to more conventional aspects of Iberian studies, even when they have some interest in Latin America. However, it is now obviously desirable that, in these departments, teaching should become—as soon as possible—more frequently associated with formal research than it has been. Until this is so the status of Latin American studies in them will remain somewhat ambiguous. Our recommendations about named posts should help to encourage this development.

The question of research into Latin American literature requires special examination since this branch of study, both at the teaching and research stage, involves peculiar problems of approach and evaluation.[2] These must be carefully considered before an academically valuable tradition of criticism can be established in this country. Our discussions with a number of universities about teaching and research in this field seemed to reveal a perhaps not wholly well-founded assumption that critical approaches found adequate for the study of the great European literatures would also be adequate for the study of Latin American literature. Many Spanish departments, too, laid great stress on the need for a thorough grounding in Spanish and Portuguese literature before Latin American literature could usefully be studied. We agree that, in general, work in the latter field ought to be associated with knowledge of another literary tradition to secure a comparative basis for evaluation. We also agree that Spanish and Portuguese literature may often serve this purpose well, though sometimes other literatures (e.g. French or North American literature) may offer a more fruitful field for critical comparison. In the case of post-colonial Latin American literature there would appear to be a risk that an excessive concentration on the Iberian tradition may lead critics engaged on teaching or research away from those elements that are new and significant in Latin American writing. We have reached no firm conclusions on these problems, nor is it our business to do so, but our visits to universities in other countries where Latin American literature has been longer established as a subject have led us to think that they require early and serious discussion here.

[2] *La Gaceta*, published in Mexico by the Fondo de Cultura Económica, printed (1963–64) a series of discussions about the status and aims of their work contributed by teachers of Latin American literature in North American universities (where the subject is long-established). These discussions draw attention to the various special problems of approach which confront the student of Latin American literature as a university subject and to the arguments these have provoked in the United States.

History

The history department at Aberystwyth and the Spanish department at Cambridge were the pioneers, in the nineteen-twenties, in the teaching of Latin American history in Great Britain.[3] The subject was introduced into the London history school and into the School of Hispanic Studies at Liverpool in the nineteen-thirties, and a Chair of Latin American History was established at University College, London, in 1948. Today Latin American history can more often be taken by undergraduates as a special or optional subject paper, or as part of a more general paper, than any other Latin American subject. There is a growing number of postgraduate students at work on British, Spanish and Latin American records, and a guide to the manuscript sources in the United Kingdom for the study of Latin American history is in process of preparation under the auspices of the International Council on Archives. The records of the Foreign Office itself are a rich, and still only partially exploited, source for nineteenth-century Latin American history, and there is besides a great variety of business archives.

Despite, however, the richness of the sources in Europe for the study of the Spanish and Portuguese empires, despite the importance of British policy, British sea-power and British trade to the infant states of Latin America at the beginning of the nineteenth century, and despite the close economic connections between Britain and Latin America in the later years of that century, this is a field in which British scholarship lags far behind that of the United States. It is a field, moreover, which is increasingly attracting attention in France, Germany and the U.S.S.R. We should not wish to advocate that the study of Latin American history be made compulsory in the history schools of our universities. We do not think that much more attention should be given to it. It is a subject of great interest in its own right. The history of Latin America, moreover, is a vital part of the history of European colonial expansion during the three centuries of Spanish and Portuguese rule and of European economic expansion thereafter, and the twentieth-century evolution of the continent, with its processes of political, social and economic change, is something which, on any consideration, we cannot afford to ignore.

Archaeology and Anthropology

The history of Latin America, in the restricted sense of the detailed study of written records, covers little more than the four-and-a-half centuries of European occupation, but the human past of the area covers a vastly longer time. Amerindian societies have a vital and exceptional interest for the students of the science of man, because they grew up in complete, or almost complete, isolation from the much more numerous societies of the Old World. With a few exceptions —the Maya, and to a limited extent some Mexican groups—they had no writing. The study of their pre-conquest development must therefore be based almost entirely on archaeology. Latin America, indeed, presents one of the most interesting and least exploited archaeological areas in the world, and one which is rightly attracting increasing systematic attention. Individual British scholars have made very distinguished contributions to its study; but little specific provision is made in this country, either in universities or elsewhere, for American archaeology. In a few instances, holders of posts in museums are enabled to pursue an interest in the subject; but the total effort is small in relation to that in comparable fields of archaeology, and very small indeed compared with that in the United States. There is little to encourage a young man to enter the field, interesting though it is; some, indeed, have had to abandon their interest in America and take up other fields simply because posts do not exist. On the other hand, archaeology in general is a study in which our universities have long excelled, and there is no shortage of well-trained young archaeologists who might be attracted into the American field. We would hope that one at

[3] Reflecting the interests of the late Cecil Jane at Aberystwyth and of the late F. A. Kirkpatrick at Cambridge.

least of the universities to be designated as Centres of Latin American Studies would propose American archaeology as a special field of interest, and that one of the chairs to be established in due course would be in this subject. We use the term "American archaeology" deliberately; the archaeology of all the Americas is one, although its most spectacular monuments are in Latin America.

The Amerindian cultures are by no means extinct. In remote parts of Latin America, notably in the great Amazonian forest region, untouched Stone Age cultures still exist; and at the other extreme, in the ancient areas of dense settlement and high civilization, in Mexico, Central America and the northern and central Andean regions, populous Amerindian societies will survive, their cultures still distinct, though naturally much modified by European influence. The study of these societies, with their complex patterns of cultural contact, is a task for the anthropologist. A school of anthropology cannot, indeed, be truly comprehensive in its range if it ignores the Amerindian field. Yet in the departments of anthropology in British universities, distinguished though many of them are, there are few facilities for research in this field and almost no provision for teaching. Even more than in archaeology, the contrast between British and North American universities is striking. In the latter, Latin American studies form part of the main stream of physical and social anthropological studies and are usually associated with continuing field work in Latin America, often carried out in collaboration with a Latin American university. In anthropology, as in archaeology, we would hope that one at least of the proposed Centres—preferably the same one—would include such studies among its activities, promote field work, develop regular trans-Atlantic contacts, serve as a focal centre for British scholars, and stimulate interest in what must be regarded as an extremely neglected subject.

In many parts of Latin America, serious anthropological study demands a knowledge of Amerindian languages; and apart from the needs of the anthropologist, this family of languages is of great interest, in its own right, to students of the problems of language. Some Amerindian languages are dying out, and the opportunity of studying them in the field may soon be gone. Others are still widely spoken, and some appear to be reviving. Many Mexicans speak Nahuatl, to say nothing of minor languages. In Peru and Bolivia several million people speak either Quechua or Aymara. Guaraní is the most commonly spoken language in Paraguay, in many rural areas almost the only language. Various forms of Maya are widely spoken in Guatemala, Yucatán and Honduras. No British university makes provision for the study of any Amerindian language, and we have been able to discover, in the universities we questioned or visited, only one scholar interested in research in this field. Modern methods both of recording and teaching by machine make the study of out-of-the-way languages a less formidable task than formerly. We would hope that a university Centre proposing to develop archaeological or anthropological studies in Latin America would be able and willing also to stimulate interest in some at least of the major Amerindian languages.

Sociology

It is difficult to distinguish precisely between the functions of the sociologist and those of the social anthropologist. The principal differences between them are differences of technique rather than of purpose; but in general, and certainly in the Latin American field, the anthropologists have tended to direct their attention to comprehensive studies of specific, usually comparatively small communities, while the sociologists have investigated specific phenomena in the context of much larger societies. Contemporary Latin America presents in the sociologist with a great range of problems, as acute as they are fascinating: in the rural areas, shortage of good land for small-scale farming, decay of traditional village communities, conflict between plantation estates and peasant squatters, suspicion of innovation, however necessary, however well-meant; in the urban areas, rapid industrialization, and the concentration in big cities of great numbers of people unaccustomed either to factory employment or to urban life; and everywhere an unprecedented rate of population growth. The problems of making ends meet in most parts of Latin America are as much sociological as economic. The sociologists and the demographers, together with the economists, can make a major contribution both to the understanding of these problems and to their practical solution. Sociology is a comparative newcomer among academic disciplines in most British universities. Development in recent years has been rapid and lively, but few British sociologists have as yet turned their attention to Latin America. In a university which is to be a Centre of Latin American Studies, sociologists should be able to devise projects both of teaching and research which would be of great intellectual interest and great practical value. We hope that such proposals will be made and will receive support.

Economics and Political Science

While it is true that there is considerable and growing interest in Latin America among economists generally and that this is reflected in the universities, where two named posts have recently been created and where research students are increasingly directing their attention to the area, the scale of activity is by no means commensurate with the much greater knowledge which is needed in the interests of trade and commerce and the provision of effective technical aid. For economists the Latin American countries present a fascinating field of study in their own right and as areas of comparative study, e.g. in the study of inflation, where the pattern presents features of peculiar interest. In the United States of America, where the economic study of Latin America is both extensive and widely spread throughout the universities, we found a clearly marked division in the attitude of economists. Those interested in short-term researches concerned with particular problems thought they could quite simply apply their techniques to any area, while those engaged on basic research more often wished to widen

their field of study, finding that they needed to know, for example, something of the past history of the area. In this country university economists and business men have told us that an understanding of the evolutionary and revolutionary economic changes taking place all over Latin America demands a knowledge of the historical and contemporary social and political backgrounds against which they are happening, and that current economic problems cannot usefully be studied in isolation. In this view we find support for our recommendations that Centres of Latin American Studies should be established providing postgraduate courses in which the student with a first degree in economics could concentrate on Latin America as the field of his specialist studies and also gain knowledge of other aspects of the area realted in some degree to them.

Latin American studies in political science, government, public administration, international relations and law are virtually non-existent in our universities, but the importance of their inclusion is obvious. These are fields in which knowledge is particularly needed for understanding contemporary Latin America. Without a supply of people possessing such understanding, British participation in projects of technical cooperation in the area cannot be fully effective.

Geography and Geology

The geographical study of the Latin American area in British universities falls far behind that of other continents; the work of Latin American geographers themselves does not appeal to be well-known to British geographers, just as that of British geographers is not well-known to Latin Americans; and, with few exceptions, regional courses on Latin America in Britain seem not to have been based on first-hand knowledge of the area.

Yet the American continent presents a rich variety of geographical phenomena, both of physical and human geography. These are not only of the greatest interest in themselves, but also it may well be thought that a study of them is indispensable to a more complete understanding of geographical phenomena in general. Enquiry into the geography of other areas of the world cannot be complete without the analogies to be drawn from this important continent. Field-work conditions and an excellent range of documentary, cartographical and statistical materials offer enormous possibilities for primary research.

A small but increasing number of university geographers has begun to offer courses based on personal experience in Latin America. Although this development is encouraging, the number of teachers, research workers and students of the continent is very much smaller than the numbers concerned with other areas of comparable size, complexity and importance.

Few geologists specialize in the area, and only a very small number of undergraduates is able to receive an introduction to the geology of the Americas.

Pure and Applied Science

The contribution that scholars in the fields of pure and applied science can make to the development of Latin American studies is not negligible and should not be overlooked. Physical scientists, engineers, metallurgists, architects and town planners, medical and veterinary scientists, agriculturalists, botanists and zoologists are among those we have in mind, and during the course of our enquiry we met, scattered about the universities, men and women who had not only found Latin America a fruitful field in relation to their own studies, but whose contact with their colleagues in departments of language and literature, history, geography and economics, had been of mutual benefit. They had been able to provide knowledge and general information not otherwise readily available and had aroused interest in the area among both staff and students.

In the Centres of Latin American Studies which we have suggested should be established, efforts to encourage these scholars and their students to co-operate as fully as possible will, we hope, be made, so that within a climate of general interest in the area there will be a growing awareness among them of Latin America as a possible field for the application of their skills. They will have at hand facilities for acquiring the language and background knowledge of Latin America, its history and culture.

We accept that the conception of a Centre crossing all disciplinary barriers cannot be taken too far. The engineer may have no natural link with the historian, or the agriculturist with the student of literature, and both will more easily make contact with other specialists in their own fields whatever their geographical area of interest. We found in the United States of America that attempts to combine too wide and too numerous a range of disciplines in a Latin American group, or within a seminar studying some particular aspect of Latin America, were not proving successful; the so-called "common interests" were found to be unreal, and the "co-operation" artificial, so that those responsible for the organization of these formal activities were questioning whether there was in fact any natural bridge between more than a few disciplines and whether any group should try to embrace more than a small number. Nor in France, Germany or Spain did we find any close links between the pure and applied scientists and the sociologists, economists, historians and the like. In some cases no attempt to find out whether any common interest in Latin America existed had been made, but it was generally thought that there was little scope for co-operation.

A more informal approach than the organized group or seminar, at any rate initially, is in our view more likely to be successful. What is needed is the focal point, which the Centre would provide, consciously creating an atmosphere of interest and including in its activities as many people as possible with a contribution to offer. It should be headed by someone specifically charged with the task of ensuring that administrative arrangements are such that everyone concerned or likely to be interested is aware of what is going on and what is available, and alive to the importance of using—and if necessary of creating—opportunities to cross disciplinary and departmental lines.

99. Universities and Latin American Studies*

Melvin J. Fox

Latin American studies as an interest of American scholars, and as special focus for training and research in U.S. universities, has probably had more inventories, diagnoses, and prescriptions for deep therapy from the academic community than any other Area Study program. Additional comment at this time on the current state of the arts in this field by an outsider and non-expert can be justified only if such a restatement carries with it some promise of active effort to bring Latin American studies more vigorously into the mainstream of change that is sweeping international and comparative studies in U.S. universities.

I would like to summarize some of the paradoxes that have struck an outsider reviewing Latin American studies in U.S. universities, and to comment on the extent to which changes currently taking place appear to be significantly different from past efforts. These comments, which are based on three years of study of this field by the Ford Foundation, will conclude with steps the Foundation is taking to help translate past blueprints into active current efforts by many U.S. universities to revitalize Latin American studies.

Although Latin American studies are the oldest of the programs devoted to separate regions or areas, they have been strikingly unsuccessful in developing the broad disciplinary base that has characterized the modern Area Studies programs. Among the Area programs, they have been the least effective in providing sustained attraction for distinguished scholars and graduate students in those disciplines that are primarily preoccupied with methodology, theory, and the search for universals, in contrast to the more ideographic concern and focus of anthropology, history, literature, and the environmental sciences. Thus they have been severely handicapped in the analysis of social, political, and economic problems of change.

When one looks into the Irving Leonard Notes of 1943, or the report of the SSRC Committee on World Area Research of 1947 (which mark the dates of the first abortive effort to establish a Joint Committee on Latin American Studies); or when one rereads the brilliant statement prepared by Bryce Wood for the National Conference on Area Studies a decade later (1957), or the Gibson-Keen reassessment of historical research (1957), or the Hispanic Foundation Survey Reports of Teaching and Research Resources and Activities in the U.S. on Latin America (1958), or indeed a substantial part of the discussion of the Palo Alto Seminar on Latin American Studies in the summer of 1963 (*Social Science Research on Latin America* edited by Charles Wagley), one is made aware of the sense of inadequacy and frustration that has been hanging over the Latin American studies field for over two decades. These gloomy reassessments have been accompanied by brave affirmations of hope that things were about to change for the better, and detailed blueprints of the steps needed to achieve such change. It is my conviction that the most recent phase of this cyclical self-analysis is beginning at long last to produce deep changes in both the disciplinary and university approaches to Latin America studies that are beginning to set in motion fundamental transformations in the field.

The most striking paradox is that the periodic efforts at inventory and diagnosis of Latin American studies, carried out in all cases by individuals inside the academic community, have underscored the dearth of bibliographical and other research tools.

* Luncheon address, Conference on Latin American History, December 28, 1964, by Associate Director, Ford Foundation.

This view of the inadequacy of Latin American bibliographical materials resulted from the tendency of U.S. scholars to compare such resources with those relating to U.S. and Europe where the experience and work of most historians and social scientists has focused until relatively recently. However, the fact is that the Latin American field offers greater resources of this kind, and on a continuing basis, than any other developing area—certainly vastly better materials in most disciplines than Africa, Asia, and the Middle East. Is there another area that can boast of a journal comparable to the *Hispanic American Historical Review* that has been published for all but four of the past forty-four years? or that has sustained for almost thirty years a bibliographical organ like the *Handbook*? or indeed that has had the benefit of a group like the Conference on Latin American History for over three decades? In the process of identifying the research gaps, the volume on *Social Science Research on Latin America* cited above provides impressive evidence of a sizable body of scholarly work and materials in geography, history, anthropology, political science, economics, sociology, and law. Thus, in dealing with the lacunae, Latin Americanists can start in all disciplines miles ahead of Africanists, and scholars concerned with most other developing areas.

Paradox number two is the persistent absence of a vigorous multi-disciplinary strength, particularly in certain of the social sciences. Yet for a variety of reasons Latin American studies have consistently required the type of extra-disciplinary stretch that is one of the objectives of, and a presumed precondition for, modern Area Studies programs. For example, Latin America has required, and produced, historical and geographic dimensions in most disciplines. Similarly the historian, as he has begun to shift his focus beyond 1850, has had to develop new disciplinary tools. Stanley Stein in the previously mentioned *Social Science Research on Latin America* states: ". . . the historian . . . [pursuing] an interdisciplinary and multicausal view of the historical process can and indeed must now call

upon research tools, analytical approaches, and the finding of scholars in allied disciplines—economics, sociology, anthropology, psychology, art and literary history . . ." Most of the social scientists participating in the Palo Alto Seminar stressed their need for more comprehensive historical reinforcement for their efforts.

Paradox number three is that despite its great head-start in teaching, in research, in the accumulation of the research materials, and in its tendency toward (or need for) an interdisciplinary outreach—and even though in certain universities Latin American studies represent much greater faculty and library resources and a larger and broader curriculum units than all other Area Studies combined—Latin American studies have not provided intellectual and disciplinary stimulation or leadership, nor have they presented a competitive challenge. On the contrary, until recently, they have not caught up with the great Area Study breakthrough of the 1950's. Indeed, to quote Professor Wagley, ". . . throughout the exciting revolution that established area studies as an integral part of the curriculum of many of our universities [in the Fifties] Latin American studies languished."

There are two additional paradoxes worth mentioning because of the extent they relate to the current renascence taking place in Latin American studies: Latin American studies are said to have suffered a perpetual and crippling short fall of funds for training, research, field-work and the build-up of other university resources. In relation to the other Area Study programs that took the center of the foundation and government attention in the Fifties, this is undoubtedly true. However, Latin American studies have received from many institutions with major centers or institutes steady and sizeable support for such bed-rock needs as faculty salaries and library and even research release time. This is noteworthy in relation to state universities such as the Universities of California, Wisconsin, Texas, and Florida, which are among the leading institutions for graduate training relating to this area and which in recent years have greatly increased their support for research, library holdings and student fellowships relating to Latin American studies.

Finally, I would point to the purported lack of university interest and support needed to mount and sustain effective contract with Latin American scholars and institutions. Yet over many years professional schools—in most cases in those very universities with major Latin American study interests—have had a continuous, extensive and in some cases massive involvement with Latin American governments, institutions of higher education, scholars and educational and political leaders. These overseas service undertakings have persisted longer than is true in relation to any other developing area, except perhaps the Philippines. They have resulted in more enduring personal and institutional professional relationships, more solid "field station" possibilities or potentialities, more accomplished and sophisticated Latin American collaborators than is true of any other region.

There are, in my view, eight reasons why the changes in Latin American studies which have begun to burst into view in major universities during the past several years are unlike the cyclical spurts of the past thirty years and promise to raise Latin American studies to a new level of effectiveness, performance, and sustained support.

1. External world realities and internal pressures are forcing countries of Latin America to an awareness of the need for fundamental social, economic, and political change; in some cases these changes are moving at pace and with the effect of revolution. Though Cuba may be regarded as a major example, and perhaps the first dramatic example of a mass-supported effort, since Mexico, it is not the most significant illustration. Latin American educators, scholars, *and* politicians are increasingly aware that for Latin America to make the trip across this historical watershed from the past into the future will require an enormous build-up of factual knowledge about their societies, and the use in the process of modern analytical tools and techniques. An increasing number of the Latin American leaders now realize that achievement of these indispensable elements, i.e. factual knowledge about their societies and their correct evaluation and use, require collaboration with outside scholars and specialists, including North Americans.

2. Outstanding North American social scientists, in the so-called nomothetic disciplines (i.e., those concerned primarily with the macrocosmic analysis) commanding the requisite disciplinary knowledge and skills, are becoming interested in the problems of Latin American countries. This is partly due to the general thrust in comparative studies that has been made possible by the substantial foundation of Area knowledge built up during the last fifteen years. Such Area knowledge was a precondition for, and is just now beginning to make possible, comparative political, economic, sociological analysis. Although Latin American studies did not share in this build-up, they are now ready to begin to reap the benefits of it. Scholars with knowledge of other developing areas have discovered the richness of the Latin terrain for the study of all levels of societal growth and development. The increasing numbers of well-trained Latin American collaborators sufficiently skilled, experienced, and sophisticated to assist at all levels of scholarly work, even the most theoretical, has helped to open the eyes of North American social scientists to the richness of this area as a field for study. This factor does not apply to the same extent in any of the other developing areas. Thus U.S. social scientists are finding for themselves and their students access to the study of problems of social change which they do not have to the same extent in most other areas.

3. The increasing contact between U.S. and Latin American scholars and educators during the past several years, partly as a result of the efforts of the SSRC-ACLS Joint Committee on Latin American Studies, the Inter-American Faculty Interchange Project, and the Committee on Higher Education in the American Republics, has increased the realization on both sides of the Rio Grande of the need for an enlarged and more systematic dialogue between educators and scholars.

4. As noted above, a number of professional fields have been continuously involved in Latin America over many years—and with increased intensity during the past five years—in the work of modernizing educational, agricultural, health, and governmental institutions and in improving public works, medical care, and other social services. Because of the short-term and practical nature of their assigned projects, and because these fields have generally lacked a research dimension in their overseas work, there has been relatively little resultant accumulated knowledge or reinvestment of this experience either in the U.S. training programs of the professions themselves or in their home university's Latin American study interests. It is worth noting that professional schools in most of the universities with major Latin American study programs have had involvement—in most cases extensive involvement—in Latin America over many years. The conviction is increasing among the professional schools involved in these efforts and on the parts of their universities that these overseas service activities cannot be sustained unless there is a greater long-term benefit both to the profession itself, and to the university. Thus a determined effort is now being made to relate this work to the basic, long-run Latin American study interests of the social sciences, humanities, and environmental sciences. Fortunately, there is an increasing awareness on the part of these social scientists, whose research interests if carried out independently may often appear esoteric, irrelevant, futuristic, or controversial to harried and oversensitive Latin American government administrators, of the advantages and desirability of seeking ways to collaborate on certain of the more practical and operationally-focused projects.

5. In the past few years the social science disciplines and their leaders have begun to give sanction to the new "hybrid" branches of research. These include such formerly untouchable (and in some cases unresearchable) subjects as the economic problems of developing areas; the sociological dimensions of educational development; the characteris-

tics of the power structure in underdeveloped countries; the sociology of political institutions; the changing character of the elites. Many senior U.S. scholars who have begun to work on these problems in Africa, Asia, and the Middle East having quite recently discovered Latin America, they have encouraged an expanding stream of lively pre- and post-doctoral research work on Latin America. Latin America has quite suddenly been discovered to be relatively accessible to North American professors and their students for depth research on social, economic, and political problems or societies involved in revolutionary change.

6. An additional piece of evidence that suggests that the new phase of Latin American studies now emerging may be more lasting than past efforts, is the extent to which the current impetus is coming from university management, and the extent to which resultant changes are being fostered as *university*, and (in the case of State institutions) legislative and regential policy. This has not just happened. It is the result of a deliberate university-wide reassessment—in many cases entailing difficult internal reorganization to pull together scattered, disconnected research units and to shift entrenched academic satrapies. This is a direct consequence of basic changes in the approach of many universities to their international programs over the past five years: e.g. (a) the absorption of Area Studies as a regular part of the university's program and budget, necessitating more systematic university planning and deployment of resources in the international sector; (b) the more recent effort by most institutions with major domestic and overseas activities to review the university's *total* international interests and commitments and to develop some type of integrated, or inter-related long-term strategy and plan of development relating overseas and domestic international studies programs; (c) the establishment of some type of university-wide instrument to plan and supervise the carrying out of such programs and to assure maximum appropriate interaction between the disciplines and components concerned with international problems whether on an

area, functional or professional training, research, or service basis.

7. The establishment of the Language Development Program in the U.S. Office of Education has represented a major breakthrough in government contribution toward basic university resources in that since 1959 it provided significant support at the four levels most basic for building stronger university programs: (a) through fiscal 1965 the Office had invested $1.3 million in the establishment of seven centers all of which had to be matched by the university recipients, and thus helped measurably to accelerate the process mentioned in point 6 above; (b) some 427 graduate fellowships totalling $52.3 million had been awarded for study of Latin American languages and area problems; (c) $1.8 million had been invested in a variety of research projects most of which relate to the study of Spanish and Portuguese and the development of new teaching materials and aids; (d) finally, some $1.3 million had been devoted to 227 institutes, 218 for the summer only and 9 for the full academic year, directed at improving the competence of 8025 high school and elementary teachers of Spanish.

8. The final difference between the current push of universities and their past efforts is the participation of the Ford Foundation.

This brings me finally to the contribution of the Ford Foundation to this new university development of Latin American studies. Operating as we do on the edge of the academic world, we in the Foundation can only support innovation and change that has already been triggered by scholars and their universities. We cannot force universities to change policy, over-all programs, or the research interests of scholars. We cannot assure that increased university funds will be channeled into particular training and research activities to reinforce those put in by the Foundation, particularly in the case of State institutions. And it is the university that must take responsibility for providing the funds to *sustain* staff, library and graduate study development. Unless such funds are available or in prospect, Foundation grants for Area Studies can in fact pour down a drain, as the past history of Latin American studies has demonstrated. Nor can Foundation funds greatly accelerate the long, arduous process necessary to produce the outstanding individual scholars who must forge new paths to research of contemporary problems of social, political, and economic change, and provide the sanction, inspiration, and guidance for students. To suggest otherwise is to demonstrate naivete about the university as an institution and the way it operates, a distortion of or contempt for the decisive role of the scholar or university executive in triggering change in the university, and ignorance about the limits to the influence and power of foundations in forcing scholarly or institutional changes. However, with the changes suggested above in progress, all of which were in process *before* major Ford Foundation funds began to flow into Latin American studies, the Foundation can give underwriting to help assure that these changes have a chance to take permanent hold.

The development plan that has finally been approved by the Foundation, after several years of study by our own staff, reinforced by special surveys and a series of conferences with scholars and government and university administrators, culminating in the Palo Alto Seminar, can be summarized as follows: First, it is our strong conviction based on a decade of experience with other Area Study programs that a substantial massing of resources is needed to achieve the research and advanced graduate training strength of a modern Area Study program. Our study disclosed no such program in Latin American studies and suggested the following priority needs: expansion in the number of the core of competent scholars and students, in a wide variety of social science, humanities, and other disciplines, with a major interest in the countries to the South of the Rio Grande; improvement of the research tools and teaching materials needed to sustain the efforts of these new scholars; increase of meaningful interaction between professional fields and the social sciences and humanities; provision of support to those universities which have the resources, the commitment, the leadership, and the organizational means to establish major university-wide Latin American studies programs.

The Foundation support, therefore, has focused on those institutions capable of generating and sustaining the necessary disciplinary breadth and depth of faculty, student, and library resources, and the revitalizing interaction between strong graduate social science interests and sustained professional involvement that are indispensable for maintaining major centers for study of Latin American societies. Such institutions will fulfill the criteria outlined in points 2 through 6 above. They will have a strong university commitment to the countries of Latin America, as a field of continuing training and research activity; they will have resources for advanced graduate training in the social sciences, humanities, and environmental sciences required for the study of contemporary problems of change in Latin America; they will have effective professional school participation and involvement both overseas and on campus in Latin American programs; they will have collaborative relations with one or more Latin American institutions, and administrative policies and instruments on campus which promote the mutual reinforcement of training, research, and overseas service.

The development of these individual centers of university strength requires a number of essential supportive activities that must be dealt with on a national rather than on an individual university basis. This relates to the work of individual scholars (who may not be located at major centers) or to the efforts of non-academic scholarly, professional, or research institutions. Most of these require some type of national or inter-university screening, selection, or decision-making process to assure expansion of training opportunities for junior and senior scholars; an increase of contact, communication, and collaboration between U.S. and Latin American scholars and professional leaders; and encouragement of experimental efforts to sharpen research and training techniques and tools and expand the research output of U.S. scholars concerned in Latin America. It is estimated that perhaps as much as one-third of the Foundation funds invested in Latin American studies may go to reinforcing and supportive training and research and materials-development activities. As of the end of calendar 1965, the Foundation had invested some $10 million in these university and ancillary efforts.

The fact that a recent Foundation grant to the Conference on Latin American History is its first foundation support in over thirty years of its history may provide evidence that the Foundation is serious about its effort to assist scholars and their universities to modernize Latin American studies. It is prepared to put enough funds into this effort to make a significant difference. Its actions will be determined by the wisdom and initiative of specialists who can assure that our grants will strengthen the main trunk of American scholarship relating to Latin American and will be significant by furthering the collaborative relation of U.S. and Latin American scholars.

It also provides a final compelling bit of evidence that Latin American studies have achieved new status among U.S. scholars and their universities.

Bibliographical Index of Items*

Basadre, Jorge
1949 Introduction, *Latin American Courses in the United States*. Washington. Pan American Union. Pp. ix–lxxiii. [Item 56]

Bernstein, Harry
1944 Regionalism in the National History of Mexico. *Acta Americana*, 2:305–314 (Oct.–Dec.). [Item 53]

Bingham, Hiram
1908 The Possibilities of South American History and Politics as a Field of Research. Washington. International Bureau of the American Republics. *Monthly Bulletin* (Feb.). [Item 10].

Bobb, Bernard E., see, Worcester, Donald E., 1953.

Bolton, Herbert E.
1912 Early Views, 1911. *American Historical Review*, 17: 460–461. [Item 26]
1933 The Epic of Greater America. *American Historical Review*, 38:448–474 (April). [Item 27]

Borah, Woodrow, and Sherburne F. Cook
1960 New Demographic Research on the Sixteenth Century in Mexico. Unpublished. [Item 88. Spanish translation: "La Despoblación del México Central en el siglo XVI." *Historia Mexicana*, 12:1–12 (jul.–sept. 1962)]

Bourne, Edward Gaylord
1906 The Relation of American History to Other Fields of Historical Study [1904]. In H. J. Rogers, ed., *Politics, Law, and Religion*. Congress of Arts and Sciences, Universal Exposition, St. Louis, 1904. 8 v. Boston. 2:172–182. [Item 8]

Burgin, Miron
1947 Research in Latin American Economics and Economic History. *Inter-American Economic Affairs*, 1/3:3–22. [Item 58]

Burr, Robert N.
1958 History: Needs and Prospects. In Howard F. Cline, ed., *Latin American Studies in the United States: Proceedings of a Meeting held in Chicago, November 6–8, 1958, Sponsored by the American Council of Learned Societies and the Newberry Library (assisted by the Hispanic Foundation)*. Washington. Hispanic Foundation, *Survey Reports*, 8:57–62. [Item 65]

Caughey, John W.
1945 Hubert Howe Bancroft, Historian of Western America. *American Historical Review*, 50:461–470 (April). [Item 5]
1964 Herbert Eugene Bolton. *American West*, 1/1:36–39, 79 (Winter). [Item 28]

Chapman, Charles E.
1918 The Founding of the *Review*. *HAHR*, 1:8–20 (Feb.). [Item 18]

Cleven, N. Andrew N., A. Curtis Wilgus, and M. W. Williams
1928 Founding: Minutes of the Washington Meeting of the Hispanic American History Group of the American Historical Association. *HAHR*, 8:293–298. [Item 42]

Cline, Howard F.
1949 Reflections on Traditionalism in the Historiography of Hispanic America. *HAHR*, 29:205–212 (May). [Item 21]
1960 Ethnohistory: A Progress Report on the Handbook of Middle American Indians. *HAHR*, 40:224–229 (May). [Item 75]
1961a Latin America. American Historical Association, *Guide to Historical Literature*. New York. Pp. 656–657. [Item 77]
1961b Clarence Henry Haring, 1885–1960. *Americas*, 17:292–297 (Jan.). [Item 16]
1962 Imperial Perspectives on the Borderlands. In K. Ross Toole, and others, eds. *Probing the American West*. Santa Fe. Pp. 168–174. [Item 34]
1964a Latin American History: Development of Its Study and Teaching in the United States Since 1898. Unpublished. [Item 2]
1964b United States Historiography of Latin America. *American Behavioral Scientist*, 7:15–18 (Sept.). [Item 70]

* The *Hispanic American Historical Review* is cited herein as *HAHR*.

1965a The Ford Foundation Grant to the Conference: A Special Report. Conference on Latin American History, *Newsletter*, n.s. 1/1:2–5 (Jan.). [Item 81]

1965b The Conference: A Fecund Decade, 1954–1964. *HAHR*, 45:434–438 (Aug.). [Item 80]

Conn, Stetson
1934 A Topical Analysis of the College Texts on Hispanic American History. *HAHR*, 14:108–113 (Feb.). [Item 36]

Cook, Sherburne F., see Borah, Woodrow.

Cox, Isaac J.
1931 Hispanic America. American Historical Association, *Guide to Historical Literature*. New York. Pp. 1051–1052. [Item 37]

Everett, Samuel, see, King, James F., 1944

Fisher, Lillian Estelle
1939 Reconstitution: Minutes of the Conference on Latin American History of the American Historical Association, Held in Chicago, December 28, 1938. *HAHR*, 19:218–221 (May). [Item 43]

Fox, Melvin J.
1964 Universities and Latin American Studies. Unpublished. [Item 99]

Gibson, Charles
1958 The Colonial Period in Latin American History. Washington. American Historical Association, Service Center for Teachers of History, *Pamphlet* 7. [Item 72]

1963 History of the New World Program: Assessment. *Handbook of Latin American Studies*, 25:197. [Item 32]

1963, 1964 History. *Handbook of Latin American Studies*, 25:195–197 (1963), 26:38–42 (1964). [Item 78]

Gibson, Charles, and Benjamin Keen
1957 Trends of United States Studies in Latin American History. *American Historical Review*, 62:855–877 (July). [Item 64]

Griffin, Charles C.
1949 Economic and Social Aspects of the Era of Spanish-American Independence. *HAHR*, 29:170–187 (May). [Item 60]

1962 History of the New World. *The National Period in the History of the New World: An Outline and Commentary*. Mexico City. Comisión de Historia, Program of the History of the New World, 3. Pan American Institute of Geography and History, 240:ix–xviii. [Item 31]

1964 An Essay on Regionalism and Nationalism in Latin American Historiography. *Journal of World History*, 8/2:37–378. [Item 85]

Hackett, Charles W.
1949 Discussion of Lesley Byrd Simpson, "Thirty Years of The Hispanic American Historical Review." *HAHR*, 29:213–218 (May). [Item 22]

Hanke, Lewis
1936 The First Lecturer on Hispanic American Diplomatic History in the United States. *HAHR*, 16:399–402 (Aug.). [Item 4]

1947 The Development of Latin-American Studies in the United States, 1939–1945. *Americas*, 4:32–64 (July). [Item 47]

1964 Development of Bolton's Theory. *Do the Americas Have a Common History? A Critique of the Bolton Theory*. New York. Pp. 10–30. [Item 29]

Haring, Clarence H.
1936 Handbook of Latin American Studies. *Handbook of Latin American Studies*, 1:xi–xii. [Item 38]

Harrison, John P., see, Worcester, Donald E., 1953

Haverstock, Nathan A.
1959 The *Handbook of Latin American Studies*, Nos. 1–21. *Handbook of Latin American Studies*, 21:xi–xvi. [Item 40]

Helguera, J. León
1961 The Changing Role of the Military in Colombia. *Journal of Inter-American Studies*, 3:351–358 (July). [Item 96]

1962 Research Opportunities: The Bolivarian Nations. *Americas*, 18:365–374 (April). [Item 68]

Humphreys, Robin A.
1950 The Fall of the Spanish American Empire. *History: The Journal of the Historical Association*, n.s. 37:213–227 (Oct.). [Item 59]

1958 Four Bibliographical Tools Needed for Latin American History. *HAHR*, 38:260–262 (May). [Item 74]

1959 William Hickling Prescott: The Man and the Historian. *HAHR*, 39:1–19 (Feb.). [Item 3]

Jameson, J. Franklin
1918 A New American Historical Journal. *HAHR*, 1:2–7 (Feb.). [Item 17]

Johnson, John J.
1961 Whither the Latin American Middle Sectors? *The Virginia Quarterly Review*, 27:508–521 (Autumn). [Item 93]

Keen, Benjamin
1957 co-author, see, Gibson, Charles
1962 Edward Gaylord Bourne's *Spain in*

America. In E. G. Bourne, *Spain in America, 1450–1580, with New Introduction and Supplementary Bibliography.* New York. [Item 9]

King, James F.
1944 Negro History in Continental Spanish America. *Journal of Negro History,* 28: 7–32 (Jan.). [Item 52]

King, James F., and Samuel Everett
1944 Latin American History Textbooks. In *Latin America in School and College Teaching Materials: Report of the Committee on the Study of Teaching Materials on Inter-American Subjects.* Washington. American Council on Education. Pp. 107–132. [Item 48]

Klein, Julius G.
1917 The Church in Spanish American History. *Catholic Historical Review,* 3:290–307 (Oct.). [Item 14]

Kroeber, Clifton B.
1953 La tradición de la historia latinoamericana en los Estados Unidos: Apreción preliminar. *Revista de Historia de América,* 35/36:21–58 (ene.–dic.), [Item 55, translated by Howard F. Cline]

Lanning, John Tate
1936 Research Possibilities in the Cultural History of Spain in America. *HAHR,* 16: 149–161 (May). [Item 45]
1944 A Reconsideration of Spanish Colonial Culture. *Americas,* 1:166–178 (Oct.). [Item 51]
1964 The Hispanist in the American Historical Association. *Americas,* 20:393–406 (April). [Item 79]

Lavretskii, I. R.
1960 A Survey of the *Hispanic American Historical Review,* 1956–1958. *HAHR,* 40: 340–360 (Aug.). [Item 24]

Leonard, Irving A.
1943 A Survey of Personnel and Activities in Latin American Aspects of the Humanities and Social Sciences at Twenty Universities of the United States. Joint Committee on Latin American Studies, *Notes on Latin American Studies,* 1:7–46 (April). [Item 46]

Lieuwen, Edwin
1961 The Changing Role of the Military in Latin America. *Journal of Inter-American Studies,* 3:559–569. [Item 95]

McAlister, Lyle N.
1961 Civil-Military Relations in Latin America. *Journal of Inter-American Studies,* 3:341–350 (July). [Item 94]

1963 Social Structure and Social Change in New Spain, *HAHR,* 43:349–370 (Aug.). [Item 92]

McGann, Thomas F.
1962 Research Opportunities: Southern South America. *Americas,* 18:375–379 (April). [Item 69]

Marchant, Alexander
1951 The Unity of Brazilian History. In Alexander Marchant and T. L. Smith, eds., *Brazil: A Portrait of Half a Continent.* New York. Pp. 37–51. [Item 86]

Mattingly, Garrett
1948 The Historian of the Spanish Empire. *American Historical Review,* 54:32–48 (Oct.). [Item 15]

Morse, Richard M.
1954 Toward a Theory of Spanish American Government. *Journal of the History of Ideas,* 15:71–93 (Jan.). [Item 63]
1955 Language as a Key to Latin American Historiography. *Americas,* 11:517–538 (April). [Item 82]
1962a Some Characteristics of Latin American Urban History. *American Historical Review,* 67:317–338 (Jan.). [Item 84]
1962b Some Themes of Brazilian History. *South Atlantic Quarterly,* 61:159–182. [Item 87]

Moses, Bernard
1898 The Neglected Half of American History. University of California (Berkeley), *University Chronicle,* 1:120–126. [Item 6]

Mosk, Sanford
1949 Latin American Economics: The Field and Its Problems. *Inter-American Economic Affairs,* 3:55–64. [Item 61]
1958 Latin American Economies: Needs and Prospects. In Howard F. Cline, ed., *Latin American Studies in the United States: Proceedings of a Meeting Held in Chicago, November 6–8, 1958, Sponsored by the American Council of Learned Societies and the Newberry Library (assisted by the Hispanic Foundation).* Washington. Hispanic Foundation, *Survey Reports,* 8:52–55. [Item 83]

Naylor, Robert A.
1962 Research Opportunities: Mexico and Central America. *Americas,* 18:352–365 (April). [Item 67]

Nicholson, Henry B.
1960 Ethnohistory: Mesoamerica. *Handbook of Latin American Studies,* 22:30–32. [Item 76]

O'Hara, John F.
1917 A Frank Word about South American History. *Catholic Historical Review*, 2: 433–436 (Jan.). [Item 13]

Oswald, J. Gregory
1960 A Soviet Criticism of the *Hispanic American Historical Review*. *HAHR*, 40:337–339 (Aug.). [Item 23]

Pariseau, Earl J.
1963, 1964 The *Handbook of Latin American Studies:* Recent Developments. *Handbook of Latin American Studies*, 25:ix–x (1963), 26:ix–x (1964). [Item 41]

Parry, John H., and Others
1965 History in British Studies of Latin America. University Grants Committee, *Report of the Committee on Latin American Studies*. London. Pp. 6–8, 40–46. [Item 98]

Pattee, Richard
1944 A Revisionist Approach to Hispanic American Studies. *Catholic Historical Review*, 29:431–444 (Jan.). [Item 50]

Phelan, John L.
1960 Authority and Flexibility in the Spanish Imperial Bureaucracy. *Administrative Science Quarterly*, 5:47–56 (June). [Item 91]

Pierson, George W., and Others
1964 The Nature of History. American Historical Association, *Newsletter*, 2/4:5–7 (April). [Item 1]

Potash, Robert A.
1961 The Changing Role of the Military in Argentina. *Journal of Inter-American Studies*, 3:571–577 (Oct.). [Item 97]

Reinsch, Paul Samuel
1910 Some Notes on the Study of South American History. In Guy Stanton Ford, ed., *Essays in American History Dedicated to Frederick Jackson Turner*. New York. Pp. 269–293. [Item 12]

Robertson, James Alexander, and Others
1919 A Symposium on the Teaching of the History of Hispanic America in Educational Institutions in the United States. *HAHR*, 2:397–418 (Aug.). [Item 35]

Robertson, William Spence
1950 *The Hispanic American Historical Review*. In Ruth Lapham Butler, comp., *Guide to the Hispanic American Historical Review*. Durham. Pp. vii–xvi. [Item 19]

Schmitt, Karl
1959 The Clergy and the Enlightenment in

Latin America: An Analysis. *Americas*, 15:381–391 (April). [Item 90]

Shelby, Charmion
1951 The *Handbook of Latin American Studies:* Its First Fifteen Years. *Revista Interamericana de Bibliografía*, 1:89–94 (abr.–jun.). [Item 39]

Shepherd, William R.
1909 The Contribution of the Romance Nations to the History of the Americas. *Annual Report of the American Historical Association for the Year 1909*. Washington. Pp. 221–227. [Item 11]
1933 Brazil as a Field for Historical Study. *HAHR*, 13:427–436 (Nov.). [Item 44]

Simpson, Lesley Byrd
1949 Thirty Years of *The Hispanic American Historical Review*. *HAHR*, 29:188–204 (May). [Item 20]
1953 Mexico's Forgotten Century. *Pacific Historical Review*, 22:113–121. [Item 62]

Steck, Francis Borgia
1942 Some Recent Trends and Findings in the History of the Spanish Colonial Empire in America. *Catholic Historical Review*, 28:13–42. [Item 49]

Stein, Stanley J.
1961 The Tasks Ahead for Latin American Historians. *HAHR*, 41:424–433 (Aug.). [Item 66]
1964 Latin American Historiography: Status and Research Opportunities. In Charles Wagley, ed., *Social Science Research on Latin America: Report and Papers of a Seminar on Latin American Studies in the United States Held at Stanford, California, July 8–August 23, 1963*. New York. Pp. 86–124. [Item 71]

Watson, James E.
1962 Bernard Moses: Pioneer in Latin American Scholarship. *HAHR*, 42:212–216 (May). [Item 7]

Whitaker, Arthur P.
1950 Developments of the Past Decade in the Writing of Latin American History. *Revista de Historia de América*, 29:123–133 (junio). [Item 54]
1951 The Americas in the Atlantic Triangle. In *Ensayos sobre la historia del Nuevo Mundo*. Mexico City. Pan American Institute of Geography and History, 118:69–95. [Item 33]
1955–1957 The Intellectual History of Eighteenth-Century Spanish America. *Relazioni del X Congresso Internazionale di*

Scienze Storiche. 7 v., Firenze and Rome. 1:187–206. [Item 89]

1961 Latin American History Since 1825. Washington. American Historical Association, Service Center for Teachers of History, *Pamphlet 42*. Second ed. 1965. [Item 73]

Wilgus, A. Curtis, see, Cleven, N. Andrew N., 1928.

Williams, Mary Wilhelmine

1929 Hispanic America at the 1928 Meeting of the American Historical Association. *HAHR*, 9:241–242. [Item 42]

Worcester, Donald E.

1961 Editorial Note: The Lavretskii Article. *HAHR*, 41:173. [Item 25]

Worcester, Donald E., Bernard E. Bobb, and John P. Harrison

1953 Report of the Committee on the Twenty-Fifth Anniversary. Mimeo. n.p. Conference on Latin American History Archives, Hispanic Foundation. [Item 57]

Zavala, Silvio

1961 A General View of the Colonial History of the New World. *American Historical Review*, 66: 913–929 (July). [Item 30]